PHILIP'S

ESSENTIAL WORLD ATLAS

Dear Liz,

Happy Travelling!

With love from Dave & Jenny.

xxx

World

Europe

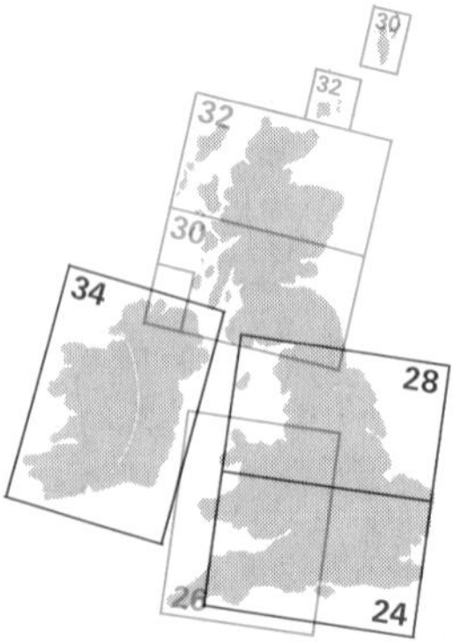

Edited by
B. M. Willett, Cartographic Editor
David Gaylard
Lilla Prince-Smith
   George Philip and Son Ltd., London

Maps prepared by
Cox Cartographic Ltd., and
George Philip Cartographic Services Ltd.,
London under the direction of Alan Poynter.

© **1990 George Philip Ltd., London**

ISBN 0-540-05582-4

Reprinted 1991

Printed in Italy

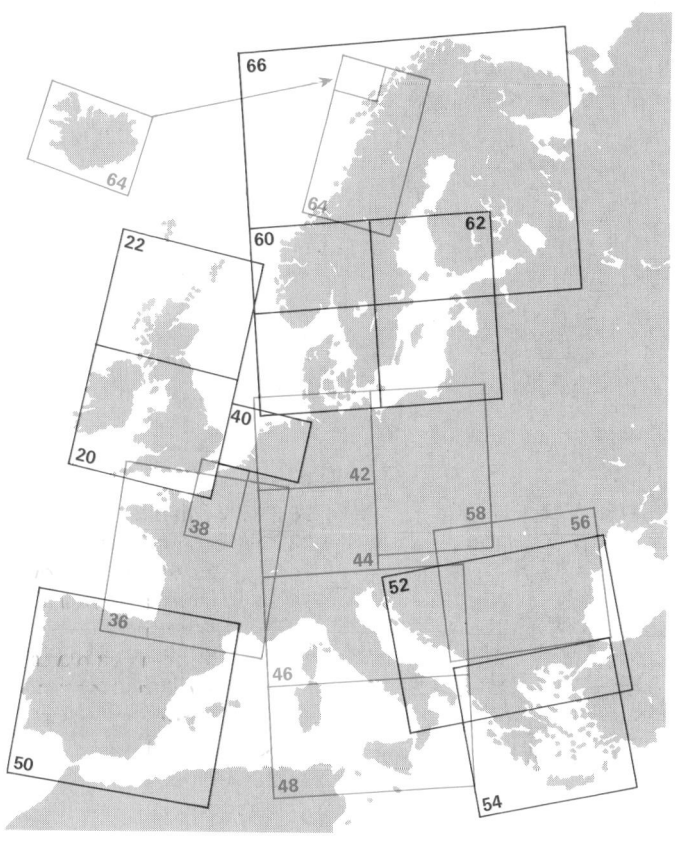

36-37	France
38-39	Northern France
40-41	Netherlands
42-43	Germany and the Low Countries
44-45	Alpine Lands
46-47	Northern Italy and Corsica
48-49	Southern Italy and Sardinia
50-51	Spain and Portugal
52-53	Danube Lands
54-55	Greece and Albania
56-57	Romania
58-59	Central Europe
60-61	Southern Scandinavia
62-63	Baltic Lands
64-65	North West Scandinavia and Iceland
66-67	Northern Scandinavia

Asia

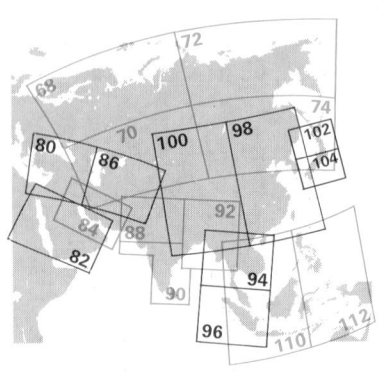

68-75 **U.S.S.R.**
68-69 West
70-71 South West
72-73 North East
74-75 South East and Mongolia

76-77 Asia: Physical
78-79 Asia: Political
80-81 Turkey and the Middle East
82-83 Arabian Peninsula
84-85 The Gulf
86-87 Central Asia and Afghanistan
88-89 Pakistan and North West India

90-91 Central and Southern India, Sri Lanka
92-93 Eastern India, Bangladesh and Burma
94-95 Mainland South East Asia
96-97 The Malay Peninsula
98-99 China: East
100-101 China: West

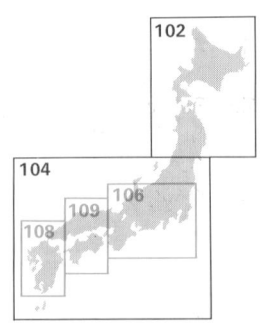

102-109 Japan
102-103 North
104-105 South
106-107 Tokyo, Kyoto, Osaka
108 Kyushu
109 West Honshu and Shikoku

110-111 Indonesia: West
112-113 Indonesia: East

Australasia

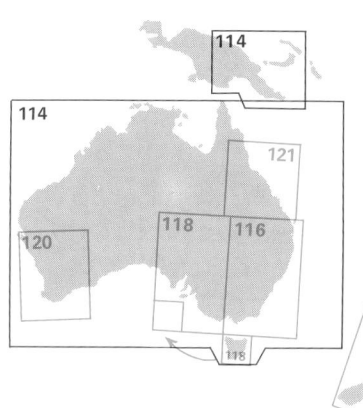

114-115 **Australia, New Zealand and Papua New Guinea**

116-121 **Australia**
116-117 Brisbane, Sydney, Melbourne
118-119 Adelaide, Melbourne, Tasmania
120 Perth
121 North East Queensland

122-123 **New Zealand, Central and South West Pacific**

Africa

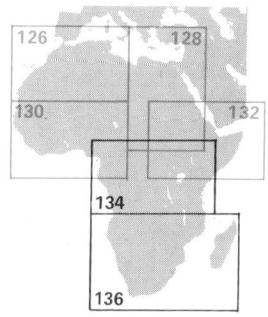

124-137 **Africa**
124 Physical
125 Political
126-127 North West
128-129 North East
130-131 West
132-133 East
134-135 Central
136-137 South

North America

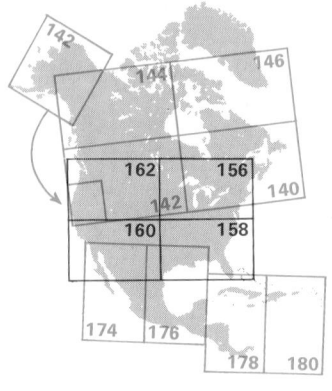
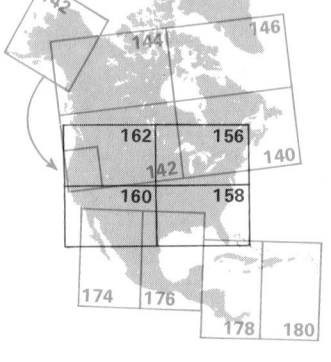

138   North America: Physical
139   North America: Political

140-155   Canada
  140-141   South East
  142-143   South West and Alaska
  144-145   North West
  146-147   North East
  148-149   Saint Lawrence Estuary
  150-151   The Great Lakes
  152-153   Southern Saskatchewan and
              Manitoba
  154-155   Southern British Columbia and
              Alberta

156-173   U.S.A.
  156-157   North East
  158-159   South East
  160-161   South West
  162-163   North West
      164   Boston, New York,
              Washington
      165   Washington, Atlanta
  166-167   Upper Mississippi
  168-169   Lower Mississippi and Gulf
              Coast
      170   Florida
      171   Columbia Basin
  172-173   California

174-175   Mexico: West
176-177   Mexico: East
178-179   Caribbean: West
180-181   Caribbean: East

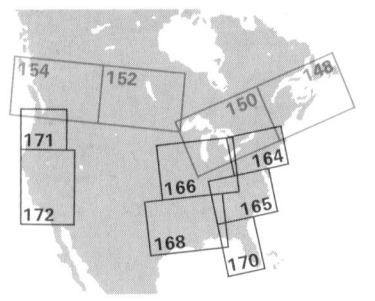

South America

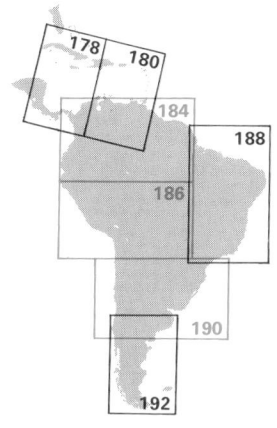

182-192 **South America**
182 Physical
183 Political
184-185 North West
186-187 West
188-189 East
190-191 Central
192 South

Index

Map Symbols

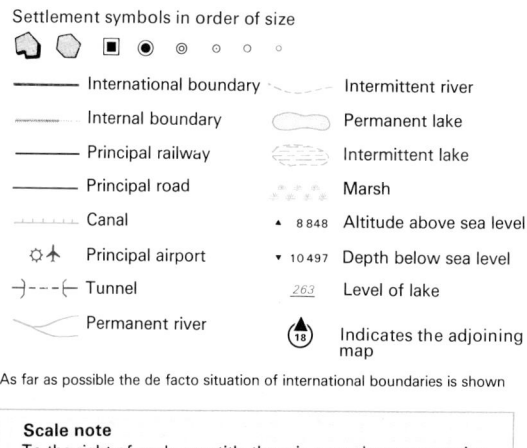

Settlement symbols in order of size

		International boundary		Intermittent river
		Internal boundary		Permanent lake
		Principal railway		Intermittent lake
		Principal road		Marsh
		Canal	▲ 8 848	Altitude above sea level
☼ ✈		Principal airport	▼ 10 497	Depth below sea level
┤---├		Tunnel	*263*	Level of lake
		Permanent river	(18)	Indicates the adjoining map

As far as possible the de facto situation of international boundaries is shown

Scale note
To the right of each map title there is a number representing the scale of the map for example, 1 : 2 000 000. This means that one centimetre on the map represents 2 million centimetres or 20 kilometres on the ground. Or, if the number is 1 : 40 000 000, one centimetre represents 40 million centimetres or 400 kilometres.

Height and depth colours
Height of land above sea level

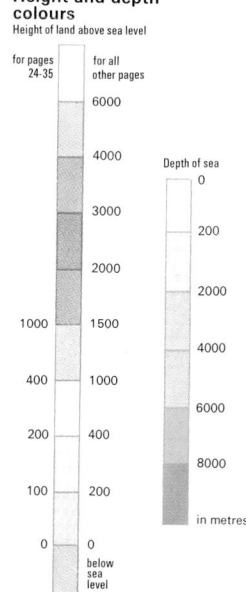

World: Northern Part

PROJECTION CENTRED ON LONDON
ARCTIC OCEAN
North Pole
Magnetic Pole
Arctic Circle
International Dateline
Tropic of Cancer
180
160
140
120
100
80
U. S. S. R.
CHINA
INDIA
MONGOLIA
JAPAN
KOREA
TAIWAN
VIETNAM
CAMBODIA
THAILAND
BURMA
BANGLADESH
NEPAL
SRI LANKA
MALDIVES
Laccadives
PAKISTAN
AFGHANISTAN
IRAN
IRAQ
KUWAIT
U.A.E.
OMAN
YEMEN
SAUDI ARABIA
JORDAN
SYRIA
ISRAEL
TURKEY
EGYPT
GREECE
TUNISIA
ITALY
GERMANY
FINLAND
SWEDEN
NORWAY
ICELAND
GREENLAND
UNITED KINGDOM
IRELAND
FRANCE
SPAIN
MOROCCO
Madeira
Canary Is.
Azores
Bermuda
CANADA
UNITED STATES
MEXICO
BAHAMAS
CUBA
JAMAICA
GUATEMALA
EL SALVADOR
HONDURAS
NICARAGUA
COSTA RICA
PANAMA
TRINIDAD & TOBAGO
VENEZUELA
COLOMBIA
ECUADOR
PERU
Tokyo
Seoul
Pyongyang
Peking
Shanghai
Hongkong
Hanoi
Bangkok
Rangoon
Dacca
Calcutta
Katmandu
Delhi
Islamabad
Kabul
Karachi
Bombay
Colombo
Muscat
Tehran
Bagdad
Riyadh
Beirut
Ankara
Jerusalem
Cairo
Tripoli
Tunis
Athens
Istanbul
Budapest
Warsaw
Moscow
Helsinki
Stockholm
Copenhagen
Berlin
Bonn
Vienna
Oslo
Amsterdam
London
Paris
Rome
Algiers
Madrid
Lisbon
Gibraltar
Rabat
Reykjavik
Godthåb
Ulan Bator
Anchorage
Vancouver
San Francisco
Los Angeles
Toronto
Ottawa
New York
Washington
Havana
Mexico City
Kingston
Caracas
Port of Spain
Bogotá
Quito

Map 8

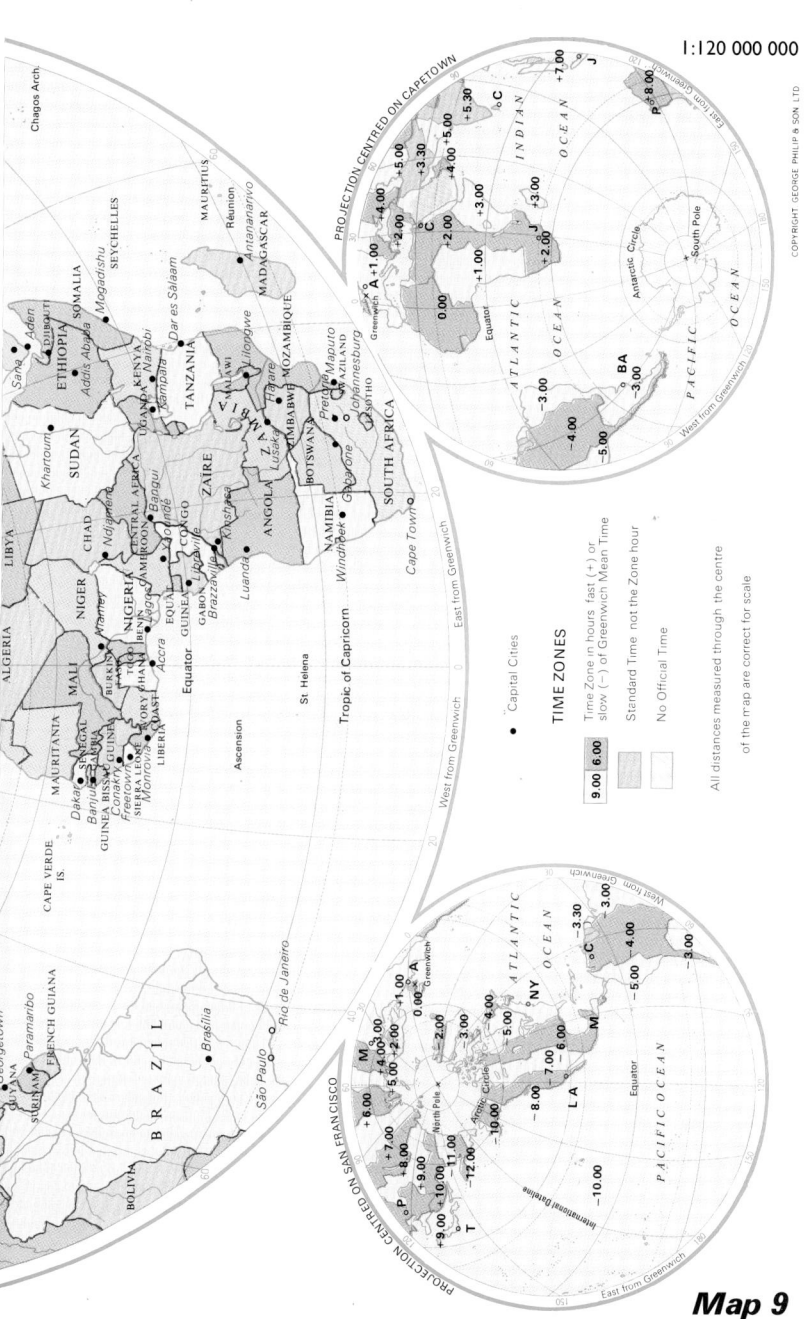

1:120 000 000

PROJECTION CENTRED ON CAPETOWN

Chagos Arch.

MAURITIUS
Réunion
SEYCHELLES
SOMALIA
Mogadishu
DJIBOUTI
Aden
Saña
ETHIOPIA
Addis Abeba
MADAGASCAR
Antananarivo
KENYA
Nairobi
UGANDA
Kampala
TANZANIA
Dar es Salaam
SUDAN
Khartoum
ZAIRE
Kinshasa
Brazzaville
CONGO
GABON
Libreville
EQUAT. GUINEA
CAMEROON
Yaoundé
CENTRAL AFRICA
Bangui
Ndjamena
CHAD
LIBYA
NIGER
NIGERIA
Lagos
BENIN
TOGO
GHANA
Accra
IVORY COAST
LIBERIA
Monrovia
SIERRA LEONE
Freetown
GUINEA
Conakry
GUINEA BISSAU
SENEGAL
Banjul
Dakar
GAMBIA
MAURITANIA
MALI
BURKINA
ALGERIA
CAPE VERDE IS.
ANGOLA
Luanda
ZAMBIA
Lusaka
MALAWI
ZIMBABWE
Harare
Lilongwe
MOZAMBIQUE
Maputo
SWAZILAND
LESOTHO
BOTSWANA
Gaborone
Pretoria
Johannesburg
NAMIBIA
Windhoek
SOUTH AFRICA
Cape Town

St Helena
Ascension
Tropic of Capricorn
Equator

BRAZIL
Brasília
São Paulo
Rio de Janeiro
BOLIVIA
GUIANA
SURINAM
Paramaribo
FRENCH GUIANA
Georgetown

INDIAN OCEAN
ATLANTIC OCEAN
PACIFIC OCEAN

Greenwich
Antarctic Circle
South Pole
Equator

+1.00 +2.00 +3.00 +4.00 +5.00 +5.30 +7.00
+3.30 +4.00 +5.00
0.00 +2.00
+1.00 +2.00 +3.00
−3.00
−4.00
−5.00
+8.00
East from Greenwich
West from Greenwich
A C C J J R BA

PROJECTION CENTRED ON SAN FRANCISCO

ATLANTIC OCEAN
PACIFIC OCEAN
Greenwich
Arctic Circle
North Pole
Equator
International Dateline
West from Greenwich
East from Greenwich

+1.00 0.00 −3.30 −3.00
+3.00 +4.00 −3.00
+2.00 +4.00 −5.00 −4.00
+5.00 −6.00
+6.00 +4.00 −5.00 −7.00
+7.00 −8.00
+8.00 −10.00
+9.00 +9.00 −11.00 −10.00
−9.00 −12.00
A M C NY LA M P T −10.00

COPYRIGHT GEORGE PHILIP & SON LTD

• Capital Cities

TIME ZONES

Time Zone in hours fast (+) or
slow (−) of Greenwich Mean Time

9.00 6.00

Standard Time not the Zone hour

No Official Time

All distances measured through the centre
of the map are correct for scale

Map 9

9

World: Southern Part

PROJECTION CENTRED ON THE ANTIPODES OF LONDON

Galapagos Is.

Easter I.

PACIFIC OCEAN

Marquesas Is.

Tuamotu Arch.

Tropic of Capricorn

Pitcairn I.

FRENCH POLYNESIA

Tahiti

Hawaiian Is.

PACIFIC OCEAN

Tropic of Cancer

Kiritimati

Cook Is.

SAMOA

Midway I.

Equator

TONGA

Wellington

NEW ZEALAND

Auckland

Antipodes I.

International Dateline

FIJI

KIRIBATI

Macquarie I.

Antarctic Circle

Victoria Land

Marshall Is.

TUVALU

Auckland I.

Wake I.

VANUATU

New Caledonia

Adélie Land

Bonin I.

SOLOMON IS.

Sydney

Canberra

Northern
Marianas

Port Moresby

AUSTRALIA

Guam

PAPUA

NEW GUINEA

Perth

Caroline Is.

PHILIPPINES

INDONESIA

Manila

VIETNAM

Jakarta

INDIAN OCEAN

BRUNEI

Ho Chi Minh City

Singapore

MALAYSIA

Kuala Lumpur

East from Greenwich

West from Greenwich

Map 10

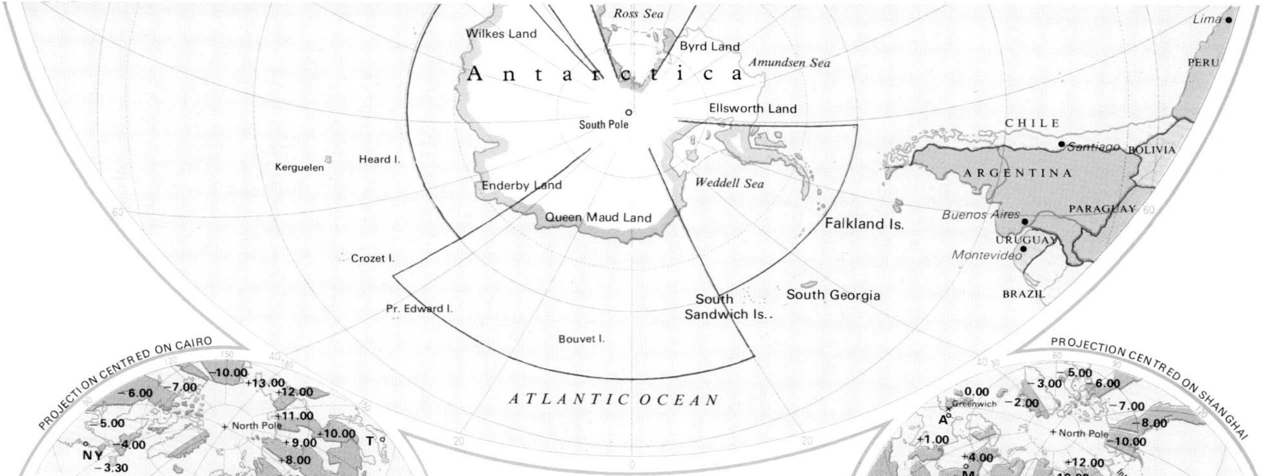

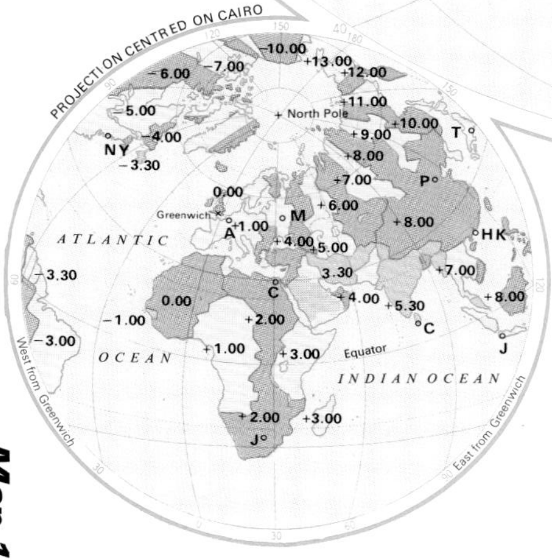

Map 11

1:120 000 000

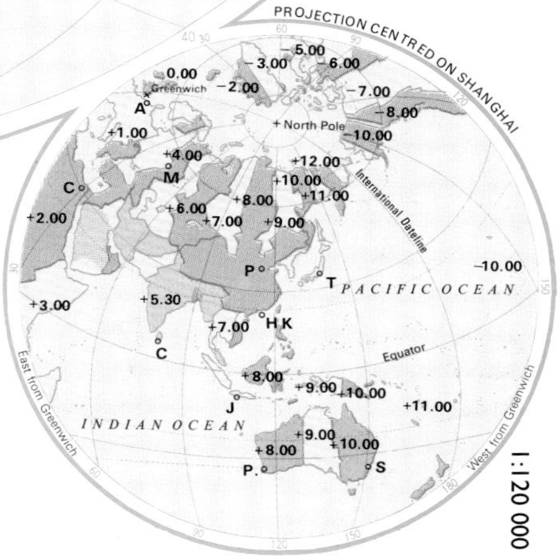

PROJECTION CENTRED ON SHANGHAI

West from Greenwich

East from Greenwich

PACIFIC OCEAN

INDIAN OCEAN

International Dateline

North Pole

Greenwich

Equator

−10.00 −8.00 −7.00 −6.00 −5.00 −3.00 −2.00 0.00 +1.00 +2.00 +3.00 +4.00 +5.30 +6.00 +7.00 +8.00 +9.00 +10.00 +11.00 +12.00

A° C° M° P° HK° T° J° C° S° P°

COPYRIGHT GEORGE PHILIP & SON LTD

TIME ZONES

• Capital Cities

| 9.00 | 6.00 | Time zone in hours fast (+) or slow (−) of Greenwich Mean Time |

Standard Time not the Zone hour

No Official Time

PERU • Lima

CHILE

BOLIVIA

Santiago •

ARGENTINA

PARAGUAY

URUGUAY

Buenos Aires •

Montevideo •

BRAZIL

Falkland Is.

South Georgia

South Sandwich Is.

Ross Sea
Byrd Land
Amundsen Sea
Ellsworth Land
Weddell Sea
Wilkes Land
Antarctica
South Pole
Queen Maud Land
Enderby Land
Bouvet I.
Pr. Edward I.
Crozet I.
Heard I.
Kerguelen

ATLANTIC OCEAN

PROJECTION CENTRED ON CAIRO

West from Greenwich

East from Greenwich

ATLANTIC OCEAN

INDIAN OCEAN

Equator

North Pole

Greenwich

−10.00 +13.00 +12.00 +11.00 +10.00 +9.00 +7.00 +6.00 +5.30 +4.00 +3.30 +3.00 +2.00 +1.00 0.00 −1.00 −3.00 −4.00 −5.00 −6.00 −7.00

NY° A° M° C° P° HK° T° J°

3.30 −3.00 −3.30

11

Arctic

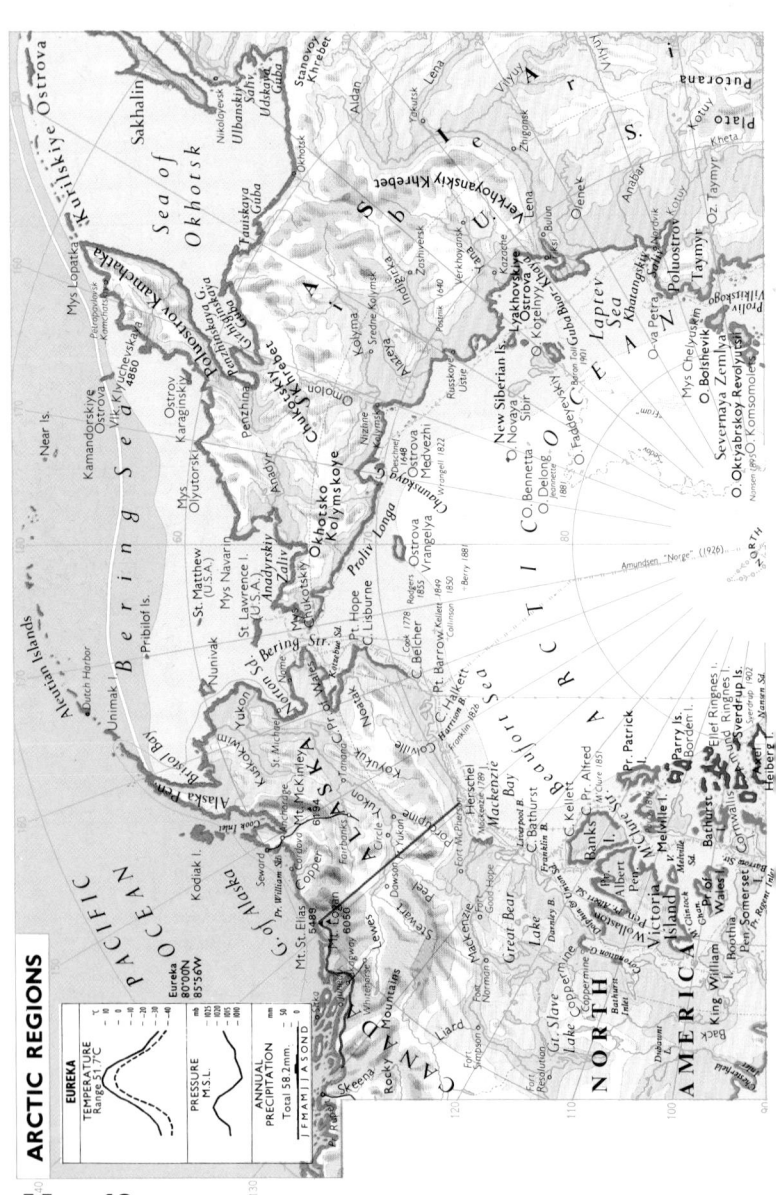

ARCTIC REGIONS

EUREKA
TEMPERATURE
Range 51.7°C

PRESSURE
M.S.L.

ANNUAL
PRECIPITATION
Total 58.2mm
J F M A M J J A S O N D

Eureka
80°00N
85°56W

Map 12

1:42 000 000

Progress of Exploration

Coasts explored before 1800
    ,,   ,, between 1800 & 1850
    ,,   ,, between 1850 & 1900
    ,,   ,, since 1900

Highest latitudes reached by explorers with date

+ Byrd 1926

Seas open all year

Extreme limits of drift-ice

Seas covered by pack-ice in Spring

Seas permanently covered by pack-ice

ice caps and permanent ice shelf

Arctic Explorers

Cook 1778
Franklin 1826-47
McClure 1850-53
Nansen (Fram) 1893-96
Sverdrup 1902
Peary 1892-1906
Amundsen 1903-6 & 1926
Bernier 1906-1913
Peary 1908-9
Knud Rasmussen 1912
Stefánsson 1914-15
Byrd 1926 (by air)
Wilkins 1928 (by air)
Lindsay 1934
Sedov 1937-40
Papanin (Drift of Soviet Expedition) 1937-8
Knuth (Danish Peary-land Expedition) 1948-49
Skate (Nuclear submarine) 1959
Manhattan (Tanker) 1969

Map 13

13

Antarctic

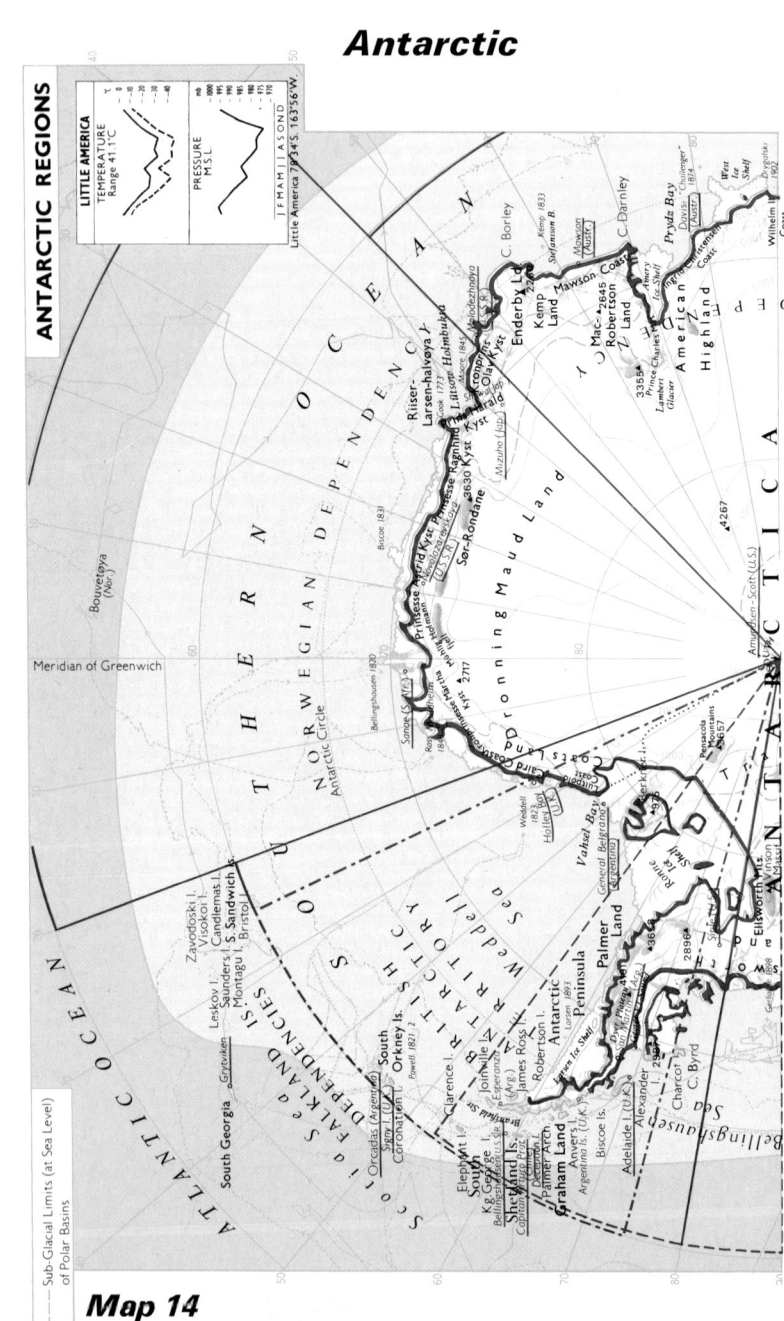
ANTARCTIC REGIONS
LITTLE AMERICA
TEMPERATURE
Range 41.1°C
PRESSURE
M.S.L.
J F M A M J J A S O N D
Little America 78°34'S. 163°56'W.
Sub-Glacial Limits (at Sea Level) of Polar Basins
Meridian of Greenwich
ATLANTIC OCEAN
SOUTHERN OCEAN
NORWEGIAN DEPENDENCY
FALKLAND IS. DEPENDENCIES
BRITISH ANTARCTIC TERRITORY
Weddell Sea
Bellingshausen Sea
ANTARCTICA
Bouvetøya
(Nor.)
South Georgia
Grytviken
S. Sandwich Is.
Zavodoski I.
Visokoi I.
Candlemas I.
Leskov I.
Saunders I.
Montagu I.
Bristol I.
South Orkney Is.
Orcadas (Argentina)
Signy I. (U.K.)
Coronation I.
Powell 1821-2
South Shetland Is.
Elephant I.
Kg. George I.
Clarence I.
Joinville I.
James Ross I.
Robertson I.
Esperanza (Arg.)
Bransfield Str.
Graham Land
Palmer Arch.
Anvers I.
Argentina Is. (U.K.)
Biscoe Is.
Adelaide I. (U.K.)
Alexander I.
Charcot I.
C. Byrd
Antarctic Peninsula
Larsen 1893
Larsen Ice Shelf
Palmer Land
Dyer Plateau
General San Martin (Arg.)
Vahsel Bay
General Belgrano (Argentina)
Holley Bay (U.K.)
Weddell 1823
Luitpold Coast
Coats Land
Caird Coast
Ronne Ice Shelf
Ellsworth Mts.
Vinson Massif
Pensacola Mountains
Amundsen-Scott (U.S.)
Dronning Maud Land
Prinsesse Martha Kyst
Prinsesse Astrid Kyst
Prinsesse Ragnhild Kyst
Prins Harald Kyst
Kronprins Olav Kyst
Sør-Rondane
Novolazarevskaya (U.S.S.R.)
Mizuho (Jap.)
Showa (Jap.)
Molodezhnaya (U.S.S.R.)
Sanae (S. Afr.)
Bellingshausen 1820
Biscoe 1831
Cook 1773
Moore 1845
Riiser-Larsen-halvøya
Lützow Holmbukta
Enderby Ld.
C. Borley
Kemp Land
Kemp 1833
Mawson Coast
Mawson (Austr.)
Robertson Land
C. Darnley
Amery Ice Shelf
Prince Charles Mts.
Lambert Glacier
Prydz Bay
Davis (Austr.)
Ingrid Christensen Coast
American Highland
West Ice Shelf
Wilhelm II Coast
Drygalski 1902
Antarctic Circle

Map 14

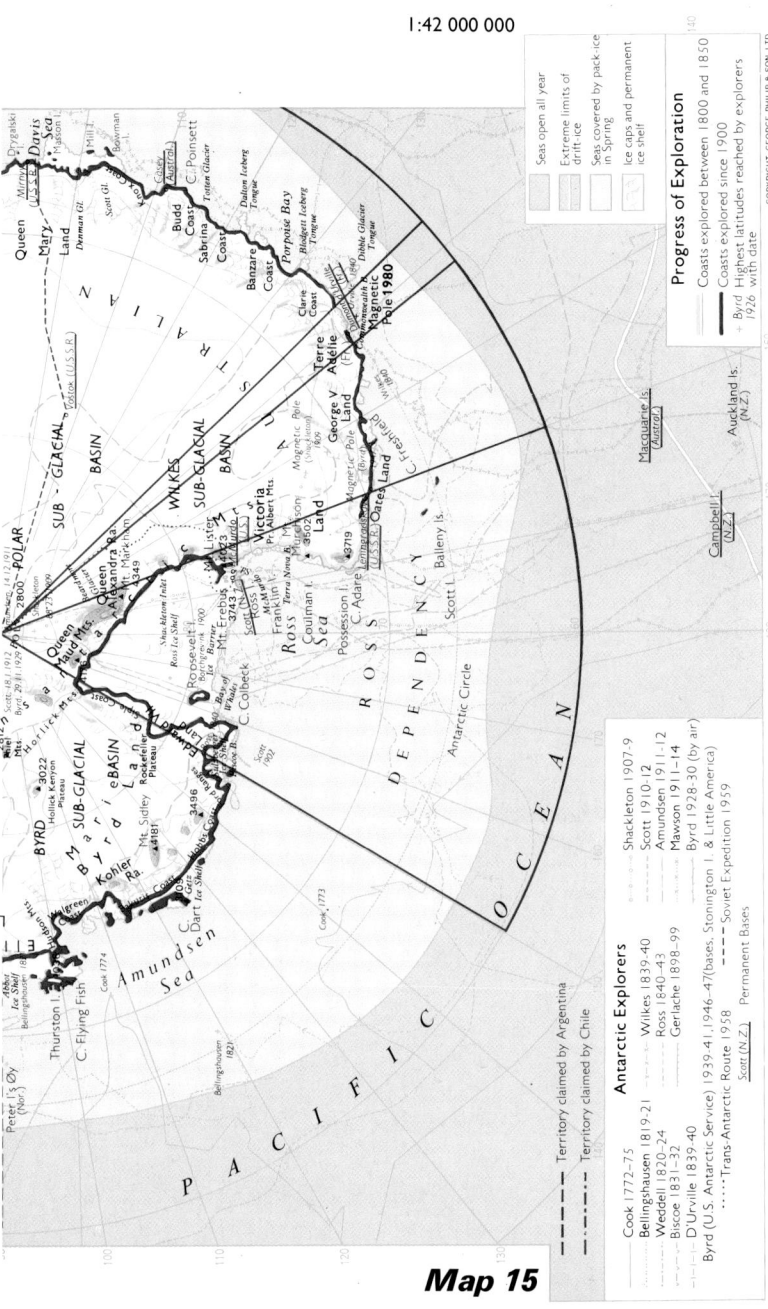

1:42 000 000

Progress of Exploration

Seas open all year

Extreme limits of
drift-ice

Seas covered by pack-ice
in Spring

Ice caps and permanent
ice shelf

Coasts explored between 1800 and 1850

Coasts explored since 1900

+Byrd Highest latitudes reached by explorers
1926 with date

COPYRIGHT GEORGE PHILIP & SON LTD

Antarctic Explorers

Cook 1772–75
Bellingshausen 1819–21
Weddell 1820–24
Biscoe 1831–32
D'Urville 1839–40
Wilkes 1839–40
Ross 1840–43
Gerlache 1898–99

Shackleton 1907–9
Scott 1910–12
Amundsen 1911–12
Mawson 1911–14
Byrd 1928–30 (by air)

Byrd (U.S. Antarctic Service) 1939–41, 1946–7(bases, Stonington I. & Little America)
Scott (N.Z.) Permanent Bases

Territory claimed by Argentina
Territory claimed by Chile

······ Trans-Antarctic Route 1958
– – – Soviet Expedition 1959

Map 15

Europe: *Physical*

Iceland
Hekla 1491▲
Öroefa Jökull 2119

NORWEGIAN SEA

Arctic Circle

Vesterålen
Lofoten
2123
Kebnek

Faroe Is.

Fisher Bank

Shetland Is.

Scandinavia
Ume
Indals
Galdhøpiggen ▲2469

Rockall

ATLANTIC

Hebrides

Orkney Is.

British Isles
Ben Nevis 1347▲

Lindesnes

Skagerrak

Kattegat

Mälaren
Vänern
Gotland
Vättern

BALTIC

Valentia I.

Irish Sea

Ireland

Great Britain

C. Clear

Snowdon 1085▲

NORTH SEA

Dogger Bank

Heligoland

Jutland

North

OCEAN

Land's End

Thames

English Channel

Netherlands

Elbe

Weser

Wista (Vistula)

Odra (Oder)

Harz 1142

Sudeten

Brittany

Loire

Seine

Meuse
Ardennes
Eifel
Wester wald
Taunus

Hunsruck

Rhine

Erz Geb.

Moravian Heights

Bay of Biscay

1861

Gironde

Vosges
Jura
Black For.
Bohemian For.
Danube
Inn

Bakony For.

C. Finisterre

Mt. Dore▲ 1886
Central Massif

Garonne

Cévennes

Rhône

Mt. Blanc ▲ 4807

ALPS

Po

Drava
Danube

Sava

Cantabrian Mts.

Pyrenees

Old Castile

Pico de Aneto 4404

Douro

Sa. da Estrela
Iberian

Sa. de Guadarrama

G. of Lions

Ligurian Sea

Apennines

Dinaric Alps

ADRIATIC SEA

Str. of Otranto

C. da Roca
Tejo (Tagus)

New Castile
Peninsula

Balearic Is.

Corsica

Str. of Bonifacio

Tiber

Gran Sasso ▲2914

Sierra Morena

C. St. Vincent

Guadalquivir

Andalusia

Sa. Nevada 3478

Sardinia

Vesuvius ▲1277

Tyrrhenian Sea

Ionian

C. Trafalgar
C. Spartel

Str. of Gibraltar

MEDITERRANEAN

C. Blanco

Str. of Messina

Calabria

Ionian Sea

Er Rif

Maritime Atlas

C. Bon

Sicily
Etna ▲3263

SEA

West from Greenwich 0 East from Greenwich

Malta

Map 16

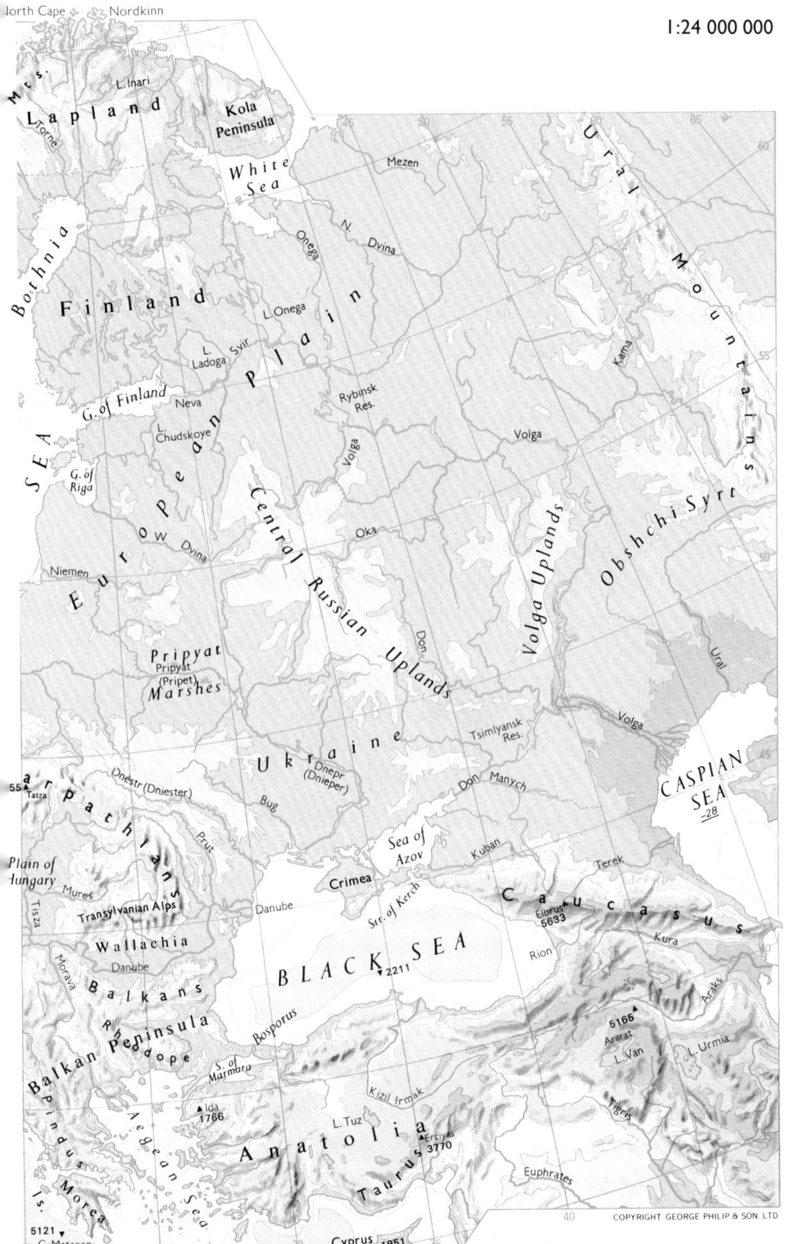

North Cape ◇ Nordkinn

1:24 000 000

Mts.
Lapland
Torne
L.Inari
Kola
Peninsula

White
Sea

Mezen

Bothnia

Finland

Onega
N. Dvina

L.Onega

Ural Mountains

L.
Ladoga
Svir

European Plain

G. of Finland
Neva

Rybinsk
Res.

SEA
L.
Chudskoye

Volga

Volga

Kama

G. of
Riga

W. Dvina

Central Russian Uplands

Oka

Volga Uplands

Obshchi Syrt

Niemen

Pripyat
Pripyat
(Pripet)
Marshes

Don

Ural

Ukraine

Volga

Tsimlyansk
Res.

CASPIAN
SEA
-28

Dnestr (Dniester)

Dnepr
(Dnieper)

Don
Manych

55

Carpathians

Tatra

Bug

Prut

Sea of
Azov

Crimea

Kuban

Terek

Plain of
Hungary

Mures

Danube

Str. of Kerch

Caucasus

Elbrus
5633

Tisza

Transylvanian Alps

Wallachia

Rion

Kura

Moraya

Danube

BLACK SEA

2211

Balkans

Bosporus

5166

Arax

Balkan Peninsula

Rhodope

S. of
Marmara

Ararat
L. Van

L. Urmia

Pindus

Aegean Sea

Kizil Irmak

Tigris

Ida
1766

L. Tuz

Is.

Morea

Anatolia

Erciyes
3770

5121
C. Matapan

Taurus

Euphrates

Crete

Cyprus
1951

COPYRIGHT GEORGE PHILIP & SON LTD

Map 17

17

Europe: Political

ICELAND
Reykjavík
Akureyri
Húsavík
Arctic Circle
ATLANTIC OCEAN
Føroyar (Den.)
Shetland Is.
Orkney Is.
Hebrides
UNITED KINGDOM
SCOTLAND
Inverness
Aberdeen
Dundee
Glasgow
Edinburgh
Londonderry
N.I.
Belfast
Isle of Man
Carlisle
Newcastle
IRELAND
Galway
Limerick
Dublin
Cork
C. Clear
Manchester
Liverpool
Leeds
York
Hull
Sheffield
WALES
Swansea
Cardiff
Birmingham
ENGLAND
Norwich
Bristol
LONDON
Southampton
Portsmouth
Plymouth
Dover
Scilly Is.
English Channel
NORTH SEA
NORWAY
Kristiansund
Trondheim
Bergen
Lillehammer
Oslo
Drammen
Stavanger
Skagerrak
Kattegat
Tromsø
Narvik
Luleälv
SWEDEN
Östersund
Indalsälven
Sundsvall
Gävle
Uppsala
STOCKHOLM
Vänern
Örebro
Eskilstuna
Göteborg
Vättern
Jönköping
Kalmar
Karlskrona
Malmö
G. of
DENMARK
Ålborg
Århus
Esbjerg
KØBENHAVN
BALTIC
Flensburg
Kiel
Rostock
Hamburg
Bremen
Elbe
Hannover
BERLIN
Groningen
NETHERLANDS
Amsterdam
's-Gravenhage
Rotterdam
Oostende
Antwerpen
BELGIUM
BRUSSEL
Lille
Calais
LUX.
Luxembourg
Metz
GERMANY
Dortmund
Essen
Köln
Bonn
Wiesbaden
Mainz
Frankfurt
Würzburg
Nürnberg
Magdeburg
Halle
Leipzig
Karl-Marx-Stadt
Dresden
Stuttgart
München
Freiburg
Strasbourg
Rhine
Meuse
POLAND
Szczecin
Gdynia
Gdańsk
Bydgoszcz
Wisła
Poznań
Łódź
Wrocław
Częstochowa
Katowice
Odra
PRAHA
Plzeň
CZECHOSLOVAKIA
Brno
Ostrava
Bratislava
Dunau
Linz
WIEN
AUSTRIA
Salzburg
Innsbruck
Graz
BUDAPEST
HUNGARY
Pécs
Cherbourg
Le Havre
Rouen
Seine
Brest
Rennes
Caen
Reims
PARIS
Le Mans
Loire
Nantes
Tours
Orléans
FRANCE
Dijon
Mulhouse
Basel
Zürich
Bern
SWITZERLAND
Genève
Limoges
Clermont-Ferrand
Périgueux
St. Étienne
Lyon
Grenoble
Bordeaux
Bayonne
Garonne
Toulouse
Montpellier
Rhône
Avignon
Perpignan
Sète
Marseille
Toulon
Nice
Monaco
BAY OF BISCAY
La Coruña
C. Finisterre
Oviedo
Santander
San Sebastián
Bilbao
Vigo
Porto
Douro
Coimbra
Duero
Valladolid
Ebro
Andorra
PORTUGAL
LISBOA
Tajo
MADRID
SPAIN
Toledo
Guadiana
Badajoz
Zaragoza
Barcelona
Valencia
Islas Baleares
Menorca
Mallorca
Palma
Ibiza
Córdoba
Sevilla
Guadalquivir
Lagos
Murcia
Alicante
Cádiz
Málaga
Granada
Almería
Cartagena
Str. of Gibraltar
Gibraltar (Br.)
Tanger
Ceuta (Sp.)
MOROCCO
Rabat
Meknes
Fès
Melilla (Sp.)
Tlemcen
Oran
Alger
Blida
ALGERIA
Constantine
Skikda
Annaba
Binzert
TUNISIA
Tunis
Milano
Trento
Bréscia
Torino
Génova
La Spezia
Trieste
Venézia
Bologna
Ravenna
San Marino
Firenze
Livorno
ITALY
Corse
Ajaccio
Sassari
Sardegna
Cagliari
ROMA
Tevere
Nápoli
Bari
Taranto
Brindisi
Tyrrhenian Sea
Palermo
Messina
Réggio
Sicilia
Catánia
Pantelleria (Ital.)
MALTA
Ionian Sea
MEDITERRANEAN SEA
ADRIATIC SEA
YUGOSLAVIA
Ljubljana
Zagreb
Rijeka
Sarajevo
Split
Dubrovnik
Tirana
ALBANIA
Kérkira
West from Greenwich
East from Greenwich

Map 18

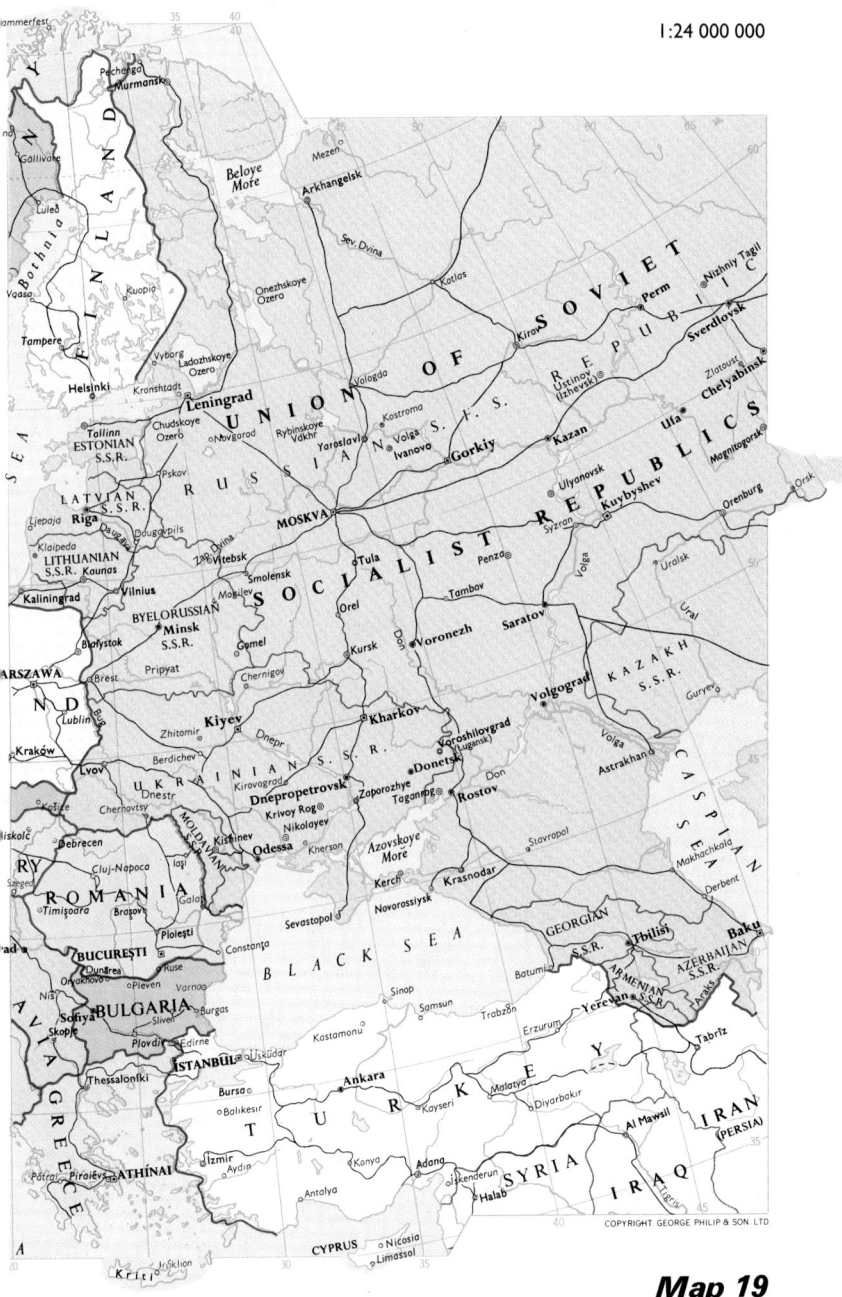

1:24 000 000

Map 19

COPYRIGHT GEORGE PHILIP & SON. LTD

C. Malin
I. Tory
Portrush
North Channel
22
Coleraine
Aran I.
Derryveagh Mts.
Londonderry
Antrim Mts.
Letterkenny
Lifford
Ballymena
Larne
Stranraer
Wigtown
Donegal
Antrim
NORTHERN IRELAND
Bangor
Donegal Bay
L. Neagh
Belfast
Mull of Galloway
Killala Bay
Bundoran
L. Erne
Omagh
Erris Hd.
Blackwater
Lisburn
Sligo
Enniskillen
Armagh
Downpatrick
Upper L. Erne
Dundrum
Ballina
ISLE OF MAN
Monaghan
Newry
Mourne Mts.
Clones
L. Conn
Douglas
Achill I.
Leitrim
Clare I.
Castlebar
Carrick-on-Shannon
Cavan
Dundalk
Greenore
Westport
Longford
L. Mask
Ceanannus Mor
Drogheda
IRISH S
Roscommon
An Uaimh
Connemara
L. Ree
Mullingar
Boyne
L. Corrib
Balbriggan
Athlone
IRELAND
Galway
Dublin
Galway Bay
Athenry
Tullamore
Anglesey
Liffey
(Baile Atha Cliath)
Holyhead
Dun Laoghaire
Bray
Naas
Kildare
Birr
Caernarfon Bay
Port Laoise
Wicklow Mts.
Athy
L. Derg
Wicklow
Ennis
Nenagh
Pwllheli
Carlow
Loop Hd.
Kilrush
Limerick
Thurles
Kilkenny
Arklow
Golden Vale
Shannon
Listowel
Cardigan Bay
Tipperary
Enniscorthy
Rath Luirc
Carrick-on-Suir
Clonmel
New Ross
Tralee
Wexford
Waterford
Rosslare
Mallow
Blackwater
Macgillycuddy's Reeks
Fermoy
Killarney
1040
Dungarvan
Cahirciveen
Carnsore Pt.
St. George's Channel
Fishguard
Cardigan
Youghal
Blarney
Cork
St. David's Hd.
Lee
Tywi
Cobh
Bandon
Bantry
Kinsale
Haverfordwest
Cork Harbour
Carmarthen
Castletown Bere
Llanelli
Milford Haven
Pembroke
C. Clear
Bristol C
Lundy I.
Hartland Point
Bude
St. Austell
Devonport
Truro
Camborne
Penzance
Falmouth
Land's End
Scilly Is.
Lizard
10
50
8

Map 20

British Isles: *South*

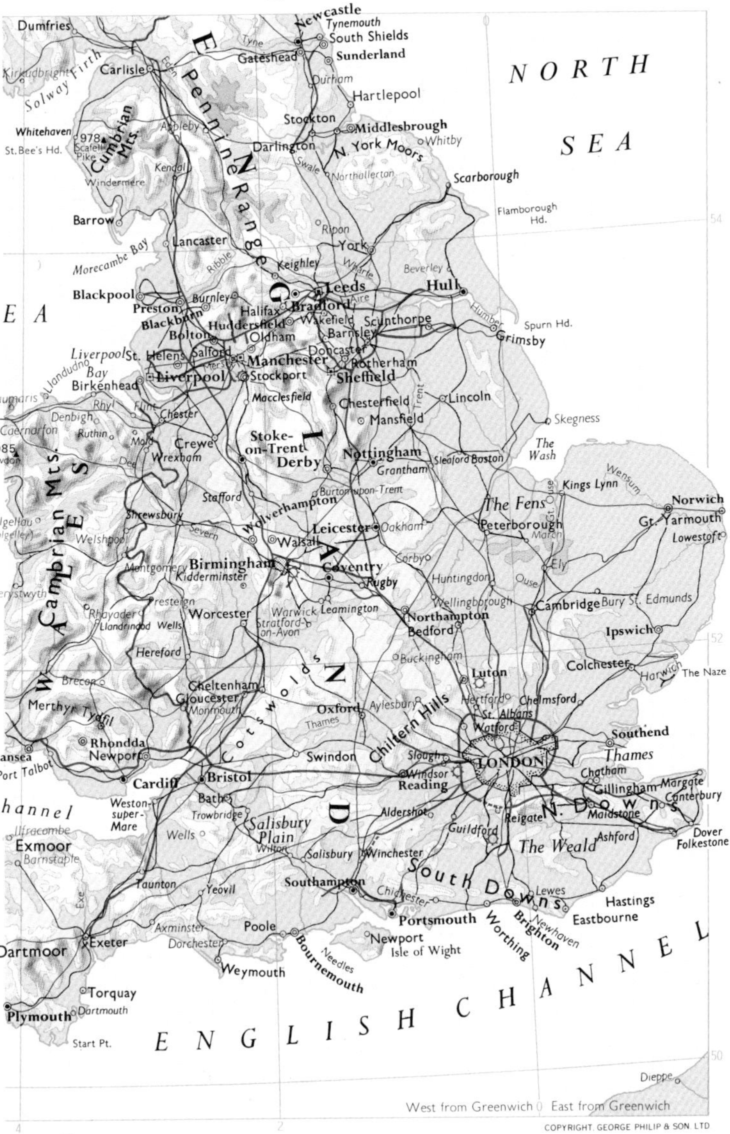

1:4 000 000

Map 21

British Isles: North

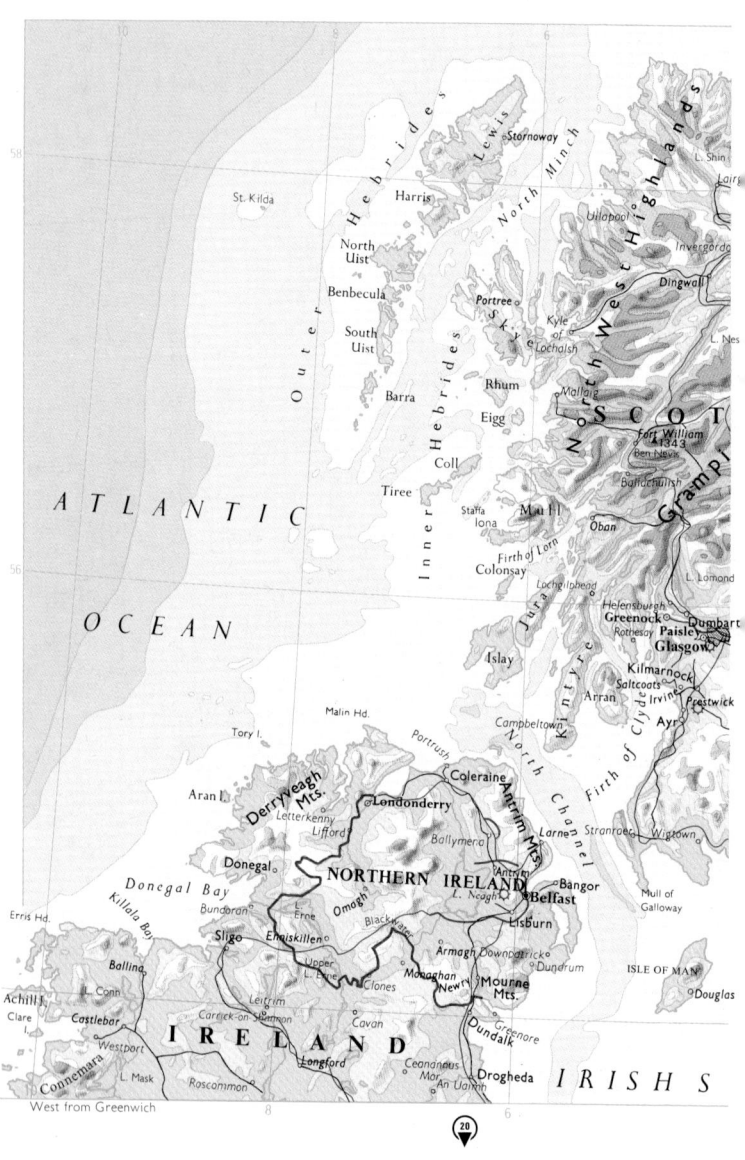

ATLANTIC
OCEAN
Outer Hebrides
Inner Hebrides
St. Kilda
Lewis
Stornoway
Harris
North Minch
North Uist
Benbecula
South Uist
Barra
Skye
Portree
Kyle of Lochalsh
Rhum
Eigg
Coll
Tiree
Staffa
Iona
Mull
Firth of Lorn
Colonsay
Jura
Islay
Kintyre
Arran
North West Highlands
L. Shin
Lairg
Ullapool
Invergordon
Dingwall
L. Ness
Mallaig
SCOT
Fort William
1343
Ben Nevis
Ballachulish
Grampi
Oban
L. Lomond
Lochgilphead
Helensburgh
Greenock
Dumbart
Rothesay
Paisley
Glasgow
Kilmarnock
Saltcoats
Irvine
Prestwick
Ayr
Campbeltown
Firth of Clyde
North Channel
Stranraer
Wigtown
Mull of Galloway
ISLE OF MAN
Douglas
Malin Hd.
Tory I.
Portrush
Coleraine
Aran I.
Derryveagh Mts.
Letterkenny
Lifford
Londonderry
Antrim Mts.
Ballymena
Larne
Donegal
Donegal Bay
NORTHERN IRELAND
Antrim
L. Neagh
Bangor
Belfast
Killala Bay
Bundoran
Omagh
L. Erne
Blackwater
Lisburn
Erris Hd.
Sligo
Enniskillen
Armagh
Downpatrick
Dundrum
Ballina
Upper L. Erne
Clones
Monaghan
Newry
Mourne Mts.
L. Conn
Achill I.
Leitrim
Clare I.
Castlebar
Carrick-on-Shannon
Cavan
Greenore
Dundalk
Westport
IRELAND
Longford
Ceanannus Mor
An Uaimh
Drogheda
IRISH S
Connemara
L. Mask
Roscommon
West from Greenwich
10
8
6
58
56
20

Map 22

1 : 4 000 000

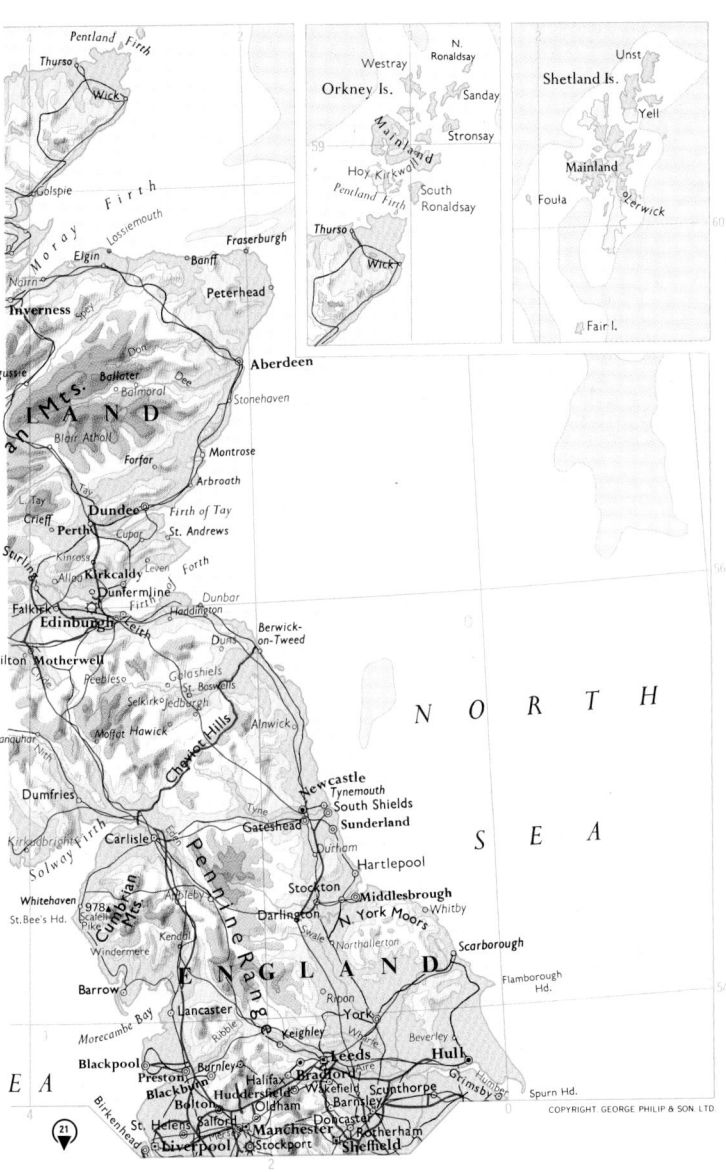

Pentland Firth
Thurso
Wick
Golspie
Moray Firth
Lossiemouth
Fraserburgh
Elgin
Nairn
Banff
Peterhead
Inverness
gussie
GRAMPIAN Mts.
Ballater
Balmoral
Stonehaven
Blair Atholl
Forfar
Montrose
Crieff
L. Tay
Dundee
Firth of Tay
Arbroath
Perth
Cupar
St. Andrews
Stirling
Kinross
Leven
Forth
Allo
Kirkcaldy
Falkirk
Dunfermline
Dunbar
ilton
Edinburgh
Leith
Haddington
Motherwell
Duns
Berwick-on-Tweed
Peebles
Galashiels
St. Boswells
Selkirk
Jedburgh
anquhar
Moffat
Hawick
Cheviot Hills
Alnwick
Dumfries
Newcastle
Tynemouth
Carlisle
Gateshead
Tyne
South Shields
Sunderland
Kirkcudbright
Solway Firth
Durham
Hartlepool
Whitehaven
978
Appleby
Stockton
Middlesbrough
St.Bee's Hd.
Scafell Pike
Cumbrian Mts.
Darlington
Swale
N. York Moors
Whitby
Kendal
Northallerton
Windermere
Scarborough
ENGLAND
Barrow
Ripon
Flamborough Hd.
Morecambe Bay
Lancaster
York
Ribble
Keighley
Wharfe
Beverley
Blackpool
Preston
Barnsley
Halifax
Bradford
Leeds
Hull
Humber
Blackburn
Huddersfield
Wakefield
Scunthorpe
Grimsby
Bolton
Oldham
Barnsley
Spurn Hd.
Birkenhead
St. Helens
Salford
Doncaster
Liverpool
Stockport
Manchester
Rotherham
Sheffield

Westray
N. Ronaldsay
Orkney Is.
Sanday
Mainland
Stronsay
Hoy
Kirkwall
South
Pentland Firth
Ronaldsay
Thurso
Wick

Shetland Is.
Unst
Yell
Mainland
Foula
Lerwick
Fair I.

NORTH

SEA

COPYRIGHT GEORGE PHILIP & SON LTD

Southern England

Map 24

1:2 000 000

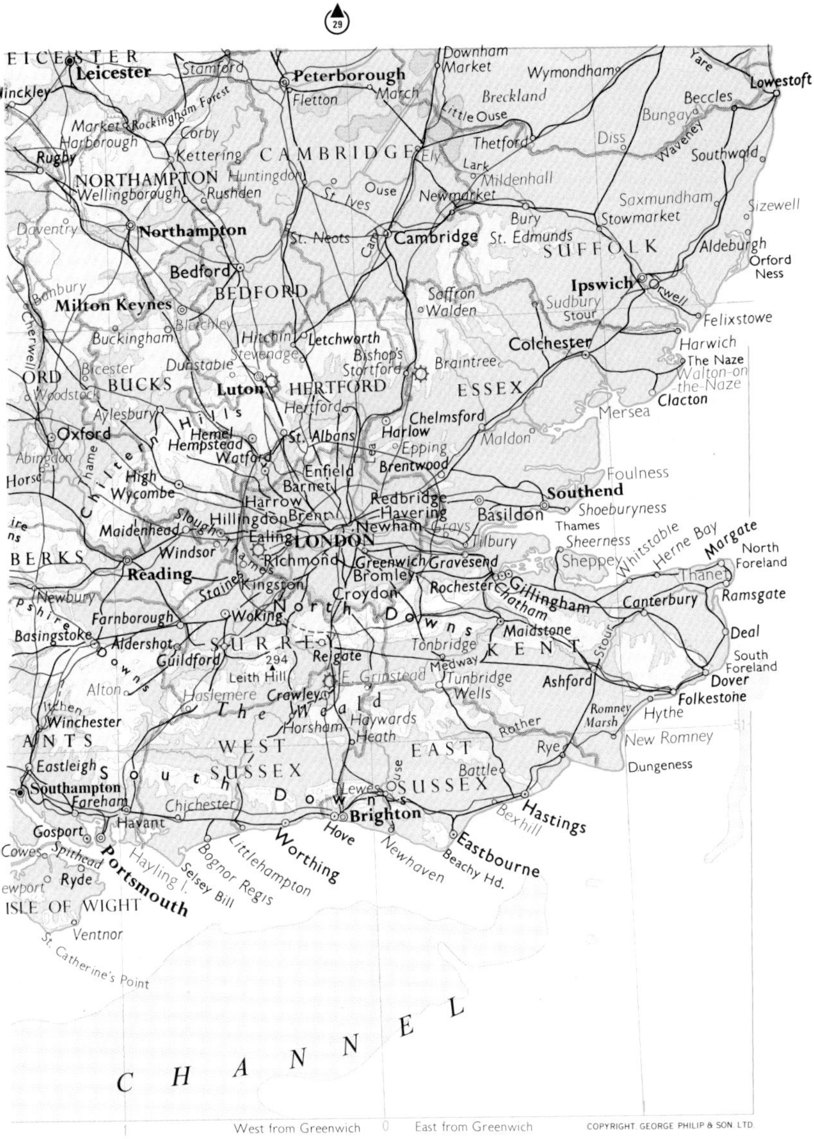

West from Greenwich   0   East from Greenwich   COPYRIGHT GEORGE PHILIP & SON LTD.

Map 25

Wales and South West England

28

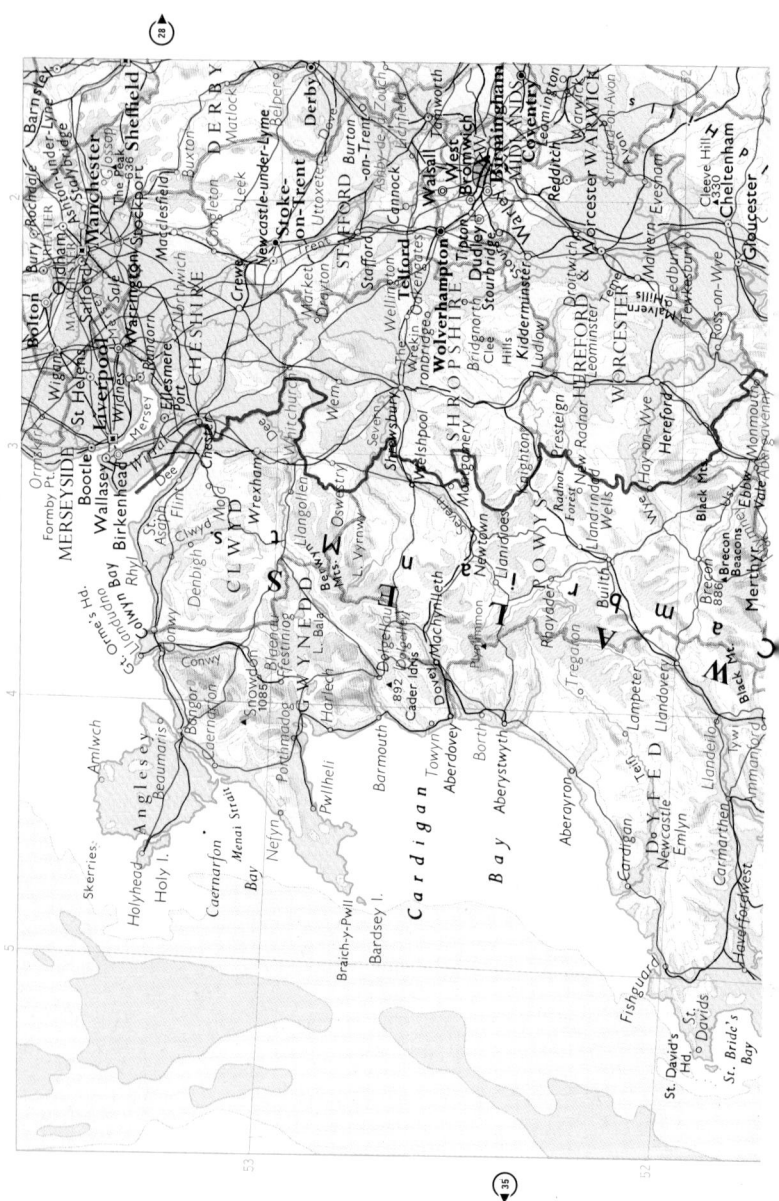

MERSEYSIDE
Liverpool
St Helens
Wigan
Bolton
Bury
Rochdale
Oldham
Manchester
Salford
Stockport
Ashton-under-Lyne
Stalybridge
Barnsley
Sheffield
Glossop
The Peak
636
Warrington
Widnes
Runcorn
Sale
Macclesfield
Ellesmere Port
Bootle
Wallasey
Birkenhead
Formby Pt.
Ormskirk
Wirral
Mersey
Dee
Chester
CHESHIRE
Northwich
Crewe
Congleton
Buxton
Leek
DERBY
Matlock
Belper
Derby
Dove
Newcastle-under-Lyme
Stoke-on-Trent
Uttoxeter
Burton-on-Trent
Trent
STAFFORD
Stafford
Cannock
Lichfield
Tamworth
Ashby-de-la-Zouch
Walsall
West Bromwich
Birmingham
Coventry
Leamington
Warwick
WARWICK
Stratford-on-Avon
Avon
Redditch
Worcester
Evesham
Cleeve Hill
330
Cheltenham
Gloucester
Tewkesbury
Malvern
Malvern Hills
Ledbury
Ross-on-Wye
Droitwich
Kidderminster
Stourbridge
Dudley
Tipton
Wolverhampton
Telford
Wellington
The Wrekin
Oakengates
Ironbridge
Bridgnorth
Clee Hills
Ludlow
Leominster
HEREFORD & WORCESTER
Teme
Hereford
Hay-on-Wye
Monmouth
Abergavenny
Market Drayton
Whitchurch
Wem
Shrewsbury
Severn
SHROPSHIRE
Welshpool
Montgomery
Oswestry
Wrexham
Llangollen
CLWYD
Mold
Flint
St. Asaph
Rhyl
Denbigh
Colwyn Bay
Llandudno
Great Orme's Hd.
Conwy
Bangor
Caernarfon
Anglesey
Amlwch
Beaumaris
Holyhead
Holy I.
Skerries
Menai Strait
Caernarfon Bay
Nefyn
Pwllheli
Porthmadog
Snowdon
1085
Blaenau Ffestiniog
GWYNEDD
Bala
L. Bala
Berwyn Mts.
L. Vyrnwy
Harlech
Barmouth
Dolgellau
892
Cader Idris
Dovey
Machynlleth
Towyn
Aberdovey
Borth
Aberystwyth
Plynlimon
Llanidloes
Newtown
Knighton
Presteign
New Radnor
Radnor Forest
Llandrindod Wells
Builth Wells
Rhayader
POWYS
Wye
Black Mts.
Brecon
Brecon Beacons
886
Usk
Ebbw Vale
Merthyr
Black Mt.
Tregaron
Lampeter
Llandovery
Llandeilo
Ammanford
Tywi
Aberayron
Teifi
DYFED
Cardigan
Newcastle Emlyn
Carmarthen
Haverfordwest
Fishguard
St. Davids
St. David's Hd.
St. Bride's Bay
Cardigan Bay
Bardsey I.
Braich-y-Pwll
WALES
53
52
2
3
4
5

35

Map 26

Map 27

1:2 000 000

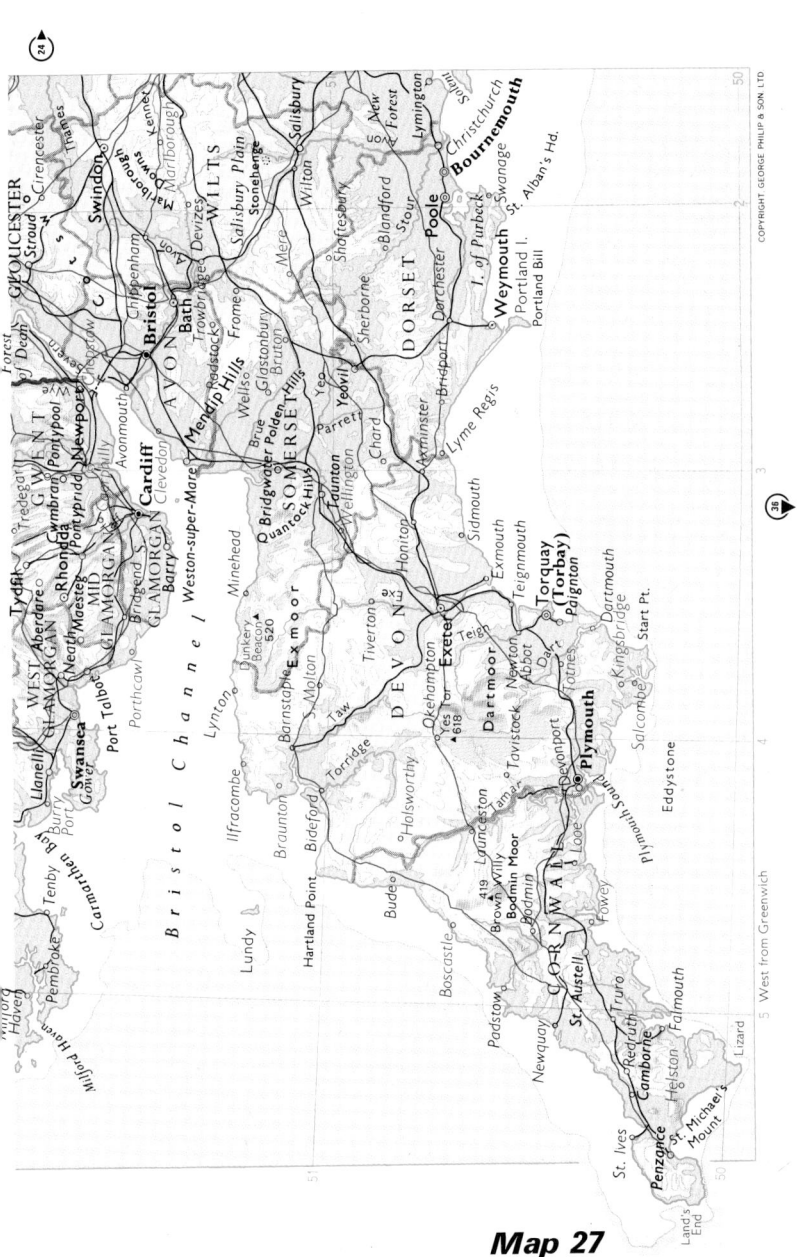

Milford Haven
Pembroke
Tenby
Carmarthen Bay
Llanelli
Burry Port
Swansea
Gower
Port Talbot
Neath
WEST GLAMORGAN
Aberdare
Tydfil
Rhondda
Maesteg
MID GLAMORGAN
Porthcawl
Bridgend
S. GLAMORGAN
Barry
Cardiff
Pontypridd
Caerphilly
Tredegar
GWENT
Cwmbran
Pontypool
Newport
Wye
Forest of Dean
Chepstow
Severn
Avonmouth
GLOUCESTER
Stroud
Cirencester
Thames
Swindon
Chippenham
Marlborough Downs
Marlborough
Kennet
Bristol
Clevedon
AVON
Bath
Weston-super-Mare
Mendip Hills
Radstock
Trowbridge
Devizes
Avon
WILTS
Frome
Salisbury Plain
Stonehenge
Bristol Channel
Lynton
Lundy
Ilfracombe
Minehead
Dunkery Beacon
520
Braunton
Barnstaple
Exmoor
Wells
Brue
Glastonbury
Bruton
Bridgwater
Polden Hills
Quantock Hills
SOMERSET
Mere
Salisbury
Wilton
Hartland Point
Bideford
S. Molton
Taunton
Wellington
Parrett
Yeo
Yeovil
Shaftesbury
Torridge
Taw
Tiverton
Chard
Sherborne
New Forest
Bude
Holsworthy
DEVON
Exe
Honiton
Blandford
Stour
DORSET
Lymington
Okehampton
Yes Tor
618
Exeter
Axminster
Bridport
Dorchester
Poole
Solent
Boscastle
Lyme Regis
Christchurch
Bournemouth
Launceston
Dartmoor
Teign
Sidmouth
I. of Purbeck
419
Brown Willy
Bodmin Moor
Padstow
Tamar
Tavistock
Exmouth
Weymouth
Swanage
Newton Abbot
Teignmouth
Portland I.
St. Alban's Hd.
Bodmin
Portland Bill
Newquay
CORNWALL
Devonport
Dart
Torquay
(Torbay)
Paignton
St. Austell
Looe
Totnes
Plymouth
Fowey
Dartmouth
St. Ives
Truro
Redruth
Plymouth Sound
Kingsbridge
Camborne
Salcombe
Start Pt.
Penzance
Helston
Falmouth
Eddystone
Land's End
St. Michael's Mount
Lizard
51
50
5
4
3
2
West from Greenwich

24

36

Northern England

31
34
26
24
NORTHUMBERLAND
Morpeth
Blyth
Newcastle
Wallsend
Blaydon
Gateshead
Sunderland
Consett
Durham
DURHAM
Bishop Auckland
Barnard Castle
Darlington
Richmond
Northallerton
Swale
Wensleydale
Ure
Nidd
Ripon
NORTH YORKSHIRE
Knaresborough
Harrogate
Keighley
Bradford
W. YORKSHIRE
Halifax
Dewsbury
Huddersfield
Barnsley
Sheffield
Chesterfield
DERBY
Matlock
Belper
Derwent
Derby
Dove
Burton -on-Trent
Lichfield
Tamworth
Nuneaton
Coventry
Birmingham
W. MIDLANDS
West Bromwich
Walsall
Dudley
Tipton
Stourbridge
Warley
Stour
Wolverhampton
Cannock
Stafford
STAFFORD
Uttoxeter
Trent
Stoke-on-Trent
Newcastle-under-Lyme
Leek
Congleton
Buxton
The Peak 636
Glossop
Macclesfield
Stockport
Manchester
GREATER MANCHESTER
Oldham
Ashton-under-Lyne
Stalybridge
Rochdale
Bury
Bolton
Salford
Sale
Calder
Accrington
Burnley
Nelson
Colne
Skipton
Settle
Ribble
Blackburn
Chorley
Wigan
St Helens
Warrington
Runcorn
Widnes
Mersey
Liverpool
Bootle
Wallasey
Birkenhead
Wirral
MERSEYSIDE
Formby Pt.
Ormskirk
Southport
Lytham-St. Annes
Preston
LANCASHIRE
Fylde
Blackpool
Cleveleys
Fleetwood
Forest of Bowland
Lancaster
Morecambe
Heysham
Morecambe Bay
Whernside 737
Ingleborough 723
Pen-y-Ghent 693
704 Gt. Whernside
Lune
Kendal
Windermere
Ambleside
Ulverston
Furness
Barrow-in-Furness
Walney I.
Millom
Seascale
Sca Fell 978
Cumbrian Mts.
Whitehaven
St. Bee's Hd.
Keswick
Derwentwater
Derwent
Workington
Maryport
Skiddaw 931
Helvellyn 950
CUMBRIA
Penrith
Ullswater
Shap
Appleby
Brough
Tees
Cross Fell 893
Alston
S. Tyne
Eden
Carlisle
Silloth
Solway Firth
Gretna Green
Annan
Dumfries
Hadrian's Wall
Hexham
Tyne
N. Tyne
Wear
Pennines
Newton Stewart
Castle Douglas
Dalbeattie
Kirkcudbright
Dee
Wigtown
Wigtown Bay
Whithorn
Pt. of Ayre
Ramsey
Snaefell 620
ISLE OF MAN
Peel
Douglas
Port Erin
Castletown
IRISH SEA
Skerries
Amlwch
Holyhead
Holy I.
Anglesey
Beaumaris
Gt. Orme's Hd.
Llandudno
Colwyn Bay
Rhyl
Conwy
Bangor
Caernarfon
Caernarfon Bay
Menai Strait
Snowdon 1085
Nefyn
Porthmadog
Blaenau Ffestiniog
Pwllheli
Bardsey I.
GWYNEDD
Harlech
L. Bala
Barmouth
892 Cader Idris
Dolgellau (Dolgelley)
Towyn
Aberdovey
Dovey
Machynlleth
WALES
Berwyn Mts.
L. Vyrnwy
Llangollen
Oswestry
Welshpool
Montgomery
Newtown
Severn
Shrewsbury
SHROPSHIRE
Bridgnorth
Ironbridge
The Wrekin
Wellington
(Telford)
Oakengates
Wem
Whitchurch
Market Drayton
Wrexham
Mold
CLWYD
Denbigh
Clwyd
St. Asaph
Flint
Dee
Chester
Ellesmere Port
CHESHIRE
Northwich
Crewe
55
54
53
4
3
West from Greenwich

Map 28

1:2 000 000

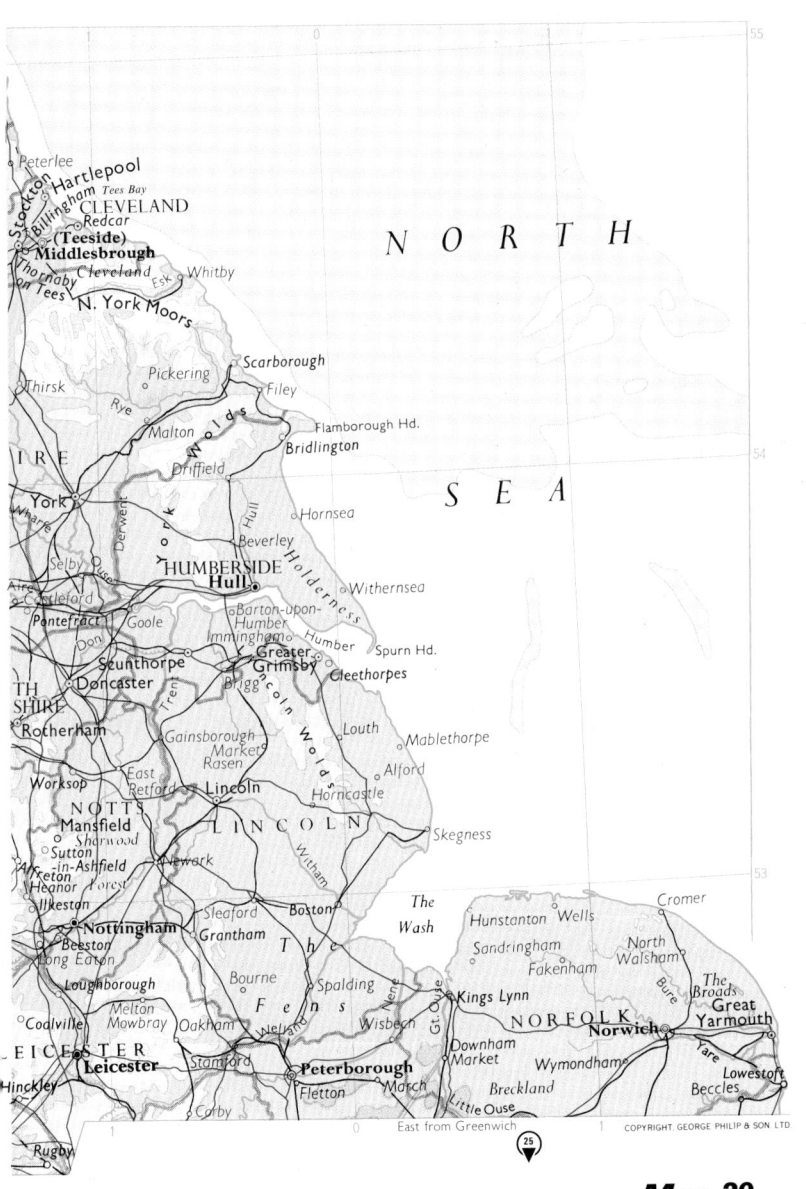
55
54
53
1
0
1
NORTH
SEA
Peterlee
Hartlepool
Stockton
Billingham
Tees Bay
CLEVELAND
Redcar
(Teeside)
Middlesbrough
Thornaby on Tees
Cleveland
Esk
Whitby
N. York Moors
Scarborough
Pickering
Thirsk
Filey
Rye
Malton
York Wolds
Flamborough Hd.
Bridlington
IRE
Driffield
York
Wharfe
Derwent
Hull
Hornsea
Beverley
Holderness
Selby
Ouse
HUMBERSIDE
Hull
Withernsea
Aire
Castleford
Pontefract
Goole
Barton-upon-Humber
Immingham
Humber
Spurn Hd.
Don
Scunthorpe
Greater Grimsby
Cleethorpes
Doncaster
Trent
Brigg
Lincoln Wolds
TH
SHIRE
Rotherham
Louth
Mablethorpe
Gainsborough
Market Rasen
Alford
East Retford
Worksop
Lincoln
Horncastle
NOTTS
Mansfield
LINCOLN
Skegness
Sherwood
Sutton-in-Ashfield
Forest
Newark
Witham
Alfreton
Heanor
Ilkeston
Nottingham
Sleaford
Boston
The Wash
Cromer
Hunstanton
Wells
Beeston
Grantham
The Fens
Long Eaton
Sandringham
North Walsham
Fakenham
Loughborough
Bourne
Spalding
Nene
Gt. Ouse
Kings Lynn
Bure
The Broads
Great Yarmouth
Melton Mowbray
Coalville
Oakham
Welland
Wisbech
NORFOLK
Norwich
LEICESTER
Leicester
Stamford
Peterborough
Downham Market
Wymondham
Yare
Lowestoft
Hinckley
March
Breckland
Beccles
Fletton
Little Ouse
Corby
Rugby
East from Greenwich
25

Map 29

Southern Scotland

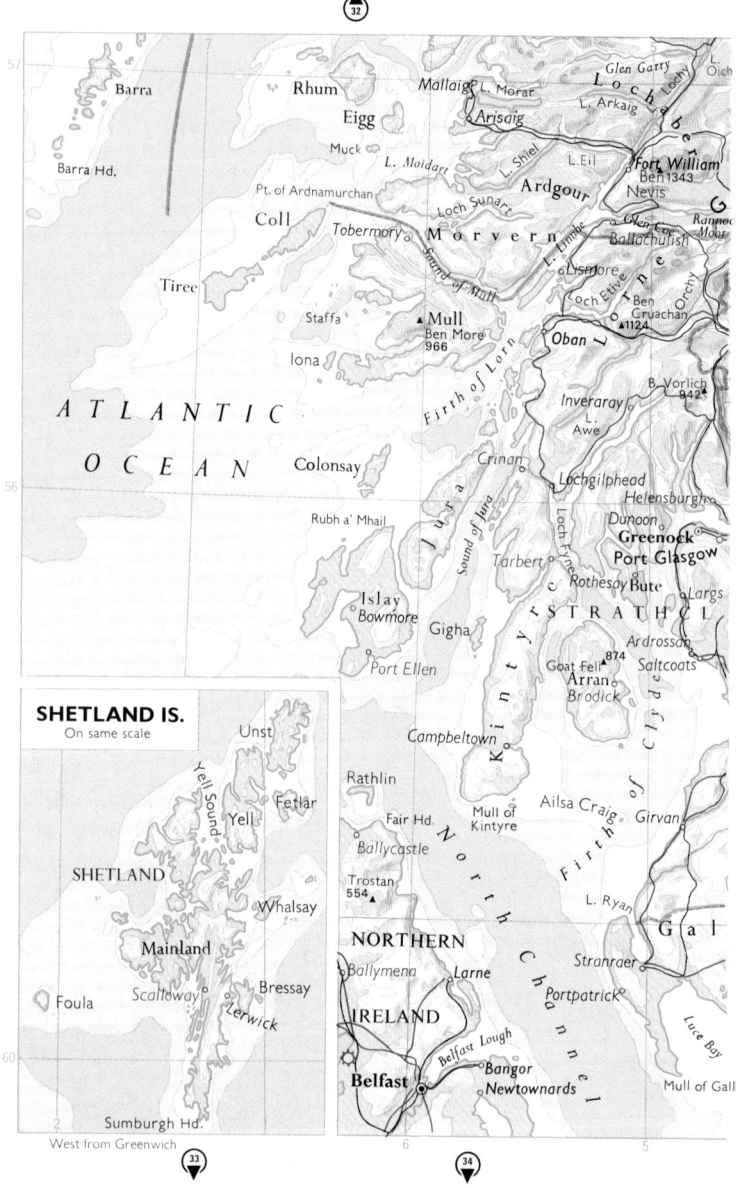

Barra

Rhum

Eigg

Mallaig L. Morar

Glen Garry

Loch

Oich

Arisaig

L. Arkaig

Barra Hd.

Muck

L. Moidart

L. Shiel

L. Eil

Fort William

Pt. of Ardnamurchan

Ben 1343

Nevis

Coll

Tobermory

Loch Sunart

Ardgour

M O R V E R N

Glen Coe

Ranno

Moor

Ballachulish

Tiree

Sound of Mull

L. Linnhe

Lismore

Loch Etive

Ben

Cruachan

▲1124

Orchy

Staffa

▲ Mull

Ben More

966

Oban

A T L A N T I C

Iona

Firth of Lorn

Inveraray

B. Vorlich

941▲

L.

Awe

O C E A N

Colonsay

Crinan

Lochgilphead

Helensburgh

Rubh a' Mhail

J u r a

Sound of Jura

Dunoon

Greenock

Port Glasgow

Tarbert

Loch Fyne

Rothesay Bute

Largs

Islay

Bowmore

Gigha

S T R A T H C L

Port Ellen

Ardrossan

Goat Fell ▲ 874

Saltcoats

Arran

Brodick

Firth of Clyde

Campbeltown

SHETLAND IS.
On same scale

Unst

Rathlin

Ailsa Craig

Girvan

Yell Sound

Fetlar

Fair Hd.

Mull of

Kintyre

Yell

Ballycastle

N o r t h   C h a n n e l

SHETLAND

Trostan

554 ▲

L. Ryan

Whalsay

NORTHERN

Stranraer

G a l

Mainland

Ballymena

Larne

Bressay

Foula

Scalloway

Lerwick

IRELAND

Portpatrick

Luce Bay

Belfast Lough

Mull of Gall

Belfast

Bangor

Newtownards

Sumburgh Hd.

West from Greenwich

Map 30

1:2 000 000

33

Kingussie
Newtonmore
Cairn Toul
1292
Ben Macdhui
1311
Ballater
Aboyne
Banchory
Balmoral
Braemar
Stonehaven
Glen Spean
Badenoch
Grampian Highlands
Lochnagar
1154
N. Esk
Forest of Atholl
Tilt
Braes of Angus
Laurencekirk
Inverbervie
Garry
Blair Atholl
Strathmore
Brechin
Montrose
L. Rannoch
L. Tummel
Pass of Killiecrankie
Pitlochry
Kirriemuir
S. Esk
Isla
Tay
Alyth
Forfar
Aberfeldy
Blairgowrie
Sidlaw Hills
Arbroath
Ben Lawers
1214
L. Tay
Dunkeld
Tay
Dundee
Broughty Ferry
NORTH SEA
Breadalbane
Killin
TAYSIDE
Scone
Carse of Gowrie
Firth of Tay
Tayport
L. Earn
Crieff
Perth
Earn
St. Andrews
Ben More
1174
B. Vorlich
983
Cupar
FIFE
Fife Ness
L. Katrine
Callander
Ochil Hills
Kinross
L. Leven
Leven
Anstruther
974
Ben Lomond
Trossachs
CENTRAL
Forth
Dunblane
Cowdenbeath
Glenrothes
Lochgelly
Buckhaven
L. Lomond
Stirling
Alloa
Bannockburn
Kirkcaldy
Firth of Forth
Dunfermline
Bass Rock
Bo'ness
Prestonpans
North Berwick
Grangemouth
Rosyth
Dunbar
Cumbernauld
Falkirk
Linlithgow
Leith
Haddington
Dumbarton
Kirkintilloch
Edinburgh
LOTHIAN
Musselburgh
St. Abbs Hd.
Eyemouth
Clydebank
Glasgow
Airdrie
Livingston
Dalkeith
Renfrew
Paisley
Coatbridge
Bathgate
Pentland Hills
Penicuik
Lammermuir Hills
Duns
Berwick-upon-Tweed
Johnstone
Rutherglen
Motherwell
Wishaw
E. Kilbride
Hamilton
Clyde
Carstairs
Moorfoot Hills
Holy I.
Peebles
Tweed
Galashiels
Coldstream
Flodden
Irvine
Kilmarnock
Lanark
Biggar
Till
Kelso
Melrose
Prestwick
Ayr
Broad Law
840
Ettrick
Selkirk
The Cheviot
816
Ayr
Cumnock
BORDERS
Jedburgh
Hawick
Leadhills
Southern Uplands
Coquet
Doon
Sanquhar
Nith
Moffat
Teviot
Cheviot Hills
Dalmellington
DUMFRIES AND GALLOWAY
Esk
Langholm
N. Tyne
Merrick
843
Lockerbie
Annan
Gretna Green
Ken
Dumfries
ENGLAND
Cree
Galloway
Annan
Hexham
HADRIAN'S WALL
Newton Stewart
Castle Douglas
Dalbeattie
Carlisle
Wigtown
Gatehouse of Fleet
Solway Firth
S. Tyne
Alston
Kirkcudbright
Wear
Wigtown Bay
Whithorn
Cross Fell
893
Derwent
Penrith
Tees
Barnard Castle
Workington
Skiddaw
931
Ullswater
Cumbrian Mts.
57
56
55
4
3
2

28

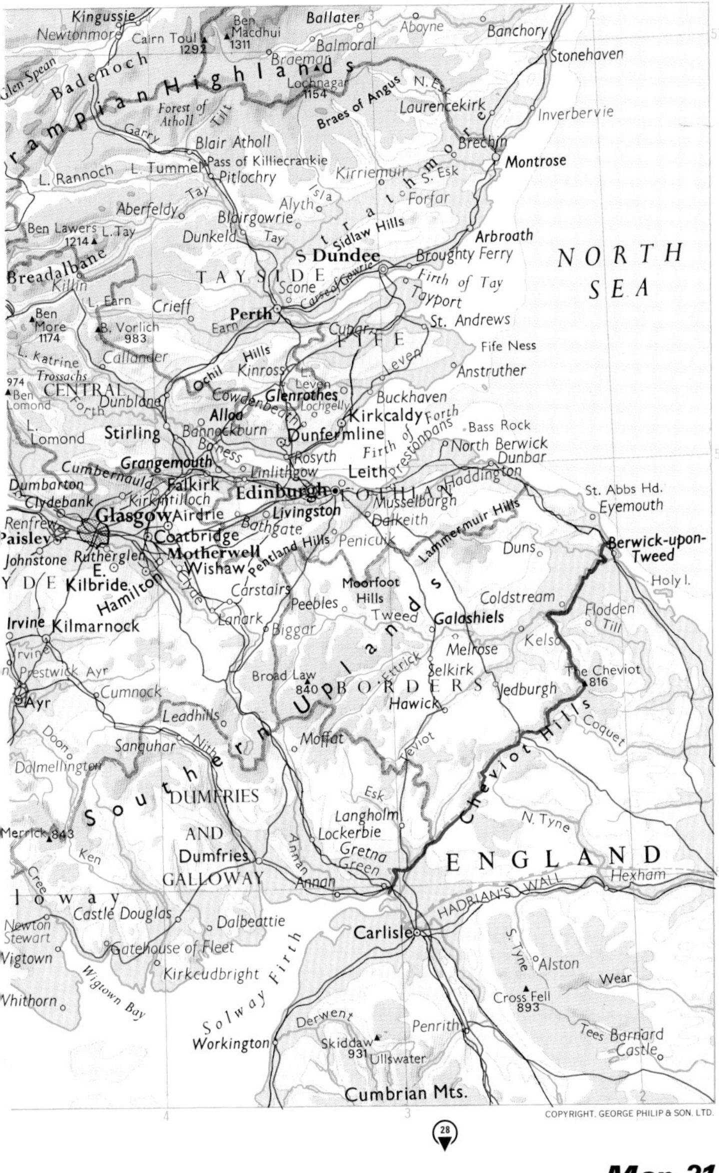

Map 31

Northern Scotland

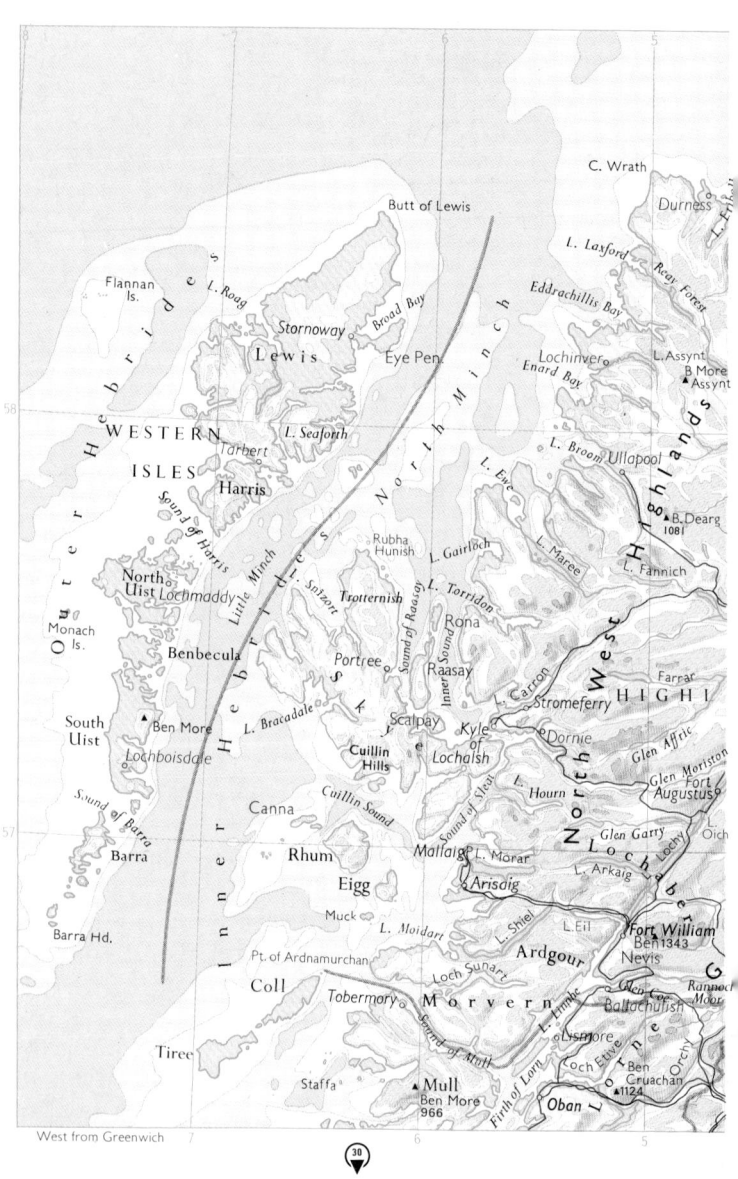

C. Wrath
Durness
L. Laxford
Butt of Lewis
Rear Forest
Eddrachillis Bay
Flannan Is.
L. Roag
Broad Bay
Lochinver
L. Assynt
Stornoway
Enard Bay
B More Assynt
Lewis
Eye Pen.
Hebrides
North Minch
WESTERN
L. Seaforth
L. Broom Ullapool
Tarbert
ISLES
L. Gairloch
L. Ewe
Harris
Rubha Hunish
L. Maree
Sound of Harris
L. Snizort
Trotternish
L. Torridon
L. Fannin
North Uist
Lochmaddy
Little Minch
Sound of Raasay
Rona
Monach Is.
Benbecula
Portree
Raasay
Sky
Inner Sound
Farrar
Carron
Stromeferry
HIGHI
South Uist
Ben More
L. Bracadale
Scalpay
Kyle
Dornie
e
of
Glen Affric
Lochboisdale
Cuillin Hills
Lochalsh
West
L. Hourn
North
Glen Moriston
Fort
Sound of Barra
Cuillin Sound
Canna
Sound of Sleat
Augustus
Barra
Rhum
Mallaig
L. Morar
Glen Garry
Lochabe
Oich
Eigg
Arisaig
L. Arkaig
Muck
L. Moidart
L. Shiel
L. Eil
Fort William
Barra Hd.
Ben 1343
Pt. of Ardnamurchan
Ardgour
Nevis
Ranno
Coll
Loch Sunart
Morvern
Glen
Moor
Tobermory
Ballachulish
Lismore
Tiree
Loch Etive
Sound of Mull
Firth of Lorn
Ben Cruachan
Staffa
Mull
1124
Ben More
966
Oban

1:2 000 000

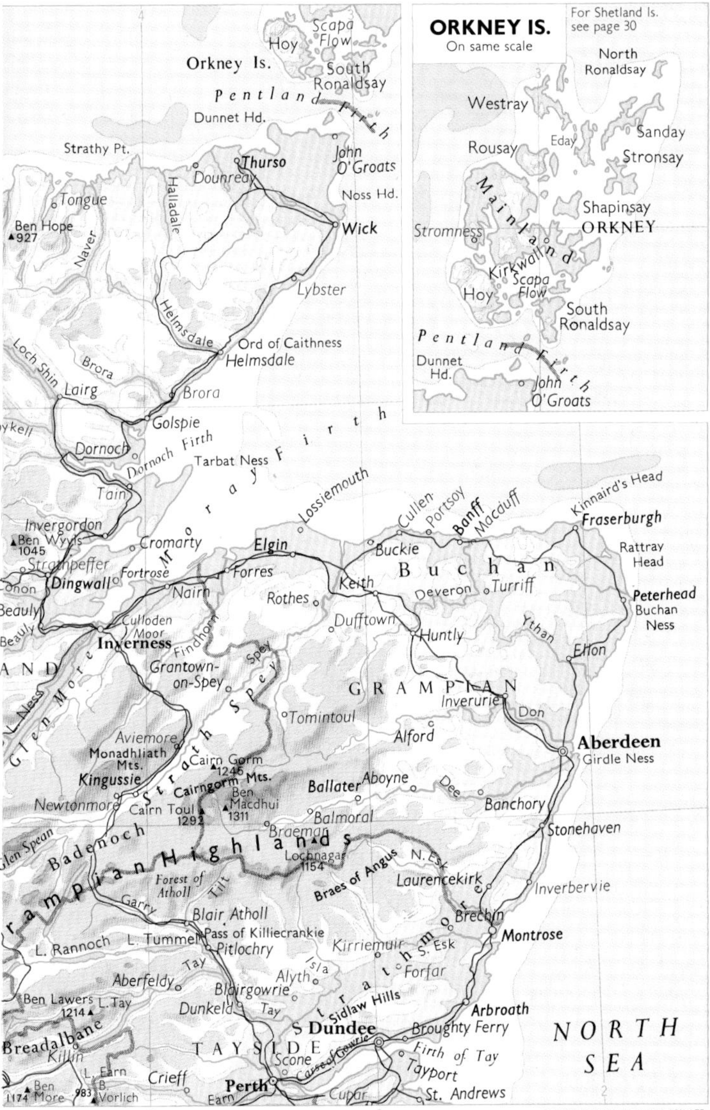

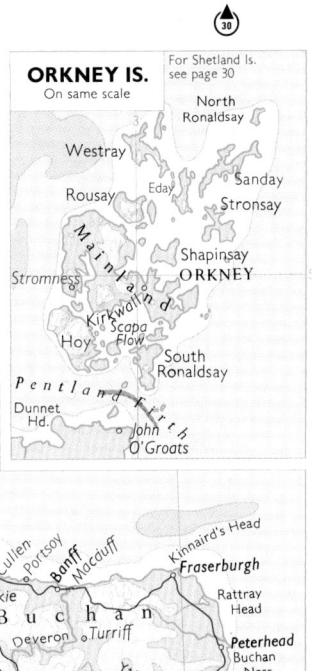

ORKNEY IS.
On same scale

For Shetland Is.
see page 30

Map 33

Ireland

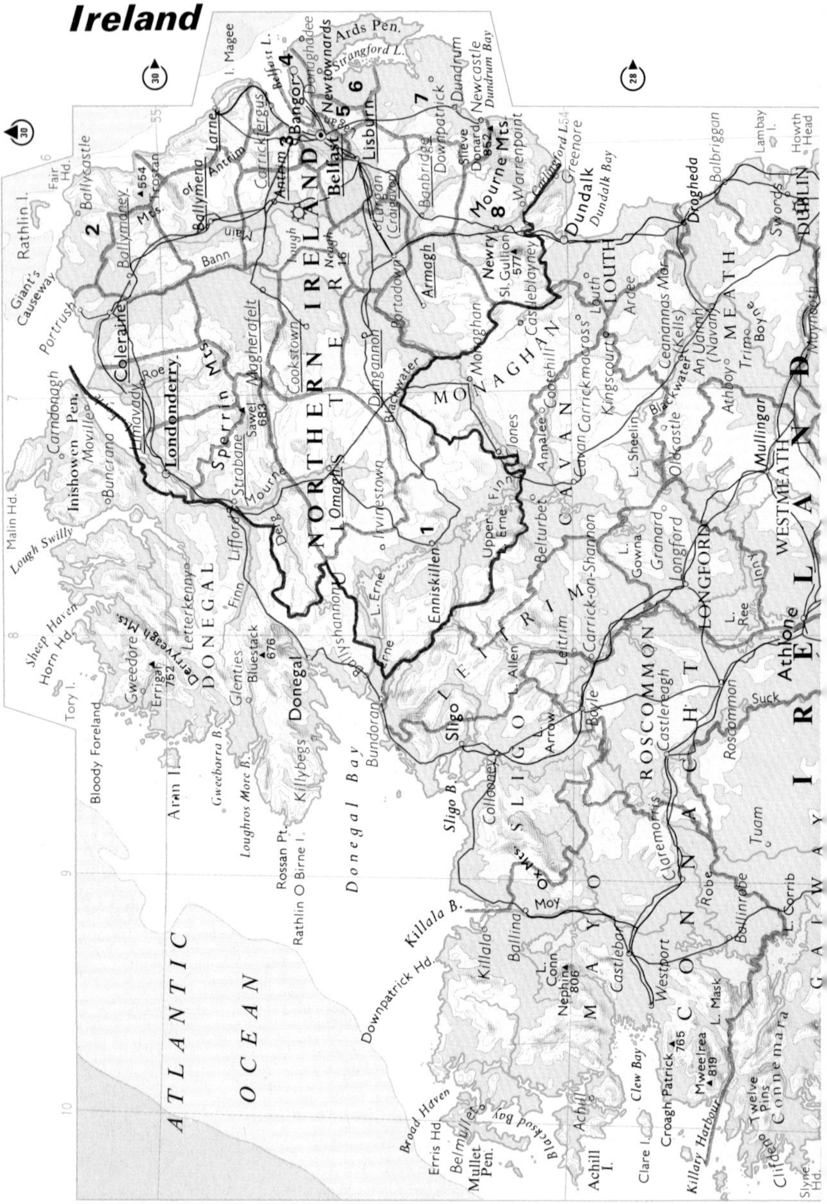

ATLANTIC
OCEAN
NORTHERN IRELAND
DONEGAL
LONDONDERRY
Londonderry
Coleraine
Ballymena
Larne
Antrim
Belfast
Bangor
Newtownards
Lisburn
Armagh
Newry
Dundalk
Drogheda
DUBLIN
Enniskillen
Omagh
Strabane
Sligo
Donegal
Donegal Bay
Killybegs
Letterkenny
Malin Hd.
Lough Swilly
Rathlin I.
Giant's Causeway
Ballycastle
Portrush
Fair Hd.
Ards Pen.
Strangford L.
Mourne Mts.
Sperrin Mts.
Dundrum Bay
Carlingford L.
Dundalk Bay
MONAGHAN
CAVAN
LEITRIM
LOUTH
MEATH
WESTMEATH
LONGFORD
ROSCOMMON
SLIGO
MAYO
CONNACHT
GALWAY
IRELAND
Athlone
Mullingar
Ballina
Castlebar
Westport
Killala B.
Clew Bay
Achill I.
Clare I.
Broad Haven
Erris Hd.
Mullet Pen.
Downpatrick Hd.
Connemara
Twelve Pins
Clifden
Killary Harbour
Croagh Patrick 765
Mweelrea 819
Nephin 806
Errigal 752
Derryveagh Mts.
Bluestack 676
Sawel 683
Slieve Donard 852
Bloody Foreland
Tory I.
Aran I.
Rossan Pt.
Inishowen Pen.
Sheep Haven
Horn Hd.
Lough Neagh
Upper L. Erne
L. Erne
Bundoran
Ballyshannon
Dungannon
Cookstown
Magherafelt
Portadown
Banbridge
Downpatrick
Carrickfergus
Tuam
Roscommon
Boyle
Carrick-on-Shannon
Longford
Granard
Cavan
Monaghan
Kells
Trim
Navan
Balbriggan
Lambay I.
Howth Head

1:2 000 000

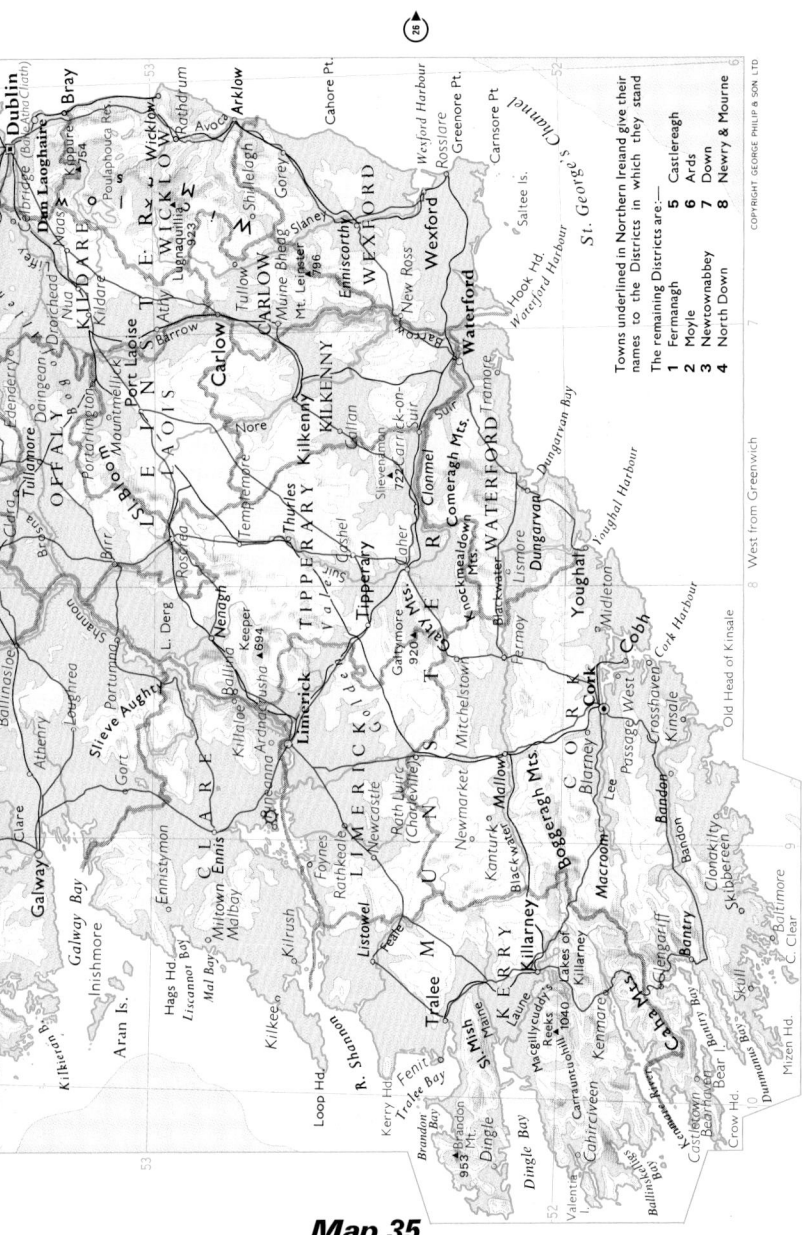

Towns underlined in Northern Ireland give their names to the Districts in which they stand

The remaining Districts are:—

1	Fermanagh	5	Castlereagh
2	Moyle	6	Ards
3	Newtownabbey	7	Down
4	North Down	8	Newry & Mourne

Map 35

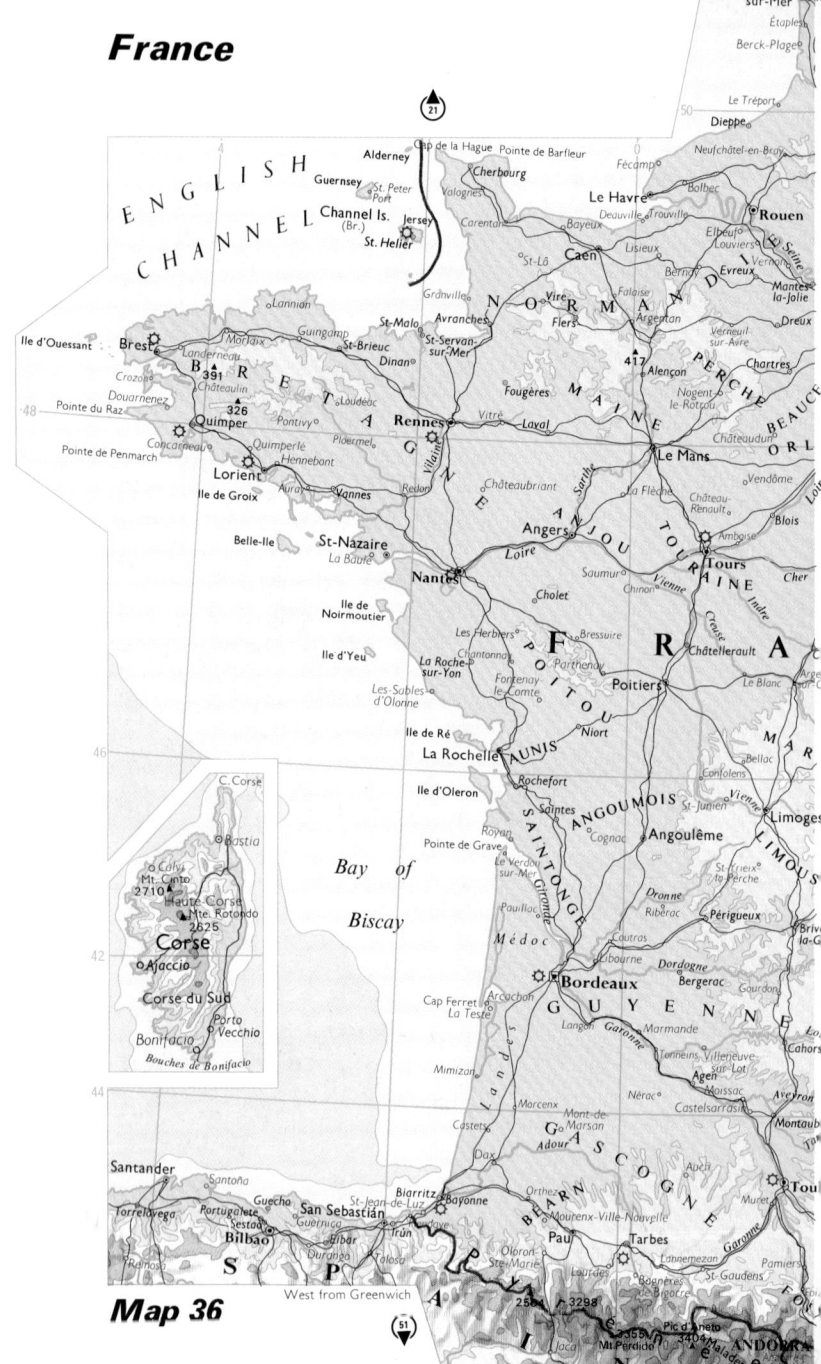

France

Map 36

Cap Gris-Nez
Boulogne-sur-Mer
Étaples
Berck-Plage
Le Tréport
Dieppe
Neufchâtel-en-Bray
50

E N G L I S H C H A N N E L

Alderney
Cap de la Hague   Pointe de Barfleur
Fécamp
Guernsey   St. Peter Port
Cherbourg
Valognes
Neufchâtel-en-Bray
Channel Is. (Br.)
Jersey
St. Helier
Carentan
Bayeux
Deauville-Trouville
Le Havre
Bolbec
Elbeuf
Louviers
Rouen
St-Lô
Caen
Lisieux
Bernay
Evreux
Mantes-la-Jolie
Dreux

Ile d'Ouessant
Brest
Lannion
Morlaix
Guingamp
St-Malo
Granville
Avranches
Virc
Flers
N O R M A N D I E
Falaise
Argentan
Verneuil-sur-Avre
Chartres
Crozon
Landerneau
Châteaulin
B R E T A G N E
Dinan
St-Brieuc
St-Servan-sur-Mer
Fougères
417
Alençon
P E R C H E
Nogent-le-Rotrou
Pointe du Raz
326
Quimper
Pontivy
Loudéac
Rennes
Vitré
Laval
M A I N E
Le Mans
Châteaudun
B E A U C E
O R L
48
Concarneau
Quimperlé
Ploërmel
Châteaubriant
Sarthe
La Flèche
Château-Renault
Vendôme
Blois
Loir
Pointe de Penmarch
Lorient
Hennebont
Auray
Redon
Vilaine
Vannes
Angers
A N J O U
T O U R A I N E
Tours
Amboise
Cher
Ile de Groix
Belle-Ile
St-Nazaire
La Baule
Loire
Saumur
Vienne
Indre
Creuse
Nantes
Cholet
Chinon
F R A N C E
Ile de Noirmoutier
Les Herbiers
Bressuire
Châtellerault
Ile d'Yeu
Chantonnay
Parthenay
P O I T O U
Le Blanc
La Roche-sur-Yon
Fontenay-le-Comte
Poitiers
46
Les Sables-d'Olonne
Niort
M A R
Ile de Ré
A U N I S
Bellac
La Rochelle
Confolens
Rochefort
Saintes
A N G O U M O I S
St-Junien
Vienne
Limoges
Ile d'Oleron
S A I N T O N G E
Cognac
Angoulême
L I M O U S
Pointe de Grave
Royan
St-Yrieix-la-Perche
Bay of Biscay
Le Verdon-sur-Mer
Pauillac
Dronne
Ribérac
Périgueux
Brive-la-G
Médoc
Coutras
Dordogne
Gourdon
Cap Ferret
Arcachon
La Teste
Bordeaux
Libourne
Bergerac
G U Y E N N E
Lo
Cahors
Langon
Garonne
Marmande
Tonneins
Villeneuve-sur-Lot
Mimizan
Nérac
Moissac
Agen
Castelsarrasin
Aveyron
Montaub
44
Morcenx
Mont-de-Marsan
G A S C O G N E
Castets
Dax
Adour
Auch
Mur
Tou
Santander
Santoña
Guecho
St-Jean-de-Luz
Biarritz
Bayonne
Orthez
Mourenx-Ville-Nouvelle
B E A R N
Garonne
Pamiers
Torrelavega
Portugalete
San Sebastián
Oloron-Ste-Marie
Pau
Tarbes
Lannemezan
St-Gaudens
F O
Reinosa
Sestao
Guernica
Irún
Lourdes
Bagnères-de-Bigorre
Bilbao
Eibar
Durango
Tolosa
S P A I N
West from Greenwich
2560
3298
P Y R E N E E S
Jaca
3355
Mt Perdido
Pic d'Aneto
3404
ANDORRA
21
51

Corse

C. Corse
Bastia
Calvi
Mt. Cinto
2710
Haute-Corse
Mte. Rotondo
2625
Corse
Ajaccio
Corse du Sud
Porto-Vecchio
Bonifacio
Bouches de Bonifacio
42

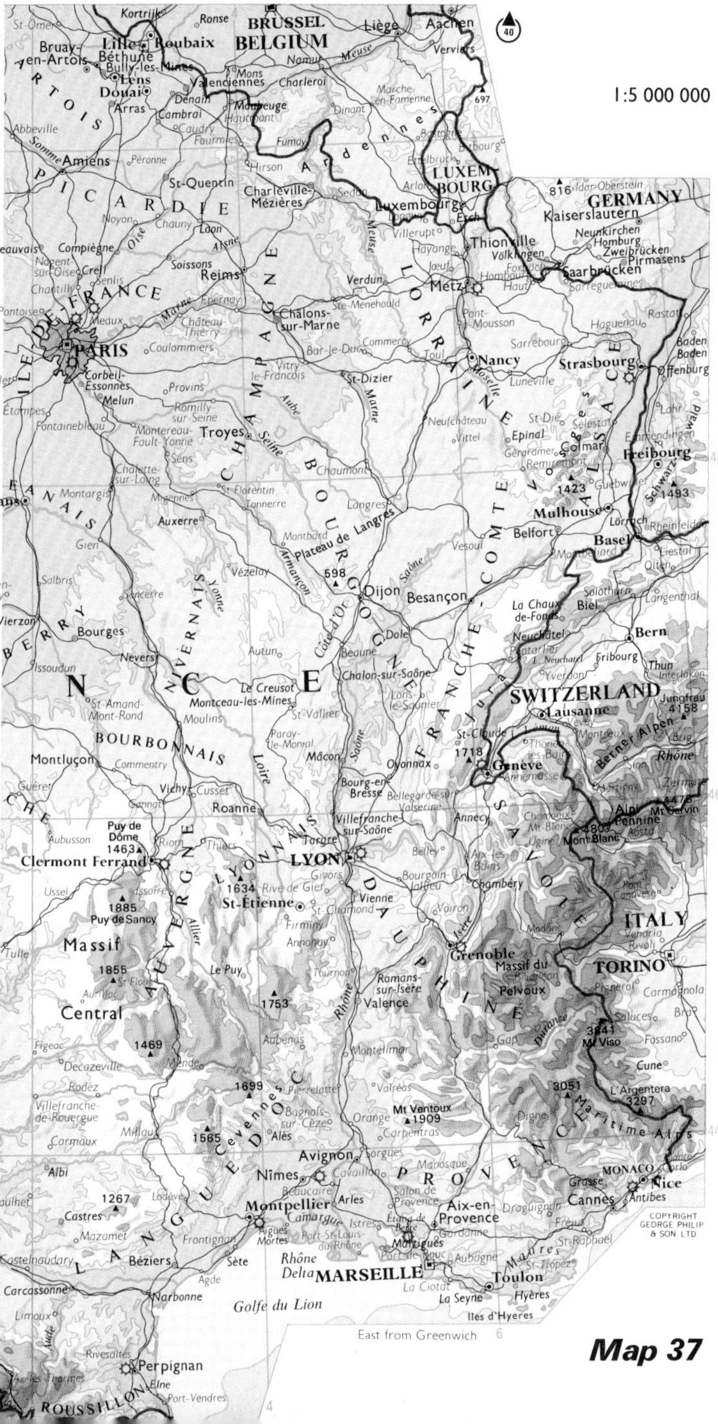
1:5 000 000
40
42
44
46
BRUSSEL
BELGIUM
Kortrijk
Ronse
Liège
Aachen
Verviers
Namur
Meuse
St-Omer
Lille
Roubaix
Bruay-en-Artois
Béthune
Bully-les-Mines
Lens
Douai
Arras
Mons
Valenciennes
Charleroi
Denain
Maubeuge
Hautmont
Cambrai
Caudry
Fourmies
Marche-en-Famenne
Dinant
697
ARTOIS
Abbeville
Somme
Amiens
Péronne
St-Quentin
Hirson
Fumay
Ardennes
Bastogne
Bitbourg
Ettelbruck
LUXEMBOURG
Arlon
Luxembourg
Esch
Longwy
Charleville-Mézières
Sedan
PICARDIE
Noyon
Chauny
Oise
Laon
Aisne
Beauvais
Compiègne
Nogent-sur-Oise
Creil
Senlis
Chantilly
Soissons
Reims
ÎLE-DE-FRANCE
Pontoise
Meaux
Marne
Epernay
Château-Thierry
Châlons-sur-Marne
PARIS
Coulommiers
Corbeil-Essonnes
Melun
Étampes
Fontainebleau
Provins
Romilly-sur-Seine
Montereau-Fault-Yonne
Troyes
Sens
CHAMPAGNE
Vitry-le-François
Bar-le-Duc
St-Dizier
Aube
Seine
Marne
Meuse
Verdun
Ste-Menehould
Commercy
Toul
Villerupt
Hayange
Jœuf
Thionville
Völklingen
Metz
Pont-à-Mousson
Nancy
Moselle
Lunéville
LORRAINE
816
Idar-Oberstein
GERMANY
Kaiserslautern
Neunkirchen
Homburg
Zweibrücken
Pirmasens
Saarbrücken
Forbach
Hombourg-Haut
Sarreguemines
Rastatt
Haguenau
Sarrebourg
Strasbourg
Baden-Baden
Offenburg
Lahr
Emmendingen
Freiburg
Schwarzwald
1493
Rheinfelden
Lörrach
Basel
Liestal
Olten
ALSACE
Vosges
St-Dié
Sélestat
Epinal
Colmar
Gérardmer
Remiremont
Guebwiller
1423
Mulhouse
Belfort
Montbéliard
Neufchâteau
Vittel
Chaumont
Langres
Plateau de Langres
Vesoul
FRANCHE-COMTÉ
BOURGOGNE
Montbard
Armançon
598
Dijon
Saône
Besançon
Côte d'Or
Dole
Beaune
Autun
Chalon-sur-Saône
Lons-le-Saunier
Le Creusot
Montceau-les-Mines
St-Vallier
Paray-le-Monial
Mâcon
Oyonnax
Bourg-en-Bresse
Bellegarde-sur-Valserine
Villefranche-sur-Saône
Tarare
Chalette-sur-Loing
Montargis
St-Florentin
Tonnerre
Migennes
Auxerre
Gien
Vézelay
Yonne
NIVERNAIS
Salbris
Sancerre
Vierzon
BERRY
Bourges
Nevers
Issoudun
St-Amand-Mont-Rond
Moulins
BOURBONNAIS
Montluçon
Commentry
Guéret
Vichy
Cusset
Gannat
Roanne
Loire
Riom
Thiers
Aubusson
Puy de Dôme
1463
Clermont Ferrand
LYONNAIS
LYON
Givors
Rive de Gier
1634
St-Étienne
St-Chamond
Firminy
Annonay
Vienne
Ussel
Issoire
1885
Puy de Sancy
Massif Central
Tulle
1855
St-Flour
Aurillac
AUVERGNE
Allier
Le Puy
1753
Tournon
1469
Figeac
Decazeville
Mende
Rodez
Villefranche-de-Rouergue
Carmaux
Millau
Albi
1699
1565
Cévennes
Aubenas
Montélimar
Pierrelatte
Bagnols-sur-Cèze
Alès
Valréas
Orange
Mt Ventoux
1909
Carpentras
Avignon
Sorgues
Cavaillon
Manosque
Nîmes
Beaucaire
Arles
Salon de Provence
Aix-en-Provence
Montpellier
Camargue
Aigues Mortes
Istres
Étang de Berre
Martigues
Port-St-Louis-du-Rhône
Gardanne
Port-de-Bouc
Aubagne
Rhône Delta
MARSEILLE
La Ciotat
La Seyne
Toulon
Hyères
Iles d'Hyères
1267
Castres
Mazamet
Lodève
Frontignan
Sète
Agde
Béziers
LANGUEDOC
Castelnaudary
Carcassonne
Narbonne
Golfe du Lion
Limoux
Aude
Rivesaltes
Perpignan
Elne
Port-Vendres
Ax-les-Thermes
ROUSSILLON
FRANCE
Romans-sur-Isère
Valence
Rhône
DAUPHINÉ
Grenoble
Isère
Voiron
Bourgoin-Jallieu
Belley
Aix-les-Bains
Chambéry
Annecy
SAVOIE
Massif du Pelvoux
Briançon
Durance
Gap
Digne
Draguignan
Grasse
Cannes
Antibes
Nice
MONACO
Menton
Fréjus
St-Raphaël
St-Tropez
Maures
PROVENCE
Maritime Alps
3051
L'Argentera
3297
Cuneo
Fossano
Bra
Saluzzo
3841
Mt Viso
Pinerolo
Carmagnola
TORINO
Venaria
Rivoli
ITALY
Modane
Gran Paradiso
Aosta
Mont Blanc
4807
Chamonix
Ugine
Alpi Pennine
Mt Cervin
4478
Zermatt
Martigny
Sion
Rhône
Brig
Berner Alpen
Jungfrau
4158
Interlaken
Thun
Montreux
Vevey
Thonon-les-Bains
Annemasse
Genève
Lausanne
SWITZERLAND
Yverdon
Fribourg
Bern
L. Neuchâtel
Pontarlier
Neuchâtel
La Chaux-de-Fonds
Biel
Solothurn
Langenthal
Jura
St-Claude
1718
L. Léman
East from Greenwich
6
4
48
46
44
COPYRIGHT GEORGE PHILIP & SON LTD

Map 37

Northern France

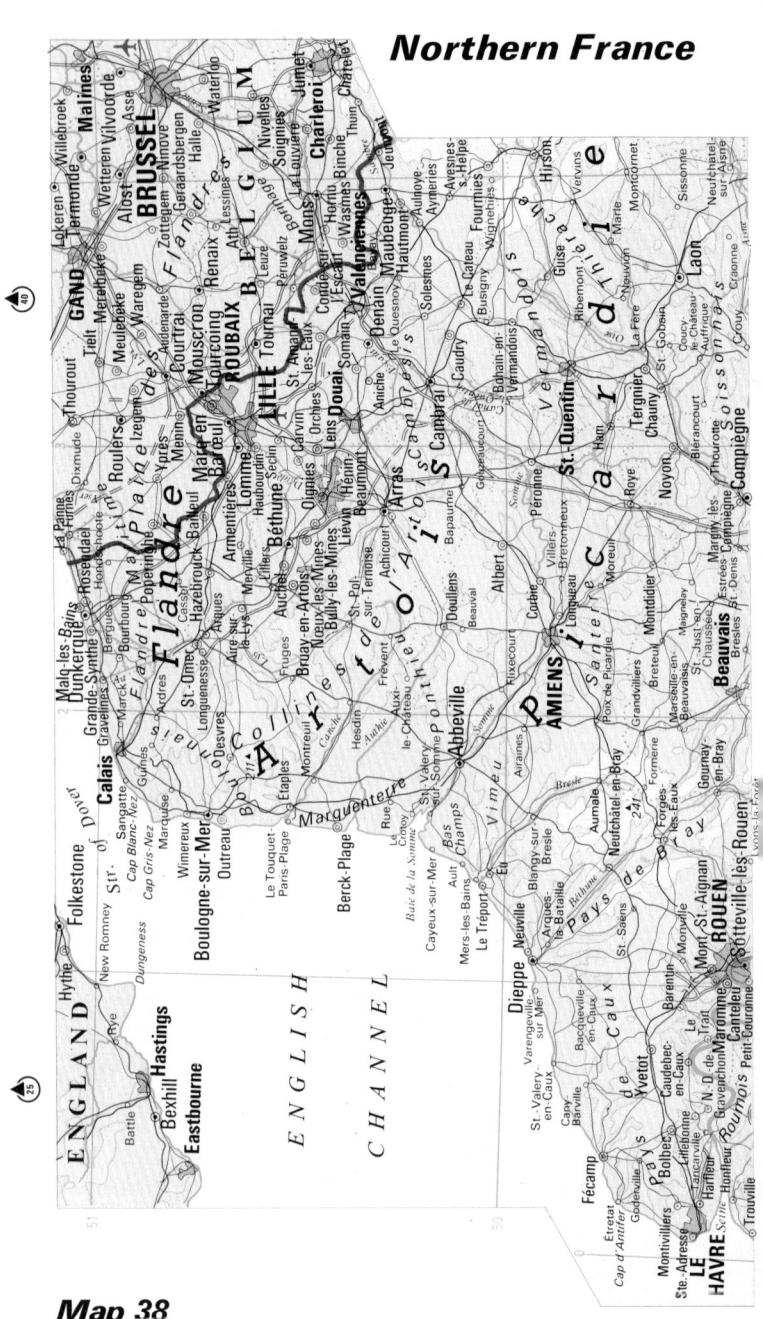
ENGLAND
Hastings
Bexhill
Eastbourne
Battle
Rye
Hythe
Folkestone
New Romney
Dungeness
Str. of Dover
ENGLISH CHANNEL
Calais
Sangatte
Cap Blanc-Nez
Cap Gris-Nez
Marquise
Wimereux
Boulogne-sur-Mer
Outreau
Le Touquet-Paris-Plage
Berck-Plage
Étaples
Montreuil
Marquenterre
Rue
Le Crotoy
Baie de la Somme
Cayeux-sur-Mer
Bas Champs
Ault
Mers-les-Bains
Le Tréport
Eu
Dieppe
Neuville
Arques-la-Bataille
Varengeville-sur-Mer
St.-Valery-en-Caux
Cany-Barville
Fécamp
Étretat
Cap d'Antifer
Goderville
Montivilliers
Ste.-Adresse
LE HAVRE
Harfleur
Honfleur
Trouville
Bolbec
Lillebonne
Tancarville
N.-D.-de-Gravenchon
Caudebec-en-Caux
Yvetot
Pays de Caux
Bacqueville-en-Caux
Barentin
Le Trait
Maromme
Canteleu
Petit-Couronne
Roumois
Monville
Mont-St.-Aignan
ROUEN
Sotteville-lès-Rouen
St.-Saëns
Pays de Bray
Neufchâtel-en-Bray
Forges-les-Eaux
Gournay-en-Bray
Blangy-sur-Bresle
Aumale
Vimeu
Abbeville
St.-Valery-sur-Somme
Airaines
AMIENS
Poix-de-Picardie
Grandvilliers
Formerie
Marseille-en-Beauvaisis
Beauvais
Bresles
St.-Just-en-Chaussée
Breteuil
Montdidier
Moreuil
Longueau
Corbie
Albert
Doullens
Beauval
Flixecourt
Ponthieu
Hesdin
Auxi-le-Château
Frévent
St.-Pol-sur-Ternoise
Artois
Picardie
Santerre
Vermandois
Thiérache
Soissonnais
Cambrésis
Flandre
Boulonnais
Collines de l'Artois
Dunkerque
Malo-les-Bains
Grande-Synthe
Gravelines
Marck
Ardres
Guînes
Desvres
St.-Omer
Longuenesse
Arques
Aire-sur-la-Lys
Hazebrouck
Cassel
Bergues
Bourbourg
Hondschoote
Rosendael
Poperinge
Bailleul
Armentières
Merville
Lillers
Béthune
Auchel
Bruay-en-Artois
Nœux-les-Mines
Bully-les-Mines
Liévin
Lens
Hénin-Beaumont
Oignies
Carvin
Seclin
Haubourdin
Lomme
LILLE
Marcq-en-Barœul
Tourcoing
ROUBAIX
Mouscron
Courtrai
Menin
Ypres
Roulers
Dixmude
Furnes
La Panne
Thourout
Tielt
GAND
Merelbeke
Lokeren
Termonde
Malines
Willebroek
Vilvoorde
BRUSSEL
Alost
Asse
Ninove
Zottegem
Geraardsbergen
Halle
Waterloo
Audenarde
Renaix
Waregem
Meulebeke
Izegem
Ath
Lessines
Leuze
Tournai
Péruwelz
Orchies
Douai
Somain
Denain
Valenciennes
Condé-sur-l'Escaut
St.-Amand-les-Eaux
Arras
Achicourt
Bapaume
Cambrai
Caudry
Le Cateau
Solesmes
Le Quesnoy
Maubeuge
Hautmont
Aulnoye-Aymeries
Jeumont
Avesnes-s.-Helpe
Fourmies
Wignehies
Hirson
Vervins
Guise
Bohain-en-Vermandois
Busigny
Gouzeaucourt
Péronne
Ham
St.-Quentin
Ribemont
La Fère
Tergnier
Chauny
Noyon
Roye
Villers-Bretonneux
Laon
Marle
Montcornet
Sissonne
Craonne
Coucy-le-Château-Auffrique
St.-Gobain
Crouy
Blérancourt
Thourotte
Compiègne
Margny-lès-Compiègne
Estrées-St.-Denis
Maignelay
Mons
Hornu
Wasmes
Binche
La Louvière
Soignies
Nivelles
Charleroi
Jumet
Châtelet
Thuin
Borinage
BELGIUM
Somme
Oise
Aisne
Sambre
Canche
Authie
Bresle
Béthune
Seine
Lys
Escaut

Map 38

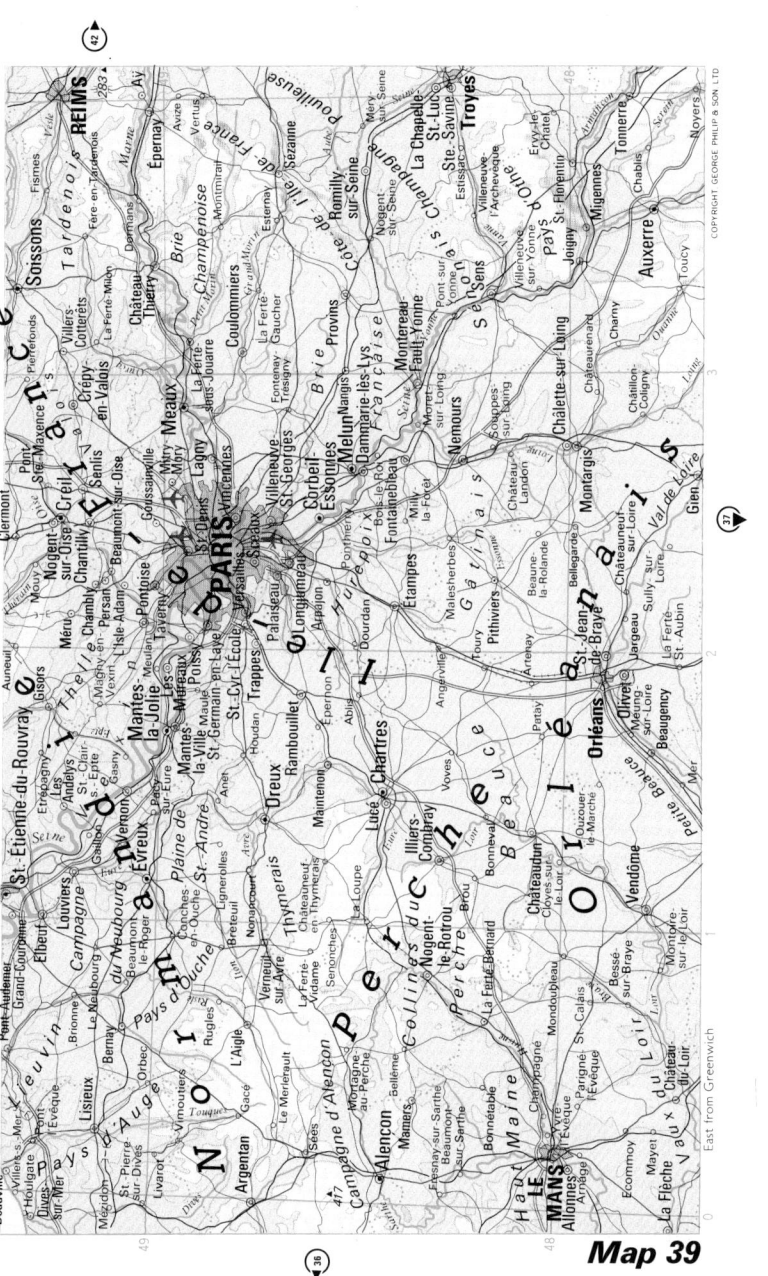

1:2 000 000

Map 39

East from Greenwich

COPYRIGHT GEORGE PHILIP & SON LTD

Netherlands

NORTH

SEA

WESTFRIESCHE

Terschelli

Vlieland

Waddenz

Texel

Den Burgo

53

Den Helder

Den Oever

Staveren

Middenmeer

Ijssel

Bergen-Binnen

Enkhuizen

Alkmaar

Hoorn

Heiloo

Castricum

Wormer

Purmerend

Edam

Beverwijk

Volendam

IJmuiden

Zaanstad

Marken

Velsen

Haarlem

AMSTERDAM

Zandvoort

Heemstede

Weesp

Huizen

Hillegom

Aalsmeer

Bussum

Laren

Noordwijk-aan-Zee

Lisse

Hilversum

Baar

Katwijk-aan-Zee

Leiden

Soest

Wassenaar

Oude

Alphen

Scheveningen

Voorburg

Rijn

UTRECHT

s'GRAVENHAGE

Waddinx

Zeist

(The Hague)

Rijswijk

veen

Utrecht

52

Delft

Gouda

Lek

Ijsselstein

Hoek van Holland

Naaldwijk

Earopoort

Maassluis

ROTTERDAM

Vlaardingen

Schiedam

Sliedrecht

Oleer

Tiel

Goeree

Hellevoetsluis

dam

Gelder

Oldorp

Overflakkee

Gorinchem

malse

Brouwershaven

Zuid

Dordrecht

Zierikzee

Waalwijk

Miaa

Schouwen

Made

E

Noord Beveland

Oosterschelde

Dongen B

's-He

R

D

N

Vught

Oosterhout

Walcheren

Oudenbosch

Breda

Boxter

Middelburg

Goes

Roosendaal

Goirle

Tilburg

Vlissingen

Bergen-op

Baarle

(Flushing)

Zoom

Nassau

Knokke

Westerschelde

Essen

Blankenberge

Zeebrugge

Terneuzen

Kalmthout

Rijkevorsel

Oostende

Hulst

Kellen

Brasschaat

Turnhout

Arendonk

(Ostend)

Brugge

Moldegem

ANTWERPEN

Lommel

(Bruges)

Beveren

Schoten

Mol

Nieuwpoort

Eernegem

Eeklo

St-

Merksem

Antwerpen

Geel

Veurne

Zelzo

Niklaas

Hoboken

Deurne

Hefentals

Leopoldsb

Torhout

Lokeren

Eier

Berlaar

Diksmuide

Ruiselede

Lede

St-Amandsberg

Boom

Duffel

Nethe

Tessende Lo

Hoogledeo

Roeselare

Tielt

Gent (Gand)

Willebroek

Mechelen

(Nete)

Lo

Ongelmunster

Izegem

Wetteren

B

Lebbeke

Aarschot

Diest

Hasselt

Poperinge

Passgeblde

Denze

Aalst

Asse

Vilvoorde

Demer

Diepenbeek

Me) Menen

Kessel-Lo

Ieper

Bocke

Zottegem

Hinove

BRUSSEL

Leuven

G

I

Kortrijk

Oudenaarde

(Bruxelles)

1:2 000 000

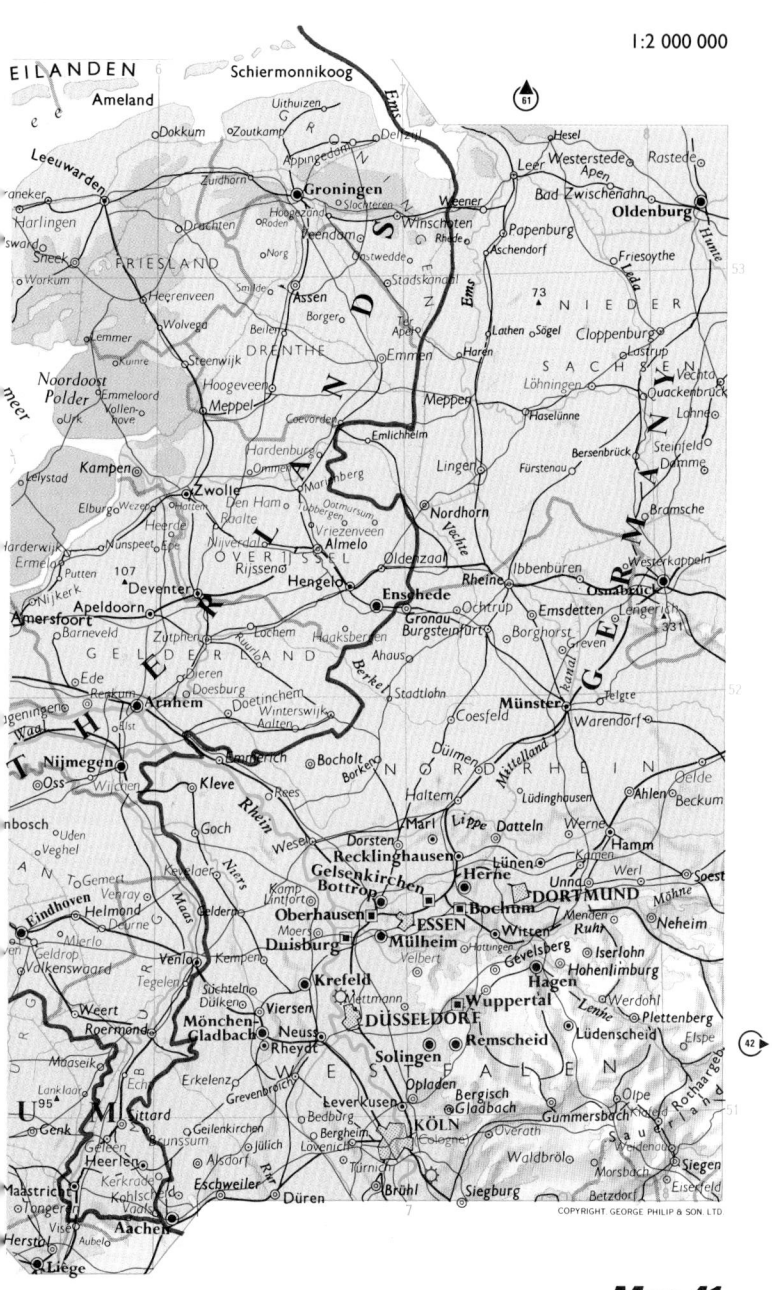
Schiermonnikoog
Ameland
EILANDEN
Dokkum
Zoutkamp
Uithuizen
Delfzijl
Appingedam
Leeuwarden
Franeker
Harlingen
Groningen
Zuidhorn
Drachten
Hoogezand
Slochteren
Roden
Veendam
Winschoten
Weener
Leer
Hesel
Westerstede
Rastede
Apen
Bad Zwischenahn
Oldenburg
Hunte
Papenburg
Aschendorf
Rhede
Friesoythe
Leda
Sneek
FRIESLAND
Workum
Norg
Onstwedde
Stadskanaal
Ems
Smilde
Assen
Heerenveen
Wolvega
Borger
Beilen
Ter Apel
Lathen
Sögel
Cloppenburg
73
NIEDER
SACHSEN
Lastrup
Vechta
Löhningen
Quakenbrück
Lemmer
Kuinre
DRENTHE
Emmen
Haren
Steenwijk
Noordoost Polder
Emmeloord
Vollenhove
Urk
Hoogeveen
Meppel
Meppen
Haselünne
Lohne
Coevorden
Emlichheim
Steinfeld
Bersenbrück
Damme
Hardenburg
Ommen
Mariënberg
Lingen
Fürstenau
Lelystad
Kampen
Zwolle
Elburg
Wezep
Hattem
Den Ham
Ootmarsum
Tubbergen
Nordhorn
Vechte
Bramsche
Heerde
Raalte
Vriezenveen
Harderwijk
Ermelo
Nunspeet
Epe
Nijverdal
Almelo
OVERIJSSEL
Oldenzaal
Westerkappeln
Putten
107
Deventer
Rijssen
Hengelo
Rheine
Ibbenbüren
Osnabrück
Nijkerk
Apeldoorn
Amersfoort
Enschede
Ochtrup
Emsdetten
Lengerich
331
Barneveld
Zutphen
Lochem
Ruurlo
Haaksbergen
Gronau
Burgsteinfurt
Borghorst
Greven
GELDERLAND
Ahaus
Ede
Dieren
Doesburg
Renkum
Berkel
Stadtlohn
Wageningen
Arnhem
Doetinchem
Winterswijk
Aalten
Münster
Telgte
Warendorf
Coesfeld
Waal
Elst
Nijmegen
Emmerich
Bocholt
Borken
Dülmen
Mittelland kanal
Oss
Wijchen
Kleve
Rees
Haltern
Lüdinghausen
Ahlen
Oelde
Beckum
NORDRHEIN
Rhein
Marl
Lippe
Datteln
Werne
Hamm
Uden
Veghel
Goch
Wesel
Dorsten
Recklinghausen
Lünen
Kamen
Werl
Soest
Gemert
Kevelaer
Niers
Gelsenkirchen
Bottrop
Herne
Unna
Möhne
Venray
Kamp Lintfort
DORTMUND
Eindhoven
Helmond
Deurne
Maas
Geldern
Oberhausen
ESSEN
Bochum
Menden
Neheim
Mierlo
Moers
Duisburg
Mülheim
Witten
Ruhr
Geldrop
Valkenswaard
Venlo
Kempen
Hattingen
Velbert
Gevelsberg
Iserlohn
Hohenlimburg
Tegelen
Krefeld
Hagen
Süchteln
Dülken
Mettmann
Wuppertal
Lenne
Werdohl
Plettenberg
Weert
Viersen
Mönchen-Gladbach
DÜSSELDORF
Roermond
Neuss
Rheydt
Remscheid
Lüdenscheid
Elspe
Maaseik
Solingen
WESTFALEN
Echt
Erkelenz
Grevenbroich
Opladen
Leverkusen
Bergisch Gladbach
Gummersbach
Olpe
Kirchhundem
Rothaargebirge
Sauerland
Lanklaar
95
Sittard
Bedburg
Genk
Geilenkirchen
Bergheim
KÖLN
(Cologne)
Overath
Geleen
Brunssum
Jülich
Lövenich
Weidenau
Heerlen
Alsdorf
Rur
Türnich
Waldbröl
Siegen
Morsbach
Kerkrade
Kohlscheid
Eschweiler
Brühl
Siegburg
Betzdorf
Eiserfeld
Maastricht
Tongeren
Vaals
Düren
Aachen
Visé
Herstal
Aubel
Liège
NETHERLANDS
GERMANY
61
42

Map 41

Germany and the Low Countries

NORTH SEA
NETHERLANDS
BELGIUM
LUX.
FRANCE
G
E
SCHLES
Helgoland
Ost-friesische Inseln
Norderney
Wangerooge
Borkum
Schiermonnikoog
Ameland
Terschelling
Texel
Deutsche Bucht
Cuxhaven
Elbe
Brunsbü
Glückstadt
Weser
Wilhelmshaven
Bremerhaven
Emden
Ems
Leeuwarden
Sneek
Groningen
Den Helder
IJsselmeer
Assen
Oldenburg
Bremen
Alkmaar
Hoorn
Meppel
NIEDERSACHSE
Verden
Aller
Nienburg
Haarlem
Zaandam
Kampen
Zwolle
Lingen
Amsterdam
'S-Gravenhage
(The Hague)
Hoek van Holland
Leiden
Gouda
Hilversum
Almelo
Deventer
Rheine
Osnabrück
Leine
Utrecht
Apeldoorn
Enschede
Teutoburger Wald
Minden
Hannover
Schiedam
Rotterdam
Arnhem
Münster
Herford
Bielefeld
Hameln
Dordrecht
Waal
Maas
Nijmegen
NORDRHEIN-WESTFALEN
Detmold
Vlissingen
Breda
's-Hertogenbosch
Bocholt
Lippe
Zeebrugge
Oostende
Tilburg
Oberhausen
Mülheim
Gelsenkirchen
Hamm
Paderborn
Brugge
Antwerpen
Turnhout
Eindhoven
Duisburg
Dortmund
Gent (Gand)
Schelde
Bochum
Göttin
Krefeld
Essen
Mönchengladbach
Hagen
Ruhr
Kortrijk
Leie
Aalst
Mechelen
Wuppertal
Kassel
Brussel
(Bruxelles)
Leuven
Düsseldorf
Remscheid
Münde
Tourcoing
Roubaix
Lille
Maastricht
Heerlen
840
Rothaargeb.
Eder
Tournai
Köln
(Cologne)
Fulda
Liège
Aachen
Douai
Mons
Namur
Bonn
Siegen
Marburg
Valenciennes
Cambrai
Charleroi
Meuse
Eupen
Verviers
Malmedy
Sieg
Westerwald
Ardennes
Rhein (Rhine)
Wetzlar
Lahn
Giessen
Koblenz
Limburg
Vogelsberg
772
950
Fulda
Rhön
RHEINLAND
St. Quentin
Hirson
Eifel
Mosel
Taunus
Frankfurt
Hanau
Charleville-Mézières
Hunsrück
Wiesbaden
Offenbach
Spessart
Hessen
Laon
Sedan
Mainz
Aschaffenburg
Soissons
Aisne
Luxembourg
Trier
Main
Darmstadt
Longwy
PFALZ
Worms
Würzburg
Château Thierry
Reims
Meuse
Thionville
Saar
Kaiserslautern
SAARLAND
Ludwigshafen
Mannheim
Neunkirchen
Épernay
Châlons-sur-Marne
Verdun
Saarbrücken
Speyer
Heidelberg
Metz
Vitry-le-François
LORRAINE
Karlsruhe
Neckar
Aube
St. Dizier
Bar-le-Duc
Nancy
Haguenau
Pforzheim
Heilbronn
BADEN-WÜRTTEMBERG
Toul
Stuttgart
Ludwigsburg
Esslingen
Troyes
Marne
Lunéville
Baden-Baden
CHAMPAGNE
Vosges
Strasbourg
Schwarzwald
ALSACE
Tübingen
Reutlingen
Ulm
Seine
Chaumont
St. Dié
Épinal
Rottweil
Schwäbische Alb
Iller
Langres
Plateau de Langres
1424
Colmar
Rhein (Rhine)
Freiburg
Biberach
(Danube)
Avallon
Donau
Tuttlingen
Mulhouse
Memm
Belfort
Schaffhausen
Ravensburg
Friedrichshafen
Basel
Konstanz
Bodensee
Kemp
Winterthur
St. Gallen
Bregenz
Biel
Aarau
Zürich
VORARLBERG
Aare
Solothurn
East from Greenwich
4
6
8
10
52
50
48
38
44

Map 42

1:5 000 000

BALTIC SEA

Map 43

COPYRIGHT GEORGE PHILIP & SON LTD

Alpine Lands

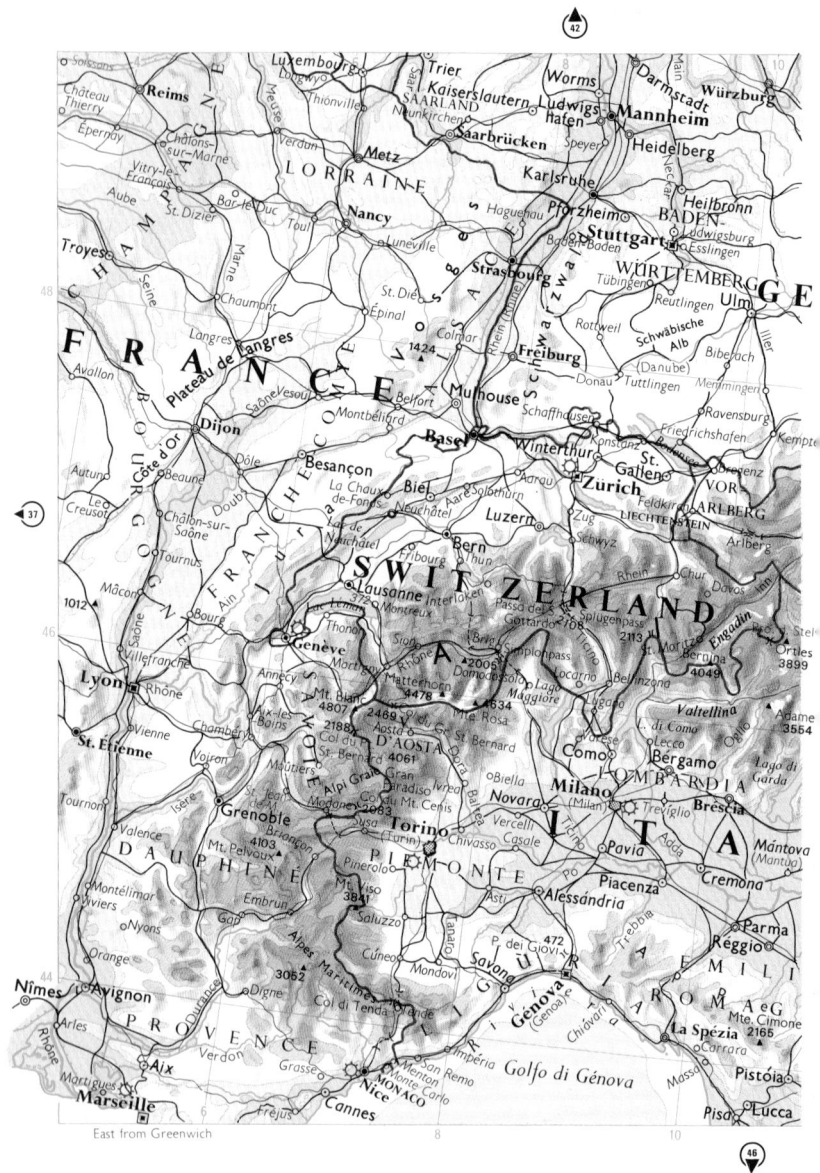
42
37
46
East from Greenwich
6
8
10
48
46
44
FRANCE
SWITZERLAND
ITALIA
GE
LORRAINE
CHAMPAGNE
BOURGOGNE
FRANCHE-COMTÉ
SAVOIE
DAUPHINÉ
PROVENCE
PIEMONTE
LOMBARDIA
LIGURIA
EMILIA-ROMAGNA
ALSACE
Vosges
BADEN-WÜRTTEMBERG
SAARLAND
VORARLBERG
LIECHTENSTEIN
MONACO
Luxembourg
Longwy
Trier
Worms
Darmstadt
Würzburg
Reims
Soissons
Château Thierry
Épernay
Châlons-sur-Marne
Thionville
Kaiserslautern
Ludwigshafen
Mannheim
Neunkirchen
Saarbrücken
Speyer
Heidelberg
Verdun
Metz
Vitry-le-François
Aube
St. Dizier
Bar-le-Duc
Toul
Nancy
Karlsruhe
Heilbronn
Pforzheim
Haguenau
Stuttgart
Ludwigsburg
Esslingen
Baden-Baden
Troyes
Seine
Marne
Lunéville
Strasbourg
Tübingen
Reutlingen
Ulm
Chaumont
St. Dié
Épinal
Schwarzwald
Rottweil
Schwäbische Alb
Langres
Plateau de Langres
Colmar
1424
Freiburg
Biberach
Iller
Avallon
Vesoul
Saône
Belfort
Mulhouse
Donau
(Danube)
Tuttlingen
Memmingen
Montbéliard
Schaffhausen
Ravensburg
Dijon
Côte d'Or
Basel
Friedrichshafen
Kempten
Konstanz
Bodensee
Winterthur
St. Gallen
Bregenz
Autun
Beaune
Dôle
Besançon
Biel
Aarau
Zürich
La Chaux-de-Fonds
Solothurn
Aare
Feldkirch
Le Creusot
Doubs
Neuchâtel
Luzern
Zug
Arlberg
Châlon-sur-Saône
Lac de Neuchâtel
Jura
Bern
Schwyz
Tournus
Fribourg
Thun
Rhein
Chur
Davos
Inn
Mâcon
1012
Lausanne
Interlaken
Ain
372
Montreux
Passo del S. Gottardo
2108
Splügenpass
2113
Engadin
Bourg
Lac Léman
Thonon
Genève
Sion
Brig
Simplonpass
Ticino
St. Moritz
Bernina
Ortles
3899
Villefranche
Martigny
Rhône
2005
Domodossola
Locarno
Bellinzona
4049
Lyon
Annecy
Matterhorn
4478
Lago Maggiore
Lugano
Mt. Blanc
4807
4634
Mte. Rosa
Valtellina
Adamello
3554
Aix-les-Bains
2469
Aosta
Col du Gr. St. Bernard
L. di Como
Vienne
2188
Col du Pt. St. Bernard
Varese
Lecco
Oglio
St. Étienne
Chambéry
Voiron
VAL D'AOSTA
4061
Como
Bérgamo
Lago di Garda
Moûtiers
Gran Paradiso
Alpi Graie
Biella
Ivrea
Dora Baltea
Milano
(Milan)
St. Jean-de-M.
Modane
Col du Mt. Cenis
2083
Novara
Treviglio
Bréscia
Tournon
Isère
Grenoble
Susa
Torino
(Turin)
Vercelli
Casale
Chivasso
Valence
Briançon
4103
Mt. Pelvoux
Pavia
Adda
Mántova
(Mantua)
Pinerolo
Po
Piacenza
Cremona
Montélimar
Viviers
Embrun
Mt. Viso
3841
Asti
Alessándria
Gap
Saluzzo
Tanaro
Trebbia
Parma
Nyons
Orange
Cúneo
Mondovì
P. dei Giovi
472
Savona
Reggio
3052
Alpes Maritimes
Nîmes
Avignon
Digne
Durance
Col di Tenda
Tende
Génova
(Genoa)
Riviera
Chiávari
Mte. Cimone
2165
Arles
Rhône
Verdon
Impéria
San Remo
La Spézia
Carrara
Aix
Grasse
Nice
Menton
Monte Carlo
Golfo di Génova
Massa
Pistóia
Martigues
Marseille
Fréjus
Cannes
Pisa
Lucca

Map 44

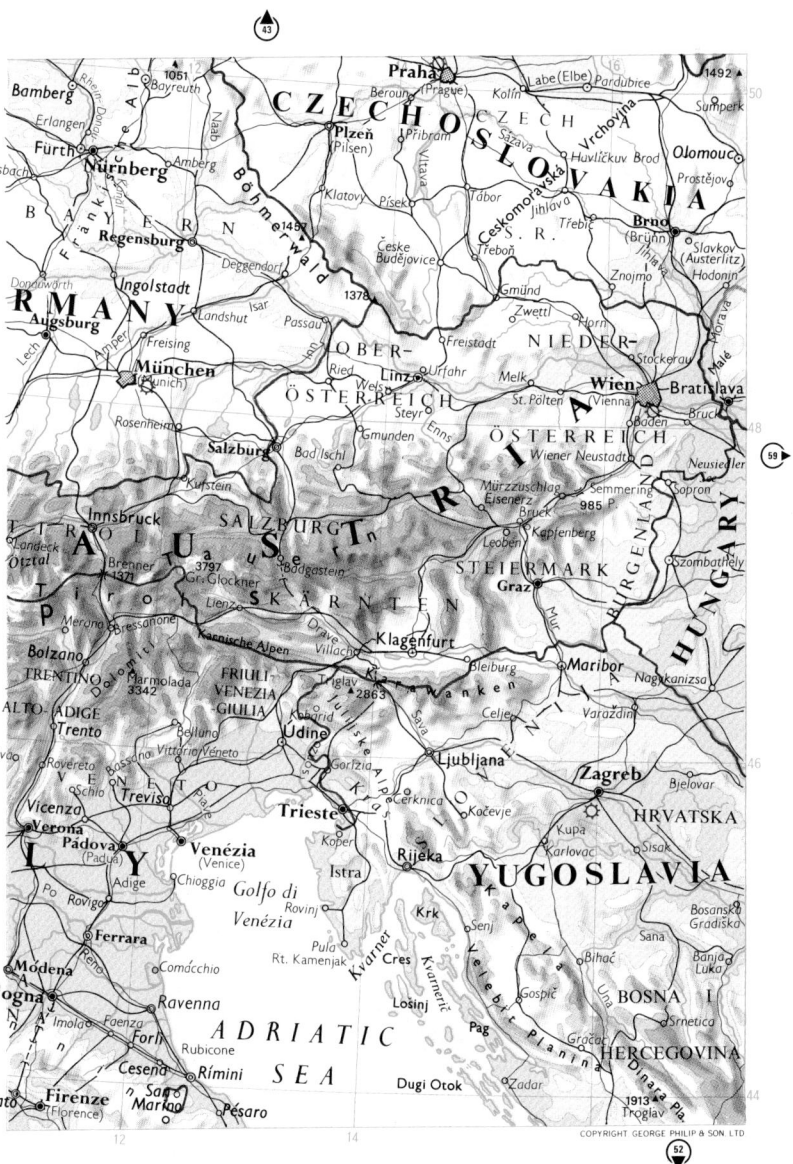

Map 45

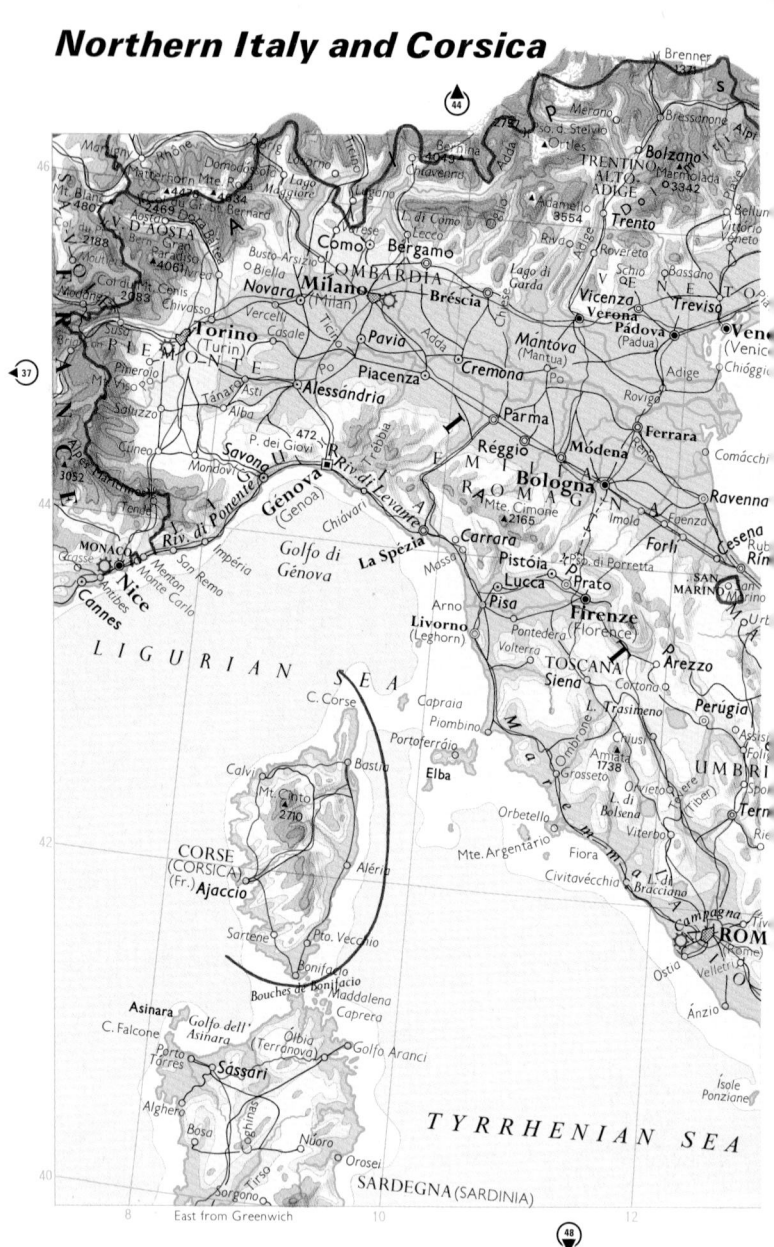

Northern Italy and Corsica

Map 46

LIGURIAN SEA

TYRRHENIAN SEA

MONACO
Nice
Cannes
Antibes
Menton
Monte Carlo
San Remo
Impéria

Riv. di Ponente
Riv. di Levante
Golfo di Génova
(Genova)
Génova
Genoa
Chiávari

Mt. Blanc
4810
Matterhorn Mte. R.
4474
Gr. Paradiso
4061
V. D'AOSTA
Aosta
Bern. Alps
Col di Gt.
Bernard
Mte. Rosa
4634
Dom. d'Ossola
Lago Maggiore
Varese
Busto-Arsizio
Novara

Torino
(Turin)
PIEMONTE
Pinérolo
Viso
3841
Saluzzo
Cúneo
Alba
Asti
Alessándria
Mondovi
Tánaro

Savona
P. dei Giovi
472

Como
Lecco
Lago di Como
Bérgamo
Milano
(Milan)
LOMBARDIA
Biella
Vercelli
Casale
Chivasso
Pavia
Piacenza
Cremona

Bréscia
Mantova
(Mantua)
Adda
Adige

Bérnina
4049
Ortles
3554
Adamello
3554
Rivo di Sol
TRENTINO
ALTO
ADIGE
Merano
Brenner
1371
Bolzano
Marmolada
3342
Trento
Rovereto
Schio
Bassano
VENETO
Vicenza
Verona
Pádova
(Padua)
Vittório Véneto
Belluno
Bressanone
S
Alpi
Ádige
Rovigo
Chióggia
Venezia
(Venice)

Párma
Réggio
Módena
EMILIA
ROMAGNA
Bologna
Mte. Cimone
2165
Comácchio
Ferrara
Imola
Faenza
Ravenna
Forlì
Cesena
Rín
SAN MARINO
S. Marino

Carrara
La Spézia
Massa
Pistóia
Lucca
Prato
Arno
Pisa
Livorno
(Leghorn)
Ponte di Porretta
Firenze
(Florence)
Arezzo

TOSCANA
Volterra
Siena
Cortona
L. Trasimeno
Perúgia
Chiusi
Amiata
1738
Grosseto
Orvieto
L. di Bolsena
UMBRIA
Assisi
Foli
Spol
Terni

Capraia
Piombino
Portoferráio
Elba
Orbetello
Mte. Argentário
Fiora
Viterbo
Civitavécchia
L. di Bracciano

C. Corse
Calvi
Bástia
Mt. Cinto
2710
CORSE
(CORSICA)
(Fr.)
Ajáccio
Aléria
Sartene
Pto. Vecchio
Bonifácio
Bouches de Bonifacio
Maddalena
Caprera

Asinara
C. Falcone
Golfo dell'
Asinara
Porto Torres
Álghero
Bosa
Olbia
(Terranova)
Golfo Aranci
Sássari
Cóghinas
Núoro
Orosei
SARDEGNA (SARDINIA)
Sórgono
Tirso

Ánzio
Velletri
Óstia
ROM
(Rome)
Campagna
Riv

Ísole Ponziane

East from Greenwich

1:5 000 000

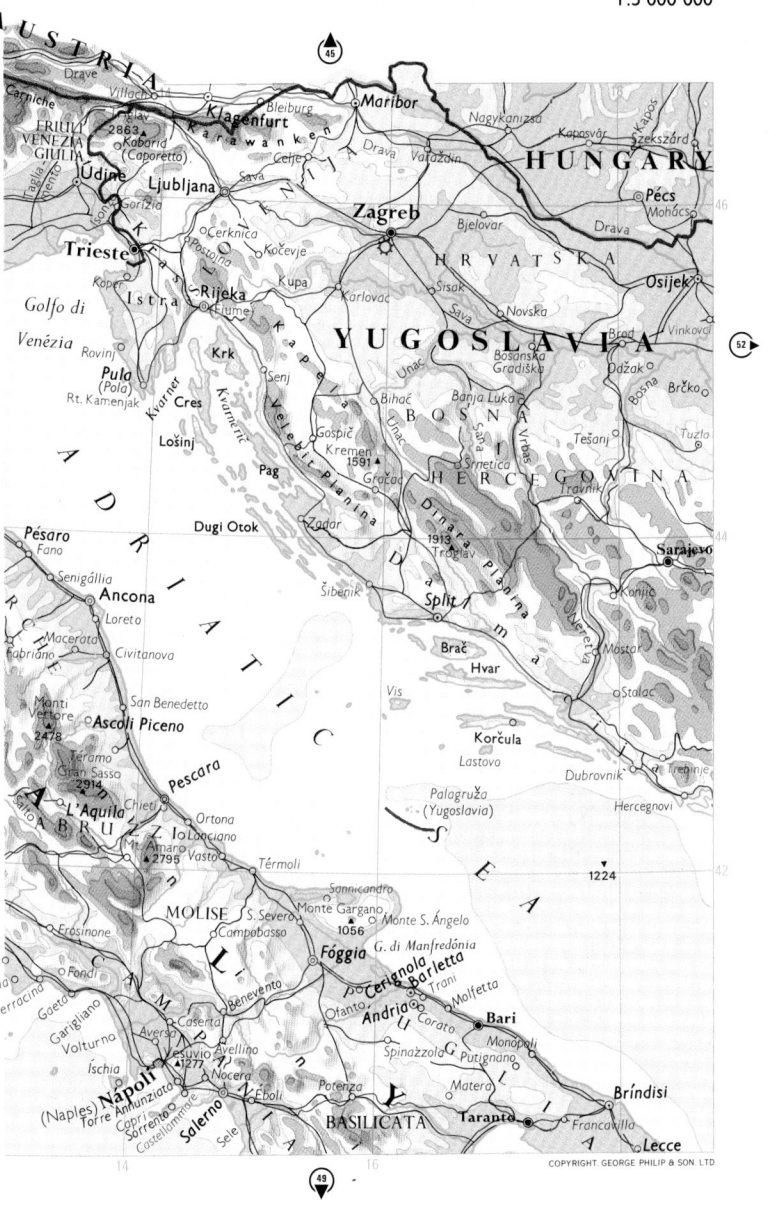
AUSTRIA
45
Drave
Carniche
Villach
Klagenfurt
Bleiburg
Maribor
Karawanken
FRIULI VENEZIA GIULIA
2863
Kobarid (Caporetto)
Celje
Drava
Varaždin
Nagykanizsa
Kaposvár
Kapos
Szekszárd
HUNGARY
Údine
Tagliamento
Ljubljana
Sava
Pécs
Mohács
Isonzo
Gorizia
Zagreb
Bjelovar
Drava
Trieste
Cerknica
Postojna
Kočevje
HRVATSKA
Koper
Rijeka
Fiume
Kupa
Sisak
Osijek
Golfo di Venézia
Istra
Karlovac
Sava
Novska
Vinkovci
Rovinj
Krk
YUGOSLAVIA
52
Brod
Bosanska Gradiška
Pula (Pola)
Senj
Unac
Đakovo
Rt. Kamenjak
Kvarner
Cres
Bihać
Banja Luka
Brčko
Bosna
Lošinj
Kvarnerić
Velebit Planina
Gospić
BOSNA I HERCEGOVINA
Sana
Vrbas
Tešanj
Tuzla
Kremen 1591
Srnetica
Pag
Gračac
Travnik
ADRIATIC SEA
Dugi Otok
Zadar
Dinara Planina
Pésaro
Fano
1913 Troglav
Sarajevo
Senigállia
Šibenik
Dalmacija
Ancona
Split
Konjic
Loreto
MARCHE
Macerata
Fabriano
Civitanova
Brač
Mostar
Hvar
Neretva
Vis
Monti Vettore 2478
San Benedetto
Ascoli Piceno
Stolac
Téramo
Korčula
Gran Sasso 2914
Lastovo
Pescara
Dubrovnik
Trebinje
ABRUZZI
L'Aquila
Chieti
Palagruža (Yugoslavia)
Herceg-novi
Salto
Ortona
Lanciano
Mt. Amaro 2795
Vasto
Términi
1224
42
Sannicandro
MOLISE
S. Severo
Monte Gargano 1056
Monte S. Ángelo
Frosinone
Campobasso
G. di Manfredónia
Fóggia
Fondi
Cerignola
Barletta
Trani
Terracina
Gaeta
Benevento
Molfetta
CAMPANIA
Ofanto
Ándria
Corato
Bari
Garigliano
Caserta
Volturno
Aversa
PUGLIA
Monópoli
Vesuvio 1277
Avellino
Spinazzola
Putignano
Íschia
Nocera
Nápoli (Naples)
Torre Annunziata
Potenza
Matera
Bríndisi
Éboli
Capri
Sorrento
Castellammare
Salerno
BASILICATA
Taranto
Francavilla
Sele
Lecce
14
16
44
46
18
49

Map 47

Southern Italy and Sardinia

46

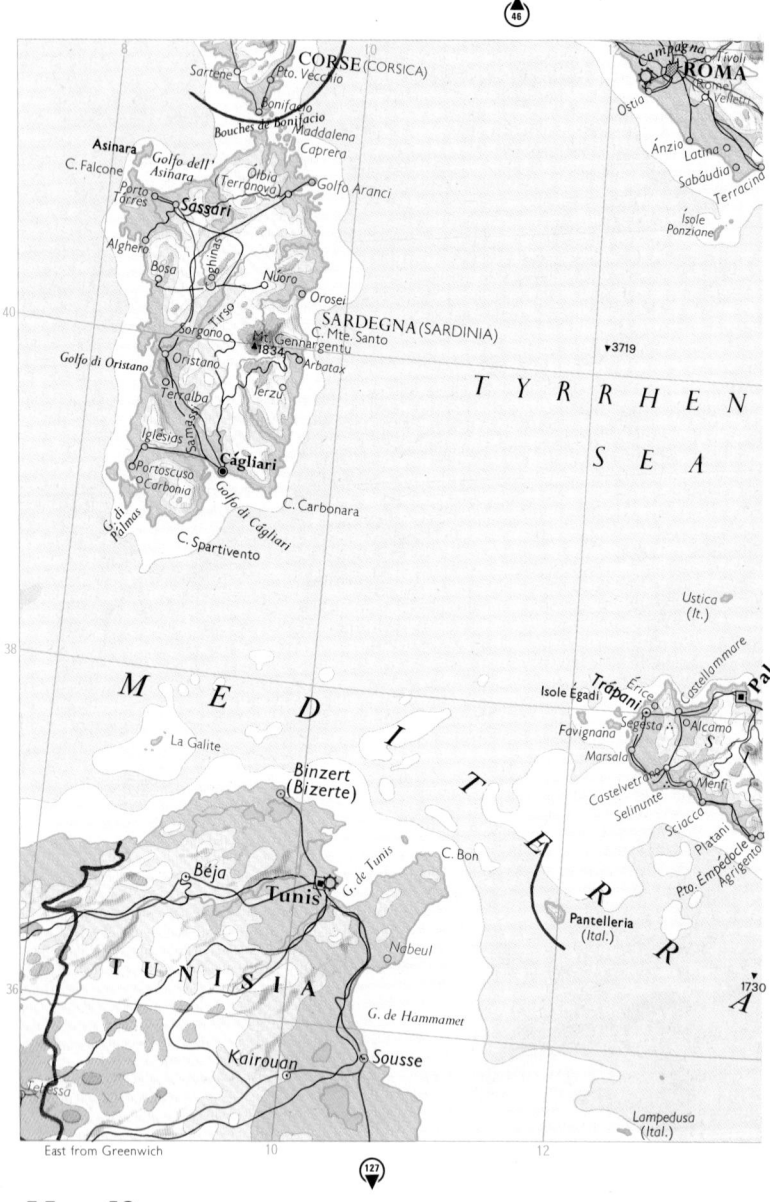

8
10
12
40
38
36
CORSE (CORSICA)
Sartene
Pto. Vecchio
Bonifacio
Bouches de Bonifacio
Maddalena
Caprera
Asinara
C. Falcone
Golfo dell' Asinara
Ólbia (Terranova)
Golfo Aranci
Porto Torres
Sássari
Alghero
Coghinas
Bosa
Núoro
Orosei
Tirso
SARDEGNA (SARDINIA)
C. Mte. Santo
Sorgono
Mt. Gennargentu
1834
Golfo di Oristano
Oristano
Arbatax
Terralba
Ierzu
Samassi
Iglesias
Cágliari
Portoscuso
Carbonia
G. di Pálmas
Golfo di Cágliari
C. Carbonara
C. Spartivento
Campagna
Tivoli
ROMA
(Rome)
Velletri
Ostia
Ánzio
Latina
Sabáudia
Terracina
Ísole Ponzione
3719
TYRRHENIAN SEA
Ustica (It.)
MEDITERRANEAN
Isole Égadi
Trápani
Érice
Castellammare
Segesta
Alcamo
Favignana
Marsala
Castelvetrano
Selinunte
Menfi
Sciacca
Platani
Pto. Empédocle
Agrigento
La Galite
Binzert (Bizerte)
C. Bon
G. de Tunis
Béja
Tunis
Pantelleria (Ital.)
Nabeul
TUNISIA
1730
G. de Hammamet
Kairouan
Sousse
Tebessa
Lampedusa (Ital.)
East from Greenwich

127

Map 48

1:5 000 000

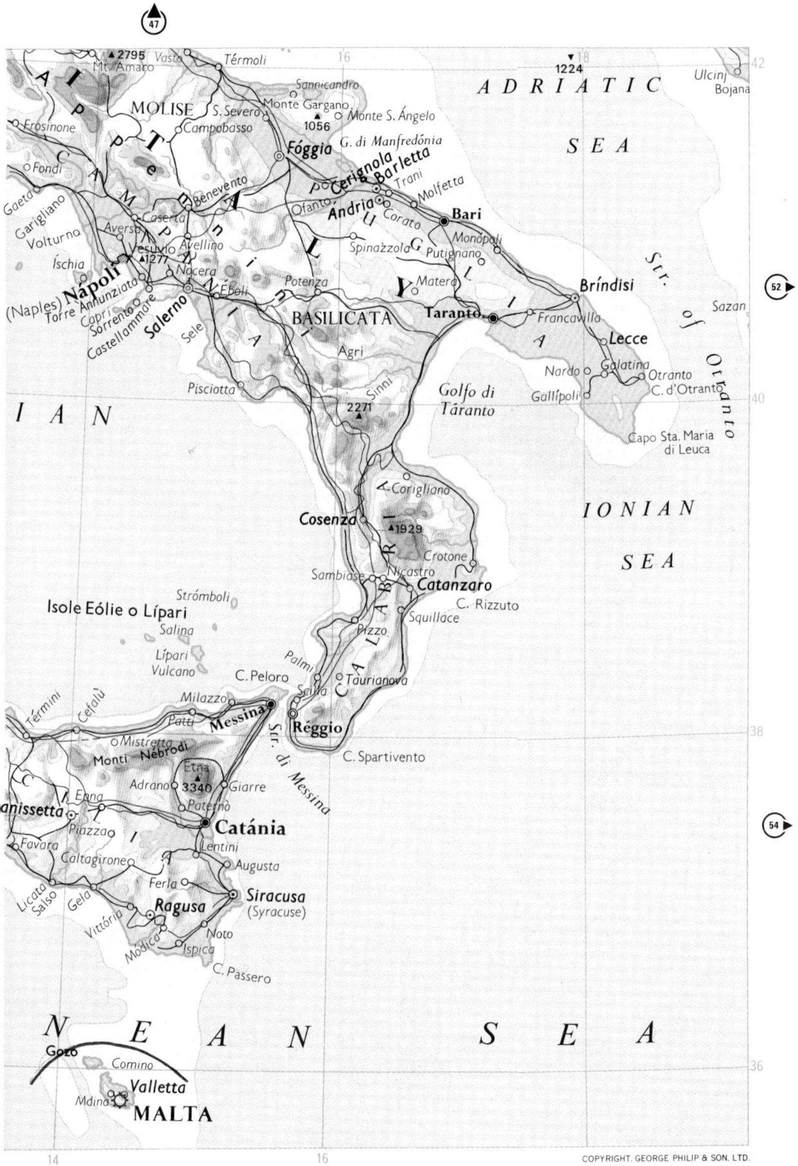
47
52
54
16
18
42
40
38
36
14
▲2795
Mt. Amaro
Vasto
Térmoli
1224
ADRIATIC
SEA
Ulcinj
Bojana
Sannicandro
Monte Gargano
1056
Monte S. Ángelo
MOLISE
S. Severo
Frosinone
Campobasso
Fóggia
G. di Manfredónia
Fondi
Cerignola
Barletta
Trani
Molfetta
Benevento
Gaeta
Garigliano
Ofanto
Andria
Corato
Bari
Caserta
Volturno
Aversa
Spinazzola
Monopoli
Putignano
Avellino
Vesuvio
▲1277
Íschia
Nocera
Nápoli
(Naples)
Torre Annunziata
Potenza
Matera
Brindisi
Str. of Otranto
Sazan
Éboli
Capri
Sorrento
Castellammare
Salerno
BASILICATA
Taranto
Francavilla
Lecce
Sele
Agri
Nardo
Galatina
Otranto
C. d'Otranto
Gallípoli
Golfo di Táranto
Pisciotta
Sinni
2271
Capo Sta. Maria di Leuca
Corigliano
IONIAN
SEA
Cosenza
1929
Crotone
Sambiase
Nicastro
Catanzaro
C. Rizzuto
Squillace
Strómboli
Isole Eólie o Lípari
Salina
Pizzo
Lípari
Vulcano
Palmi
C. Peloro
Taurianova
Milazzo
Scilla
Términi
Cefalù
Patti
Messina
Réggio
Mistretta
Monti Nébrodi
Str. di Messina
C. Spartivento
Etna
3340
Adrano
Giarre
Enna
Paternò
anissetta
Catánia
Piazza
Favara
Lentini
Caltagirone
Augusta
Ferla
Licata
Salso
Gela
Siracusa
(Syracuse)
Ragusa
Vittória
Noto
Módica
Ispica
C. Passero
N
E
A
N
S
E
A
Gozo
Comino
Valletta
Mdina
MALTA
APPENNINO
CAMPANIA
PUGLIA
CALABRIA
SICILIA
I A N

Spain and Portugal

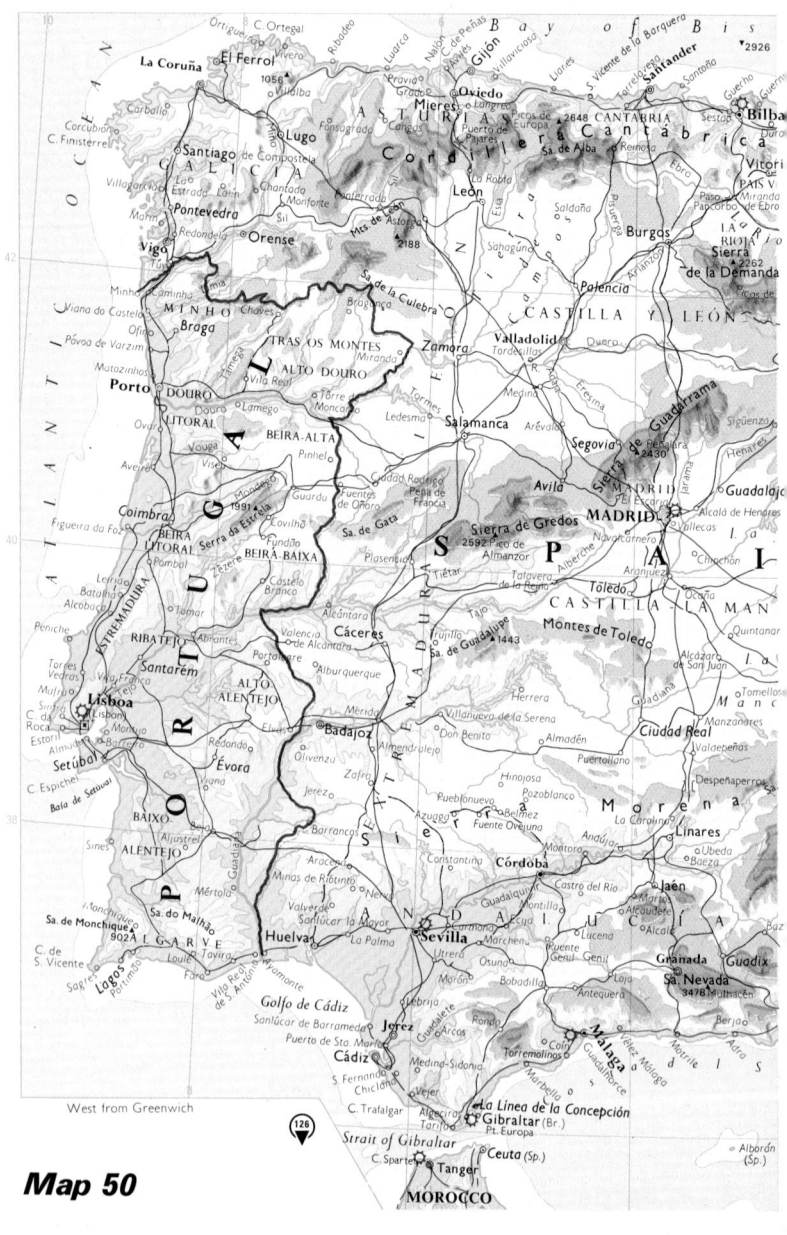

Bay of Bis
ATLANTIC OCEAN
La Coruña
El Ferrol
C. Ortegal
Ortigueira
Vivero
Ribadeo
Luarca
Avilés
Gijón
Villaviciosa
Llanes
S. Vicente de la Barquera
Torrelavega
Santander
Santoña
Bilba
Oviedo
Mieres
Langreo
Pravia
Grado
Cangas
Fonsagrada
Lugo
Villalba
Carballo
Corcubión
C. Finisterre
Santiago de Compostela
GALICIA
Villagarcía
La Estrada
Lalín
Chantada
Monforte
Ponferrada
Sil
Pontevedra
Marín
Redondela
Orense
Vigo
Tuy
ASTURIAS
Picos de Europa
Puerto de Pajares
2648
CANTABRIA
Cordillera Cantábrica
Sa. de Alba
Reinosa
Ebro
Vitori
PAIS V
Paso Pancorbo
Miranda de Ebro
LA RIOJA
Sierra de la Demanda
2262
2926
La Robla
León
Astorga
Mts. de León
2188
Esla
Saldaña
Pisuerga
Burgos
Arlanzón
Sahagún
Tierra de Campos
Palencia
Minho
Caminha
Viana do Castelo
MINHO
Chaves
Bragança
Sa. de la Culebra
Braga
Ofir
Póvoa de Varzim
TRAS OS MONTES
Miranda
ALTO DOURO
Matozinhos
Tâmega
Vila Real
Porto
DOURO
Torre de Moncorvo
Zamora
Valladolid
Tordesillas
Duero
CASTILLA Y LEÓN
Medina
Eresma
Tormes
Ledesma
Salamanca
Arévalo
Segovia
Sierra de Guadarrama
Peñalara
2430
Sigüenza
Henares
Lamego
Ovar
LITORAL
BEIRA-ALTA
Pinhel
Vouga
Viseu
Aveiro
Ciudad Rodrigo
Peña de Francia
Avila
MADRID
El Escorial
Jarama
Guadalaja
Alcalá de Henares
Mondego
1991
Guarda
Fuentes de Oñoro
Coimbra
Figueira da Foz
Serra da Estrela
Covilhã
Sa. de Gata
Sierra de Gredos
2592 Pico de Almanzor
Vallecas
BEIRA LITORAL
Fundão
Zêzere
BEIRA-BAIXA
Plasencia
Tiétar
Navalcarnero
Alberche
Aranjuez
Chinchón
Pombal
Castelo Branco
Talavera de la Reina
Toledo
Ocaña
Leiria
Batalha
Alcobaça
Tomar
Alcántara
Tajo
CASTILLA-LA MAN
Peniche
ESTREMADURA
RIBATEJO
Abrantes
Valencia de Alcántara
Cáceres
Trujillo
Sa. de Guadalupe
1443
Montes de Toledo
Quintanar
Torres Vedras
Santarém
Portalegre
Alburquerque
Alcázar de San Juan
Mafra
Vila Franca
ALTO ALENTEJO
Herrera
Guadiana
Tomellos
Sintra
Lisboa
(Lisbon)
C. da Roca
Estoril
Almada
Montijo
Barreiro
Elvas
Mérida
Badajoz
Villanueva de la Serena
Don Benito
Almadén
Ciudad Real
Manzanares
Setúbal
Redondo
Évora
Olivenza
Almendralejo
Puertollano
Valdepeñas
C. Espichel
Baía de Setúbal
Viana
Zafra
Hinojosa
Despeñaperros
Jerez
Pozoblanco
Pueblonuevo
Belmez
Fuente Ovejuna
Azuaga
Sierra Morena
La Carolina
BAIXO-ALENTEJO
Beja
Barrancos
Andújar
Linares
Sines
Aljustrel
ALENTEJO
Guadiana
Aracena
Constantina
Montoro
Córdoba
Ubeda
Baeza
Minas de Riotinto
Nerva
Castro del Río
Jaén
Mértola
Guadalquivir
Montilla
Martos
Alcaudete
Monchique
Sa. do Malhão
Valverde
Sanlúcar la Mayor
Carmona
Écija
Lucena
Alcalá
ANDALUCÍA
Sa. de Monchique
902
ALGARVE
Huelva
La Palma
Sevilla
Marchena
Puente Genil
Genil
Granada
Guadix
C. de S. Vicente
Loulé
Tavira
Utrera
Osuna
Loja
Sa. Nevada
3478 Mulhacén
Sagres
Lagos
Portimão
Faro
Vila Real de S. António
Ayamonte
Morón
Bobadilla
Antequera
Golfo de Cádiz
Lebrija
Sanlúcar de Barrameda
Jerez
Guadalete
Arcos
Ronda
Coín
Málaga
Vélez Málaga
Berja
Adra
Motril
Puerto de Sta. María
Cádiz
Torremolinos
Guadalhorce
Marbella
S. Fernando
Chiclana
Medina-Sidonia
Vejer
C. Trafalgar
Algeciras
Tarifa
La Linea de la Concepción
Gibraltar (Br.)
Pt. Europa
Strait of Gibraltar
C. Spartel
Tanger
Ceuta (Sp.)
MOROCCO
Alborán (Sp.)
West from Greenwich
126
10
8
6
42
40
38

Map 50

1:6 000 000

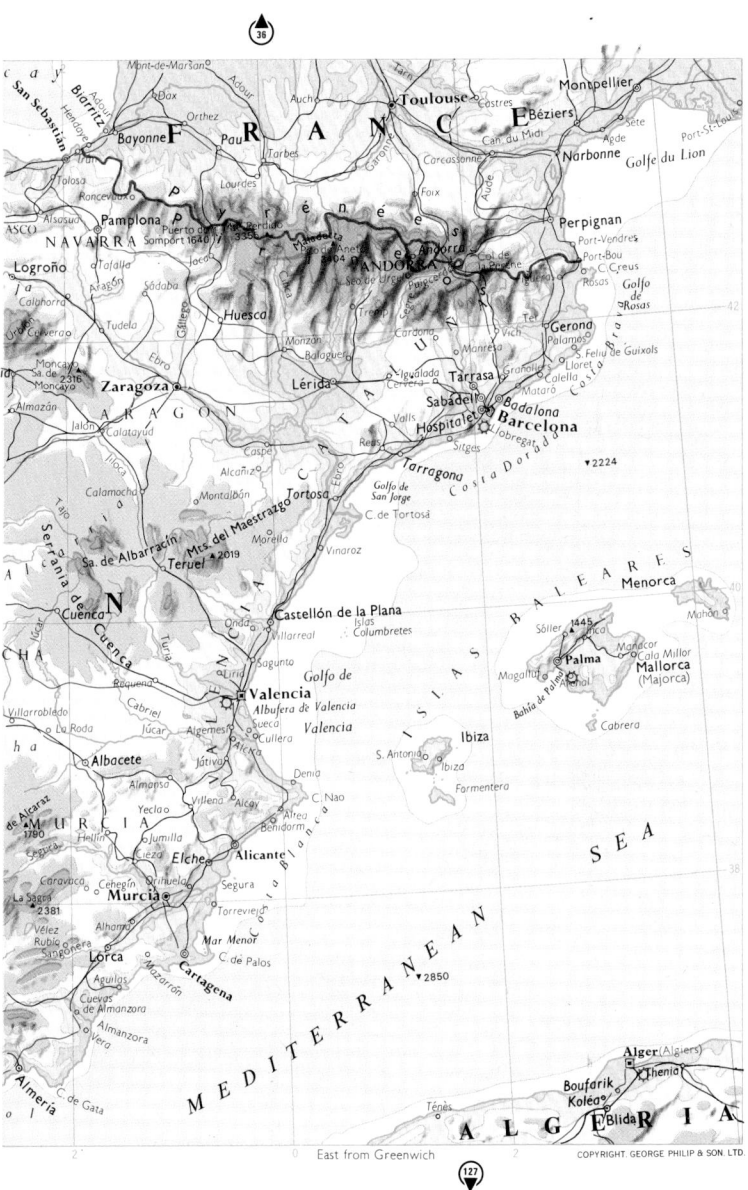

COPYRIGHT GEORGE PHILIP & SON. LTD.

Map 51

36
Mont-de-Marsan
Dax
Adour
Biarritz
Hendaye
San Sebastián
Bayonne
Orthez
Pau
Tarbes
Lourdes
Auch
Toulouse
Castres
Tarn
Garonne
FRANCE
Béziers
Montpellier
Sète
Agde
Port-St-Louis
Can. du Midi
Carcassonne
Narbonne
Golfe du Lion
Aude
Foix
Tolosa
Roncevaux
Alsasua
Pamplona
NAVARRA
Puerto de Somport 1640
Pyrénées
Perdido 3355
Maladetta
Pico de Aneto 3404
ANDORRA
Andorra
Col de la Perche
Perpignan
Port-Vendres
Port-Bou
C. Creus
Rosas
Golfo de Rosas
Logroño
Tafalla
Aragón
Sádaba
Jaca
Seo de Urgel
Puigcerdá
Calahorra
Cervera
Tudela
Gállego
Huesca
Cinca
Segre
Tremp
Ter
Vich
Gerona
Palamós
S. Feliu de Guixols
Costa Brava
Lloret
Calella
Mataró
Granollers
Manresa
Cardona
Monzón
Balaguer
CATALUÑA
Moncayo
Sa. de Moncayo 2316
Ebro
Zaragoza
Lérida
Igualada
Cervera
Tarrasa
Sabadell
Badalona
Barcelona
Hospitalet
Llobregat
Sitges
Costa Dorada
2224
Almazán
ARAGON
Jalón
Calatayud
Valls
Reus
Caspe
Tarragona
Alcañiz
Jiloca
Calamocha
Montalbán
Tortosa
Golfo de San Jorge
C. de Tortosa
Tajo
Serranía de Cuenca
Sa. de Albarracín
Mts. del Maestrazgo
Morella
Teruel
2019
Vinaroz
ISLAS BALEARES
Menorca
Mahón
Cuenca
Júcar
Turia
Onda
Castellón de la Plana
Islas Columbretes
Villarreal
Sóller
1445
Inca
Manacor
Cala Millor
Palma
Mallorca
(Majorca)
Magalluf
Arenal
Bahía de Palma
Cabrera
Sagunto
Liria
Requena
Golfo de Valencia
Valencia
Albufera de Valencia
VALENCIA
Cabriel
Villarrobledo
La Roda
Júcar
Algemesí
Sueca
Cullera
Alcira
Játiva
Albacete
Ibiza
S. Antonio
Formentera
Denia
Almansa
C. Nao
Villena
Alcoy
Altea
Benidorm
Yecla
MURCIA
1790
Hellín
Jumilla
Segura
Cieza
Elche
Alicante
SEA
Caravaca
Cehegín
Orihuela
Segura
La Sagra 2381
Murcia
Torrevieja
Costa Blanca
Vélez Rubio
Alhama
Sangonera
Mar Menor
C. de Palos
MEDITERRANEAN
Lorca
Mazarrón
Cartagena
2850
Aguilas
Cuevas de Almanzora
Almanzora
Vera
Almería
C. de Gata
Alger (Algiers)
Thenia
Boufarik
Koléa
Ténès
Blida
ALGERIA
42
40
38
2
2
East from Greenwich
127

Danube Lands

59
47
49
HUNGARY
HRVATSKA
BOSNA I HERCEGOVINA
YUGOSLAVIA
SERBIA
CRNA GORA
ALBANIA
ITALY
MOLISE
CAMPANIA
BASILICATA
PUGLIA
ADRIATIC SEA
IONIAN SEA
Str. of Otranto
Golfo di Táranto
G. di Manfredónia
Villach
Triglav
2863
Kobarid (Caporetto)
Klagenfurt
Bleiburg
Karawanken
Maribor
Nagykanizsa
Kaposvár
Kapos
Szekszárd
Kiskőrös
Kalocsa
Kiskunhalas
Szentes
Békéscsaba
Hódmezővásárhely
Makó
Arad
Szeged
Baja
Subotica
Pécs
Mohács
Drava
Varaždin
Celje
Sava
Ljubljana
Gorizia
Zagreb
Bjelovar
Trieste
Koper
Istra
Cerknica
Postojna
Kočevje
Kupa
Rijeka (Fiume)
Karlovac
Sisak
Novska
Osijek
Sombor
Senta
Kikinda
Timişoara
Bečej
Zrenjanin
Novi Sad
Petrovaradin
Vinkovci
Brod
Vršac
Pančevo
Bela Crkva
Sremska Mitrovica
Zemun
Beograd (Belgrade)
Smederevo
Požarevac
Rovinj
Pula (Pola)
Rt. Kamenjak
Kvarner
Cres
Lošinj
Krk
Senj
Kapela
Velebit Planina
Kvarnerić
Pag
Gospić
Kremen
1591
Gračac
Dugi Otok
Zadar
Bihać
Unac
Bosanska Gradiška
Banja Luka
Vrbas
Sana
Srnetica
Odžak
Bosna
Brčko
Bijeljina
Drina
Tešanj
Tuzla
Travnik
Valjevo
Morava
Kragujevac
Han Pijesak
Titovo Užice
Čačak
Kraljevo
Kruševac
Dinara Planina
1913
Troglav
Dalmacija
Sarajevo
Višegrad
Šibenik
Split
Konjic
Neretva
Brač
Hvar
Vis
Mostar
Stolac
Pljevlja
Tara
2522
Durmitor
Novi Pazar
Ibar
Kopaonik Pl.
Kuršumlija
Kosovska Mitrovica
Korčula
Lastovo
Nikšić
Dubrovnik
Trebinje
Peć
Priština
Palagruža (Yugoslavia)
Hercegnovi
Kotor
Cetinje
Titograd (Podgorica)
Đakovica
Beli Drim
Prizren
Šar Pl.
2496
Crna Gora
Skadarsko Jezero
Shkodra
Drini
Bar
Ulcinj
Bojana
Tetovo
Korab
2764
Solunska
2540
Debar
Kep-i-Rodonit
Kep-i-Palit
Durrësi
Tirana
2259
Jablanica
Ohrid
Shkumbini
Elbasani
Ohridsko Jezero
Prespansko Jezero
Semani
Berati
Tomorit
2480
Korça
Sazan
Vlora
Vjosa
Smólikas
2637
Pindos
Gjirokastra
Ioánnina
Ipiros
Kérkira (Corfu)
Árta
Ortona
Lanciano
Vasto
Térmoli
1224
Sannicandro
Monte Gargano
S. Severo
Campobasso
1056
Monte S. Ángelo
Fóggia
Cerignola
Barletta
Trani
Molfetta
Ofanto
Andria
Corato
Bari
Benevento
Caserta
Aversa
Vesuvio
1277
Avellino
Ischia
Nápoli (Naples)
Capri
Sorrento
Castellammare
Nocera
Salerno
Éboli
Potenza
Spinazzola
Putignano
Monopoli
Matera
Bríndisi
Táranto
Francavilla
Lecce
Galatina
Otranto
C. d'Otranto
Nardo
Gallípoli
Capo Sta. Maria di Leuca
Sele
Agri
Sinni
2271
Pisciotta
Corigliano
Cosenza
1929
44
42
40
18
20
East from Greenwich

1:6 000 000

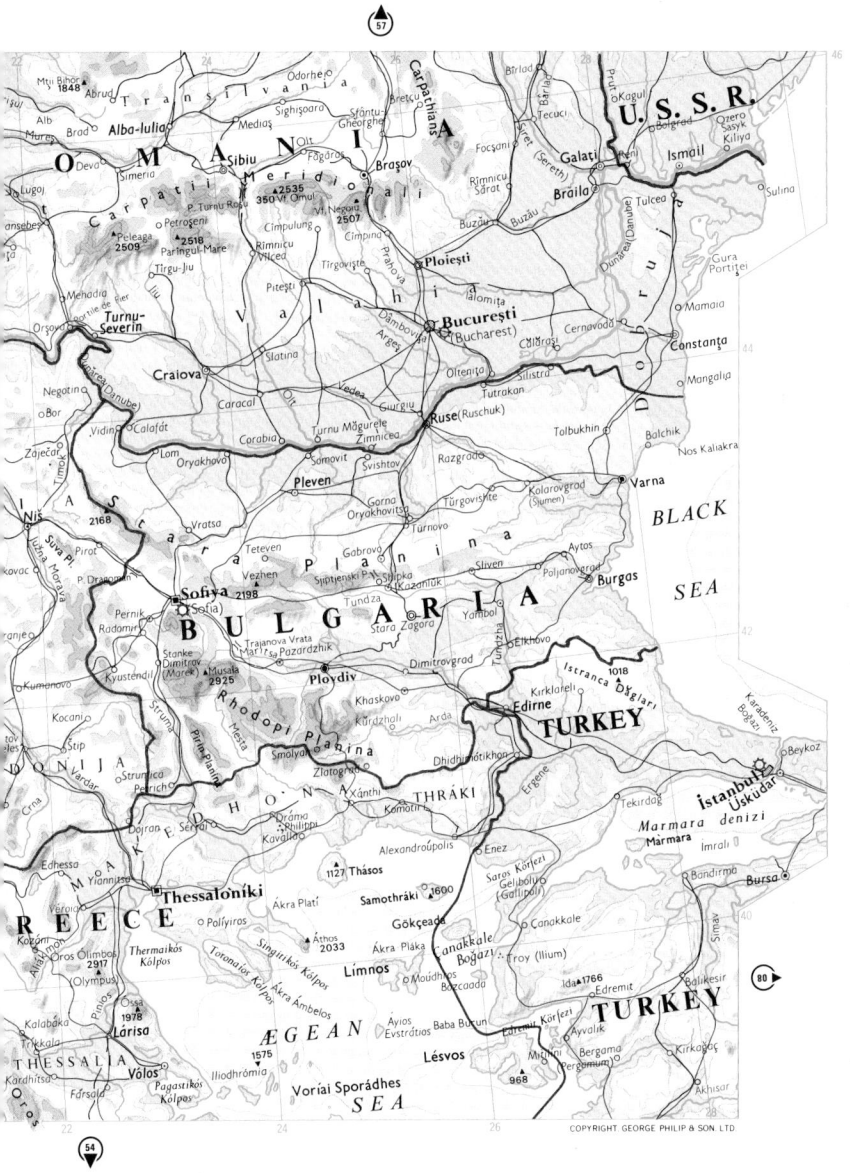

Map 53

Greece and *Albania*

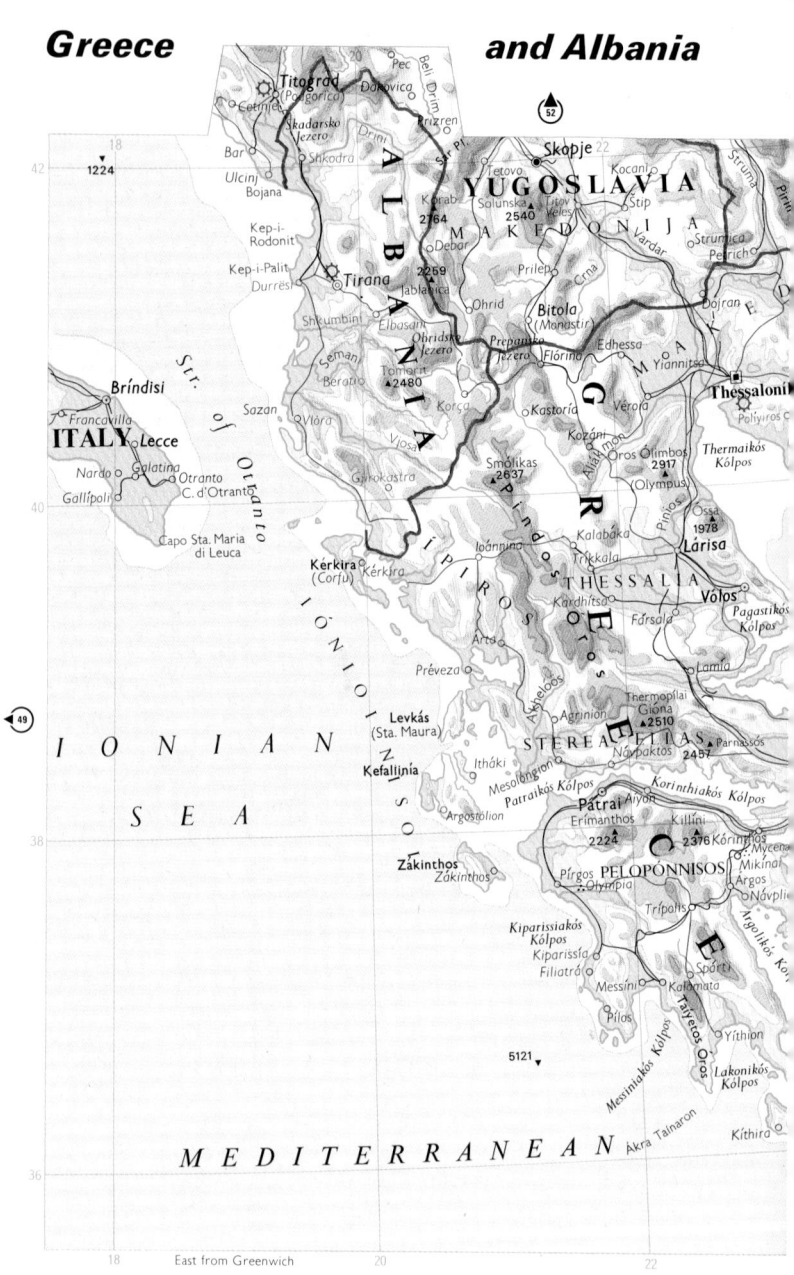

Titograd
(Podgorica)
Cetinje
Pec
Beli Drim
Danovica
Skadarsko
Jezero
Drim
Prizren
52
Bar
Shkodra
Sar Pl.
Skopje
22
42
18
1224
Ulcinj
Bojana
Korab
2764
Tetovo
Solunska
2540
Urov Veles
Kocani
Stip
YUGOSLAVIA
MAKEDONIJA
Kep-i-
Rodonit
Debar
Vardar
Strumica
Petrich
Kep-i-Palit
Durrës
Tirana
2269
Jablanica
Prilep
Crna
Strma
Shkumbin
Elbasan
Ohrid
Bitola
(Monastir)
Dojran
ED
Ohridsko
Jezero
Prespa
Jezero
Florína
Edhessa
Yiannitsá
MA
Thessaloni
Polyiros
Seman
Berona
Tomorit
2480
Vjosa
Kastoria
Véroia
Kozáni
G
Oros Ólimbos
2917
(Olympus)
Thermaïkós
Kólpos
Sazan
ITALY
Lecce
Bríndisi
Francavilla
Nardo
Galatina
Otranto
C. d'Otranto
Gallípoli
Capo Sta. Maria
di Leuca
Str. of Otranto
Vlóra
Gjirokastra
Smólikas
2637
Pindos
R
Kalabáka
Pínios
Óssa
1978
Lárisa
Kérkira
(Corfu)
Kérkira
Ioánnina
THESSALIA
Vólos
49
IONIAN
Levkás
(Sta. Maura)
Kefallinía
Itháki
Préveza
Árta
Agrínion
Akhelóos
Farsala
Pagastikós
Kólpos
Kardhítsa
Oros
Thermopílai
Giona
2510
Návpaktos
Parnassós
2457
STEREA ELLAS
Lamía
Mesolóngion
Patraïkós Kólpos
Korinthiakós Kólpos
SEA
Argostólion
Pátrai
Erímanthos
2224
Aiyion
Killíni
2376
Kórinthos
Mikínai
Argos
Návplia
Mycenae
Zákinthos
Zákinthos
Pírgos
Olympia
PELOPÓNNISOS
Kiparissiakós
Kólpos
Kiparissía
Filiatró
Trípolis
Argolikós Kól
38
Messíni
Kalamáta
Spárti
Taïyetos Oros
Pílos
5121
Messiniakós Kólpos
Lakonikós
Kólpos
Yíthion
MEDITERRANEAN
Akra Taínaron
Kíthira
36
18
East from Greenwich
20
22

Map 54

1:5 000 000

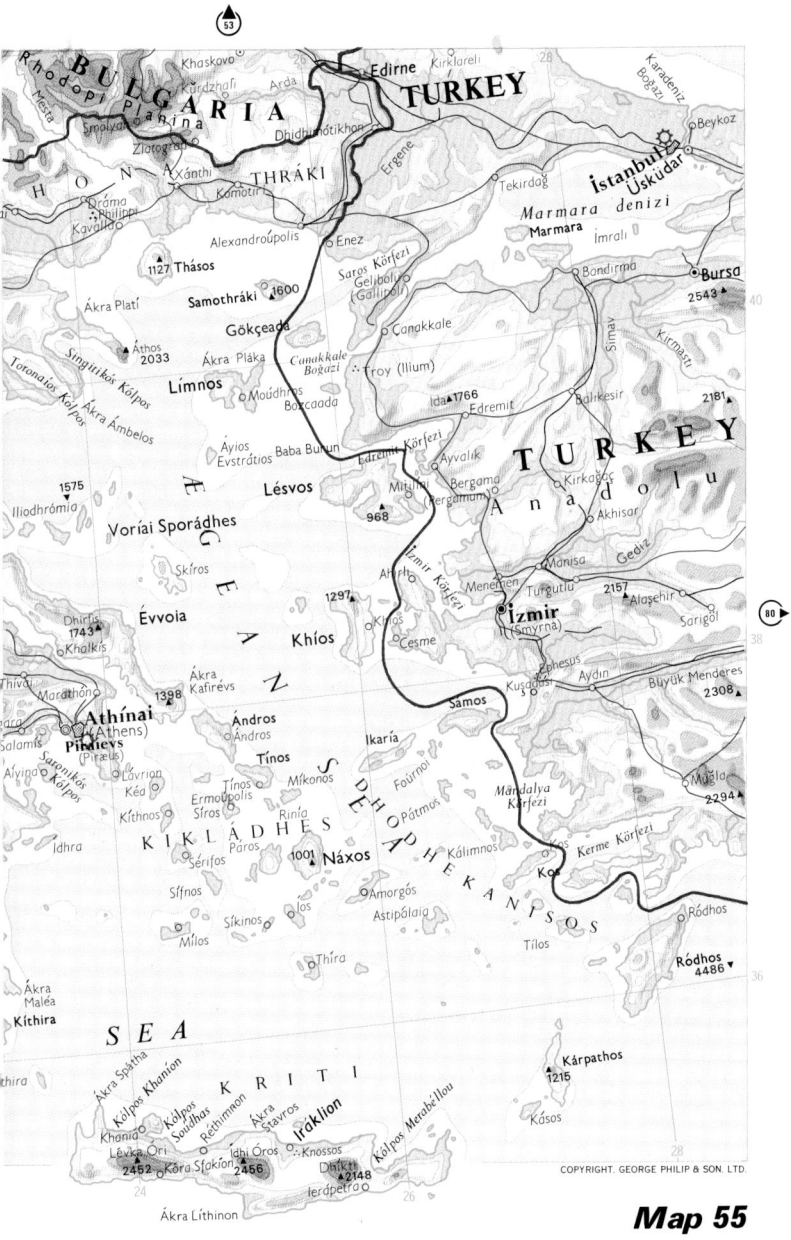

Map 55

Romania

58

59

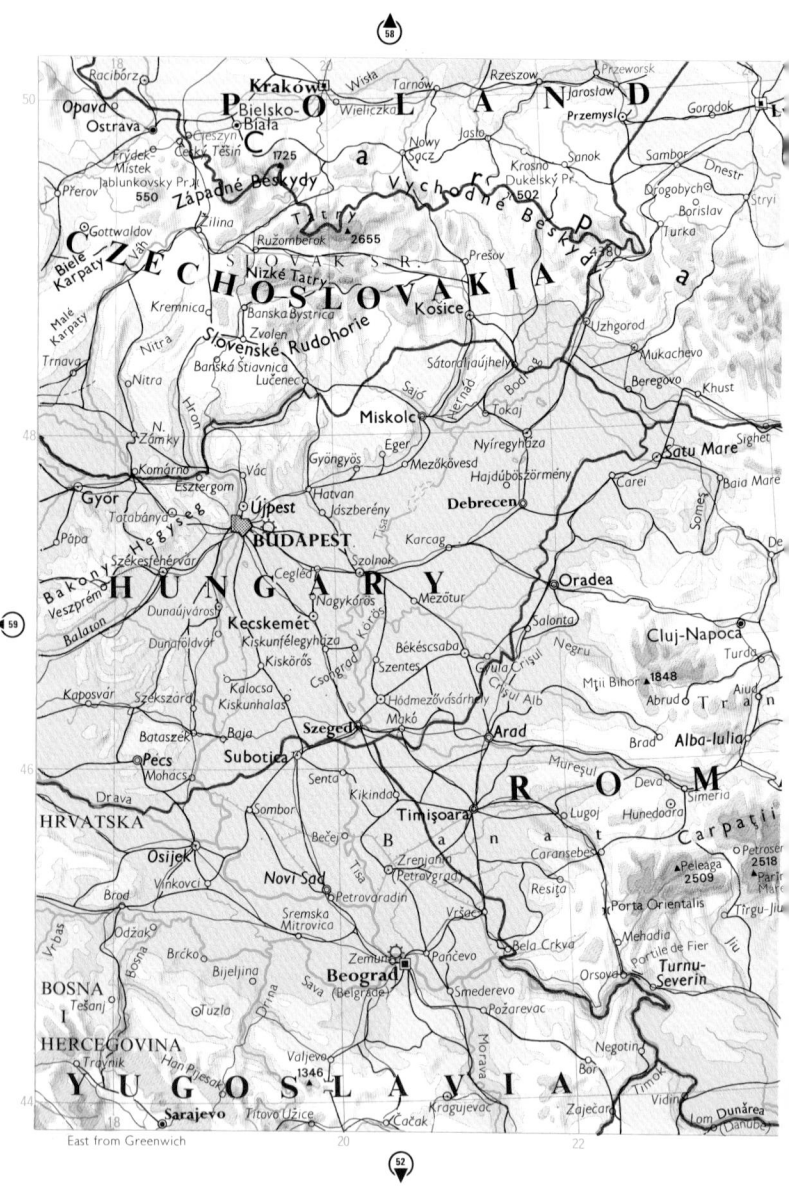
POLAND
CZECHOSLOVAKIA
HUNGARY
ROM
YUGOSLAVIA
HRVATSKA
BOSNA I HERCEGOVINA
Racibórz
Opava
Ostrava
Kraków
Bielsko-Biała
Cieszyn
Český Těšín
Frýdek-Místek
Jablunkovský Pr.
550
Přerov
Západné Beskydy
1725
Wisła
Tarnów
Wieliczka
Nowy Sącz
Rzeszow
Jaslo
Przeworsk
Jarosław
Przemysl
Gorodok
Sanok
Krosno
Dukelský Pr.
502
Východné Beskydy
Sambor
Dnestr
Drogobych
Borislav
Stryi
Turka
Tatry
2655
Žilina
Ružomberok
Gottwaldov
Biele Karpaty
Váh
SLOVAK S.R.
Nizké Tatry
Prešov
438
Kremnica
Banská Bystrica
Košice
Malé Karpaty
Zvolen
Slovenské Rudohorie
Uzhgorod
Nitra
Mukachevo
Trnava
Banská Štiavnica
Lučenec
Sátoraljaújhely
Bodrog
Beregovo
Khust
Hron
Sajó
Hernád
Tokaj
Miskolc
N. Zámky
Eger
Nyíregyháza
Satu Mare
Sighet
Komárno
Gyöngyös
Mezőkövesd
Hajdúböszörmény
Carei
Baia Mare
Vác
Esztergom
Győr
Hatvan
Debrecen
Someş
Újpest
Tatabánya
Jászberény
Hegység
Tisza
Pápa
BUDAPEST
Karcag
Székesfehérvár
Szolnok
Bakony
Cegléd
Oradea
Veszprém
Nagykőrös
Mezőtúr
Dunaújváros
Balaton
Kecskemét
Salonta
Cluj-Napoca
Dunaföldvár
Kiskunfélegyháza
Körös
Negru
Kiskőrös
Békéscsaba
Turda
Csongrád
Szentes
Gyula
Crişul
Mţii Bihor
1848
Kalocsa
Crişul Alb
Aiud
Abrud
Kaposvár
Szekszárd
Kiskunhalas
Hódmezővásárhely
Szeged
Makó
Arad
Brad
Alba-Iulia
Bataszék
Baja
Pécs
Subotica
Mureşul
Mohács
Senta
Deva
Simeria
Drava
Kikinda
Timişoara
Lugoj
Hunedoara
Sombor
Banat
Carpaţii
Bečej
Caransebeş
Petroşeni
2518
Osijek
Zrenjanin (Petrovgrad)
Peleaga
2509
Vinkovci
Novi Sad
Reşiţa
Brod
Petrovaradin
Porta Orientalis
Tîrgu-Jiu
Vrbas
Sremska Mitrovica
Vršac
Odžak
Mehadia
Bosna
Brčko
Zemun
Pančevo
Bela Crkva
Portile de Fier
Jiu
Bijeljina
Beograd (Belgrade)
Orşova
Turnu-Severin
Sava
Drina
Smederevo
Tešanj
Tuzla
Požarevac
Morava
Negotin
Travnik
Valjevo
Bor
Han Pijesak
1346
Timok
Sarajevo
Titovo Užice
Kragujevac
Zaječar
Vidin
Čačak
Lom
Dunărea (Danube)
50
48
46
44
18
20
22
East from Greenwich

52

Map 56

1:5 000 000

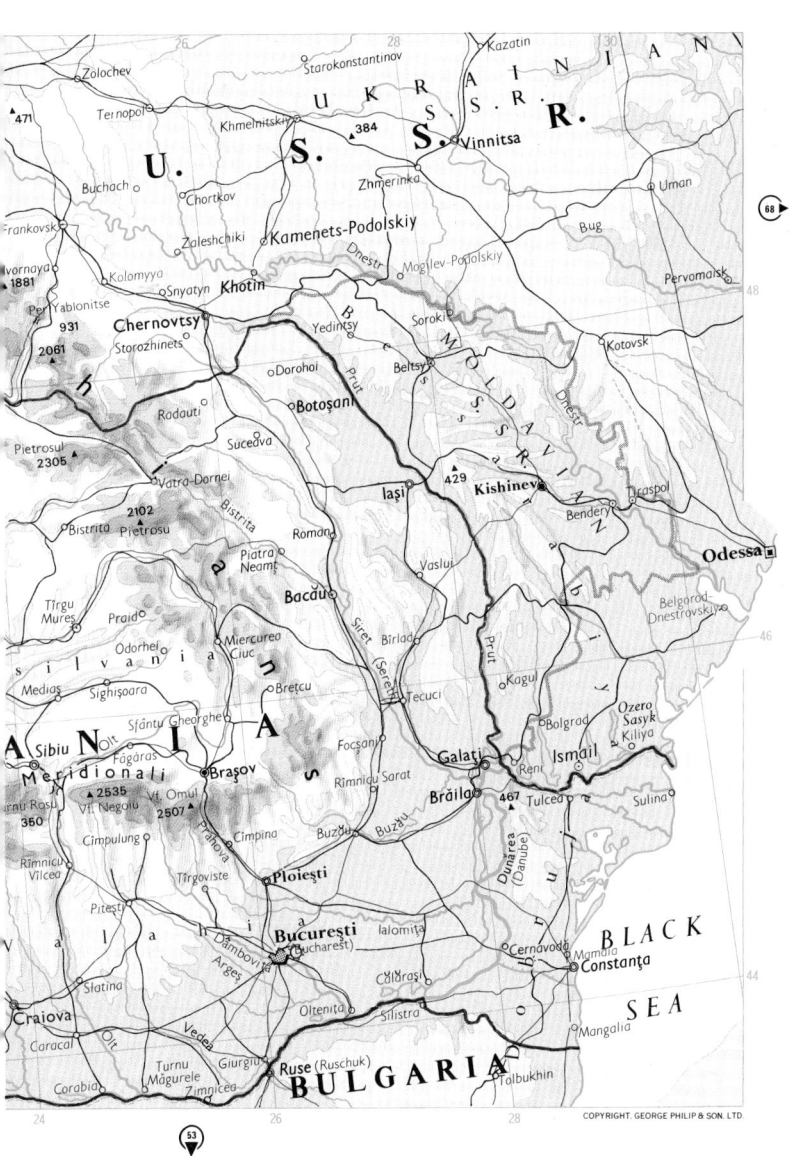

Map 57

Central Europe

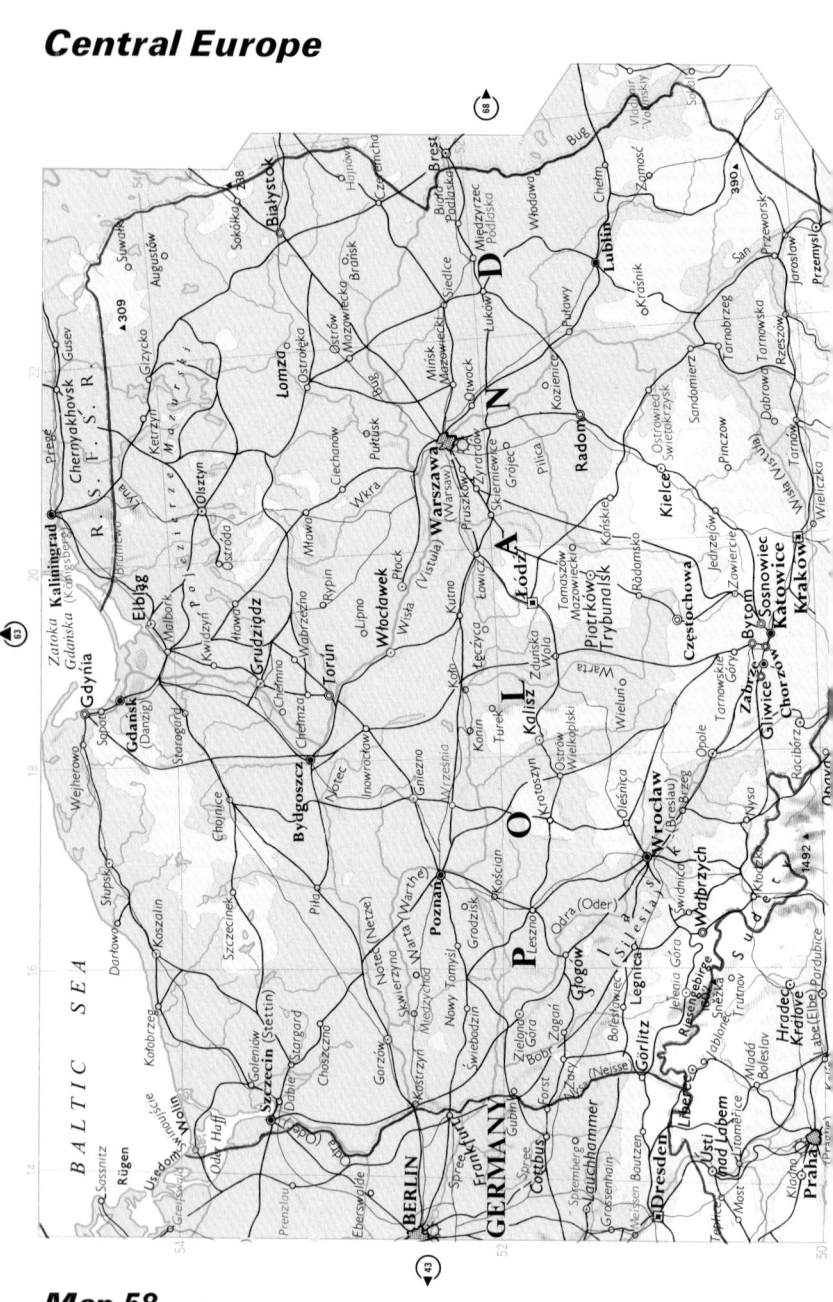

BALTIC SEA
Rügen
Sassnitz
Usedom
Wolin
Świnoujście
Oder Haff
Szczecin (Stettin)
Goleniów
Stargard
Kołobrzeg
Koszalin
Darłowo
Słupsk
Wejherowo
Gdynia
Sopot
Gdańsk (Danzig)
Zatoka Gdańska
Kaliningrad (Königsberg)
Chernyakhovsk
Gusev
Pregel
R. S. F. S. R.
Elbląg
Braniewo
Malbork
Kwidzyń
Iława
Ostróda
Olsztyn
Kętrzyn
Giżycko
Mazurski
Suwałki
Augustów
Sokółka
Białystok
Hajnówka
Bielsk
Brest
Biała Podlaska
Międzyrzec Podlaski
Łomża
Ostrołęka
Ostrów Mazowiecka
Ciechanów
Pułtusk
Mława
Grudziądz
Chełmno
Chełmża
Toruń
Bydgoszcz
Inowrocław
Włocławek
Płock
Lipno
Rypin
Brodnica
Wkra
Bug
Warszawa (Warsaw)
Wisła (Vistula)
Pruszków
Żyrardów
Grójec
Otwock
Mińsk Mazowiecki
Siedlce
Łuków
Puławy
Lublin
Kraśnik
Chełm
Włodawa
Zamość
Kozienice
Radom
Pilica
Skierniewice
Łowicz
Kutno
Łęczyca
Łódź
Tomaszów Mazowiecki
Piotrków Trybunalski
Radomsko
Końskie
Kielce
Ostrowiec Świętokrzyski
Sandomierz
Tarnobrzeg
Stalowa Wola
San
Przeworsk
Jarosław
Przemyśl
Rzeszów
Tarnów
Dębica
Pińczów
Jędrzejów
Zawiercie
Częstochowa
Kraków
Wieliczka
Sosnowiec
Katowice
Bytom
Chorzów
Zabrze
Gliwice
Tarnowskie Góry
Racibórz
Opole
Nysa
Brzeg
Kłodzko
Wałbrzych
Świdnica
Wrocław (Breslau)
Oleśnica
Krotoszyn
Ostrów Wielkopolski
Kalisz
Wieluń
Warta
Zduńska Wola
Turek
Konin
Koło
Gniezno
Września
Poznań
Kościan
Grodzisk
Leszno
Nowy Tomyśl
Świebodzin
Międzychód
Skwierzyna
Gorzów
Noteć (Netze)
Warta (Warthe)
Piła
Chojnice
Szczecinek
Starogard
Choszczno
Kostrzyn
Zielona Góra
Żagań
Głogów
Legnica
Bolesławiec
Jelenia Góra
Riesengebirge
Sněžka
Sudety
Silesia
Odra (Oder)
Bóbr
Nysa (Neisse)
Görlitz
Zgorzelec
Forst
Gubin
Frankfurt
Spree
Cottbus
Spremberg
Lauchhammer
Grossenhain
Bautzen
Dresden
Meissen
Teplice
Most
Ústí nad Labem
Litoměřice
Liberec
Jablonec
Mladá Boleslav
Trutnov
Hradec Králové
Pardubice
Labe (Elbe)
Kladno
Praha (Prague)
Ostrava
Eberswalde
Prenzlau
Greifswald
BERLIN
GERMANY
POLAND
1492
390
309
238
14
16
18
20
22
50
52
54
63
68
43

Map 58

1:5 000 000

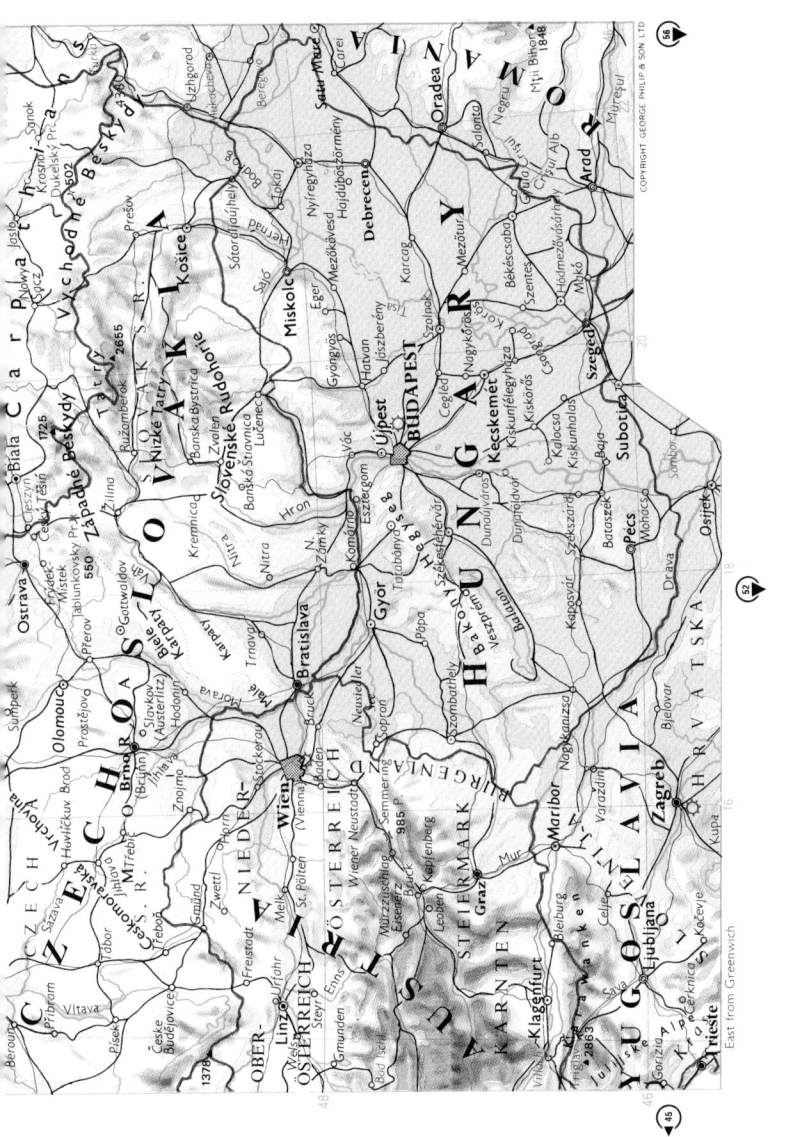
CZECHOSLOVAKIA
AUSTRIA
HUNGARY
YUGOSLAVIA
ROMANIA
OBER-ÖSTERREICH
NIEDER-ÖSTERREICH
BURGENLAND
STEIERMARK
KÄRNTEN
SLOVENSKÁ S.R.
ČESKÁ S.R.
HRVATSKA
Carpathians
Východné Beskydy
Západné Beskydy
Tatry
Nízke Tatry
Slovenské Rudohorie
Biele Karpaty
Malé Karpaty
Bakony
Julijske Alpe
Karawanken
Českomoravská Vrchovina
Ostrava
Olomouc
Brno
Bratislava
Košice
Miskolc
Debrecen
Oradea
Arad
Szeged
Subotica
Kecskemét
BUDAPEST
Újpest
Győr
Pécs
Wien (Vienna)
Linz
Graz
Maribor
Zagreb
Ljubljana
Klagenfurt
Trieste
Uzhgorod
Žilina
Nitra
Trnava
Prešov
Eger
Szolnok
Nyíregyháza
Békéscsaba
Székesfehérvár
Veszprém
Szombathely
Sopron
Balaton
Dunaújváros
Osijek
Sombor
Vltava
Morava
Hron
Tisza
Drava
Sava
Mur
1725
2655
1378
2863
1848
985
550
502
East from Greenwich
COPYRIGHT GEORGE PHILIP & SON LTD
56
52
45

Map 59

Southern Scandinavia

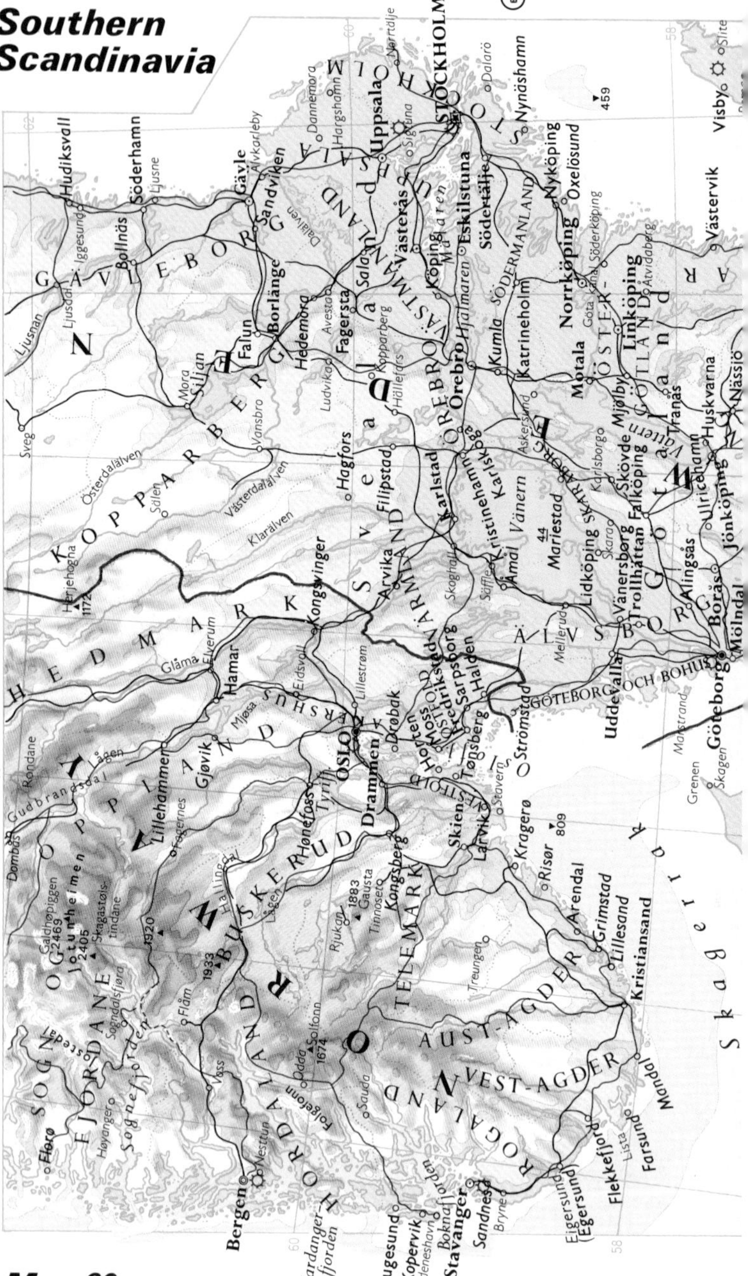
Hudiksvall
Söderhamn
Bollnäs
Gävle
Sandviken
Falun
Borlänge
Hedemora
Fagersta
Sala
Uppsala
Västerås
Köping
Eskilstuna
Södertälje
STOCKHOLM
Nynäshamn
Nyköping
Oxelösund
Norrköping
Linköping
Motala
Mjölby
Tranås
Örebro
Kumla
Katrineholm
Karlstad
Kristinehamn
Karlskoga
Filipstad
Hagfors
Arvika
Mariestad
Lidköping
Skövde
Falköping
Vänersborg
Trollhättan
Alingsås
Borås
Jönköping
Huskvarna
Västervik
Visby
Uddevalla
Göteborg
Mölndal
Strömstad
Kongsvinger
Hamar
Gjøvik
Lillehammer
OSLO
Drammen
Hønefoss
Kongsberg
Skien
Larvik
Tønsberg
Horten
Moss
Fredrikstad
Sarpsborg
Halden
Kragerø
Arendal
Grimstad
Lillesand
Kristiansand
Mandal
Farsund
Flekkefjord
Egersund
Sandnes
Stavanger
Haugesund
Kopervik
Bergen
Florø
Mora
Siljan
Vänern
Vättern
Hjälmaren
Mälaren
Mjøsa
Skagerrak
Jotunheimen
SOGN OG FJORDANE
HORDALAND
ROGALAND
VEST-AGDER
AUST-AGDER
TELEMARK
BUSKERUD
OPPLAND
HEDMARK
AKERSHUS
VESTFOLD
ØSTFOLD
VÄRMLAND
KOPPARBERG
GÄVLEBORG
UPPSALA
STOCKHOLM
VÄSTMANLAND
SÖDERMANLAND
ÖREBRO
SKARABORG
ÄLVSBORG
GÖTEBORG OCH BOHUS
ÖSTERGÖTLAND
NORWAY
SWEDEN
65
66
62

Map 60

1:5 000 000

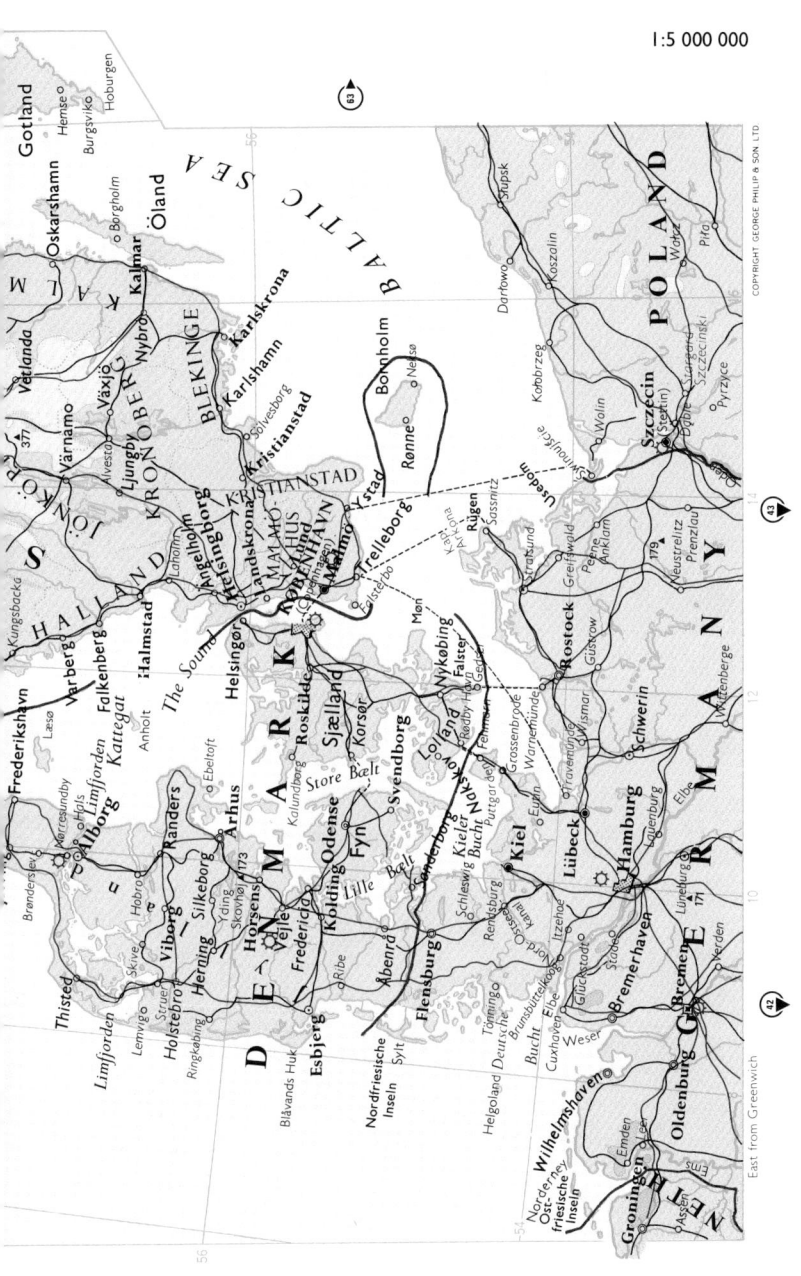

DENMARK
SWEDEN
GERMANY
POLAND
BALTIC SEA
Kattegat
Skagerrak
The Sound
Store Bælt
Lille Bælt
Limfjorden
Kieler Bucht
Deutsche Bucht
Nordfriesische Inseln
Ostfriesische Inseln
Frederikshavn
Ålborg
Thisted
Viborg
Randers
Århus
Silkeborg
Herning
Holstebro
Horsens
Vejle
Fredericia
Kolding
Esbjerg
Ribe
Odense
Fyn
Svendborg
Sjælland
Roskilde
Korsør
Helsingør
København (Copenhagen)
Lolland
Falster
Nykøbing
Møn
Bornholm
Rønne
Nexø
Helsingborg
Landskrona
Malmö
Lund
Trelleborg
Ystad
Kristianstad
Karlshamn
Karlskrona
Halmstad
Falkenberg
Varberg
Växjö
Värnamo
Vetlanda
Kalmar
Öland
Oskarshamn
Gotland
Flensburg
Kiel
Lübeck
Hamburg
Rostock
Schwerin
Stralsund
Rügen
Greifswald
Usedom
Szczecin (Stettin)
Koszalin
Słupsk
Bremerhaven
Bremen
Oldenburg
Wilhelmshaven
Emden
Groningen
Cuxhaven
Helgoland
Elbe
Weser
East from Greenwich
COPYRIGHT GEORGE PHILIP & SON LTD.

Map 61

Baltic Lands

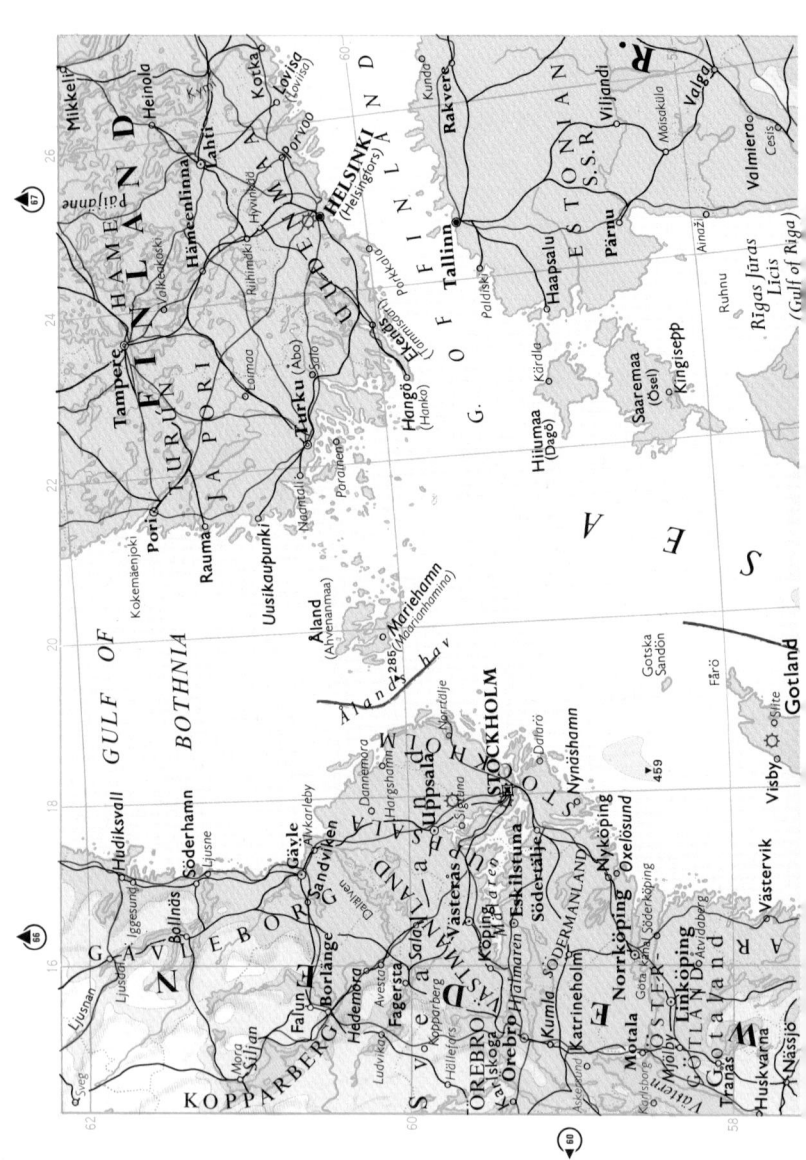

Map 62

1:5 000 000

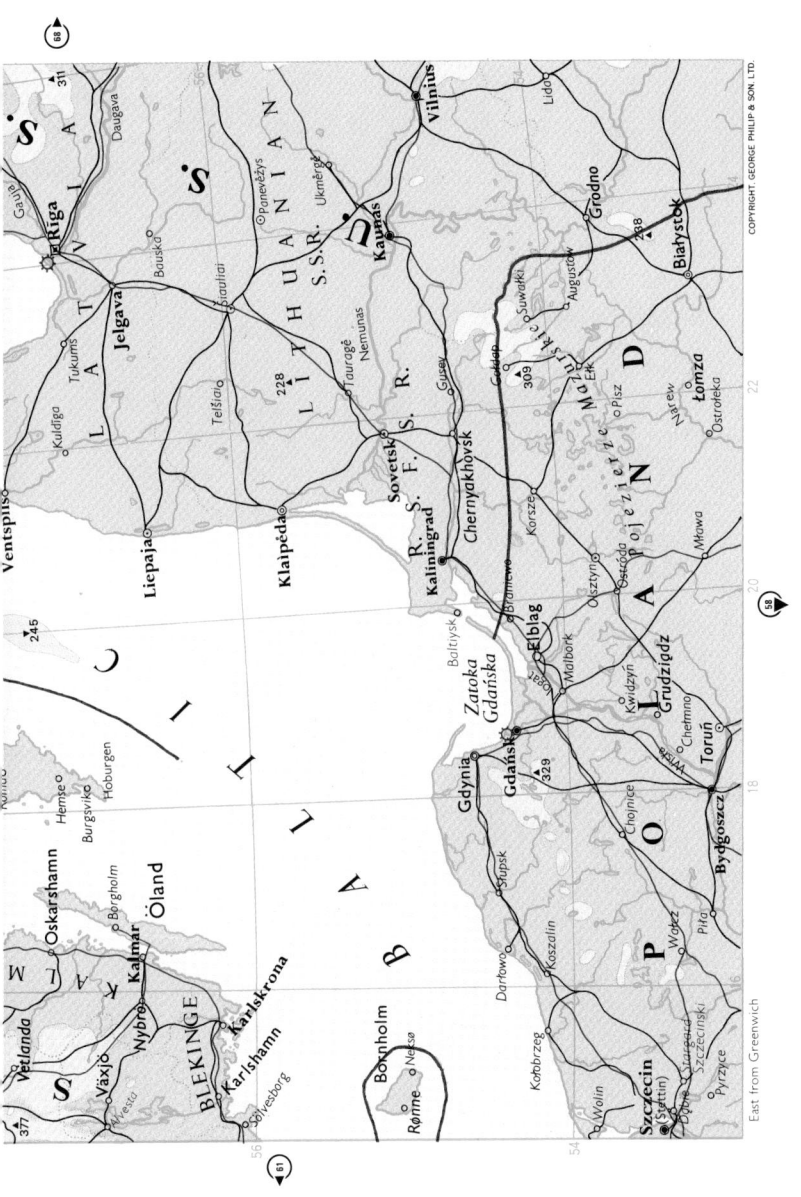
68
58
61
Ventspils
Liepaja
Klaipėda
Kaliningrad
Sovetsk
Chernyakhovsk
Riga
Jelgava
Tukums
Kuldīga
Bauska
Šiauliai
Telšiai
Tauragė
Panevėžys
Ukmergė
Kaunas
Vilnius
Lida
Grodno
Białystok
Suwałki
Augustów
Gołdap
Ełk
Pisz
Łomża
Ostrołęka
Narew
Mława
Olsztyn
Ostróda
Korsze
Braniewo
Elbląg
Malbork
Baltiysk
Gusev
Nemunas
Daugava
Gauja
Zatoka Gdańska
Gdańsk
Gdynia
Kwidzyn
Grudziądz
Chełmno
Toruń
Wisła
Bydgoszcz
Chojnice
Słupsk
Koszalin
Darłowo
Wałcz
Piła
Kołobrzeg
Szczecin (Stettin)
Stargard Szczeciński
Pyrzyce
Wolin
Dąbie
Bornholm
Rønne
Nexø
Karlshamn
Karlskrona
Sölvesborg
Växjö
Nybro
Kalmar
Vetlanda
Oskarshamn
Öland
Borgholm
Alvesta
BLEKINGE
Hemse
Burgsvik
Hoburgen
L A T V I A N S.S.R.
L I T H U A N I A N S.S.R.
R. S. F. S. R.
P O L A N D
B A L T I C
S
K A L M
Pojezierze Mazurskie
Łyna
377
245
311
228
309
238
329
56
54
18
20
22
East from Greenwich

Map 63

North West Scandinavia and Iceland

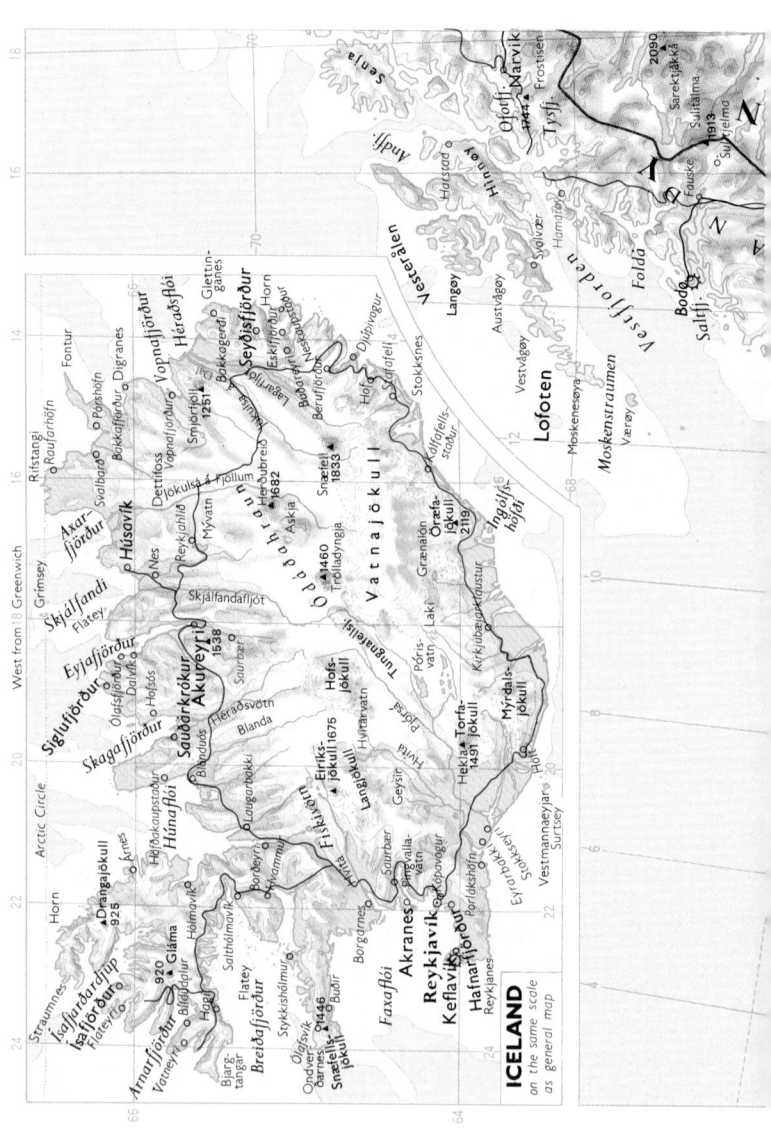

Map 64

1:5 000 000

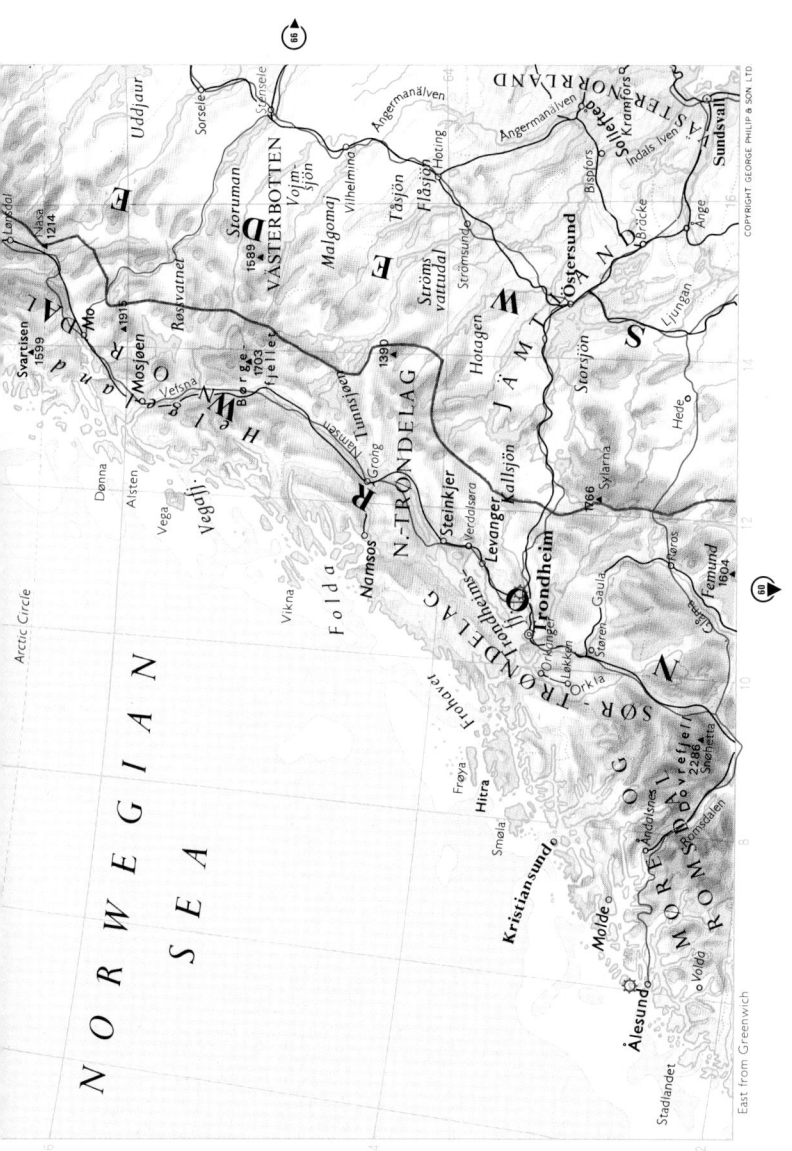
NORWEGIAN SEA
Arctic Circle
NORWAY
SWEDEN
Dønna
Alsten
Vega
Vegafj.
Vikna
Folda
Namsos
Frohavet
Frøya
Hitra
Smøla
Kristiansund
Molde
Ålesund
Stadlandet
Volda
Åndalsnes
Romsdalen
MØRE OG ROMSDAL
Dovrefjell
2286
Snøhetta
SØR-TRØNDELAG
Orkla
Løkken
Orkanger
Trondheim
Trondheimsfjorden
Levanger
Verdalsøra
Steinkjer
N.-TRØNDELAG
Grong
Namsen
Tunnsjøen
1390
Støren
Gaula
Røros
Femund
1604
Glomma
Sylarna
1766
Kallsjön
Storsjön
Hede
JÄMTLAND
Hotagen
Östersund
Ljungan
Bräcke
Ånge
Sundsvall
Indals älven
Kramfors
Sollefteå
Bispfors
Ångermanälven
VÄSTERNORRLAND
Strömsund
Ströms vattudal
Flåsjön
Hoting
Tåsjön
Vilhelmina
Malgomaj
Vojmsjön
VÄSTERBOTTEN
Storuman
1589
Sorsele
Stensele
Uddjaur
Røssvatnet
Lønsdal
Nasa
1214
Svartisen
1599
Mo
1915
Mosjøen
Vefsna
Helgeland
Børgefjellet
1703
East from Greenwich
COPYRIGHT GEORGE PHILIP & SON LTD

Map 65

Northern Scandinavia

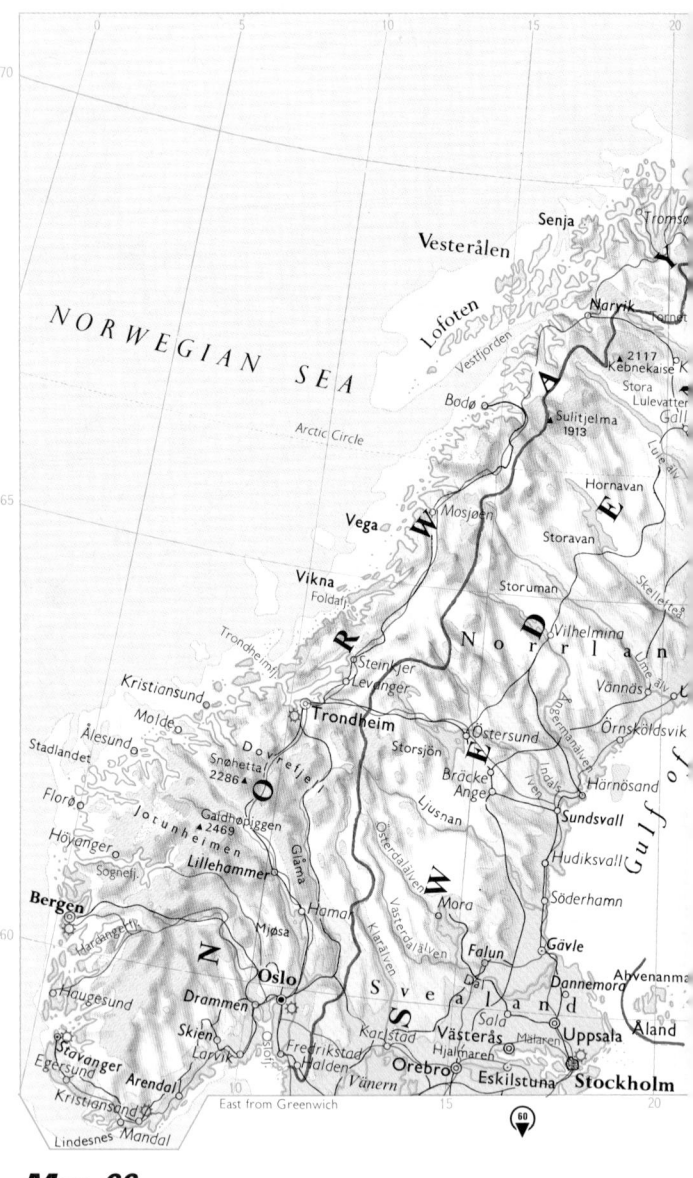
NORWEGIAN SEA
Senja
Tromsø
Vesterålen
Lofoten
Vestfjorden
Narvik
2117
Kebnekaise
Stora Lulevatten
Bodø
Sulitjelma 1913
Arctic Circle
Lule älv
Hornavan
Mosjøen
Vega
Storavan
Vikna
Foldafj.
Storuman
Skellefteå
Vilhelmina
Trondheimfj.
Norrland
Steinkjer
Levanger
Kristiansund
Vännäs
Ume älv
Trondheim
Molde
Ålesund
Stadlandet
Östersund
Ångermanälven
Örnsköldsvik
Storsjön
Dovrefjell
Snøhetta 2286
Bräcke
Ange
Indals
Härnösand
Florø
Jotunheimen
Galdhøpiggen 2469
Ljusnan
Sundsvall
Höyanger
Sognefj.
Lillehammer
Glåma
Österdalälven
Hudiksvall
Gulf of
Bergen
Hamar
Mora
Söderhamn
Hardangerfj.
Mjøsa
Västerdalälven
Klarälven
Falun
Gävle
Oslo
Dal
Dannemora
Ahvenanmaa
Haugesund
Drammen
Svealand
Sala
Åland
Skien
Karlstad
Västerås
Mälaren
Uppsala
Stavanger
Larvik
Oslofj.
Fredrikstad
Hjälmaren
Egersund
Halden
Orebro
Eskilstuna
Stockholm
Arendal
Vänern
Kristiansand
East from Greenwich
Lindesnes
Mandal
NORWAY
SWEDEN
0
5
10
15
20
70
65
60
60

Map 66

1:10 000 000

BARENTS
SEA

Hammerfest
orøya
Nordkapp
Nordkinn
Vardø
Vardsø
Varangerfj.
Pechenga
Tana
Inari
Inari
●Murmansk
Porttipahta
Lokka
L a p p l a n d
Kirovsk
Kolskiy
Poluostrov
Tornetrask
Kemijoki
Kandalaksha
Rovaniemi
B e l o y e   M o r e
Tornio
Kemi
oden
Luleå
Haparanda
Kem
Piteå
Arkhangelsk●
Skellefteå
Raahe
Oulu
Belomorsk
Onega
Oulu-
järvi
Kajaani
Onega
Bothnia
Iisalmi
Karelia
Vaasa
Kuopio
U. S. S. R.
F I N L A N D
Joensuu
Onezhskoye
Ozero
Jyväskylä
Petrozavodsk
Tampere
Imatra
Saimaa
ori
Uusikaupunki
Ladozhskoye
Ozero
Oz.
Beloye
Hämeenlinna
Lahti
Turku
Helsinki
Kotka
Vyborg
Tikhvin
Hangö
Porkkala
Kronstadt
●Leningrad
Gulf of Finland
Cherepovets
●Tallinn
Kohtla-Järve
Narva
Malaya Vishera

Map 67

U.S.S.R.: West

58

57

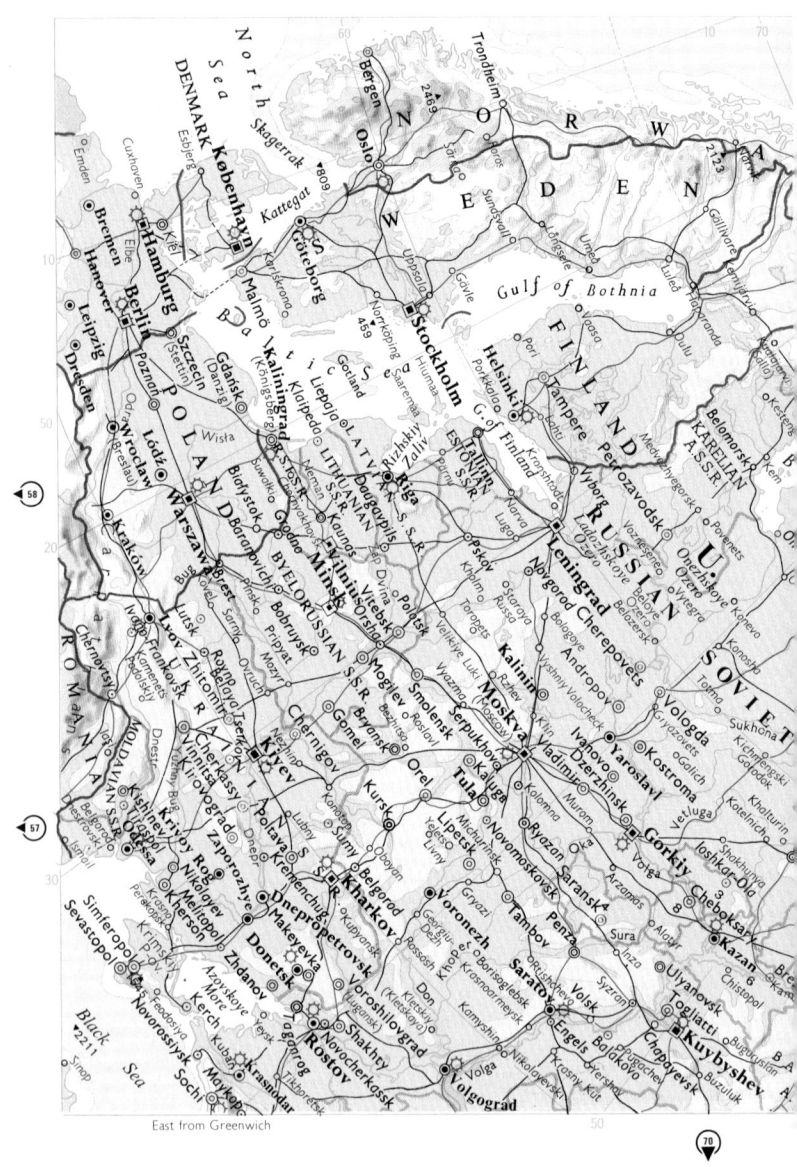
North Sea
DENMARK
København
Skagerrak
Kattegat
Oslo
Bergen
Trondheim
NORWAY
SWEDEN
Stockholm
Göteborg
Malmö
Gulf of Bothnia
FINLAND
Helsinki
Tampere
G. of Finland
Baltic Sea
Hamburg
Berlin
Bremen
Hanover
Leipzig
Dresden
POLAND
Warszawa
Łódź
Wrocław
Kraków
Gdańsk
Szczecin
Kaliningrad
LITHUANIAN S.S.R.
LATVIAN S.S.R.
ESTONIAN S.S.R.
Riga
Tallinn
Vilnius
Minsk
BYELORUSSIAN S.S.R.
UKRAINIAN S.S.R.
Kiyev
Kharkov
Odessa
Dnepropetrovsk
Donetsk
Rostov
Volgograd
Voronezh
Moskva
(Moscow)
Leningrad
Gorkiy
Kazan
Kuybyshev
Saratov
MOLDAVIAN S.S.R.
ROMANIA
KARELIAN A.S.S.R.
RUSSIAN SOVIET
Black Sea

East from Greenwich

70

Map 68

1:20 000 000

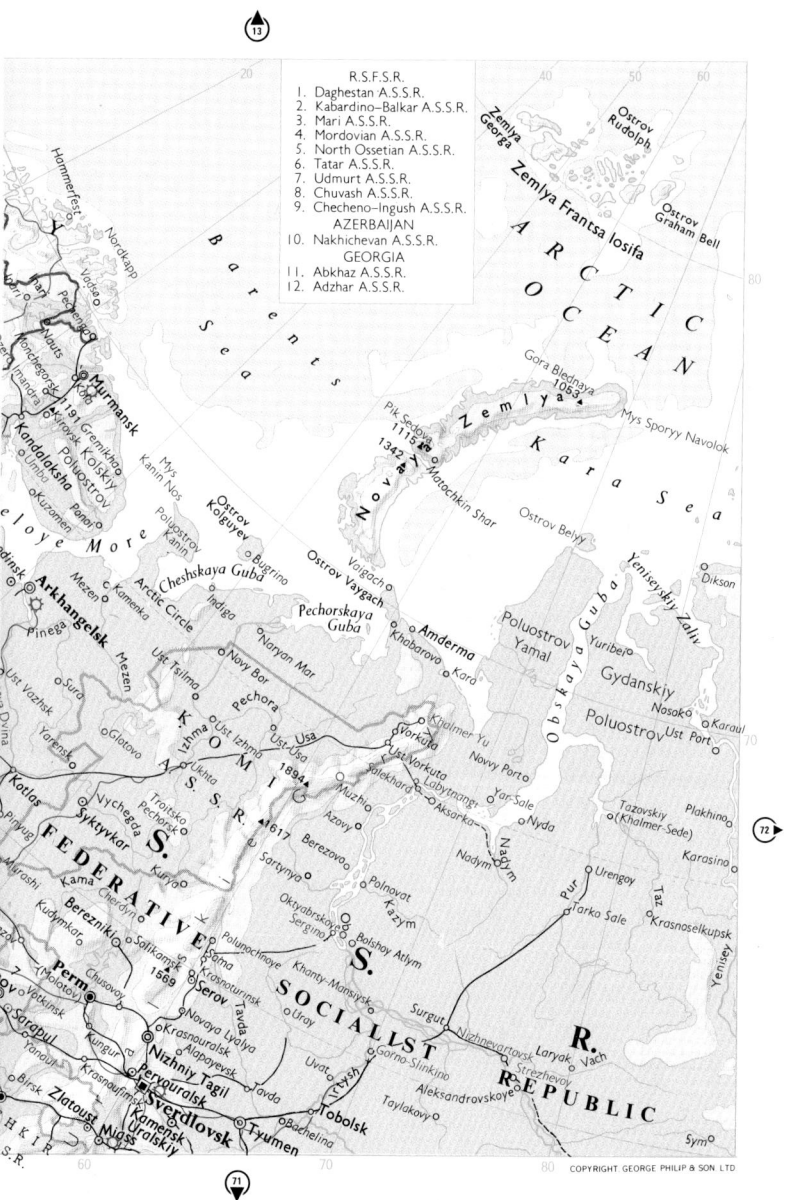

R.S.F.S.R.
1. Daghestan A.S.S.R.
2. Kabardino–Balkar A.S.S.R.
3. Mari A.S.S.R.
4. Mordovian A.S.S.R.
5. North Ossetian A.S.S.R.
6. Tatar A.S.S.R.
7. Udmurt A.S.S.R.
8. Chuvash A.S.S.R.
9. Checheno–Ingush A.S.S.R.
    AZERBAIJAN
10. Nakhichevan A.S.S.R.
    GEORGIA
11. Abkhaz A.S.S.R.
12. Adzhar A.S.S.R.

COPYRIGHT GEORGE PHILIP & SON LTD

Map 69

U.S.S.R.: South West

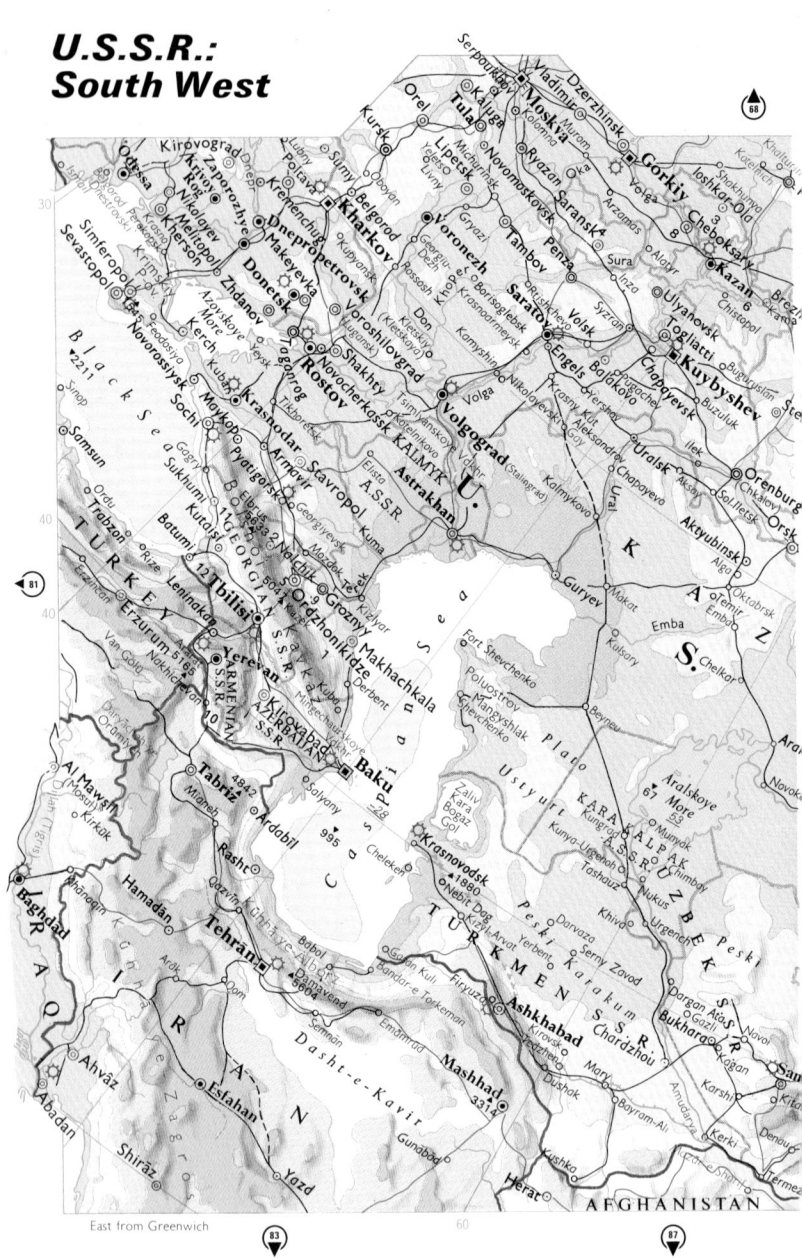
68
81
83
87
East from Greenwich
30
40
60
Moskva
Vladimir
Dzerzhinsk
Gorkiy
Serpukhov
Kaluga
Tula
Orel
Kursk
Kolomna
Murom
Ryazan
Lipetsk
Novomoskovsk
Michurinsk
Yelets
Livny
Oka
Volga
Arzamas
Saransk
Ioshkar-Ola
Cheboksary
Kazan
Kama
Chistopol
Shakhunya
Kotelnich
Sura
Alatyr
Inza
Ulyanovsk
Togliatti
Kuybyshev
Syzran
Penza
Tambov
Voronezh
Gryazi
Kirovograd
Odessa
Izmail
Dnestrovski
Zaporozhye
Krivoy Rog
Nikolayev
Kherson
Melitopol
Dnepr
Lubny
Poltava
Sumy
Kremenchug
Kharkov
Belgorod
Oboyan
Kupyansk
Dnepropetrovsk
Makeyevka
Donetsk
Zhdanov
Voroshilovgrad
(Lugansk)
Simferopol
Sevastopol
Krimskiy P-ov
Kerch
Feodosiya
Azovskoye More
Yeysk
Taganrog
Rostov
Novocherkassk
Shakhty
Novorossiysk
Kuban
Krasnodar
Tikhoretsk
Maykop
Sochi
Armavir
Stavropol
Pyatigorsk
Elbrus 5633
Nalchik
Mozdok
Terek
Kuma
Georgiyevsk
Elista
KALMYK A.S.S.R.
Astrakhan
Volgograd
(Stalingrad)
Kotelnikovo
Tsimlyanskoye Vdkhr.
Don
Kletskiy
(Kletskaya)
Rossosh
Georgiu-Dezh
Khoper
Borisoglebsk
Krasnoarmeysk
Kamyshin
Rtishchevo
Saratov
Volsk
Engels
Balakovo
Nikolayevsk
Krasny Kut
Aleksandrov Gay
Yershov
Pugachev
Chapayevsk
Buzuluk
Buguruslan
Uralsk
Chapayevo
Ilek
Aksay
Sol-Iletsk
Orenburg
(Chkalov)
Orsk
Aktyubinsk
Alga
Kalmykovo
Ural
Guryev
Makat
Temir
Oktabrsk
Emba
Kulsary
Chelkar
Black Sea
2211
Sinop
Samsun
Ordu
Trabzon
Rize
Gagry
Sukhumi
Kutaisi
Batumi
GEORGIAN S.S.R.
TURKEY
Erzincan
Erzurum
Leninakan
Tbilisi
Ordzhonikidze
Grozny
Kizlyar
Makhachkala
Kavkaz
Kazbek 5047
Yerevan
ARMENIAN S.S.R.
Ararat 5165
Van Gölü
Nakhichevan
Kirovabad
AZERBAIJAN S.S.R.
Mingechaurskoye Vdkhr.
Kuba
Derbent
Baku
-28
Caspian Sea
Salyany
995
Cheleken
Krasnovodsk
1880
Nebit Dag
Fort Shevchenko
Poluostrov Mangyshlak
Shevchenko
Zaliv Kara Bogaz Gol
Plato Ustyurt
Beyneu
KARAKALPAK A.S.S.R.
Kungrad
Muynak
Aralskoye More
53
67
Chimbay
Nukus
Kunya-Urgench
Tashauz
Khiva
Urgench
Darvaza
Yerbent
Serny Zavod
Peski Karakum
Kizyl-Arvat
TURKMEN S.S.R.
Ashkhabad
Firyuza
Kirovsk
Tedzhen
Dushak
Mary
Bayram-Ali
Chardzhou
Bukhara
Dargan Ata
Gazli
Navoi
Kagan
Karshi
Kerki
Amudarya
Kushka
Herat
Termez
Denau
Kitab
Samarkand
UZBEK S.S.R.
Peski
KAZ S.
U.
Daryacheh-ye Orumiyeh
Tabriz
4842
Mianeh
Ardabil
Rasht
Qazvin
Kuhha-ye Alborz
Tehran
Damavend 5604
Babol
Gorgan
Bandar-e Torkeman
Gonbad-e Kavus
Emamrud
Semnan
Dasht-e-Kavir
Mashhad
3314
Gunabad
Qom
Arak
Hamadan
Al Mawsil
(Mosul)
Kirkuk
Dijlah (Tigris)
Khanaqin
Baghdad
IRAQ
IRAN
Kuhha-ye Zagros
Ahvaz
Abadan
Esfahan
Shiraz
Yazd
AFGHANISTAN

Map 70

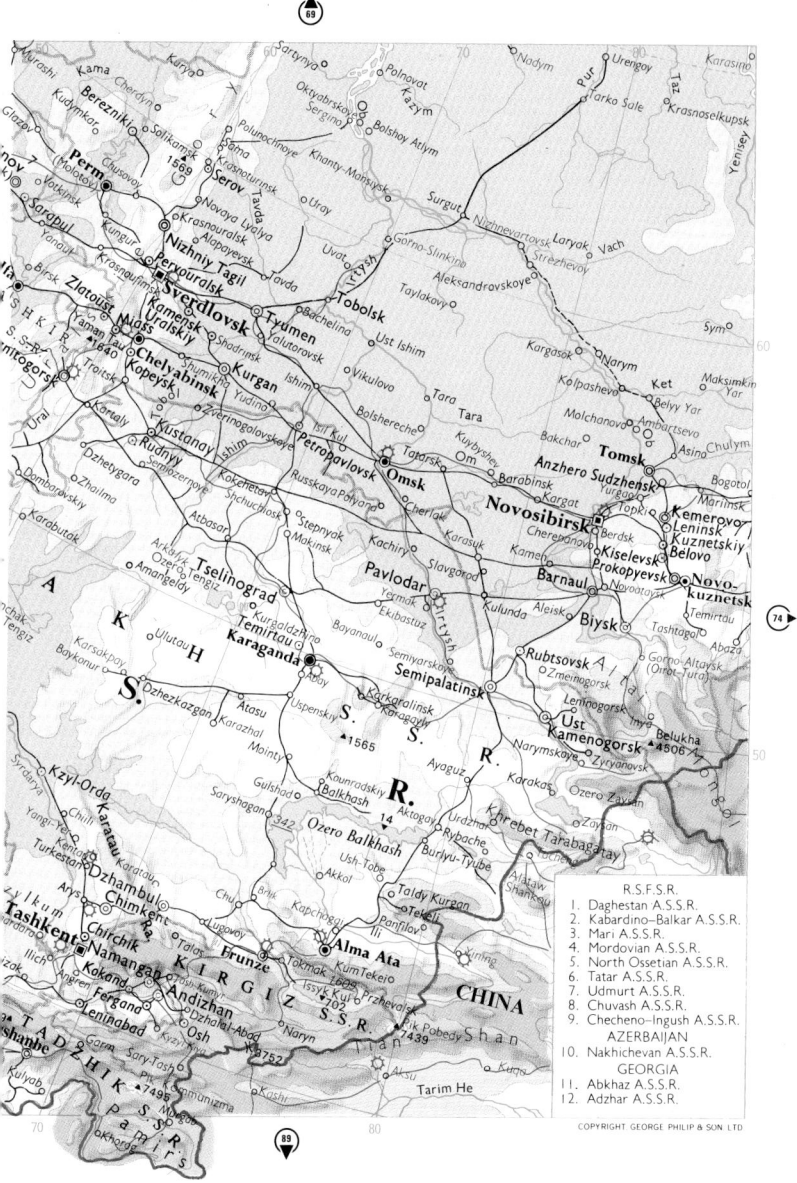

1:20 000 000

R.S.F.S.R.
1. Daghestan A.S.S.R.
2. Kabardino–Balkar A.S.S.R.
3. Mari A.S.S.R.
4. Mordovian A.S.S.R.
5. North Ossetian A.S.S.R.
6. Tatar A.S.S.R.
7. Udmurt A.S.S.R.
8. Chuvash A.S.S.R.
9. Checheno–Ingush A.S.S.R.
AZERBAIJAN
10. Nakhichevan A.S.S.R.
GEORGIA
11. Abkhaz A.S.S.R.
12. Adzhar A.S.S.R.

COPYRIGHT GEORGE PHILIP & SON LTD

Map 71

U.S.S.R.: North East

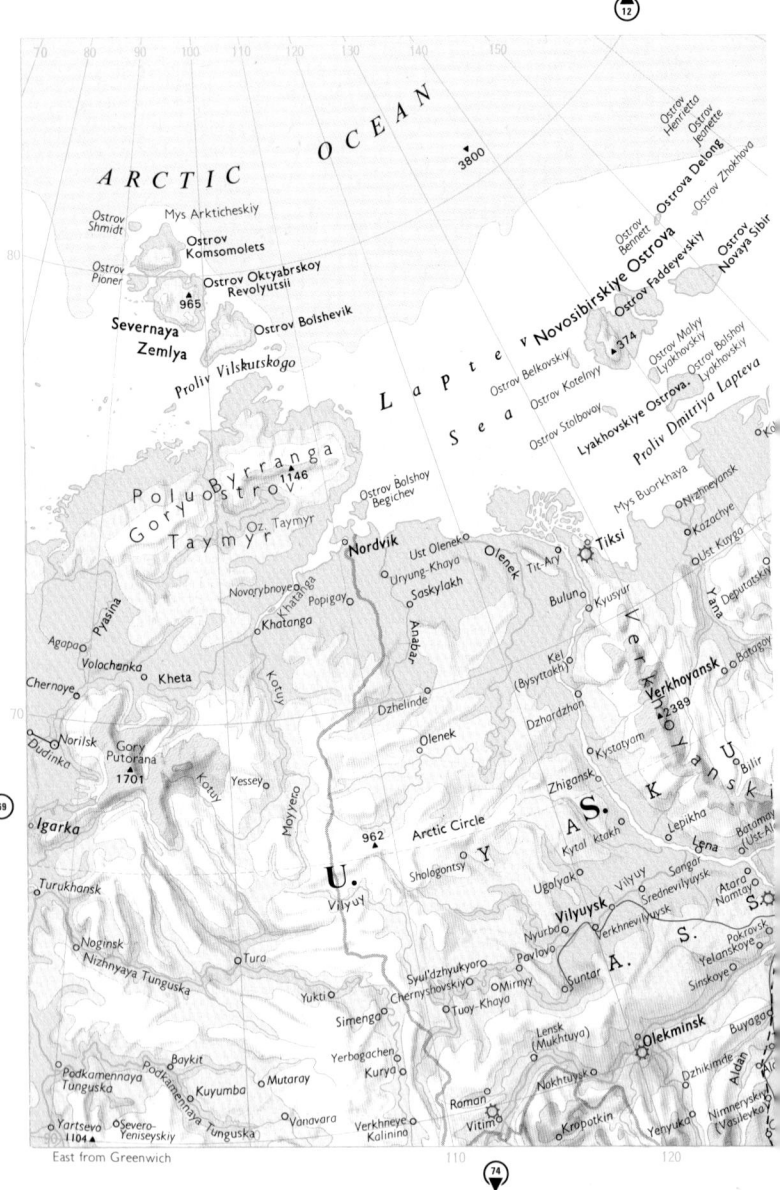
12
ARCTIC OCEAN
3800
Ostrov Henrietta
Ostrov Jeanette
Ostrova Delong
Ostrov Zhokhova
Ostrov Shmidt
Mys Arkticheskiy
Ostrov Komsomolets
Ostrov Pioner
Ostrov Oktyabrskoy Revolyutsii
965
Severnaya Zemlya
Ostrov Bolshevik
Proliv Vilskutskogo
Ostrov Bennett
Novosibirskiye Ostrova
Ostrov Faddeyevskiy
Ostrov Novaya Sibir
374
Laptev Sea
Ostrov Belkovskiy
Ostrov Kotelnyy
Ostrov Malyy Lyakhovskiy
Ostrov Bolshoy Lyakhovskiy
Ostrov Stolbovoy
Lyakhovskiye Ostrova
Proliv Dmitriya Lapteva
Gory Byrranga
1146
Poluostrov Taymyr
Oz. Taymyr
Ostrov Bolshoy Begichev
Nordvik
Ust Olenek
Olenek
Tit-Ary
Tiksi
Mys Buorkhaya
Nizhneyansk
Kazachye
Ust Kuyga
Uryung-Khaya
Saskylakh
Novorybnoye
Popigay
Khatanga
Bulun
Kyusyur
Yana
Deputatskiy
Pyasina
Agapa
Volochanka
Kheta
Kotuy
Anabar
Kel (Bysyttakh)
Verkhoyansk
Batagay
Chernoye
Dzhelinde
Dzhardzhan
2389
Norilsk
Dudinka
Gory Putorana
1701
Olenek
Kystatyam
Verkhoyanskiy
Bilir
Yessey
Moyyero
Zhigansk
69
Igarka
962
Arctic Circle
Kytal ktakh
Lepikha
Batamay (Ust-Aldan)
Lena
Y A K U T S K
Sholagontsy
U. S. S. R.
A. S. S. R.
Turukhansk
Vilyuy
Ugolyak
Vilyuysk
Vilyuy
Sangar
Srednevilyuysk
Atara
Namtay
Nyurba
Verkhnevilyuysk
Noginsk
Nizhnyaya Tunguska
Tura
Pavlovo
Pokrovsk
Yelanskoye
Syul'dzhyukyoro
Chernyshovskiy
Mirnyy
Suntar
Sinskoye
Yukti
Tuoy-Khaya
Simenga
Lensk (Mukhtuya)
Olekminsk
Buyaga
Baykit
Yerbogachen
Podkamennaya Tunguska
Kurya
Dzhikimde
Aldan
Kuyumba
Mutaray
Nokhtuysk
Roman
Yartsevo
Severo-Yeniseyskiy
Vanavara
Verkhneye Kalinino
Vitim
Kropotkin
Yenyuka
Nimneryskiy (Vasilevka)
1104
East from Greenwich
70
80
90
100
110
120
130
140
150
74

Map 72

1:20 000 000

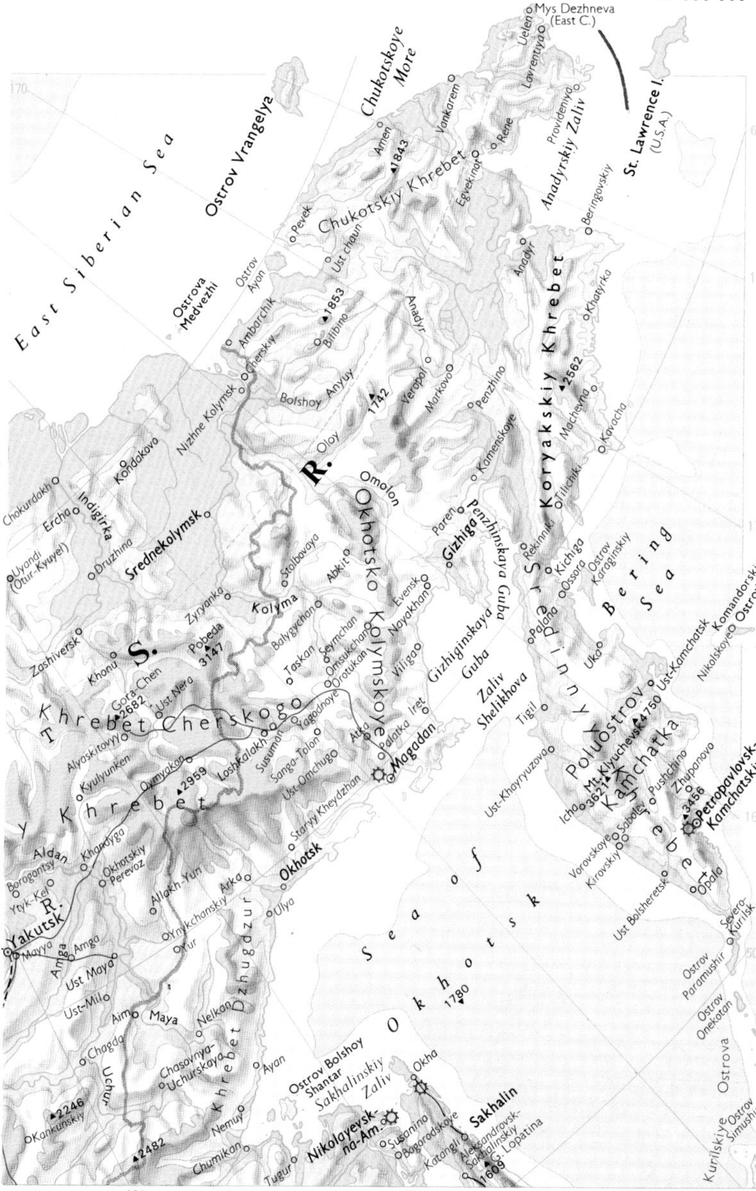

Mys Dezhneva
(East C.)

St. Lawrence I.
(U.S.A.)

Chukotskoye
More

East Siberian Sea

Ostrov Vrangelya

Ostrova
Medvezhi

Chukotskiy Khrebet

Anadyrskiy Zaliv

Koryakskiy Khrebet
▲2562

Bering
Sea

Chokurdakh
Ercho Indigirka
Uyandi
(Otur-Kyuyel)
Druzhina
Zashiversk
Khonu
Gora Chen
2682
Alyaskitovyy
Kryulyunken
Omchikandya ▲2959
Khrebet Cherskogo
y Khrebet
Aldan
Khangolya
Okhotskiy
Perevoz
Borogontsy
Ytyk-Kyel
Yakutsk
Mayya
Amga
Ust Maya
Ust-Milo
Chagda
Aimo Maya
▲2246
OKankunskiy
▲2282
Uchur
Chumikan

Koddakovo
Srednekolymsk
Zyryanka
Kolyma
Balygychan
Taskan Seymchan
Omsukchan
Emtygey Omchak
Atka Palatka Iret
Song-Tolon
Ust-Omchug
Staryy Kheydzhan

Nizhne Kolymsk
Ambarchik
Cherskiy
Ostrov Ayon

R. Oloy
▲1853
Bilibino
Omolon
Bolshoy Anyuy
▲1742

Pevek
Ust Chaun

Amen ▲1843
Vankarem

Uelen
Lavrentiya

Lelen

Ryrka

Egvekinot
Providenya
Beringovskiy

Anadyr
Markovo
Penzhino
Kamenskoye
Poren
Gizhiga
Penzhinskaya Guba
Gizhiginskaya Guba
Evensk Naykhandran
Viligino

Zaliv
Shelikhova

Sredinnyy
Khrebet

Okhotsko Kolymskoye

R. Omolon

Balakareto
Kidinga
Oranga Ostrov
Karaginskiy
Ossora
Palana
Tigil

Poluostrov
Kamchatka

Khrebet

Kamandorskiye
Ostrova

Nikolskoye
Ust-Kamchatsk
▲4750 Klyuchevskaya
Mt. Keuchevskaya ▲4750
Ushki Pushchino
Ichopka Sopochnoye Zhupanovo
Voronskoye ▲456
Kirovskiy Petropavlovsk-
Kamchatskiy

Ust Khayryuzovo
Ust Bolsheretsk
Severo-
Kurilsk

Sea of
Okhotsk

▲1790

Ostrov
Paramushir

Ostrov
Onekotan

Ostrova

Kurilskiye Ostrov
Shimushir

Ostrov Bolshoy
Shantar
Uchurskaya
Chasovnya
Ayan
Nelkan
Nemuyo
Tuguro

Khrebet Dzhugdzur
Ulya
Okhotsk
Arka
Aldoma-Yun

Sakhalinskiy
Zaliv

Okha
Bogorodskoye
Katangli
Nikolayevsk-
na-Am.
Sofroni
Dioma
Aleksandrovsk-
Sakhalinskiy
Lopatina
▲1609
Sakhalin

S.
Khrebet
T

COPYRIGHT GEORGE PHILIP & SON. LTD

Map 73

U.S.S.R.: South East and Mongolia

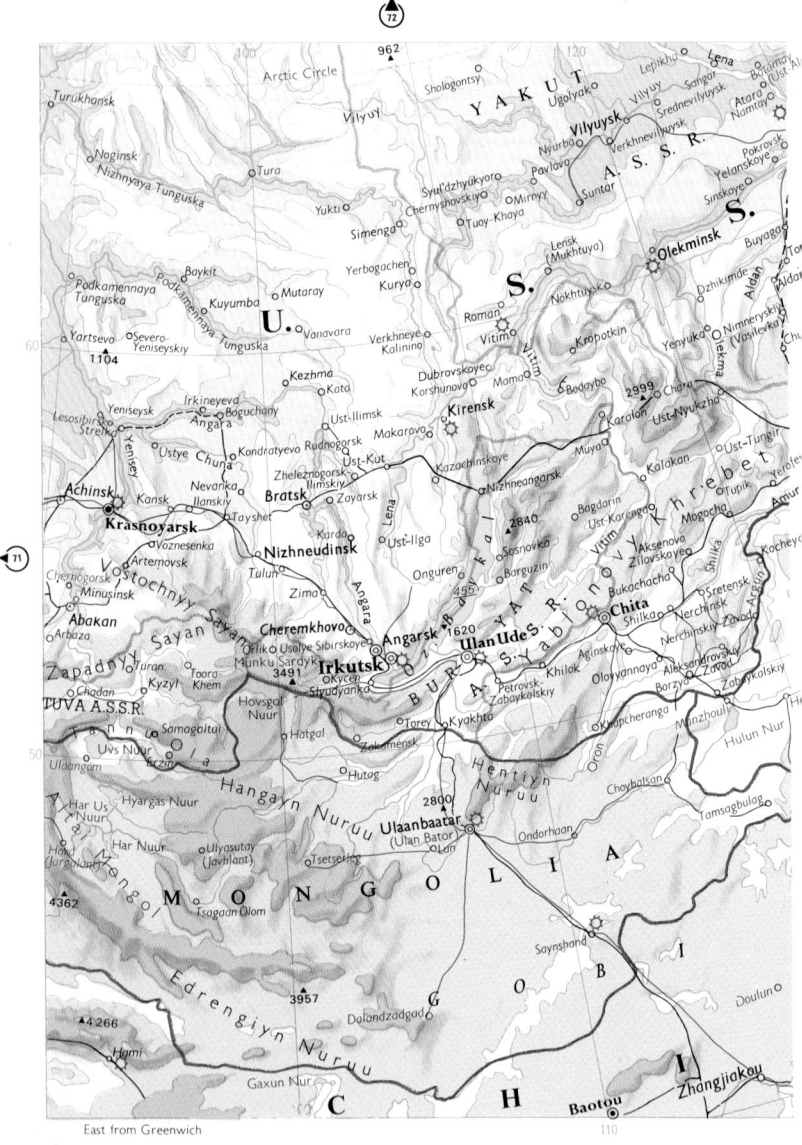

Arctic Circle

YAKUT

A.S.S.R.

U. S. S. R.

Turukhansk
Noginsk
Nizhnyaya Tunguska
Podkamennaya Tunguska
Yartsevo
1104
Achinsk
Krasnoyarsk
Abakan
Arbaza
Chernogorsk
Minusinsk
Zapadnyy Sayan
Chadan
Kyzyl
TUVA A.S.S.R.
Uvs Nuur
Ulaangom
Har Us Nuur
Hyargas Nuur
Har Nuur
4362
MONGOLIA
Tsagaan Olom

962
Shologontsy
Vilyuy
Vilyuysk
Nyurba
Verkhnevilyuysk
Srednevilyuysk
Sangar
Namtsy
Atara
Pokrovsk
Yelanskoye
Sinekoye
Olekminsk
Buyaga
Dzhikimde
Nimnyrsky
Yenyuka
Vasilevsky
2999
Chara
Ust-Nyukzha
Tura
Yukti
Simenga
Tuoy-Khaya
Lensk (Mukhtuya)
Nokhtuysk
Baykit
Kuyumba
Mutoray
Vanavara
Verkhneye-Kalinino
Roman
Vitimo
Vitim
Podkamennaya Tunguska
Severo-Yeniseyskiy
Kezhma
Kata
Dubrovskoye
Korshunovo
Mama
Bodaybe
Krobotkin
Karolon
Yeniseysk
Irkineyeva
Boguchany
Angara
Ust-Ilimsk
Makarovo
Kirensk
Muya
Ust-Tungir
Lesosibirsk
Strelka
Ustye Chuna
Nevanka
Rudnogorsk
Ust-Kut
Kazachinskoye
Nizhneangarsk
Bogdarin
Kalakan
Tupik
Yerofey
Kansk
Ilanskiy
Zheleznogorsk-Ilimskiy
Zayarsk
Kardoy
Ust-Ilga
Onguren
Barguzin
Vitim
Ust-Karenga
Mogocha
Amur
Bratsk
Tayshet
Nizhneudinsk
Voznesenka
Artemovsk
Tulun
Zima
Angara
Sosnovka
Bukachacha
Aksenova
Zilovskoye
Shilka
Kocheno
Vostochnyy Sayan
Cheremkhovo
Orlik
Usolye Sibirskoye
Angarsk
UlanUde
Khilok
Aginskoye
Nerchinsk
Nerchinskiy Zavod
Sretensk
Chita
Shilka
Munku Sardyk
3491
Irkutsk
Slyudyanka
1620
BURYATA
Petrovsk-Zabaykalskiy
Oloyyannaya
Aleksandrovskiy Zavod
Borzya
Zabaykalsk
Hovsgol Nuur
Hatgal
Torey
Kyakhta
Zakamensk
Oron
Chopcheranga
Manzhouli
Hulun Nuur
Samagaltay
Mondy
YABLONOVYY Khrebet
Hentiyn Nuruu
2800
Ulaanbaatar (Ulan Bator)
Ondorhaan
Choybalsan
Tamsagbulag
Ulyasutay (Javhlant)
Tsetserleg
Lun
Saynshand
GOBI
4266
Hami
Edrengiyn Nuruu
3957
Dalandzadgad
Doulun
Gaxun Nur
Zhangjiakou
Baotou
CHINA

Map 74

1:20 000 000

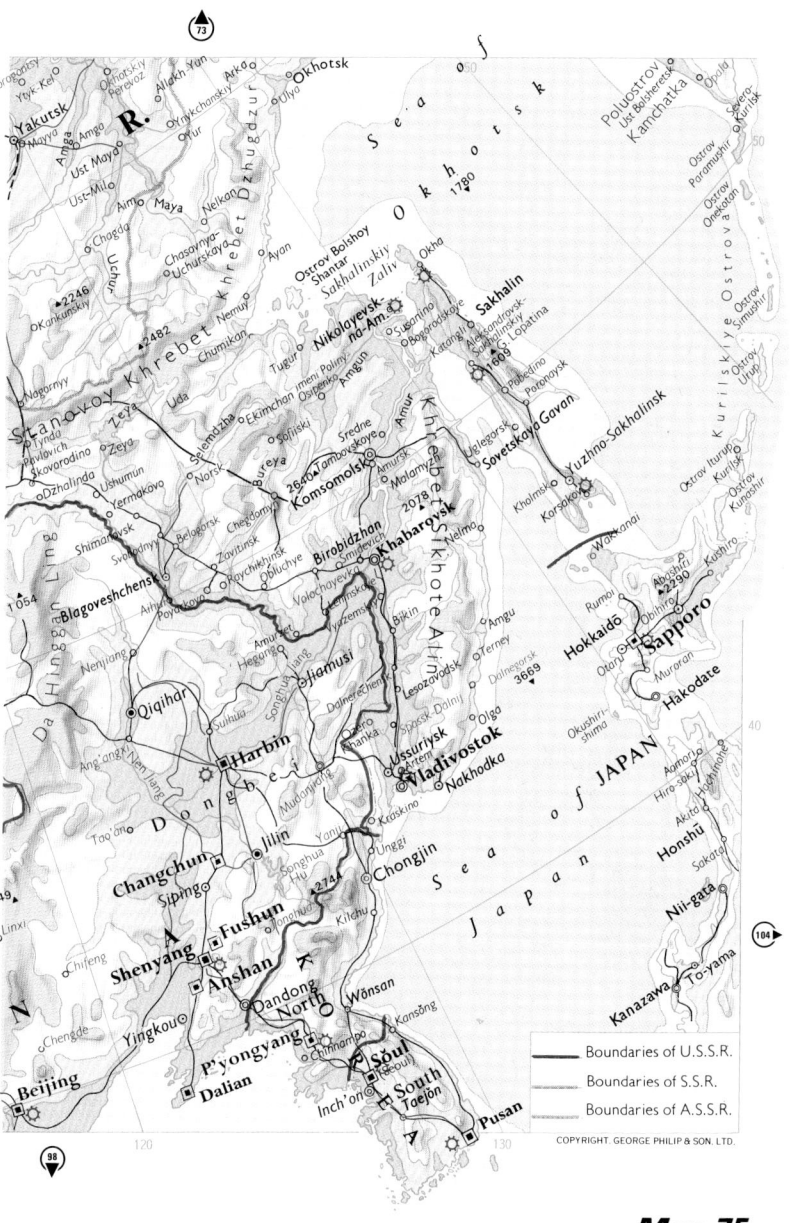

Boundaries of U.S.S.R.
Boundaries of S.S.R.
Boundaries of A.S.S.R.

COPYRIGHT. GEORGE PHILIP & SON. LTD.

Map 75

Asia: Physical

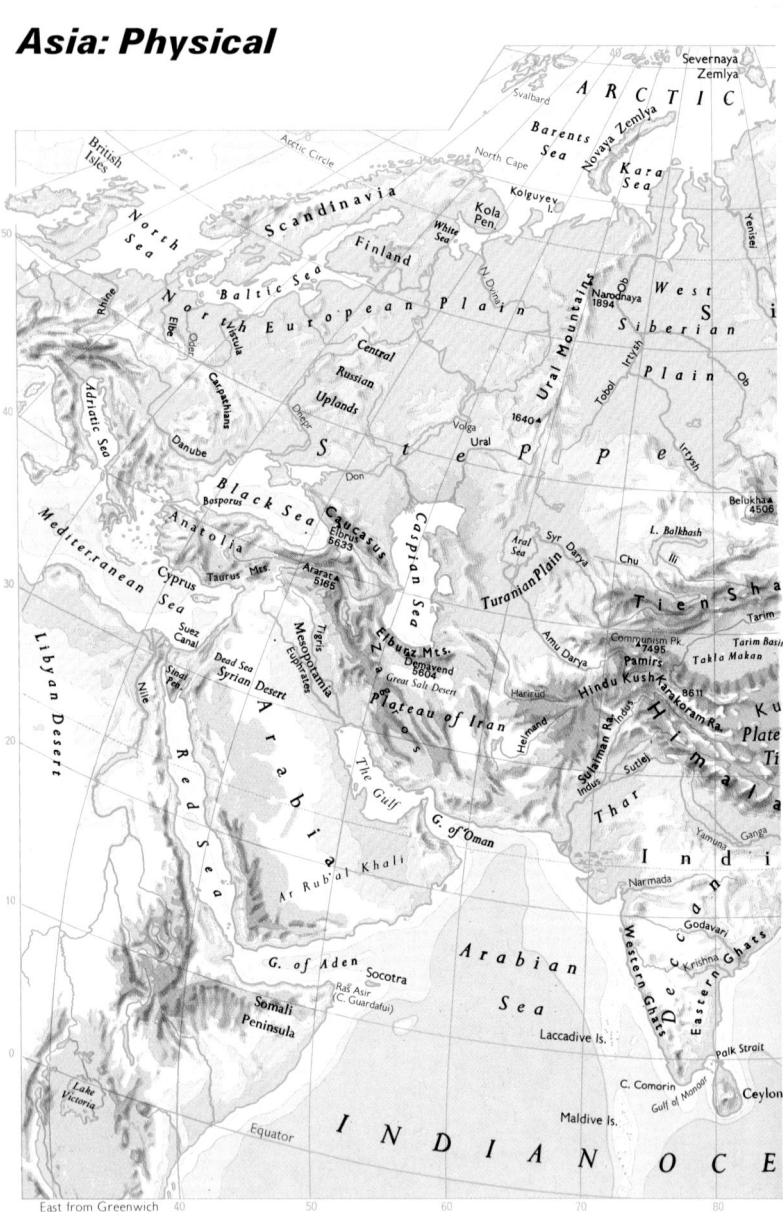

ARCTIC

Severnaya Zemlya

Svalbard

Barents Sea

Novaya Zemlya

Kara Sea

North Cape

Kolguyev I.

British Isles

Arctic Circle

Scandinavia

Kola Pen.

White Sea

West Siberian

Yenisei

North Sea

Finland

N. Dvina

Ural Mountains

Narodnaya 1894

Ob

Plain

Rhine

Baltic Sea

North European Plain

Elbe

Oder

Vistula

Central Russian Uplands

Dnepr

Volga

Ural

1640

Tobol

Irtysh

Ob

Irtysh

Carpathians

Adriatic Sea

Danube

Don

S t e p p e

Belukha 4506

Black Sea

Caucasus

Elbruz 5633

Caspian Sea

Aral Sea

Syr Darya

L. Balkhash

Bosporus

Chu

Ili

Mediterranean Sea

Anatolia

Cyprus

Taurus Mts.

Ararat 5165

Turanian Plain

Tien Shan

Tarim

Elburz Mts.

Demavend 5604

Amu Darya

Communism Pk. 7495

Tarim Basin

Suez Canal

Tigris

Euphrates

Dead Sea

Syrian Desert

Mesopotamia

Great Salt Desert

Pamirs

Takla Makan

Ku

Libyan Desert

Plateau of Iran

Z a g r o s

Hariirud

Hindu Kush

Karakoram Ra. 8611

Himalaya

Plate

Nile

Sinai Pen.

Helmand

Indus

Sulaiman Ra.

Sutlej

Ti

A r a b i a

Red Sea

The Gulf

G. of Oman

Thar

Indus

Yamuna

Ganga

I n d i

Narmada

Ar Rub'al Khali

Godavari

Western Ghats

Krishna

Eastern Ghats

G. of Aden

Socotra

Ras Asir (C. Guardafui)

A r a b i a n

S e a

Somali Peninsula

Laccadive Is.

Palk Strait

D e c c a n

Lake Victoria

C. Comorin

Gulf of Mannar

Ceylon

Maldive Is.

Equator

I N D I A N   O C E

Map 76

1:60 000 000

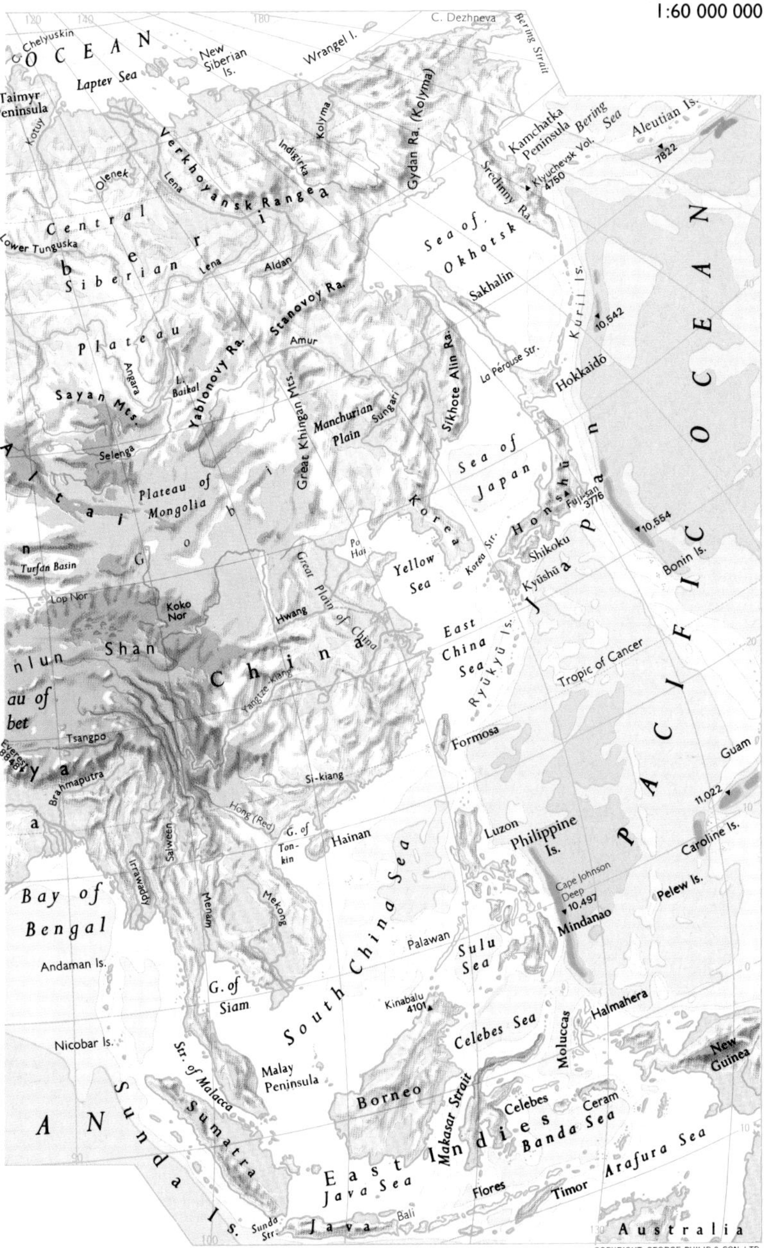

ARCTIC OCEAN

Chelyuskin
Taimyr Peninsula
Kotuy
Laptev Sea
Olenek
New Siberian Is.
Wrangel I.
C. Dezhneva
Bering Strait

Lower Tunguska
Central
Siberian
Plateau

Verkhoyansk Range
Indigirka
Kolyma
Gydan Ra. (Kolyma)

Kamchatka Peninsula
Bering Sea
Aleutian Is.
7822

Lena
Aldan
Sredinny Ra.
Klyuchevsk Vol. 4750

Sayan Mts
Angara
L. Baikal
Yablonovy Ra.
Stanovoy Ra.
Amur

Sea of Okhotsk
Sakhalin
10,542

Selenga
Plateau of Mongolia
Gobi
Great Khingan Mts.
Manchurian Plain
Sungari
Sikhote Alin Ra.
La Pérouse Str.
Hokkaidō

Turfan Basin
Lop Nor
Koko Nor
Kunlun Shan

Pa Hai
Hwang
Yellow Sea
Korea
Korea Str.

Sea of Japan
Honshu
Fuji San 3776
10,564
Bonin Is.

Plateau of Tibet
Tsangpo
Great Plain of China
Yangtse Kiang

East China Sea
Ryūkyū Is.
Tropic of Cancer
Shikoku
Kyūshū

PACIFIC OCEAN

Himalaya
Brahmaputra
Salween
Si-kiang
Hong (Red)
G. of Tonkin
Hainan
Formosa

Guam
11,022

Bay of Bengal
Andaman Is.

Irrawaddy
Menam
Mekong
G. of Siam

Luzon
Philippine Is.
Cape Johnson Deep 10,497
Mindanao
Caroline Is.
Pelew Is.

Nicobar Is.
Str. of Malacca
Malay Peninsula
South China Sea
Palawan
Sulu Sea
Kinabalu 4101

SUNDA Is.
Sumatra
Borneo
Celebes Sea
Makassar Strait
Celebes
Moluccas
Halmahera
Ceram
Banda Sea
New Guinea

ANDAMAN
Sunda Str.
East Indies
Java Sea
Java
Bali
Flores
Timor
Arafura Sea
Australia

Map 77

Asia: Political

ARCTIC
Severnaya Zemlya
Svalbard
Barents Sea
Novaya Zemlya
Kara Sea
Arctic Circle
UNITED KINGDOM
North Sea
London
Baltic Sea
Berlin
Paris
Rhine
EUROPE
Murmansk
Beloje More
Arkhangelsk
Leningrad
Moskva
Warszawa
Wisla
Wien
Roma
Beograd
Danube
Odessa
Dnepr
Rostov
Don
Volga
Orenburg
Ural Mts.
U.S.S.R.
Ob
Irtysh
Tobolsk
Sverdlovsk
Chelyabinsk
Magnitogorsk
Omsk
Novosibirsk
Yenisey
Igark
Toms
Barnau
Semipalatin
Ural
Thessaloniki
Istanbul
Black Sea
Bursa
Athinai
Izmir
Ankara
Erzurum
Batumi
Tbilisi
TURKEY
Yerevan
Astrakhan
Caspian Sea
Baku
Aralskoye More
Ozero Balkhash
Syr Darya
Ining
Alma Ata
Mediterranean Sea
El Iskandariya
Bayrut
LEB
SYRIA
Halab
Dimashq
ISRAEL
Jerusalem
JORDAN
LIBYA
El Qâhira
Euphrates
Tigris
IRAQ
Baghdad
Tabriz
Krasnovodsk
Khiva
Tashkent
Kokand
Bukhara
Ashkhabad
Mary
Samarkand
Kashi
Shache
Tarim
XINJIANG UYG
Mashhad
Tehrān
IRAN
Esfahān
Shīrāz
Herāt
Kabul
Peshawar
AFGHANISTAN
Qandahar
Quetta
KASHMIR
XIZ (TI
Himalaya
Lahore
Simla
NEP
Delhi
Agra
Lucknow
Kanpur
Allahabad
Varana
INDIA
Nile
EGYPT
Aswân
Al Basrah
Kuwait
The Gulf
Bandar e Bushehr
Zāhedān
PAKISTAN
Indus
Bahrain
Ar Riyād
SAUDI ARABIA
Al Madīnah
Makkah (Mecca)
U.A.E.
Gwādar
G. of Oman
Muscat
Karachi
Red Sea
Bûr Sûdân
Suakin
El Khartûm
El Obeid
SUDAN
AFRICA
Mitsiwa
Eritrea
Kamaran
Gondar
OMAN
Ahmadabad
Narmada
YEMEN
Bombay
Godavari
Hyderabad
Djibouti
Zeila
G. of Aden
Addis Abeba
Socotra (Yemen)
Arabian Sea
Goa
Harer
ETHIOPIA
SOMALI REP
Madras
Pondicherry
Laccadive Is. (India)
Calicut
UGANDA
Kampala
KENYA
Obbia
Giuba
ZAIRE
RWANDA
BURUNDI
Colombo
SRI LA (CEYL
MALDIVES
Muqdisho
Nairobi
Kigoma
TANZANIA
Mombasa
Equator
INDIAN OC
East from Greenwich

Map 78

1:60 000 000

O C E A N

Chelyuskin

Laptev Sea

Novosibirskiye Ostrova

Ostrova Vrangelya

Bering Sea

Aleutian Is.

Nizhnyaya Tunguska

Lena

S. Lena

Yakutsk

Aldan

Okhotsk

Sea of Okhotsk

Sakhalin

Kuril Is.

Petropavlovsk-Kamchatskiy

Angara

Krasnoyarsk

Ozero Baykal

Chita

Amur

Khabarovsk

Nikolayevsk

Hokkaidō

Sapporo

Hakodate

P A C I F I C

O C E A N

Irkutsk

Kyakhta

Manchuria

Vladivostok

Sea of Japan

Hovd

Ulaanbaatar (Ulan Bator)

Harbin

Changchun

Shenyang (Mukden)

N. KOREA

Tōkyō

Yokohama

M O N G O L I A

INNER MONGOLIA

Beijing

Tianjin

Dalian

Seoul

S. KOREA

Pusan

Kyōto

Osaka

J A P A N

Ürümqi (Urumchi)

Qingdao

Yellow Sea

Kitakyūshū

Bonin Is.

ANG

UR

Xi'an

Huang

Nanjing

Nagasaki

Shanghai

Suzhou

East China Sea

Ryūkyū-rettō

Tropic of Cancer

ANG (TIBET)

C H I N A

Chang

Wuhan

Lhasa

Chengdu

Chongqing

Xiangtan

Fuzhou

Taiwan (Formosa)

Guam (U.S)

Kunming

Guangzhou

HONG KONG (Br.)

Macau (Port.)

Zhanjiang

P A C I F I C

Y

BHU

Brahmaputra

Myitkyina

Hanoi

G. of Tongking

Hainan

Luzon

PHILIPPINES

Caroline Is.

Ganges

Dhaka

BURMA

Mandalay

Irrawaddy

Manila

Calcutta

V I E T N A M

Belau

Bay of Bengal

Andaman Is. (India)

THAILAND

Hué

South China Sea

Palawan

Mindanao

Davao

Rangoon (Yangon)

Bangkok

CAMBODIA

Gulf of Thailand

Thanh Pho Ho Chi Minh

Sulu Sea

Zamboanga

Sulu Arch.

Sabah

Nicobar Is. (India)

George Town

Str. of Malacca

Kuala Lumpur

BRUNEI

SARAWAK

MALAYSIA

Kuching

Celebes Sea

Maluku (Moluccas)

Halmahera

New Guinea

Meloka

Borneo

Sulawesi

Ceram

Banda Sea

E A N

Sumatra

Singapore

Jakarta

Selat Sunda

Ujung Pandang

J a v a

Flores

Timor

Darwin

AUSTRALIA

Thursday I.

I N D O N E S I A

Java Sea

COPYRIGHT. GEORGE PHILIP & SON. LTD.

Map 79

Turkey and the Middle East

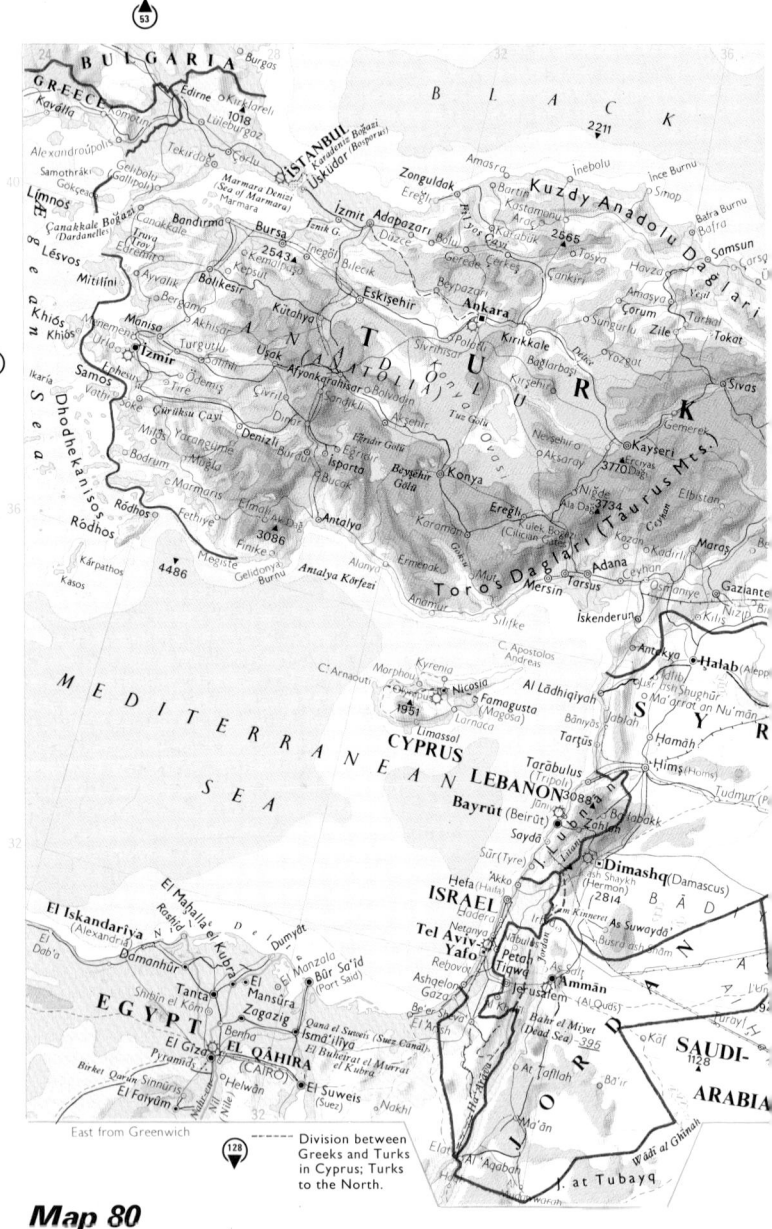

East from Greenwich

- - - - - Division between
Greeks and Turks
in Cyprus; Turks
to the North.

Map 80

1:10 000 000

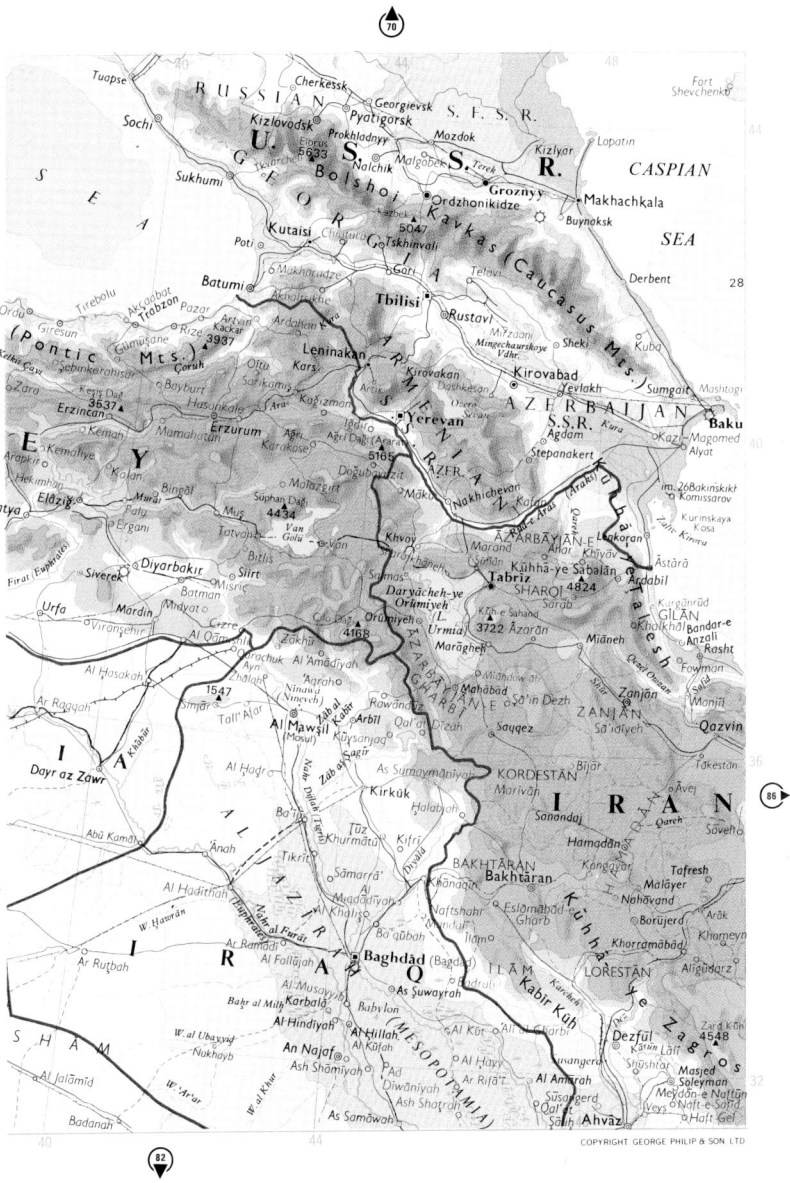

COPYRIGHT GEORGE PHILIP & SON LTD

Map 81

Arabian Peninsula

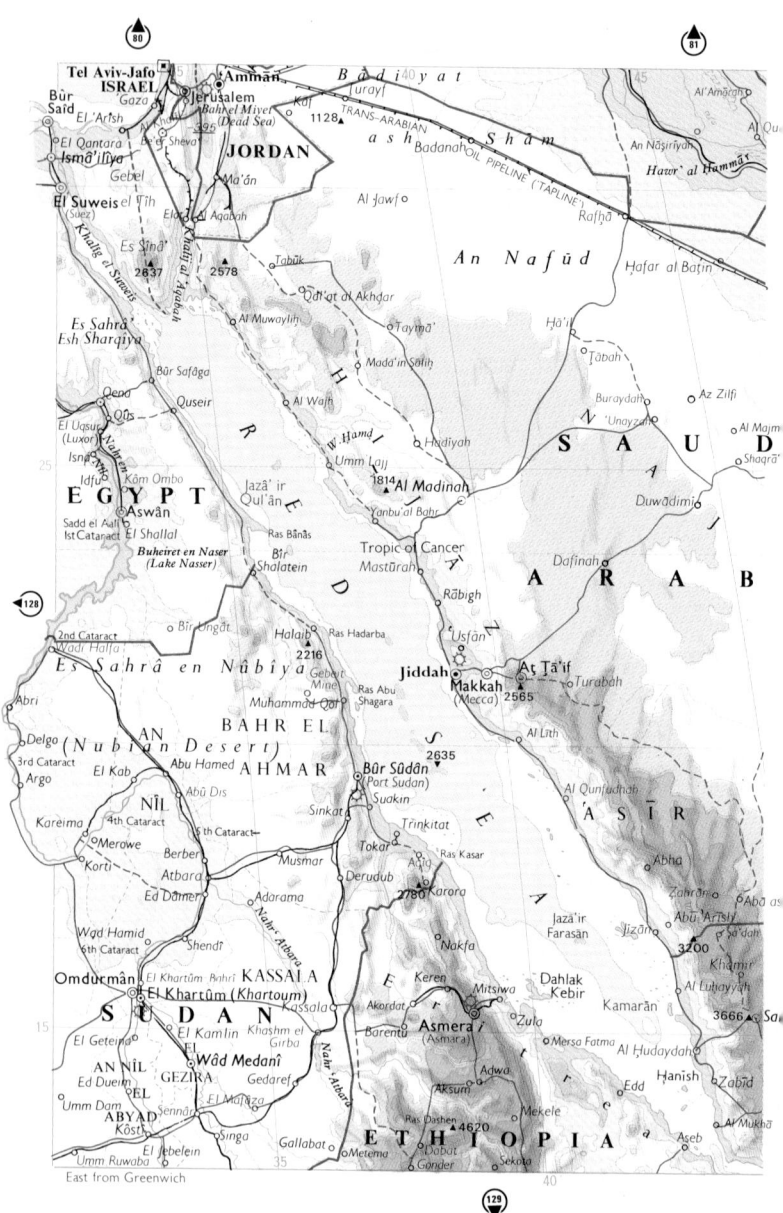

Tel Aviv-Jafo
ISRAEL
Amman
B ā d i y a t
Bûr
Saîd
Gaza
Jerusalem
El 'Arîsh
Bahr el Miyet
(Dead Sea)
Turayf
Kaf
1128
TRANS-ARABIAN
An Nāşirīyah
Al 'Amādīs
Ḥawr al Ḥammār
El Qantara
Ismâ'ilîya
Sheva
Badanah
OIL PIPELINE (TAPLINE)
a s h
S h a m
El Suweis
(Suez)
Gebel
el Tih
Eloi
Aqaba
Ma'ān
Al Jawf
Rafḥā
Es Sînai
Khalîg el Suweis
2637
2578
Khalîg el 'Aqaba
Tabūk
Qal'at al Akhḍar
A n   N a f ū d
Ḥafar al Bāţin
Es Sahrâ'
Esh Sharqîya
Al Muwaylih
Taymā'
Madā'in Şāliḥ
Ḥā'il
Ṭābah
Az Zilfî
Bûr Safâga
Ḥaidīyah
Burayḍah
Al Majm
Qena
Qûs
Quseir
Al Wajh
W. Ḥamḍ
Umm Lajj
'Unayzah
Shaqrā'
El Uqsur
(Luxor)
Nubia
Jazā'ir
Qul'ān
1814
Al Madīnah
Duwādimī
S A U D
Isna
Idfu
Kôm Ombo
E G Y P T
Aswân
Yanbu'al Baḥr
A R A B
Sadd el Aâli
1st Cataract
El Shallal
Ras Bânâs
Tropic of Cancer
Mastūrah
Dafinah
Buheiret en Naser
(Lake Nasser)
Bîr
Shalatein
Rābigh
128
2nd Cataract
Wadi Halfa
Bîr Ungat
Es Sahrâ en Nûbiya
2216
Gebeit
Mine
Halaib
Ras Hadarba
Usfān
Jiddah
At Tā'if
Turabah
Abri
Muhammad Qol
Ras Abu
Shagara
Makkah
(Mecca)
2565
Delgo
BAHR EL
Delgo
(N u b i a n   D e s e r t)
Al Lith
3rd Cataract
Argo
El Kab
Abu Hamed
AHMAR
Bûr Sûdân
(Port Sudan)
2635
Al Qunfudhah
A S Ī R
Kareima
4th Cataract
NÎL
Abû Dîs
Suakin
Merowe
5th Cataract
Sinkat
Trinkitat
Abha
Korti
Berber
Musmar
Tokar
Ras Kasar
Atbara
Derudub
2780
Zahrān
Abā
Ed Damer
Adarama
Karora
Jizān
Abū 'Arish
3200
Wad Hamid
Nakfa
Jazā'ir
Farasān
Khamī
6th Cataract
Shendî
KASSALA
Keren
Mitsiwa
Dahlak
Kebir
Al Luḥayyah
Omdurmân
El Khartûm Baḥri
El Khartûm (Khartoum)
Kassala
Akordat
Asmera
(Asmara)
Zula
Kamarân
3666
Sa
S U D Â N
El Getena
El Kamlin
Khashm el
Girba
Barentu
Mersa Fatma
Al Ḥudaydah
AN NÎL
Ed Dueim
EL
GEZIRA
Gedaref
Wâd Medanî
El Manâqil
Adwa
Aksum
Edd
Hanish
Zabīd
ABYAD
Kôstî
Umm Ruwaba
Sennâr
Singa
Gallabat
Ras Dashen
4620
Mekele
Aseb
Al Mukhā
El Jebelein
Metema
Debat
Gonder
Sekota
E T H I O P I A

Map 82

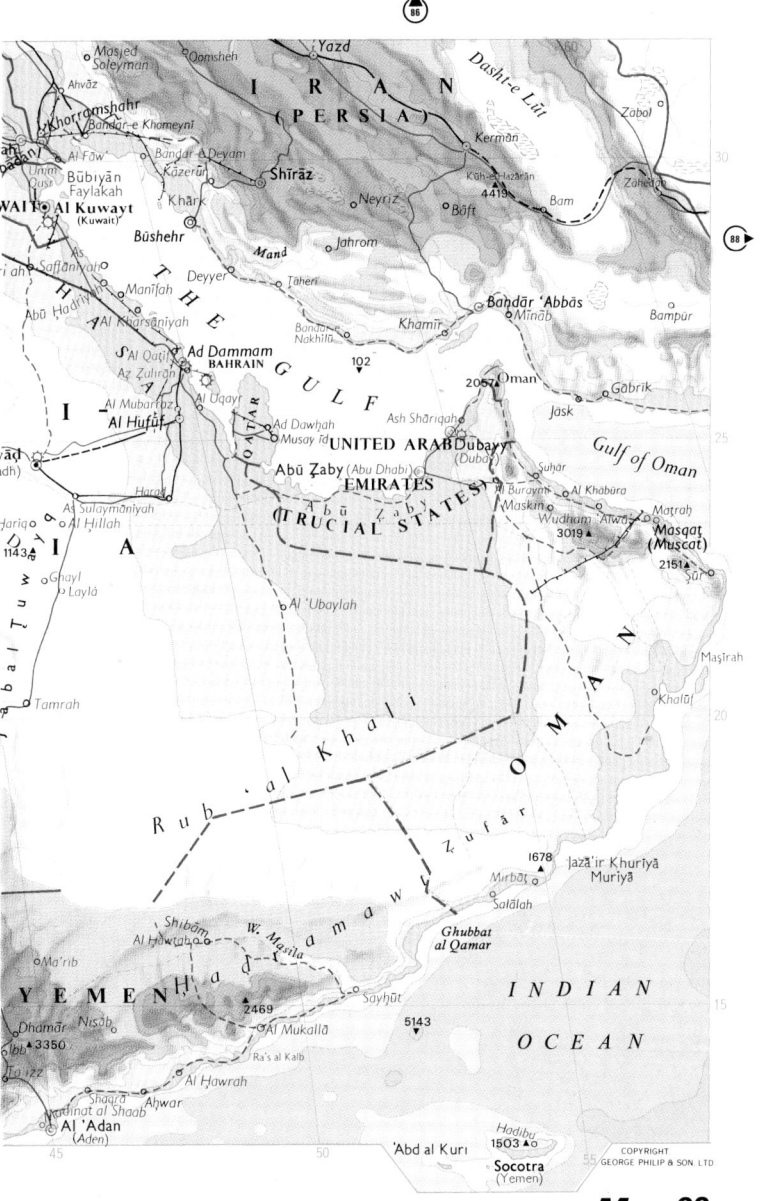

1:15 000 000

86

88 ►

I R A N
(P E R S I A)

Yazd
Qomsheh
Masjed
Soleymän
Ahväz
Bandar-e Khomeyni
Khorramshahr
Dasht-e Lūt
Zābol
Al Fāw
Bandar-e Deyam
Kāzerūn
Kermān
Umm Qasr
Būbiyān
Faylakah
Shīrāz
Kūh-e Hazārān
4419
Bam
Zāhedān
WAIT
Al Kuwayt
(Kuwait)
Al Khārk
Neyrīz
Būft
Būshehr
Jahrom
As Saffānīyah
Mand
Manīfah
Deyyer
Tāheri
Bandār 'Abbās
Bampūr
Abū Ḥadrīya
Al Kharsānīyah
Bandar-e
Nakhīlū
Khamīr
Mīnāb
THE
Ad Dammam
BAHRAIN
Az Zulrāh
102
20571 Oman
Gābrik
Al Qaṭīf
S
GULF
Ash Shāriqah
Jask
'āḍ
Al Mubarrez
Al Hufūf
Al Uqayr
QATAR
Ad Dawḥah
Musay'īd
UNITED ARAB
Dubayy
(Dubai)
Gulf of Oman
Harad
Abū Ẓaby (Abu Dhabi)
EMIRATES
Şuḥār
Jariqa
As Sulaymānīyah
Al Ḥillah
TRUCIAL STATES
Al Buraymī
Maskin
Al Khabūra
Wudhum Aṭwah
Maṭrah
Masqaṭ
(Muscat)
1143
Ghayl
Laylā
Abū Ẓaby
3019
2151
Şūr
Tamrah
Al 'Ubaylah
O M A N
Maşīrah
Khalūf
R u b   ' a l   K h a l i
Ḥaḍramawt
Ẓufār
1678
Jazā'ir Khurīyā
Muriyā
Mirbāṭ
Shibām
Al Ḥawtah
W. Masīla
Ghubbat
al Qamar
Ma'rib
Salālah
Y E M E N
2469
Sayḥūt
I N D I A N
Dhamār
Niṣāb
5143
O C E A N
Ibb
3350
Al Mukallā
Ta'izz
Ra's al Kalb
Shaqra
Ahwar
Al Ḥawrah
Madīnat al Shaab
Al 'Adan
(Aden)
'Abd al Kuri
Ḥadību
1503
Socotra
(Yemen)

Map 83

The Gulf

81

82

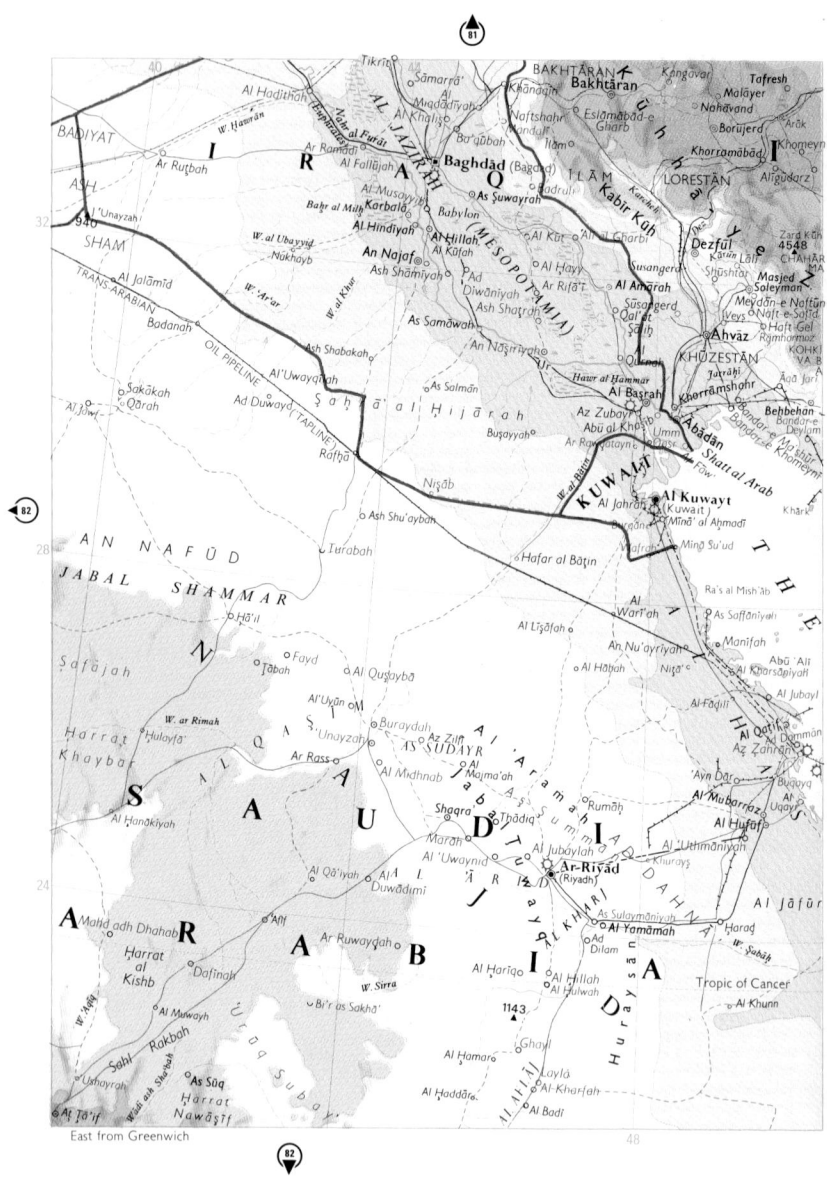
Tikrit
Sāmarrā'
Al Miqdādīyah
Al Khāliş
Al Ḩadīthah
BADIYAT ASH SHAM
W. Ḩawrān
Ar Ramādī
Al Fallūjah
Ar Ruţbah
AL JAZĪRAH
Nahr al Furāt (Euphrates)
Baghdād (Bagdad)
Ba'qūbah
BAKHTĀRAN
Bakhtāran
Kangāvar
Tafresh
Malāyer
Nahāvand
Borūjerd
Arāk
Khorramābād
Khomeyn
Alīgūdarz
LORESTĀN
ĪLĀM
Īlām
Eslāmābād-e Gharb
Naftshahr
Kabīr Kūh
Karkheh
IRAQ
IRAN
Al 'Unayzah
940
Al Musayyib
Karbalā'
Baḩr al Milḩ
Babylon
As Şuwayrah
Badrah
Al Hindīyah
Al Ḩillah
Al Kūfah
An Najaf
Ash Shāmīyah
(MESOPOTAMIA)
Al Kūt
'Alī al Gharbī
Al Ḩayy
Ar Rifā'ī
Ad Dīwānīyah
Ash Shaţrah
Al 'Amārah
Dezfūl
Zard Kūh
4548
CHAHĀR MAḨĀL
Lālī
Shūshtar
Masjed Soleymān
Meydān-e Naftūn
Naft-e Safīd
Haft Gel
Rāmhormoz
KOHKĪLŪYEH VA BŪYER AḨMADĪ
Veys
Ahvāz
KHŪZESTĀN
Sūsangerd
Qal'at Şāliḩ
Al Qurnah
Jarrāhī
Āqā Jarī
W. al Ubayyid
Nukhayb
W. 'Ar'ar
W. al Khur
Al Jalāmīd
TRANS-ARABIAN OIL PIPELINE ("TAPLINE")
Badanah
As Samāwah
An Nāşirīyah
Ur
Hawr al Ḩammār
Al Başrah
Khorramshahr
Behbehān
Bandar-e Deylam
Bandar-e Ma'shūr
Bandar-e Khomeynī
Ash Shabakah
Al 'Uwayqīlah
As Salmān
Sakākah
Qārah
Al Jawf
Ad Duwayd
Şaḩrā' al Ḩijārah
Buşayyah
Az Zubayr
Abū al Khaşīb
Umm Qaşr
Ābādān
Shaţţ al Arab
Al Fāw
Ar Rawḑatayn
Rafḩā
Nişāb
W. al Bāţin
KUWAIT
Al Kuwayt (Kuwait)
Al Jahrah
Khārk
Mīnā' al Aḩmadī
Burgān
Mīnā Su'ud
Wafrah
Ash Shu'aybah
AN NAFŪD
Turabah
Hafar al Bāţin
JABAL SHAMMAR
Ḩā'il
Al Wari'ah
Al Līşāfah
Ra's al Mish'āb
As Saffānīyah
Manīfah
An Nu'ayrīyah
Nişā'
Al Ḩābah
Abū 'Alī
Al Kharsānīyah
Al Jubayl
Fayd
Ţābah
Şafājah
Al Quşaybā
Al 'Uyūn
Al Fāḑilī
THE GULF
Buraydah
W. ar Rimah
Ḩulayfā'
Ḩarrat Khaybar
AL QAŞĪM
'Unayzah
Az Zilfī
AS SUDAYR
Al Qaţīf
Ad Dammān
Az Zahrān
Ar Rass
Al Midhnab
Al Majma'ah
AL 'ARAMAH
AŞ ŞUMMĀN
'Ayn Dār
Buqayq
Al Mubarraz
Al 'Uqayr
Rumāḩ
Shaqrā'
Thādiq
Al Hufūf
Al Ḩanākīyah
SAUDI ARABIA
Marāh
Al 'Uwaynid
Al Jubaylah
Al 'Uthmānīyah
Khurays
Ar Riyāḑ (Riyadh)
'ĀRIḐ
JABAL ŢUWAYQ
AD DAHNĀ'
Al Qā'iyah
Al Duwādimī
Al Jāfūrah
Mahd adh Dhahab
'Afīf
As Sulaymānīyah
Al Yamāmah
AL KHARJ
Ad Dilam
Ḩaraḑ
W. Şabāḩ
Ḩarrat al Kishb
Dafīnah
Ar Ruwayḑah
W. Sirra
Al Ḩarīq
Al Ḩillah
Al Ḩulwah
Tropic of Cancer
Al Khunn
Ḩuraysān
Bi'r as Sakhā'
1143
Al Muwayh
W. 'Aqīq
'Urūq Subay'
Sahl Rakbah
Ghayl
Al Ḩamar
Laylā
Al Kharfah
'Ushayrah
Wādī ash Sha'bah
As Sūq
Ḩarrat Nawāşīf
Al Ḩaddār
AL AFLĀJ
Al Badī'
Aţ Ţā'if
40
44
48
32
28
24
East from Greenwich

82

Map 84

1:10 000 000

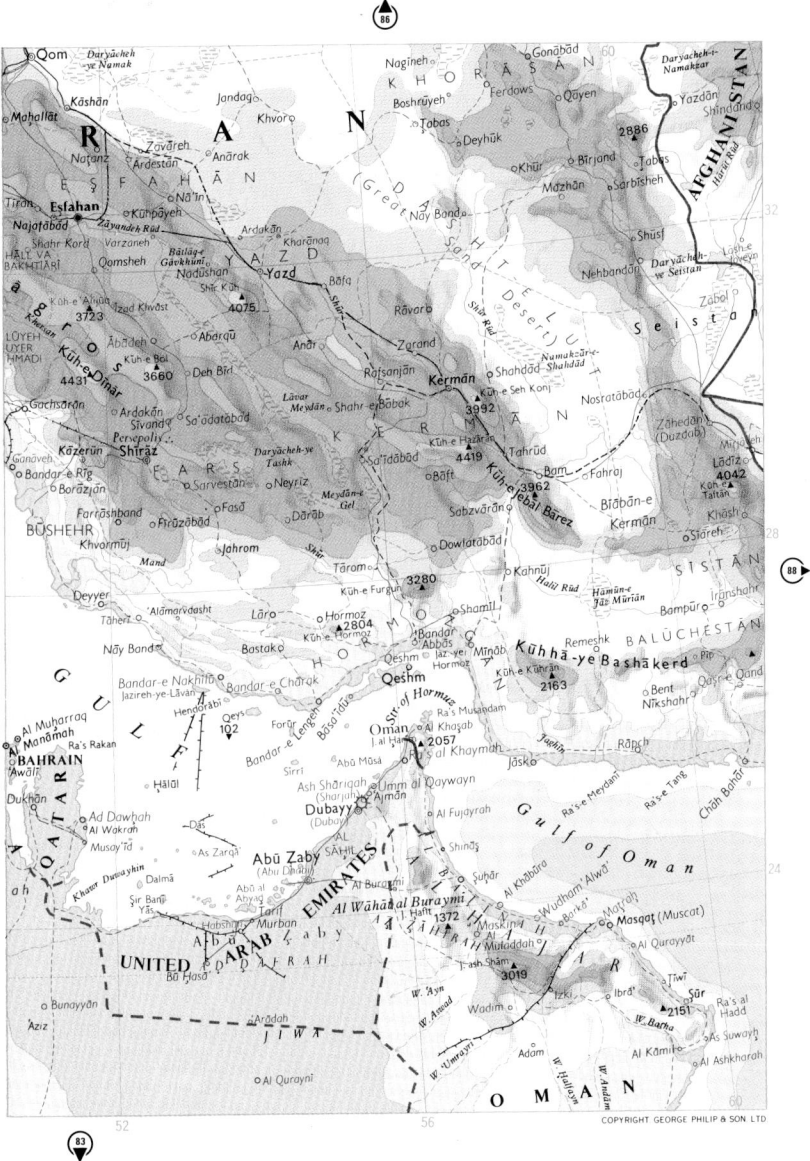

°Qom *Daryācheh-ye Namak* Nagīneh Gonābād 60 *Daryācheh-i-Namakzar*

KHORĀSĀN

Mahallāt° Kāshān Jandaq° Khvor° Boshrūyeh° Ferdows° Qāyen° Yazdān° Shindand° AFGHĀNISTĀN

R Zavāreh °Ardestān Anārak° Tabas° Deyhūk° 2886 Bīrjand° Tabas° Hari Rūd

Natanz° °Ardestān Khūr° Mazhān° Sarbīsheh°

A Tirāno *DASHT-E* Shūs°

Esfahān Nā'īn° N (Great Nāy Band Sūs° Lashe Veyn°

Najafābād° Kūhpāyeh° Nehbandān° Daryācheh-i-w Seistan

HĀLT VA *Zāyandeh Rūd* Ardakān Kharānaq° Zābol°

BAKHTĪĀRĪ Shahr Kord Varzaneh YAZD Seistan

°Qomsheh Bāfluq°Gōkhūni Nadushān °Yazd Bāfq° Sāb Rūd

Kūh-e 'Ainūn 'Izad Khvāst Shīr Kūh 4075 Rāvar° Namaksar-e Shahdād

3723 °Ābādeh Abarqū° Anār° Zarand° Shahdād° Seh Konj Nosratābād°

LŪYEH Kūh-e Bol Deh Bīd° Rafsanjān° Kermān Zāhedān° (Duzdāb)

UYER Kūh-e Dīnār 3660 Lāvar KERMAN Mirjāveh°

HMADI 4431 Ardakān° Sīvand° Mewlān° Shahr-e Bābak° 3992 Kūh-e Hazārān Tahrūd° 4042 Koh Taftān

°Gachsārān Persepolis° Sa'ādatābād° 4419 3962 Bam° Fahraj°

°Gunāveh Kāzerūn° Shīrāz Sa'īdābād° Kūh-e Jebāl Barez Blābān-e Khāsh°

°Bandar-e Rīg FARS *Daryācheh-ye Tashk* Bāft° Kermān SISTĀN Stārch°

°Borāzjān Sarvestān° Neyrīz° Meydān-e Sabzvārān° 28

BŪSHEHR Farrāshband° Fasā° Gel Dowlatābād° BALŪCHESTĀN

Khvormūj° Fīrūzābād° Dārāb° Kahnūj° Hāmūn-e Irānshahr°

°Deyyer Mand Jahrom° Shūr Tārom° Halil Rūd Jāz Mūrīān Bampūr° 88

°Tāherī 'Alāmarvdasht° Kūh-e Furgūn 3280 Remeshk Qasr-e Qand°

Nāy Band° Lārō °Hormoz Shamīl° Kūhhā-ye Bashākerd Pīp°

Bastak° 2804 Bandar 2163 Bent° Nīkshahr°

°Hormoz 'Abbās° Mīnāb° Kūh-e Kūhrān

Bandar-e Nakhīlū° Qeshm° Jaz-yeh Kūhhā-ye Bashākerd

Jazīreh-ye Lāvān° Bandar-e Chārak° Hormoz°

Hendurābī° Qeshm Str. of Hormuz Jāsk° Ras'e Merdān Ras'e Tang Chāh Bahār°

G Qers Forūr° Bāsa'īdū° Oman °Al Khasab Jaghin° Rānch°

°Al Muharraq 102 Bandar-e Lengeh° °al Hamr 2057 Ras'al Khaymah Wudham Alwā°

Manāmah Ra's Rakan Sirri° Abū Mūsā° Ash Shāriqah Umm al Qaywayn° Masqat (Muscat)

BAHRAIN Hālūl° (Sharjah) °Ajmān Gulf of Oman Masqat

°'Awālī Dukhān° Dubayy° °Al Fujayrah Shināş°

Ad Dawhah° (Dubai) °Al Khabūra Al Qurayyāt°

QATAR Al Wakrah° Abū Zaby SĀHIL °Suhār

Musay'īd° Dalmā° (Abū Dhabī) Mayfah°

°As Zarqā UNITED Al Wāhat al Buraymī 2151

Khawr Duwayhin Şīr Banī Yās° Abū al Hatt° 1372 Maskin° ‘Ibrā° Tīwī°

ah °Habshān Murban ARAB Al Muladdah° As Suwayh°

Ţarīf° ABŪ ZABY EMIRATES JABAL Adam° Izkī° Tāsh Sham° 3019 Ra's al Hadd

UNITED Bū Hasa° AZ ZAFRAH OMAN W. Bahla Ra's al Hadd

°Bunayyān 'Aziz° °Arādah JIWĀ W. 'Ayn Wadim° Al Kāmīl° Al Ashkharah°

60

°Al Qurayn Adam° OMAN Al Ashkharah°

52 56 COPYRIGHT GEORGE PHILIP & SON LTD

Map 85

Central Asia and Afghanistan

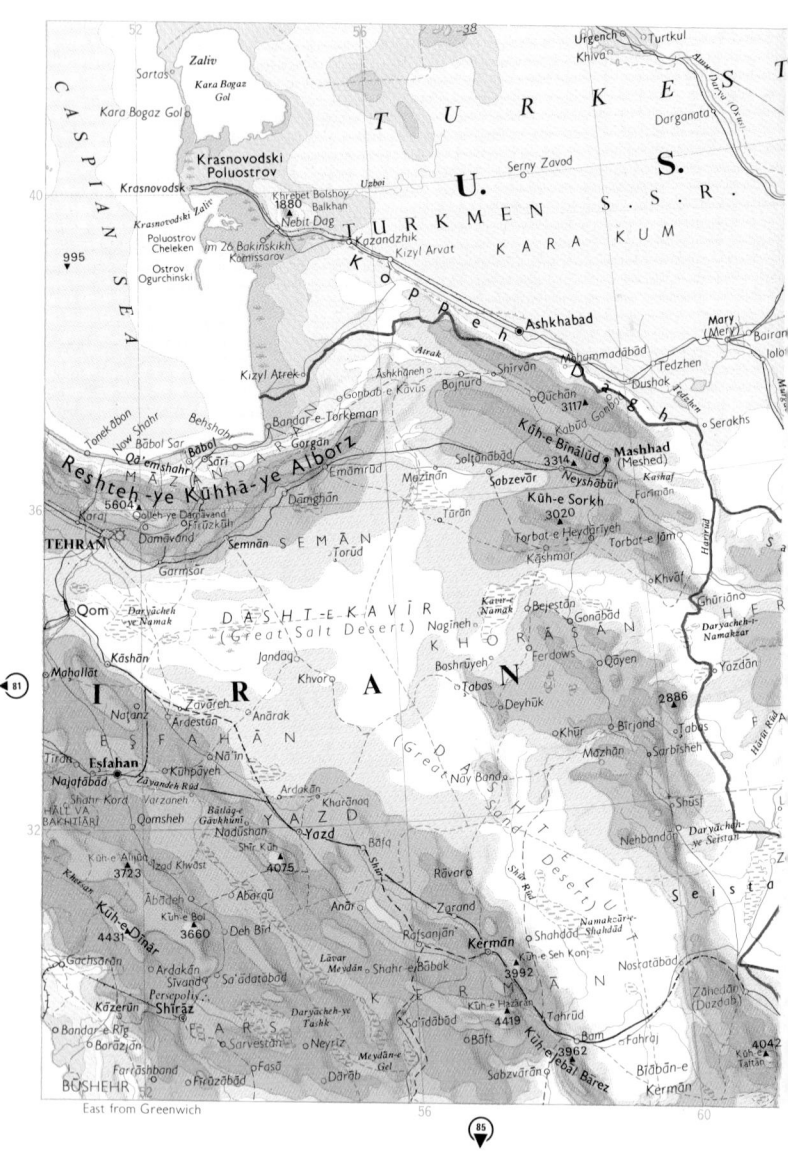

East from Greenwich

Map 86

1:10 000 000

70

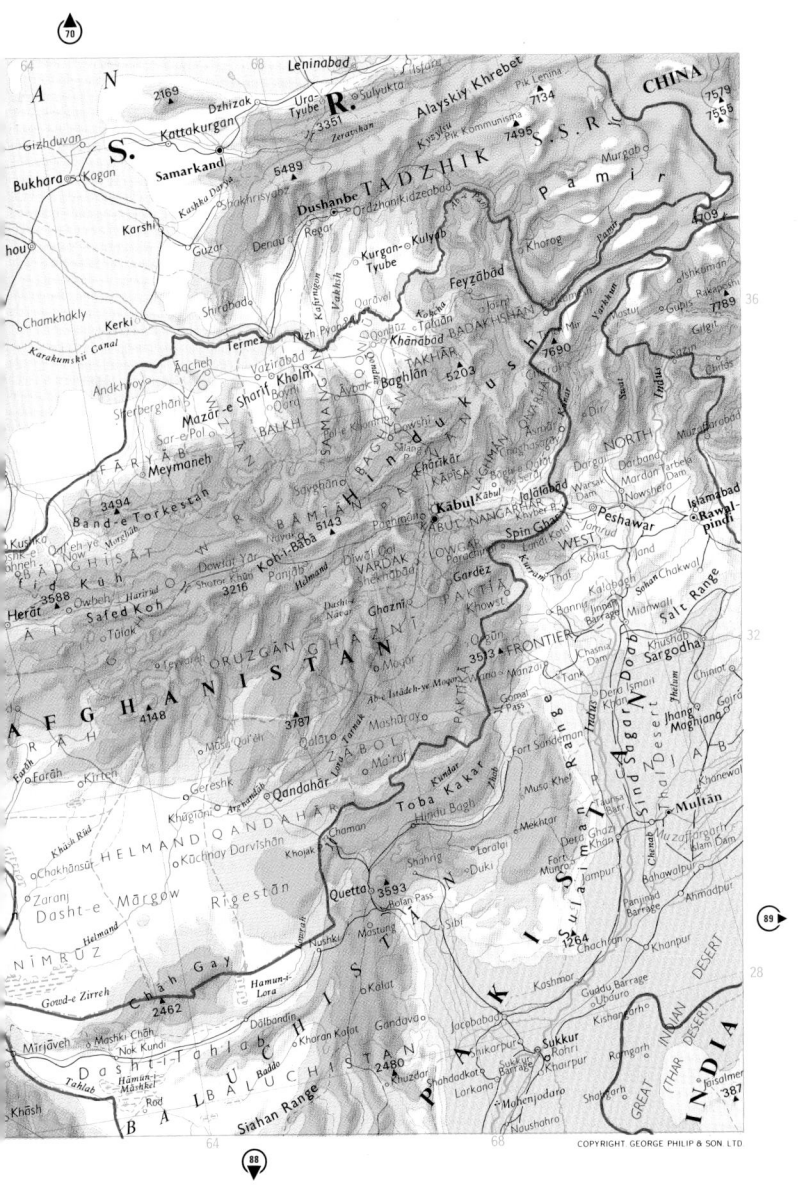

Leninabad
Isfara
Sulyukta
Ura-Tyube
R.
Dzhizak
Kattakurgan
Gizhduvan
S.
Samarkand
Bukhara
Kagan
Alayskiy Khrebet
Pik Lenina
7134
Pik Kommunisma
7495
CHINA
7579
7555
TADZHIK
S.S.R.
Dushanbe
Ordzhonikidzeabad
Murgab
Pamir
Shakhrisyabz
Kashka Darya
Karshi
Guzar
Denau
Regar
Kurgan-Tyube
Kulyab
Khorog
4709
Feyzābād
Chamkhakly
Kerki
Shirabad
Termez
Karakumskii Canal
Kholm
Kunduz
Khānābād
BADAKHSHĀN
TAKHĀR
Baghlān
Mazār-e Sharīf
Andkhvoy
Sherberghān
Sar-e Pol
BALKH
Meymaneh
FĀRYĀB
JOWZJĀN
SAMANGĀN
BAGHLĀN
Hindu Kush
Tirich Mir
7690
Gilgit
Rakaposhi
7789
Ishkuman
Gupis
Chilas
Indus
Swat
Dir
NORTH
Muzaffarabad
Chārīkār
KĀPĪSĀ
LAGHMĀN
Jalālābād
Kābul
Peshawar
Islamabad
Rawalpindi
Mardan
Tarbela Dam
Nowshera
Warsak Dam
Khyber P.
Spin Ghar
WEST
Kohat
Jand
Sohan
Chakwal
Salt Range
Band-e Torkestan
3494
Kushka
Qal'eh-ye Now
BĀDGHĪSĀT
BĀMĪĀN
5143
Koh-i-Bābā
Dowlat Yār
Shotor Khūn
3216
Panjāb
VARDAK
Gardēz
PAKTĪĀ
LOWGAR
Helmand
Herāt
3588
Owbeh
Harirud
Safed Koh
Ghaznī
GHAZNĪ
Khowst
Bannu
Kalabagh
Jinnah Barrage
Mianwali
FRONTIER
3513
ORUZGĀN
AFGHANISTAN
Moqor
Wana
Tank
Chasma Dam
Sargodha
Khushab
Chiniot
Sind Sagar Doab
Ab-e Istādeh-ye Moqor
Gomal Pass
4148
3787
Qalāt
ZĀBOL
Fort Sandeman
Jhang Maghiana
Thal Desert
Jhelum
Farāh
FARĀH
Gereshk
Qandahār
Toba Kakar
Hindu Bagh
Musa Khel
Multān
Khanewal
KANDAHĀR
HELMAND
Khāsh Rūd
Chakhānsūr
Kūchnay Darvīshān
Khojak
Chaman
Mekhtar
Dera Ghazi Khan
Muzaffargarh
Chenab
Zaranj
Dasht-e Mārgow
Rīgestān
Quetta
3593
Shahrig
Loralai
Duki
Fort Munro
Bolan Pass
Sibi
Jampur
Bahawalpur
Panjnad Barrage
Ahmadpur
Helmand
NĪMRŪZ
Nushki
Mastung
Sulaiman Range
1264
Chachran
Khanpur
Chāh Gay
2462
Gowd-e Zirreh
Hamun-i-Lora
Kalat
Kashmor
Guddu Barrage
Ubauro
Mīrjāveh
Mashki Chāh
Nok Kundi
Dālbandin
Kharan Kalat
Gandava
Jacobabad
Kishangarh
Dasht-i-Tahlab
Shikarpur
Sukkur
Rohri
Khairpur
Ramgarh
INDIAN DESERT
(THAR DESERT)
INDIA
Tahlab
Hāmūn-i-Māshkel
Baddo
BALUCHISTAN
2480
Khuzdar
Shahdadkot
Sukkur Barrage
Larkana
Mohenjodaro
Shahgarh
GREAT
Jaisalmer
387
Khāsh
Siahan Range
PAKISTAN
Naushahro
36
32
28
64
68

89

88

Map 87

Pakistan and North West India

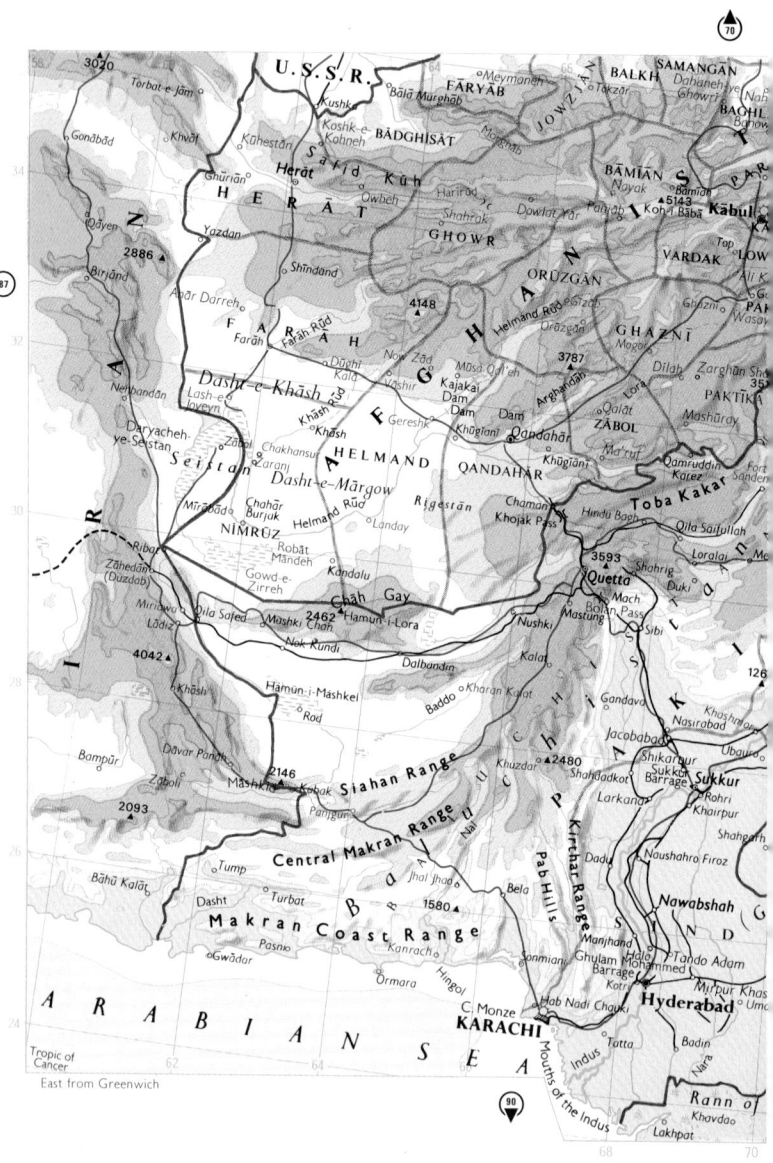

Map 88

1:10 000 000

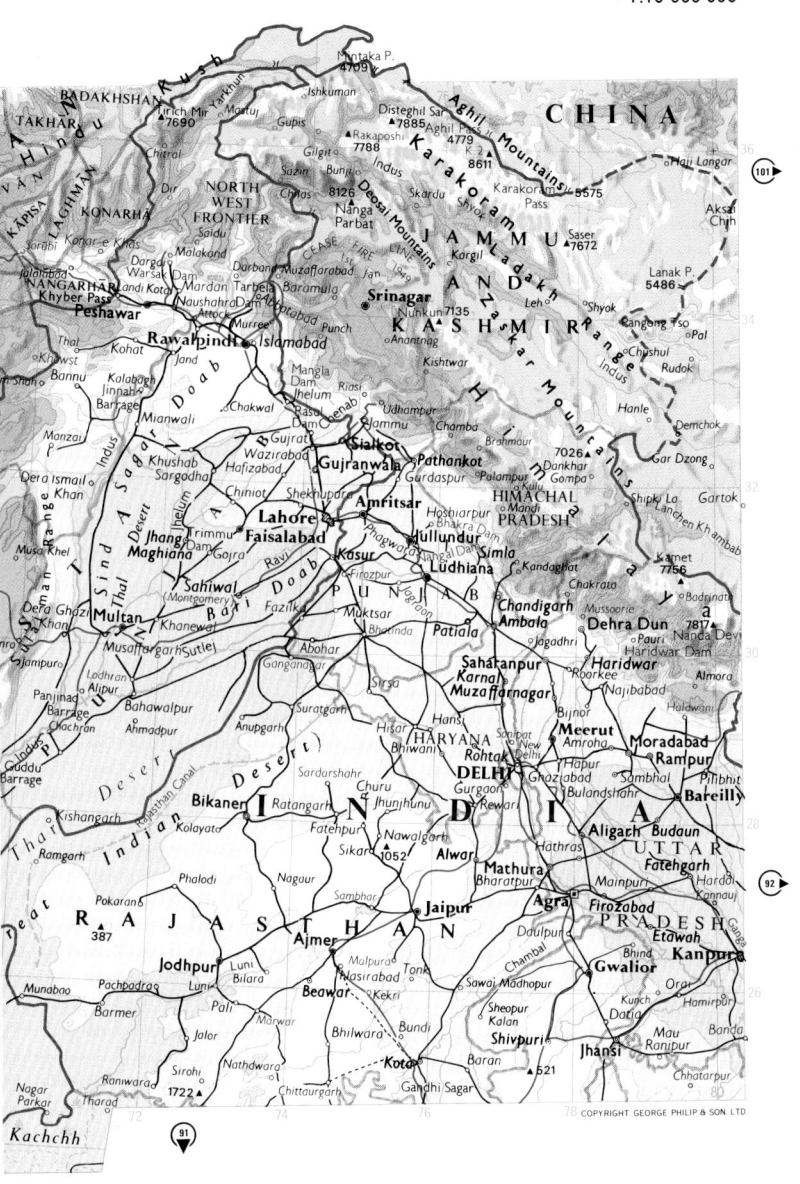
CHINA
Mintaka P.
4709
Ishkuman
BADAKHSHAN
TAKHAR
Hindu Kush
Tirich Mir
7690
Yarkhun
Mastuj
Gupis
Disteghil Sar
7885
Aghil Pass
4779
Aghil Mountains
Rakaposhi
7788
K-2
8611
Karakoram
Gilgit
Indus
Haji Langar
Chitral
Sazin
Bunji
Karakoram Pass
5575
Aksai Chin
NORTH WEST FRONTIER
Dir
Chilas
8126
Nanga Parbat
Deosai Mountains
Skardu
Shyok
KONARHA
KAPISA
LAGHMAN
Saidu
Malakand
CEASE FIRE LINE 1949
JAMMU AND KASHMIR
Saser
7672
Ladakh Range
Kargil
Sorubi
Konar-e Khas
Jalalabad
Darga
Warsak Dam
Darband
Muzaffarabad
Jhelum
Lanak P.
5486
NANGARHAR
Khyber Pass
Landi Kotal
Mardan
Tarbela Dam
Baramula
Srinagar
Leh
Shyok
Peshawar
Naushahra
Attock
Abbottabad
Murree
Nunkun 7135
Zaskar Mountains
Pangong Tso
Pal
Punch
Anantnag
Thal
Kohat
Rawalpindi
Islamabad
Chushul
Rudok
Khowst
Jand
Kishtwar
Indus
Bannu
Kalabagh
Jinnah Barrage
Mangla Dam
Jhelum
Riasi
Chakwal
Udhampur
Hanle
Himalaya
Mianwali
Rasul Dam
Chenab
Jammu
Chamba
Demchok
Manzai
Gujrat
Sialkot
Brahmaur
Wazirabad
Gujranwala
Pathankot
7026
Dankhar Gompa
Gar Dzong
Dera Ismail Khan
Indus
Khushab
Sargodha
Hafizabad
Gurdaspur
Palampur
Kulu
Chiniot
Shekhupura
Amritsar
HIMACHAL PRADESH
Mandi
Shipki La
Gartok
Lanchen Khambab
Sulaiman Range
Thal Desert
Sind Sagar Doab
Jhelum
Lahore
Hoshiarpur
Bhakra Dam
Jhang
Trimmu Dam
Faisalabad
Jullundur
Musa Khel
Maghiana
Gojra
Phagwara
Nangal Dam
Simla
Ravi
Kasur
Ludhiana
Kandaghat
Kamet
7756
Firozpur
Sahiwal
(Montgomery)
Bari Doab
PUNJAB
Jagraon
Chakrata
Badrinath
Dera Ghazi Khan
Multan
Khanewal
Fazilka
Muktsar
Chandigarh
Ambala
Mussoorie
Dehra Dun
7817
Nanda Devi
Bhatinda
Patiala
Pauri
Haridwar Dam
Musaffargarh
Sutlej
Abohar
Jagadhri
Jampur
Ganganagar
Saharanpur
Haridwar
Almora
Lodhran
Alipur
Roorkee
Karnal
Panjinad Barrage
Sirsa
Muzaffarnagar
Najibabad
Bahawalpur
Suratgarh
Bijnor
Haldwani
Chachran
Ahmadpur
Anupgarh
Hisar
Hansi
HARYANA
Sonipat
Meerut
Moradabad
Indus
Bhiwani
Rohtak
New Delhi
Amroha
Rampur
Guddu Barrage
Sardarshahr
DELHI
Hapur
Ghaziabad
Sambhal
Pilibhit
Desert
Churu
Gurgaon
Bulandshahr
Bareilly
Rajasthan Canal
Bikaner
Ratangarh
Jhunjhunu
Rewari
Kishangarh
Indian Desert
INDIA
Thar
Kolayat
Fatehpur
Nawalgarh
Aligarh
Budaun
Ramgarh
Sikar
1052
Alwar
Hathras
UTTAR PRADESH
Fatehgarh
Mathura
Phalodi
Nagaur
Bharatpur
Mainpuri
Hardoi
Sambhar
Kannauj
Pokaran
Agra
Firozabad
Great
RAJASTHAN
Jaipur
387
Daulpur
Etawah
Ajmer
Ganga
Jodhpur
Luni
Bilara
Malpura
Tonk
Chambal
Bhind
Kanpur
Nasirabad
Sawai Madhopur
Gwalior
Munabao
Pachpadra
Luni
Beawar
Kekri
Orai
Barmer
Pali
Sheopur Kalan
Kunch
Hamirpur
Marwar
Bundi
Datia
Jalor
Bhilwara
Shivpuri
Mau Ranipur
Banda
Jhansi
Sirohi
Nathdwara
Kota
Baran
521
Raniwara
1722
Chittaurgarh
Gandhi Sagar
Chhatarpur
Nagar Parkar
Tharad
Kachchh
101
92
91
36
34
32
30
28
26
72
74
76
78
80
COPYRIGHT GEORGE PHILIP & SON LTD.

Map 89

Central and Southern India, Sri Lanka

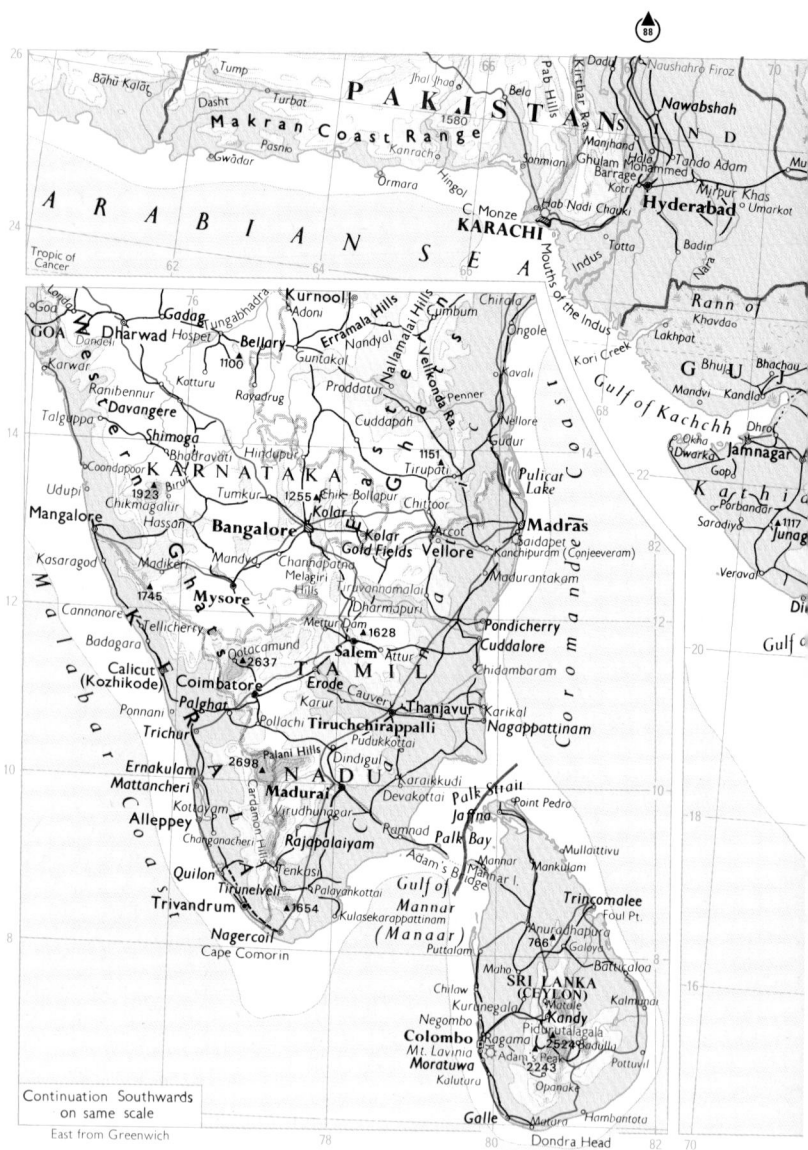

PAKISTAN

Bāhū Kalāt   Tump   Jhal Jhao   Pab Hills   Dadu   Naushahro Firoz
Dasht   Turbat   Bela   SIND   Nawabshah
Makran Coast Range   1580   Manjhand
Pasni   Kanrach   Sonmiani   Ghulam   Hala   Tando Adam   Mu
Gwadar   Ormara   Hingol   Barrage   Kotri   Mirpur Khas   Umarkot
C. Monze   Hab Nadi Chauki   Indus   Totta   Badin   Nara
ARABIAN   KARACHI   Mouths of the Indus

Tropic of Cancer

SEA

Rann of   Khavdao   Lakhpat   Kori Creek   Bhuj   GUJ   Bhachau
God   Long   Gadag   Kurnool   Adoni   Erramala Hills   Cumbum   Chitala   Ongole   Gulf of Kachchh   Mandvi   Kandla
GOA   Dharwad   Hospet   Bellary   Nandyal   Velkonda Ra.   Kavali   Okha   Dwarka   Jamnagar
Dandeli   Kattura   Proddatur   Penner   Nellore   Porbandar   Sarodiyo   Junag
Karwar   Ranibennur   Rayadrug   Cuddapah   Sudur   Veraval   Di
Davangere   Talguppa   Shimoga   1151   Pulicat Lake   KATHIA
Coondapoor   Bhadravati   Hindupur   Tirupati   Madras
Udupi   1923   KARNATAKA   Tumkur   1255   Chik   Bollapur   Chittoor   Saidapet   Kanchipuram (Conjeeveram)
Mangalore   Chikmagalur   Kolar   Arcot   Vellore   Madurantakam
Kasaragod   Hassan   Madikeri   Channapatna   Gold Fields   Tiruvannamalai
Bangalore   Mandya   Melagiri Hills
745   Mysore   Dharmapuri   Pondicherry   Cuddalore
Cannanore   Tellicherry   Mettur Dam   1628   Chidambaram   Coromandel
Badagara   Ootacamund   Salem   Attur   TAMIL
Calicut (Kozhikode)   2637   Erode   Cauvery   Thanjavur   Karikal
Coimbatore   Karur   Tiruchirappalli   Nagappattinam
Ponnani   Palghat   Pollachi   Pudukkottai
Trichur   Palani Hills   Dindigul   NADU   Karaikkudi
Ernakulam   2698   Madurai   Devakottai   Palk Strait   Point Pedro
Mattancheri   Cardamom   Virudhunagar   Jaffna   Mullaittivu
Alleppey   Changanacheri   Ramnad   Palk Bay   Mannar I.   Mankulam
Quilon   Rajapalaiyam   Adam's Bridge   Gulf of   Trincomalee
Tirunelveli   Tenkasi   Palayankottai   Mannar   766   Anuradhapura   Foul Pt.
Trivandrum   654   Kulasekarappattinam   (Manaar)   Galoya   Batticaloa
Nagercoil   Puttalam   Maho
Cape Comorin   Chilaw   SRI LANKA (CEYLON)   Kalmunai
Kurunegala   Matale
Negombo   Kandy   2524   Badulla
Colombo   Ragama   Adam's Peak   Pidurutalagala
Mt. Lavinia   2243   Pottuvil
Moratuwa   Opanake
Kalutara
Galle   Matara   Hambantota
Dondra Head

Continuation Southwards
on same scale

East from Greenwich

Map 90

1:10 000 000

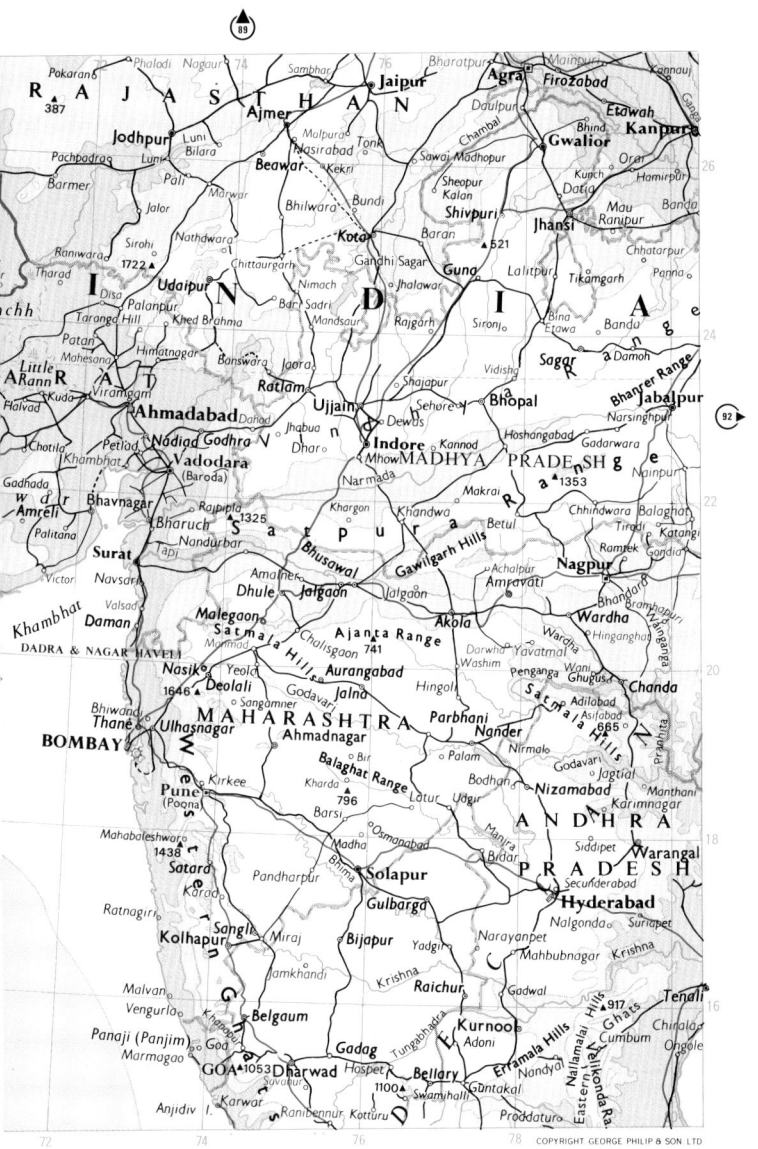

Map 91

Eastern India, Bangladesh and Burma

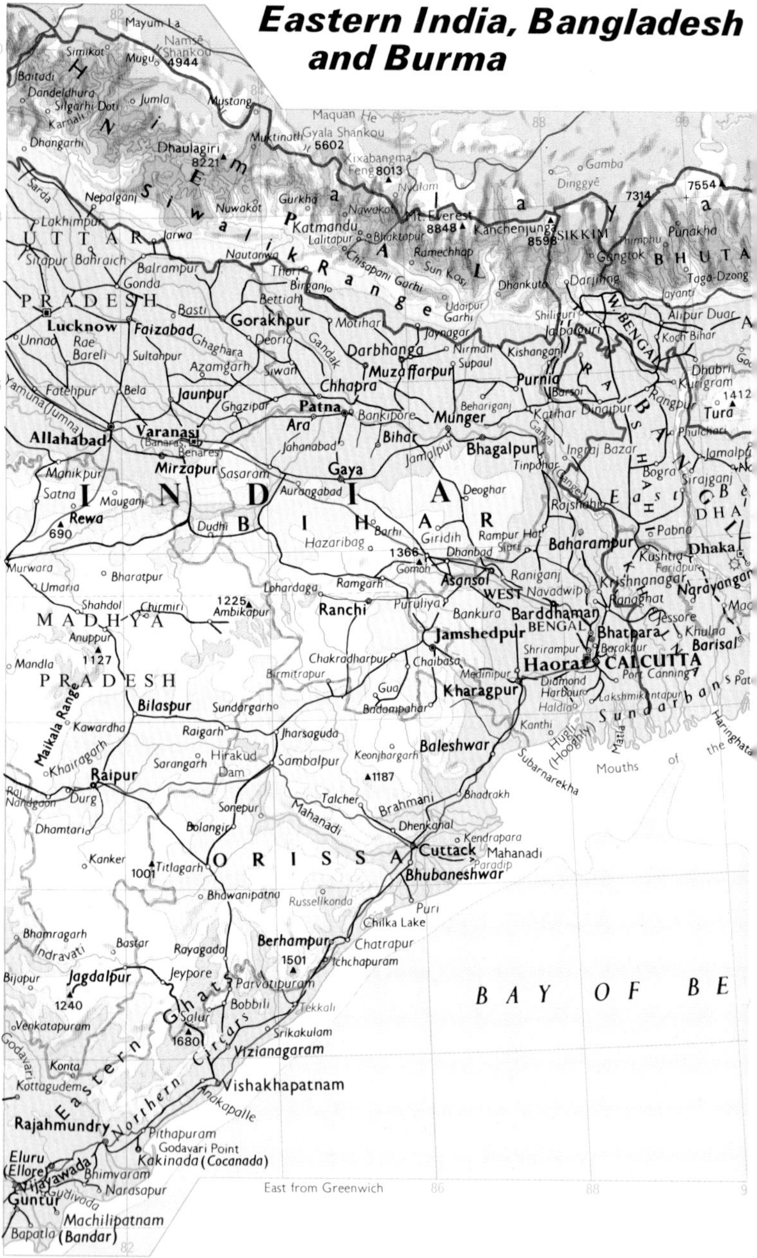
Mayum La
Namsê Shankou
4944
Simikot
Mugu
Baitadi
Dandeldhura
Silgarhi Doti
Jumla
Karnali
Mustang
Dhangarhi
Muktinath
Maquan He
Gyala Shankou
5602
Dhaulagiri
8221
Xixabangma Feng 8013
Nyalam
Gamba
Dinggyê
7554
7314
HIMALAYA
NEPAL
Sarda
Nepalganj
Nuwakot
Gurkha
Nawakot
Mt. Everest
8848
Kanchenjunga
8598
SIKKIM
Thimphu
Punakha
Siwalik Range
Lakhimpur
UTTAR PRADESH
Jarwa
Katmandu
Lalitapur
Bhaktapur
Ramechhap
Gangtok
BHUTA
Sitapur
Bahraich
Nautanwa
Chisapani Garhi
Sun Kosi
Dhankuta
Darjiling
Taga-Dzong
Balrampur
Gonda
Thori
Birganj
Udaipur Garhi
Jayanti
Bettiah
Basti
Shiliguri
Jalpaiguri
W. BENGAL
Alipur Duar
Lucknow
Faizabad
Gorakhpur
Motihari
Jaynagar
Koch Bihar
Unnao
Rae Bareli
Sultanpur
Ghaghara
Deoria
Gandak
Darbhanga
Nirmali
Kishanganj
Azamgarh
Siwan
Muzaffarpur
Supaul
Dhubri
Kurigram
Yamuna (Jumna)
Fatehpur
Bela
Jaunpur
Chhapra
Purnia
Barsoi
RAJSHAHI
BANGLA
Rangpur
1412
Tura
Ghazipur
Patna
Bankipore
Munger
Beharigani
Katihar
Dinajpur
Allahabad
Varanasi (Banaras, Benares)
Ara
Bihar
Ganga
Phulchari
Jahanabad
Bhagalpur
Ingraj Bazar
Jamalpur
Mirzapur
Sasaram
Gaya
Jamalpur
Tinpahar
Manikpur
Bogra
Sirajganj
Satna
INDIA
Mauganj
Aurangabad
Deoghar
(Ganges)
Rajshahi
East
Rewa
690
BIHAR
Dudhi
Barhi
Giridih
Rampur Hat
Pabna
DHAKA
Hazaribag
Suri
Baharampur
Dhaka
1366
Dhanbad
Kushtia
Faridpur
Murwara
Bharatpur
Gomoh
Asansol
Raniganj
Krishnanagar
Narayanganj
Umaria
Lohardaga
Ramgarh
WEST
Navadwip
Ranaghat
Shahdol
Chirmiri
1225
Ambikapur
Ranchi
Puruliya
Bankura
Barddhaman
Jessore
MADHYA PRADESH
BENGAL
Khulna
Anuppur
Jamshedpur
Bhatpara
KHULNA
Barisal
Shrirampur
Barakpur
1127
Mandla
Chakradharpur
Chaibasa
Haora
CALCUTTA
Birmitrapur
Medinipur
Diamond Harbour
Port Canning
Gua
Kharagpur
Maikala Range
Bilaspur
Sundargarh
Badampahar
Haldia
Lakshmikantapur
Sundarbans
Kawardha
Kanthi
Raigarh
Jharsaguda
Hugli (Hooghly)
Matla
Haringhata
Khairagarh
Hirakud Dam
Baleshwar
Sarangarh
Keonjhargarh
Mouths of the
Raipur
Sambalpur
Subarnarekha
1187
Rajnandgaon
Durg
Bhadrakh
Talcher
Brahmani
Sonepur
Mahanadi
Dhamtari
Bolangir
Dhenkanal
Kendrapara
ORISSA
Cuttack
Mahanadi
Kanker
Paradip
1001
Titlagarh
Bhubaneshwar
Bhawanipatna
Russellkonda
Puri
Chilka Lake
Bhamragarh
Bastar
Berhampur
Chatrapur
Indravati
Rayagada
1501
Ichchapuram
Bijapur
Jagdalpur
Jeypore
Parvatipuram
BAY OF BE
1240
Eastern Ghats
Bobbili
Tekkali
Salur
Venkatapuram
1680
Northern Circars
Srikakulam
Godavari
Vizianagaram
Konta
Kottagudem
Vishakhapatnam
Anakapalle
Rajahmundry
Pithapuram
Godavari Point
Eluru (Ellore)
Kakinada (Cocanada)
Vijayawada
Bhimavaram
Narasapur
Guntur
Gudivada
Machilipatnam (Bandar)
Bapatla
East from Greenwich
82
84
86
88
90
30
28
26
24
22
20
16
89
91

Map 92

1:10 000 000

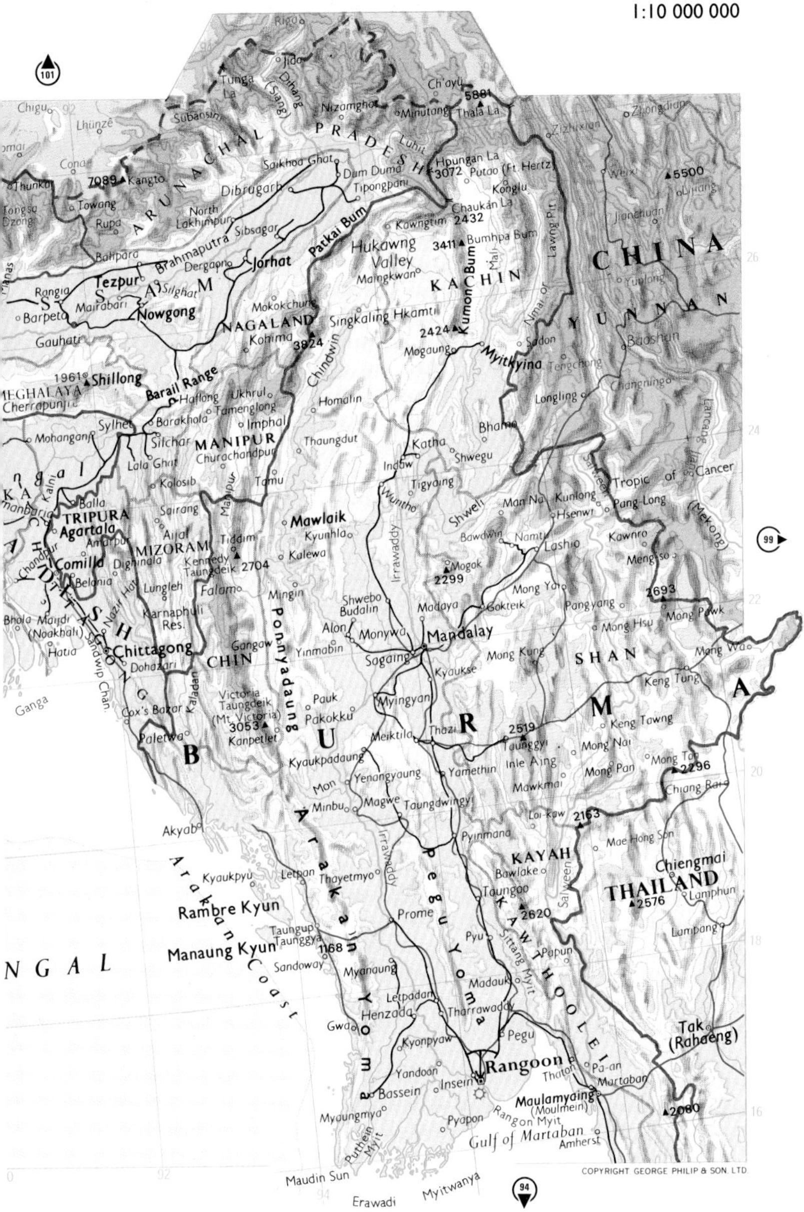
101
99
94
CHINA
YUNNAN
KACHIN
SHAN
KAYAH
CHIN
BURMA
THAILAND
ARUNACHAL PRADESH
ASSAM
NAGALAND
MANIPUR
MIZORAM
TRIPURA
MEGHALAYA
BANGLADESH
KAWTHOOLEI
NGAL
Tropic of Cancer
Tunga La
Jido
Dihang (Siang)
Ch'ayü
5881
Thala La
Nizamghat
Minutang
Subansiri
Chigu
Lhünzê
Cona
7089
Kangto
Thunka
Towang
Tongsa Dzong
Rupa
Balipara
Saikhoa Ghat
Dum Duma
Tipongpani
Lohit
Hpungan La
3072
Putao (Ft. Hertz)
Konglu
Chaukan La
2432
Kawngtim
Dibrugarh
North Lakhimpur
Sibsagar
Brahmaputra
Dergaon
Jorhat
Patkai Bum
Hukawng Valley
Maingkwan
3411
Bumhpa Bum
Kumon Bum
Mali
Lawng Pit
Zhongdian
Zizhixian
Weixi
5500
Lijiang
Jianchuan
Yulong
Baoshan
Tezpur
Silghat
Rangia
Barpeta
Mairabari
Nowgong
Gauhati
Mokokchung
Singkaling Hkamti
Kohima
3824
Chindwin
2424
Mogaung
Myitkyina
Nmai
Sadon
Tengchong
Changning
Lancang Jiang
1961
Shillong
Cherrapunji
Barail Range
Haflong
Ukhrul
Tamenglong
Imphal
Barakhola
Silchar
Sylhet
Mohanganj
Homalin
Longling
Bhamo
Thaungdut
Churachandpur
Lala Ghat
Katha
Shwegu
Indaw
Tigyaing
Tamu
Kolosib
Wuntho
Shweli
Man Na
Kunlong
Hsenwi
Pang-Long
Salween
Balla
Agartala
Sairang
Aijal
Mawlaik
Kyunhla
Bawdwin
Namtu
Lashio
Kawnro
(Mekong)
Amarpur
Tiddim
Manipur
Irrawaddy
Kennedy Taungdeik
2704
Kalewa
Mogok
2299
Mengliso
Chandpur
Comilla
Belonia
Lungleh
Falam
Mingin
Shwebo
Budalin
Madaya
Mong Yai
Gokteik
2693
Mong Pawk
Pangyang
Karnaphuli Res.
Pondaung
Alon
Monywa
Mandalay
Mong Hsu
Bhola
Maijdi (Noakhali)
Hatia
Sandwip Chan.
Chittagong
Dohazari
Gangaw
Yinmabin
Sagaing
Kyaukse
Mong Kung
Mong Wa
Keng Tung
Ganga
Cox's Bazar
Kaladan
Victoria Taungdeik (Mt. Victoria)
3053
Kanpetlet
Pauk
Pakokku
Myingyan
2519
Taunggyi
Keng Tawng
Paletwa
Meiktila
Thazi
Mong Nai
Kyaukpadaung
Yenangyaung
Yamethin
Inle Aing
Mong Pan
Mong Tan
2296
Chiang Rai
Minbu
Magwe
Taungdwingyi
Mawkmai
Loi-kaw
2163
Akyab
Pyinmana
Mae Hong Son
Arakan Coast
Kyaukpyu
Letpan
Thayetmyo
Bawlake
Chiengmai
Toungoo
2620
2576
Lamphun
Rambre Kyun
Prome
Arakan Yoma
Pegu Yoma
Taungup
Taunggya
Pyu
Lampang
Manaung Kyun
1168
Sandoway
Sittang Myit
Papun
Myanaung
Madauk
Letpadan
Henzada
Tharrawaddy
Gwa
Pegu
Tak (Raheng)
Kyonpyaw
Rangoon
Thaton
Pa-an
Yandoon
Insein
Martaban
Bassein
Maulamyaing (Moulmein)
2080
Myaungmya
Pyapon
Rangoon Myit
Gulf of Martaban
Amherst
Puthein Myit
Maudin Sun
Erawadi
Myitwanya
92
94
26
24
22
20
18
16

Mainland South East Asia

Map 94

1:10 000 000

CHINA

Gejiu Mengzi
Jinping
2431
3076 Cha Pa Ha Giang Gao Bang
Lai Chau Lao Cai Ha Huyen Longzhou
Yibang 3143 **Bac Phan** Bac Quang Nanning
Mengla Luan **(Tongking)** Bac Kan Pingxiang Qinzhou Hepu
Phong Saly Chau Ngai Lo Phu Thai Nguyen Langson Mong Cai Beihai Haikang
Muong Sing Nam Tha Dien Bien Son La Hanoi Bac Ninh Quang Leizhou Bandao
Vien Pou Kha Muong Ngoi Ha Dong Haiphong Lingao
Muong Sam Neua Hoa Binh Nam Dinh **Gulf of**
Pak Beng Nam Phu Lo Phu Ly Xinzhou Dan Xian
2061 DongMuong Sou 2257 Hoi Xuan Ninh Binh **Tongkin** Changjiang **Hainan**
Luang Prabang Chu Thanh Hoa Dongfang **Dao**
Cao Nguyen Wuzhi Shan 1867
Vang Tran Ninh Ban Ban Thai Hoa Gancheng Ledong Lingao
Vieng Xieng 2711 Ban Khe Bo Huanglu Yacheng Tianda
Khouang 2820 Vinh Chinmu
Pak Sane Kam Keut Vinh Cam Yulins Chiao
Theun Ho Tinh
Vientiane Tuyen Hoa
Pak Vang Ban Don
Lay Mong Nong Khai Dong Hoi
2306 Loei Wang Saphung Udon Thani Nakhon Thakhek Dong Hene 701 Quang Tri **VIETNAM**
2320 Uboiratna Phanom Savannakhet Sepon Hue
Phetchabun Phong Nam Sakon Nakhon Bang Hieng Da Nang (Tourane)
ILAND Phong Pao Lam Khemmarat Hoi An Thang Binh
Khan Kaen Kalasin Saravane Quang Ngai
Chaiyaphum Roi Et 1572 Ban Thateng
Ban Phai Yasothon Ubon Se Done Cao Nguyen 3280 Hoai Nhon
Ban Bua **Khorat** Ratchathani Pakse Boloven (Bong Son)
Yai Mun Sisaket Hat Nhao Attopeu Kontum An Nhon
1328 Buriram Surin Khong San Pleiku (Binh Dinh) Qui
Nong Prachin Buri Nakhon **Phanom Dang Rack** Gia Lai Nhon
Khae Ratchasima Cheom Ksan Stung Cheo Reo Song
Ban Aranyaprathet (Khorat) Phnom Theng Meanchey Khong Cau
Chachoengsao Sisophon Koulen Srepok Tuy
Samut Prakan (Paknam) Angkor Cheo Reo Hoa
Chon Buri Siem Reap Stung-Treng Buon Me Thuot
Si Racha **Tonie Sap** 2405 Nha
Ban Lamung Battambang **CAMBODIA** Trang
Rayang Sandan (Sanbor) Cao Nguyen Cam
Chanthaburi Pursat Kratie Senmonorom Gia Nghia Da Lat Di Linh
Ko Chang Trat 1784 Kompong Kompong Chhlong Loc Ninh Phan
Koh Kut 1813 Chhnang Cham Djiringne Rang
. of Thailand Kas Kong Koulen Budop Phan Da
Koh Kong Prek Thnot **Phnom Penh** Prey-Veng Tay Ninh (Phan Ri)
Kompong Banam Hoa Da
Sre Umbell Speu Kompong Bien Hoa Phan Thiet
Koh Rong Som Taken Svay **Thanh Pho** Vung Tau
1075 Kampot Rieng **Ho Chi Minh** (Saigon)
Phu Hon Long My Cong COPYRIGHT
Quoc Chong Xuyen Sa Dec GEORGE PHILIP & SON LTD
Rach Gia Can Tho
Khanh Hung
(Soc Trang)
Ca Mau Bac Lieu
Mui Ca Mau Con Dao

Map 95

The Malay Peninsula

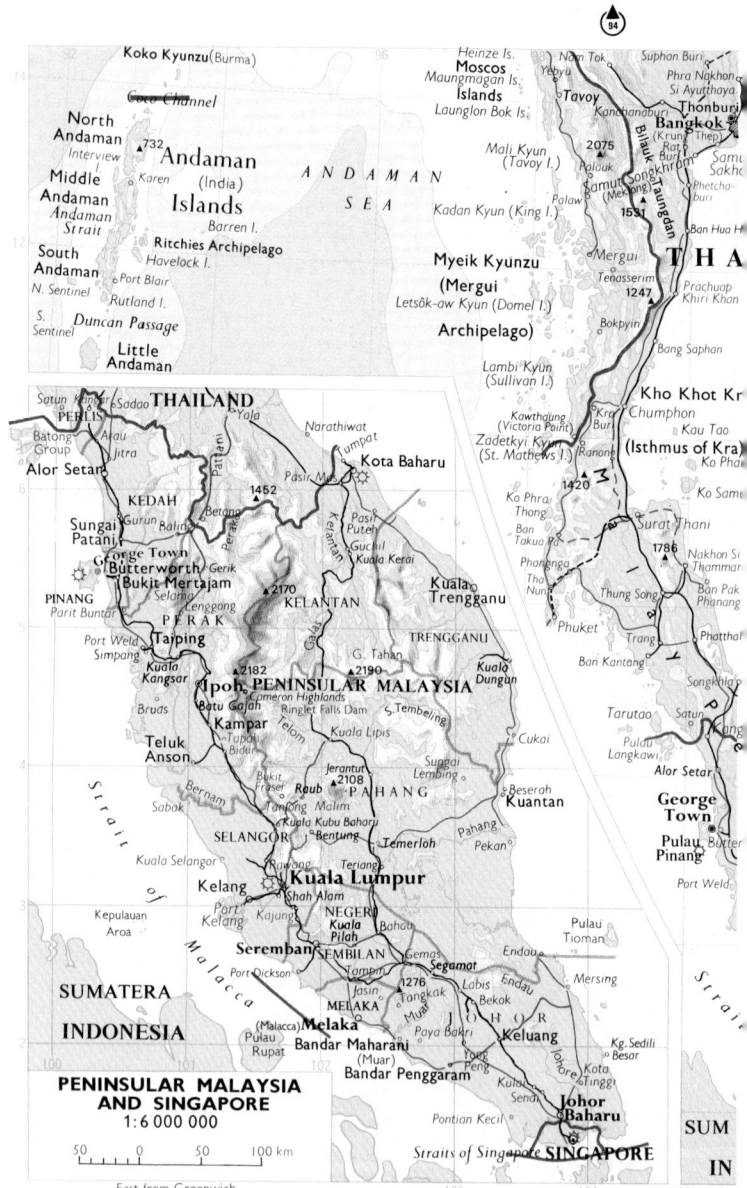

94

Koko Kyunzu (Burma)
Coco Channel

North
Andaman
Interview I.
Middle   732   Andaman
Andaman   Karen   (India)
Andaman   Islands
Strait   Barren I.
          Ritchies Archipelago
South   Havelock I.
Andaman   Port Blair
N. Sentinel   Rutland I.
S.   Duncan Passage
Sentinel
          Little
          Andaman

Heinze Is.   Nan Tok   Suphan Buri
Moscos   Yebyu   Phra Nakhon
Maungmagan Is.   Si Ayutthaya
Islands   Tavoy   Thonburi
Launglon Bok Is.   Kanchanaburi   (Krun   Bangkok
                    Thep)
        Mali Kyun   2075   Samut
A N D A M A N   (Tavoy I.)   Palauk   Rat   Sakhe
        Palaw   Mekong Songkhram   Phetcha-
    S E A   Kadan Kyun (King I.)   1531   buri
                    Ban Hua H

Myeik Kyunzu   Mergui   T H A
(Mergui)   Tenasserim   1247   Prachuap
Letsôk-aw Kyun (Domel I.)   Khiri Khan
Archipelago)   Bokpyin

          Bang Saphan
Lambi Kyun
(Sullivan I.)

          Kho Khot Kr
Satun   Sadao THAILAND   Kra   Chumphon
PERLIS   Yala   Buri   Kau Tao
Batong Arau   Zadetkyi Kyun   (Isthmus of Kra)
Group Jitra   Narathiwat   (St. Mathews I.)   Ranong   Ko Pha
Alor Setar   Victoria Point   1420   Ko Same
              Kawthaung   Ko Phra
      1452   Kota Baharu   Thong   Surat Thani
KEDAH   Betong   Pasir Ma   Ban
Sungai Gurun Baling   Takua Pa   1786   Nakhon Si
Patani   Pasir   Phangnga   Thammar
    George Town   Puteh   Tha   Ban Ban
Butterworth Gerik   Guchil Nun   Thung Song   Phanga
Bukit Mertajam   Kuala Kerai
PINANG Selom   Kuala   Phuket   Trang   Phatthal
Parit Buntar   Lenggong KELANTAN Trengganu
    PERAK   TRENGGANU   Ban Kantang
Port Weld Taiping   G. Tahan
Simpang   Kuala   Tarutao Satu
Kuala   2182 2190   Dungun
Kangsar Ipoh PENINSULAR MALAYSIA   Pulau
Batu Gajah Cameron Highlands   Langkawi   Alor Setar
Bruas   Kampar Ringlet Falls Dam S.Tembeling
Telok   Tapah   Kuala Lipis   Cukai   George
Anson   Bidur   Town
        Jerantut Sungai
    Bukit 2108 Lembing   Pulau   Bixter
Bernam Fraser Raub PAHANG Beserah   Pinang
Sabak Tanjong Malim   Kuantan
    Kuala Kubu Baharu   Pahang   Port Weld
SELANGOR Bentong Temerloh
Kuala Selangor Rawang Teriang Pekan
Kelang Shah Alam Kuala Lumpur
Kepulauan Port Kajang NEGERI   Pulau
Aroa   Kelang   Kuala Bahau   Tioman
      Pilah   Endau
    Seremban SEMBILAN Gemas
    Port Dickson Tampin Segamat Mersing
SUMATERA   1276 Labis Bekok
        Jasin Tongkak Muar   J O H O R
INDONESIA   MELAKA   Paya Bakri
    (Malacca) Melaka J O H O R Keluang
    Pulau Bandar Maharani   Kg. Sedili
    Rupat   (Muar)   Pong   Besar
      Bandar Penggaram Kota
            Kuala Tinggi
            Senai
PENINSULAR MALAYSIA   Johor
AND SINGAPORE   Pontian Kecil Baharu   SUM
1:6 000 000
50 0 50 100 km   Straits of Singapore SINGAPORE   IN

East from Greenwich

Map 96

1:10 000 000

1328
Nong Khae ▲   Prachin Buri   Phanom Dang Rack   Cheom Ksan   Phnom Penh   Koulen   Khong   Khong   San   Kantum   An Nhon (Binh Dinh)
Chachoengsao   Ban Aranyaprathet Sisophon   Pleiku   Gia Lai   Qui Nhon
Samut Prakan(Paknam)   Angkor   Siem Reap   Srepok   Cheo Reo   Song Cau   Tuy Hoa
Chon Buri
Si Racha   Battambang   Tonlé Sap   Stung-Treng   C A M B O D I A   Buon Me Thuot   Ba
Ban Lamung   Pailin   San   Sandan(Sanbor)   Kratie   Senmonorom   2405   Nha Trang
Rayong   Pursat   Kompong   Chhnang   Chhlong   Cao Nguyen   Di Linh   Com   Rhan
Chanthaburi   Trat ▲1744   Kompong   Cham   Budop   Gia Nghia Da Lat   Cao Lanh
Ko Chang   1813   Loc Ninh   Djirlagne   Phan Rang
I L A N D   Phnom Kravanh   Prey-Veng   Tay Ninh   Biên Hoa   Hoa Da (Phan Ri)
of Thailand   Ko Kut   Kas Kong   Phnom Penh   Prek Thnot   Kompong   Speu   Banam   Phan Thiet
Koh Kong   Sre Umbell   Takeo   Svay   Rieng   Thanh Pho   Ho Chi Minh (Saigon)
Koh Rong   1075   Kampot   Long   Xuyen   My Tho   Ba Ria   Cu Lao Hon
Kompong Som   (Sihanoukville)   Reum   Sa Dec   Vung Tau
Phu Quoc   Hon Chong   Rach-Gia   Can Tho   Go Cong
Khanh Hung (Soc Trang)
Bac Lieu
Mui Ca Mau   Ca Mau   Côn Dao

S O U T H   C H I N A   S E A

Pattani
Yala   Narathiwat   Tumpat
Betong   Kota Baharu
Gerik   2170   Kepulauan   Perhentian
Taiping 2182   Kuala Trengganu   Laut
Ipoh   Kuala Dungun   P E N I N S U L A R   Telukbutun   959
Kelantan   Gunong Tahan ▲2190   Kepulauan   Natuna Besar
Cameron Highlands   M A L A Y S I A   Binjai
Kuala Lipis   Kuantan   Matok   Subi
Raub   Siantan   Midai
Kuala   Pahang   Jemaja   Kuala   Kepulauan   Natuna Selatan
Selangor   Kuala Lumpur   Tioman
Port   Kelang   Seremban   Mersing   Kepulauan   Anambas
Kelang   Gemas
Port Dickson   Melaka   Keluang
Bandar   Maharani   Malacca   Kepulauan   Tambelan
T E R A   Bandar   Penggaram   Johor Baharu
O N E S I A   SINGAPORE   I N D O N E S I A

COPYRIGHT GEORGE PHILIP & SON. LTD

Map 97

China: East

74

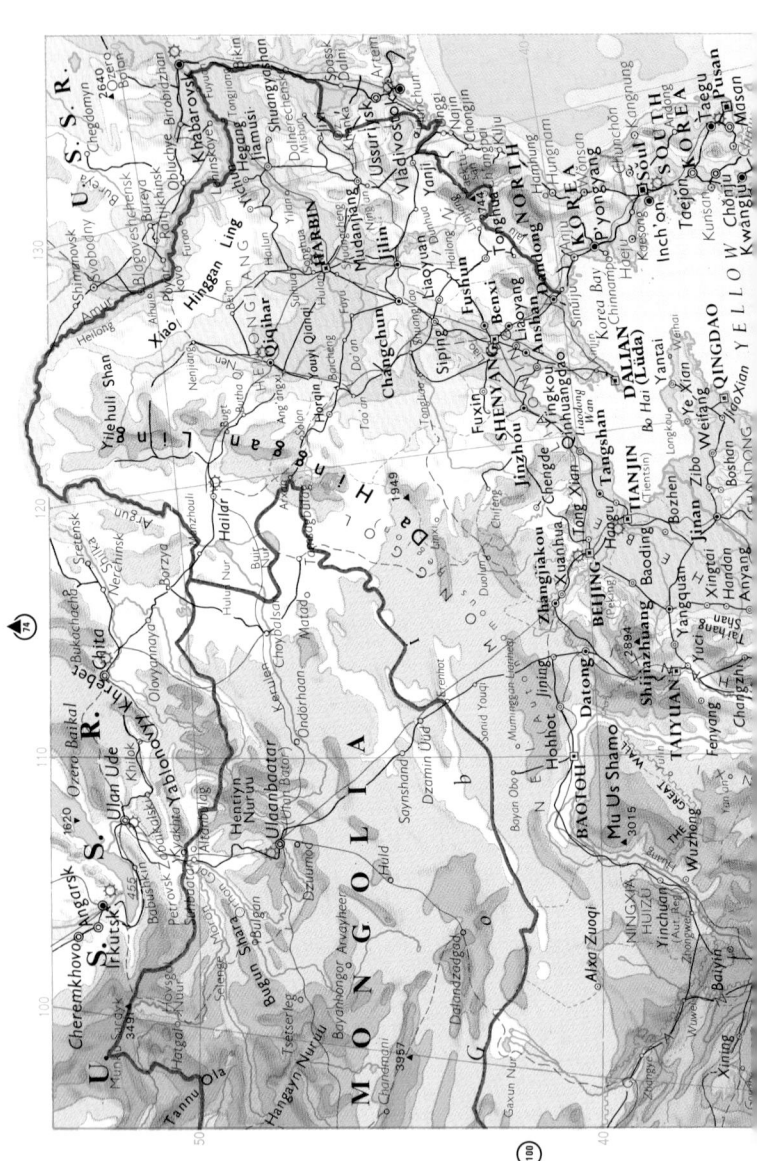
U. S. S. R.
MONGOLIA
Irkutsk
Angarsk
Cheremkhovo
Ulan Ude
Ozero Baikal
Chita
Ulaanbaatar
(Ulan Bator)
Hentiyn Nuruu
Choybalsan
Kerulen
Hailar
Yilehuli Shan
Da Hinggan Ling
Xiao Hinggan Ling
Heilong
Amur
Blagoveshchensk
Khabarovsk
Birobidzhan
Vladivostok
Ussuriysk
HARBIN
Qiqihar
Jiamusi
Hegang
Mudanjiang
Jilin
Changchun
Siping
Liaoyuan
Fushun
SHENYANG
Benxi
Liaoyang
Anshan
Dandong
Yingkou
Jinzhou
Fuxin
Qinhuangdao
DALIAN
(Lüda)
Korea Bay
NORTH KOREA
P'yongyang
SOUTH KOREA
Sŏul
Inch'ŏn
Taejŏn
Taegu
Pusan
Kwangju
Chŏnju
YELLOW
Bo Hai
Yantai
QINGDAO
Weifang
Zibo
Jinan
TIANJIN
(Tientsin)
Tangshan
BEIJING
(Peking)
Zhangjiakou
Xuanhua
Baoding
Shijiazhuang
TAIYUAN
Datong
Hohhot
Jining
BAOTOU
Mu Us Shamo
THE GREAT WALL
Yinchuan
NINGXIA HUIZU
Alxa Zuoqi
Baiyin
Xining
Wuzhong
Handan
Anyang
Xingtai
Yangquan
Changzhi
Fenyang
Saynshand
Dzamin Üüd
Erenhot
Gobi
Dalandzadgad
Hangayn Nuruu
Tannu Ola
Bugun
Selenge
Sharaa
Tsetserleg
Bayanhongor
Arvayheer
Huld
Dzuunmod
Öndörhaan
Matad
Chifeng
Yablonovyy
Khrebet
Shimanovsk
Svobodny
Chegdomyn
Nerchinsk
Sretensk
Borzya
Argun
Tongliao
Tao'an
Baicheng
Horqin Youyi Qianqi
Yanji
Tonghua
Chengde
Tong Xian
Hangu
Bozhen
Boshan
Jiaoxian
Ye Xian
Longkou
Weihai
Wŏnsan
Hamhung
Chongjin
Nakhodka
Artem
Spassk Dal'niy
Yuci
Taihang Shan
Sonid Youqi
Bayan Obo
Gaxun Nur
Chandmani
Hulun Nur
Buir Nur
120
110
100
130
50
40

100

Map 98

1:20 000 000

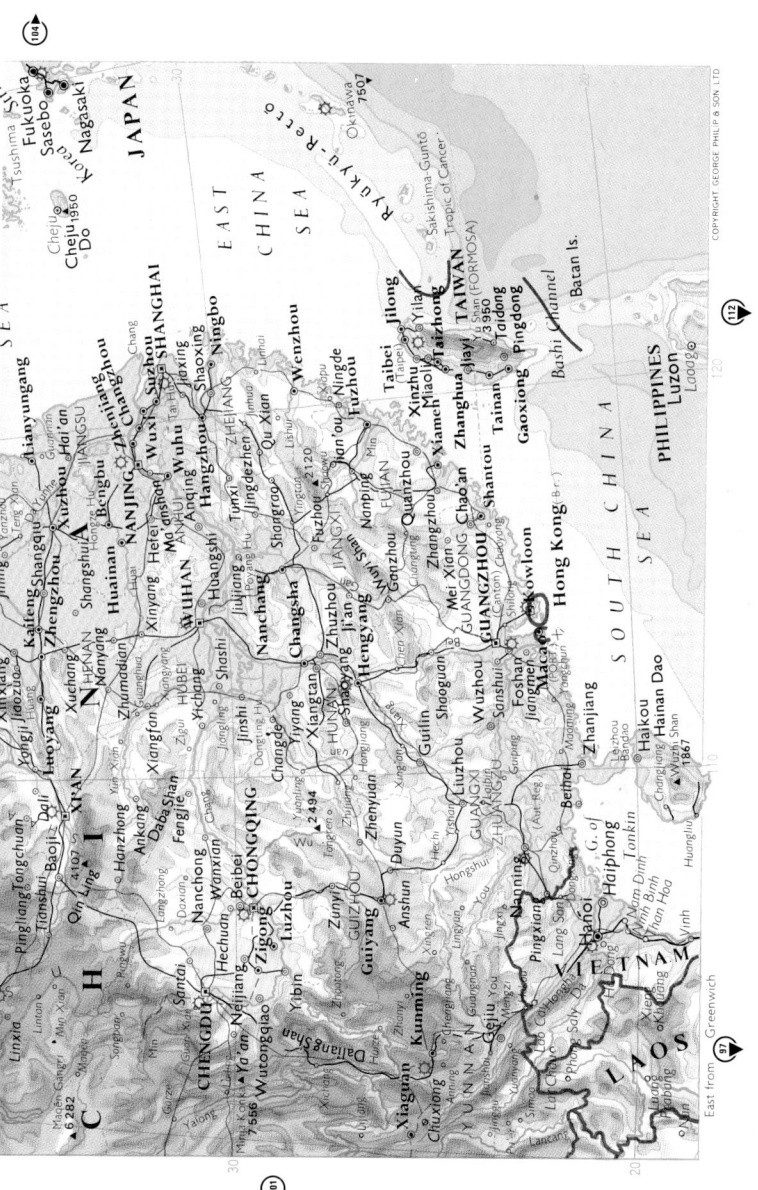

Map 99

COPYRIGHT GEORGE PHILIP & SON LTD

China: West

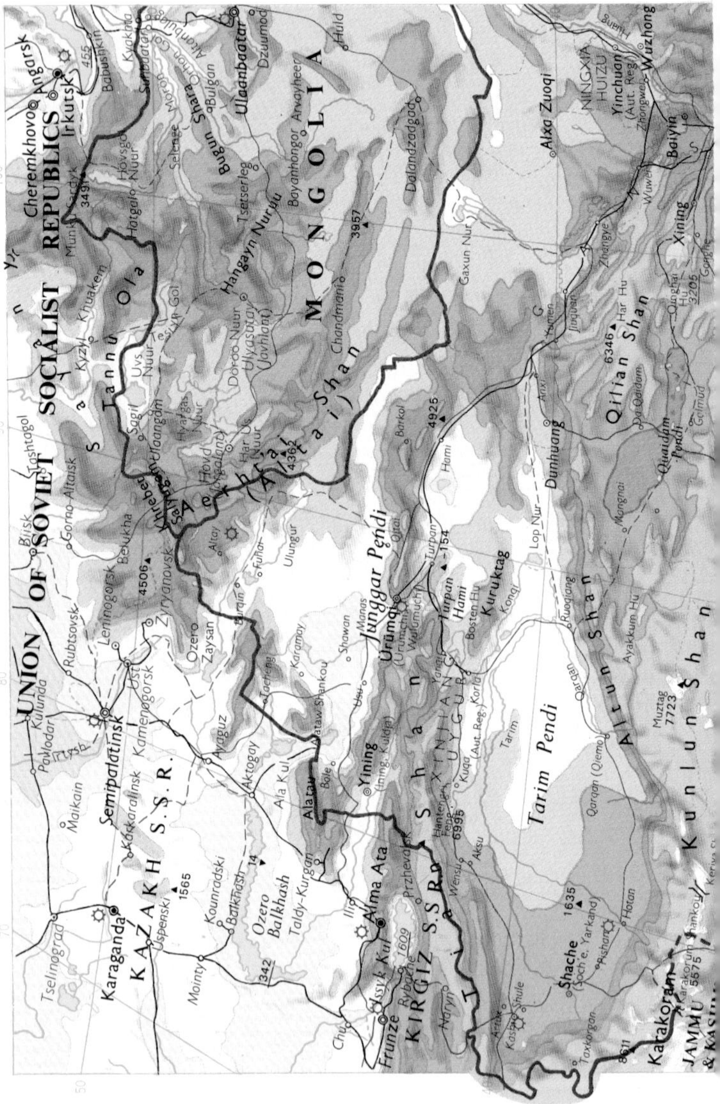

UNION OF SOVIET SOCIALIST REPUBLICS
KAZAKH S.S.R.
KIRGIZ S.S.R.
MONGOLIA
XINJIANG UYGUR (Aut. Reg.)
NINGXIA HUIZU (Aut. Reg.)
JAMMU & KASHMIR
Tianshan
Tarim Pendi
Junggar Pendi
Altun Shan
Kunlun Shan
Qilian Shan
Qaidam Pendi
Karakoram
Aerhtai Shan (Altai Shan)
Sayan Ola
Tannu Ola
Hangayn Nuruu
Kuruktag
Turpan Hami
Ozero Balkhash
Ozero Zaysan
Issyk Kul
Alma Ata
Frunze
Karaganda
Semipalatinsk
Irkutsk
Ulaanbaatar
Ürümqi
Yining
Shache
Hotan
Aksu
Kuqa
Korla
Hami
Dunhuang
Yinchuan
Xining
Baiyin
Wuzhong
Alxa Zuoqi
Yumen
Jiuquan
Zhangye
Wuwei
Golmud
Da Qaidam
Mangnai
Ruoqiang
Qarqan
Lop Nur
Bosten Hu
Karamay
Altay
Ulungur
Tacheng
Bole
Kashi
Taxkorgan
Pishan
Khovd
Ulaangom
Uliastay
Tsetserleg
Bayanhongor
Dalandzadgad
Chandmani
Bugun Shara
Bulgan
Cheremkhovo
Angarsk
Kyzyl
Gorno-Altaisk
Biisk
Barnaul
Rubtsovsk
Leninogorsk
Zyryanovsk
Ust-Kamenogorsk
Pavlodar
Kulunda
Tselinograd
Maikain
Ayaguz
Aktogay
Ala Kul
Alatau
Taldy-Kurgan
Balkhash
Kounradski
Uspenski
Mointy
Chu
Przhevalsk
Rybache
Naryn
Muztag 7723
Hantengri Feng 6995
4506
3491
3957
4362
4925
6346
5575
8611
1635
1565
-154

1:20 000 000

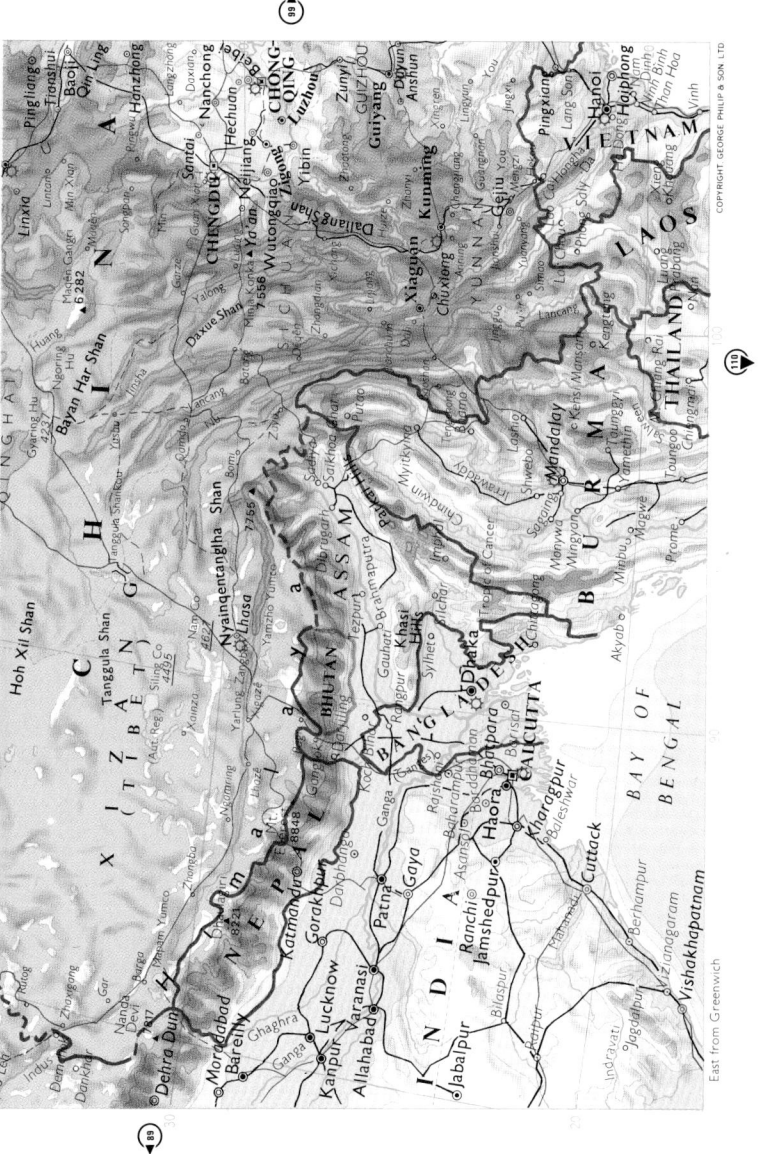

East from Greenwich

Map 101

Japan: North

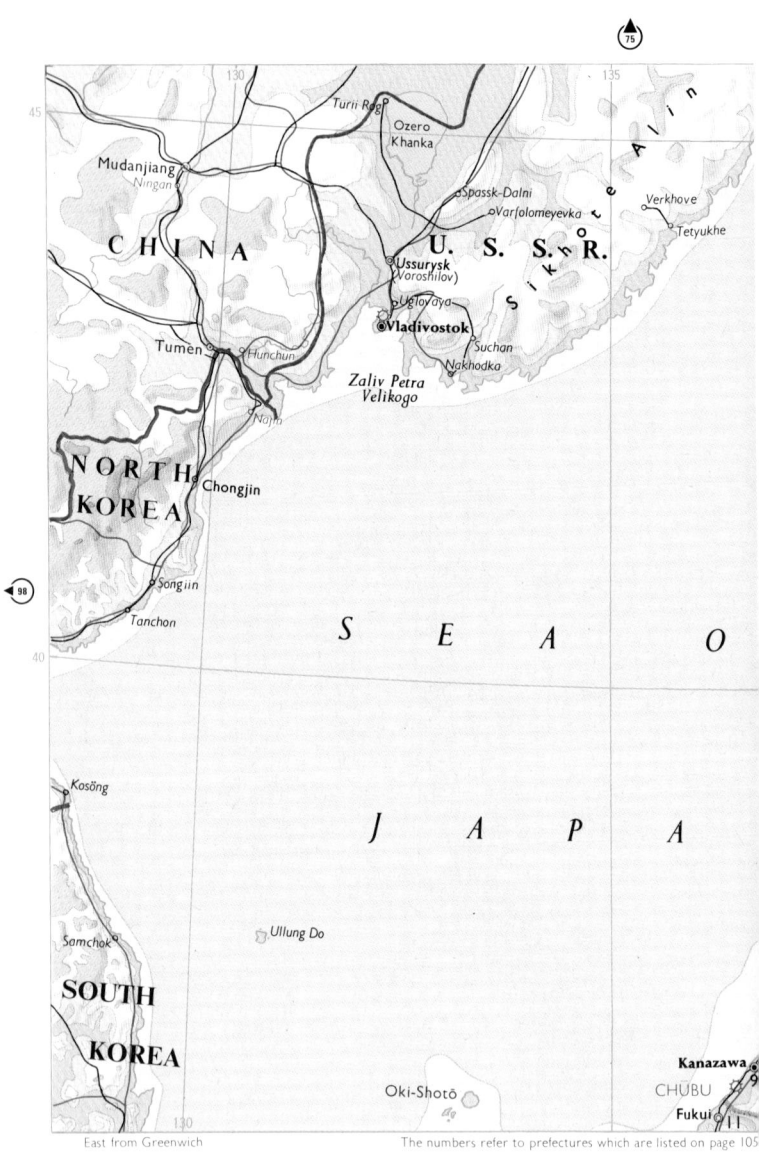

Map 102

1:7 500 000

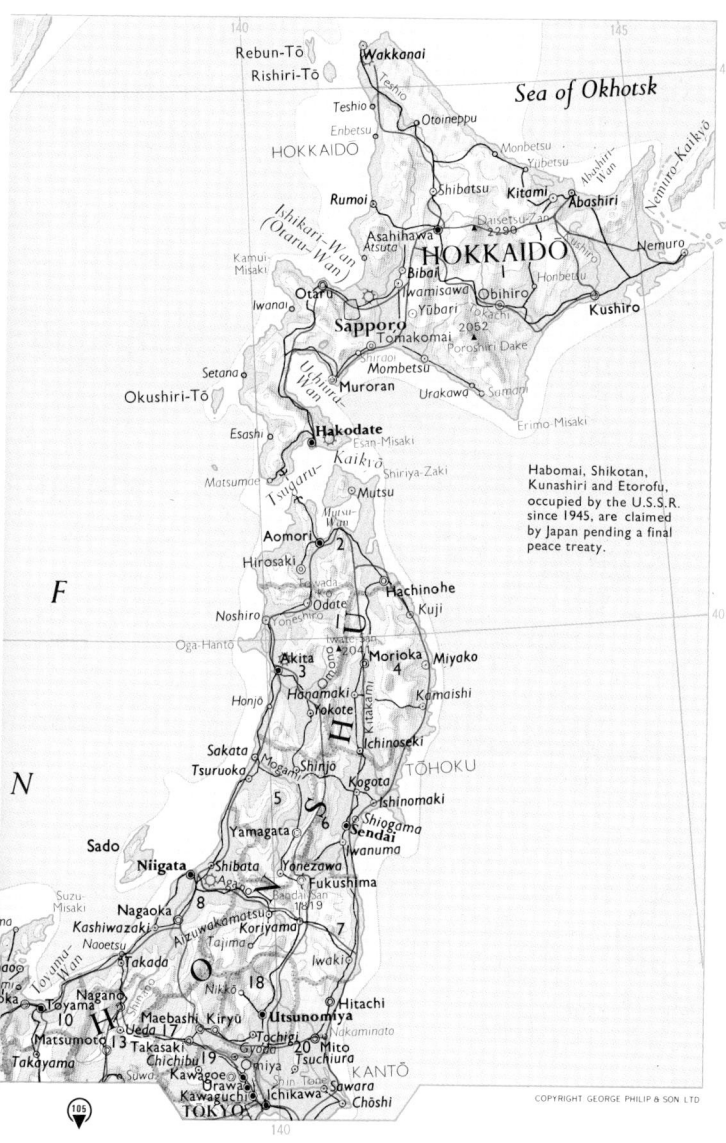

Habomai, Shikotan,
Kunashiri and Etorofu,
occupied by the U.S.S.R.
since 1945, are claimed
by Japan pending a final
peace treaty.

COPYRIGHT GEORGE PHILIP & SON LTD

Map 103

Japan: South

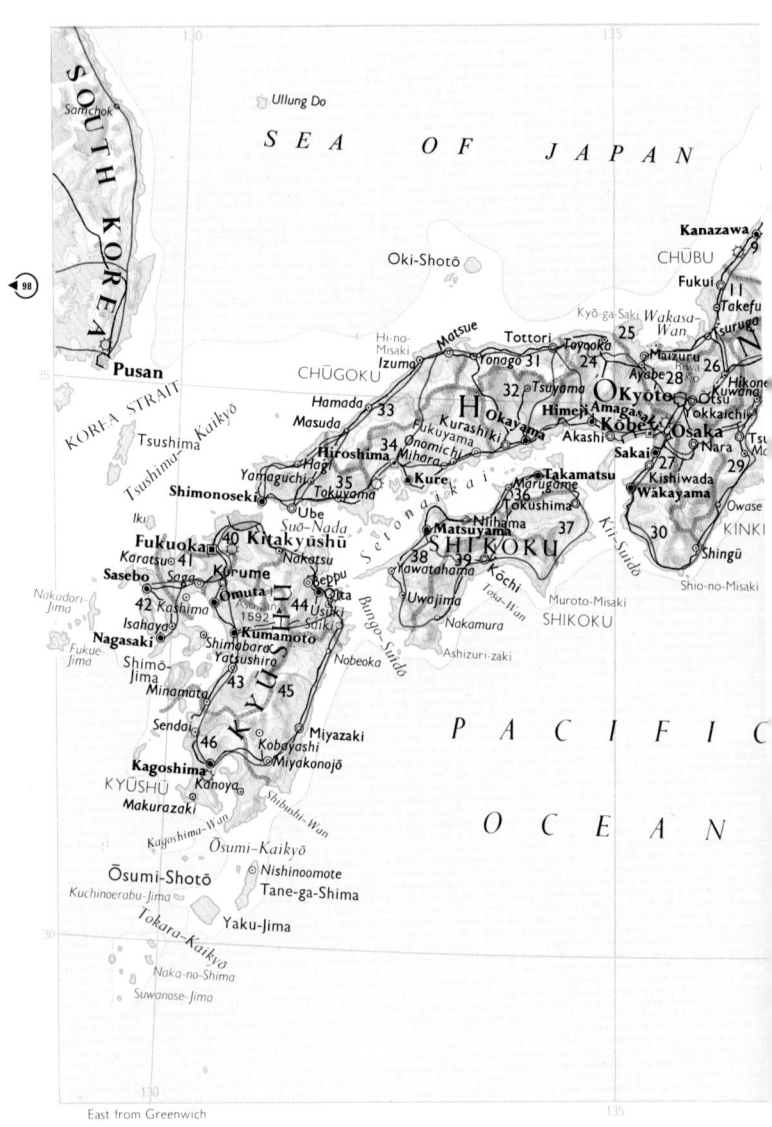

SEA OF JAPAN

SOUTH KOREA

Samchok

Ullung Do

Oki-Shotō

Kanazawa

CHŪBU

Fukui

Takefu

Tsuruga

98

Kyō-ga-Saki

Wakasa-Wan

Hi-no-Misaki

Matsue

Tottori

25

Maizuru

Ayabe 28

Hikone

Kuwana

Pusan

CHŪGOKU

Izumo

Yonago 31

Toyooka

24

Okayama

Himeji

Amaga

Kōbe

Okkaichi

Hamada 33

Masuda

Hōkayama

Akashi

Osaka

Tsu

Tsuyama

32

Tsuyama

Kurashiki

Fukuyama

Ōsaka

Nara

29

KOREA STRAIT

Hiroshima

Hagi

34

Ōnomichi

Mihara

Sakai

27

Kishiwada

Wakayama

Tsushima

Tsushima-Kaikyō

Yamaguchi

35

Tokuyama

Kure

Takamatsu

36

Marugame

Tokushima

Owase

KINKI

Shimonoseki

Iki

Ube

Suō-Nada

Seto-naikai

Niihama

Matsuyama

37

Shingū

Shio-no-Misaki

Fukuoka

40

Kitakyūshū

Nakatsu

Beppu

SHIKOKU

38

39

Kōchi

Muroto-Misaki

Karatsu 41

Kurume

Ōita

Kawatahama

Sasebo

Saga

Ōmuta

44

Usuki

Uwajima

SHIKOKU

Isahaya

42

Kashima

Aso-san 1592

Saiki

Nakamura

Ashizuri-zaki

Nagasaki

Kumamoto

Shimabara

Yatsushiro

Nobeoka

Nakudori-Jima

Fukue-Jima

Shimo-Jima

43

45

PACIFIC

Minamata

Miyazaki

Sendai

46

Kobayashi

Miyakonojō

Kagoshima

KYŪSHŪ

Kanoya

OCEAN

Makurazaki

Kagoshima-Wan

Shibushi-Wan

Ōsumi-Kaikyō

Ōsumi-Shotō

Nishinoomote

Kuchinoerabu-Jima

Tane-ga-Shima

Yaku-Jima

Tokara-Kaikyō

Naka-no-Shima

Suwanose-Jima

Map 104

1:7 500 000

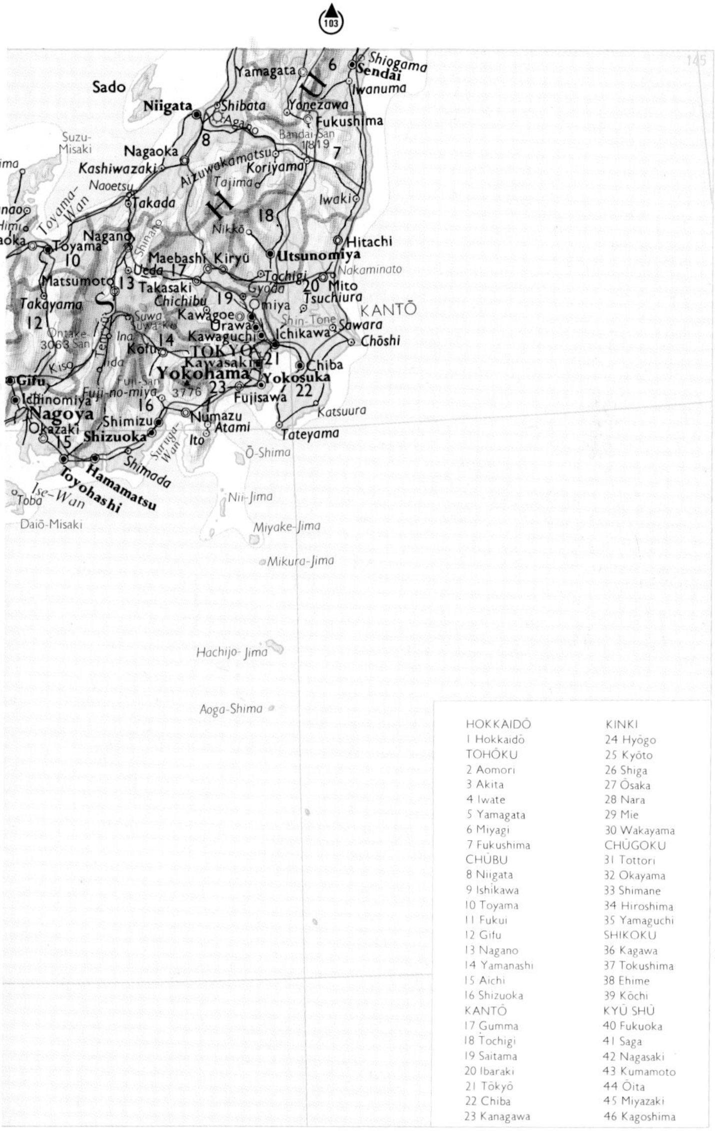

103

145

Sado
Yamagata
Shiogama
Sendai
Iwanuma
Niigata
Shibata
Yonezawa
Suzu-
Misaki
Nagaoka
Agano
Bandai-San
Fukushima
1819
7
Kashiwazaki
Aizuwakamatsu
Koriyama
ma
Naoetsu
Tajima
Takada
Iwaki
18
Nikko
nao
Nagano
Hitachi
aka
Toyama
Chikuma
Maebashi Kiryu
Utsunomiya
Nakaminato
Matsumoto
Ueda
Tochigi
Mito
Takayama
Chichibu
19
Omiya
Tsuchiura
KANTO
Ontake
Suwa
Kawagoe
Urawa
Shin-Tone
Sawara
3063 San
Ina
Kawaguchi
Ichikawa
Choshi
Kiso
Iida
Kofu
TOKYO
21
Chiba
Gifu
Fuji-run-San
Kawasaki
Yokosuka
Ichinomiya
16
3776
Yokohama
22
Nagoya
Numazu
Fujisawa
Katsuura
Okazaki
Shimizu
Atami
Tateyama
15
Shizuoka
Ito
O-Shima
Shimada
Hamamatsu
Toyohashi
Toba
Ise-Wan
Nii-Jima
Daio-Misaki
Miyake-Jima

Mikura-Jima

Hachijo-Jima

Aoga-Shima

HOKKAIDO	KINKI
1 Hokkaido	24 Hyogo
TOHOKU	25 Kyoto
2 Aomori	26 Shiga
3 Akita	27 Osaka
4 Iwate	28 Nara
5 Yamagata	29 Mie
6 Miyagi	30 Wakayama
7 Fukushima	CHUGOKU
CHUBU	31 Tottori
8 Niigata	32 Okayama
9 Ishikawa	33 Shimane
10 Toyama	34 Hiroshima
11 Fukui	35 Yamaguchi
12 Gifu	SHIKOKU
13 Nagano	36 Kagawa
14 Yamanashi	37 Tokushima
15 Aichi	38 Ehime
16 Shizuoka	39 Kochi
KANTO	KYUSHU
17 Gumma	40 Fukuoka
18 Tochigi	41 Saga
19 Saitama	42 Nagasaki
20 Ibaraki	43 Kumamoto
21 Tokyo	44 Oita
22 Chiba	45 Miyazaki
23 Kanagawa	46 Kagoshima

Map 105

Japan: Tokyo, Kyoto, Osaka

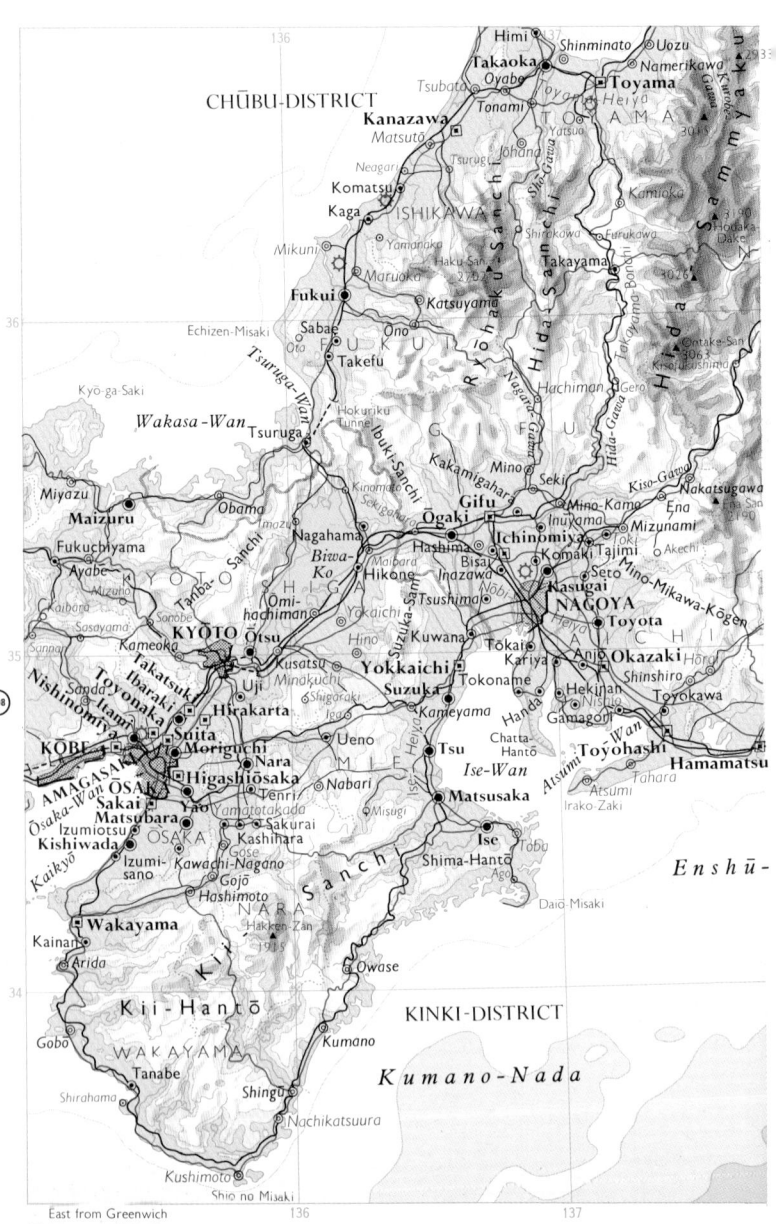
136
137
36
35
34
CHŪBU-DISTRICT
KINKI-DISTRICT
Himi
Shinminato
Uozu
Takaoka
Namerikawa
Toyama
Tsubata
Oyabe
Tonami
Kanazawa
Matsutō
Neagari
Komatsu
Kaga
ISHIKAWA
Mikuni
Maruoka
Fukui
Katsuyama
Haku-San 2702
Yamanaka
Echizen-Misaki
Sabae
Ōno
Takefu
FUKUI
Tsuruga-Wan
Kyō-ga-Saki
Wakasa-Wan
Tsuruga
Hokuriku Tunnel
Ibuki-Sanchi
Ryōhaku-Sanchi
Hida-Sanchi
Hida-Sammyaku
Jōhana
Shirakawa
Furukawa
Takayama
Kamioka
Hodaka-Dake 3190
3026
Ontake-San 3063
Takayama-Bonchi
Hachiman
Gero
Hida-Gawa
Nagara-Gawa
GIFU
Kakamigahara
Mino
Seki
Gifu
Ōgaki
Kiso-Gawa
Nakatsugawa
Ena-San 2190
Mino-Kamo
Ena
Inuyama
Mizunami
Ichinomiya
Komaki
Tajimi
Akechi
Seto
Kasugai
Mino-Mikawa-Kōgen
NAGOYA
Toyota
Miyazu
Maizuru
Obama
Fukuchiyama
Ayabe
KYOTO
Tamba-Sanchi
Nagahama
Biwa-Ko
Maibara
Hikone
SHIGA
Ōmi-hachiman
Yōkaichi
Sekigahara
Kinomoto
Hashima
Bisai
Inazawa
Tsushima
Nōbi-Heiya
Kaibara
Sasayama
Sonobe
Kameoka
KYŌTO
Ōtsu
Kusatsu
Minakuchi
Hino
Suzuka-Sanmyaku
Kuwana
Yokkaichi
Tōkai
Kariya
Anjō
Okazaki
AICHI
Shinshiro
Tokoname
Suzuka
Kameyama
Hekinan
Nishio
Handa
Gamagōri
Toyokawa
Takatsuki
Ibaraki
Toyonaka
Itami
Nishinomiya
Sanda
Hirakarta
Uji
Shigaraki
Iga
Suita
Moriguchi
Nara
Ueno
MIE
KŌBE
AMAGASAKI
Higashiōsaka
ŌSAKA
Ōsaka-Wan
Sakai
Yao
Tenri
Nabari
Matsubara
Yamatotakada
Sakurai
Misugi
Tsu
Chatta-Hantō
Ise-Wan
Toyohashi
Hamamatsu
Atsumi
Tahara
Irako-Zaki
Matsusaka
Izumiotsu
Kishiwada
Kashihara
Gose
Ise
Toba
Kaikyō
Izumi-sano
Kawachi-Nagano
Gojō
Shima-Hantō
Ago
Hashimoto
Daiō-Misaki
Enshū-
NARA
Hakken-Zan 1915
Kii-Sanchi
Wakayama
Kainan
Arida
Owase
Kii-Hantō
Gobō
WAKAYAMA
Kumano
Tanabe
Kumano-Nada
Shirahama
Shingū
Nachikatsuura
Kushimoto
Shio no Misaki
East from Greenwich

108

1:2 500 000

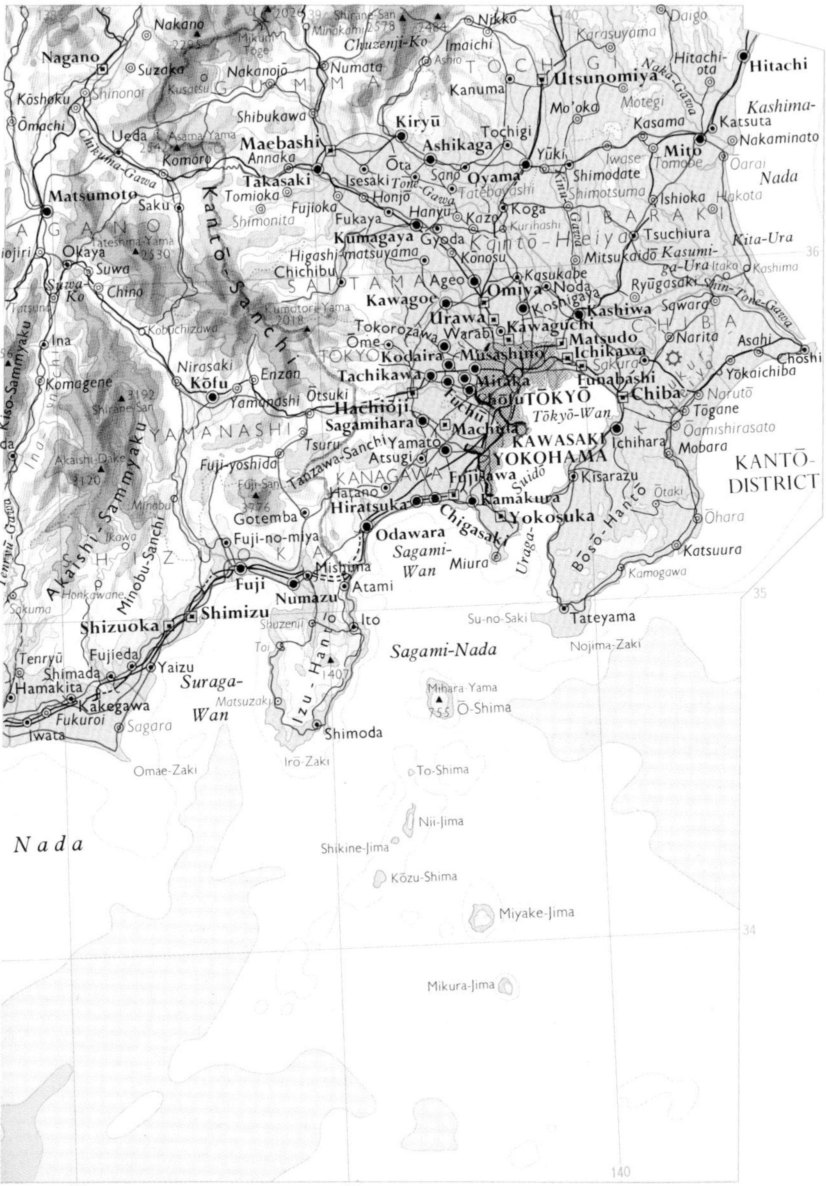

Map 107

Japan: Kyushu

1:2 500 000

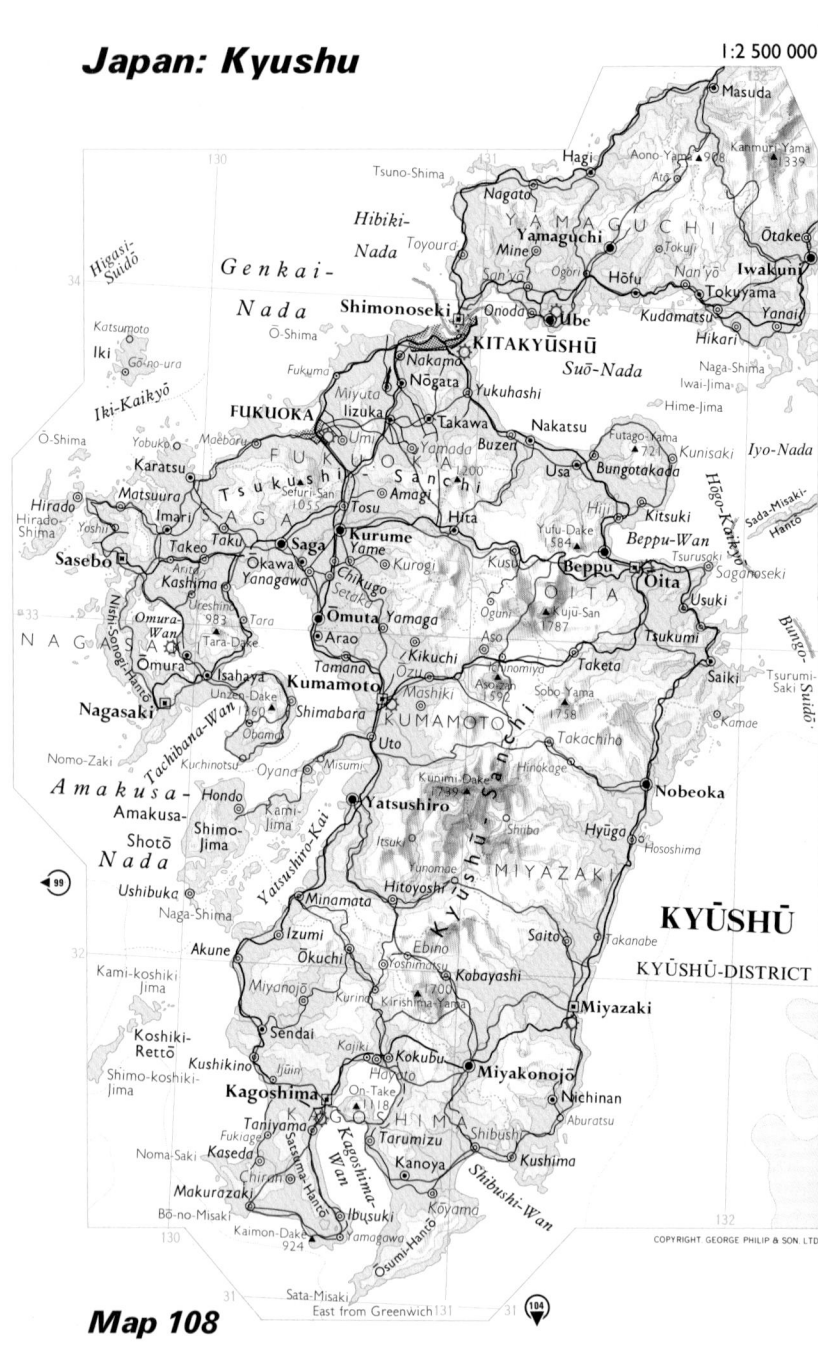

Map 108

West Honshu and Shikoku

1:2 500 000

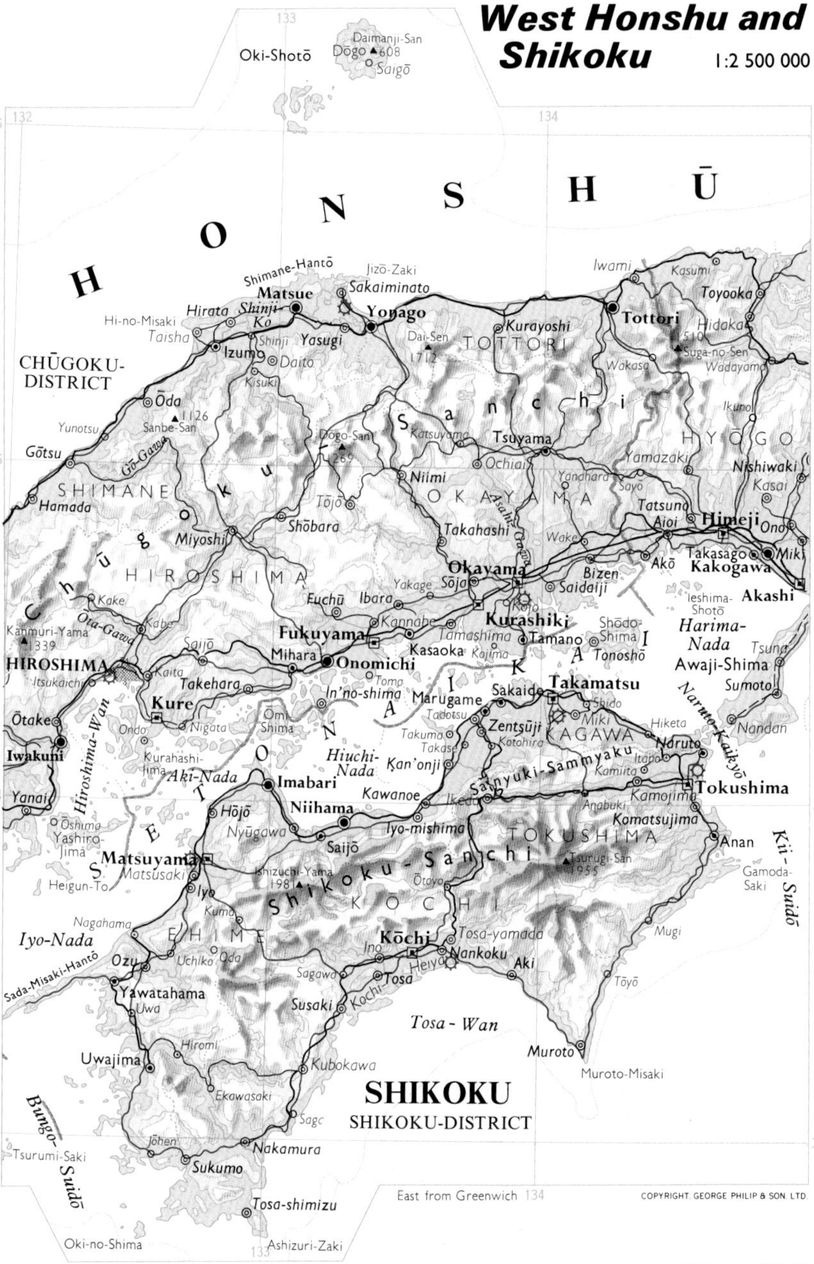

Oki-Shotō

Daimanji-San
Dōgo ▲608
Saigō

H O N S H Ū

H O

CHŪGOKU-DISTRICT

Shimane-Hantō
Jizō-Zaki
Iwami
Kasumi
Toyooka

Hi-no-Misaki
Hirata **Matsue** Sakaiminato
Yonago **Tottori** Hidaka

Taisha Shinji Yasugi Dai-Sen **TOTTORI** Suga-no-Sen Wadayama

Izumo Shinji-Ko Daito Kurayoshi Wakasa Ikuno

Ōda Kisuki S Katsuyama Ochiai Yamazaki **HYŌGO**

Yunotsu ▲1126 Dōgo-San Tsuyama Yonahara Sayō Nishiwaki

Gōtsu Sanbe-San 1269° Niimi OKAYAMA Tatsuno Kasai

SHIMANE Tōjō Takahashi Wake Aioi **Himeji** Miki

Hamada Shōbara Sōja Bizen Takasago Kakogawa

Miyoshi Yakage Saidaiji Akō Ieshima-Shotō **Akashi**

HIROSHIMA Ibara **Okayama** Shōdo-Shima I **Harima-Nada**

Kōke Ota-Gawa Fuchū Kannabe Tamashima Tamano Tonoshō Tsuna

Kanmuri-Yama Saijō Mihara Kasaoka Kajima A **Takamatsu** Awaji-Shima Sumoto

HIROSHIMA Kaita **Fukuyama** **Onomichi** Marugame Sakaide **KAGAWA** Naruto-Kaikyō Nandan

Itsukaichi Takehara Tomo In'no-shima Takuma Takase Zentsūji Miki Hiketa Naruto

Ōtake Kure Nigata Ōmi Shima Kotohira Kamito Itano **Tokushima**

Ondo Kurahashi- Hiuchi- Kan'onji Sanyuki-Sammyaku Kamojima Komatsujima

Iwakuni Jima Aki-Nada Nada Ikeda Anabuki **Anan**

Yanai Ōshima **Imabari** Kawanoe Gamoda-Saki

Yashiro- Hōjō **Niihama** **TOKUSHIMA**

Jima Nyūgawa Iyo-mishima Tsurugi-San Kii-Suidō

Matsuyama Saijō Shikoku-Sanchi ▲955

Matsusaki Ishizuchi-Yama **KŌCHI**

Iyo 1981 Ōtoyo

Nagahama Kuma **EHIME** Inō Tosa-yamada

Iyo-Nada Uchiko Ōda Sagawa Heiya **Kōchi** Aki Mugi

Ōzu Uwa Susaki Tosa Tōyō

Yawatahama Kochi

Sada-Misaki-Hantō Tosa - Wan **Muroto**

Uwajima Hiromi Kubokawa Muroto-Misaki

Bungo- Ekawasaki

Tsurumi-Saki Sage **SHIKOKU**

Jōhen Nakamura **SHIKOKU-DISTRICT**

Sukumo

Tosa-shimizu

Oki-no-Shima Ashizuri-Zaki

East from Greenwich 134

COPYRIGHT GEORGE PHILIP & SON LTD

Map 109

Indonesia: West

112

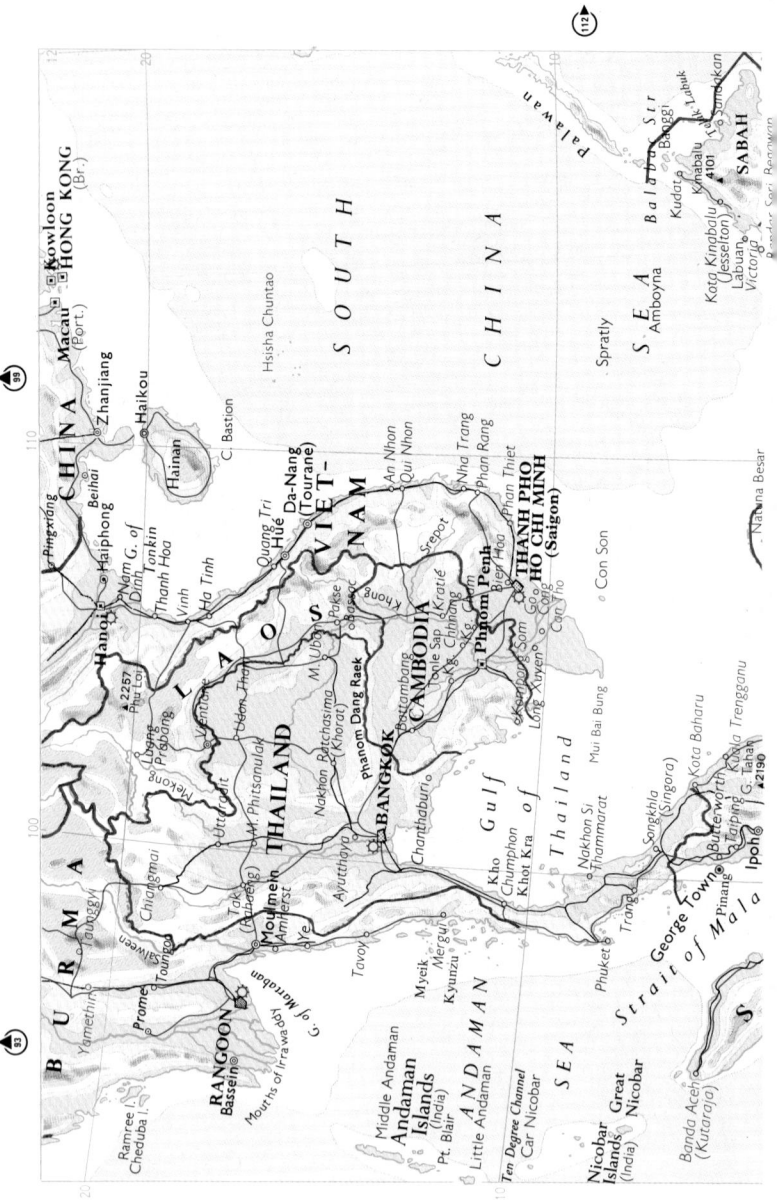

BURMA
CHINA
HONG KONG
(Br.)
Kowloon
Macau
(Port.)
Zhanjiang
Haikou
Hainan
Beihai
Pingxiang
Haiphong
Hanoi
G. of Tonkin
Nam Dinh
Thanh Hoa
Vinh
Ha Tinh
Quang Tri
Hue
Da-Nang
(Tourane)
VIET-NAM
LAOS
Vientiane
Luang Prabang
Phu Loi
2257
Mekong
Udon Thani
Uttaradit
M. Phitsanulok
THAILAND
Nakhon Ratchasima
(Khorat)
Phanom Dang Raek
M. Ubon
Pakse
Bassac
Khong
CAMBODIA
Battambang
Tonle Sap
Kg. Chhnang
Kg. Cham
Kratié
Phnom Penh
Kompong Som
Long Xuyen
Can Tho
Go Cong
Bien Hoa
THANH PHO
HO CHI MINH
(Saigon)
Phan Thiet
Phan Rang
Nha Trang
Qui Nhon
An Nhon
Srepok
C. Bastion
Hsisha Chuntao
SOUTH CHINA SEA
Palawan
Spratly
Amboyna
Balabac Str.
Banggi
Kudat
Kota Kinabalu
(Jesselton)
Kinabalu
4101
SABAH
Labuan
Victoria
Natuna Besar
Con Son
Mui Bai Bung
Gulf of Thailand
BANGKOK
Chanthaburi
Ayutthaya
Tak
(Rahaeng)
Chiangmai
Taunggyi
Yamethin
Prome
Toungoo
Salween
RANGOON
Bassein
Mouths of Irrawaddy
G. of Martaban
Moulmein
Amherst
Ye
Tavoy
Mergui
Myeik
Kyunzu
Kho Khot Kra
Chumphon
Nakhon Si Thammarat
Songkhla
(Singora)
Kota Baharu
Kuala Trengganu
G. Tahan
2190
Ipoh
Taiping
Butterworth
George Town
Pinang
Trang
Phuket
Strait of Malacca
ANDAMAN SEA
Ramree I.
Cheduba I.
Middle Andaman
Andaman Islands
(India)
Pt. Blair
Little Andaman
Ten Degree Channel
Car Nicobar
Nicobar Islands
(India)
Great Nicobar
Banda Aceh
(Kutaraja)

93
99

Map 110

1:20 000 000

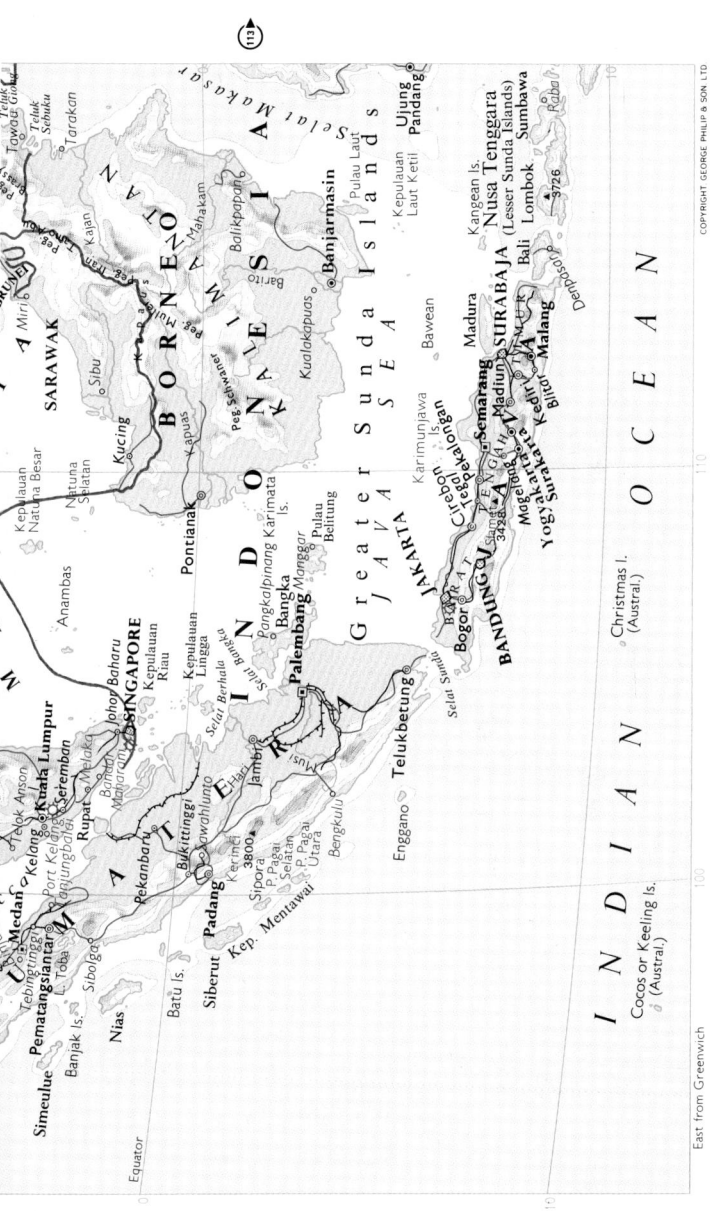

East from Greenwich

Map 111

Indonesia: East

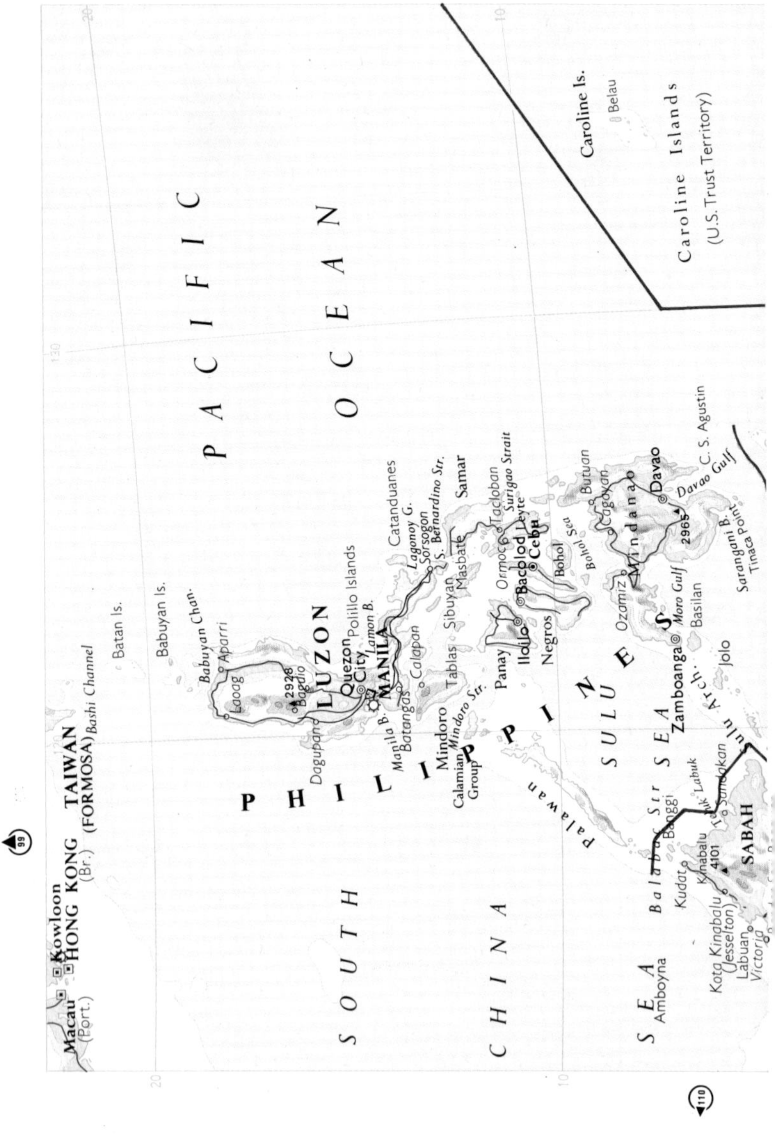

Map 112

1 : 20 000 000

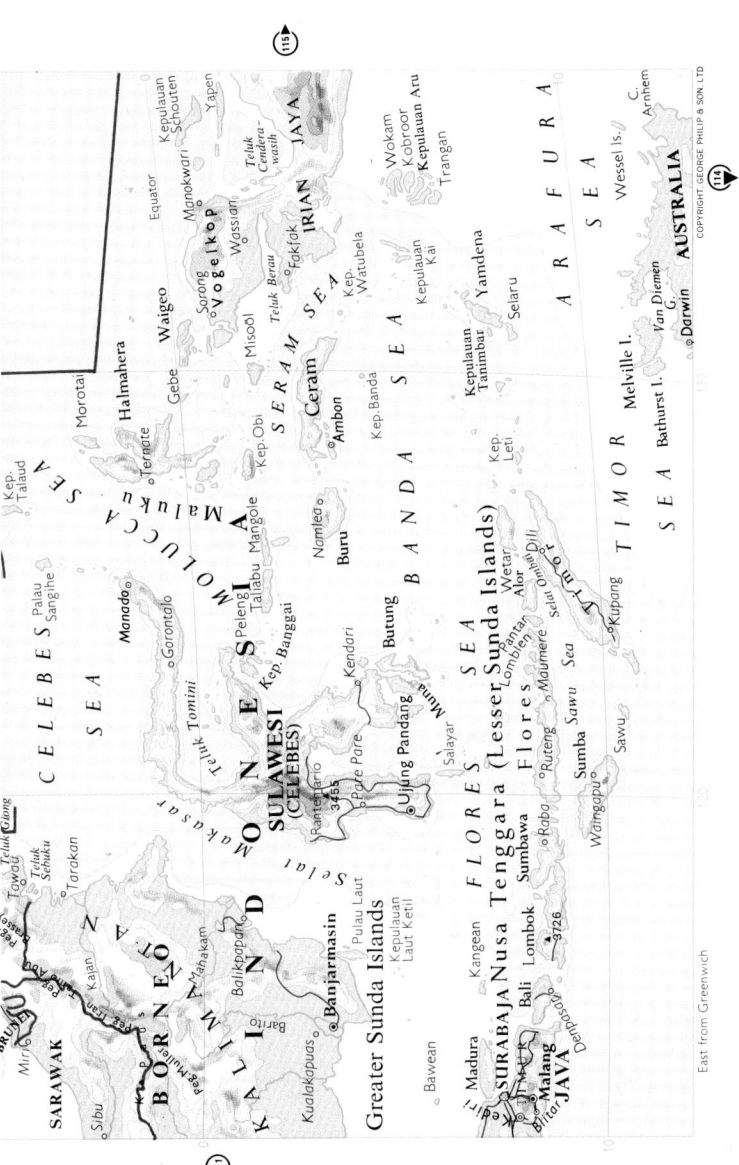

East from Greenwich

COPYRIGHT GEORGE PHILIP & SON LTD

Map 113

Australia, New Zealand and Papua New Guinea

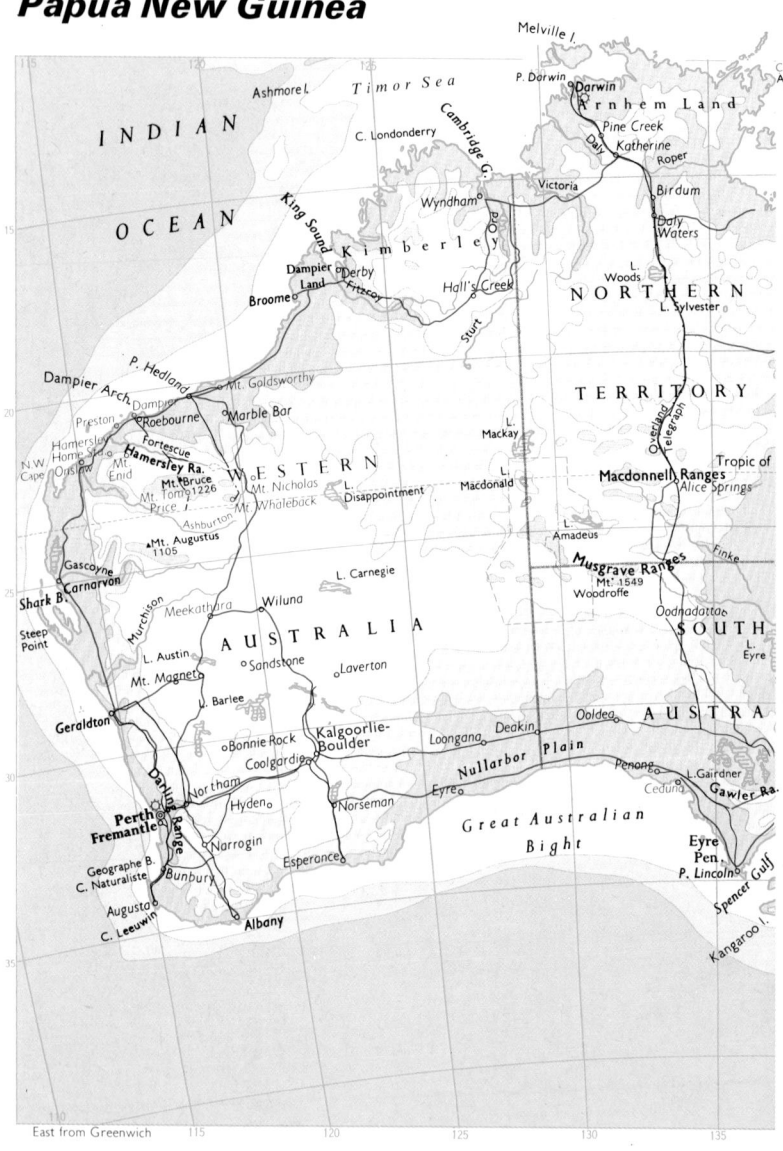

Map 114

1:24 000 000

PAPUA NEW GUINEA
On same scale as general map

NEW ZEALAND
On same scale as main map

COPYRIGHT. GEORGE PHILIP & SON. LTD.

Map 115

121

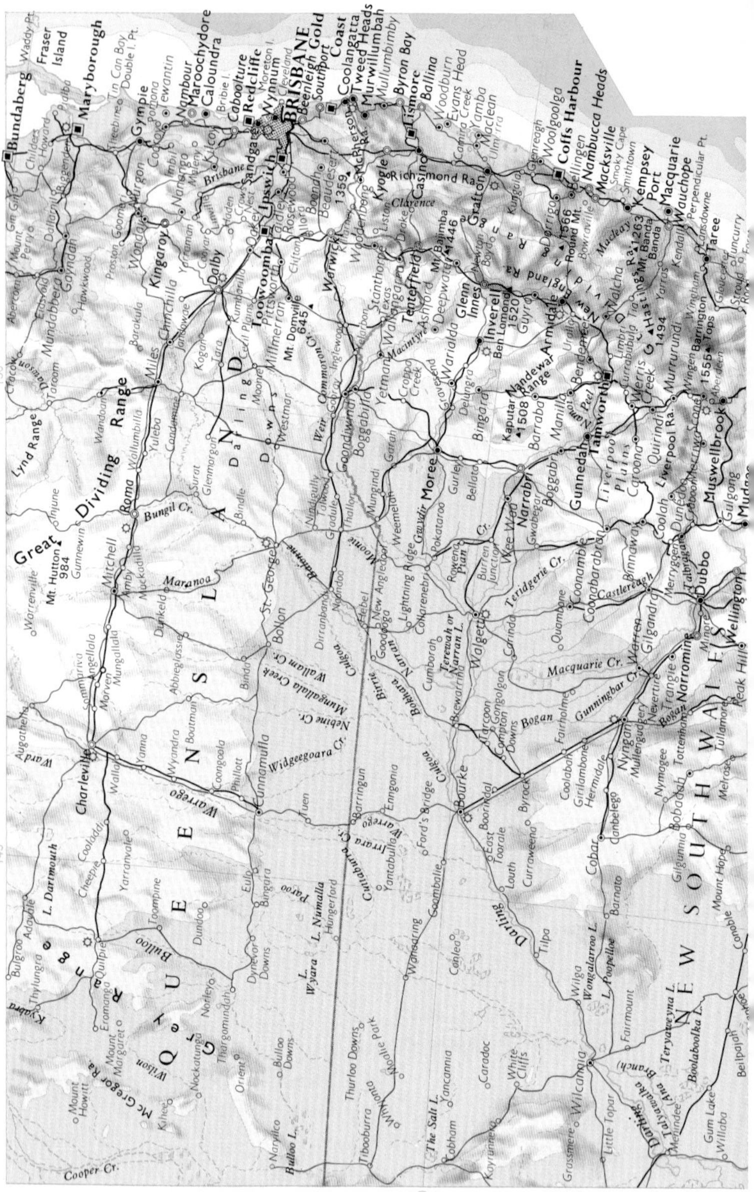
QUEENSLAND
NEW SOUTH WALES
Great Dividing Range
Darling Downs
Grey Range
BRISBANE
Gold Coast
Bundaberg
Maryborough
Fraser Island
Gympie
Nambour
Maroochydore
Caloundra
Redcliffe
Caboolture
Ipswich
Toowoomba
Dalby
Kingaroy
Warwick
Tweed Heads
Coolangatta
Murwillumbah
Byron Bay
Lismore
Ballina
Casino
Grafton
Coffs Harbour
Nambucca Heads
Macksville
Kempsey
Port Macquarie
Wauchope
Taree
Tenterfield
Glenn Innes
Inverell
Armidale
Tamworth
Gunnedah
Narrabri
Moree
Goondiwindi
St. George
Roma
Mitchell
Charleville
Cunnamulla
Bourke
Walgett
Coonamble
Dubbo
Wellington
Narromine
Nyngan
Cobar
Wilcannia
Muswellbrook
Mudgee
Warrego
Darling
Barwon
Mt. Hutton 984
Kaputar 1508
Ben Lomond 1520
Barrington Tops 1555
145
150
30

118

Map 116

Australia: Brisbane, Sydney, Melbourne

1:8 000 000

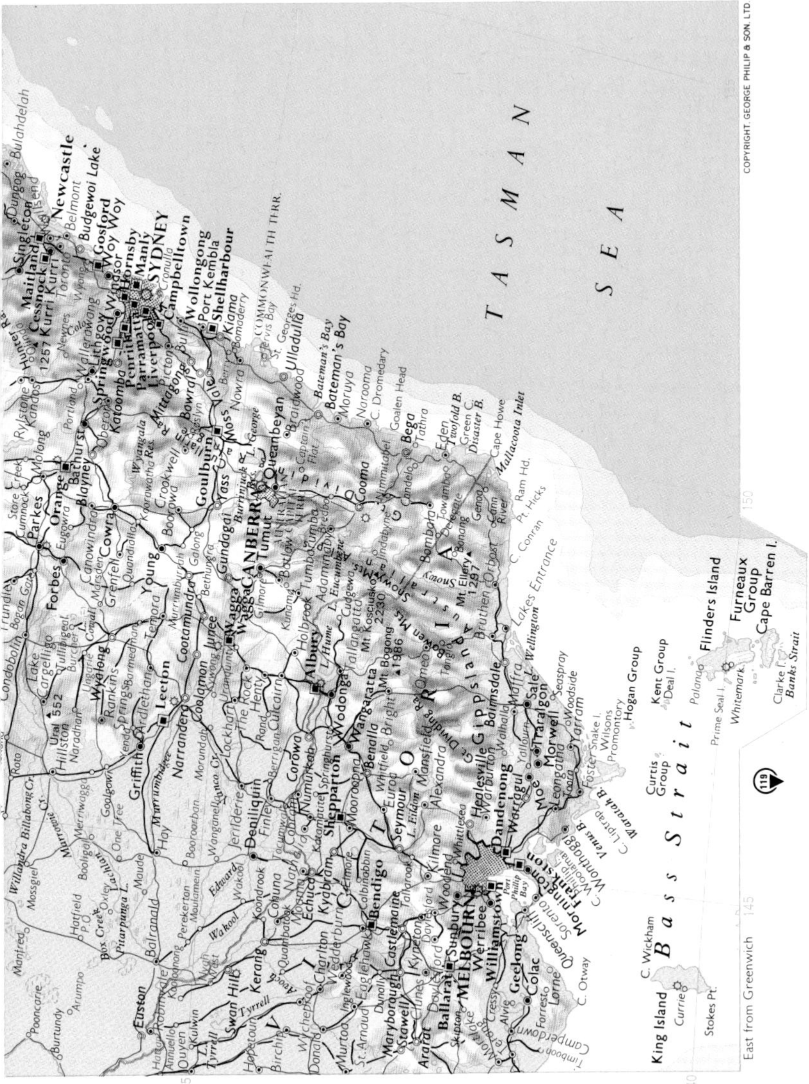

East from Greenwich

Map 117

Australia: Adelaide, Melbourne, Tasmania

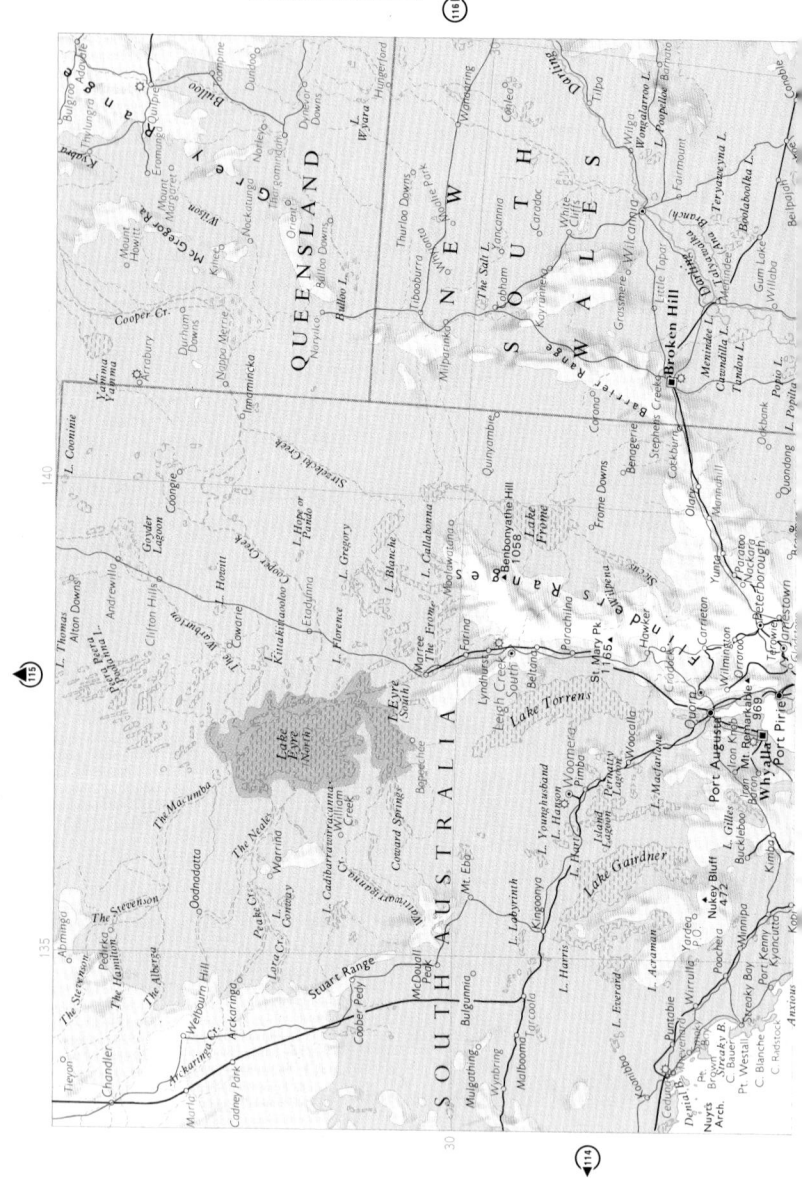

Map 118

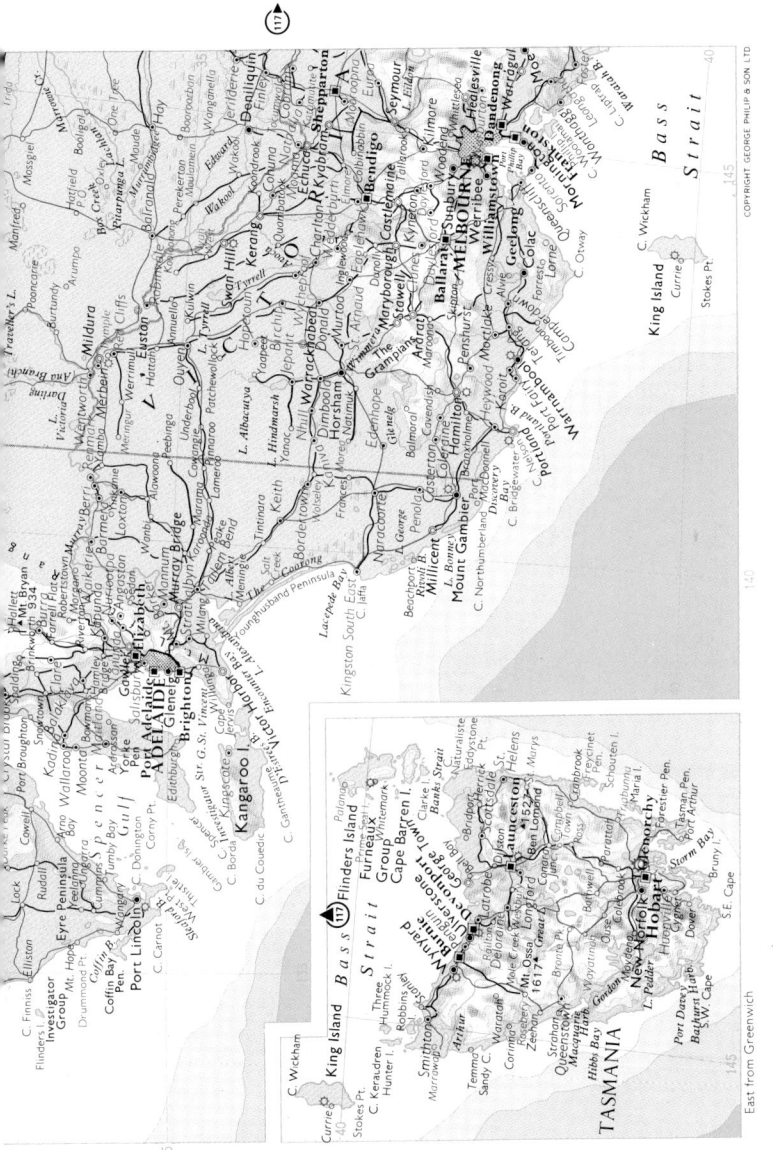

COPYRIGHT GEORGE PHILIP & SON LTD

East from Greenwich

Map 119

Australia: Perth

1:8 000 000

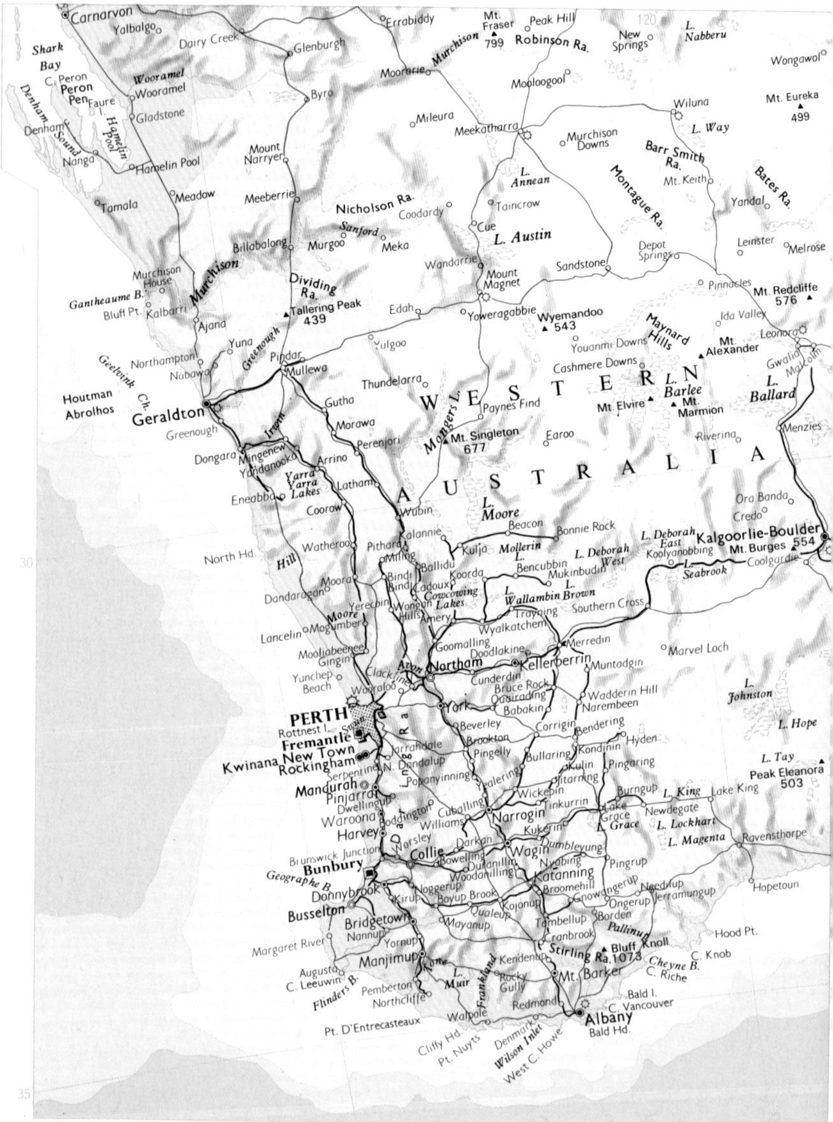

East from Greenwich

COPYRIGHT GEORGE PHILIP & SON. LTD.

Map 120

Australia: North East Queensland

1:8 000 000

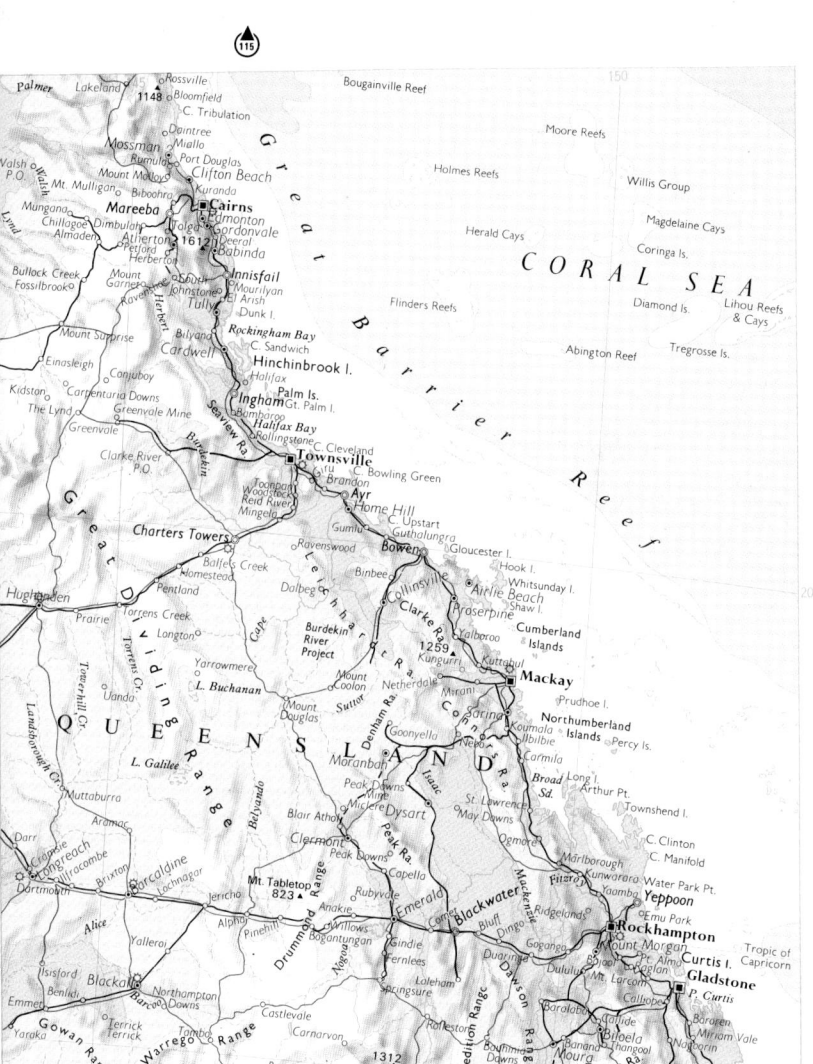

East from Greenwich

Map 121

New Zealand, Central and South West Pacific

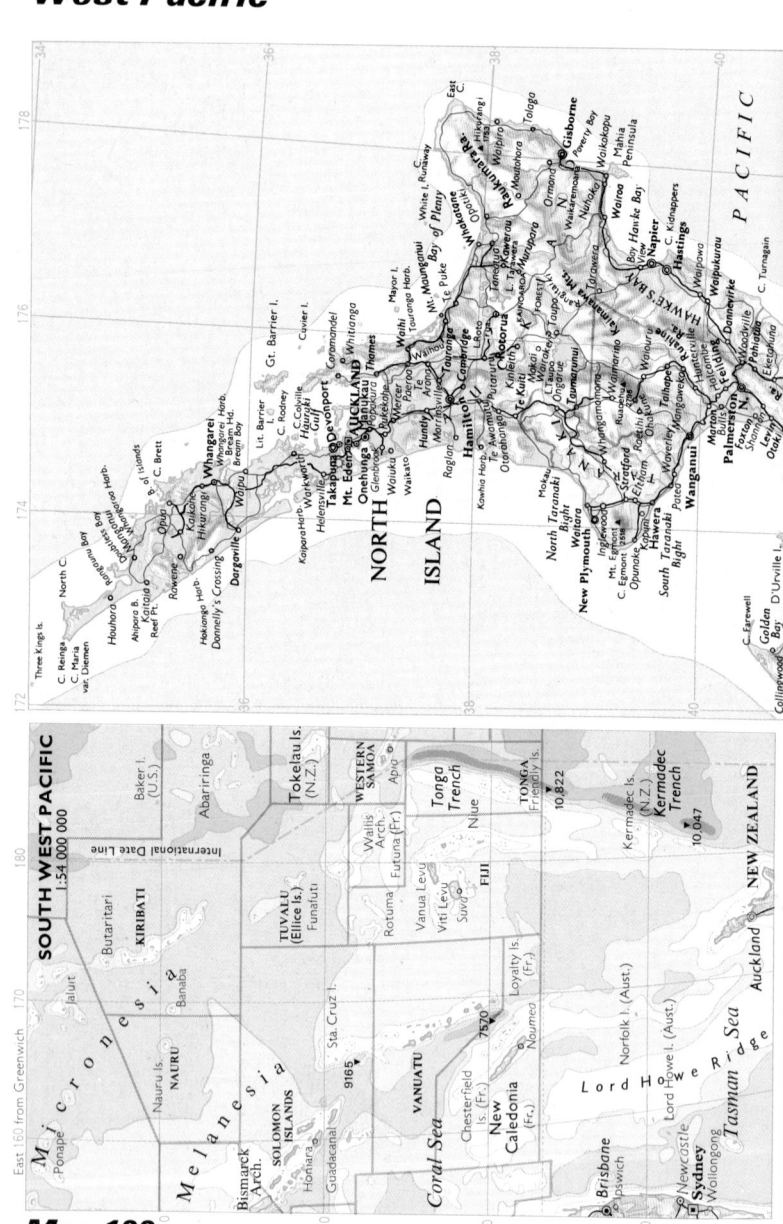

Map 122

115

Map 123

1:7 000 000

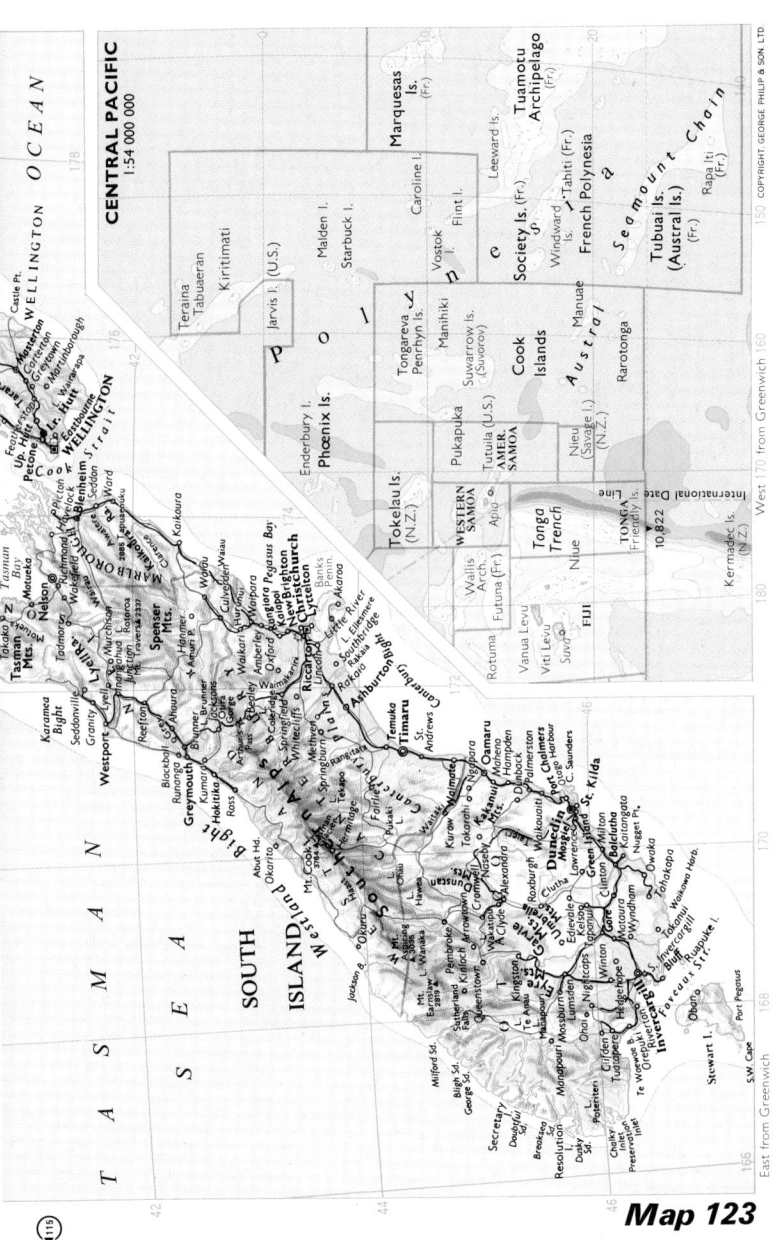
TASMAN SEA
SOUTH ISLAND
Southern Alps
Westland Bight
Karamea Bight
Tasman Bay
Tasman Mts.
Spenser Mts.
MARLBOROUGH
CANTERBURY
Canterbury Plains
Canterbury Bight
Pegasus Bay
Banks Penin.
Cook Strait
Foveaux Str.
OTAGO
Nelson
Westport
Greymouth
Hokitika
Blenheim
Kaikoura
Christchurch
Lyttelton
New Brighton
Ashburton
Timaru
Oamaru
Dunedin
Port Chalmers
Invercargill
Bluff
Queenstown
Gore
Balclutha
Mt. Cook 3764
Mt. Aspiring 3036
Mt. Earnslaw 2819
Stewart I.
WELLINGTON
Lr. Hutt
Up. Hutt
Petone
Masterton
Castle Pt.
OCEAN
East from Greenwich
CENTRAL PACIFIC
1:54 000 000
Polynesia
Teraina
Tabuaeran
Kiritimati
Jarvis I. (U.S.)
Enderbury I.
Phœnix Is.
Malden I.
Starbuck I.
Tokelau Is. (N.Z.)
Tongareva
Penrhyn Is.
Manihiki
Caroline I.
Vostok I.
Flint I.
Marquesas Is. (Fr.)
Wallis Arch.
Futuna (Fr.)
WESTERN SAMOA
Apia
Pukapuka
Suwarrow Is. (Suvorov)
Tutuila (U.S.)
AMER. SAMOA
Rotuma
Vanua Levu
Viti Levu
Suva
FIJI
Tonga Trench
Niue
Nieu (Savage I.) (N.Z.)
Cook Islands
Rarotonga
Manuae
Society Is. (Fr.)
Leeward Is.
Windward Is.
Tahiti (Fr.)
French Polynesia
Tuamotu Archipelago (Fr.)
Austral Seamount Chain
Tubuai Is. (Austral Is.) (Fr.)
Rapa Iti (Fr.)
TONGA
Friendly Is.
10,822
International Date Line
Kermadec Is. (N.Z.)
West 170 from Greenwich 160

Africa: Physical

1:70 000 000

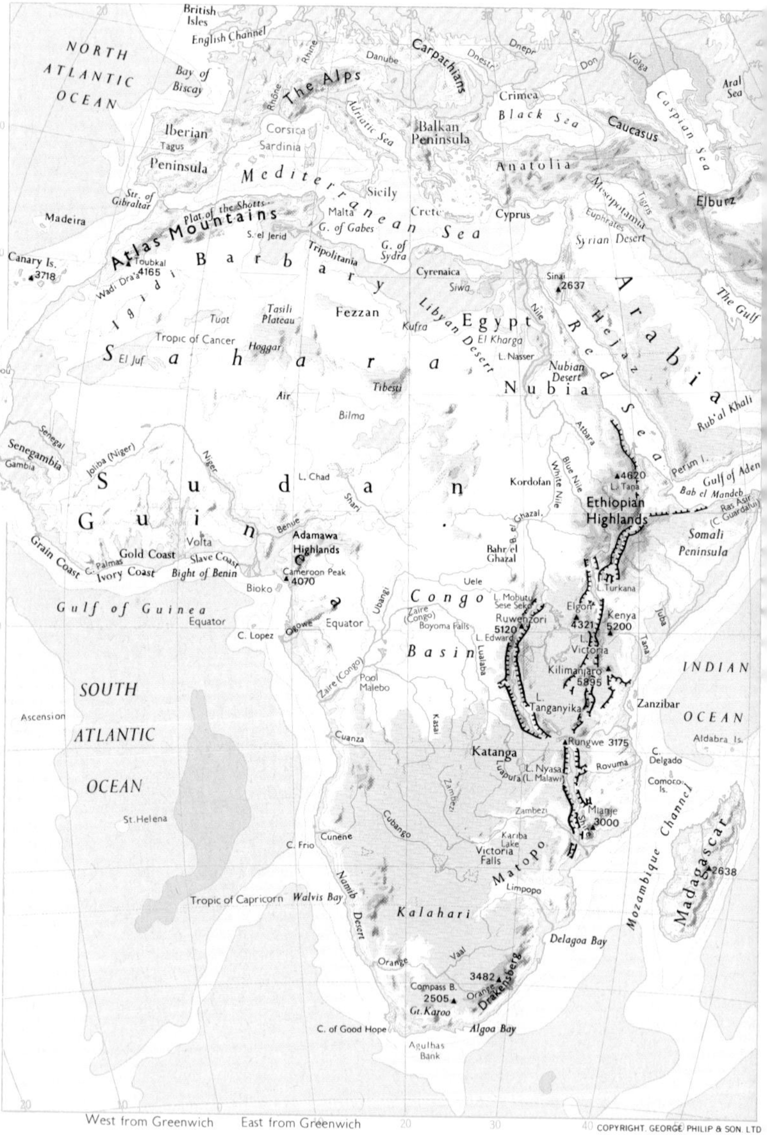

NORTH
ATLANTIC
OCEAN

British
Isles
English Channel

Bay of
Biscay

Rhône
Danube

The Alps

Carpathians

Dnepr
Dniester
Don

Volga

Aral
Sea

Crimea

Black Sea

Caucasus

Caspian Sea

Iberian
Peninsula

Corsica
Sardinia

Balkan
Peninsula

Anatolia

Elburz

Tagus

Madeira

Str. of
Gibraltar

Atlas Mountains

Mediterranean Sea

Sicily

Malta

Crete

Cyprus

Mesopotamia

Tigris
Euphrates

Syrian Desert

The Gulf

Canary Is.
▲3718

Toubkal
4165

Plat. of the Shotts

Wadi Dra'a

S. el Jerid

G. of Gabes

Tripolitania

Cyrenaica

Siwa

Sinai
▲2637

Hejaz

Arabia

Barbary

Tuat

Tasili
Plateau

Fezzan

Kufra

Libyan Desert

Egypt

El Kharga

L. Nasser

Nubian
Desert

Red Sea

Rub' al Khali

Tropic of Cancer

Hoggar

Ras
Nouadhibou

El Juf

Sahara

Air

Tibesti

Nubia

Atbara

Persian G.

Gulf of Aden

Bab el Mandeb

Ras Asir
(C. Guardafui)

Bilma

C.
Verde

Senegal

Senegambia

Gambia

Joliba (Niger)

Niger

L. Chad

Kordofan

Blue Nile

White Nile

▲4620
L. Tana

Ethiopian
Highlands

Somali
Peninsula

Sudan

Guinea

Grain Coast

C. Palmas

Ivory Coast

Gold Coast

Slave Coast

Volta

Benue

Adamawa
Highlands

Shari

Bight of Benin

Cameroon Peak
▲4070

Bioko

Ghazal

Bahr el
Ghazal

Uele

Congo

L. Mobutu

Rise Seko

Ruwenzori
5120▲

Elgon
4321▲

Kenya
5200▲

Turkana

L.
Victoria

INDIAN

OCEAN

Gulf of Guinea

C. Lopez

Ogwe

Equator

Equator

Boyoma Falls

L. Edward

Zaire
(Congo)

L. Kivu

Lualaba

Basin

Kilimanjaro
▲5895

Zanzibar

Aldabra Is.

SOUTH

ATLANTIC

OCEAN

Ascension

Pool
Maiebo

Zaire (Congo)

Kasai

L.
Tanganyika

Kwanza

Katanga

Lapura (L. Malawi)

L. Nyasa

Rungwe 3175▲

Rovuma

C.
Delgado

Comoro
Is.

St. Helena

Cubango

Zambezi

Kariba
Lake

Victoria
Falls

Mlanje
▲3000

Mozambique Channel

Madagascar

▲2638

Cunene

Matopo

Limpopo

Tropic of Capricorn

Walvis Bay

Namib Desert

Kalahari

Delagoa Bay

Orange

Vaal

Drakensberg

3482▲

Compass B.
2505▲

Gt. Karoo

Orange

Algoa Bay

C. Frio

C. of Good Hope

Agulhas
Bank

COPYRIGHT. GEORGE PHILIP & SON LTD

Map 124

Africa: Political

1 : 70 000 000

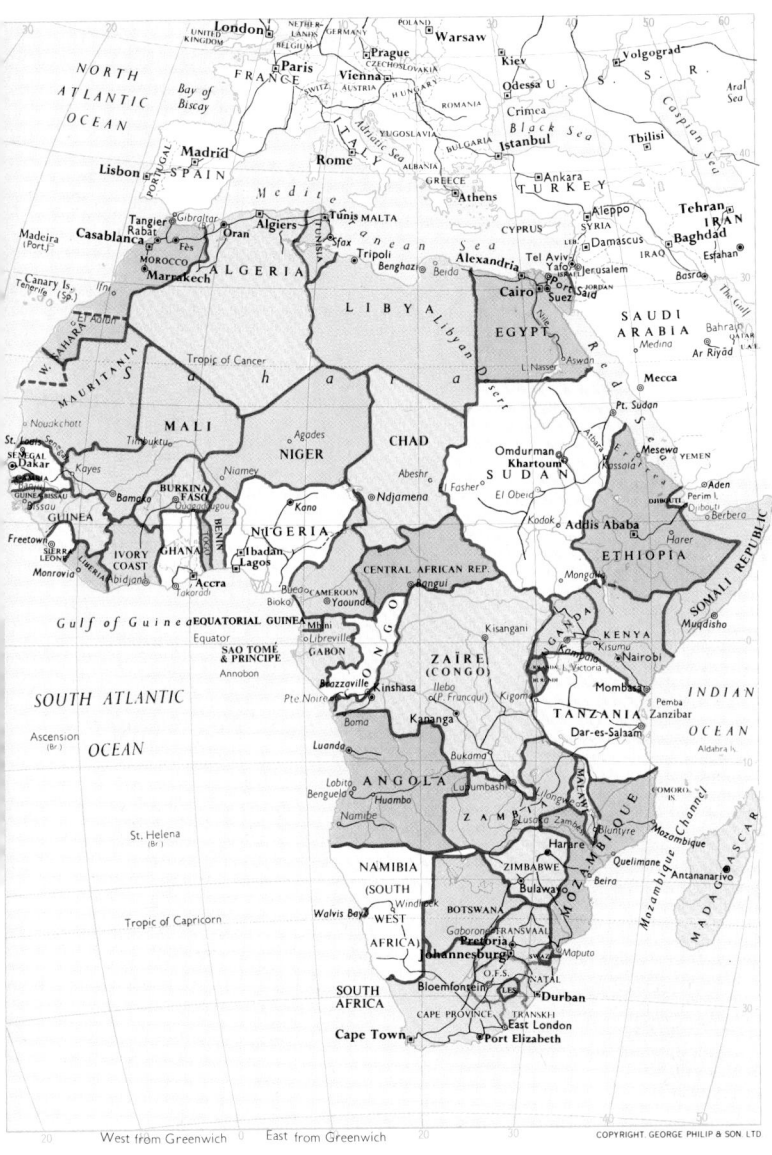

West from Greenwich   East from Greenwich

Map 125

Africa: North West

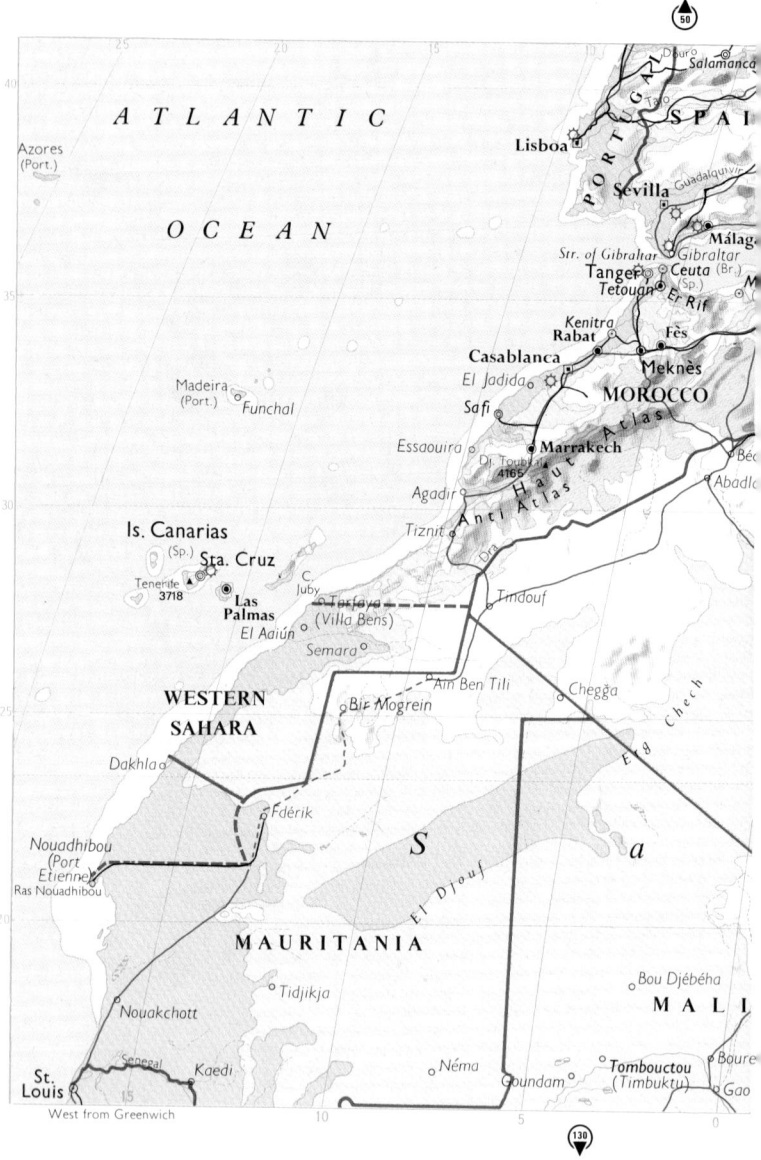

ATLANTIC

OCEAN

Azores
(Port.)

Madeira
(Port.) Funchal

Is. Canarias
(Sp.) Sta. Cruz
Tenerife C.
3718 Juby
Las Tarfaya
Palmas (Villa Bens)
El Aaiún
Semara

WESTERN
SAHARA

Dakhla

Nouadhibou
(Port
Etienne)
Ras Nouadhibou

MAURITANIA

Nouakchott Tidjikja

St. Senegal Kaedi
Louis Néma
West from Greenwich

Douro Salamanca
Lisboa SPAI
PORTUGAL
Sevilla Guadalquivir
Málaga
Str. of Gibraltar Gibraltar
Tanger Ceuta (Br.)
(Sp.)
Tetouan El Rif M
Kenitra
Rabat Fès
Casablanca
El Jadida Meknès
Safi MOROCCO
Essaouira Haut Atlas
Dj. Toubkal Marrakech Béc
4165
Agadir Anti Atlas Abadl
Tiznit Dra
Tindouf
Ain Ben Tili Chegga
Bir Mogrein Erg Chech
Fdérik
S a
El Djouf

Bou Djébéha
MALI
Tombouctou Boure
Goundam (Timbuktu) Gao

Map 126

126

1:20 000 000

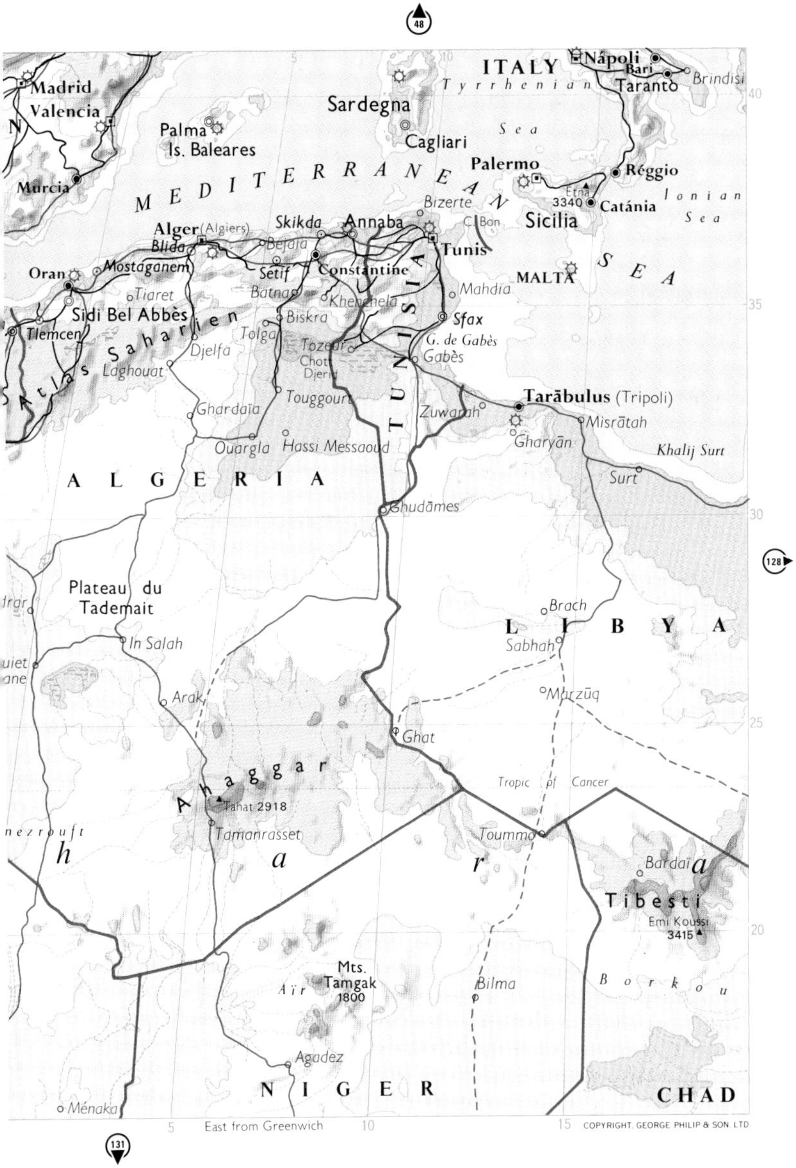

ITALY •Nápoli
•Bari
Tyrrhenian Taranto •Brindisi
Sardegna
Sea
•Cagliari
Palma ▫ Is. Baleares **Palermo**
Murcia **Réggio**
M E D I T E R R A N E A N Etna *Ionian*
3340 •Catánia *Sea*
Alger (Algiers) Skikda **Annaba** Bizerte C. Bon **Sicília**
Blida Bejaïa Tunis
Oran ▫Mostaganem Sétif Constantine **MALTA** *S E A*
Sidi Bel Abbès Tiaret Bátna Khenchela Mahdia
Tlemcen *Atlas* Biskra Sfax
Saharien Tolga G. de Gabès
Djelfa Tozeur Gabès
Laghouat Chott
Djerid
Ghardaïa Touggourt **Tarābulus** (Tripoli)
Zuwārah •Misrātah
Ouargla •Hassi Messaoud Gharyān Khalij Surt
Surt
A L G E R I A
•Ghudāmes

Plateau du
Tademaït L I B Y A
•Brach
•In Salah Sabhah
•Marzūq
Arak
•Ghat

A h a g g a r *Tropic of Cancer*

Tahat 2918 Toumma •Bardaï
•Tamanrasset *r* *a*
h *a* **Tibesti**
Emi Koussi
3415 ▲
B o r k o u
Mts.
Aïr Tamgak •Bilma
1800

•Agadez

•Ménaka **N I G E R** **CHAD**

East from Greenwich COPYRIGHT GEORGE PHILIP & SON LTD

Map 127

Africa: North East

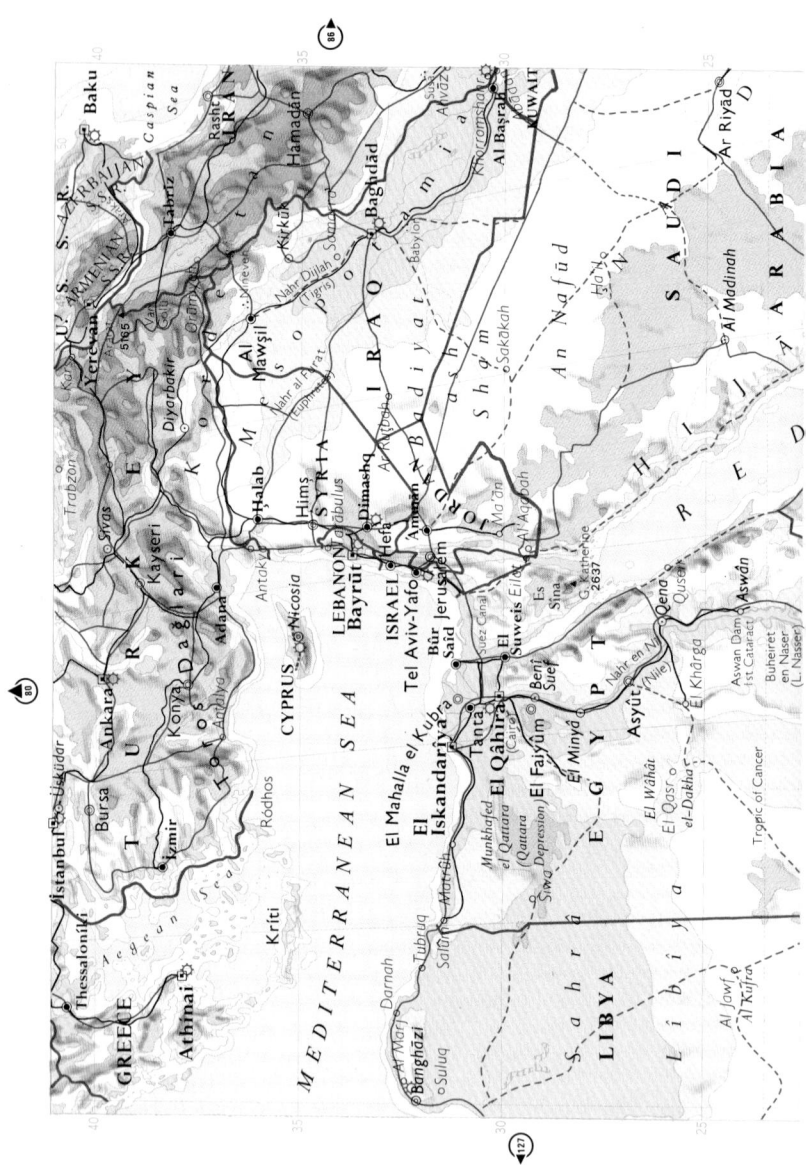
86
80
127
MEDITERRANEAN SEA
Aegean Sea
Caspian Sea
TURKEY
Toros Dağlari
Istanbul
Üsküdar
Bursa
Izmir
Ankara
Konya
Antalya
Adana
Kayseri
Sivas
Trabzon
Diyarbakir
Kars
Yerevan
ARMENIAN S.S.R.
AZERBAIJAN S.S.R.
U. S. S. R.
Baku
Tabriz
Rasht
IRAN
Hamadān
Kirkūk
Al Mawşil
Nineveh
Nahr Dijlah (Tigris)
Nahr al Furat (Euphrates)
Baghdād
Babylon
Al Başrah
Khorromshahr
KUWAIT
IRAQ
Mesopotamia
SYRIA
Ḥalab
Ḥimş
Dimashq
LEBANON
Bayrūt
ISRAEL
Tel Aviv-Yafo
Jerusalem
Hefa
JORDAN
'Ammān
Ma'ān
Al 'Aqabah
Badiyat ash Sham
Sakākah
An Nafūd
SAUDI ARABIA
Al Madinah
Ar Riyād
HIJAZ
RED SEA
CYPRUS
Nicosia
Antakya
Ródhos
Kríti
GREECE
Thessaloníki
Athínai
Banghāzī
Suluq
Al Marj
Darnah
Tubruq
Salûm
Matrûh
LIBYA
Sahrâ Lîbîya
Al Jawf
Al Kufra
EGYPT
El Iskandarîya
El Mahalla el Kubra
Tanta
El Qâhira (Cairo)
Bûr Saîd
Suez Canal
El Suweis
Es Sina
G. Katherîna 2637
El Faiyûm
Beni Suef
El Minyâ
Asyût
Nahr en Nil (Nile)
Qena
Quseir
Aswân
Aswan Dam 1st Cataract
Buheiret en Naser (L. Nasser)
El Khârga
El Wâhât
El Qasr el-Dakhla
Munkhafed el Qattara (Qattara Depression)
Siwa
Tropic of Cancer
5165
40
35
30
25

Map 128

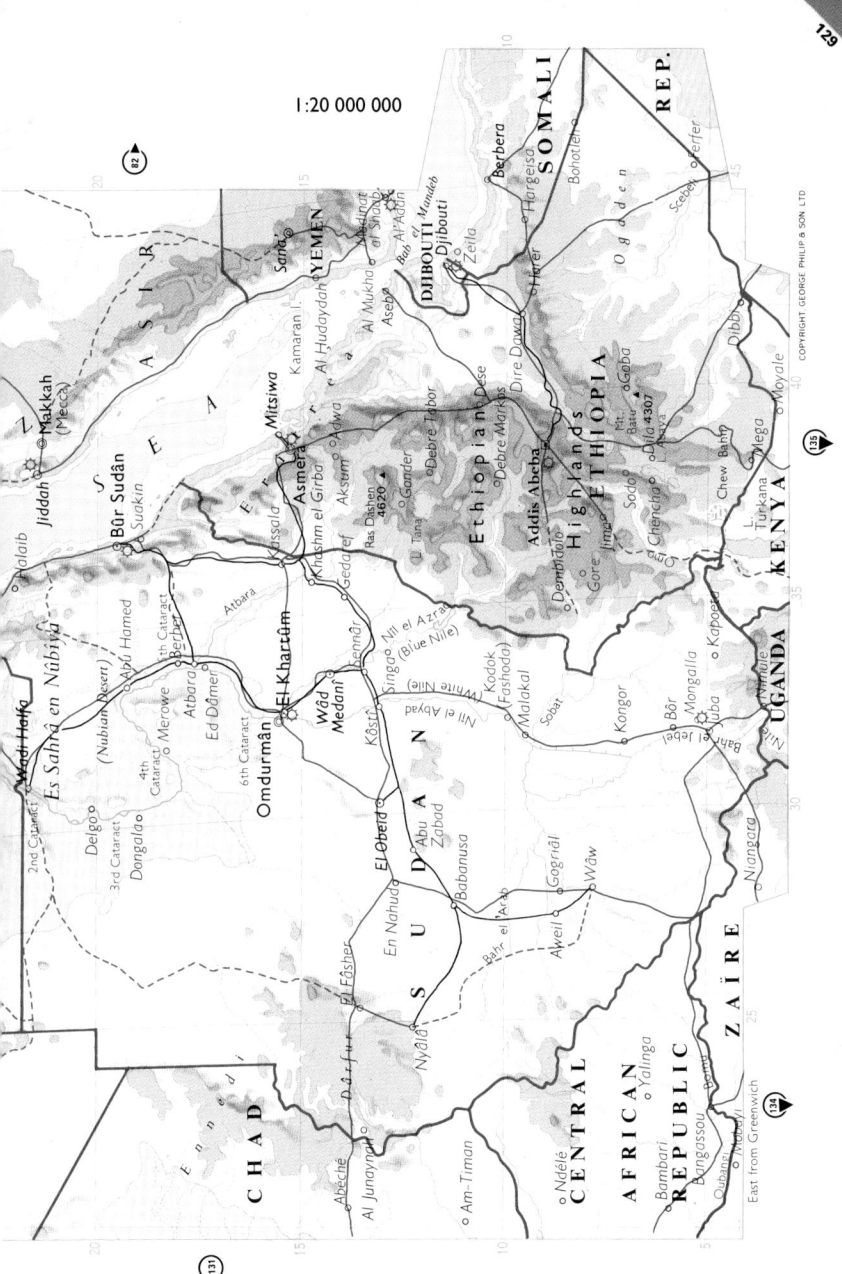

1:20 000 000

SOMALI REP.

Berbera

Berbera

Bohotere

Hargeisa

O g a d e n

Seseba

DJIBOUTI

Djibouti

Zeila

Awash

Dire Dawa

ETHIOPIA

Harer

Dibbi

Moyale

Geba

Mt. Batu 4307

Dala

Dava

ETHIOPIA Highlands

Addis Abeba

Debre Markos

Debre Tabor

Dese

Nega

Chew Bahir

L. Turkana

Chenkibe

Sodo

Jima

Gore

Dembidolo

Gonder

Aksum

Ras Dashen 4620

L. Tana

Khashm el Girba

KENYA

UGANDA

Kapoeta

Bor

Mongalla

Juba

Niangara

Bahr el Jebel

Nile

Kongor

Sobat

Malakal

Fashoda

Kodok

Nil el Azraq (Blue Nile)

Singa

Sennar

Nil el Abyad (White Nile)

Gogrial

Wāw

Aweil

Bahr el Arab

Babanusa

Abu Zabad

ZAIRE

Bambari

Bangassou

Ouango

YALINGA

Ndélé

AFRICAN REPUBLIC

CENTRAL

Am-Timan

Al Junaynah

Abéché

CHAD

E n n e d i

D a r f u r

El Fasher

Nyala

En Nahud

El Obeid

S U D A N

Ed Dueim

Wad Medani

Kosti

El Khartūm

Omdurmān

Ed Damer

Atbara

Berber

6th Cataract

5th Cataract

Abū Hamed

Atbara

Merowe

4th Cataract

Dongola

3rd Cataract

Delgo

2nd Cataract

Es Sahâ en Nûbiya

(Nubian Desert)

Wadi Halfa

Halaib

Jiddah

Makkah (Mecca)

H E J A Z

A S I R

YEMEN

Sana

Kamaran I.

Al Hudaydah

Al Mukha

Bab el Mandab

Aseb

Mitsiwa

Asmera

Kassala

Gedaref

Sudan

Bûr Sûdân

RED SEA

ERITREA

Akordat

East from Greenwich

COPYRIGHT GEORGE PHILIP & SON LTD

Map 129

Africa: West

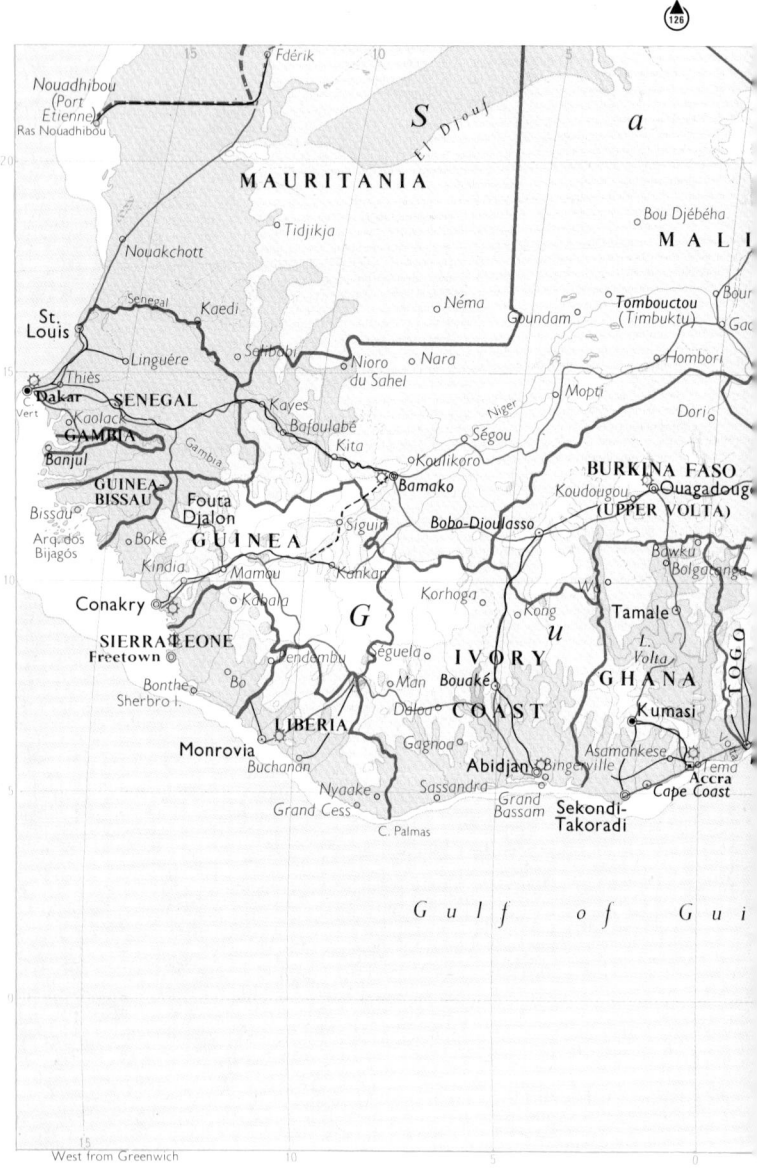

Map 130

1:20 000 000

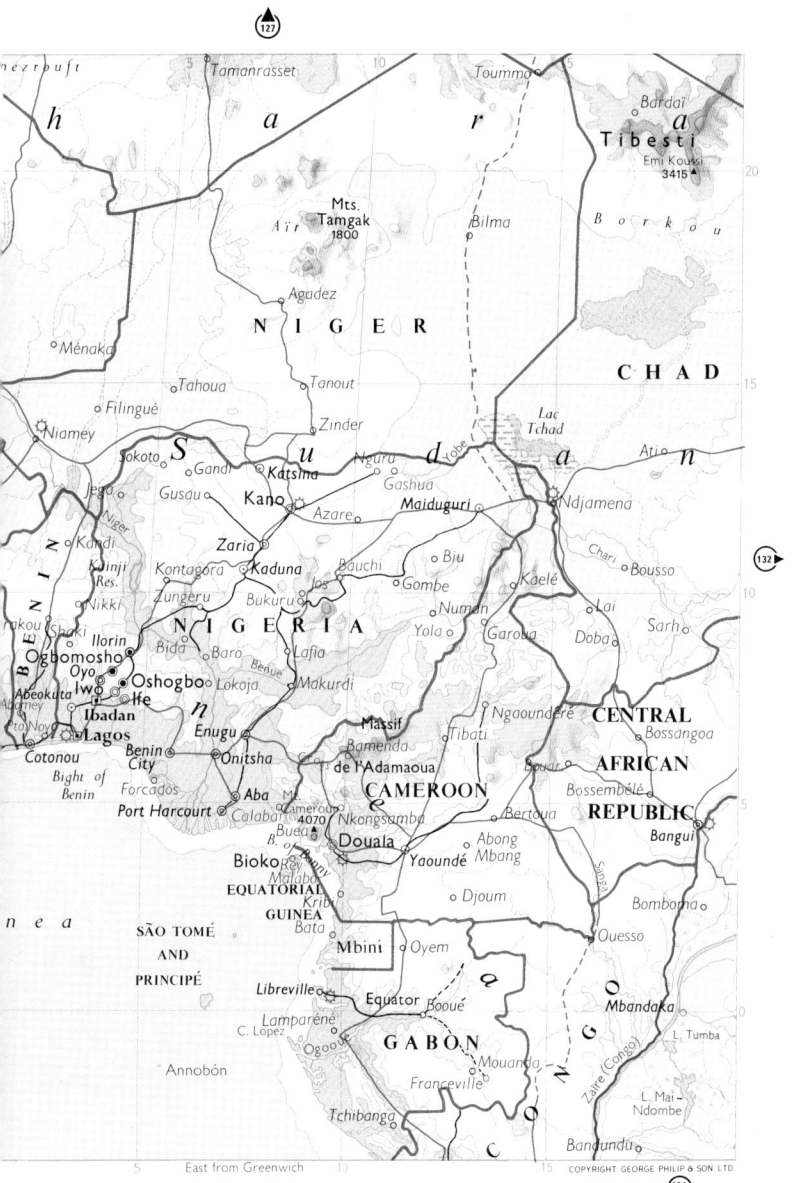
127
132
134
Tamanrasset
Toummo
Bardaï
Tibesti
Emi Koussi
3415
Sahara
Mts. Tamgak 1800
Aïr
Bilma
Borkou
Agadez
NIGER
Ménaka
CHAD
Tahoua
Tanout
Filingué
Zinder
Lac Tchad
Niamey
Sudan
Sokoto
Gandi
Katsina
Nguru
Gashua
Yobe
Ati
Jega
Gusau
Kano
Azare
Maiduguri
Ndjamena
Niger
Kandi
Zaria
Chari
Bousso
Kainji Res.
Kontagora
Kaduna
Bauchi
Biu
Gombe
Kaelé
BENIN
Nikki
Zungeru
Bukuru
Jos
Numan
Lai
Sarh
Shaki
NIGERIA
Yola
Garoua
Doba
Ilorin
Bida
Baro
Lafia
Ogbomosho
Oyo
Benue
Oshogbo
Lokoja
Makurdi
Iwo
Ife
Abeokuta
Ibadan
Ngaoundéré
CENTRAL AFRICAN REPUBLIC
Lagos
Enugu
Massif de l'Adamaoua
Tibati
Bossangoa
Cotonou
Benin City
Onitsha
Bamenda
Bouar
Bight of Benin
Forcados
Aba
CAMEROON
Bossembélé
Port Harcourt
Calabar
Mt. Cameroun 4070
Nkongsamba
Bertoua
Bangui
Buea
B. of Bonny
Douala
Abong Mbang
Bioko
Rey Malabo
Yaoundé
EQUATORIAL GUINEA
Kribi
Djoum
Bata
Bomboma
Sanga
SÃO TOMÉ AND PRINCIPÉ
Mbini
Oyem
Ouesso
Libreville
Equator
Booué
CONGO
Mbandaka
Lambaréné
C. Lopez
GABON
L. Tumba
Ogooué
Zaïre (Congo)
Annobón
Mouanda
Franceville
L. Mai-Ndombe
Tchibanga
Bandundu
East from Greenwich
COPYRIGHT GEORGE PHILIP & SON LTD

Map 131

Africa: East

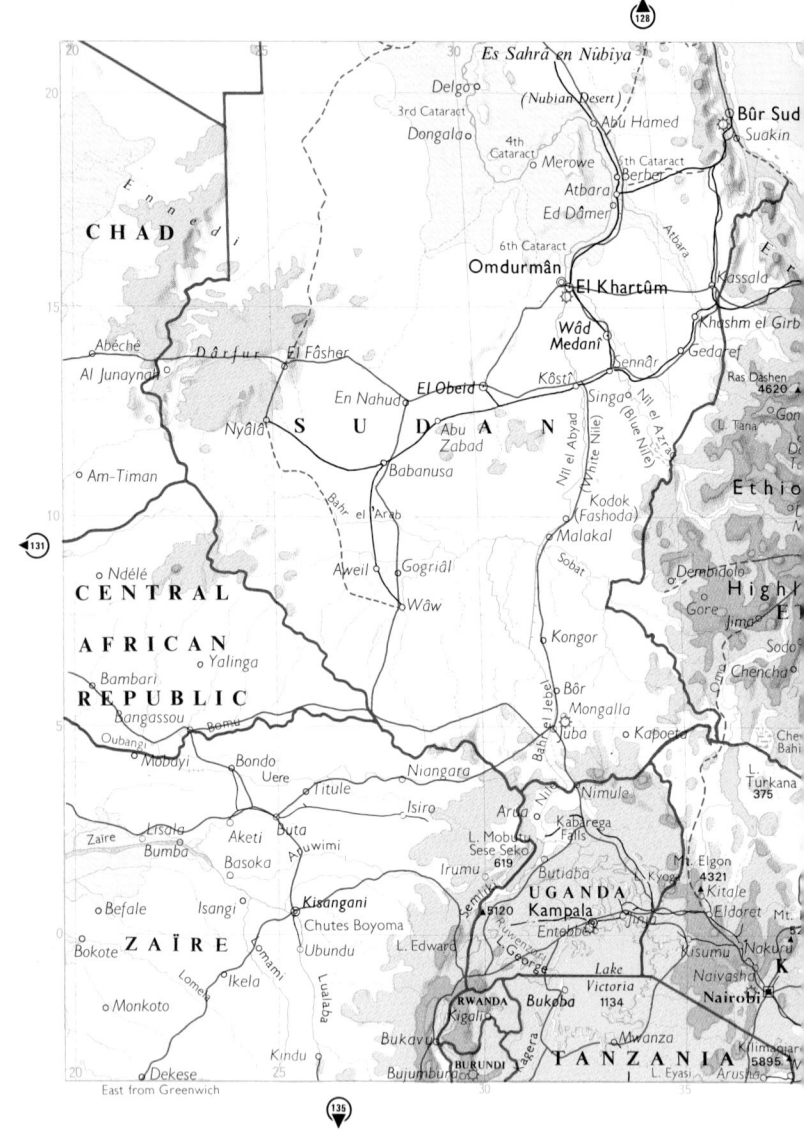

20   25   30

Es Sahrâ en Nûbiya
Delgo
(Nubian Desert)
3rd Cataract   Abu Hamed   **Bûr Sud**
Dongala   Suakin
4th
Cataract   Merowe   5th Cataract
Berber
CHAD   Atbara
Ennedi   Ed Dâmer   Atbara
6th Cataract   Kassala
Omdurmân
El Khartûm   Khashm el Girb
Wâd
Medanî
Abéché   Dârfur   El Fâsher   Sennâr   Gedaref
Al Junaynah   Ras Dashen
En Nahud   El Obeid   Kôstî   4620
Nyâlâ   **S   U   D   A   N**   L. Tana   Gon
Abu
Zabad   **Ethio**
Am-Timan   Babanusa   of
Bahr el Arab   Kodok   **High**
(Fashoda)   Dembidolo
Ndélé   Malakal   Gore   Jima   **E**
CENTRAL   Aweil   Gogriâl   Sobat
Wâw   Sodo
AFRICAN   Yalinga   Chencha
Bambari   Kongor
REPUBLIC   Bôr   Che
Bangassou   Mongalla   Bahi
Oubangi   Bomu   Juba   Kapoeta
Mobayi   Bondo   Niangara   Nimule   L. Turkana
Uere   375
Titule   Isiro   Arua   Kabarega
Lisala   Aketi   Buta   Falls
Bumba   Uwimi   L. Mobutu   Butiaba   Mt. Elgon
Basoka   Sese Seko   4321
Irumu   619   Kyoga   Kitale
Befale   Isangi   Kisangani   **UGANDA**   Eldoret   Mt.
Bokote   Chutes Boyoma   5120   Kampala
ZAÏRE   Ubundu   Entebbe   Kisumu   Nakuru
Ikela   L. Edward   Naivasha   **K**
Monkoto   George   Lake   **Nairobi**
RWANDA   Bukoba   Victoria
Kigali   1134
Bukavu   Mwanza   Kilimanjaro
Kindu   Kagera   5895
Dekese   **BURUNDI**   **TANZANIA**
Bujumbura   L. Eyasi   Arusha

Map 132

1:20 000 000

82

SAUDI   ARABIA

OMAN

Rub 'al Khali

A S I R

R E D   S E A

Mitsiwa

Kamaran I.

Sana'

YEMEN *Hadramaw*

Al Hudaydah

Al Mukallā

Al Mukha

Madinat ash Sha'b

Socotra
(Yemen)

Asebo

Al 'Adan (Aden)

Bab el Mandeb *Gulf of*

DJIBOUTI *Aden*

Candala

Ras Asir
(C. Guardafui)

Djibouti

Zeila

pian Dese

Berbera

Bender Beila

Dire Dawa

Hargeisa

Harer

Bohotleh

SOMALI

ddis Abeba

HIOPIA

Ogaden

Eil

Mt.
Batu

Goba

Scebei

REPUBLIC

Dila 4307

L. Abaya

Ferfer

Obbia

Dibb

El Dere

I N D I A N

Mega

Moyale

Bardera

Merca

Muqdisho
(Mogadishu)

Marsabit

Wajir

Brava

Giuba

Equator

N Y A

Chisimaio

Tana

O C E A N

Lamu

Voi

Malindi

COPYRIGHT GEORGE PHILIP & SON LTD.

Map 133

Africa: Central

131

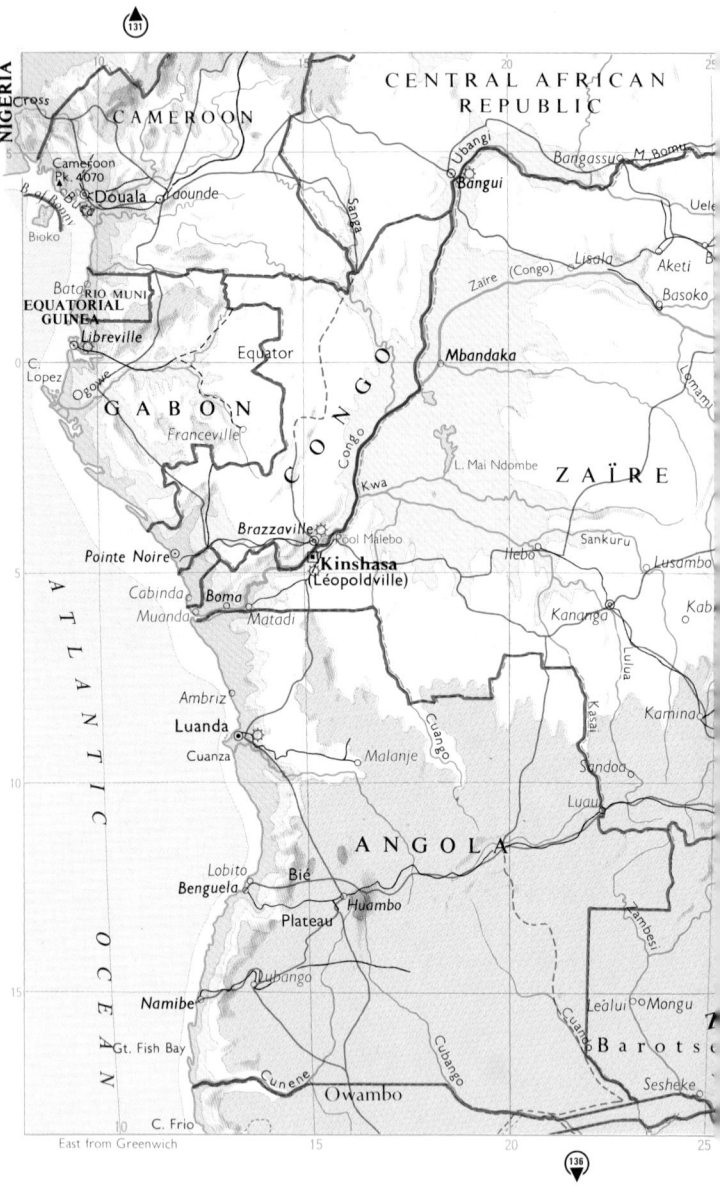

CENTRAL AFRICAN REPUBLIC
CAMEROON
NIGERIA
Cross
Cameroon Pk. 4070
Buea
Douala
Yaounde
B. of Bonny
Bioko
Bata
RIO MUNI
EQUATORIAL GUINEA
Libreville
C. Lopez
Ogowe
GABON
Equator
Franceville
CONGO
Congo
Sanga
Ubangi
Bangui
Bangassu
M. Bomu
Uele
Lisala
Aketi
Zaïre (Congo)
Basoko
Mbandaka
Lomami
L. Mai Ndombe
ZAÏRE
Kwa
Brazzaville
Pool Malebo
Kinshasa
(Léopoldville)
Pointe Noire
Cabinda
Boma
Muanda
Matadi
Ilebo
Sankuru
Lusambo
Kananga
Lulua
Kasai
Kamina
ATLANTIC OCEAN
Ambriz
Luanda
Cuanza
Malanje
Cuango
Sandoa
Luau
ANGOLA
Lobito
Benguela
Bié
Huambo
Plateau
Zambesi
Lubango
Namibe
Lealui
Mongu
Gt. Fish Bay
Cuando
Barots
Cubango
Cunene
Owambo
Sesheke
C. Frio
East from Greenwich

136

Map 134

1:20 000 000

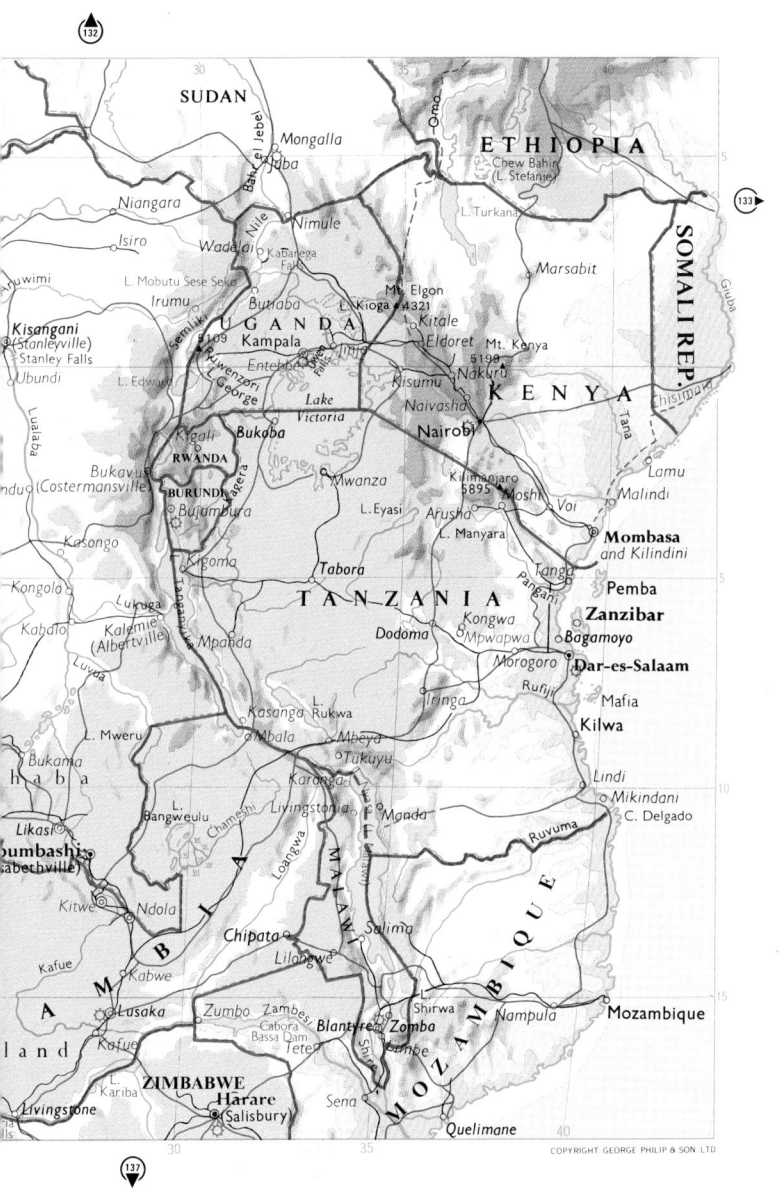

SUDAN

Mongalla
Juba
Nimule
Niangara
Isiro
Wadala
Irumu
L. Mobutu Sese Seko
Butiaba
Kisangani
(Stanleyville)
Stanley Falls
Ubundi

UGANDA
Kampala
Entebbe
Jinja
L. Edward
L. George
Kigali
RWANDA
Bukoba
Lake
Victoria

ETHIOPIA
Chew Bahir
(L. Stefanie)
L. Turkana
Marsabit

L. Kioga
Mt. Elgon
4321
Kitale
Eldoret
Mt. Kenya
5198
Nakuru
Kisumu
Naivasha
K E N Y A
Nairobi

SOMALI REP.
Guuba
Chisimav

Lamu
Malindi

Bukavu
(Costermansville)
BURUNDI
Bujumbura
Mwanza
Kasongo
Kongolo
Kigoma
Kabalo
L. Eyasi
Arusha
L. Manyara
Moshi
Kilimanjaro
5895
Voi
Tabora

T A N Z A N I A
Dodoma
Kongwa
Mpwapwa
Morogoro
Mombasa
and Kilindini
Tanga
Pemba
Zanzibar
Bagamoyo
Dar-es-Salaam
Iringa
Rufiji
Mafia
Kilwa

L. Mweru
Bukama
L. Bangweulu
Kasanga
L. Rukwa
Mbala
Mbeya
Tukuyu
Karonga
Livingstonia
Manda
Ruvuma
Lindi
Mikindani
C. Delgado

Likasi
umbashi
abethville)
Kitwe
Ndola
M O Z A M B I Q U E

Kafue
Kabwe
Z A M B I A
Chipata
Lilongwe
Salima
Lusaka
Zumbo
Zambezi
Cabora
Bassa Dam
Tete
Blantyre
Shirwa
Zomba
Nampula
Mozambique

Kafue
Livingstone
L. Kariba
ZIMBABWE
Harare
(Salisbury)
Sena
Quelimane

M A L A W I
L. Malawi

COPYRIGHT GEORGE PHILIP & SON LTD

Map 135

Africa: South

A N G O L A

Ludu

Lobito
Benguela
Bié
Huambo
Plateau

Lubango

A T L A N T I C

Namibe

Zambesi

Lealui ᵒᵒMongu

Cunene

Cubango

B a r o t s e

Gt. Fish Bay

Cuando

Sesheke

C. Frio

Owambo

Etosha
Pan

Otavi
Grootfontein

Botle

Makgadikgadi
Salt pan

D a m a r a l a n d

B O T S W A

Swakopmund
Walvis Bay
Windhoek

Tropic of Capricorn

K a l a h a r i

NAMIBIA

Nossob

O C E A N

Hardap Dam

Namaland

Mafikeng

Molopo

Lüderitz
Possession I.

Keetmanshoop
Karas
Mts.

Vryburg

Upington

Kimberley

Orange
Port Nolloth
Bushmanland

Orange

De Aar
Stor

SOUTH AFRICA
St. Helena Bay

Calvinia

CAPE PROVI

Kompasberg 2504
Graaff-Rein

Nuweveldberge
Karoo
Swartberg

Cape Town
Table Mountain
C. of Good Hope

Paarl
Oudtshoorn

Mosselbaai

Port
Elizabe

C. Agulhas

East from Greenwich

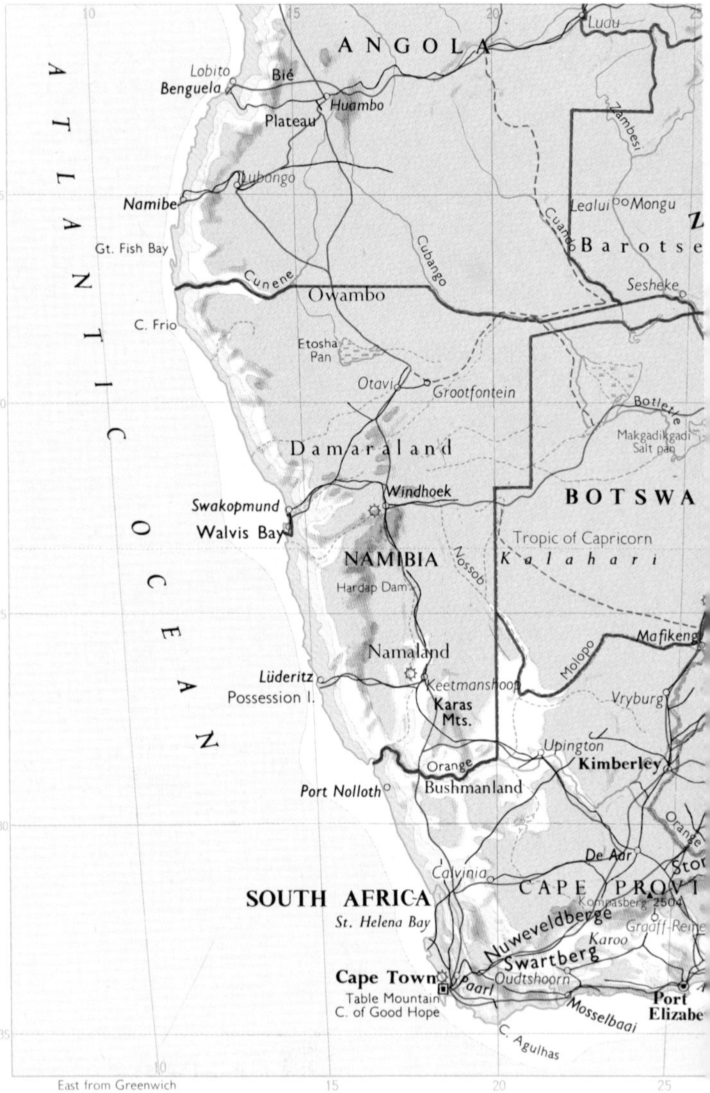

Map 136

1:20 000 000

Karonga
Livingstonia
Mandui
Ruvuma
C. Delgado
Likasi
Lubumbashi
(Isabethville)
Bangweulu
Chameshi
Loangwa
Kitwe
Ndola
Chipata
Lilongwe
Salima
Kafue
Kabwe
Z A M B I A
Lusaka
Zumbo
Zambezi
Shirwa
Nampula
Mozambique
Kafue
Cabora
Bassa Dam
Blantyre
Zomba
L a n d
Kariba
Tete
Limbe
Livingstone
L. Kariba
Harare
(Salisbury)
Sena
Quelimane
alls
ange
Z I M B A B W E
Mutare
Chinde
Zambesi
Gweru
Matabeleland
Sabi
Beira
Bulawayo
Matopo
Hills
Masvingo
Zimbabwe
Sofala
M o z a m b i q u e   C h a n n e l
wanda
West
Nicholson
Sabi
M O Z A M B I Q U E
C. Bobraomby
Serowe
NA
Palapye
Messina
Antsiranano
hong
Limpopo
Inhambane
Nossi-Bé
Andoany
Vohimarina
2876
Tsaratanana
Andapa
borone
Pietersburg
Olifants
Maroantsetra
T R A N S V A A L
Lydenburg
Barberton
Mahajanga
Marovoay
Pretoria
akpan
Maputo
Delagoa Bay
Besalampy
ugersdorp
Springs
SWAZI
LAND
Maevatanana
Fenoarivo
Alaotra
Ambatondrazaka
nnesburg
Germiston
Vereeniging
Maintirano
Belo-Tsiribhina
2643
Antananarivo
Toamasina
RANGE
REE
Mt. aux Sources
Kroonstad
NATE:
Ladysmith
St. Lucia Bay
Mahanoro
nfontein
Maseru
3482
Ntenyana
LESOTHO
Pietermaritzburg
Antsirabe
mberg
Dr
Durban
Morondava
Mananjary
NGE
Umtata
Morombé
Fianarantsoa
Manakara
East London
I N D I A N
Mangoky
Ihosy
William's Town
Ankazoabo
Betroka
Farafangana
Grahamstown
O C E A N
Toliara
Tropic of Capricorn
Bekily
1956
Ambovombé
Faradofay
C. Vohimena
MADAGASCAR
On same scale.
COPYRIGHT. GEORGE PHILIP & SON LTD

Map 137

North America: Physical

1:60 000 000

Map 138

West from Greenwich 100 90

COPYRIGHT GEORGE PHILIP & SON LTD

North America: Political

1:60 000 000

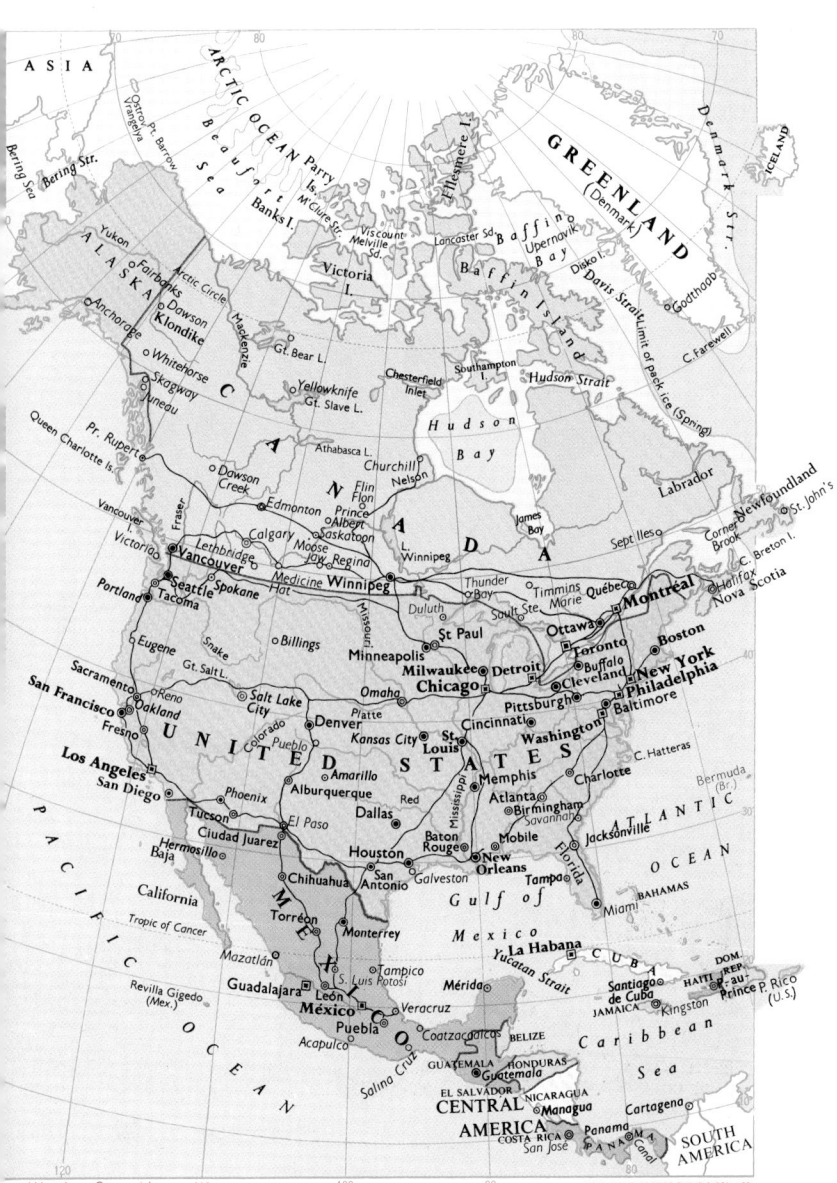
ASIA
ARCTIC OCEAN
Beaufort Sea
Ostrov Vrangelya
Pt. Barrow
Bering Sea
Bering Str.
Parry Is.
M'Clure Str.
Banks I.
Viscount Melville Sd.
Victoria I.
Ellesmere I.
Lancaster Sd.
Baffin Bay
Upernavik
Disko I.
Baffin Island
GREENLAND (Denmark)
Denmark Str.
ICELAND
Davis Strait
Godthaab
C. Farewell
Limit of pack ice (Spring)
Yukon
ALASKA
Fairbanks
Anchorage
Arctic Circle
Dawson
Klondike
Whitehorse
Skagway
Juneau
Mackenzie
Gt. Bear L.
Yellowknife
Gt. Slave L.
Chesterfield Inlet
Southampton I.
Hudson Strait
Hudson Bay
CANADA
Pr. Rupert
Queen Charlotte Is.
Dawson Creek
Athabasca L.
Churchill
Nelson
Flin Flon
Labrador
Newfoundland
St. John's
Edmonton
Prince Albert
Saskatoon
James Bay
Sept Iles
Corner Brook
C. Breton I.
Vancouver I.
Victoria
Fraser
Calgary
Lethbridge
Moose Jaw
Regina
L. Winnipeg
Vancouver
Medicine Hat
Winnipeg
Thunder Bay
Timmins
Québec
Halifax
Nova Scotia
Seattle
Spokane
Portland
Tacoma
Duluth
Sault Ste. Marie
Montréal
Ottawa
Missouri
St Paul
Minneapolis
Toronto
Boston
Billings
Eugene
Snake
Gt. Salt L.
Buffalo
New York
Milwaukee
Detroit
Cleveland
Philadelphia
Chicago
Sacramento
Reno
San Francisco
Oakland
Salt Lake City
Omaha
Platte
Pittsburgh
Baltimore
Fresno
Denver
Colorado
Pueblo
Cincinnati
Washington
UNITED STATES
Kansas City
St. Louis
C. Hatteras
Los Angeles
San Diego
Amarillo
Memphis
Bermuda (Br.)
Alburquerque
Red
Mississippi
Charlotte
Phoenix
Atlanta
Birmingham
Savannah
Tucson
El Paso
Dallas
ATLANTIC OCEAN
Ciudad Juarez
Baton Rouge
Mobile
Jacksonville
Hermosillo
Baja California
Houston
New Orleans
Florida
Chihuahua
San Antonio
Galveston
Tampa
PACIFIC OCEAN
MEXICO
Gulf of Mexico
BAHAMAS
Miami
Torreón
Tropic of Cancer
Monterrey
La Habana
CUBA
Yucatan Strait
DOM. REP.
HAITI
P. au-Prince
P. Rico (U.S.)
Mazatlán
Tampico
S. Luis Potosí
Mérida
Santiago de Cuba
JAMAICA
Kingston
Revilla Gigedo (Mex.)
Guadalajara
León
México
Veracruz
Puebla
Coatzacoalcos
BELIZE
Caribbean Sea
Acapulco
GUATEMALA
HONDURAS
Guatemala
Salina Cruz
EL SALVADOR
NICARAGUA
CENTRAL AMERICA
Managua
Cartagena
COSTA RICA
San José
Panama
PANAMA
Canal
SOUTH AMERICA
West from Greenwich

Map 139

Canada: South East

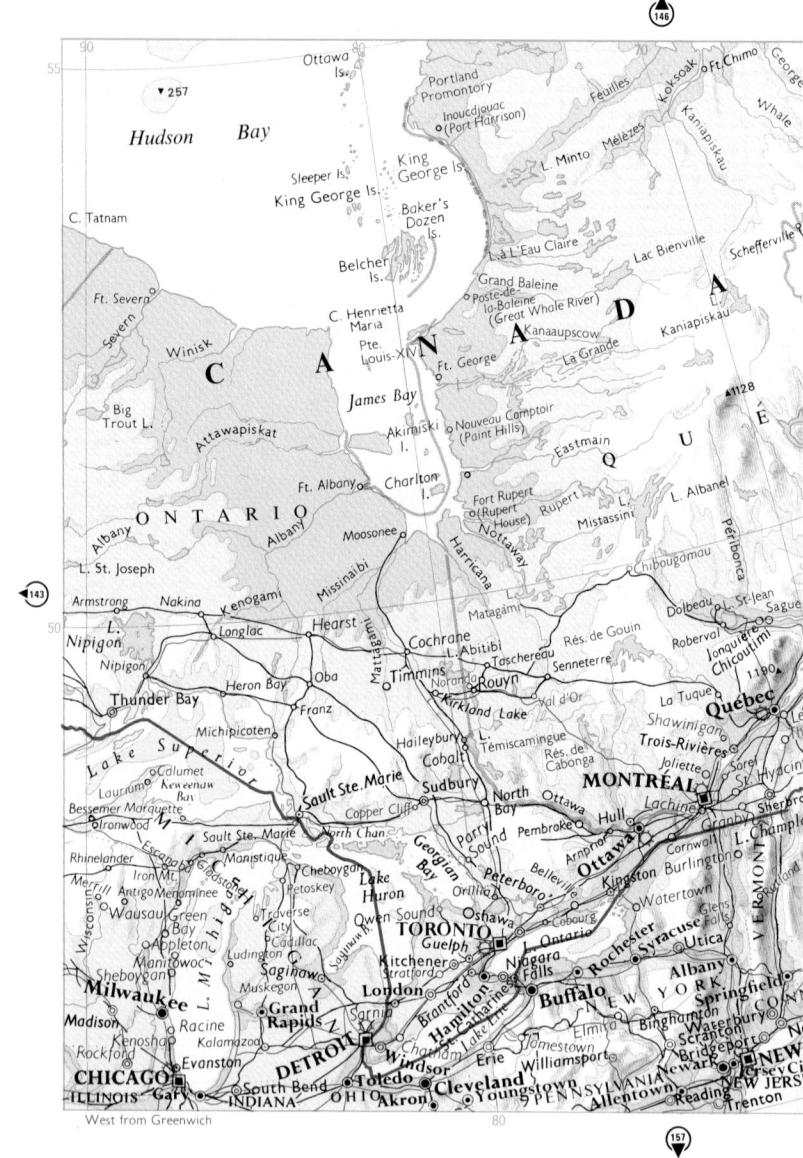

90

55

Ottawa Is.

▼257

Portland
Promontory

Inoucdjouac
(Port Harrison)

Hudson   Bay

Feuilles

Koksoak Ft. Chimo George

Whale

Sleeper Is.   King
George Is.

King George Is.

Baker's
Dozen
Is.

L. Minto Mélèzes

Kaniapiskau

C. Tatnam

Belcher
Is.

Là L'Eau Claire

Lac Bienville

Schefferville

Ft. Severn

C. Henrietta
Maria

Pte.
Louis-XIV

Grand Baleine

Poste-de-
la-Baleine
(Great Whale River)

Kanaaupscow

La Grande

Kaniapiskau

Severn

Winisk

C   A   N   A   D   A

Ft. George

Big
Trout L.

Attawapiskat

James Bay

Akimiski
I.

Nouveau Comptoir
(Paint Hills)

Eastmain

Q   U   É

▲1128

Albany

O   N   T   A   R   I   O

Ft. Albany

Charlton
I.

Fort Rupert
(Rupert
House)

Rupert

L.

L. Albanel

Albany

Moosonee

Nottaway

Mistassini

Péribonca

L. St. Joseph

Missinaibi

Harricana

Chibougamau

143

Armstrong   Nakina   Kenogami

Matagami

Dolbeau

St-Jean

Sague

L.
Nipigon

Longlac

Hearst

Cochrane

L. Abitibi Taschereau

Rés. de Gouin

Roberval

Jonquière
Chicoutimi

Nipigon

Timmins   Noranda Rouyn

Senneterre

1190

Thunder Bay

Heron Bay

Oba

Franz

Val d'Or

La Tuque

Québec

Michipicoten

Kirkland Lake

Shawinigan

Lake   Superior

Haileybury

Témiscamingue

Rés. de
Cabonga

Trois-Rivières

Calumet Keweenaw
Bay

Cobalt

Joliette

Sorel St-Hyacin

Laurium
Bessemer Marquette

Sault Ste. Marie

Sudbury

North
Bay

Ottawa

Hull

MONTRÉAL

Lachine

Sherbr

Ironwood

Sault Ste. Marie

Copper Cliffs

North Chan.

Parry
Sound

Pembroke

Arnpro

Cornwall

L. Champla

Rhinelander

Manistique

Georgian

Belleville

Ottawa

Kingston Burlington

VERMONT

Iron Mt.

Escanaba

Cheboygan

Bay

Orillia

Peterboro

Watertown

Glens
Falls

Merrill
Antigo Menominee

Petoskey

Lake
Huron

Owen Sound

Cobourg

L. Ontario

Rochester

Syracuse

Utica

Albany

Springfield

Wausau Green
Bay

Traverse
City

Oshawa

Niagara

Brantford

Buffalo

Binghamton

Scranton

Waterbury
Bridgeport

Appleton

Cadillac

TORONTO

Guelph

Falls

N   E   W   Y   O   R   K

CON

Sheboygan

Manitowoc

Saginaw

Kitchener
Stratford

Hamilton

St. Catharines

Elmira

Williamsport

Reading

NEW

NEW JERS

Milwaukee

Muskegon

London

Lake Erie

Jamestown

Madison

Grand
Rapids

Sarnia

Erie

Williamsport

Allentown

Trenton

Kenosha Racine

Kalamazoo

Rockford

Evanston

South Bend

Toledo

Cleveland

Youngstown

PENNSYLVANIA

CHICAGO   Gary

ILLINOIS   INDIANA

DETROIT

Windsor

Akron

OHIO

50

80

West from Greenwich

157

Map 140

1:15 000 000

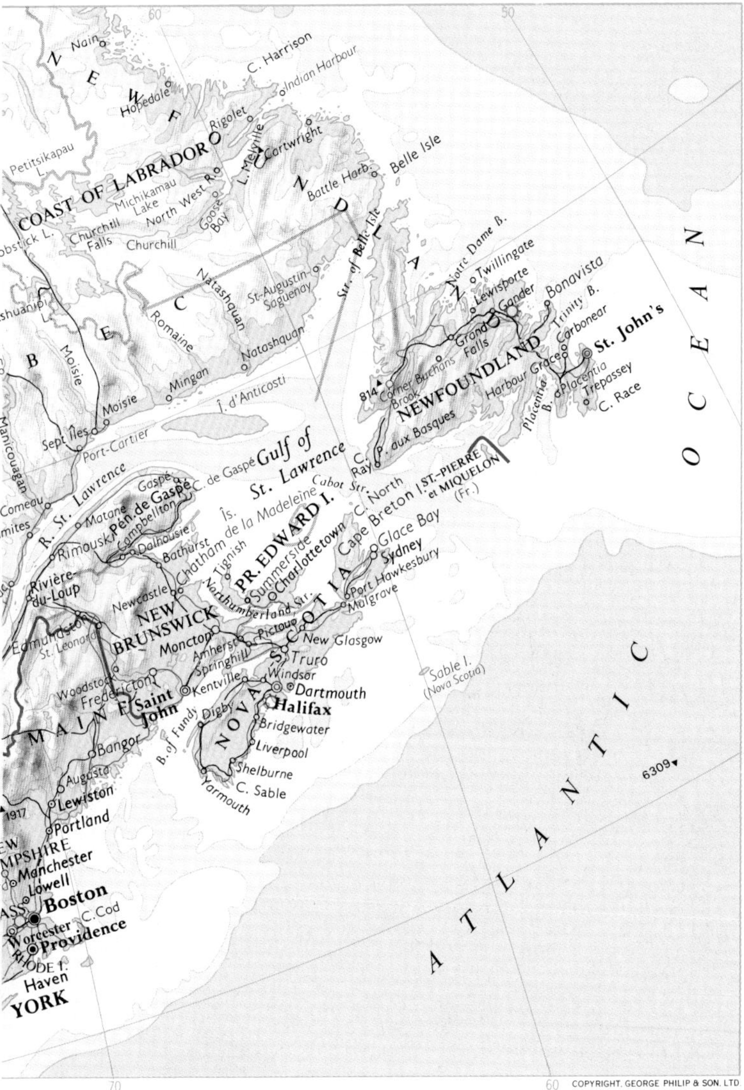

COPYRIGHT. GEORGE PHILIP & SON. LTD

Map 141

Canada: South West and Alaska

ALASKA
1 : 30 000 000

100   0   200   400 km

Map 142

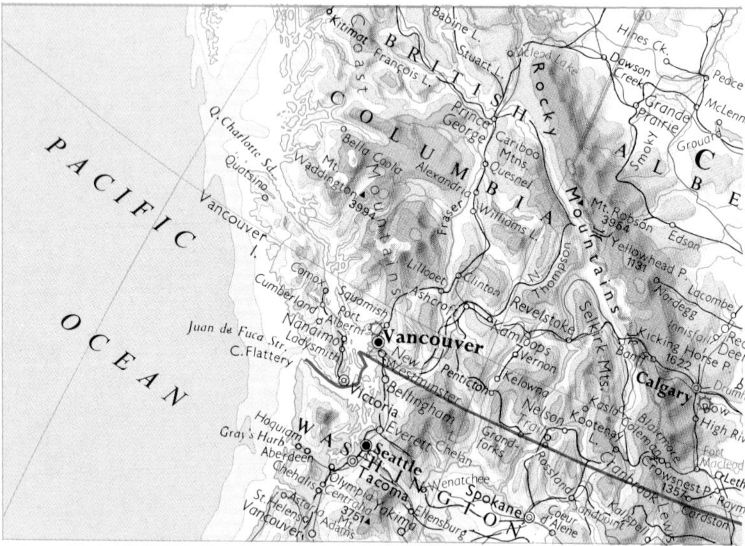

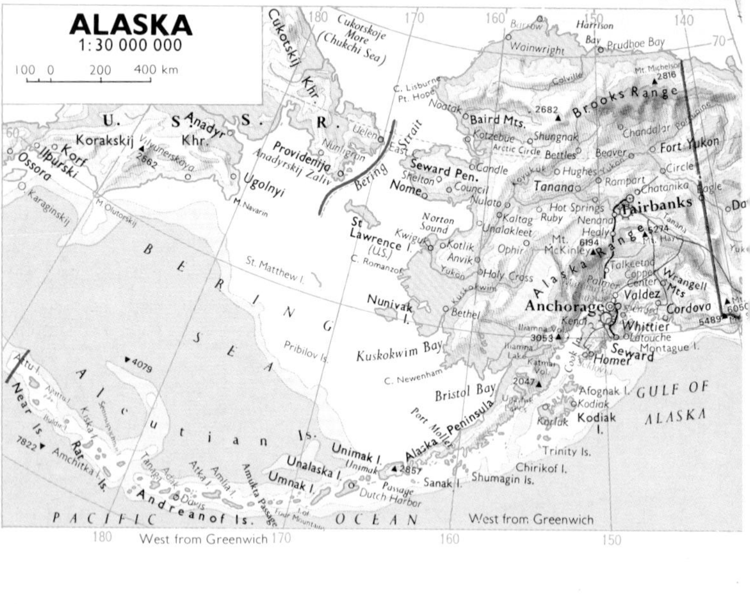

1:15 000 000

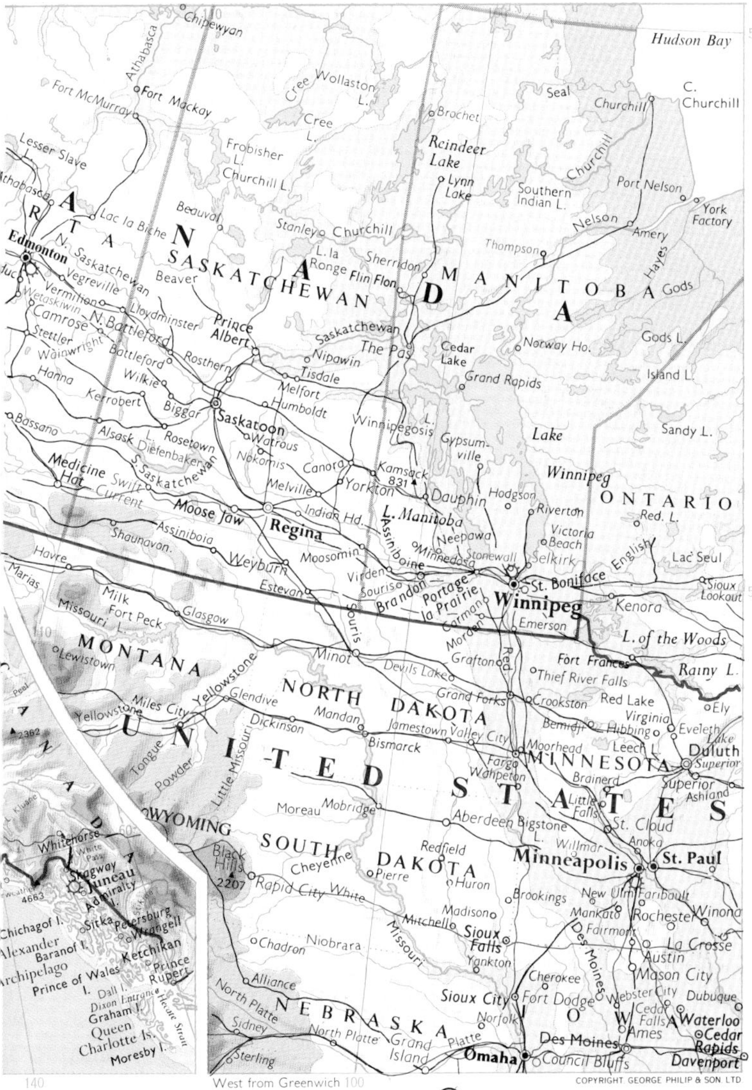

Map 143

Canada: North West

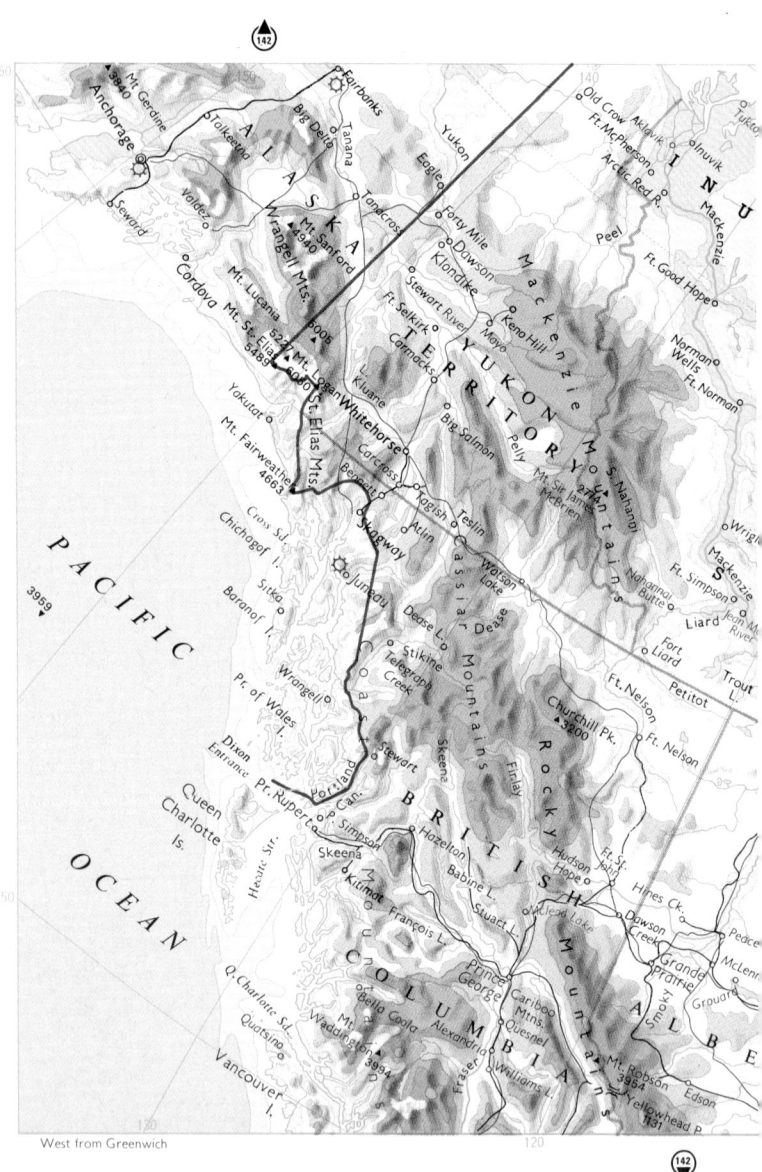

PACIFIC OCEAN

A L A S K A

Y U K O N   T E R R I T O R Y

B R I T I S H   C O L U M B I A

A L B E

Anchorage
Mt Gerdine
Seward
Stalkeyna
Valdez
Cordova
Big Delta
Fairbanks
Tanana
Tanacross
Mt Sanford
Wrangell Mts.
Mt Lucania
Mt. St. Elias 5489
Mt. Logan
St. Elias Mts.
Yokutat
Mt. Fairweather 4663
Chichagof I.
Cross Sd.
Sitka
Baranof I.
Wrangell
Pr. of Wales I.
Dixon Entrance
Queen Charlotte Is.
Hecate Str.
Q. Charlotte Sd.
Quatsino
Vancouver I.
Bella Coola
Mt. Waddington 3994
Alexandria
Fraser
Williams L.
Quesnel
Cariboo Mtns.
Prince George
Francois L.
Stuart L.
Skeena
Kitimat
Hazelton
Babine L.
McLeod Lake
Prince Rupert
Pt. Simpson
Portland Can.
Stewart
Telegraph Creek
Stikine
Dease L.
Cassiar Mountains
Deese
Atlin
Watson Lake
Teslin
Big Salmon
Pelly
Mt. St. James McBrien
Yukon Mts.
Mackenzie Mts. Nahanni
Whitehorse
Carcross
Bennett
Skagway
Juneau
Tagish
Kluane
Carmacks
Ft. Selkirk
Stewart River
Mayo
Keno Hill
Klondike
Dawson
Forty Mile
Eagle
Yukon
Old Crow
Aklavik
Ft. McPherson
Arctic Red
Inuvik
Yukon
I N U
Mackenzie
Peel
Ft. Good Hope
Norman Wells
Ft. Norman
Wrigl
Mackenzie
Ft. Simpson
Nahanni Butte
Jean M
Liard
Fort Liard
Trout L.
Petitot
Ft. Nelson
Churchill Pk. 3600
Finlay
Ft. St. John
Hudson Hope
Hines Ck.
Dawson Creek
Grande Prairie
Grouard
McLenr
Pedce
Mt. Robson 3954
Yellowhead P. 1131
Edson
Rocky Mountains
Skeena
3959
West from Greenwich
120

Map 144

1:15 000 000

12

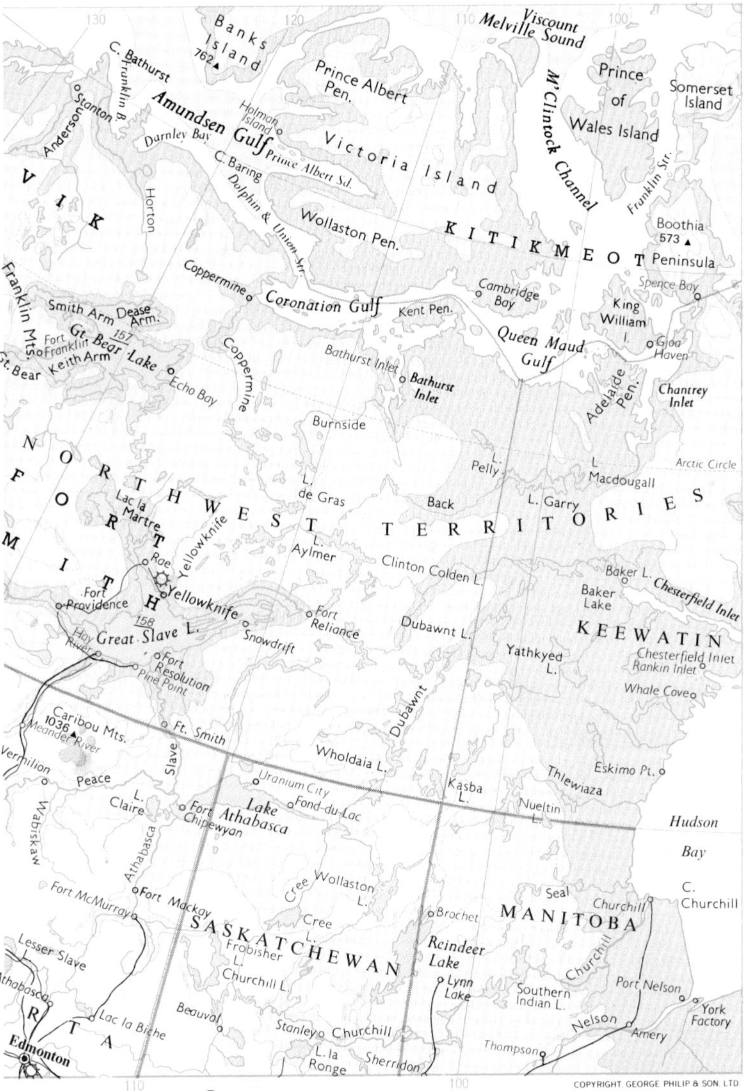

Banks
Island
782 ▲

C. Bathurst

C. Franklin R.

Stanton

Anderson

Prince Albert
Pen.

Amundsen Gulf

Holman
Island

Durnley Bay

C. Baring

Prince Albert Sd.

Dolphin & Union Str.

Victoria Island

Wollaston Pen.

Viscount
Melville Sound

M'Clintock Channel

Prince
of
Wales Island

Somerset
Island

Franklin Str.

Boothia
573 ▲

Spence Bay

King
William
I.

Gjoa
Haven

KITIKMEOT Peninsula

Chantrey
Inlet

V
I
K

Franklin Mts.

Smith Arm

Dease
Arm.

Fort
Franklin

157

Keith Arm

Gt. Bear

Gt. Bear Lake

Echo Bay

Horton

Coppermine

Coronation Gulf

Coppermine

Kent Pen.

Cambridge
Bay

Queen Maud
Gulf

Adelaide
Pen.

Bathurst Inlet

Bathurst
Inlet

Burnside

L.
de Gras

Pelly

Back

L. Garry

Macdougall

Arctic Circle

N
O
R
T
H
W
E
S
T

Lac la
Martre

Rae

Yellowknife

Aylmer

Clinton Colden L.

T
E
R
R
I
T
O
R
I
E
S

Baker L.

Chesterfield Inlet

F
O
R
T

S
M
I
T
H

Fort
Providence

Yellowknife

Snowdrift

158

Fort
Reliance

Dubawnt L.

Baker
Lake

KEEWATIN

Chesterfield Inlet

Rankin Inlet

146

Hay
River

Great Slave L.

Fort
Resolution

Pine Point

Ft. Smith

Wholdaia L.

Dubawnt

Yathkyed
L.

Whale Cove

Caribou Mts.
1036

Meander River

Vermilion

Peace

Slave

Uranium City

Fond-du-Lac

Kasba
L.

Nueltin
L.

Thlewiaza

Eskimo Pt.

Hudson

Bay

Wabiskaw

L.
Claire

Fort
Chipewyan

Athabasca

Lake
Athabasca

Wollaston
L.

Seal

Brochet

MANITOBA

Churchill

C.
Churchill

Fort McMurray

Fort Mackay

Cree

Cree

SASKATCHEWAN

Reindeer
Lake

Churchill

Port Nelson

York
Factory

Lesser Slave

A
L
T
A

Athabasca

Beauval

Lac la Biche

Frobisher
L.

Churchill L.

Stanley

Churchill

L. la
Ronge

Sherridon

Lynn
Lake

Southern
Indian L.

Thompson

Nelson

Amery

R

COPYRIGHT GEORGE PHILIP & SON LTD

Edmonton

130

120

110

100

70

60

110

100

143

Map 145

Canada: North East

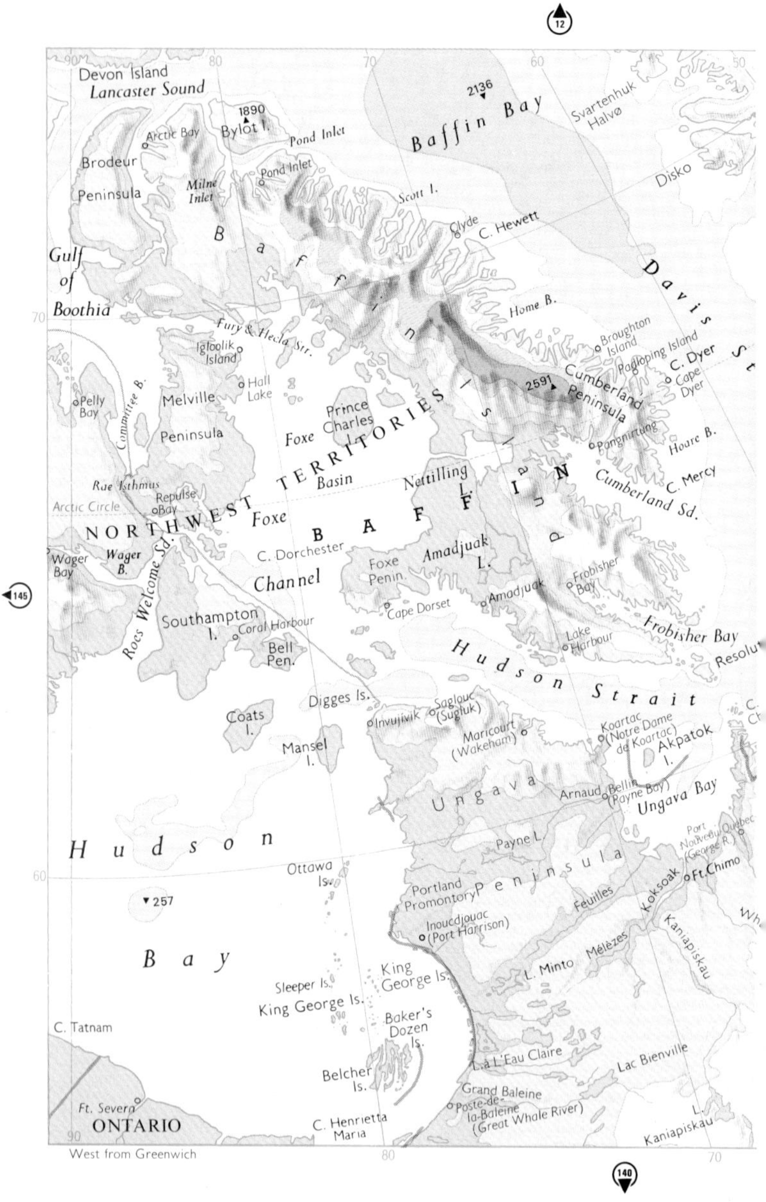

12

Devon Island
Lancaster Sound

2136

Baffin Bay

Svartenhuk Halvø

1890
Arctic Bay
Bylot I.
Pond Inlet

Brodeur

Milne
Inlet

Pond Inlet

Scott I.

Disko

B

Clyde
C. Hewett

Davis Str.

Peninsula

Gulf
of
Boothia

a

f

f

Home B.

Broughton
Island
Padloping Island
C. Dyer
Cape
Dyer

Fury & Hecla Str.

Igloolik
Island

n

Cumberland
Peninsula

Pelly
Bay

Committee B.

Melville

Hall
Lake

2591

Pangnirtung

Hoare B.

Prince
Charles

Peninsula

Foxe

I

s

l

a

Cumberland Sd.

Rae Isthmus
Repulse
Bay

Arctic Circle

NORTHWEST

TERRITORIES

Basin

Nettilling

C. Mercy

Wager
Bay
Wager
B.

Foxe

B
A
F
F
I
N

n

d

Coral Harbour
Southampton
I.

Roe's Welcome Sd.

Channel

C. Dorchester

Foxe
Penin.

Amadjuak
L.

Amadjuak

Cape Dorset

Frobisher
Bay

Lake
Harbour

Frobisher Bay

Resolut

Bell
Pen.

Coats
I.

Digges Is.

Invujivik
Sagluk
(Sugluk)

H u d s o n   S t r a i t

Mansel
I.

Maricourt
(Wakeham)

Koartac
(Notre Dame
de Koartac)

Akpatok
I.

H u d s o n

U n g a v a

Arnaud
Bellin
(Payne Bay)

Ungava Bay

Payne L.

Port
Nouveau-Québec
(George R.)

Ottawa
Isve

60

257

Portland
Promontory

P e n i n s u l a

Ft. Chimo

B a y

Inoucdjouac
(Port Harrison)

Feuilles

Mélèzes

Koksoak

Kaniapiskau

Wh

Sleeper Is.
King George Is.

King
George Is.

Baker's
Dozen
Is.

L. Minto

C. Tatnam

Ft. Severn
ONTARIO

Belcher
Is.

C. Henrietta
Maria

L'Eau Claire

Grand Baleine
Poste-de-
la-Baleine
(Great Whale River)

Lac Bienville

L.

Kaniapiskau

West from Greenwich

90

80

70

140

Map 146

146

1:15 000 000

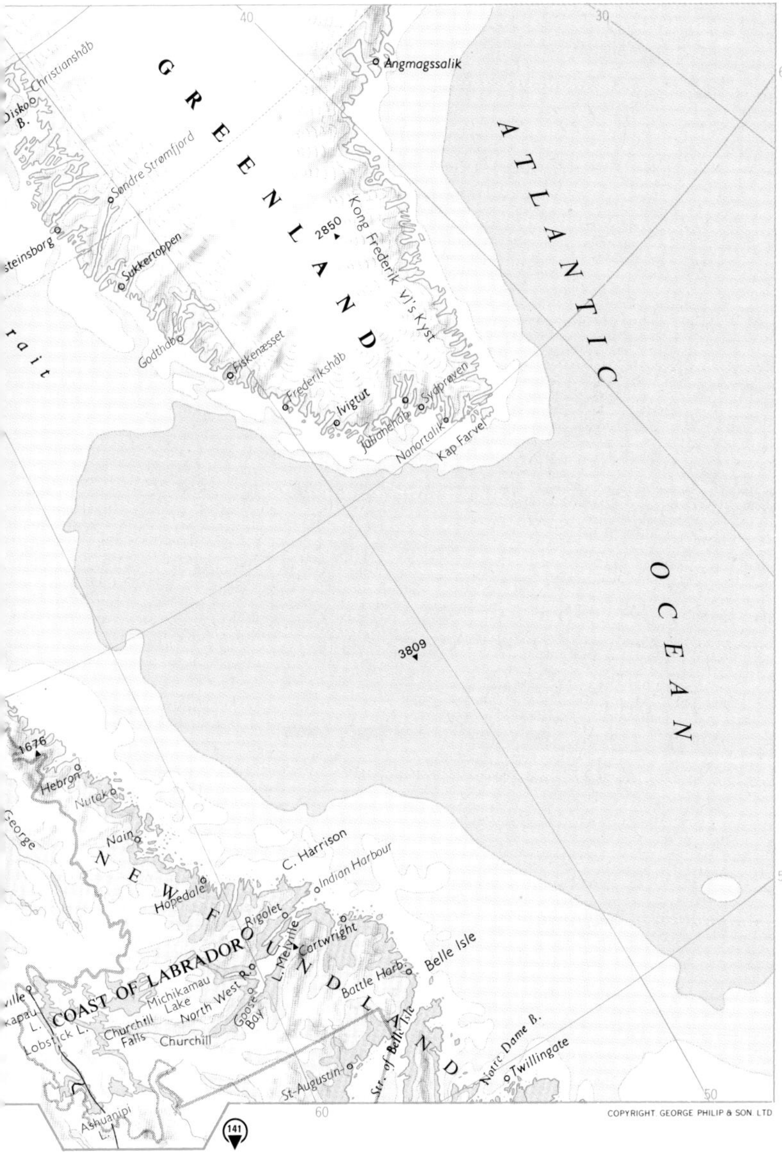
40
30
60
50
GREENLAND
ATLANTIC
OCEAN
Angmagssalik
Christianshåb
Disko B.
Søndre Strømfjord
steinsborg
Sukkertoppen
Godthåb
Fiskenæsset
Frederikshåb
Ivigtut
Julianehåb
Sydprøven
Nanortalik
Kap Farvel
Kong Frederik VI's Kyst
2850
3809
1676
Hebron
Nutak
Nain
George
NEWFOUNDLAND
Hopedale
C. Harrison
Indian Harbour
Rigolet
L. Melville
Cartwright
COAST OF LABRADOR
Michikamau Lake
North West R.
Goose Bay
Battle Harb.
Belle Isle
Lobstick L.
Churchill Falls
Churchill
Str. of Belle Isle
Notre Dame B.
Twillingate
St-Augustin
Ashuanipi L.
141

Canada: Saint Lawrence Estuary

West from Greenwich

Map 148

1:7 000 000

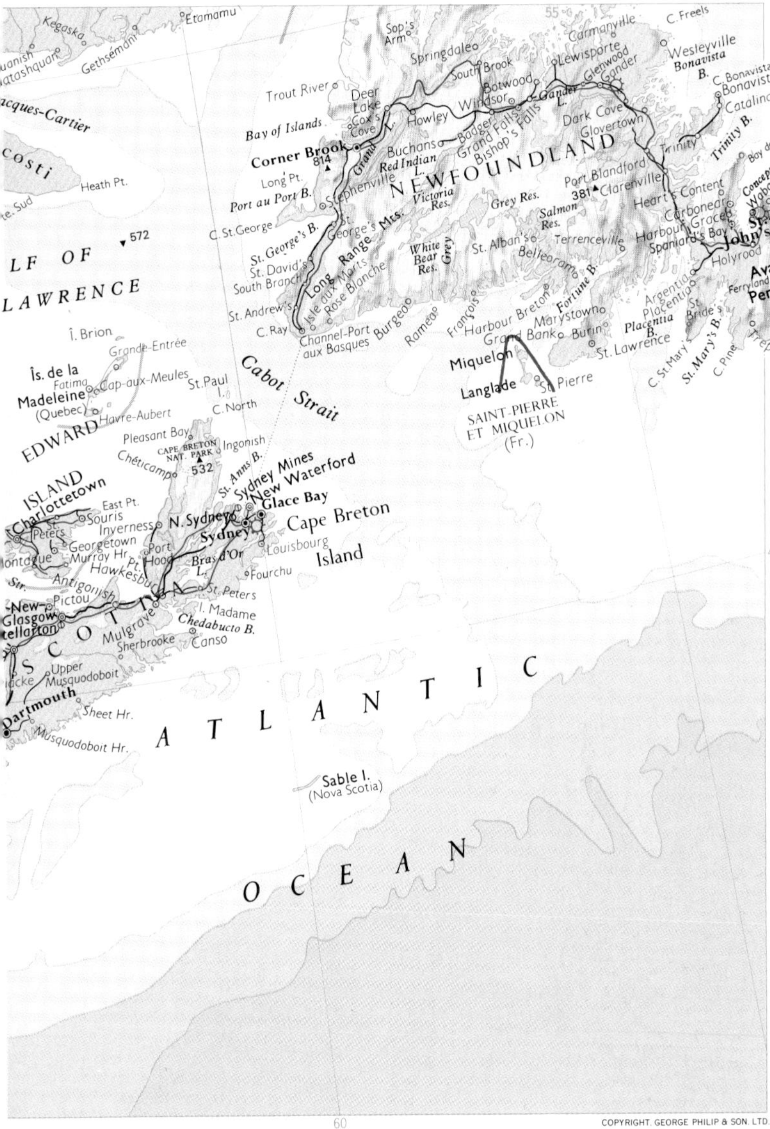

COPYRIGHT. GEORGE PHILIP & SON. LTD.

Map 149

Canada: The Great Lakes

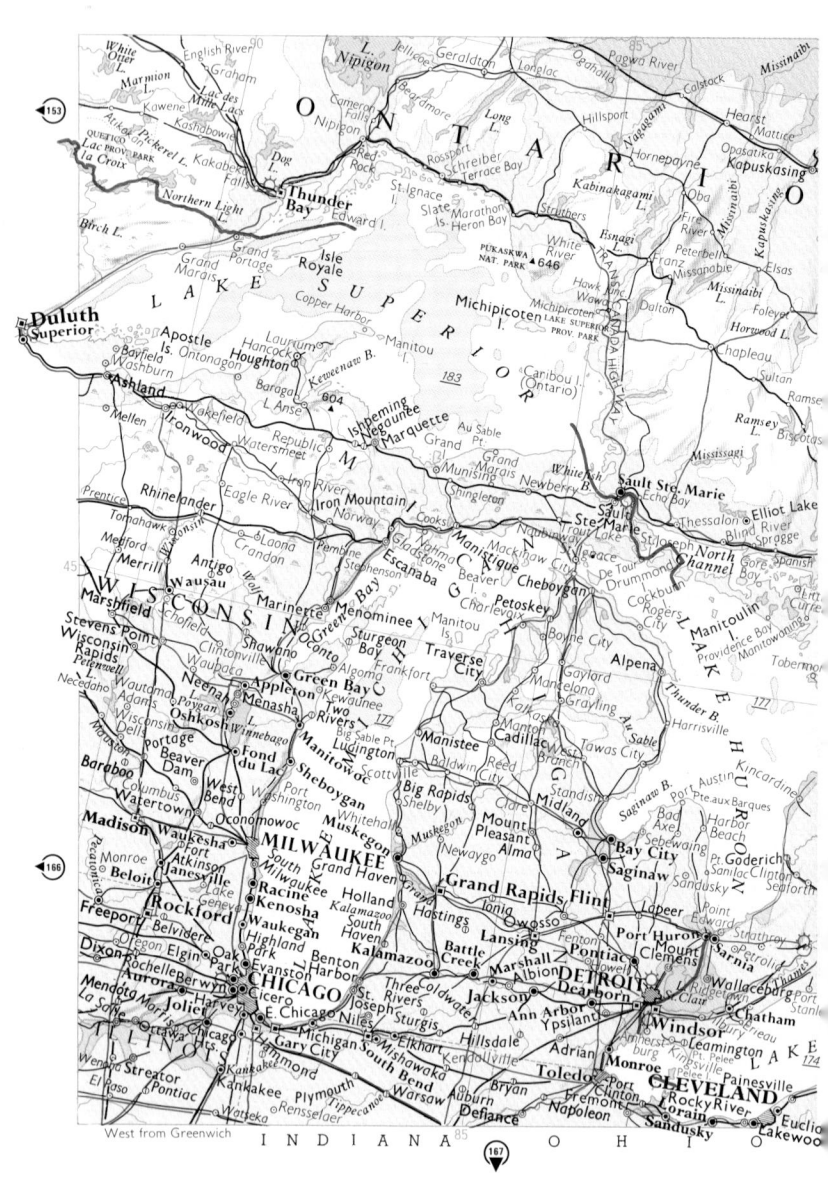
ONTARIO
LAKE SUPERIOR
MICHIGAN
WISCONSIN
ILLINOIS
LAKE MICHIGAN
LAKE HURON
LAKE ERIE
INDIANA
OHIO
L. Nipigon
Nipigon
Thunder Bay
Duluth
Superior
Sault Ste. Marie
Marquette
Ishpeming
Negaunee
Green Bay
Appleton
Oshkosh
Milwaukee
Racine
Kenosha
Waukegan
Chicago
Gary City
Hammond
Joliet
Aurora
Elgin
Rockford
Madison
Beloit
Janesville
Grand Rapids
Flint
Saginaw
Bay City
Lansing
Kalamazoo
Battle Creek
Jackson
Ann Arbor
Detroit
Dearborn
Windsor
Pontiac
Port Huron
Sarnia
Toledo
Cleveland
Sandusky
Lorain
Lakewood
South Bend
Elkhart
Muskegon
Traverse City
Alpena
Cheboygan
Petoskey
Escanaba
Menominee
Iron Mountain
Ironwood
Ashland
Houghton
Wausau
Marshfield
Stevens Point
Sheboygan
Manitowoc
Fond du Lac
Midland
Chatham
Leamington
Goderich
Manitoulin I.
Isle Royale
Keweenaw B.
Apostle Is.
Saginaw B.
Thunder B.
North Channel
Wawa
Chapleau
Hearst
Kapuskasing
Geraldton
Marathon
Schreiber
Elliot Lake
Michipicoten I.
Caribou I. (Ontario)
TRANS CANADA HIGHWAY
PUKASKWA NAT. PARK
646
604
183
177
174
West from Greenwich
90
85
45
153
166
167

Map 150

1:7 000 000

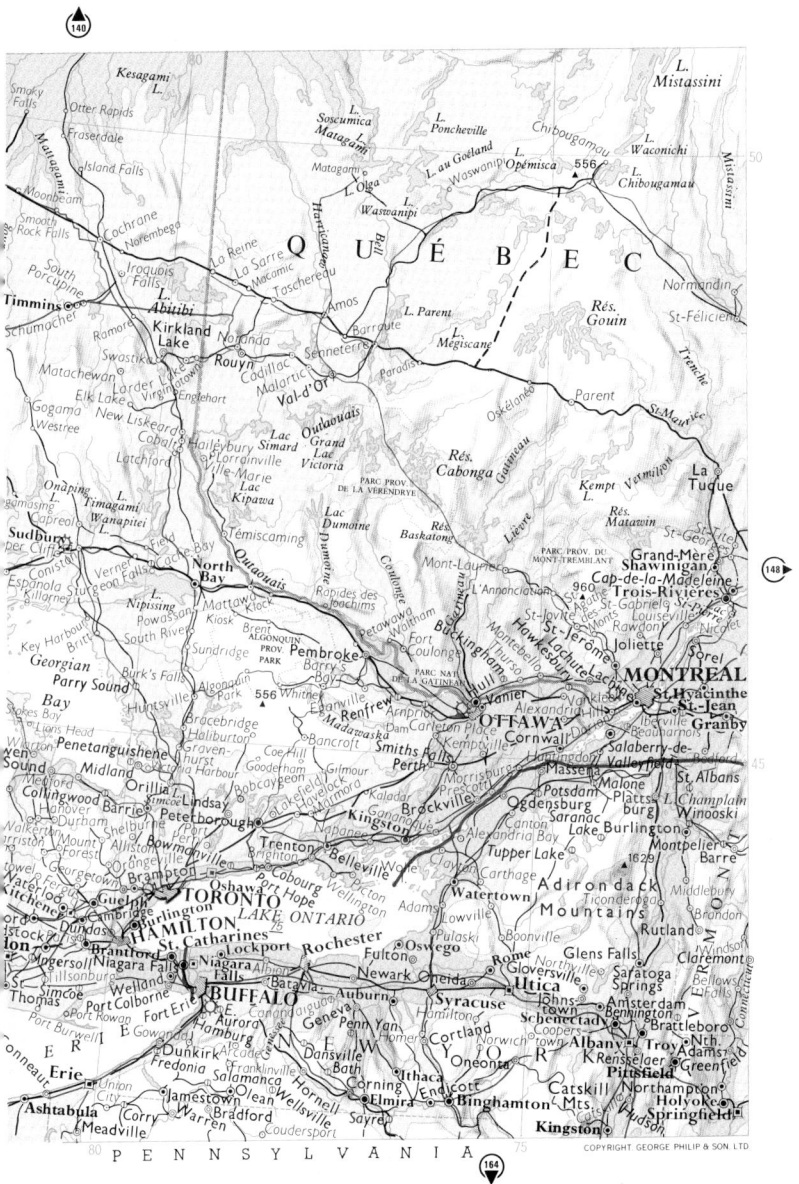

140

148 ►

Kesagami
L. Mistassini
Smoky Falls
Otter Rapids
Fraserdale
Island Falls
Moonbeam
Smooth Rock Falls
Cochrane
Norembega
South Porcupine
Iroquois Falls
Timmins
Schumacher
L. Abitibi
Ramore
Swastika
Matachewan
Kirkland Lake
Larder Lake
Elk Lake
Virginiatown
Englehort
Gogama
Westree
New Liskeard
Cobalt
Haileybury
Latchford
Lorrainville
Ville-Marie
Onaping
L. Timagami
Capreol
L. Wanapitei
Sudbury
Copper Cliff
Espanola
Killarney
Vernet
French River
North Bay
Mattawa
Nipissing
Powassan
Kiosk
Klock
Key Harbour
Britt
South River
Sundridge
Brent
ALGONQUIN PROV. PARK
Georgian Bay
Burk's Falls
Algonquin Park
556
Parry Sound
Huntsville
Whitney
Stokes Bay
Lions Head
Bracebridge
Haliburton
Eganville
Renfrew
Penetanguishene
Graven-hurst
Bancroft
Arnprior
Wiarton
Midland
Orillia
Coe Hill
Smiths Falls
Owen Sound
Collingwood
Barrie
Lindsay
Fenelon Falls
Perth
Meaford
Durham
Shelburne
Peterborough
Bobcaygeon
Kaladar
Kingston
Hanover
Walkerton
Alliston
Port Perry
Trenton
Belleville
Napanee
Mount Forest
Orangeville
Bowmanville
Cobourg
Picton
Watford
Georgetown
Brampton
Oshawa
Port Hope
Wellington
Listowel
Guelph
TORONTO
Kitchener
Cambridge
HAMILTON
LAKE ONTARIO
Stratford
Dundas
Burlington
Ingersoll
Brantford
St. Catharines
Rochester
Woodstock
Paris
Niagara Falls
Lockport
Fulton
Tillsonburg
Simcoe
Welland
Batavia
BUFFALO
Geneva
Auburn
Syracuse
Port Colborne
Fort Erie
Hamburg
Penn Yan
Cortland
St. Thomas
Port Rowan
Gowanda
Dunkirk
Dansville
Bath
Norwich
Ithaca
Conneaut
Erie
Fredonia
Franklinville
Hornell
Corning
Elmira
Endicott
Binghamton
Ashtabula
Union City
Jamestown
Salamanca
Olean
Wellsville
Sayre
Meadville
Corry
Warren
Bradford
Coudersport

QUÉBEC
Soscumica
Matagami
Poncheville
L. au Goéland
Waswanipi
Opémisca
556
Waconichi
Chibougamau
Matagami
Olga
Waswanipi
Chibougamou
La Reine
La Sarre
Macamic
Taschereau
Amos
Normandin
St-Félicien
Noranda
Rouyn
Cadillac
Malartic
Val-d'Or
Senneterre
Paradis
Barraute
L. Parent
Méganga
Rés. Gouin
Oskélaneo
Parent
St-Maurice
Lac Simard
Grand Lac Victoria
Outaouais
Parc Prov. de la Vérendrye
Rés. Cabonga
Guineau
Kempt
Vermilon
La Tuque
Lac Kipawa
Témiscaming
Lac Dumoine
Rés. Baskatong
Rés. Matawin
St-Georges
Mont-Laurier
Parc Prov. du Mont-Tremblant
Grand-Mère
Shawinigan
Cap-de-la-Madeleine
Trois-Rivières
Nicolet
L'Annonciation
St-Jovite
St-Jérôme
St-Gabriel
Louiseville
Joliette
Sorel
Pembroke
Petawawa
Fort Coulonge
Buckingham
Montebello
Hawkesbury
Lachute
Rawdon
MONTREAL
St-Hyacinthe
St-Jean
Granby
Hull
Vanier
OTTAWA
Alexandria
Cornwall
Salaberry-de-Valleyfield
Beauharnois
St Albans
Carleton Place
Kemptville
Huntingdon
Malone
L. Champlain
Winooski
Morrisburg
Prescott
Potsdam
Plattsburg
Burlington
Brockville
Ogdensburg
Canton
Saranac
Montpelier
Gananoque
Alexandria Bay
Tupper Lake
Lake
1629
Barre
Clayton
Carthage
Watertown
Adirondack Mountains
Ticonderoga
Middlebury
Brandon
Rutland
Adams
Lowville
Boonville
Pulaski
Oswego
Rome
Northville
Glens Falls
Saratoga Springs
Claremont
Bellows Falls
Utica
Johnstown
Amsterdam
Bennington
Brattleboro
Newark
Oneida
Schenectady
Cooperstown
Albany
Troy
Pittsfield
Greenfield
Homer
Norwich
Rensselaer
Northampton
Holyoke
Springfield
Catskill Mts.
Hudson
Kingston

PENNSYLVANIA

164

Map 151

Canada: Southern Saskatchewan and Manitoba

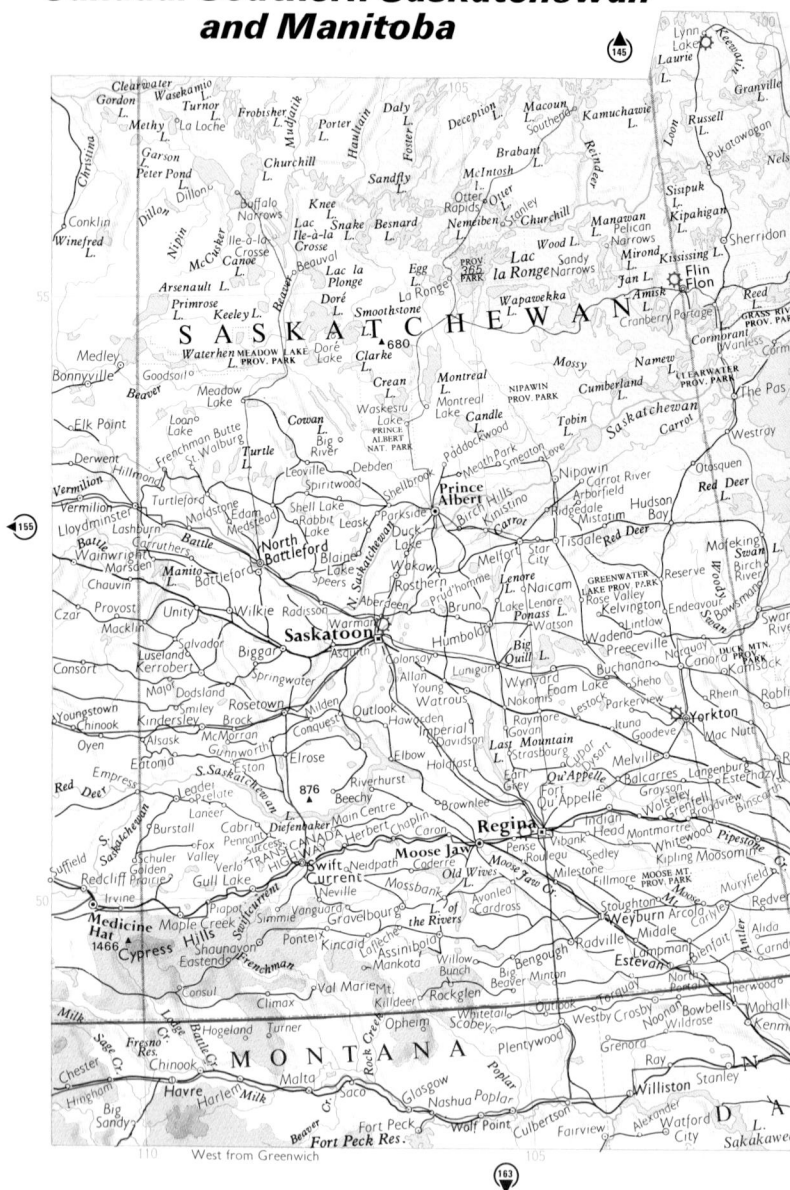

West from Greenwich

Map 152

1:7 000 000

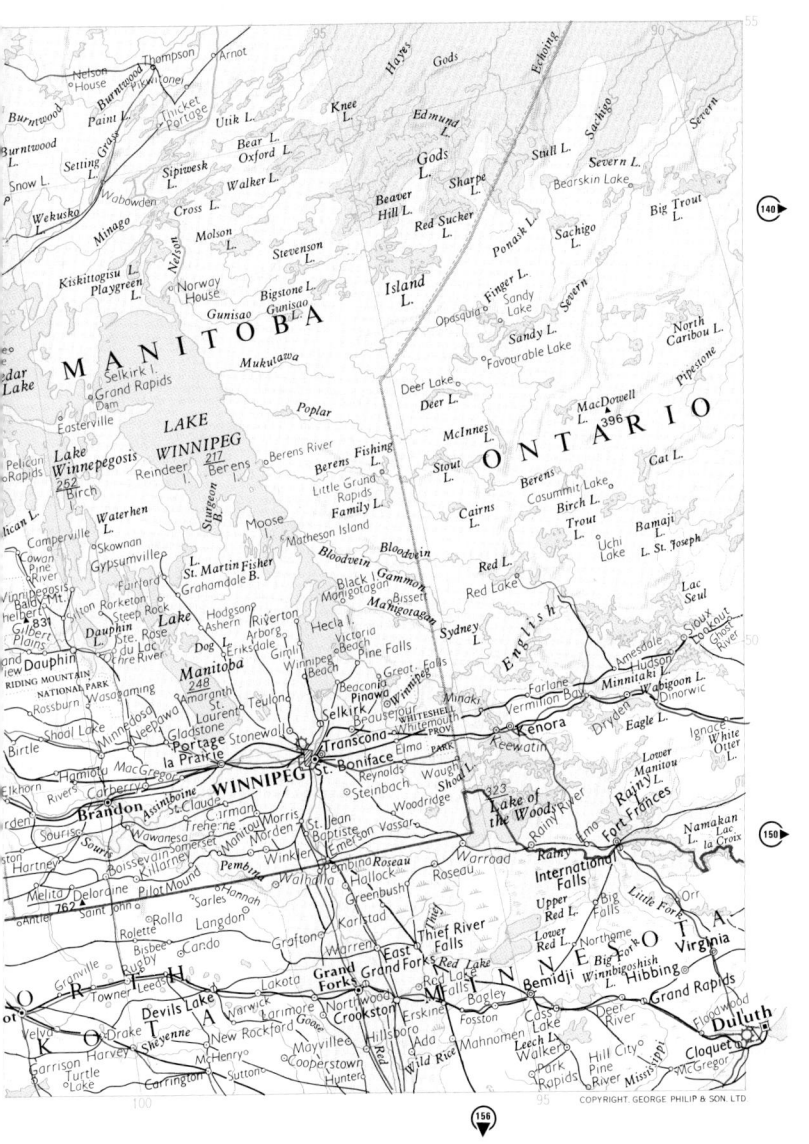

COPYRIGHT. GEORGE PHILIP & SON. LTD.

Map 153

Canada: Southern British Columbia and Alberta

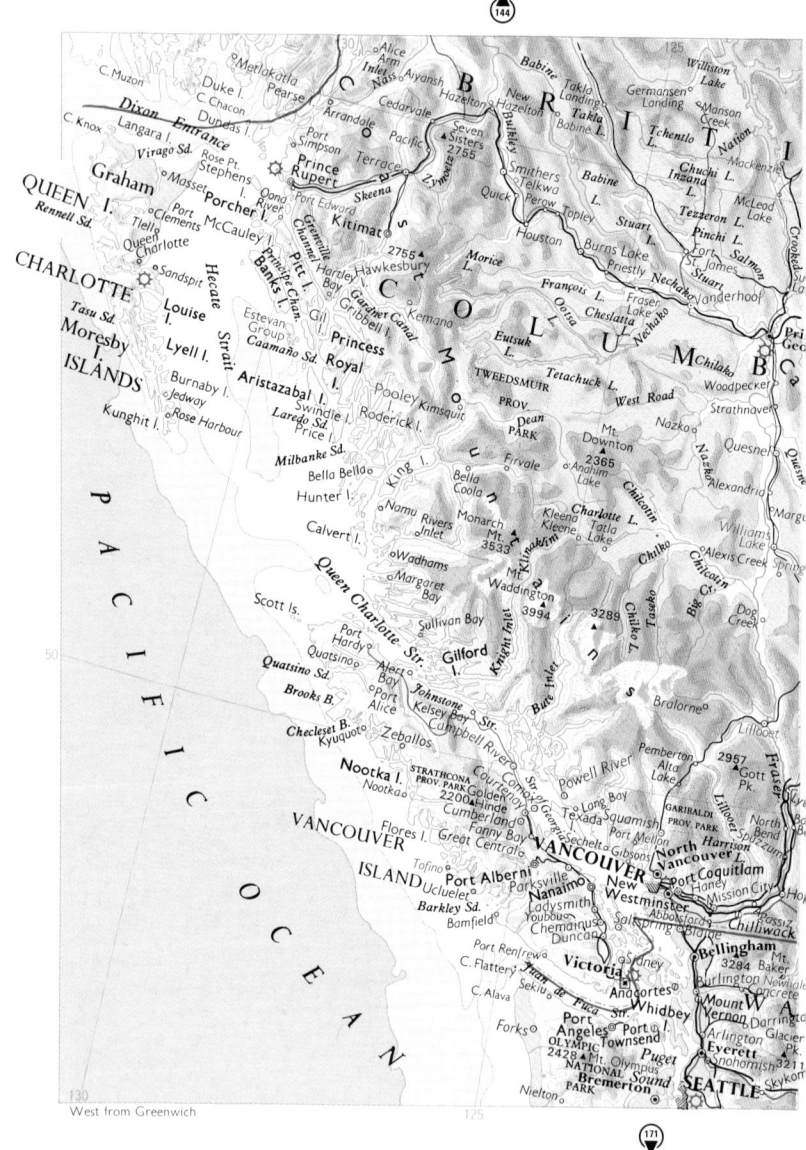

Map 154

1:7 000 000

145

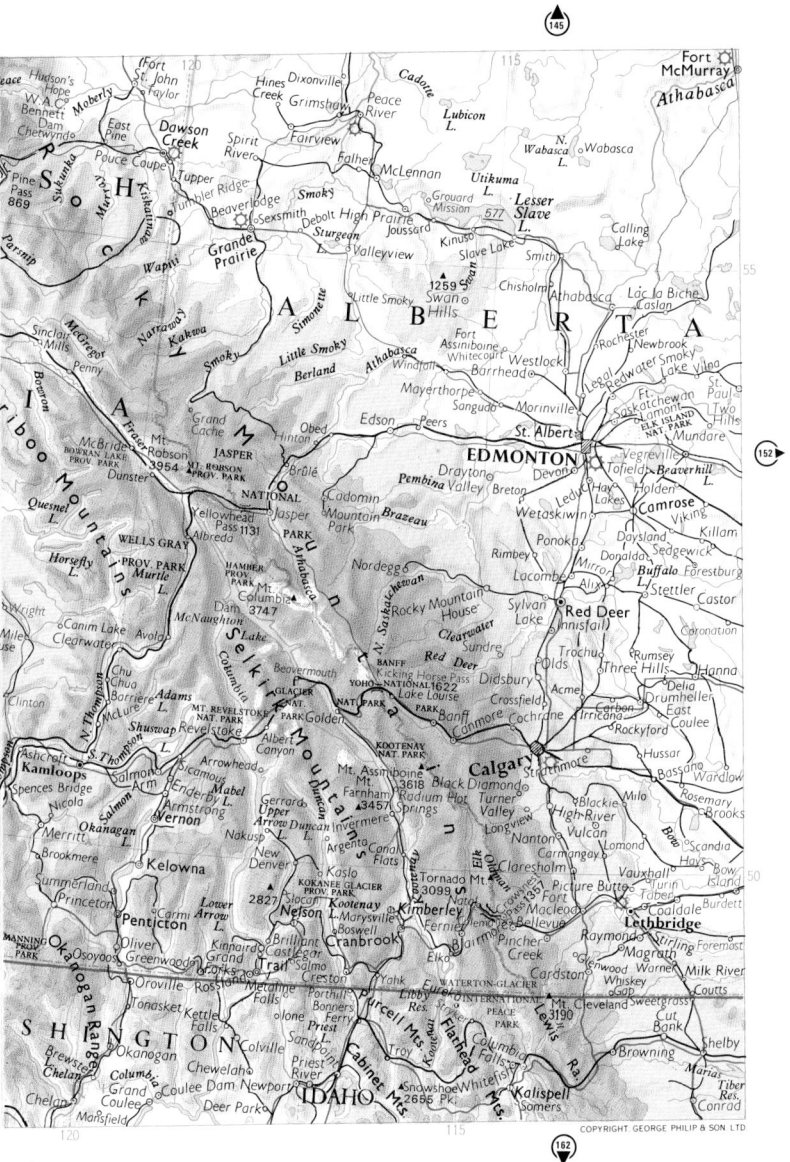

Fort McMurray
Athabasca
Fort St. John
Taylor
Hudson's Hope
W.A.C. Bennett Dam
Chetwynd
Moberly
East Pine
Dawson Creek
Pouce Coupe
Tupper
Tumbler Ridge
Pine Pass 869
Sukunka
Murray
Kiskatinaw
Parsnip
Hines Creek
Dixonville
Grimshaw
Peace River
Cadotte
Lubicon L.
Fairview
Spirit River
Falher
McLennan
N. Wabasca L.
Wabasca
Utikuma L.
Grouard Mission
Lesser Slave L.
Beaverlodge
Sexsmith
Smoky
Debolt
High Prairie
Joussard
Kinuso
Grande Prairie
Sturgeon L.
Valleyview
Slave Lake
Smith
Calling Lake
Wapiti
Swan
1259
Swan Hills
Little Smoky
Chisholm
Athabasca
Lac la Biche
Caslan
ALBERTA
Simonette
McGregor
Sinclair Mills
Narraway
Kakwa
Penny
Fort Assiniboine
Whitecourt
Westlock
Rochester
Newbrook
Little Smoky
Berland
Athabasca
Windfall
Barrhead
Redwater
Smoky Lake
Vilna
Legal
Bowron
Smoky
Mayerthorpe
Sangudo
Morinville
Ft. Saskatchewan
Lamont
St. Paul
Two Hills
ELK ISLAND NAT. PARK
Mundare
Grand Cache
Obed
Hinton
Edson
Peers
St. Albert
EDMONTON
Vegreville
McBride
BOWRAN LAKE PROV. PARK
Fraser
Mt. Robson 3954
MT. ROBSON PROV. PARK
JASPER
Dunster
Brûlé
Drayton Valley
Pembina
Breton
Devon
Tofield
Beaverhill L.
Holden
Quesnel L.
NATIONAL
Cadomin
Hay Lakes
Leduc
Camrose
Yellowhead Pass 1131
Jasper
Mountain Park
Brazeau
Wetaskiwin
Viking
PARK
Albreda
WELLS GRAY
Daysland
Killam
Horsefly L.
PROV. PARK
Murtle L.
HAMBER PROV. PARK
Ponoka
Rimbey
Sedgewick
Donalda
Nordegg
Mirror
Buffalo L.
Forestburg
Athabasca
Mt. Columbia 3747
N. Saskatchewan
Lacombe
Alix
Stettler
Castor
Wright
Rocky Mountain House
Sylvan Lake
Red Deer
Innisfail
Coronation
Mica Dam
McNaughton Lake
Canim Lake
Avola
Clearwater
Clearwater
Sundre
Trochu
Rumsey
Selkirk
Columbia
Red Deer
Three Hills
Hanna
Chu Chua
Beavermouth
BANFF
Kicking Horse Pass
Didsbury
Olds
Delia
Clinton
N. Thompson
Barrière
Adams L.
GLACIER NAT. PARK
YOHO NATIONAL PARK
Lake Louise 1622
Crossfield
Acme
Drumheller
McLure
MT. REVELSTOKE NAT. PARK
Golden
Banff
Carbon
Irricana
East Coulee
Shuswap L.
Revelstoke
Canmore
Cochrane
Rockyford
Ashcroft
S. Thompson
Albert Canyon
KOOTENAY NAT. PARK
Calgary
Strathmore
Hussar
Kamloops
Salmon Arm
Sicamous
Arrowhead
Mt. Assiniboine 3618
Black Diamond
Bassano
Wardlow
Spences Bridge
Enderby
Mabel L.
Mt. Farnham 3457
Radium Hot Springs
Turner Valley
Blackie
Milo
Rosemary
Salmon
Nicola
Armstrong
Gerrard
Duncan
Upper Arrow L.
Duncan L.
Longview
High River
Brooks
Vernon
Okanagan L.
Invermere
Vulcan
Bow
Merritt
Nakusp
Argenta
Canal Flats
Nanton
Lomond
Scandia
Brookmere
Kelowna
New Denver
Kootenay
Kaslo
Elk
Oldman
Carmangay
Claresholm
Hays
Bow Island
Summerland
KOKANEE GLACIER PROV. PARK
Tornado Mt. 3099
Vauxhall
Turin
Princeton
Lower Arrow L.
2827
Slocan
Nelson
Kootenay L.
Marysville
Kimberley
Crowsnest Pass 1357
Picture Butte
Taber
Coaldale
Burdett
Carmi
Penticton
Natal
Fort Macleod
Lethbridge
Boswell
Fernie
Michel
Bellevue
MANNING PROV. PARK
Oliver
Kinnaird
Brilliant
Cranbrook
Blairmore
Pincher Creek
Raymond
Stirling
Foremost
Okanogan
Osoyoos
Greenwood
Grand Forks
Castlegar
Trail
Salmo
Elko
Magrath
Glenwood
Warner
Milk River
Creston
Yahk
Cardston
Whiskey Gap
Oroville
Rossland
Metaline Falls
Porthill
Eureka
WATERTON-GLACIER INTERNATIONAL PEACE PARK
Coutts
Libby Res.
Mt. Cleveland 3190
Sweetgrass
Tonasket
Kettle Falls
Bonners Ferry
Stryker
Lewis Ra.
Ione
Priest L.
Cut Bank
Range
Purcell Mts.
Flathead
Columbia Falls
Colville
Sandpoint
Kootenai
Troy
Shelby
Brewster
Okanogan
Browning
Chelan
Chewelah
Priest River
Cabinet Mts.
Whitefish
Marias
Columbia
Grand Coulee
Coulee Dam
Newport
IDAHO
Snowshoe Pk. 2655
Kalispell
Tiber Res.
Chelan
Mansfield
Deer Park
Somers
Mts.
Conrad
120
115
55
50

152

162

Map 155

U.S.A.: North East

140

163

Lake Winnipeg
MANITOBA
Trout Lake
L. St. Joseph
Albany
O N T A R I O
C A N A D A
English
L. Seul
Nakina
Kenogami
Missinaibi
Moosonee
Abitibi
Gimli
Winnipeg
Sioux Lookout
Lake Nipigon
Longlac
Hearst
Mattagami
Winnipeg
Kenora
Lake of the Woods
Ignace
Seine
Rainy L.
Oba
Nipigon
White River
Franz
Timmins
Emerson
Thunder Bay
I. St. Ignace
Wawa
Michipicoten
Michipicoten I.
Grafton
Fort Frances
Thief River Falls
Red
I. Royale
Lake Superior
183 above S. L.
Whitefish Bay
Grand Forks
Red Lake
Bemidji
Hibbing
Virginia
Calumet
Laurium
Keweenaw Bay
Two Harbors
Sault Ste. Marie
Leech L.
Moorhead
Fargo
MINNESOTA
Duluth
Apostle Is.
Marquette
Sault Ste. Marie
Superior
Bessemer
Ironwood
Ishpeming
North Chan.
Ashland
Escanaba
Manistique
Mississippi
Fergus Falls
Brainerd
Cheboygan
Rhinelander
Iron Mt.
Big Stone Lake
St. Cloud
Anoka
Merrill
Antigo
Menominee
Lake Huron
Coteau des Prairies
Willmar
Stillwater
Chippewa Falls
Wausau
Traverse City
Saginaw Bay
Watertown
Minneapolis
St. Paul
Stevens Point
Green Bay
Red Wing
Eau Claire
Manistee
Cadillac
Minnesota
New Ulm
Faribault
Wisconsin Rapids
Appleton
Brookings
Winona
WISCONSIN
Manitowoc
Ludington
Midland
Bay City
Mankato
Owatonna
Rochester
La Crosse
Fond du Lac
Lake Michigan
177
Muskegon
Saginaw
Madison
Fairmont
Sheboygan
Flint
Port Huron
Austin
Beaver Dam
Albert Lea
Baraboo
Muskegon
Owosso
Pontiac
Sioux Falls
Worthington
Watertown
Lansing
Spencer
Mason City
Charles City
Wisconsin
Madison
Milwaukee
Grand Rapids
Yankton
Des Moines
Janesville
Racine
Battle Creek
Ann Arbor
Big Sioux
Cherokee
Webster City
Waterloo
Beloit
Kenosha
Kalamazoo
Jackson
Windsor
Monroe
Sioux City
Fort Dodge
Cedar Falls
Dubuque
Rockford
Waukegan
Evanston
St. Joseph
IOWA
Cedar Rapids
CHICAGO
Elkhart
Toledo
Norfolk
Ames
Marshalltown
Clinton
Dixon
Elgin
South Bend
Columbus
Iowa City
Aurora
Joliet
Fremont
Des Moines
Newton
Davenport
Moline
Ottawa
Gary
Findlay
Hammond
Ft. Wayne
Omaha
Council Bluffs
Oskaloosa
Rock Island
Kewanee
Streator
Kankakee
Wabash
Huntington
Lima
Marion
Ottumwa
Lincoln
Red Oak
Creston
Galesburg
Kokomo
Marion
OHIO
Burlington
Peoria
Lafayette
Muncie
Piqua
Nebraska City
Shenandoah
Bloomington
Keokuk
Pekin
Danville
Frankfort
Anderson
Beatrice
Illinois
Champaign
Urbana
Dayton
Springfield
Kirksville
Jacksonville
Springfield
Richmond
Kettering
Decatur
Indianapolis
Quincy
Mississippi
INDIANA
Hamilton
St. Joseph
Chillicothe
ILLINOIS
Terre Haute
Cincinnati
Atchison
Hannibal
Mattoon
Newport
Moberly
Marshall
Bloomington
Covington
Manhattan
Leavenworth
Kansas City
Mexico
Bedford
Maysville
Junction City
Kansas
Columbia
Alton
Granite City
Wabash
Vincennes
Jeffersonville
Missouri
St. Charles
Topeka
Kansas City
St. Louis
E. St. Louis
New Albany
Frankfort
Lawrence
Sedalia
Jefferson City
Centralia
Winchester
Ottawa
Belleville
Mt. Vernon
Evansville
Louisville
Lexington
Emporia
MISSOURI
Richmond
W. Frankfort
Owensboro
Danville
KANSAS
Osage
L. of the Ozarks
Rolla
Henderson
KENTUCKY
Newton
Nevada
El Dorado
Fort Scott
Lebanon
Plateau
Marion
Somerset
Cape Girardeau
Wichita
Parsons
Pittsburg
Ozark
Springfield
Ohio
Green
Bowling Green
Winfield
Cairo
Hopkinsville
Middlesboro
Paducah
West from Greenwich

158

Map 156

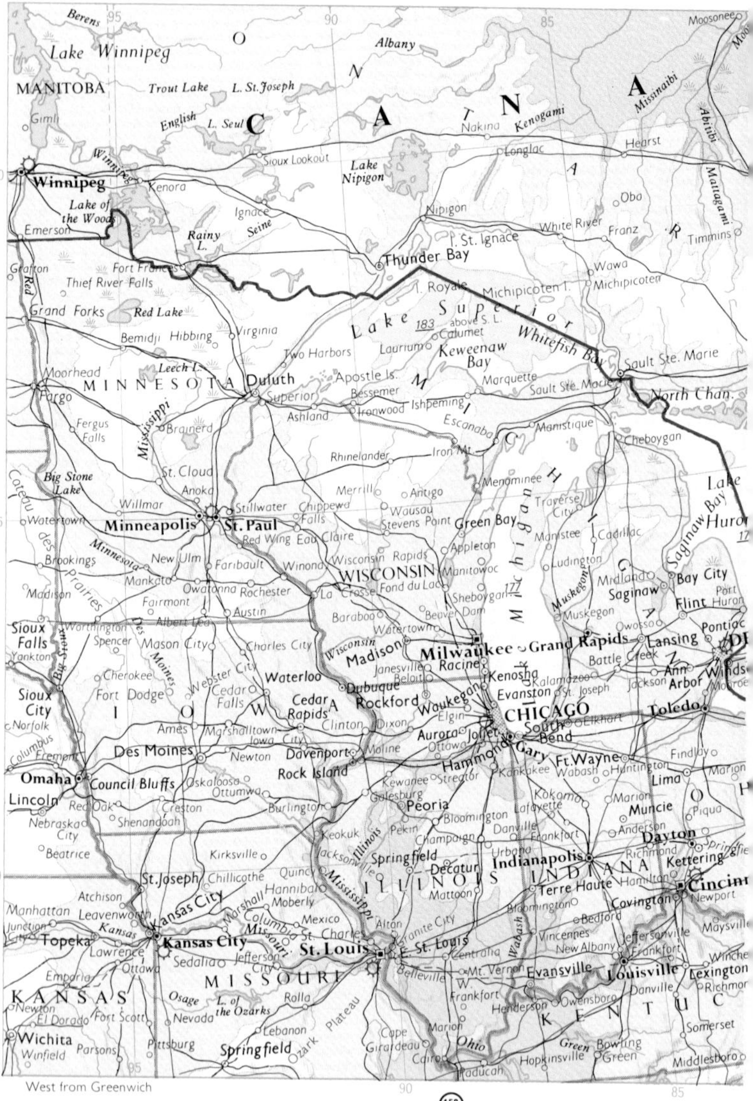

1:12 000 000

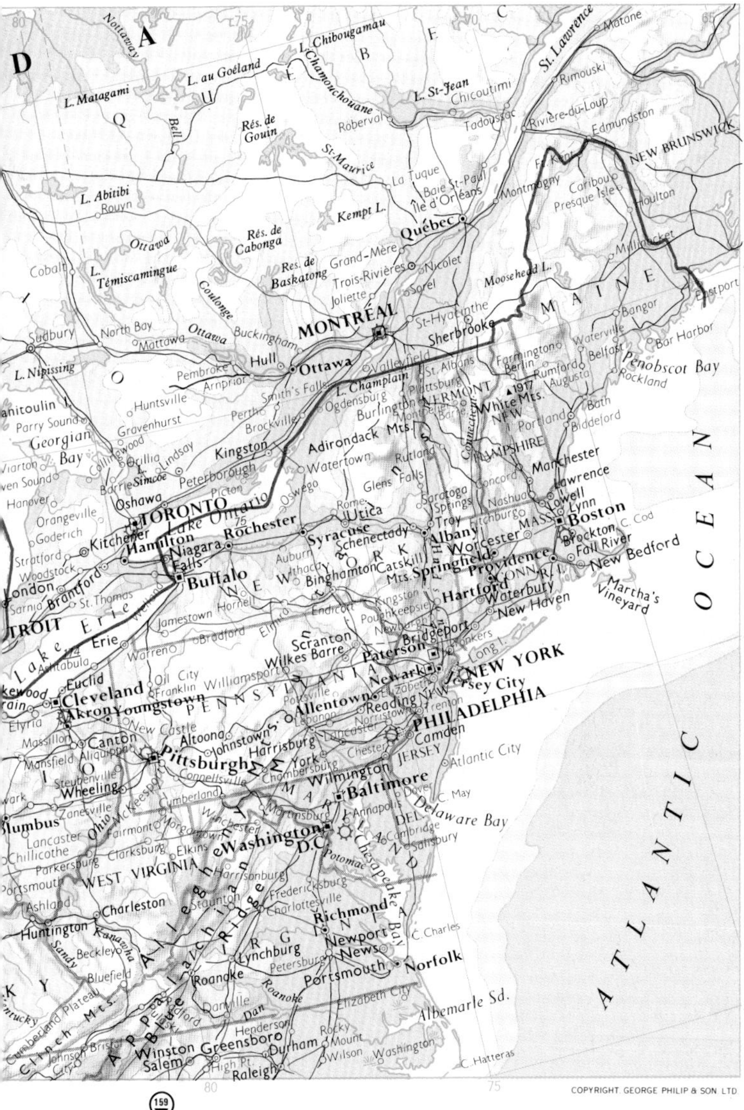

COPYRIGHT GEORGE PHILIP & SON LTD

Map 157

U.S.A.: South East

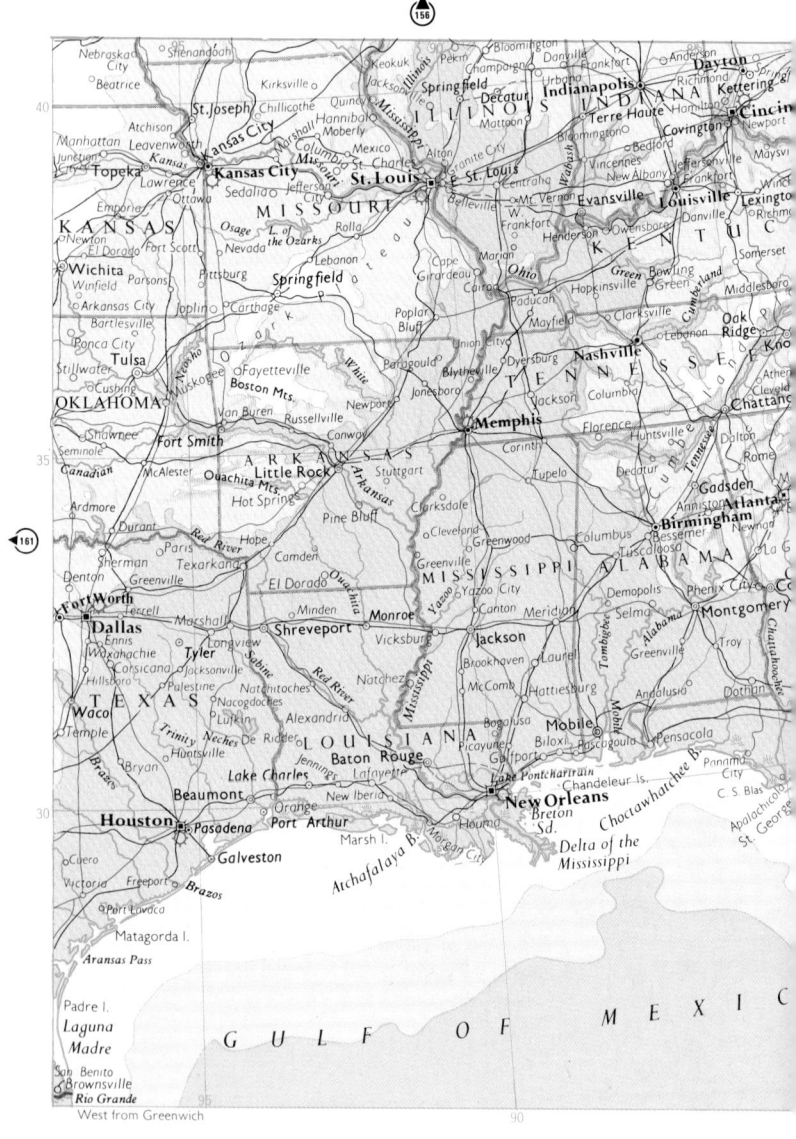

Map 158

1:12 000 000

COPYRIGHT GEORGE PHILIP & SON LTD

Map 159

U.S.A.: South West and Hawaii

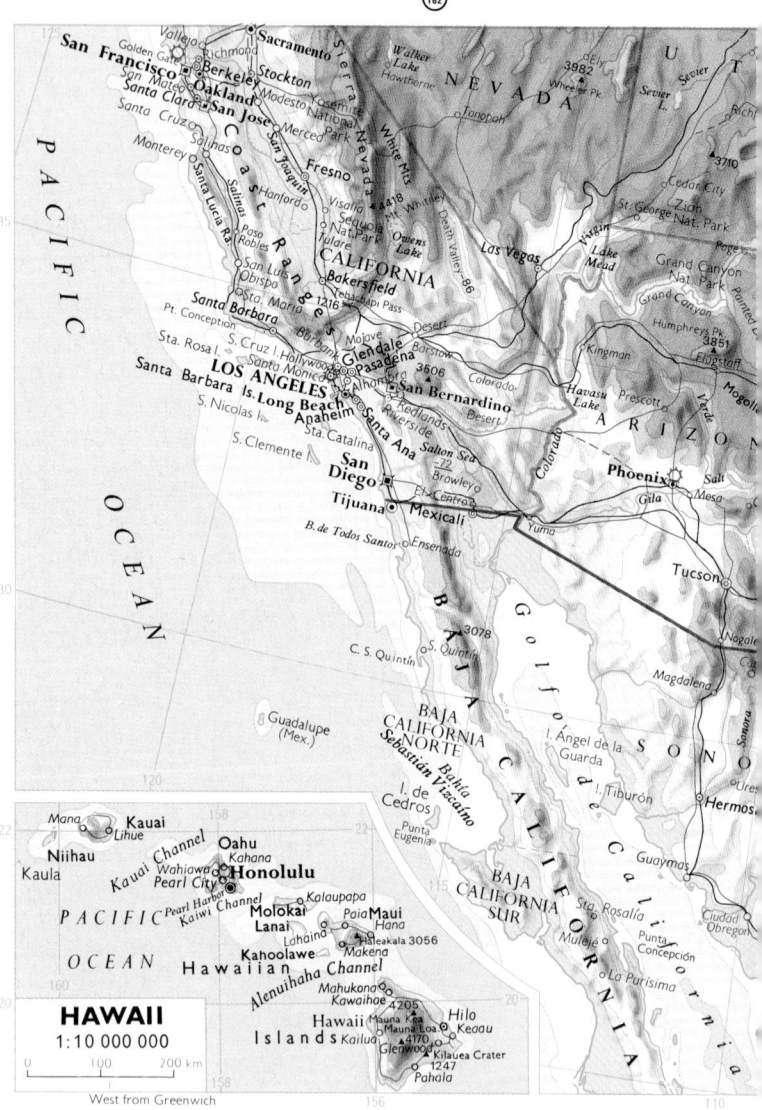

Map 160

1:12 000 000

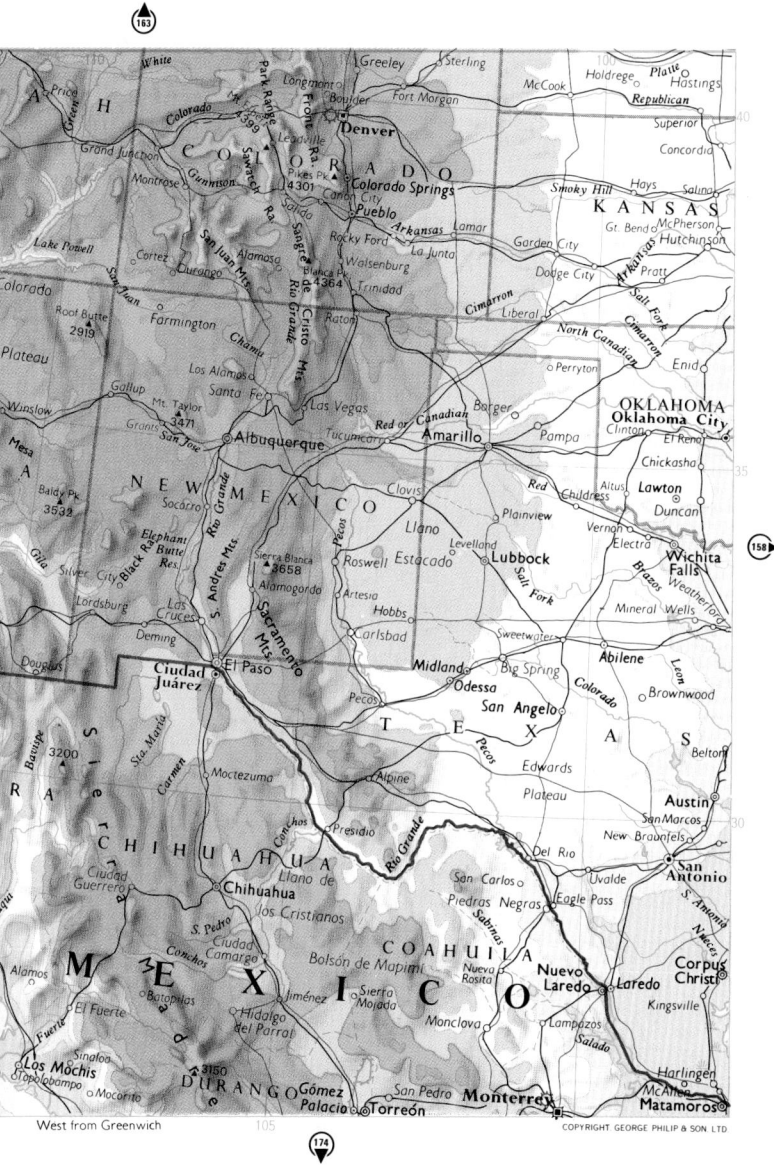

West from Greenwich

COPYRIGHT GEORGE PHILIP & SON LTD

Map 161

U.S.A.: North West

142

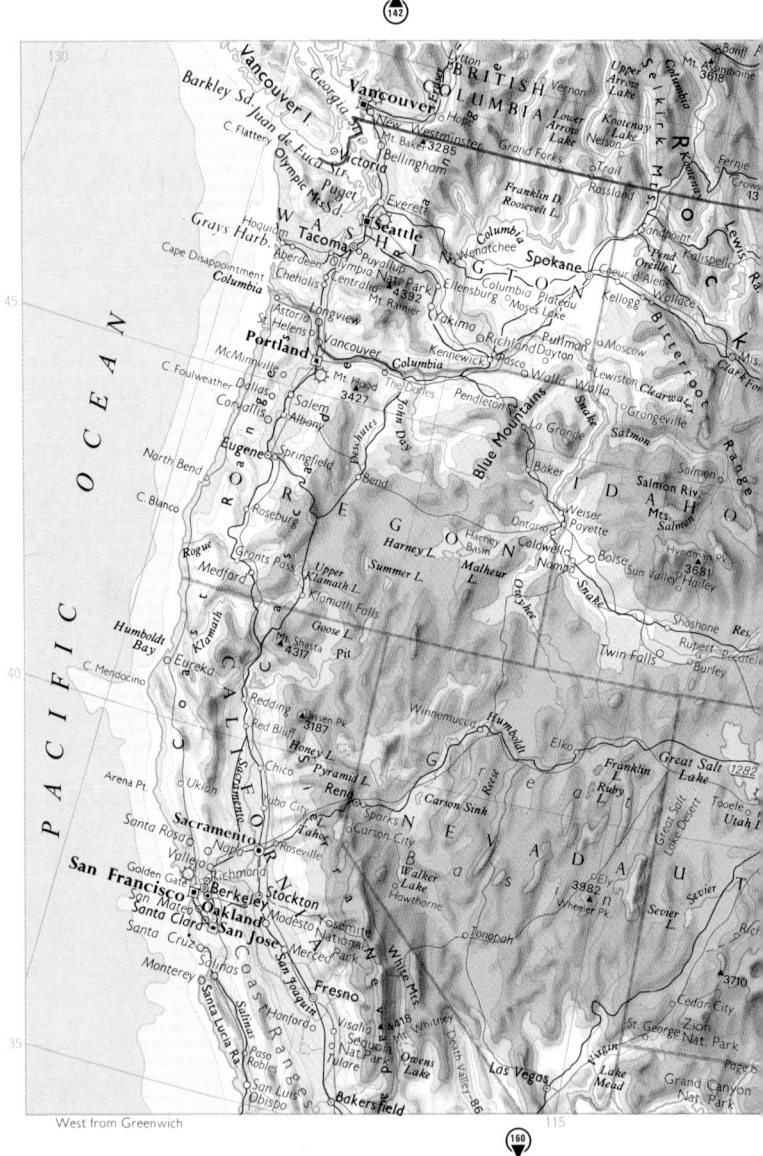

West from Greenwich

160

Map 162

1:12 000 000

Map 163

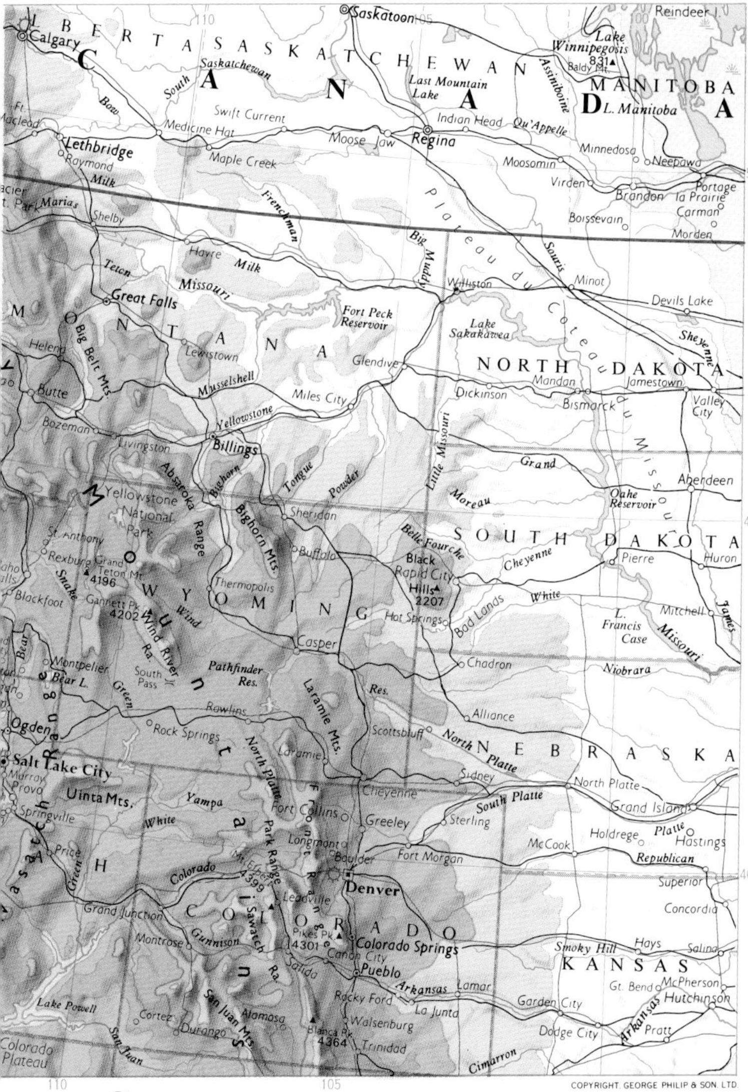

COPYRIGHT GEORGE PHILIP & SON LTD.

U.S.A.: Boston, New York, Washington

1:6 000 000

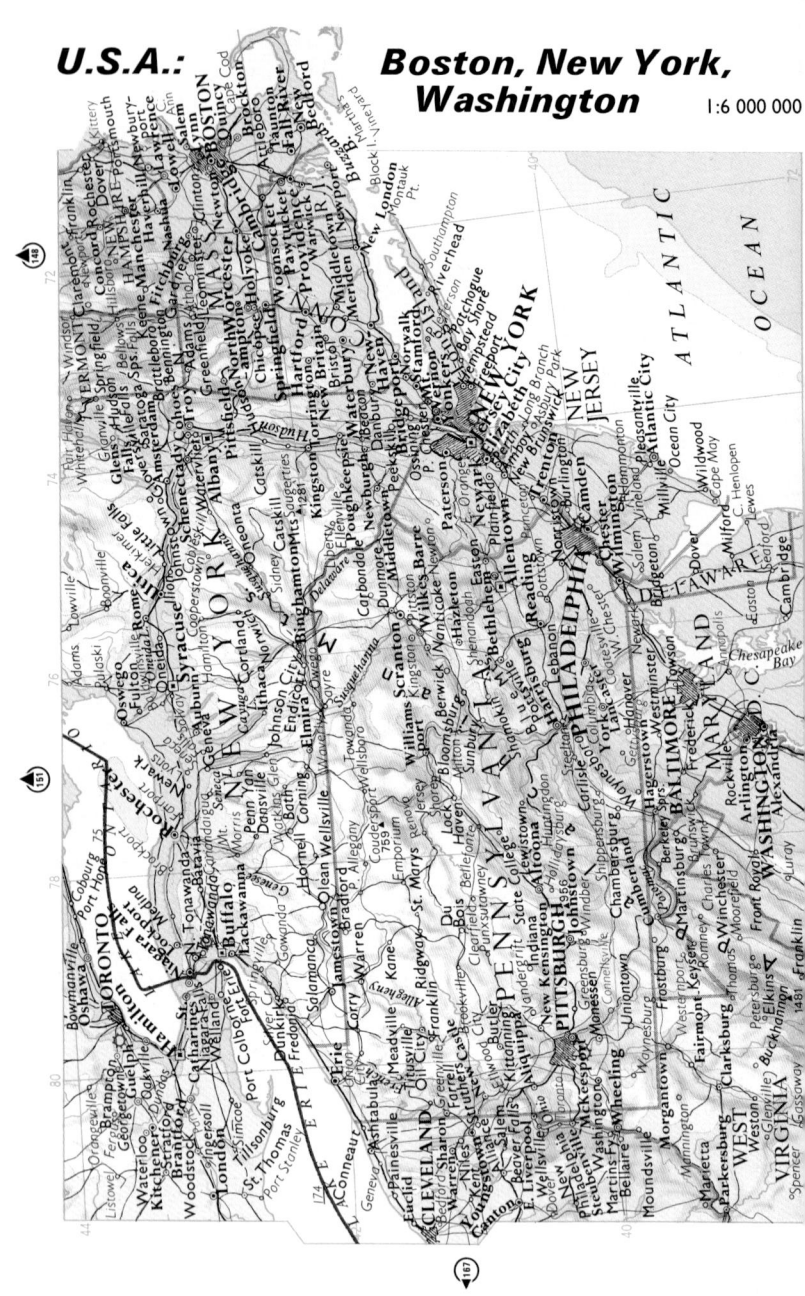

Map 164

U.S.A.: *Washington, Atlanta*

1:6 000 000

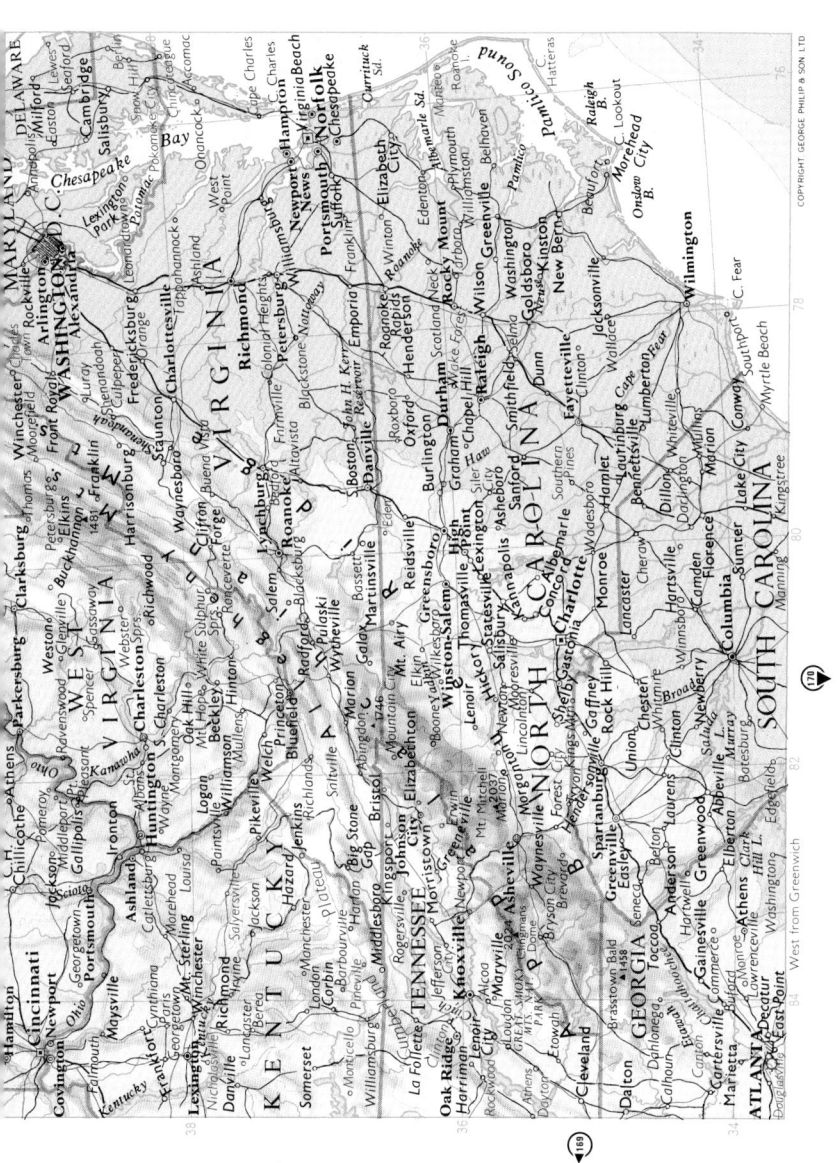

COPYRIGHT GEORGE PHILIP & SON LTD

Map 165

165

U.S.A.: Upper Mississippi

156

163

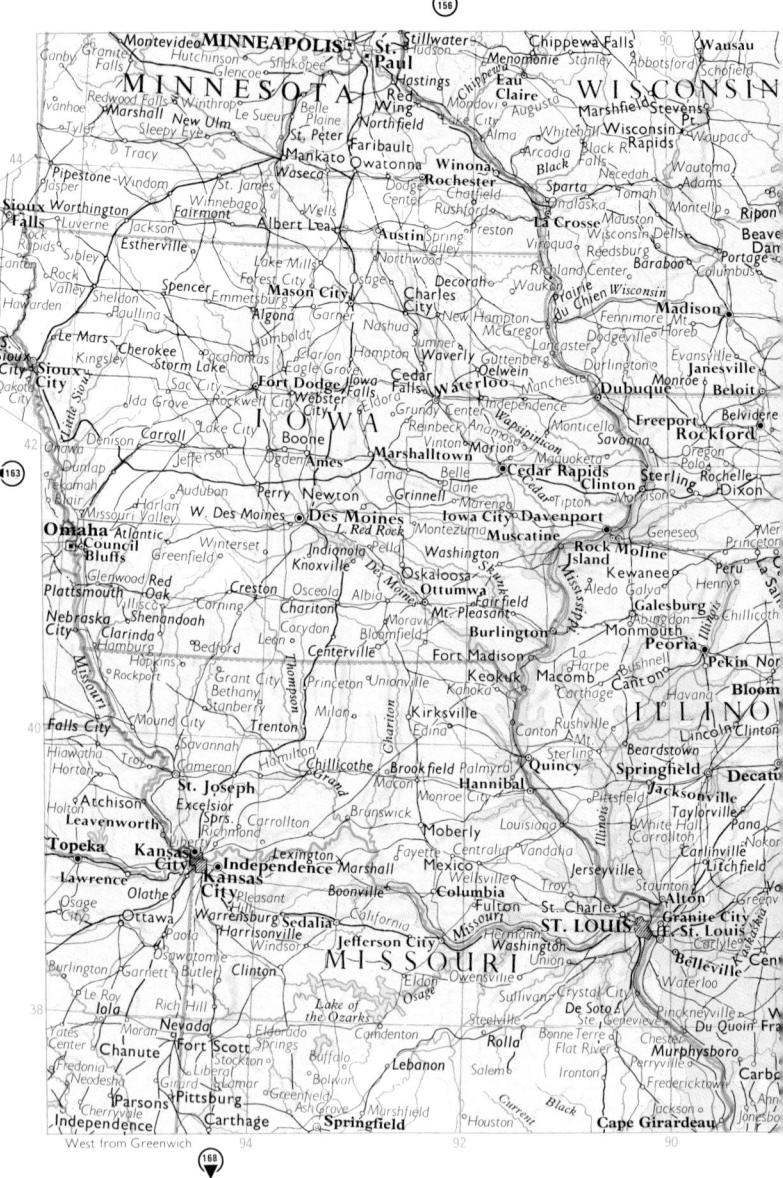

MINNESOTA
WISCONSIN
IOWA
ILLINOIS
MISSOURI
MINNEAPOLIS
St. Paul
Montevideo
Hutchinson
Glencoe
Shakopee
Stillwater
Hudson
Chippewa Falls
Menomonie
Stanley
Abbotsford
Wausau
Schofield
Canby
Granite Falls
Hastings
Red Wing
Eau Claire
Augusta
Mondovi
Chippewa
Ivanhoe
Redwood Falls
Winthrop
Marshall
New Ulm
Le Sueur
Belle Plaine
Northfield
Lake City
Marshfield
Stevens Pt.
Tyler
Sleepy Eye
St. Peter
Alma
Whitehall
Wisconsin Rapids
Waupaca
Tracy
Mankato
Faribault
Arcadia
Black R. Falls
Black
Waseca
Owatonna
Winona
Necedah
Wautoma
Pipestone
Jasper
Windom
St. James
Dodge Center
Rochester
Sparta
Tomah
Adams
Chatfield
Onalaska
Sioux Falls
Worthington
Winnebago
Fairmont
Wells
Rushford
La Crosse
Mauston
Montello
Ripon
Luverne
Jackson
Albert Lea
Austin
Spring Valley
Preston
Wisconsin Dells
Rock Rapids
Estherville
Viroqua
Reedsburg
Portage
Sibley
Lake Mills
Northwood
Baraboo
Columbus
Canton
Rock Valley
Forest City
Osage
Richland Center
Spencer
Mason City
Charles City
Decorah
Waukon
Prairie du Chien
Wisconsin
Hawarden
Sheldon
Emmetsburg
Algona
Garner
New Hampton
Madison
Paullina
Nashua
McGregor
Fennimore
Mt. Horeb
Humboldt
Dodgeville
Le Mars
Sumner
Lancaster
S. Sioux City
Cherokee
Pocahontas
Clarion
Hampton
Waverly
Guttenberg
Evansville
Kingsley
Storm Lake
Eagle Grove
Oelwein
Darlington
Janesville
Sioux City
Sac City
Fort Dodge
Iowa Falls
Cedar Falls
Manchester
Monroe
Beloit
Dakota City
Little Sioux
Ida Grove
Rockwell City
Webster City
Eldora
Waterloo
Dubuque
Independence
Grundy Center
Wapsipinicon
Freeport
Rockford
Belvidere
Lake City
Reinbeck
Anamosa
Monticello
Savanna
Onawa
Denison
Carroll
Boone
Vinton
Marion
Oregon
Jefferson
Ogden
Ames
Marshalltown
Maquoketa
Polo
Dunlap
Cedar Rapids
Clinton
Sterling
Rochelle
Tekamah
Tama
Belle Plaine
Dixon
Blair
Audubon
Perry
Newton
Grinnell
Cedar
Tipton
Morrison
Harlan
Marengo
Missouri Valley
W. Des Moines
Des Moines
Iowa City
Davenport
Omaha
Atlantic
L. Red Rock
Montezuma
Muscatine
Geneseo
Council Bluffs
Winterset
Pella
Rock Island
Moline
Princeton
Greenfield
Indianola
Washington
Knoxville
Des Moines
Skunk
Peru
La Salle
Glenwood
Red Oak
Oskaloosa
Kewanee
Henry
Plattsmouth
Creston
Osceola
Albia
Ottumwa
Fairfield
Aledo
Galva
Villisca
Corning
Chariton
Mississippi
Galesburg
Nebraska City
Shenandoah
Mt. Pleasant
Abingdon
Chillicothe
Clarinda
Corydon
Moravia
Monmouth
Hamburg
Bedford
Leon
Bloomfield
Burlington
Illinois
Peoria
Hopkins
Centerville
Fort Madison
La Harpe
Bushnell
Pekin
Rockport
Grant City
Thompson
Princeton
Unionville
Keokuk
Macomb
Canton
Bloomington
Bethany
Kahoka
Carthage
Havana
Missouri
Stanberry
Milan
Chariton
Kirksville
Falls City
Mound City
Trenton
Edina
Canton
Rushville
Lincoln
Clinton
Mt. Sterling
Beardstown
Savannah
Hiawatha
Troy
Cameron
Hamilton
Chillicothe
Brookfield
Palmyra
Quincy
Springfield
Decatur
Horton
St. Joseph
Grand
Macon
Hannibal
Pittsfield
Jacksonville
Atchison
Excelsior Sprs.
Monroe City
Holton
Taylorville
Carrollton
Brunswick
Leavenworth
Richmond
Louisiana
White Hall
Pana
Liberty
Moberly
Carrollton
Topeka
Kansas City
Lexington
Fayette
Centralia
Vandalia
Carlinville
Nokomis
Independence
Marshall
Mexico
Litchfield
Kansas City
Lawrence
Jerseyville
Wellsville
Olathe
Boonville
Columbia
Troy
Staunton
Pleasant Hill
Osage City
Fulton
St. Charles
Alton
Ottawa
Warrensburg
Sedalia
California
Missouri
ST. LOUIS
Granite City
E. St. Louis
Paola
Harrisonville
Jefferson City
Hermann
Carlyle
Osawatomie
Windsor
Washington
Kaskaskia
Union
Belleville
Burlington
Garnett
Butler
Clinton
Eldon
Owensville
Waterloo
Le Roy
Osage
Crystal City
Sullivan
Iola
Rich Hill
Lake of the Ozarks
De Soto
Pinckneyville
Du Quoin
Yates Center
Moran
Nevada
Eldorado Springs
Camdenton
Steelville
Ste. Genevieve
Rolla
Bonne Terre
Chester
Chanute
Fort Scott
Stockton
Flat River
Murphysboro
Fredonia
Liberal
Buffalo
Lebanon
Salem
Ironton
Perryville
Carbondale
Neodesha
Girard
Lamar
Bolivar
Fredericktown
Parsons
Pittsburg
Greenfield
Current
Black
Cherryvale
Ash Grove
Marshfield
Jackson
Anna
Independence
Carthage
Springfield
Houston
Cape Girardeau
Jonesboro
44
42
40
38
96
94
92
90
West from Greenwich

168

Map 166

1:6 000 000

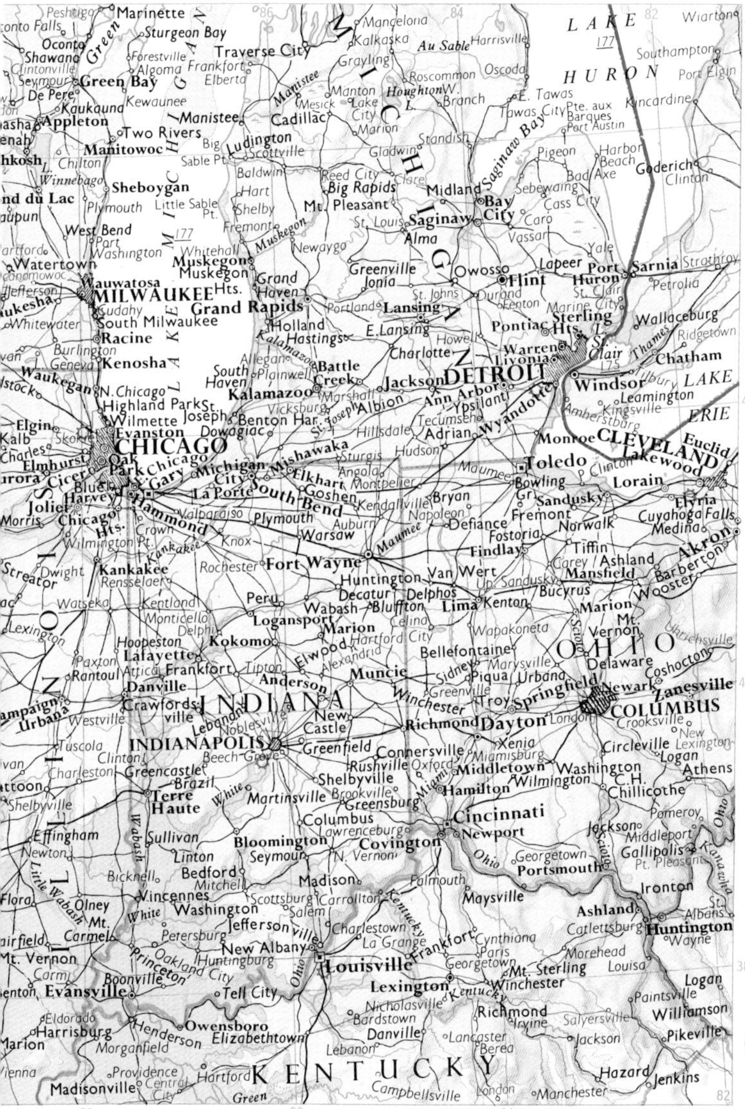

Map 167

U.S.A.: Lower Mississippi and Gulf Coast

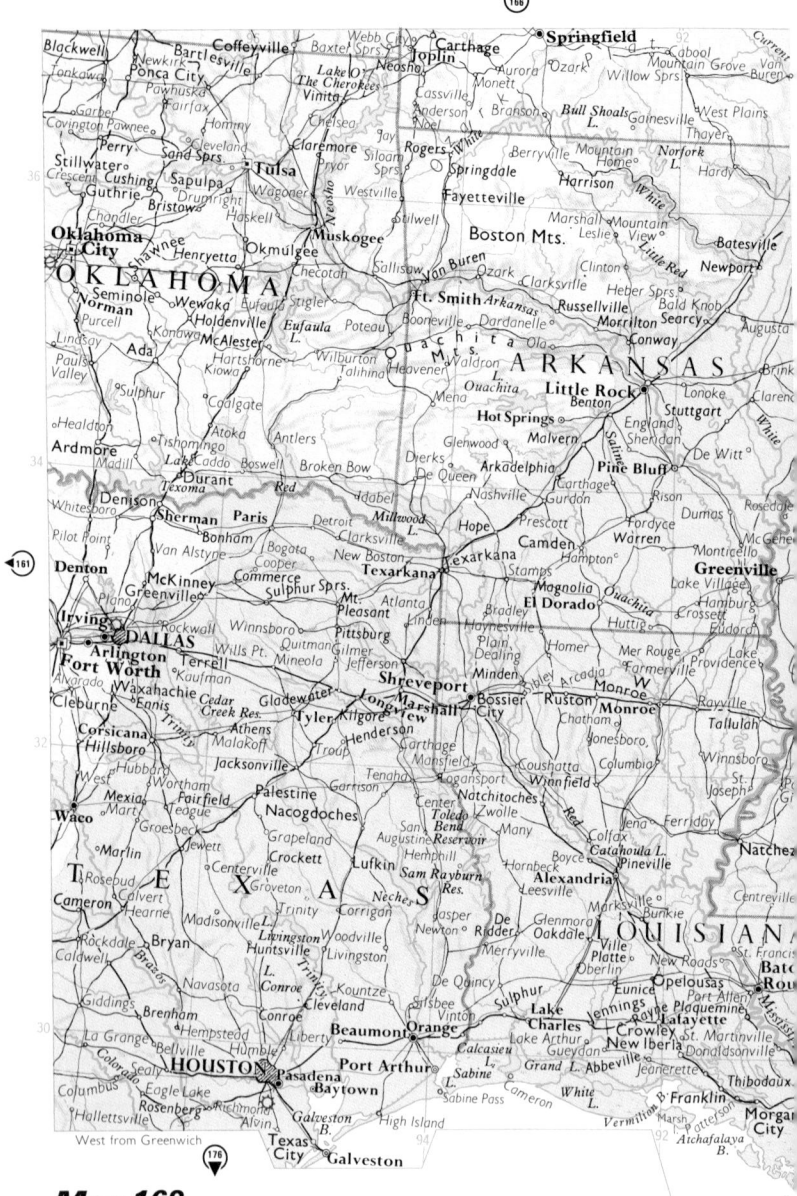

West from Greenwich

Map 168

1:6 000 000

167

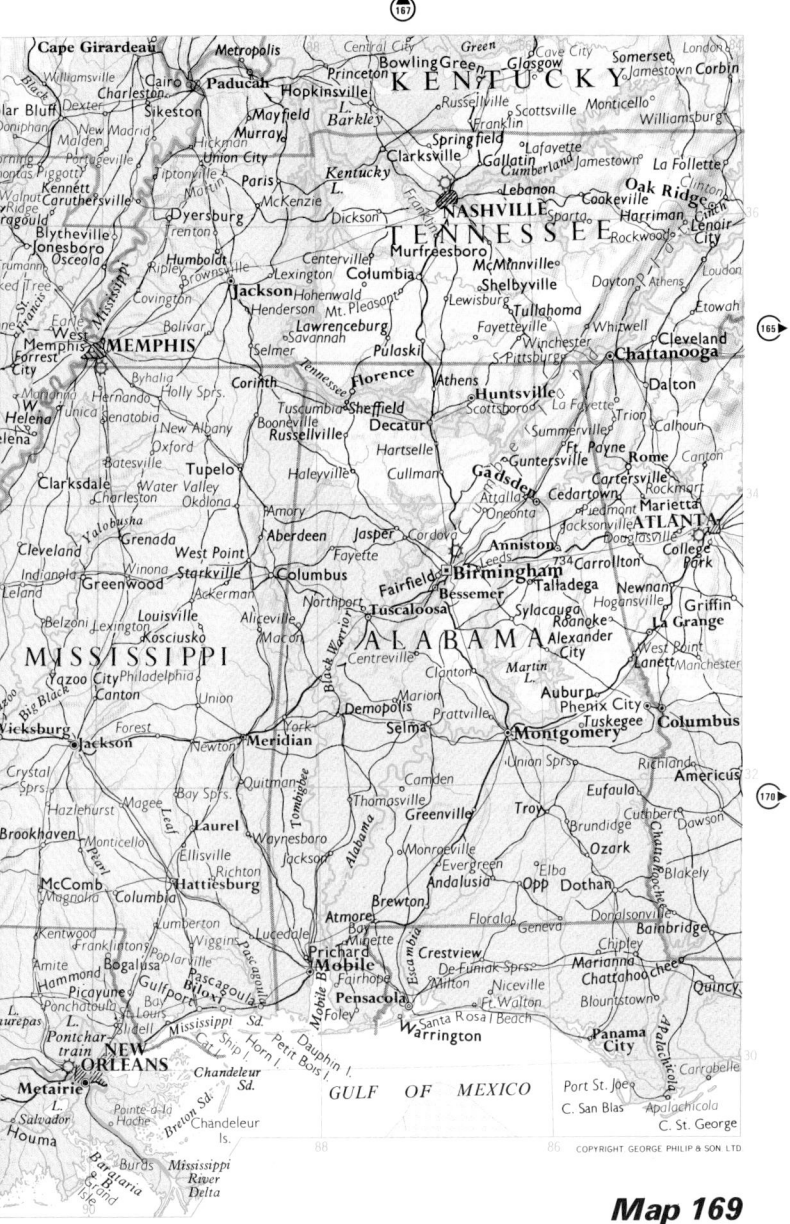

Cape Girardeau
Metropolis
Paducah
Cairo
Charleston
Sikeston
Williamsville
Poplar Bluff
Dexter
Doniphan
New Madrid
Malden
Portageville
Piggott
Kennett
Caruthersville
Walnut Ridge
Paragould
Blytheville
Jonesboro
Osceola
Trumann
St. Francis
Black
Hickman
Union City
Tiptonville
Martin
Dyersburg
Trenton
Humboldt
Ripley
Brownsville
Covington
Jackson
Bolivar
Earle
West Memphis
MEMPHIS
Forrest City
Mississippi
Byhalia
Holly Sprs.
Hernando
Marianna
Tunica
W. Helena
Helena
Senatobia
New Albany
Oxford
Batesville
Clarksdale
Charleston
Water Valley
Okolona
Tupelo
Yalobusha
Grenada
Cleveland
Indianola
Leland
Greenwood
Winona
Starkville
West Point
Ackerman
Columbus
Louisville
Belzoni
Lexington
Kosciusko
MISSISSIPPI
Yazoo City
Philadelphia
Canton
Big Black
Vicksburg
Jackson
Forest
Newton
Meridian
Union
Crystal Sprs.
Hazlehurst
Magee
Bay Sprs.
Quitman
Brookhaven
Monticello
Pearl
Leaf
Laurel
Ellisville
Waynesboro
Richton
McComb
Magnolia
Columbia
Hattiesburg
Lumberton
Wiggins
Lucedale
Kentwood
Franklinton
Poplarville
Amite
Hammond
Bogalusa
Picayune
Ponchatoula
Gulfport
Biloxi
Pascagoula
Bay St. Louis
Slidell
L. Maurepas
L. Pontchartrain
NEW ORLEANS
Metairie
L. Salvador
Houma
Pointe-a-la Hache
Breton Sd.
Chandeleur Is.
Chandeleur Sd.
Mississippi Sd.
Cat I.
Ship I.
Horn I.
Petit Bois I.
Dauphin I.
Barataria B.
Grand Isle
Burds
Mississippi River Delta
GULF OF MEXICO
Mayfield
Murray
Paris
McKenzie
Hopkinsville
Princeton
L. Barkley
Kentucky L.
Clarksville
Dickson
Centerville
Lexington
Hohenwald
Henderson
Selmer
Corinth
Tennessee
Savannah
Lawrenceburg
Mt. Pleasant
Columbia
Pulaski
Florence
Sheffield
Tuscumbia
Booneville
Russellville
Decatur
Hartselle
Haleyville
Cullman
Amory
Aberdeen
Jasper
Cordova
Fayette
Fairfield
Birmingham
Bessemer
Northport
Tuscaloosa
Aliceville
Macon
Black Warrior
Centreville
ALABAMA
Clanton
Marion
Demopolis
Prattville
Selma
York
Montgomery
Camden
Tombigbee
Thomasville
Greenville
Alabama
Jackson
Monroeville
Evergreen
Andalusia
Brewton
Atmore
Bay Minette
Prichard
Mobile
Mobile B.
Fairhope
Foley
Escambia
Pensacola
Milton
Crestview
De Funiak Sprs.
Niceville
Ft. Walton
Santa Rosa I. Beach
Warrington
Central City
Green
Bowling Green
Glasgow
Cave City
Somerset
London
Jamestown
Corbin
KENTUCKY
Russellville
Scottsville
Monticello
Franklin
Williamsburg
Springfield
Gallatin
Lafayette
Cumberland
Jamestown
La Follette
Clinton
Oak Ridge
Lebanon
Cookeville
NASHVILLE
Franklin
Sparta
Harriman
Clinch
Lenoir City
TENNESSEE
Rockwood
Murfreesboro
McMinnville
Shelbyville
Lewisburg
Tullahoma
Dayton
Athens
Loudon
Etowah
Fayetteville
Winchester
Whitwell
Cleveland
Chattanooga
S. Pittsburg
Athens
Huntsville
Dalton
Scottsboro
La Fayette
Trion
Calhoun
Summerville
Ft. Payne
Rome
Canton
Guntersville
Gadsden
Cartersville
Rockmart
Attalla
Oneonta
Cedartown
Piedmont
Marietta
ATLANTA
Jacksonville
Douglasville
Anniston
College Park
Leeds
734
Carrollton
Talladega
Newnan
Hogansville
Griffin
Sylacauga
Roanoke
La Grange
Alexander City
West Point
Lanett
Manchester
Martin L.
Auburn
Phenix City
Columbus
Tuskegee
Union Sprs.
Richland
Americus
Eufaula
Troy
Cuthbert
Dawson
Brundidge
Ozark
Elba
Opp
Dothan
Blakely
Chattahoochee
Florala
Geneva
Donalsonville
Bainbridge
Chipley
Marianna
Chattahoochee
Quincy
Blountstown
Panama City
Apalachicola
Carrabelle
Port St. Joe
C. San Blas
Apalachicola
C. St. George
88
86
84
90
36
34
32
30
COPYRIGHT GEORGE PHILIP & SON LTD

165

170

Map 169

U.S.A.: Florida

1:6 000 000

Map 170

COPYRIGHT GEORGE PHILIP & SON LTD.

U.S.A.: Columbia Basin

1:6 000 000

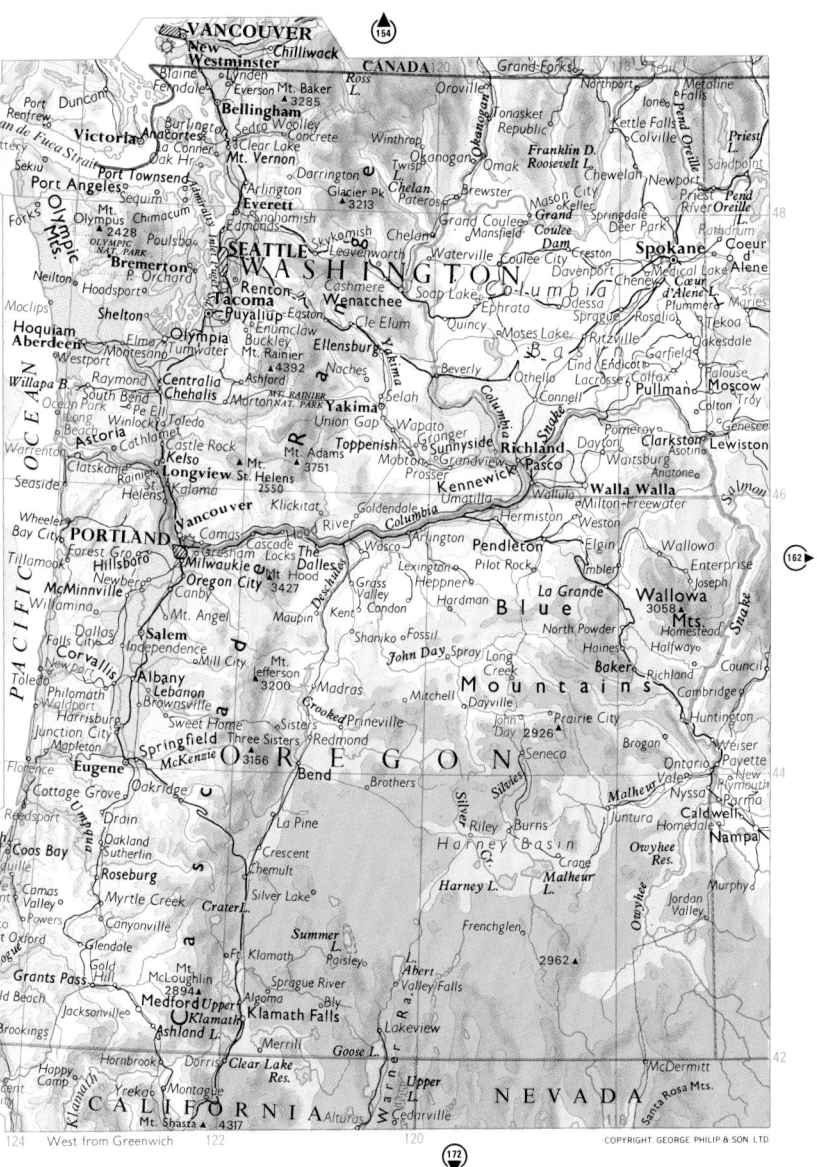

Map 171

U.S.A.: California

Map 172

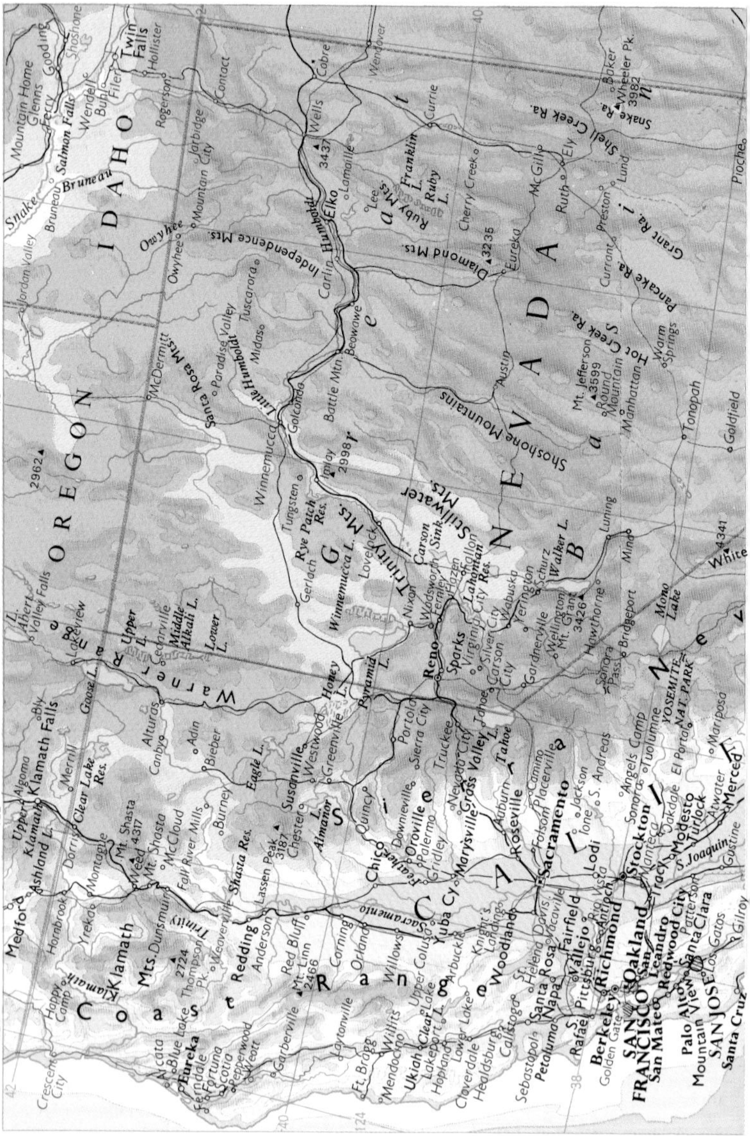

1:6 000 000

160
174
PACIFIC
OCEAN
MEXICO
ARIZONA
Coast Ranges
Sierra Nevada
Mojave Desert
LOS ANGELES
SAN DIEGO
SAN BERNARDINO
Long Beach
Santa Ana
Bakersfield
Fresno
Santa Barbara
San Luis Obispo
Monterey
Salinas
Las Vegas
Lake Mead
Hoover Dam
Death Valley
DEATH VALLEY NAT. MON.
Mt. Whitney 4418
Santa Lucia Range
Salton Sea
Colorado Aqueduct
Gila Bend Mts.
Imperial Dam
All American Canal
Mexicali
Tijuana
Yuma
Channel Is.
San Clemente I.
Santa Catalina I.
San Nicolas I.
Santa Rosa I.
Santa Cruz I.
West from Greenwich
114
116
118
120
32
34
36
38
© COPYRIGHT. GEORGE PHILIP & SON. LTD

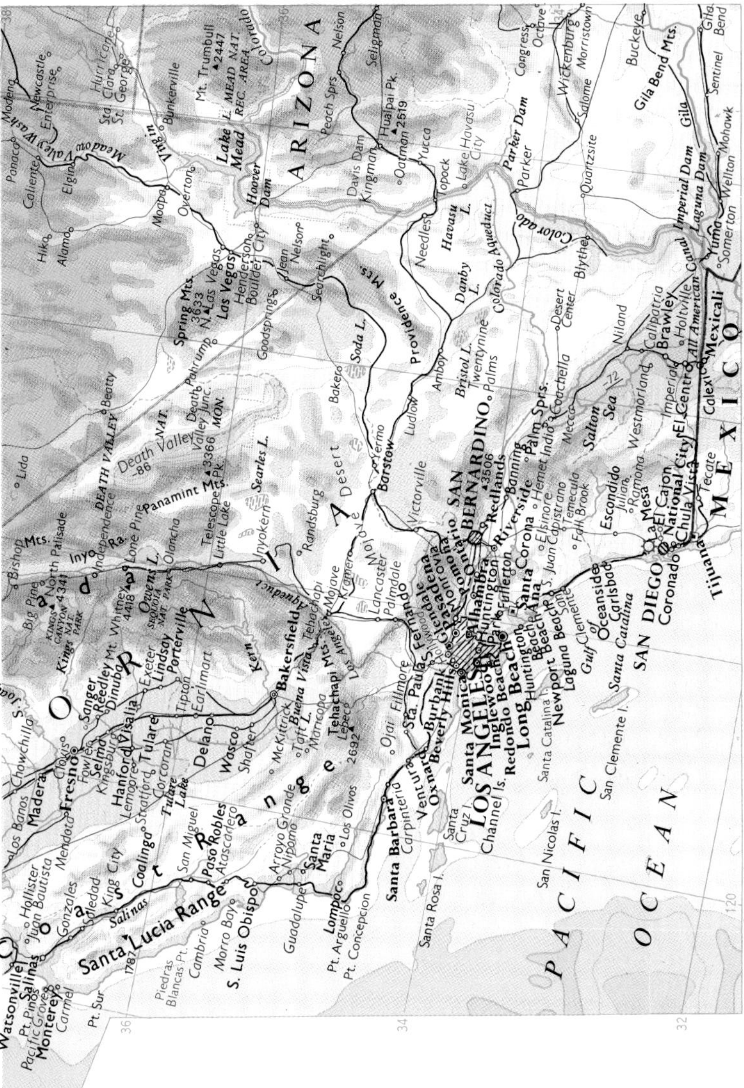

Map 173

Mexico: West

Map 174

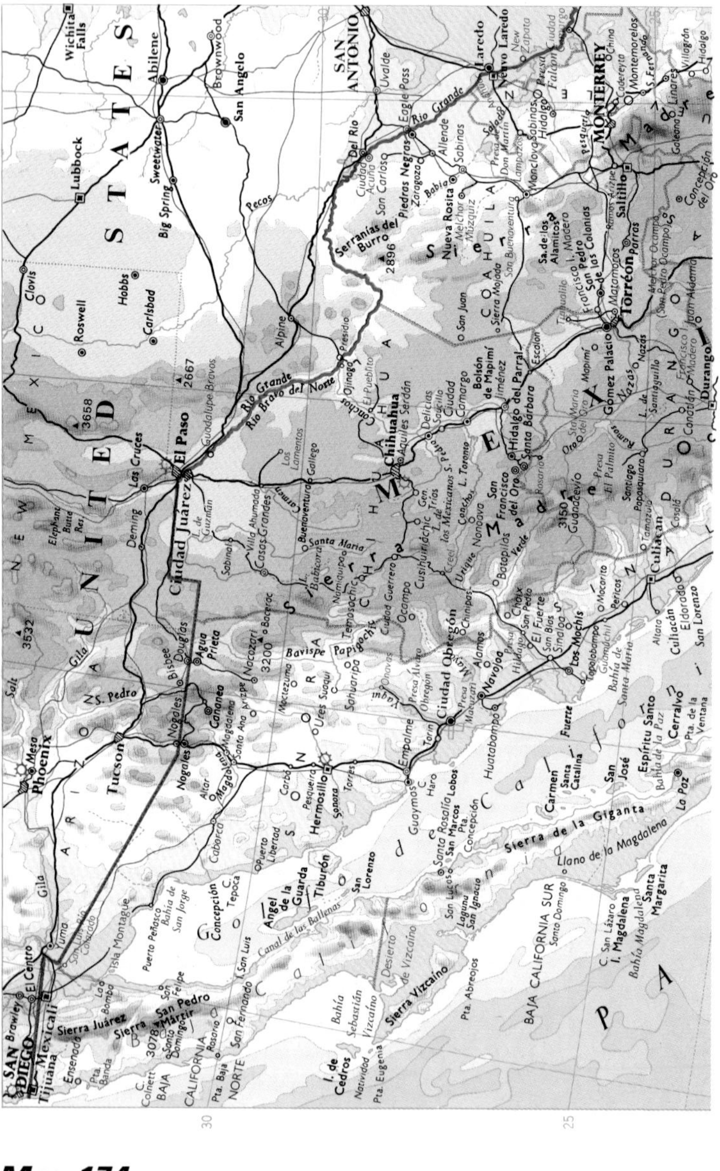

1:12 000 000

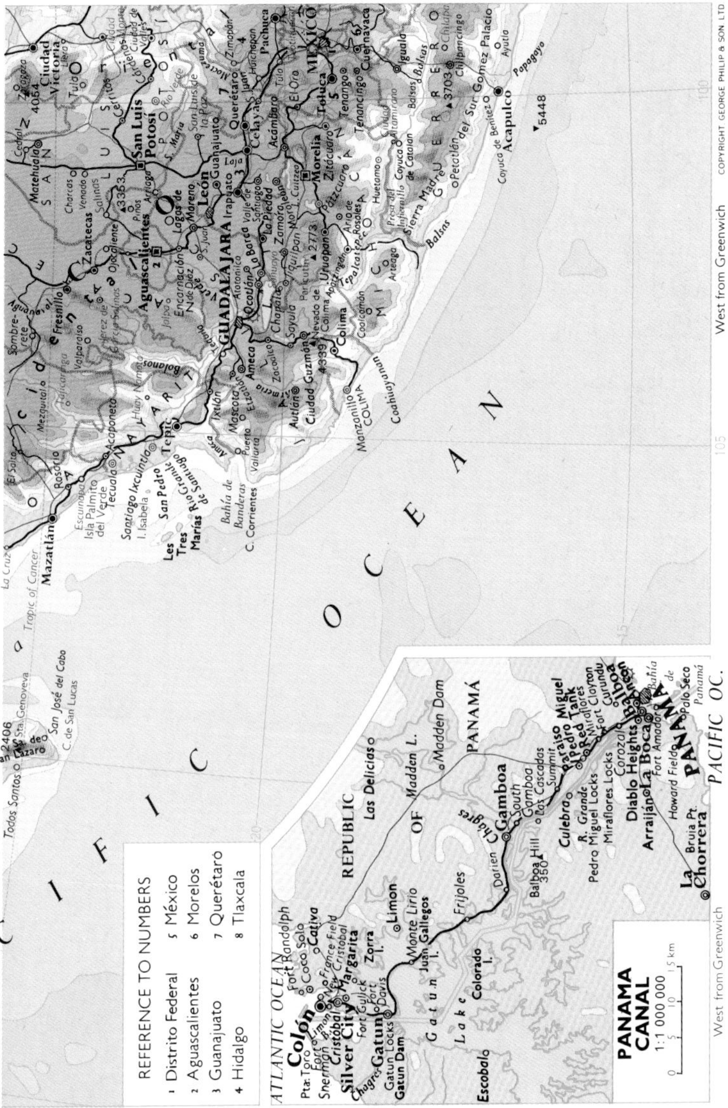

West from Greenwich

105

COPYRIGHT GEORGE PHILIP & SON LTD

MÉXICO

GUADALAJARA

San Luis Potosí

Ciudad Victoria

Aguascalientes

León · Guanajuato

Morelia

Toluca

Querétaro

Pachuca

Acapulco

Mazatlán

COLIMA

Colima

Manzanillo

Tepic

Zacatecas

Fresnillo

Irapuato

Tres Marías

I. Isabela

Islas de Revillagigedo

Tropic of Cancer

San José del Cabo

C. de San Lucas

Todos Santos

Bahía de Banderas

C. Corrientes

▲5448

▲3703

P A C I F I C   O C E A N

REFERENCE TO NUMBERS

1 Distrito Federal
2 Aguascalientes
3 Guanajuato
4 Hidalgo
5 México
6 Morelos
7 Querétaro
8 Tlaxcala

PANAMA CANAL

1:1 000 000

0   5   10   15 km

West from Greenwich

ATLANTIC OCEAN

Colón

Cristóbal

Silver City

Gatun Locks

Gatun Dam

Gatun Lake

Limón

Monte Lirio

Juan Gallegos

Frijoles

Colorado I.

Escobala

Madden L.

Madden Dam

Las Delicias

REPUBLIC

OF

PANAMÁ

Gamboa

Culebra

Pedro Miguel Locks

Miraflores Locks

Diablo Heights

Balboa

PANAMA

Fort Amador

Bahía de Panamá

La Bruja Pt.

Chorrera

PACIFIC OC.

West from Greenwich

Map 175

Mexico: East

158

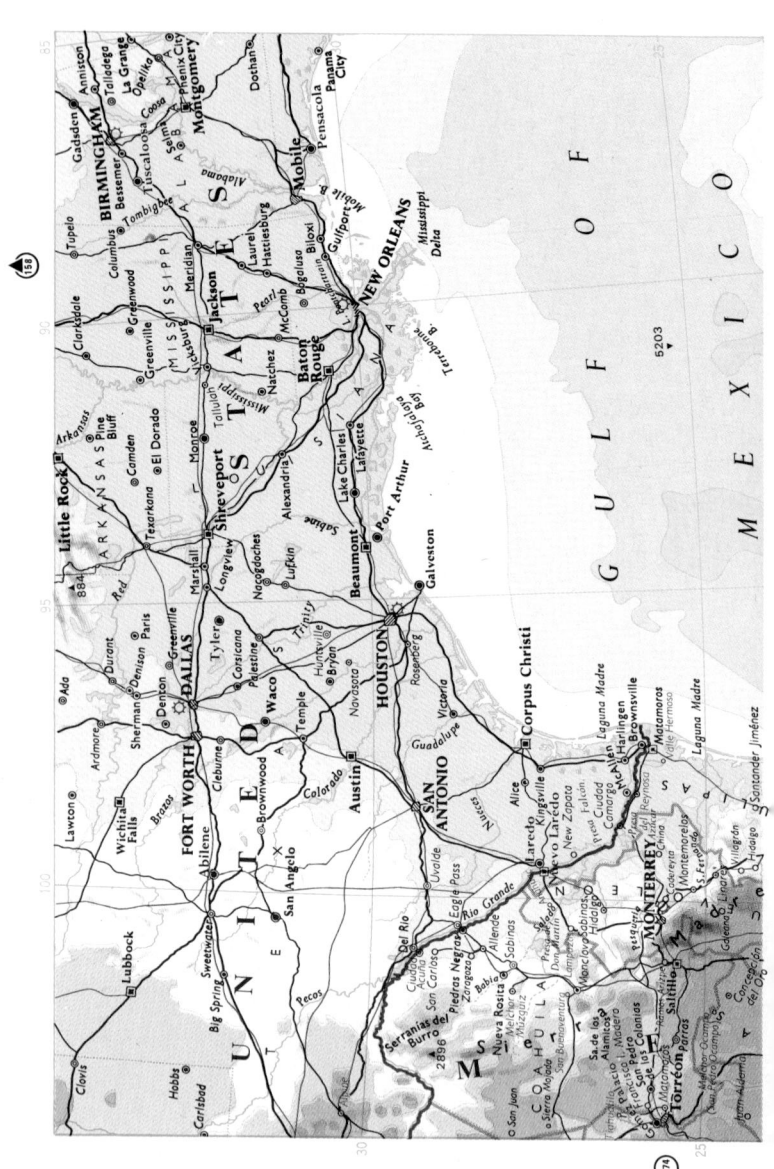
Little Rock
ARKANSAS
Pine Bluff
Camden
El Dorado
Texarkana
MISSISSIPPI
Clarksdale
Greenwood
Greenville
Vicksburg
Jackson
Meridian
Tupelo
Columbus
BIRMINGHAM
Bessemer
Tuscaloosa
Gadsden
Anniston
Talladega
La Grange
Opelika
Phenix City
Montgomery
Selma
ALABAMA
Dothan
Pensacola
Panama City
Mobile
Mobile B.
Biloxi
Gulfport
Hattiesburg
Laurel
Natchez
McComb
Bogalusa
Baton Rouge
NEW ORLEANS
Mississippi Delta
L. Pontchartrain
Terrebonne B.
Atchafalaya Bay
Lafayette
Lake Charles
Alexandria
Monroe
Tallulah
Shreveport
LOUISIANA
Port Arthur
Beaumont
Galveston
HOUSTON
Rosenberg
Lufkin
Nacogdoches
Longview
Marshall
Tyler
Corsicana
Palestine
Huntsville
Bryan
Navasota
Waco
Temple
Austin
DALLAS
FORT WORTH
Denton
Sherman
Denison
Paris
Greenville
Durant
Ardmore
Ada
Lawton
Wichita Falls
Abilene
Cleburne
Brownwood
San Angelo
Sweetwater
Big Spring
Lubbock
Clovis
Hobbs
Carlsbad
Pecos
UNITED STATES
TEXAS
SAN ANTONIO
Victoria
Corpus Christi
Alice
Kingsville
Laredo
Nuevo Laredo
Uvalde
Eagle Pass
Del Rio
Ciudad Acuña
Piedras Negras
Rio Grande
Brownsville
Harlingen
McAllen
Matamoros
Reynosa
MONTERREY
Saltillo
Torreón
COAHUILA
MEXICO
Monclova
Sabinas
Nueva Rosita
Serranías del Burro
2896
884
5203
GULF OF MEXICO
Laguna Madre
Red
Brazos
Colorado
Trinity
Sabine
Nueces
Guadalupe
Pearl
Alabama
Tombigbee
Coosa
Arkansas
Mississippi
85
90
95
100
30
25

174

Map 176

1:12 000 000

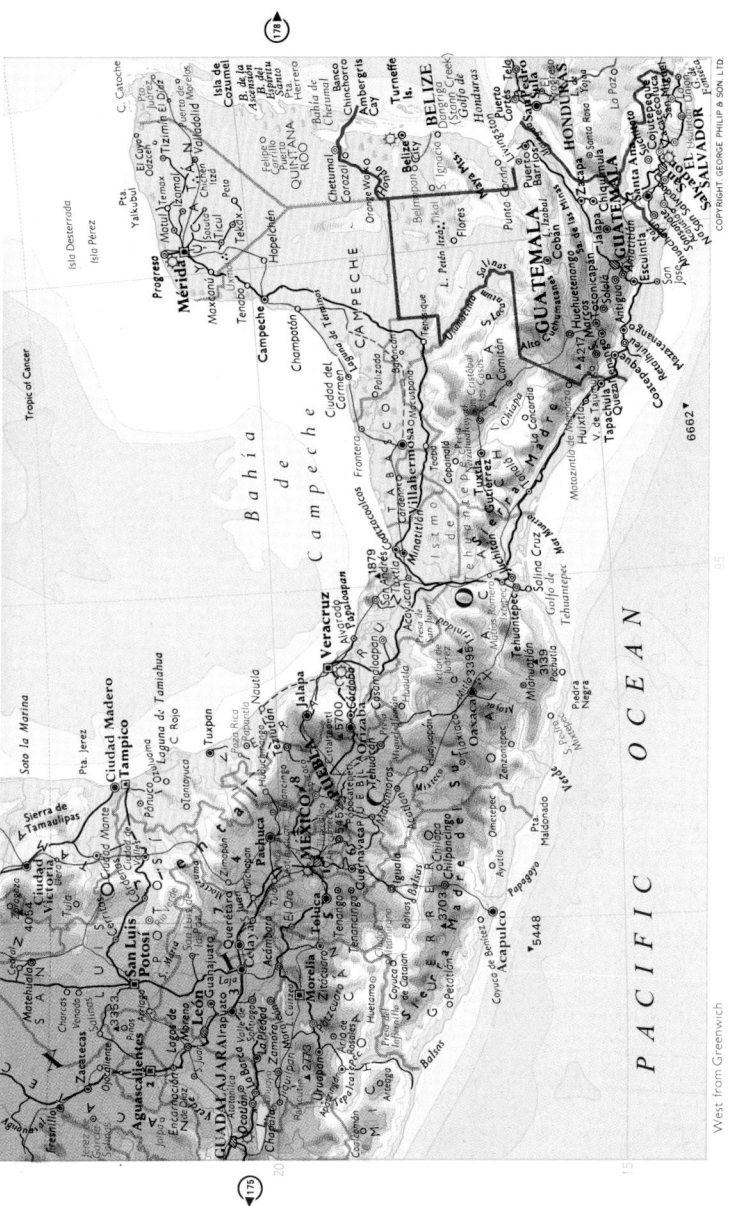

West from Greenwich

COPYRIGHT. GEORGE PHILIP & SON, LTD.

Map 177

Caribbean: West

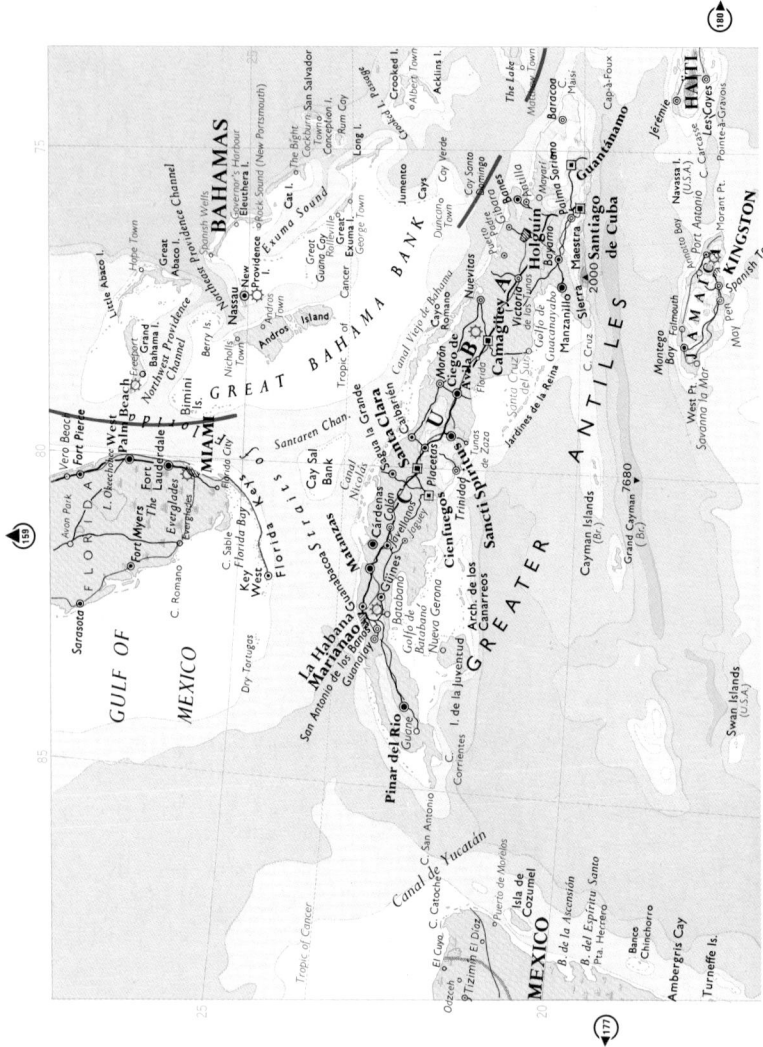

Map 178

1:12 000 000

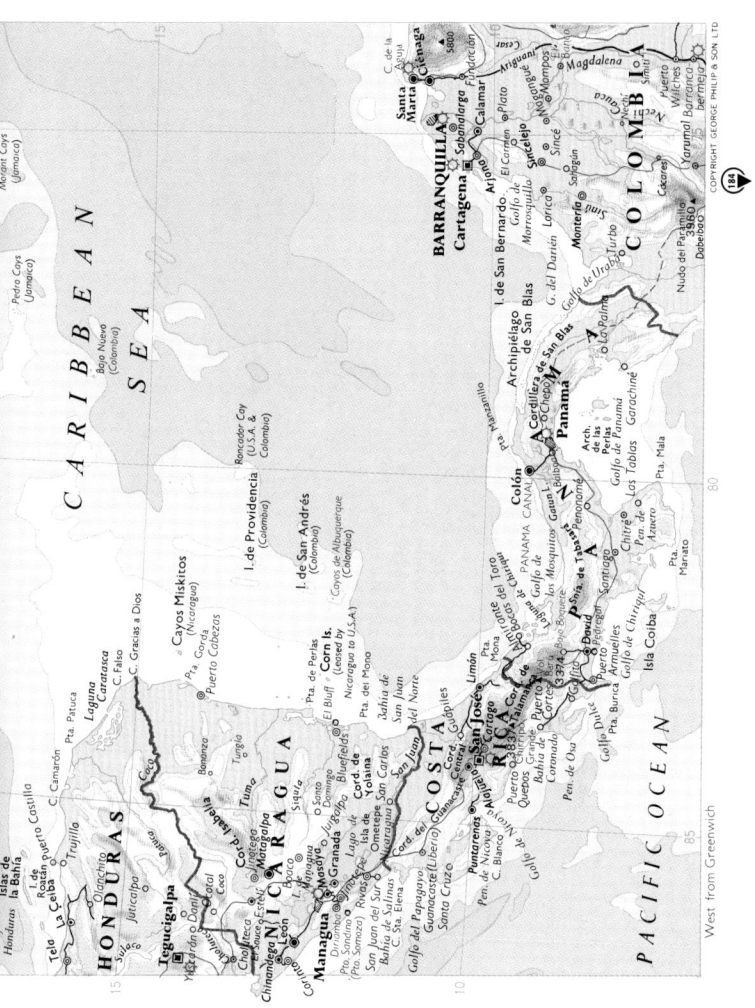
CARIBBEAN SEA
PACIFIC OCEAN
HONDURAS
NICARAGUA
COSTA RICA
PANAMA
COLOMBIA
Tegucigalpa
Managua
San José
Panamá
BARRANQUILLA
Cartagena
Santa Marta
Ciénaga
Colón
PANAMA CANAL
Limón
Puntarenas
León
Granada
Bluefields
Corn Is.
I. de Providencia
I. de San Andrés
Cayos Miskitos
C. Gracias a Dios
Pedro Cays (Jamaica)
Morant Cays (Jamaica)
Bajo Nuevo (Colombia)
Roncador Cay (U.S.A. & Colombia)
Golfo de Panamá
Golfo de Urabá
Golfo de Chiriquí
Golfo de Nicoya
Golfo del Papagayo
Lago de Nicaragua
Isla Coiba
Pen. de Azuero
Pen. de Osa
Archipiélago de San Blas
Arch. de las Perlas
David
Santiago
Chitré
Montería
Sincelejo
Magdalena
West from Greenwich
COPYRIGHT GEORGE PHILIP & SON LTD

Map 179

Caribbean: East

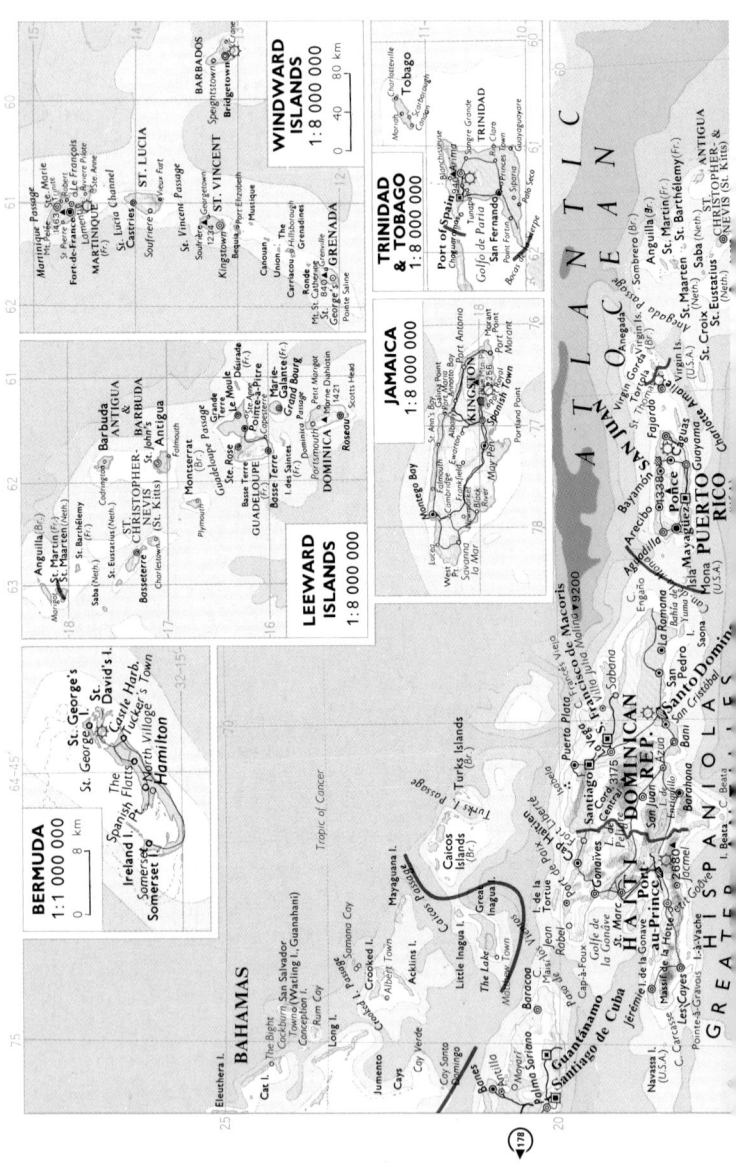

BERMUDA
1:1 000 000
0   8 km

St. George's
St. George I.
St. David's I.
Castle Harb.
The
Spanish Point
Flatts
Tucker's Town
Ireland I.
North Village
Hamilton
Somerset I.
Somerset

BAHAMAS

Eleuthera I.
Cat I.
The Bight
Cockburn Town
San Salvador
(Watling I. Guanahani)
Conception I.
Rum Cay
Long I.
Crooked I. Passage
Samana Cay
Jumento
Cays
Crooked I.
Albert Town
Acklins I.
Little Inagua I.
Mayaguana I.
Great
Inagua
Matthew Town
Cay Verde
Cay Santo
Domingo

Tropic of Cancer

Caicos Islands (Br.)

Turks Islands (Br.)

Turks I. Passage

LEEWARD ISLANDS
1:8 000 000

Anguilla (Br.)
St. Martin (Fr.)
St. Maarten (Neth.)
St. Barthélemy (Fr.)
Saba (Neth.)
St. Eustatius (Neth.)
Basseterre
Charlestown
ST. CHRISTOPHER-
NEVIS
(St. Kitts)
Barbuda
ANTIGUA &
BARBUDA
St. John's
Antigua
Plymouth
Montserrat

GUADELOUPE
Basse Terre
Basse Terre
Grande
Terre
Pointe-à-Pitre
Marie-
Galante (Fr.)
Grand Bourg
Les Saintes
1421
Petit Mangot
DOMINICA
Portsmouth
Roseau
Scotts Head
Dominica Passage

Martinique Passage
St. Pierre
Ste. Marie
Montagne
Pelée 1463
Fort-de-France
Le François
Rivière Pilote
Ste. Anne
MARTINIQUE
St. Lucia Channel
Castries
ST. LUCIA
Soufrière
Vieux Fort
St. Vincent Passage
Kingstown
ST. VINCENT
Georgetown
Bequia
Port Elizabeth
Mustique
Canouan
Union I.
The
Carriacou
Grenadines
Hillsborough
Mt. St. Catherine
840
Grenville
St.
George's
GRENADA
Pointe Saline

WINDWARD ISLANDS
1:8 000 000
0   40   80 km

BARBADOS
Speightstown
Bridgetown

TRINIDAD & TOBAGO
1:8 000 000

Charlotteville
Tobago
Scarborough
Port of Spain
Chaguaramas
Arima
Sangre Grande
TRINIDAD
Rio Claro
San Fernando
Siparia
Princes Town
Guayaguayare
Galfo de Paria
Icacos Point
Bocas del Dragón

JAMAICA
1:8 000 000

Montego Bay
Lucea
Falmouth
Savanna
la Mar
West End
St. Ann's Bay
Ocho Rios
Oracabessa
Port Maria
Port Antonio
Spanish Town
KINGSTON
May Pen
Portland Point
Morant Bay
Morant Point

A T L A N T I C   O C E A N

SAN JUAN

Virgin Gorda (Br.)
Anegada (Br.)
Sombrero (Br.)
Virgin Islands
St. Thomas
Tortola (Br.)
St. John
Virgin Is.
(U.S.A.)
St. Croix (U.S.A.)
Anguilla (Br.)
St. Martin (Fr.)
St. Barthélemy (Fr.)
St. Maarten (Neth.)
Saba (Neth.)
St. Eustatius (Neth.)
ANTIGUA
CHRISTOPHER-
NEVIS (St. Kitts)

PUERTO
RICO
(U.S.A.)
Arecibo
Bayamón
1338
San Juan
Fajardo
Aguadilla
Mayagüez
Caguas
Guayama
Ponce
Mona I.

HISPANIOLA

DOMINICAN
REP.
Puerto Plata
Santiago
3175
San Francisco de Macorís
Moca
3087
La Vega
San Juan
Barahona
C. Beata
I. Beata
Azua
Bani
San Cristóbal
Santo Domingo
San Pedro
La Romana
Higüey
C. Engaño
Saona
Bahía de
Ocoa

HAITI
Port-de-Paix
Tortue
Môle St. Nicolas
Gonaïves
St. Marc
Golfe de
la Gonâve
I. de la
Gonâve
Port-au-Prince
2680
Jacmel
Les Cayes
Jérémie
Massif de la Hotte
I. à Vache
Pointe-à-Gravois
Cap-à-Foux

GREATER   ANTILLES

Santiago de Cuba
Guantánamo
Baracoa
Punta de Maisí
9200
Maestra Palma Soriano
Windward Passage

Navassa I. (U.S.A.)

Map 180

1:12 000 000

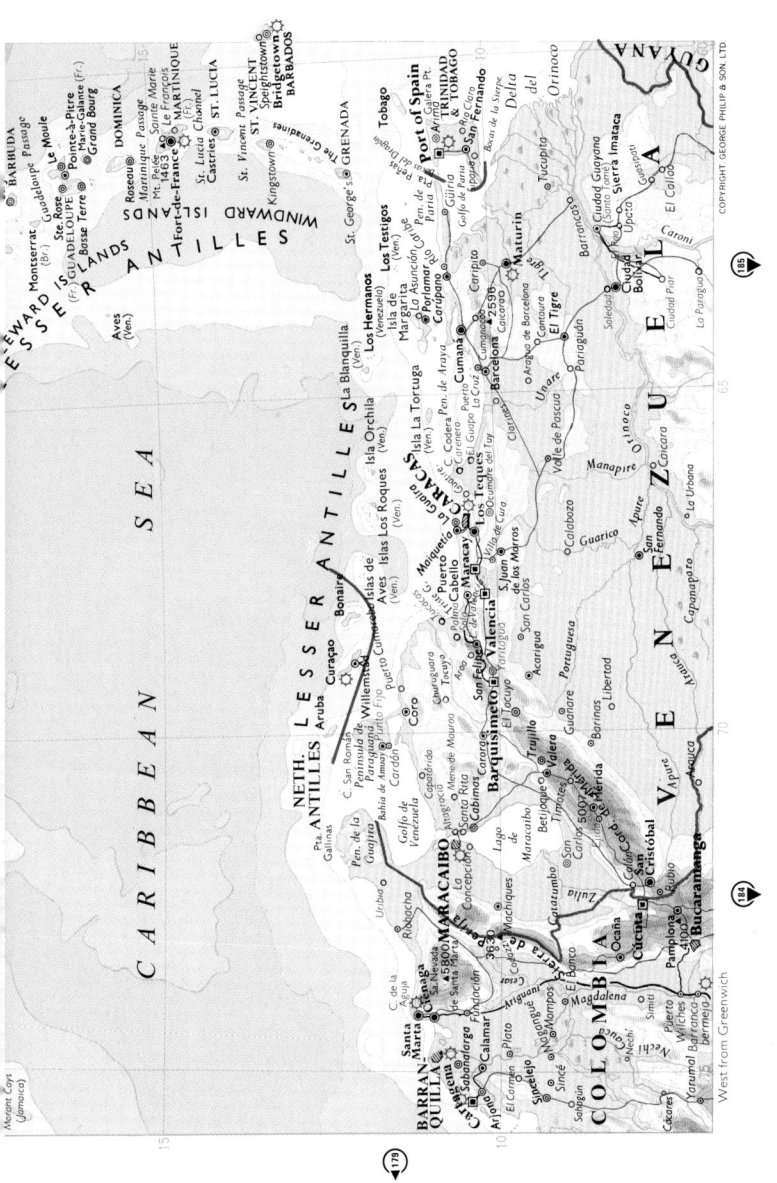

CARIBBEAN SEA
LESSER ANTILLES
NETH. ANTILLES
LEEWARD ISLANDS
WINDWARD ISLANDS
BARBUDA
Montserrat (Br.)
Guadeloupe Passage
GUADELOUPE (Fr.)
Le Moule
Ste. Rose
Pointe-à-Pitre
Basse Terre
Marie-Galante (Fr.)
Grand Bourg
DOMINICA
Roseau
Martinique Passage
Mt. Pelée 1463
Sainte Marie
Le François
Fort-de-France
MARTINIQUE (Fr.)
St. Lucia Channel
Castries
ST. LUCIA
St. Vincent Passage
ST. VINCENT
Kingstown
Speightstown
Bridgetown
BARBADOS
The Grenadines
St. George's
GRENADA
Tobago
Port of Spain
Galera Pt.
Arima
TRINIDAD & TOBAGO
San Fernando
Bocas del Dragón
Pen. de Paria
Golfo de Paria
Bocas de la Sierpe
Delta del Orinoco
Aves (Ven.)
Los Hermanos (Venezuela)
Los Testigos (Ven.)
La Blanquilla (Ven.)
Isla de Margarita
Porlamar
La Asunción
Carúpano
Güiria
Isla Orchila (Ven.)
Isla La Tortuga (Ven.)
Islas Los Roques (Ven.)
Islas de Aves (Ven.)
Bonaire
Curaçao
Willemstad
Aruba
Pta. Gallinas
C. San Román
Península de Paraguaná
Punto Fijo
Cardón
Pen. de la Guajira
Golfo de Venezuela
Bahía de Amuay
Coro
CARACAS
La Guaira
Maiquetía
Los Teques
Maracay
Valencia
Puerto Cabello
Barquisimeto
San Felipe
Carora
Cumaná
Barcelona
Maturín
Caripito
El Tigre
Ciudad Guayana
Ciudad Bolívar
Sierra Imataca
El Callao
Tucupita
Barrancas
Caroní
Orinoco
Apure
San Fernando
Calabozo
Valle de Pascua
Guarico
Manapire
Caicara
Capanaparo
Arauca
Barinas
Guanare
Acarigua
Portuguesa
Trujillo
Valera
Mérida
San Cristóbal
Lago de Maracaibo
MARACAIBO
Cabimas
Santa Rita
Machiques
Zulia
Catatumbo
Cúcuta
Pamplona
Bucaramanga
Ocaña
El Banco
Magdalena
Barrancabermeja
Puerto Wilches
Cartagena
BARRANQUILLA
Santa Marta
Ciénaga
Sa. Nevada de Santa Marta 5800
Riohacha
Uribia
Sincelejo
Sincé
Mompós
Calamar
Plato
Fundación
Cesar
COLOMBIA
VENEZUELA
GUYANA
Morant Cays (Jamaica)
West from Greenwich
COPYRIGHT. GEORGE PHILIP & SON. LTD.

184

185

179

Map 181

South America: Physical

1:50 000 000

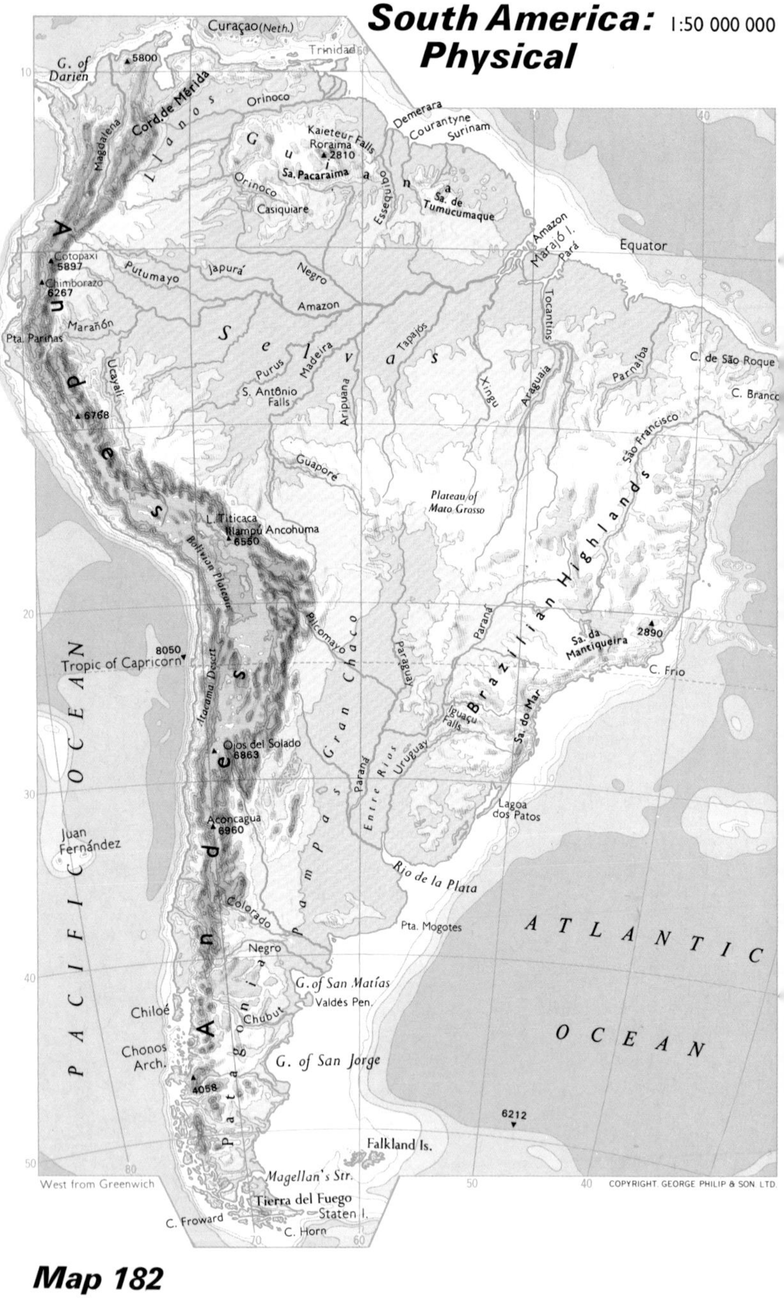

Curaçao (Neth.)

Trinidad

G. of Darién ▲5800

Orinoco

Llanos

Kaieteur Falls

Roraima ▲2810

Demerara

Courantyne

Surinam

G u i a n a

Orinoco

Sa. Pacaraima

Sa. de Tumucumaque

Casiquiare

Amazon

Marajó I.

Pará

Equator

Cotopaxi 5897

Putumayo

Japurá

Negro

Tocantins

▲Chimborazo 6267

Marañón

Amazon

Pta. Pariñas

S e l v a s

Purus

Madeira

Tapajós

C. de São Roque

Ucayali

▲6768

S. António Falls

Aripuaná

Xingu

Araguaia

Parnaiba

C. Branco

Guaporé

Plateau of Mato Grosso

São Francisco

A n d e s

L. Titicaca

Illampú Ancohuma 6550

Bolivian Plateau

Alto mayo

B r a z i l i a n   H i g h l a n d s

Tropic of Capricorn

8050

Gran Chaco

Paraguay

Paraná

Sa. da Mantiqueira ▲2890

C. Frio

Atacama Desert

Ojos del Solado 6863

Pampas

Sa. do Mar

Iguaçu Falls

Aconcagua ▲6960

Paraná

Entre Rios

Uruguay

Lagoa dos Patos

Juan Fernández

Colorado

Río de la Plata

Negro

Pta. Mogotes

A T L A N T I C

Chiloé

G. of San Matías

Valdés Pen.

P a t a g o n i a

Chubut

Chonos Arch.

G. of San Jorge

O C E A N

P A C I F I C   O C E A N

A n d e s

▲4058

6212

Falkland Is.

West from Greenwich

Magellan's Str.

Tierra del Fuego

Staten I.

C. Froward

C. Horn

Map 182

South America: Political

1:50 000 000

Map 183

Barranquilla
Maracaibo
G. of Darien
Cartagena
La Guaira
Curaçao (Neth.)
Trinidad & Tobago
Caracas
Barquisimeto
Bucaramanga
Orinoco
VENEZUELA
Georgetown
GUYANA
Paramaribo
Medellín
Manizales
Bogotá
SURINAM
FR. GUIANA
Cayenne
Cali
COLOMBIA
Orinoco
Casiquiare
Quito
ECUADOR
Guayaquil
Cuenca
Marañón
Putumayo
Japurá
Negro
Amazon
Pará
Equator
Belém
São Luís (Maranhão)
Iquitos
Ucayali
Manaus
Tocantins
Teresina
Parnaíba
Fortaleza (Ceará)
Natal
Chiclayo
Trujillo
Purus
Madeira
Aripuana
Tapajós
Xingu
Araguaia
Paulistana
São Francisco
João Pessoa
Recife (Pernambuco)
Maceió
PERU
Callão
Lima
Cuzco
Guaporé
B R A Z I L
Salvador (Bahia)
Titicaca
BOLIVIA
Cuiabá
Goiânia
Brasília
Arequipa
La Paz
Mollendo
Tacna
Oruro
Cochabamba
Santa Cruz
Sucre
Corumbá
Pirapora
Belo Horizonte
Arica
Iquique
Tropic of Capricorn
Antofagasta
PARAGUAY
Paraná
Ribeirão Prêto
Campinas
Niteroi
São Paulo
Curitiba
Santos
Rio de Janeiro
Pilcomayo
Asunción
Iguaçu Falls
Paraná
Tucumán
20
Juan Fernández (Chile)
ARGENTINA
Córdoba
Mendoza
Rosario
Santa Fé
Paraná
URUGUAY
Pôrto Alegre
Lagoa dos Patos
Rio Grande do Sul
Viña del Mar
Valparaíso
Santiago
Talca
Buenos Aires
La Plata
Montevideo
Río de la Plata
Concepción
Colorado
Temuco
Bahía Blanca
Pta. Mogotes
Valdivia
Negro
Chubut
G. of San Matías
Puerto Montt
Chiloé
Chonos Arch.
G. of San Jorge
A T L A N T I C   O C E A N
Patagonia
Arenas
Magellan's Str.
Falkland Is. (Br.)
Stanley
Tierra del Fuego
Staten I.
C. Horn

P A C I F I C   O C E A N

West from Greenwich

COPYRIGHT GEORGE PHILIP & SON. LTD

Map 183

South America: North West

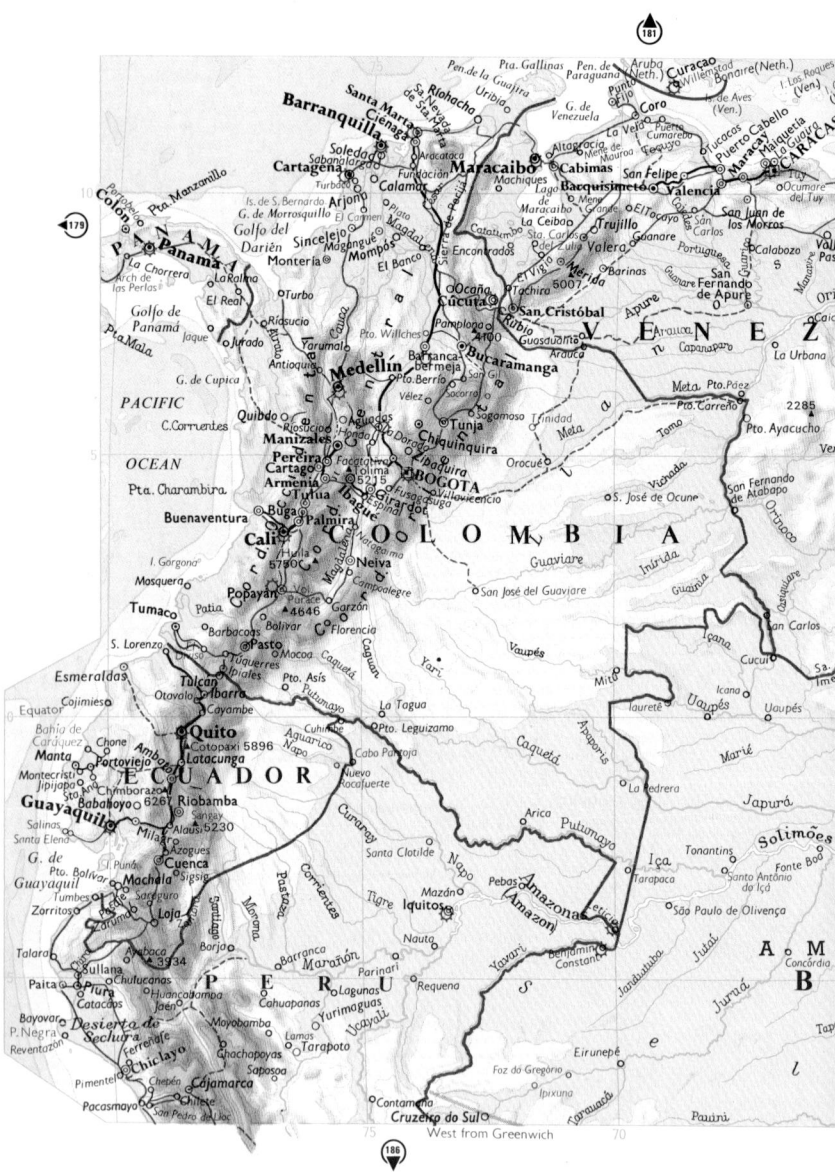

Pta. Gallinas
Pen. de la Guajira
Pta. Gallinas
Pen. de Paraguaná
Aruba
Curaçao
I. Los Roques (Ven.)
Uribia
Punta Fijo
Willemstad
Bonaire (Neth.)
I. de Aves (Ven.)

Santa Marta
Riohacha
S. Nevada
de Sta. Marta
G. de Venezuela
Coro
Pto. Cumarebo
Puerto Cabello
Maiquetía
CARACAS
Barranquilla
Ciénaga
Altagracia
La Vela
Maracay
Ocumare del Tuy

Soledad
Aracataca
Fundación
Maracaibo
Machiques
Lago de Maracaibo
Cabimas
San Felipe
Valencia
San Juan de los Morros

Cartagena
Calamar
Pivijay
Bacquisimeto
Val
Pas

Is. de S. Bernardo
Arjona
El Carmen
Turbaco
Magangue
Plato
La Ceiba
Sta. Carlos del Zulia
Trujillo
Valera
Barinas

Colón
Pta. Manzanillo
Sincelejo
Mompós
El Banco
Catatumbo
Mérida 5007
Guanare
San Fernando de Apure

PANAMÁ
Panamá
Golfo del Darién
Montería
Encontrados
Portuguesa

La Chorrera
La Palma
Arch. de las Perlas
El Real
Turbo
Ocaña
Pto. Willches
Pamplona
Cúcuta
San Cristóbal
Táchira 5007
Rubio
Guasdualito
Arauca
La Urbana

Golfo de Panamá
Pta. Mala
Jaque
Jurado
Riosucio
Yarumal
Barranca bermeja
San Gil
Socorro
Bucaramanga
Meta
Pto. Páez
Pto. Carreño
2285

PACIFIC
C. Corrientes
Quibdó
Riosucio
Antioquia
Medellín
Pto. Berrío
Vélez
Chiquinquirá
Tunja
Sogamoso
Trinidad
Meta
Orocué
San José de Ocune
Pto. Ayacucho
Ver

OCEAN
Pta. Charambira
Manizales
Pereira
Cartago
Armenia
Tuluá
Ibagué
Facatativá
BOGOTÁ
Villavicencio
Fusagasugá
Guáitara

Buenaventura
I. Gorgona
Buga
Palmira
Cali
COLOMBIA
Huila 5750
Neiva
Campoalegre
Guaviare
Guainía
Inírida
San Fernando de Atabapo

Mosquera
Popayán
Puracé 4646
Garzón
Florencia
San José del Guaviare
Orinoco
San Carlos

Tumaco
Patía
Barbacoas
Bolívar
Mocoa
Caquetá
Yarí
Vaupés
Mitú
Içana
San Carlos

S. Lorenzo
Túquerres
Ipiales
Pto. Asís
Putumayo
La Tagua
Cuçuí
Sa.
Íme

Esmeraldas
Cojimíes
Tulcán
Otavalo
Ibarra
Cayambe
Pto. Leguizamo
Caquetá
Apaporis
Iaureté
Uaupés
Uaupés

Equator
Bahía de Caráquez
Chone
Amba
Quito
Cotopaxi 5896
Latacunga
Aguarico
Napo
Nuevo Rocafuerte
Cabo Pantoja
Marié

Manta
Montecristi
Jipijapa
Sto. Ana
Portoviejo
ECUADOR
Riobamba
Chimborazo 6267
Curaray
Santa Clotilde
Arica
Putumayo
Içá
Japurá
La Pedrera
Santo Antônio do Içá
Solimões
Fonte Boa

Guayaquil
Salinas
Santa Elena
Milagro
Alausí 5230
Azogues
Sigsig
Cuenca
Pastaza
Mazán
Napo
Pebas
Amazonas
(Amazon)
Iça
Tarapacá
Tonantins
São Paulo de Olivença

G. de Guayaquil
Pto. Bolívar
Machala
Zorritos
Tumbes
Sozoranga
Loja
Santiago
Tigre
Iquitos
Nauta
Yavarí
Benjamim Constant
Jutaí
A.
M
B

Talara
Sullana
Ayabaca 3934
Morona
Borjo
Marañón
Barranca
Parinari
Requena
Juruá
Concórdia

Paita
Piura
Catacaos
Huancabamba
Jaén
Lagunas
Cahuapanas
Yurimaguas
Ucayali
Janduaíba

Bayovar
P. Negra
Reventazón
Desierto de Sechura
Ferreñafe
Moyobamba
Lamas
Tarapoto
Saposoa
PERU
S.
Eirunepé

Pimentel
Chiclayo
Chepén
Cajamarca
Chachapoyas
Ipixuna
Foz do Gregório
Pauiní

Pacasmayo
San Pedro de Lloc
Chilete
Contamana
Cruzeiro do Sul
Tarauacá

West from Greenwich

75 · · · · · · 70

Map 184

184

1:16 000 000

Map 185

COPYRIGHT GEORGE PHILIP & SON LTD

South America: West

184

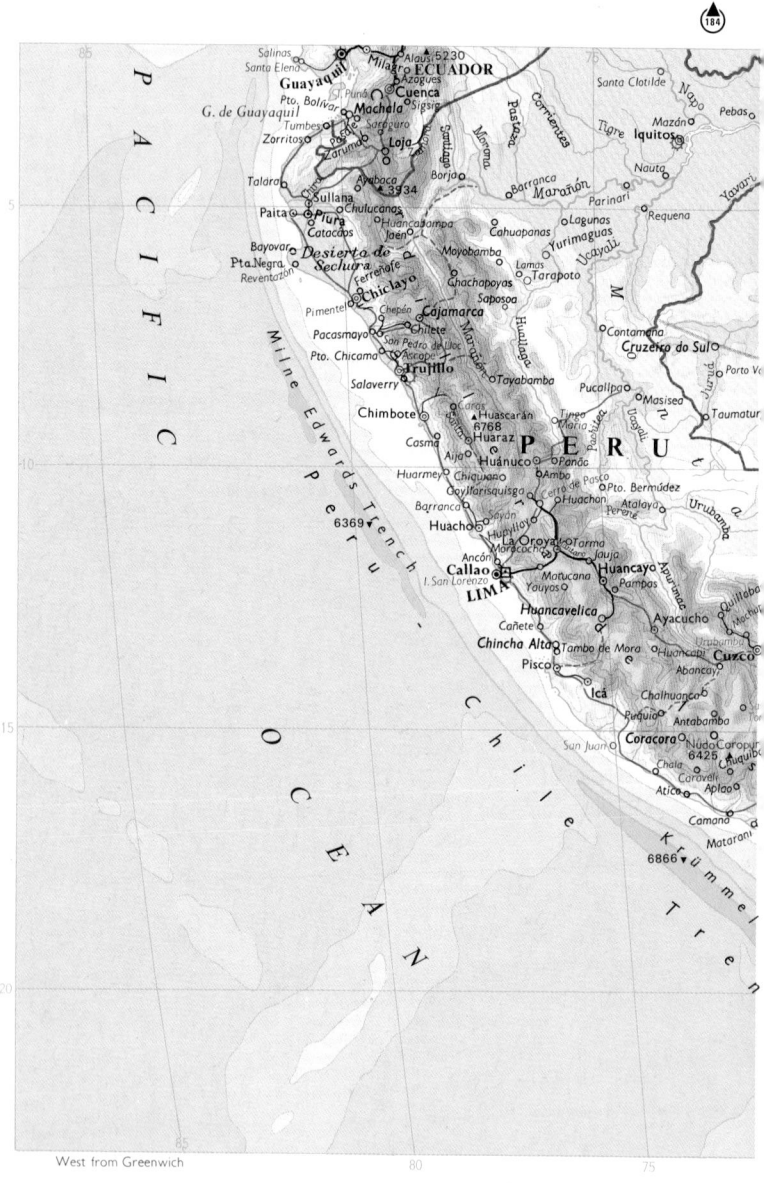

PACIFIC
OCEAN
Milne Edwards Trench
Peru - Chile Trench
Krümmel Trench
ECUADOR
PERU
Guayaquil
Salinas
Santa Elena
G. de Guayaquil
Pto. Bolívar
Machala
Cuenca
Azogues
Alausí 5230
Milagro
Sigsig
Saraguro
Tumbes
Zorritos
Zaruma
Loja
Talara
Sullana
Ayabaca
3934
Paita
Piura
Catacaos
Chulucanas
Huancabamba
Jaén
Bayovar
Pta.Negra
Reventazón
Desierto de Sechura
Ferreñafe
Chiclayo
Pimentel
Chepén
Cajamarca
Chilete
Pacasmayo
San Pedro de Lloc
Pto. Chicama
Ascope
Trujillo
Salaverry
Chimbote
Casma
Huaraz
Huascarán 6768
Aija
Huarmey
Chiquián
Barranca
Huacho
Sayán
Huaylloy
Ancón
Callao
LIMA
I. San Lorenzo
Matucana
Yauyos
La Oroya
Morococha
Tarma
Jauja
Huancayo
Pampas
Huancavelica
Cañete
Chincha Alta
Tambo de Mora
Pisco
Icá
San Juan
Coracora
Chala
Atico
Caravelí
Aplao
Camaná
Matarani
6866
6369
Huánuco
Ambo
Panao
Goyllarisquisga
Cerro de Pasco
Huachón
Pto. Bermúdez
Atalaya
Perené
Urubamba
Apurimac
Ayacucho
Huancapí
Andahuaylas
Abancay
Cuzco
Chalhuanca
Puquio
Antabamba
Nudo Coropuna
6425
Chuquibamba
Tayabamba
Pucallpa
Masisea
Tingo María
Pachitea
Ucayali
Huallaga
Marañón
Contamana
Cruzeiro do Sul
Porto Velho
Taumaturgo
Juruá
Saposoa
Chachapoyas
Moyobamba
Lamas
Tarapoto
Yurimaguas
Lagunas
Cahuapanas
Borja
Barranca
Parinari
Requena
Nauta
Iquitos
Mazán
Pebas
Napo
Santa Clotilde
Tigre
Corrientes
Pastaza
Morona
Santiago
Zamora
Yavari
West from Greenwich
85
80
75
5
10
15
20

Map 186

1:16 000 000

185

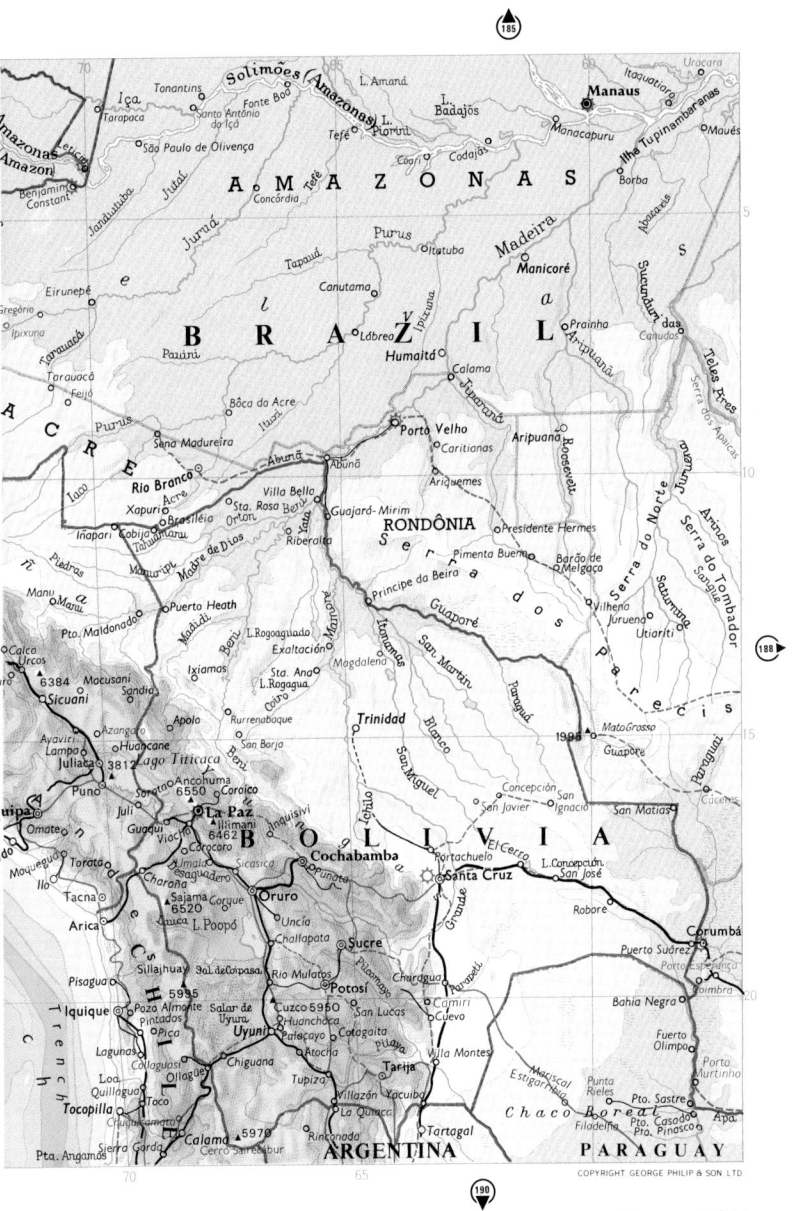

Solimões (Amazonas)
Amazonas (Amazon)
Tonantins
Içá
Tarapacá
Fonte Boa
Santo Antônio do Içá
L. Amaná
L. Badajós
L. Piorini
Tefé
São Paulo de Olivença
Leticia
Benjamin Constant
Coari
Codajás
Manaus
Itaquatiara
Manacapuru
Uracara
Maués
Ilha Tupinambaranas
Borba
AMAZONAS
Concórdia
Jandiatuba
Jutaí
Juruá
Purus
Itatuba
Madeira
Manicoré
Abacaxis
Sucunduri
Tapauá
Canutama
Eirunepé
Ipixuna
Tarauacá
Feijó
Pauini
Lábrea
Humaitá
Prainha
Aripuanã
Calama
Jiparaná
Canudos
Teles Pires
Serra dos Apiacás
BRAZIL
Bôca do Acre
Ituxi
Sena Madureira
Porto Velho
Caritianas
Aripuanã
Roosevelt
ACRE
Abunã
Rio Branco
Iaco
Acre
Xapuri
Brasiléia
Villa Bella
Sta. Rosa
Orton
Beni
Guajará-Mirim
Ariquemes
RONDÔNIA
Presidente Hermes
Juruena
Arinos
Serra do Norte
Serra do Tombador
Sangue
Iñapari
Cobija
Tahuamanu
Manuripi
Madre de Dios
Riberalta
Yata
Piedras
Pimenta Bueno
Barão de Melgaço
Serra dos Parecis
Principe da Beira
Vilhena
Juruena
Utiariti
Saturnina
Manu
Puerto Heath
Pto. Maldonado
Madidi
L.Rogoaguado
Mamoré
Itonamas
Guaporé
San Martin
Exaltación
Magdalena
Paraguá
Calca
Urcos
6384
Macusani
Sandia
Sicuani
Ixiamas
Sta. Ana
L.Rogagua
Coíro
Rurrenabaque
Apolo
Azángaro
Ayaviri
Lampa
Huancane
Juliaca
3812
Lago Titicaca
Puno
Trinidad
Blanco
San Borja
San Miguel
Mato Grosso
1995
Guaporé
Paraguai
Cáceres
Ichilo
Concepción
San Javier
San Ignacio
San Matias
Sorata
Ancohuma
6550
Coroico
La Paz
Illimani
6462
Inquisivi
Juli
Guaqui
Viacha
Omate
Corocoro
BOLIVIA
El Cerro
Portachuelo
Cochabamba
Santa Cruz
L. Concepción
San José
Moquegua
Torata
Ilo
Umala
Desaguadero
Sicasica
Punata
Charaña
Tacna
Sajama
6520
Corque
Oruro
Grande
Roboré
Arica
Lauca
L. Poopó
Uncía
Challapata
Sucre
Corumbá
Puerto Suárez
Porto Esperança
Pisagua
Sillajhuay
Sal. de Coipasa
Rio Mulatos
Potosí
Charagua
Parapeti
Pilcomayo
Coimbra
5995
Iquique
Pozo Almonte
Pintados
Pica
Salar de Uyuni
Cuzco 5950
Huanchaca
Uyuni
Pulacayo
San Lucas
Camiri
Cuevo
Bahia Negra
Fuerte Olimpo
Lagunas
Collaguasi
Ollagüe
Chiguana
Cotagaita
Pilaya
Atocha
Villa Montes
Tarija
Mariscal Estigarribia
Porto Murtinho
Loa
Quillagua
Toco
Tupiza
Villazón
Yacuiba
Punta Rieles
Pto. Sastre
Tocopilla
Chuquicamata
La Quiaca
Chaco Boreal
Pto. Casado
Apa
Filadelfia
Pto. Pinasco
Calama
5970
Rinconada
Tartagal
Sierra Gorda
Cerro Sairecabur
Pta. Angamos
ARGENTINA
PARAGUAY
Trench
CHILE
Andes
70
65
60
5
10
15
20

188

190

Map 187

185

187

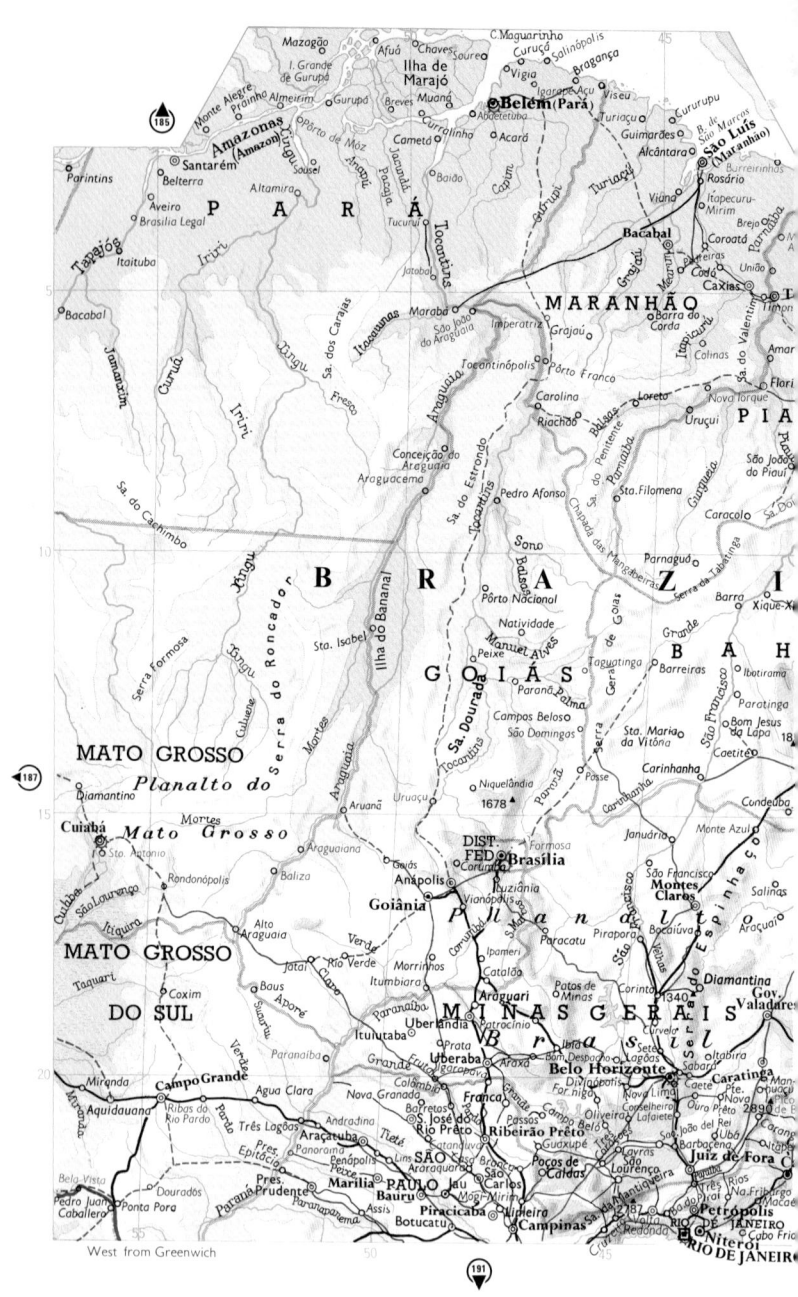
Mazagão
Afuá
Chaves
Soure
C. Maguarinho
Curuçá
Salinópolis
Bragança
Vigia
I. Grande de Gurupá
Ilha de Marajó
Viseu
Monte Alegre
Prainha
Almeirim
Gurupá
Breves
Muaná
Belém (Pará)
Abaetetuba
Cururupu
Turiaçu
Guimarães
Alcântara
São Luís (Maranhão)
B. de São Marcos
Amazonas (Amazon)
Xingu
Pôrto de Móz
Curralinho
Cametá
Acará
Parintins
Santarém
Belterra
Sousel
Anapú
Pacajá
Jacundá
Baião
Capim
Gurupi
Turiaçu
Rosário
Itapecuru-Mirim
Altamira
Aveiro
Brasília Legal
P A R Á
Tucuruí
Tocantins
Viana
Brejo
Parnaíba
Bacabal
Coroatá
Grajaú
Mearim
Pedreiras
Codó
União
Caxias
Tapajós
Itaituba
Iriri
Jatobal
Timon
5
Bacabal
Itacaiunas
Marabá
São João do Araguaia
Imperatriz
MARANHÃO
Barra do Corda
Grajaú
Itapicuru
Colinas
Sa. do Valentim
Jamanxim
Curuá
Xingu
Sa. dos Carajas
Tocantinópolis
Pôrto Franco
Fresco
Araguaia
Carolina
Loreto
Nova Iorque
Riachão
Balsas
Uruçuí
P I A
Iriri
Sa. do Penitente
Parnaíba
Conceição do Araguaia
São João do Piauí
Araguacema
Sa. do Estrondo
Pedro Afonso
Sta. Filomena
Gurgueia
Sa. do Cachimbo
Tocantins
Chapada das Mangabeiras
Caracol
10
Sono
Parnaguá
Xingu
Balsas
Serra da Tabatinga
B R A Z I
Serra do Roncador
Ilha do Bananal
Pôrto Nacional
Barra
Xique-Xique
Natividade
Sta. Isabel
Serra Formosa
Xingu
Manuel Alves
Peixe
Serra Geral de Goiás
Grande
B A H
Taguatinga
Barreiras
Ibotirama
G O I Á S
Paranã
Palma
São Francisco
Culuene
Paratinga
Campos Belos
Bom Jesus da Lapa
São Domingos
Sta. Maria da Vitória
Mortes
Sa. Dourada
Tocantins
Caetité
MATO GROSSO
Araguaia
Posse
Carinhanha
Planalto do
Diamantino
Niquelândia
Paranã
Carinhanha
Uruaçu
Aruanã
1678
Condeúba
15
Mortes
Cuiabá
Mato Grosso
Januária
Monte Azul
Sto. Antonio
DIST. FED.
Formosa
Corumbá
Brasília
Araguaiana
Goiás
Espinhaço
São Francisco
Baliza
Anápolis
Luziânia
Montes Claros
Salinas
Cuiabá
Rondonópolis
São Lourenço
Goiânia
Vianópolis
Planalto
Itiquira
Alto Araguaia
Corumbá
S. Marcos
Paracatu
Pirapora
Bocaiúva
Araçuaí
Verde
São Francisco
Velhas
MATO GROSSO
Ipameri
Jataí
Rio Verde
Morrinhos
Catalão
Taquari
Claro
Serra do Espinhaço
Diamantina
Coxim
Baus
Itumbiara
Patos de Minas
Corinto
1340
Gov. Valadares
Aporé
Araguari
DO SUL
Sucuriú
Paranaíba
MINAS GERAIS
Uberlândia
Patrocínio
Ituiutaba
Curvelo
Brasil
Verde
Paranaíba
Prata
Ibiá
Sete Lagoas
Itabira
Grande
Uberaba
Araxá
Bom Despacho
Sabará
20
Miranda
Campo Grande
Frutal
Igarapava
Belo Horizonte
Caratinga
Divinópolis
Caeté
Colômbia
Formiga
Pte. Nova
Manhuaçu
Pardo
Agua Clara
Nova Granada
Franca
Nova Lima
Miranda
Aquidauana
Ribas do Rio Pardo
Barretos
Grande
Passos
Campo Belo
Conselheiro Lafaiete
Ouro Prêto
2890
Andradina
S. José do Rio Prêto
Ribeirão Prêto
Oliveira
São João del Rei
Três Lagôas
Araçatuba
Pardo
Ubá
Tietê
Três Corações
Guaxupé
Lavras
Barbacena
Pres. Epitácio
Panorama
Catanduva
Penápolis
Lins
SÃO
Araraquara
Casa Branca
São Lourenço
Juiz de Fora
Poços de Caldas
Bela Vista
Peixe
Pres. Prudente
Marília
PAULO
Jau
São Carlos
Sa. da Mantiqueira
Paraíba
Três Rios
Dourados
Paraná
Bauru
Mogi-Mirim
Nova Friburgo
Pedro Juan Caballero
Ponta Pora
Paranapanema
Assis
Piracicaba
Limeira
2787
Barra do Piraí
Petrópolis
Macaé
Botucatu
Campinas
Volta Redonda
RIO DE JANEIRO
Cabo Frio
Cruzeiro
Niterói
RIO DE JANEIRO
55
50
45
West from Greenwich

191

Map 188

South America: East

1:16 000 000

Tutóia
Luis Correia
Comocim
alba
Granja
racurcua
Sobral
Maranguape
Fortaleza (Ceará)
diri
Baturité
Ipu
Aracati
Maior
Quixadá
Russas
Areia Branca
Macau
Qitícica
Crateús
Limoeiro do Norte
Mossoró
Ceará Mirín
C. de São Roque
CEARÁ
RIO GRANDE
Natal
Senador Pompeu
Caraúbas
DO NORTE
Valença do
Piauí
Iguatu
Oros
Soure
Caicó
Currais Novos
Nova Cruz
Canguaretama
Oeiras
Crato
Cedro
Pombal
Patos
Alagoa Grande
Mamanguape
Cabedelo
João Pessoa
(Paraíba)
UI
Chap. do Araripe
Juazeiro do Norte
PARAÍBA
Campina Grande
Itabaiana
Paulistana
Ouricuri
Sertânia
Caruaru
Limoeiro
RECIFE
(Pernambuco)
Arcoverde
Pesqueira
Feira de Santo Antão
PERNAMBUCO
Garanhuns
Barreiros
São Francisco
Petrolândia
Viçosa
Palmares
Petrolina
Delmiro Gouveia
Rio Largo
Juazeiro
Paulo Afonso
Pal das Indias
Maceió
Remanso
ALAGOAS
Campo Formoso
Senhor do Bonfim
Vaza Barris
Propriá
Penedo
L
Queimadas
Itapicuru
Cabelo
SERGIPE
Jacobina
Jacuípe
Serrinha
Capela
São Cristóvão
Estância
Aracaju
Mundo Novo
Feira de Santana
Alagoinhas
Itaberaba
Cachoeira
Castro Alves
Santo Amaro
Itaeté
Baixa
Amargosa
Valença
Salvador (Bahia)
Sincorá
Jequié
Baía de Todos os Santos
Contas
Ubaitaba
Itacaré
Vitória da Conquista
Itabuna
Ilhéus
Pedra Azul
Canavieiras
itinhonha
Belmonte
Jequitinhonha
Pôrto Seguro
Teófilo Otoni
Nanuque
Prado
Caravelas
Banka
Mucuri
Abrolhos
Nova Venécia
Conceição da Barra
São Mateus
Doce
ESPÍRITO SANTO
Vitória
da Bandeira
Cachoeira de Itapemirim

Rocas
Fernando de Noronha
(Braz.)

ATLANTIC OCEAN

6059

Trindade
(Braz.)

COPYRIGHT. GEORGE PHILIP & SON, LTD.

Map 189

South America: Central

187

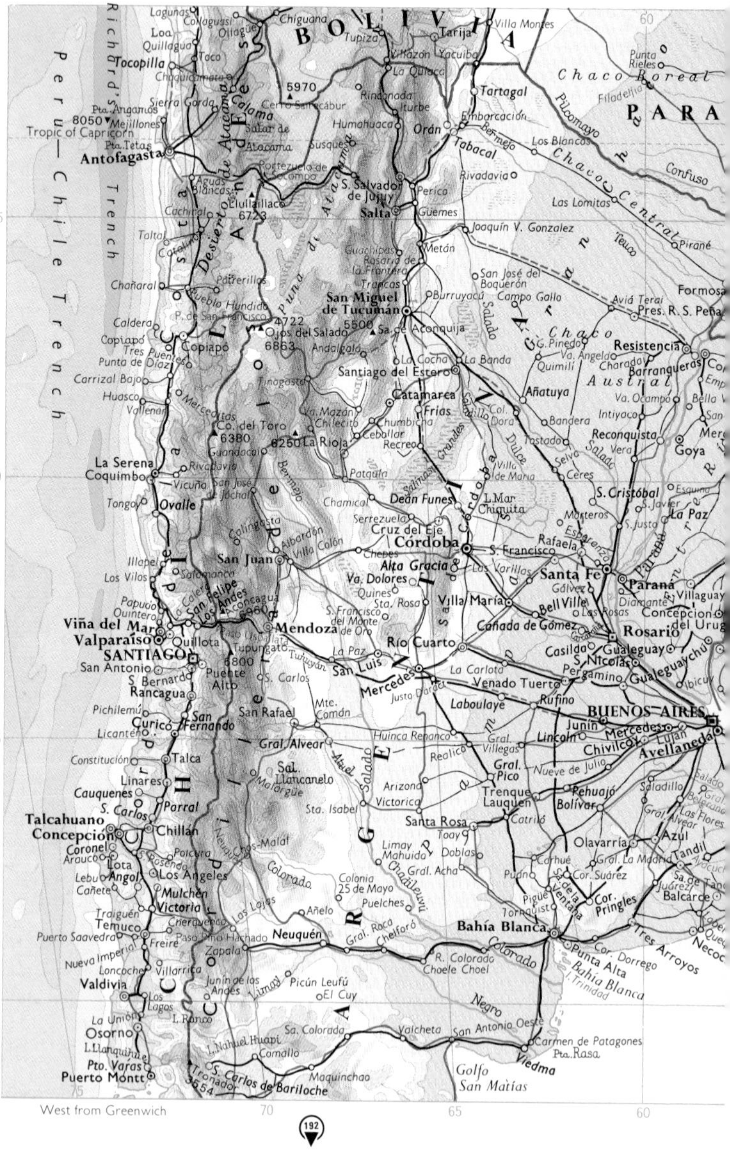

192

Map 190

1:16 000 000

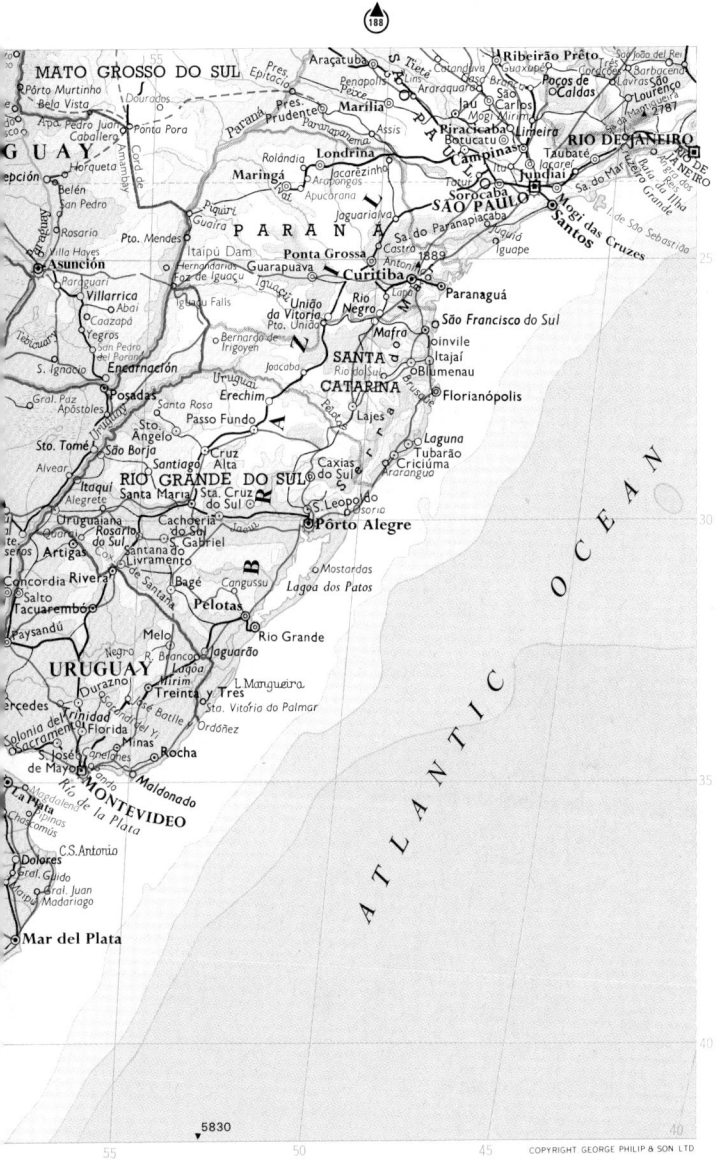

5830

Map 191

South America: South

1:16 000 000

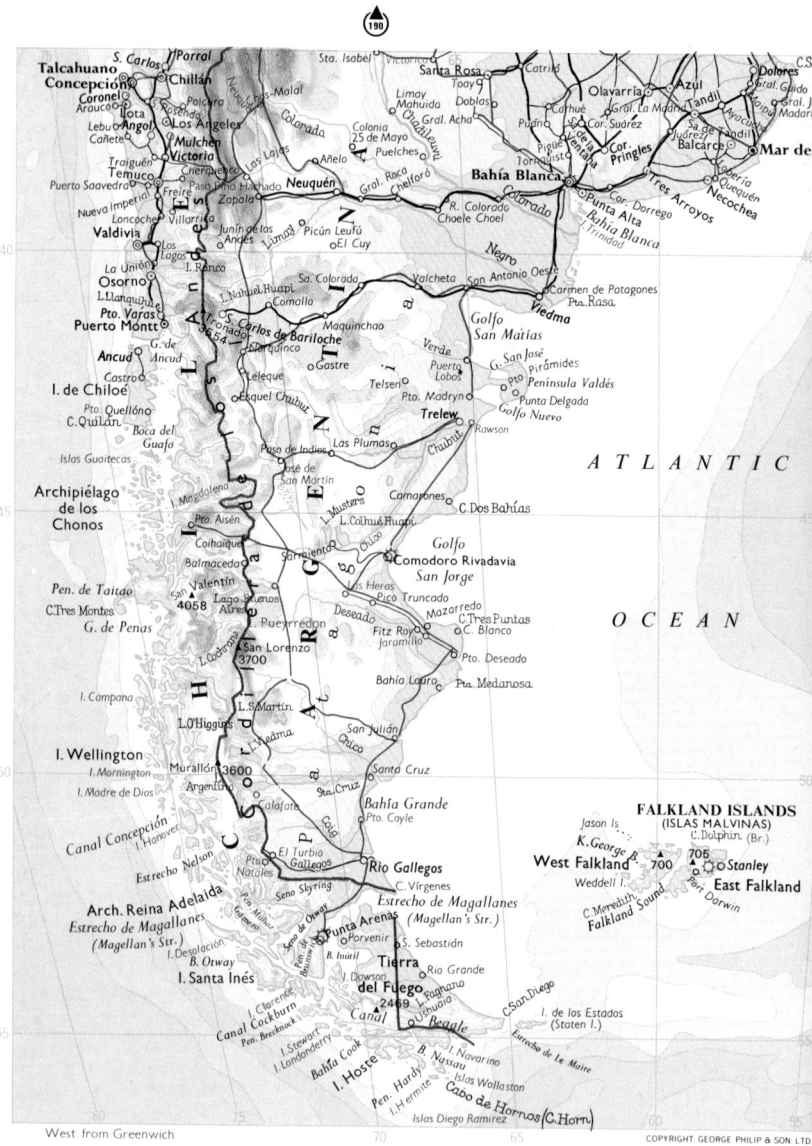

ATLANTIC

OCEAN

FALKLAND ISLANDS
(ISLAS MALVINAS)

West Falkland   East Falkland

Stanley

West from Greenwich

COPYRIGHT GEORGE PHILIP & SON LTD.

Map 192

Index

Introduction to Index

The number printed in bold type against each entry indicates the map page where the feature can be found. This is followed by its geographical coordinates. The first coordinate indicates latitude, i.e. distance north or south of the Equator. The second coordinate indicates longitude, i.e. distance east or west of the meridian of Greenwich in England (shown as 0° longitude). Both latitude and longitude are measured in degrees and minutes (with 60 minutes in a degree), and appear on the map as horizontal and vertical gridlines respectively. Thus the entry for Paris in France reads.

Paris, France........**39**   48 50N   2 20 E

This entry indicates that Paris is on page **39,** at latitude 48 degrees 50 minutes north (approximately five-sixths of the distance between horizontal gridlines 48 and 49 , marked on either side of the page) and at longitude 2 degrees 20 minutes east (approximately one-third of the distance between vertical gridlines 2 and 3, marked at top and bottom of the page). Paris can be found where lines extended from these two points cross on the page. The geographical coordinates are sometimes only approximate but are close enough for the place to be located. Rivers have been indexed to their mouth or confluence.

An open square □ signifies that the name refers to an administrative subdivision of a country while a solid square ■ follows the name of a country. An arrow ⇢ follows the name of a river.

The alphabetical order of names composed of two or more words is governed primarily by the first word and then by the second. This rule applies even if the second word is a description or its abbreviation, R., L., I. for example.

> North Walsham
> Northallerton
> Northampton
> Northern Circars
> Northumberland Is.
> Northumberland Str.

Names composed of a proper name (Gibraltar) and a description (Strait of) are positioned alphabetically by the proper name. This is the case where the definite article follows a proper name (Mans, Le). If the same word occurs in the name of a town and a geographical feature, the town name is listed first followed by the name or names of the geographical features.

Names beginning with M', Mc are all indexed as if they were spelled Mac. All names beginning St. are alphabetised under Saint, but Sankt, Sint, Santa and San are all spelt in full and are alphabetised accordingly.

If the same place name occurs twice or more times in the index and all are in the same country, each is followed by the name of the administrative subdivision in which it is located. The names are placed in the alphabetical order of the subdivisions. If the same place name occurs twice or more in the index and the places are in different countries they will be followed by their country names, the latter governing the alphabetical order. In a mixture of these situations the primary order is fixed by the alphabetical sequence of the countries and the secondary order by that of the country subdivisions.

Abbreviations used

A.S.S.R. – *Autonomous Soviet Socialist Republic*
Ala. – *Alabama*
Arch. – *Archipelago*
Ark. – *Arkansas*
Austral. – *Australia*
B. – *Baie, Bahia, Bay, Boca, Bucht, Bugt*
B.C. – *British Columbia*
Bangla. – *Bangladesh*
Br. – *British*
C. – *Cabo, Cap, Cape, Coast, Costa*
C. Rica – *Costa Rica*
Calif. – *California*
Cap. Terr. – *Capital Territory*
Cat. – *Cataract*
Cent. – *Central*
Chan. – *Channel*
Colo. – *Colorado*
Conn. – *Connecticut*
Cord. – *Cordillera*
D.C. – *District of Columbia*
Del. – *Delaware*
Dét. – *Détroit*
Dom. Rep. – *Dominican Republic*
Domin. – *Dominica*
E. – *East, Eastern*
Est. – *Estrecho*
Falk. Is. – *Falkland Is.*
Fla. – *Florida*
Fr. Gui. – *French Guiana*
G. – *Golfe, Golfo, Gulf, Guba, Gebel*
Ga. – *Georgia*
Gt. – *Great*
Guat. – *Guatemala*
Hants. – *Hampshire*
Hd. – *Head*
Hond. – *Honduras*
Hts. – *Heights*
I.(s) – *Ile, Ilha, Insel, Isla, Island(s)*
I. of W. – *Isle of Wight*
Ill. – *Illinois*
Ind. – *Indiana*
Ind. Oc. – *Indian Ocean*
J. – *Jabal, Jazira*
K. – *Kap. Kapp*
Kans. – *Kansas*

Ky. – *Kentucky*
L. – *Lac, Lacul, Lago, Lagoa, Lake, Limni, Loch, Lough*
La. – *Louisiana*
Lag. – *Laguna*
Lancs. – *Lancashire*
Man. – *Manitoba*
Mass. – *Massachusetts*
Md. – *Maryland*
Mich. – *Michigan*
Minn. – *Minnesota*
Miss. – *Mississippi*
Mo. – *Missouri*
Mont. – *Montana*
Mt.(s) – *Mont, Monta, Monti, Muntii, Montaña, Mount, Mountain(s)*
N. – *North, Northern*
N.B. – *New Brunswick*
N.C. – *North Carolina*
N. Dak. – *North Dakota*
N.H. – *New Hampshire*
N.J. – *New Jersey*
N. Mex. – *New Mexico*
N.S.W. – *New South Wales*
N.W.T. – *North West Territories*
N.Y. – *New York*
N.Z. – *New Zealand*
Nebr. – *Nebraska*
Neth. – *Netherlands*
Nev. – *Nevada*
Nfld. – *Newfoundland*
Nic. – *Nicaragua*
Okla. – *Oklahoma*
Ont. – *Ontario*
Oreg. – *Oregon*
Os. – *Ostrov*
Oz. – *Ozero*
P. – *Pass, Passo, Pasul, Pulau*
P.E.I. – *Prince Edward Island*
Pa. – *Pennsylvania*
Pac. Oc. – *Pacific Ocean*
Papua N.G. – *Papua New Guinea*
Pen. – *Peninsula*
Pk. – *Peak*
Plat. – *Plateau*
P-ov. – *Poluostrov*
Pt. – *Point*
Pta. – *Ponta, Punta*
Queens. – *Queensland*

R. – *Rio, River, Rivière*
R.I. – *Rhode Island*
R.S.F.S.R. – *Russian Soviet Federative Socialist Republic*
Ra.(s) – *Range(s)*
Raj. – *Rajasthan*
Rep. – *Republic*
Res. – *Reserve, Reservoir*
S. – *South, Southern, Sea, Sur*
S.C. – *South Carolina*
S.S.R. – *Soviet Socialist Republic*
S. Africa – *South Africa*
S. Dak. – *South Dakota*
Sa. – *Serra, Sierra*
Salop. – *Shropshire*
Sard. – *Sardinia*
Sask. – *Saskatchewan*
Sd. – *Sound*
Sev. – *Severnaya*
Si. Arabia – *Saudi Arabia*
St. – *Saint*
Sta. – *Santa*
Ste. – *Sainte*
Str. – *Strait, Stretto*
Switz. – *Switzerland*
Tas. – *Tasmania*
Tenn. – *Tennessee*
Terr. – *Territory*
Tex. – *Texas*
Tipp. – *Tipperary*
Trin. & Tob. – *Trinidad and Tobago*
U.K. – *United Kingdom*
U.S.A. – *United States of America*
U.S.S.R. – *Union of Soviet Socialist Republics*
Ut. P. – *Uttar Pradesh*
Va. – *Virginia*
Vic. – *Victoria*
Vol. – *Volcano*
Vt. – *Vermont*
Wash. – *Washington*
W. – *West, Western, Wadi*
W. Va. – *West Virginia*
Wis. – *Wisconsin*
Worcs. – *Worcestershire*
Yorks. – *Yorkshire*

Aachen	**42**	50 47N	6 4 E
Aalborg = Ålborg	**61**	57 2N	9 54 E
Aalsmeer	**40**	52 17N	4 43 E
Aalst	**42**	50 56N	4 2 E
Aalten	**41**	51 56N	6 35 E
Aarhus = Århus	**61**	56 8N	10 11 E
Aba	**131**	5 10N	7 19 E
Ābādān	**84**	30 22N	48 20 E
Ābādeh	**85**	31 8N	52 40 E
Abadla	**126**	31 2N	2 45W
Abai	**191**	25 58S	55 54W
Abakan	**74**	53 40N	91 10 E
Abancay	**186**	13 35S	72 55W
Abariringa I.	**122**	2 50S	171 40W
Abashiri	**103**	44 0N	144 15 E
Abashiri-Wan	**103**	44 0N	144 30 E
Abaya, L.	**133**	6 30N	37 50 E
Abbay = Nîl el Azraq →	**129**	15 38N	32 31 E
Abbeville, France	**38**	50 6N	1 49 E
Abbeville, U.S.A.	**165**	34 12N	82 21W
Abéché	**129**	13 50N	20 35 E
Abeokuta	**131**	7 3N	3 19 E
Aberaeron	**26**	52 15N	4 16W
Aberayron = Aberaeron	**26**	52 15N	4 16W
Aberdare	**27**	51 43N	3 27W
Aberdeen, U.K.	**33**	57 9N	2 6W
Aberdeen, S. Dak., U.S.A.	**163**	45 30N	98 30W
Aberdeen, Wash., U.S.A.	**171**	47 0N	123 50W
Aberdovey	**26**	52 33N	4 3W
Aberfeldy	**33**	56 37N	3 50W
Abergavenny	**26**	51 49N	3 1W
Aberystwyth	**26**	52 25N	4 6W
Abha	**82**	18 0N	42 34 E
Abidjan	**130**	5 26N	3 58W
Abilene	**161**	32 22N	99 40W
Abington	**25**	55 30N	3 42W
Abkhaz A.S.S.R. □	**70**	43 0N	41 0 E
Abohar	**89**	30 10N	74 10 E
Abomèy	**131**	7 10N	2 5 E
Abong-Mbang	**131**	4 0N	13 8 E
Abrud	**56**	46 19N	23 5 E
Abruzzi □	**47**	42 15N	14 0 E
Absaroka Ra.	**163**	44 40N	110 0W
Abū al Khaṣīb	**84**	30 25N	48 0 E
Abū 'Alī	**84**	27 20N	49 27 E
Abū 'Arīsh	**82**	16 58N	45 20 E
Abu Dhabi = Abū Ẓāby	**85**	24 28N	54 22 E
Abu Hamed	**129**	19 32N	33 13 E
Abū Ẓāby	**85**	24 28N	54 22 E
Abunã	**187**	9 40S	65 20W
Abunã →	**187**	9 41S	65 20W
Abut Hd.	**123**	43 7S	170 15 E
Acámbaro	**177**	20 2N	100 44W
Acaponeta	**175**	22 30N	105 22W
Acapulco	**177**	16 51N	99 56W
Acatlán	**177**	18 10N	98 3W
Acayucan	**177**	17 57N	94 55W
Accra	**130**	5 35N	0 6W
Accrington	**28**	53 46N	2 22W
Achill I.	**34**	53 58N	10 5W
Achinsk	**74**	56 20N	90 20 E
Aconcagua, Cerro	**190**	32 39S	70 0W
Aconquija, Mt.	**190**	27 0S	66 0W
Açores, Is. dos = Azores	**126**	38 44N	29 0W
Acre = 'Akko	**80**	32 55N	35 4 E
Acre □	**187**	9 1S	71 0W
Ad Dawhah	**85**	25 15N	51 35 E
Ada	**168**	34 50N	96 45W
Adamaoua, Massif de l'	**131**	7 20N	12 20 E
Adamawa Highlands = Adamaoua, Massif de l'	**131**	7 20N	12 20 E
Adaminaby	**117**	36 0S	148 45 E
Adams, Mt.	**171**	46 10N	121 28W
Adam's Bridge	**90**	9 15N	79 40 E
Adana	**80**	37 0N	35 16 E
Adapazarı	**80**	40 48N	30 25 E
Adare, C.	**15**	71 0S	171 0 E
Addis Ababa = Addis Abeba	**133**	9 2N	38 42 E
Addis Abeba	**133**	9 2N	38 42 E
Adelaide	**119**	34 52S	138 30 E
Adelaide Pen.	**145**	68 15N	97 30W
Adélie, Terre	**15**	68 0S	140 0 E
Aden = Al 'Adan	**83**	12 45N	45 0 E
Aden, G. of	**133**	13 0N	50 0 E
Adige →	**47**	45 9N	12 20 E
Adirondack Mts.	**151**	44 0N	74 15W
Admiralty Is.	**115**	2 0S	147 0 E
Adoni	**90**	15 33N	77 18W
Adrian	**167**	41 55N	84 0W
Adriatic Sea	**52**	43 0N	16 0 E
Adwa	**132**	14 15N	38 52 E
Adzhar A.S.S.R. □	**70**	42 0N	42 0 E
Ægean Sea	**55**	37 0N	25 0 E
Æolian Is. = Eólie, I.	**49**	38 30N	14 50 E
Aerht'ai Shan	**100**	46 40N	92 45 E
Afars & Issas, Terr. of = Djibouti ■	**133**	12 0N	43 0 E
Afghanistan ■	**87**	33 0N	65 0 E
Afuá	**188**	0 15S	50 20W
Afyonkarahisar	**80**	38 45N	30 33 E
Agadir	**126**	30 28N	9 35W
Agano →	**103**	37 57N	139 8 E
Agartala	**93**	23 50N	91 23 E
Agen	**36**	44 12N	0 38 E
Ageo	**107**	35 58N	139 36 E
Aghil Pass	**89**	36 15N	76 35 E
Agra	**89**	27 17N	77 58 E
Ağri Daği	**81**	39 50N	44 15 E
Água Clara	**188**	20 25S	52 45W
Agua Prieta	**174**	31 18N	109 34W
Aguadas	**184**	5 40N	75 38W
Aguadilla	**180**	18 27N	67 10W
Aguas Blancas	**190**	24 15S	69 55W
Aguascalientes	**175**	21 53N	102 18W
Aguascalientes □	**175**	22 0N	102 30W
Agulhas, Kaap	**136**	34 52S	20 0 E
Ahaggar	**127**	23 0N	6 30 E
Ahaura →	**123**	42 21S	171 34 E
Ahmadabad	**91**	23 0N	72 40 E
Ahmadnagar	**91**	19 7N	74 46 E
Ahmedabad = Ahmadabad	**91**	23 0N	72 40 E
Ahmednagar = Ahmadnagar	**91**	19 7N	74 46 E
Ahvāz	**84**	31 20N	48 40 E
Ahvenanmaa = Åland	**66**	60 15N	20 0 E
Ahwar	**83**	13 30N	46 40 E
Aigle, L'	**39**	48 46N	0 38 E
Aigues-Mortes	**37**	43 35N	4 12 E
Aiken	**170**	33 34N	81 50W
Ailsa Craig	**30**	55 15N	5 7W
Aimorés	**189**	19 30S	41 4W
Aïn Ben Tili	**126**	25 59N	9 27W
Aioi	**109**	34 48N	134 28 E
Aïr	**127**	18 30N	8 0 E
Airdrie	**31**	55 53N	3 57W
Aire →	**29**	53 42N	0 55W
Airlie Beach	**121**	20 16S	148 43 E
Aisne →	**37**	49 26N	2 50 E
Aix-en-Provence	**37**	43 32N	5 27 E
Aix-la-Chapelle = Aachen	**42**	50 47N	6 4 E
Aix-les-Bains	**37**	45 41N	5 53 E
Aizuwakamatsu	**105**	37 30N	139 56 E
Ajaccio	**36**	41 55N	8 40 E
Ajanta Ra.	**91**	20 28N	75 50 E
Ajmer	**91**	26 28N	74 37 E
Akaishi-Dake	**107**	35 27N	138 9 E
Akaishi-Sammyaku	**107**	35 25N	138 10 E
Akashi	**109**	34 45N	135 0 E
Akershus fylke □	**60**	60 0N	11 10 E
Akhelóös →	**54**	38 36N	21 14 E
Akhisar	**80**	38 56N	27 48 E
Aki	**109**	33 30N	133 54 E
Aki-Nada	**109**	34 5N	132 40 E
Akita	**103**	39 45N	140 7 E
'Akko	**80**	32 55N	35 4 E
Aklavik	**144**	68 12N	135 0W
Akō	**109**	34 45N	134 24 E
Akola	**91**	20 42N	77 2 E
Akranes	**64**	64 19N	21 58W
Akron	**167**	41 7N	81 31W
Aksaray	**80**	38 25N	34 2 E
Aksarka	**69**	66 31N	67 50 E
Akşehir	**80**	38 18N	31 30 E

Name						
Aksum	132	14	5N	38	40	E
Aktyubinsk	70	50	17N	57	10	E
Akune	108	32	1N	130	12	E
Akureyri	64	65	40N	18	6	W
Al 'Adan	83	12	45N	45	0	E
Al Amādīyah	81	37	5N	43	30	E
Al Amārah	84	31	55N	47	15	E
Al 'Aqabah	80	29	31N	35	0	E
Al Başrah	84	30	30N	47	50	E
Al Hadīthah	81	31	28N	37	8	E
Al Hāmad	80	31	30N	39	30	E
Al Hasakah	81	36	35N	40	45	E
Al Hawrah	83	13	50N	47	35	E
Al Hayy	84	32	5N	46	5	E
Al Hillah, Iraq	84	32	30N	44	25	E
Al Hillah, Si. Arabia	83	23	35N	46	50	E
Al Hindīyah	84	32	30N	44	10	E
Al Hudaydah	82	14	50N	43	0	E
Al Hūfuf	84	25	25N	49	45	E
Al Jāfūrah	84	25	0N	50	15	E
Al Jawf, Libya	128	24	10N	23	24	E
Al Jawf, Si. Arabia	82	29	55N	39	40	E
Al Jazirah	81	33	30N	44	0	E
Al Khafji	80	31	32N	35	6	E
Al Kūt	84	32	30N	46	0	E
Al Kuwayt	84	29	30N	47	30	E
Al Lādhiqīyah	80	35	30N	35	45	E
Al Lidām	82	20	33N	44	45	E
Al Luhayyah	82	15	45N	42	40	E
Al Madīnah	82	24	35N	39	52	E
Al Manāmāh	85	26	10N	50	30	E
Al Marj	128	32	25N	20	30	E
Al Mawşil	81	36	15N	43	5	E
Al Mubarraz	84	25	30N	49	40	E
Al Muharraq	85	26	15N	50	40	E
Al Mukallā	83	14	33N	49	2	E
Al Qaţif	84	26	35N	50	0	E
Al Quds = Jerusalem	80	31	47N	35	10	E
Al Qunfudhah	82	19	3N	41	4	E
Al Qurnah	84	31	1N	47	25	E
Al 'Ubaylah	83	21	59N	50	57	E
Al 'Uthmānīyah	84	25	5N	49	22	E
Al Wajh	82	26	10N	36	30	E
Alabama □	169	33	0N	87	0	W
Alabama →	169	31	8N	87	57	W
Alagoas □	189	9	0S	36	0	W
Alagoinhas	189	12	7S	38	20	W
Alajuela	179	10	2N	84	8	W
Alamogordo	161	32	59N	106	0	W
Alamos	174	27	1N	108	56	W
Alamosa	163	37	30N	106	0	W
Åland	66	60	15N	20	0	E
Alaska □	142	65	0N	150	0	W
Alaska, G. of	142	58	0N	145	0	W
Alaska Pen.	142	56	0N	160	0	W
Alaska Range	142	62	50N	151	0	W
Alba Iulia	56	46	8N	23	39	E
Albacete	51	39	0N	1	50	W
Albania ■	52	41	0N	20	0	E
Albany, Australia	120	35	1S	117	58	E
Albany, Ga., U.S.A.	170	31	40N	84	10	W
Albany, N.Y., U.S.A.	164	42	35N	73	47	W
Albany, Oreg., U.S.A.	171	44	41N	123	0	W
Albany →	140	52	17N	81	31	W
Albemarle	165	35	27N	80	15	W
Albemarle Sd.	165	36	0N	76	30	W
Albert	38	50	0N	2	38	E
Albert, L. = Mobutu Sese Seko, L.	132	1	30N	31	0	E
Albert Lea	166	43	32N	93	20	W
Alberta □	155	54	40N	115	0	W
Albertville = Kalemie	135	5	55S	29	9	E
Albi	37	43	56N	2	9	E
Albion	167	42	15N	84	45	W
Ålborg	61	57	2N	9	54	E
Alborz, Reshteh-ye Kūhhā-ye	86	36	0N	52	0	E
Albuquerque	161	35	5N	106	47	W
Alburquerque	50	39	15N	6	59	W
Albury	117	36	3S	146	56	E
Alcântara	188	2	20S	44	30	W
Alcázar de San Juan	50	39	24N	3	12	W
Alcira	51	39	9N	0	30	W
Aldan →	75	63	28N	129	35	E
Aldeburgh	25	52	9N	1	35	E
Alderney	36	49	42N	2	12	W
Aldershot	25	51	15N	0	43	W
Alençon	39	48	27N	0	4	E
Aleppo = Halab	80	36	10N	37	15	E
Alès	37	44	9N	4	5	E
Alessándria	46	44	54N	8	37	E
Ålesund	65	62	28N	6	12	E
Aleutian Is.	142	52	0N	175	0	W
Alexander Arch.	143	57	0N	135	0	W
Alexander City	169	32	58N	85	57	W
Alexandra, Australia	117	37	8S	145	40	E
Alexandra, N.Z.	123	45	14S	169	25	E
Alexandretta = Iskenderun	80	36	32N	36	10	E
Alexandria = El Iskandarîya	128	31	0N	30	0	E
Alexandria, La., U.S.A.	168	31	20N	92	30	W
Alexandria, Va., U.S.A.	164	38	47N	77	1	W
Alexandrina, L.	119	35	25S	139	10	E
Alexandroúpolis	55	40	50N	25	54	E
Alexis Creek	154	52	10N	123	20	W
Alfreton	29	53	6N	1	22	W
Algarve	50	36	58N	8	20	W
Alger	127	36	42N	3	8	E
Algeria ■	127	35	10N	3	11	E
Algiers = Alger	127	36	42N	3	8	E
Algoa B.	136	33	50S	25	45	E
Alhambra	173	34	2N	118	10	W
Alicante	51	38	23N	0	30	W
Alice Springs	114	23	40S	133	50	E
Aligarh	89	27	55N	78	10	E
Alipur Duar	92	26	30N	89	35	E
Aliquippa	164	40	38N	80	18	W
Alkmaar	40	52	37N	4	45	E
Allahabad	92	25	25N	81	58	E
Allegheny Mts.	165	38	0N	80	0	W
Allen, Bog of	35	53	15N	7	0	W
Allende	174	28	20N	100	51	W
Allentown	164	40	36N	75	30	W
Alleppey	90	9	30N	76	28	E
Aller →	42	52	57N	9	10	E
Allier →	37	46	57N	3	4	E
Alloa	31	56	7N	3	49	W
Alma, Canada	148	48	35N	71	40	W
Alma, U.S.A.	167	43	25N	84	40	W
Alma Ata	71	43	15N	76	57	E
Almada	50	38	40N	9	9	W
Almelo	41	52	22N	6	42	E
Almería	51	36	52N	2	27	W
Almirante	179	9	10N	82	30	W
Alor	113	8	15S	124	30	E
Alor Setar	96	6	7N	100	22	E
Alpena	150	45	6N	83	24	W
Alphen	40	51	29N	4	58	E
Alpine	161	30	25N	103	35	W
Alps	16	47	0N	8	0	E
Alsace	37	48	15N	7	25	E
Alsask	152	51	21N	109	59	W
Alston	28	54	48N	2	26	W
Alta Gracia	190	31	40S	64	30	W
Altagracia	184	10	45N	71	30	W
Altai = Aerht'ai Shan	100	46	40N	92	45	E
Altamaha →	170	31	19N	81	17	W
Altamira	188	3	12S	52	10	W
Alto Adige = Trentino-Alto Adige □	47	46	30N	11	0	E
Alton	166	38	55N	90	5	W
Altona	43	53	32N	9	56	E
Altoona	164	40	32N	78	24	W
Altun Shan	100	38	30N	88	0	E
Alvarado	177	18	46N	95	46	W
Älvsborgs län □	60	58	30N	12	30	E
Alwar	89	27	38N	76	34	E
Alxa Zuoqi	98	38	50N	105	40	E
Am-Timan	129	11	0N	20	10	E
Amadjuak	146	64	0N	72	39	W
Amadjuak L.	146	65	0N	71	8	W
Amagasaki	106	34	42N	135	20	E
Amagi	108	33	25N	130	39	E
Amakusa-Nada	108	32	35N	130	5	E

Amalner	**91**	21 5N	75 5 E
Amapá	**185**	2 5N	50 50W
Amapá □	**185**	1 40N	52 0W
Amarillo	**161**	35 14N	101 46W
Amasya	**80**	40 40N	35 50 E
Amatitlán	**177**	14 29N	90 38W
Amazon = Amazonas →	**185**	0 5S	50 0W
Amazonas □	**185**	4 0S	62 0W
Amazonas →	**185**	0 5S	50 0W
Ambala	**89**	30 23N	76 56 E
Ambato	**184**	1 5S	78 42W
Ambikapur	**92**	23 15N	83 15 E
Ambleside	**28**	54 26N	2 58W
Ambo	**186**	10 5S	76 10W
Ambon	**113**	3 35S	128 20 E
Amboyna I.	**112**	7 50N	112 50 E
Amderma	**69**	69 45N	61 30 E
Ameca	**175**	20 33N	104 2W
Ameca, R. →	**175**	20 41N	105 18W
Ameland	**41**	53 27N	5 45 E
American Highland	**14**	73 0S	75 0 E
American Samoa ■	**123**	14 20S	170 40W
Americus	**170**	32 0N	84 10W
Amersfoort	**40**	52 9N	5 23 E
Amery	**143**	56 34N	94 3W
Ames	**166**	42 0N	93 40W
Amga →	**75**	62 38N	134 32 E
Amgu	**75**	45 45N	137 15 E
Amgun →	**75**	52 56N	139 38 E
Amherst	**148**	45 48N	64 8W
Amherstburg	**150**	42 6N	83 6W
Amiens	**38**	49 54N	2 16 E
Amlwch	**26**	53 24N	4 21W
'Ammān	**80**	31 57N	35 52 E
Amorgós	**55**	36 50N	25 57 E
Amos	**151**	48 35N	78 5W
Amoy = Xiamen	**99**	24 25N	118 4 E
Amravati	**91**	20 55N	77 45 E
Amreli	**91**	21 35N	71 17 E
Amritsar	**89**	31 35N	74 57 E
Amsterdam, Neth.	**40**	52 23N	4 54 E
Amsterdam, U.S.A.	**164**	42 58N	74 10W
Amudarya →	**70**	43 40N	59 0 E
Amundsen Gulf	**145**	71 0N	124 0W
Amundsen Sea	**15**	72 0S	115 0W
Amur →	**75**	52 56N	141 10 E
An Nafūd	**82**	28 15N	41 0 E
An Najaf	**84**	32 3N	44 15 E
An Nāşiriyah	**84**	31 0N	46 15 E
An Nhon	**95**	13 55N	109 7 E
An Nu'ayrīyah	**84**	27 30N	48 30 E
An Uaimh	**34**	53 39N	6 40W
Anabar →	**72**	73 8N	113 36 E
Anaconda	**163**	46 7N	113 0W
Anacortes	**171**	48 30N	122 40W
Anadolu	**80**	38 0N	30 0 E
Anadyr →	**73**	64 55N	176 5 E
Anadyrskiy Zaliv	**73**	64 0N	180 0 E
Anaheim	**173**	33 50N	118 0W
Anambas Is.	**111**	3 20N	106 30 E
Anamur	**80**	36 8N	32 58 E
Anan	**109**	33 54N	134 40 E
Anápolis	**188**	16 15S	48 50W
Anārak	**85**	33 25N	53 40 E
Anatolia = Anadolu	**80**	38 0N	30 0 E
Añatuya	**190**	28 20S	62 50W
Anchorage	**142**	61 10N	149 50W
Ancohuma, Nevada	**187**	16 0S	68 50W
Ancona	**47**	43 37N	13 30 E
Ancud	**192**	42 0S	73 50W
Ancud, G. de	**192**	42 0S	73 0W
Åndalsnes	**65**	62 35N	7 43 E
Andalucía □	**50**	37 35N	5 0W
Andalusia	**169**	31 19N	86 30W
Andalusia □ = Andalucía □	**50**	37 35N	5 0W
Andaman Is.	**94**	12 30N	92 30 E
Andaman Sea	**94**	13 0N	96 0 E
Andaman Str.	**94**	12 15N	92 20 E
Andelys, Les	**39**	49 15N	1 25 E
Anderson, Ind., U.S.A.	**167**	40 5N	85 40W
Anderson, S.C., U.S.A.	**165**	34 32N	82 40W
Andes, Cord. de los	**182**	20 0S	68 0W
Andhra Pradesh □	**91**	16 0N	79 0 E
Andikíthira	**55**	35 52N	23 15 E
Andizhan	**71**	41 10N	72 0 E
Andorra ■	**36**	42 30N	1 30 E
Andover	**24**	51 13N	1 29W
Andreanof Is.	**142**	52 0N	178 0W
Andrewilla	**118**	26 31S	139 17 E
Ándria	**49**	41 13N	16 17 E
Andropov	**68**	58 5N	38 50 E
Ándros	**55**	37 50N	24 57 E
Andros I.	**178**	24 30N	78 0W
Angara →	**74**	58 30N	97 0 E
Angarsk	**74**	52 30N	104 0 E
Angaston	**119**	34 30S	139 8 E
Ånge	**66**	62 31N	15 35 E
Ängelholm	**61**	56 15N	12 58 E
Angels Camp	**172**	38 8N	120 30W
Ångerman →	**66**	64 0N	17 20 E
Angers	**36**	47 30N	0 35W
Angkor	**95**	13 22N	103 50 E
Anglesey	**26**	53 17N	4 20W
Angmagssalik	**147**	65 40N	37 20W
Angol	**190**	37 56S	72 45W
Angola ■	**134**	12 0S	18 0 E
Angoulême	**36**	45 39N	0 10 E
Angoumois	**36**	45 50N	0 25 E
Anguilla	**180**	18 14N	63 5W
Angus, Braes of	**33**	56 51N	3 10W
Anhui □	**99**	32 0N	117 0 E
Anhwei □ = Anhui □	**99**	32 0N	117 0 E
Anin	**94**	15 36N	97 50 E
Anjō	**106**	34 57N	137 5 E
Anjou	**36**	47 20N	0 15W
Anju	**98**	39 36N	125 40 E
Ankang	**99**	32 40N	109 1 E
Ankara	**80**	40 0N	32 54 E
Ann Arbor	**167**	42 17N	83 45W
Annaba	**127**	36 50N	7 46 E
Annam = Trung-Phan	**95**	16 0N	108 0 E
Annamitique, Chaîne	**95**	17 0N	106 0 E
Annan	**31**	55 0N	3 17W
Annapolis	**164**	39 0N	76 30W
Annecy	**37**	45 55N	6 8 E
Anniston	**169**	33 45N	85 50W
Annobón	**131**	1 25S	5 36 E
Annonay	**37**	45 15N	4 40 E
Annotto Bay	**180**	18 17N	77 3W
Anqing	**99**	30 30N	117 3 E
Anse, L'	**150**	46 47N	88 28W
Anshan	**98**	41 3N	122 58 E
Anshun	**99**	26 18N	105 57 E
Anstruther	**31**	56 14N	2 40W
Antabamba	**186**	14 40S	73 0W
Antakya	**80**	36 14N	36 10 E
Antalya	**80**	36 52N	30 45 E
Antalya Körfezi	**80**	36 15N	31 30 E
Antananarivo	**137**	18 55S	47 31 E
Antarctic Pen.	**14**	67 0S	60 0W
Antarctica	**14**	90 0S	0 0 E
Anti Atlas	**126**	30 0N	8 30W
Antibes	**37**	43 34N	7 6 E
Anticosti, Î. d'	**148**	49 30N	63 0W
Antigo	**150**	45 8N	89 5W
Antigua, Guat.	**177**	14 34N	90 41W
Antigua, W. Indies	**180**	17 0N	61 50W
Antigua and Barbuda ■	**180**	17 20N	61 48W
Antilla	**178**	20 40N	75 50W
Antioch	**172**	38 7N	121 45W
Antioquia	**184**	6 40N	75 55W
Antipodes Is.	**11**	49 45S	178 40 E
Antofagasta	**190**	23 50S	70 30W
Antrim	**34**	54 43N	6 13W
Antrim, Mts. of	**34**	54 57N	6 8W
Antsiranana	**137**	12 25S	49 20 E
Antwerp = Antwerpen	**42**	51 13N	4 25 E
Antwerpen	**42**	51 13N	4 25 E
Anvers = Antwerpen	**42**	51 13N	4 25 E
Anvik	**142**	62 37N	160 20W
Anxious B.	**119**	33 24S	134 45 E
Anyang	**98**	36 5N	114 21 E

Anzhero-Sudzhensk .... **71** 56 10N 86 0 E
Ánzio .... **46** 41 28N 12 37 E
Aoga-Shima .... **105** 32 28N 139 46 E
Aomori .... **103** 40 45N 140 45 E
Apalachee B. **170** 30 0N 84 0W
Apalachicola **170** 29 40N 85 0W
Apalachicola → **170** 29 40N 85 0W
Aparri .... **112** 18 22N 121 38 E
Apatzingan **175** 19 5N 102 21W
Apeldoorn .... **41** 52 13N 5 57 E
Apennines .... **16** 44 20N 10 20 E
Apizaco **177** 19 25N 98 9W
Aplao **186** 16 0S 72 40W
Apolo **187** 14 30S 68 30W
Apostle Is. **150** 47 0N 90 30W
Apostolos Andreas, C. .... **80** 35 42N 34 35 E
Appalachian Mts. **138** 38 0N 80 0W
Appingedam .... **41** 53 19N 6 51 E
Appleby **28** 54 35N 2 29W
Appleton **167** 44 17N 88 25W
Apulia = Púglia □ .... **49** 41 0N 16 30 E
Apure → **184** 7 37N 66 25W
Aqabah = Al 'Aqabah .... **80** 29 31N 35 0 E
Aquidauana **188** 20 30S 55 50W
Áquila, L' .... **47** 42 21N 13 24 E
Aquiles Serdán **174** 28 36N 105 53W
Ar Riyāḍ .... **83** 24 41N 46 42 E
Ar Ruṭbah .... **81** 33 0N 40 15 E
Ara .... **92** 25 35N 84 32 E
Arab, Bahr el → .... **129** 9 50N 29 0 E
Arab, Shatt al .... **84** 30 0N 48 31 E
Arabia .... **76** 25 0N 45 0 E
Arabian Gulf = Gulf, The .... **85** 27 0N 50 0 E
Arabian Sea .... **76** 16 0N 65 0 E
Aracaju **189** 10 55S 37 4W
Aracati **189** 4 30S 37 44W
Araçatuba **188** 21 10S 50 30W
Arad .... **56** 46 10N 21 20 E
Arafura Sea .... **113** 9 0S 135 0 E
Aragón □ **51** 41 25N 1 0W
Araguacema **188** 8 50S 49 20W
Araguaia → **188** 5 21S 48 41W
Araguari **188** 18 38S 48 11W
Arāk .... **84** 34 0N 49 40 E
Arakan Coast .... **93** 19 0N 94 0 E
Arakan Yoma .... **93** 20 0N 94 40 E
Araks = Aras, Rūd-e → .... **81** 39 10N 47 10 E
Aral Sea = Aralskoye More .... **70** 44 30N 60 0 E
Aralsk .... **70** 46 50N 61 20 E
Aralskoye More .... **70** 44 30N 60 0 E
Aran I. **34** 55 0N 8 30W
Aran Is. **35** 53 5N 9 42W
Aranjuez **50** 40 1N 3 40W
Aransas Pass **158** 27 55N 97 9W
Arao .... **108** 32 59N 130 25 E
Araraquara **188** 21 50S 48 0W
Ararat .... **119** 37 16S 143 0 E
Ararat, Mt. = Ağri Daği .... **81** 39 50N 44 15 E
Aras, Rūd-e → .... **81** 39 10N 47 10 E
Araya, Pen. de **185** 10 40N 64 0W
Arbīl .... **81** 36 15N 44 5 E
Arbroath **31** 56 34N 2 35W
Arcachon **36** 44 40N 1 10W
Arcadia **170** 27 20N 81 50W
Archangel = Arkhangelsk .... **69** 64 40N 41 0 E
Arcot .... **90** 12 53N 79 20 E
Arctic Bay **146** 73 1N 85 7W
Arctic Ocean **12** 78 0N 160 0W
Arctic Red River **144** 67 15N 134 0W
Ardabīl .... **81** 38 15N 48 18 E
Ardennes .... **42** 50 0N 5 10 E
Ardgour **32** 56 45N 5 25W
Ardlethan .... **117** 34 22S 146 53 E
Ardmore **168** 34 10N 97 5W
Ardnacrusha **35** 52 43N 8 38W
Ardnamurchan, Pt. of **32** 56 44N 6 14W
Ards Pen. **34** 54 30N 5 25W
Arecibo **180** 18 29N 66 42W
Arequipa **187** 16 20S 71 30W
Arezzo .... **46** 43 28N 11 50 E
Argentan **39** 48 45N 0 1W
Argentário, Mte. .... **46** 42 23N 11 11 E
Argentina ■ **190** 35 0S 66 0W
Argentino, L. **192** 50 10S 73 0W
Árgos .... **54** 37 40N 22 43 E
Argostólion .... **54** 38 12N 20 33 E
Argun → .... **74** 53 20N 121 28 E
Århus .... **61** 56 8N 10 11 E
Arica, Chile **187** 18 32S 70 20W
Arica, Colombia **184** 2 0S 71 50W
Arida .... **106** 34 5N 135 8 E
Arima **180** 10 38N 61 17W
Ario de Rosales **175** 19 12N 101 43W
Aripuanã **187** 9 25S 60 30W
Aripuanã → **187** 5 7S 60 25W
Ariquemes **187** 9 55S 63 6W
Arisaig **32** 56 55N 5 50W
Aristazabal I. **154** 52 40N 129 10W
Arizona □ **160** 34 20N 111 30W
Arjona **184** 10 14N 75 22W
Arkadelphia **168** 34 5N 93 0W
Arkansas □ **168** 35 0N 92 30W
Arkansas → **168** 33 48N 91 4W
Arkansas City **158** 37 4N 97 3W
Arkhangelsk .... **69** 64 40N 41 0 E
Arklow **35** 52 48N 6 10W
Arkticheskiy, Mys .... **72** 81 10N 95 0 E
Arles .... **37** 43 41N 4 40 E
Arlington **164** 38 52N 77 5W
Armagh **34** 54 22N 6 40W
Armavir .... **70** 45 2N 41 7 E
Armenia **184** 4 35N 75 45W
Armenia S.S.R. □ .... **70** 40 0N 41 0 E
Armentières .... **38** 50 40N 2 50 E
Armidale .... **116** 30 30S 151 40 E
Armstrong **155** 50 25N 119 10W
Arnaouti, C. .... **80** 35 6N 32 17 E
Arnaud → **146** 59 59N 69 46W
Arnhem .... **41** 51 58N 5 55 E
Arnhem, C. .... **115** 12 20S 137 30 E
Arnhem Land .... **114** 13 10S 134 30 E
Arnprior **151** 45 26N 76 21W
Arran **30** 55 34N 5 12W
Arras .... **38** 50 17N 2 46 E
Arriaga **177** 16 14N 93 54W
Árta .... **54** 39 8N 21 2 E
Artigas **191** 30 20S 56 30W
Artois .... **38** 50 20N 2 30 E
Aru, Kepulauan .... **113** 6 0S 134 30 E
Arua .... **132** 3 1N 30 58 E
Aruanã **188** 14 54S 51 10W
Aruba **181** 12 30N 70 0W
Arusha .... **135** 3 20S 36 40 E
Arvida **148** 48 25N 71 14W
Arys .... **71** 42 26N 68 48 E
'As Saffānīyah .... **84** 28 5N 48 50 E
As Samāwah .... **84** 31 15N 45 15 E
As Sulaymānīyah .... **83** 24 9N 47 18 E
As Sumaymānīyah .... **81** 35 35N 45 29 E
As Suwaydā' .... **80** 32 40N 36 30 E
As Şuwayrah .... **84** 32 55N 45 0 E
Asahi .... **107** 35 43N 140 39 E
Asahi-Gawa → .... **109** 34 36N 133 58 E
Asahigawa .... **103** 43 46N 142 22 E
Asama-Yama .... **107** 36 24N 138 31 E
Asamankese **130** 5 50N 0 40W
Asansol .... **92** 23 40N 87 1 E
Asbestos **148** 45 47N 71 58W
Ascension I. **125** 8 0S 14 15W
Áscoli Piceno .... **47** 42 51N 13 34 E
Aseb .... **133** 13 0N 42 40 E
Ash Shām, Bādiyat .... **80** 32 0N 40 0 E
Ash Shāmīyah .... **84** 31 55N 44 35 E
Ash Shāriqah .... **85** 25 23N 55 26 E
Ash Shaṭrah .... **84** 31 30N 46 10 E
Ashburton .... **123** 43 53S 171 48 E
Ashby-de-la-Zouch **28** 52 45N 1 29W
Ashcroft **155** 50 40N 121 20W
Asheboro **165** 35 43N 79 46W
Asheville **165** 35 39N 82 30W
Ashford, Australia .... **116** 29 15S 151 3 E
Ashford, U.K. .... **25** 51 8N 0 53 E

Ashikaga	**107**	36 28N	139 29 E
Ashizuri-Zaki	**109**	32 44N	133 0 E
Ashkhabad	**70**	38 0N	57 50 E
Ashland, Kans., U.S.A.	**156**	37 13N	99 43W
Ashland, Ky., U.S.A.	**165**	38 25N	82 40W
Ashland, Oreg., U.S.A.	**171**	42 10N	122 38W
Ashland, Wis., U.S.A.	**150**	46 40N	90 52W
Ashq'elon	**80**	31 42N	34 35 E
Ashtabula	**164**	41 52N	80 50W
Ashton-under-Lyne	**28**	53 30N	2 8W
Ashuanipi, L.	**147**	52 45N	66 15W
Asinara I.	**48**	41 5N	8 15 E
'Asīr □	**82**	18 40N	42 30 E
Asir, Ras	**133**	11 55N	51 10 E
Asmara = Asmera	**132**	15 19N	38 55 E
Asmera	**132**	15 19N	38 55 E
Aso	**108**	33 0N	131 5 E
Aso-Zan	**108**	32 53N	131 6 E
Aspiring, Mt.	**123**	44 23S	168 46 E
Assam □	**93**	26 0N	93 0 E
Assen	**41**	53 0N	6 35 E
Assiniboia	**152**	49 40N	105 59W
Assiniboine →	**153**	49 53N	97 8W
Assisi	**46**	43 4N	12 36 E
Asti	**46**	44 54N	8 11 E
Astipálaia	**55**	36 32N	26 22 E
Astoria	**171**	46 16N	123 50W
Astrakhan	**70**	46 25N	48 5 E
Asturias □	**50**	43 15N	6 0W
Asunción	**191**	25 10S	57 30W
Aswân	**128**	24 4N	32 57 E
Asyût	**128**	27 11N	31 4 E
At Ţafīlah	**80**	30 45N	35 30 E
At Ta'if	**82**	21 5N	40 27 E
Atacama, Desierto de	**190**	24 0S	69 20W
Atacama, Salar de	**190**	23 30S	68 20W
Atalaya	**186**	10 45S	73 50W
Atami	**107**	35 5N	139 4 E
Atbara	**129**	17 42N	33 59 E
'Atbara →	**129**	17 40N	33 56 E
Atchafalaya B.	**168**	29 30N	91 20W
Atchison	**166**	39 40N	95 10W
Athabasca	**155**	54 45N	113 20W
Athabasca →	**145**	58 40N	110 50W
Athabasca, L.	**145**	59 15N	109 15W
Athenry	**35**	53 18N	8 45W
Athens = Athínai	**55**	37 58N	23 46 E
Athens, Ala., U.S.A.	**169**	34 49N	86 58W
Athens, Ga., U.S.A.	**165**	33 56N	83 24W
Athens, Ohio, U.S.A.	**167**	39 25N	82 6W
Athens, Tenn., U.S.A.	**169**	35 45N	84 38W
Athens, Tex., U.S.A.	**168**	32 11N	95 48W
Atherton	**121**	17 17S	145 30 E
Athínai	**55**	37 58N	23 46 E
Athlone	**34**	53 26N	7 57W
Atholl, Forest of	**33**	56 51N	3 50W
Áthos	**55**	40 9N	24 22 E
Athy	**35**	53 0N	7 0W
Atico	**186**	16 14S	73 40W
Atlanta	**170**	33 50N	84 24W
Atlantic	**166**	41 25N	95 0W
Atlantic City	**164**	39 25N	74 25W
Atlantic Ocean	**9**	0 0	20 0W
Atlas Mts. = Haut Atlas	**126**	32 30N	5 0W
Atmore	**169**	31 2N	87 30W
Atsugi	**107**	35 25N	139 21 E
Atsumi	**106**	34 35N	137 4 E
Atsumi-Wan	**106**	34 44N	137 13 E
Attawapiskat →	**140**	52 57N	82 18W
Attleboro	**164**	41 56N	71 18W
Aubagne	**37**	43 17N	5 37 E
Aube →	**37**	48 34N	3 43 E
Aubenas	**37**	44 37N	4 24 E
Auburn, Ala., U.S.A.	**169**	32 37N	85 30W
Auburn, N.Y., U.S.A.	**164**	42 57N	76 39W
Auckland	**122**	36 52S	174 46 E
Auckland Is.	**15**	50 40S	166 5 E
Aude →	**37**	43 13N	3 14 E
Augsburg	**43**	48 22N	10 54 E
Augusta, Ga., U.S.A.	**170**	33 29N	81 59W
Augusta, Maine, U.S.A.	**148**	44 20N	69 46W
Aunis	**36**	46 5N	0 50W
Aurangabad	**91**	19 50N	75 23 E
Aurillac	**37**	44 55N	2 26 E
Aurora	**167**	41 42N	88 12W
Aust-Agder fylke □	**60**	58 55N	7 40 E
Austin, Minn., U.S.A.	**166**	43 37N	92 59W
Austin, Tex., U.S.A.	**161**	30 20N	97 45W
Austral Is. = Tubuai Is.	**123**	25 0S	150 0W
Australia ■	**114**	23 0S	135 0 E
Australian Alps	**117**	36 30S	148 30 E
Australian Cap. Terr. □	**117**	35 30S	149 0 E
Austria ■	**45**	47 0N	14 0 E
Autlán	**175**	19 40N	104 30W
Auvergne	**37**	45 20N	3 15 E
Auxerre	**39**	47 48N	3 32 E
Avalon Pen.	**149**	47 30N	53 20W
Aveiro	**185**	3 10S	55 5W
Avellaneda	**190**	34 50S	58 10W
Aves, I. de	**181**	15 45N	63 55W
Avesnes-sur-Helpe	**38**	50 8N	3 55 E
Aveyron →	**36**	44 7N	1 5 E
Aviemore	**33**	57 11N	3 50W
Avignon	**37**	43 57N	4 50 E
Ávila	**50**	40 39N	4 43W
Avon □	**27**	51 30N	2 40W
Avon →, Avon, U.K.	**24**	51 30N	2 43W
Avon →, Hants., U.K.	**24**	50 44N	1 45W
Avonmouth	**27**	51 30N	2 42W
Avranches	**36**	48 40N	1 20W
Awaji-Shima	**109**	34 30N	134 50 E
Aweil	**129**	8 42N	27 20 E
Axel Heiberg I.	**12**	80 0N	90 0W
Axminster	**27**	50 47N	3 1W
Ayabe	**106**	35 20N	135 20 E
Ayacucho	**186**	13 0S	74 0W
Ayíos Evstrátios	**55**	39 34N	24 58 E
Ayon, Ostrov	**73**	69 50N	169 0 E
Ayr, Australia	**121**	19 35S	147 25 E
Ayr, U.K.	**31**	55 28N	4 37W
Ayre, Pt. of	**28**	54 27N	4 21W
Aytos	**53**	42 42N	27 16 E
Ayutla	**177**	16 58N	99 17W
Aẓ Ẓahrān	**84**	26 10N	50 7 E
Az Zubayr	**84**	30 20N	47 50 E
Azamgarh	**92**	26 5N	83 13 E
Azbine = Aïr	**127**	18 30N	8 0 E
Azerbaijan S.S.R. □	**70**	40 20N	48 0 E
Azores	**126**	38 44N	29 0W
Azov Sea = Azovskoye More	**68**	46 0N	36 30 E
Azovskoye More	**68**	46 0N	36 30 E
Azúa de Compostela	**180**	18 25N	70 44W
Azuero, Pen. de	**179**	7 30N	80 30W
Azul	**190**	36 42S	59 43W

Ba Ngoi = Cam Lam	**95**	11 54N	109 10 E
Baarn	**40**	52 12N	5 17 E
Bāb el Māndeb	**133**	12 35N	43 25 E
Babahoyo	**184**	1 40S	79 30W
Babinda	**121**	17 20S	145 56 E
Babine L.	**154**	54 48N	126 0W
Bābol	**86**	36 40N	52 50 E
Babuyan Is.	**112**	19 10N	121 40 E
Babylon	**84**	32 40N	44 30 E
Bac Ninh	**95**	21 13N	106 4 E
Bac Phan	**95**	22 0N	105 0 E
Bac Quang	**95**	22 30N	104 48 E
Bacabal	**188**	4 15S	44 45W
Bacău	**57**	46 35N	26 55 E
Back →	**145**	65 10N	104 0W
Bacolod	**112**	10 40N	122 57 E
Bad Lands	**163**	43 40N	102 10W
Badajoz	**50**	38 50N	6 59W
Badakhshān □	**87**	36 30N	71 0 E
Badalona	**51**	41 26N	2 15 E
Badanah	**82**	30 58N	41 30 E
Baden-Baden	**42**	48 45N	8 15 E
Baden-Württemberg □	**42**	48 40N	9 0 E
Bādghīsāt □	**87**	35 0N	63 0 E
Badin	**88**	24 38N	68 54 E

Name	Page	Lat°	Lat′	N/S	Long°	Long′	E/W
Baffin □	146	70	0	N	80	0	W
Baffin B.	13	72	0	N	64	0	W
Baffin I.	146	68	0	N	75	0	W
Bafra	80	41	34	N	35	54	E
Bāft	85	29	15	N	56	38	E
Bagé	191	31	20	S	54	15	W
Baghdād	84	33	20	N	44	30	E
Baghlān	87	36	12	N	69	0	E
Baghlān □	87	36	0	N	68	30	E
Bahamas ■	178	24	0	N	75	0	W
Baharampur	92	24	2	N	88	27	E
Bahawalpur	89	29	24	N	71	40	E
Bahía = Salvador	189	13	0	S	38	30	W
Bahía □	189	12	0	S	42	0	W
Bahía Blanca	190	38	35	S	62	13	W
Bahr el Jebel ~►	129	7	30	N	30	30	E
Bahraich	92	27	38	N	81	37	E
Bahrain ■	85	26	0	N	50	35	E
Baia Mare	56	47	40	N	23	35	E
Baie Comeau	148	49	12	N	68	10	W
Baie-St-Paul	148	47	28	N	70	32	W
Ba'ijī	81	35	0	N	43	30	E
Baikal, L. = Baykal, Oz.	74	53	0	N	108	0	E
Baile Atha Cliath = Dublin	35	53	20	N	6	18	W
Bailleul	38	50	44	N	2	41	E
Bainbridge	170	30	53	N	84	34	W
Baird Mts.	142	67	10	N	160	15	W
Bairnsdale	117	37	48	S	147	36	E
Baiyin	98	36	45	N	104	14	E
Baja	59	46	12	N	18	59	E
Baja California	174	31	10	N	115	12	W
Baja California Norte □	174	30	0	N	115	0	W
Baja California Sur □	174	25	50	N	111	50	W
Bajimba, Mt.	116	29	17	S	152	6	E
Baker	171	44	50	N	117	55	W
Baker I.	122	0	10	N	176	35	W
Baker Lake	145	64	20	N	96	3	W
Bakersfield	173	35	25	N	119	0	W
Bākhtarān	84	34	23	N	47	0	E
Bakony Forest = Bakony Hegység	59	47	10	N	17	30	E
Bakony Hegység	59	47	10	N	17	30	E
Baku	70	40	25	N	49	45	E
Bala	26	52	54	N	3	36	W
Balabac, Str.	112	7	53	N	117	5	E
Balabakk	80	34	0	N	36	10	E
Balaghat	91	21	49	N	80	12	E
Balaghat Ra.	91	18	50	N	76	30	E
Balaklava	119	34	7	S	138	22	E
Balakovo	68	52	4	N	47	55	E
Balaton	59	46	50	N	17	40	E
Balboa	179	9	0	N	79	30	W
Balbriggan	34	53	35	N	6	10	W
Balcarce	190	38	0	S	58	10	W
Balclutha	123	46	15	S	169	45	E
Baldy Peak	161	33	50	N	109	30	W
Baleares, Islas	51	39	30	N	3	0	E
Balearic Is. = Baleares, Islas	51	39	30	N	3	0	E
Bali	111	8	20	S	115	0	E
Balikesir	80	39	35	N	27	58	E
Balikpapan	111	1	10	S	116	55	E
Balkan Mts. = Stara Planina	53	43	15	N	23	0	E
Balkan Pen.	17	42	0	N	22	0	E
Balkh □	87	36	30	N	67	0	E
Balkhash	71	46	50	N	74	50	E
Balkhash, Ozero	71	46	0	N	74	50	E
Ballachulish	32	56	40	N	5	10	W
Ballarat	117	37	33	S	143	50	E
Ballard, L.	120	29	20	S	120	10	E
Ballater	33	57	2	N	3	2	W
Ballina, Australia	116	28	50	S	153	31	E
Ballina, Mayo, Ireland	34	54	7	N	9	10	W
Ballina, Tipp., Ireland	35	52	49	N	8	27	W
Ballinasloe	35	53	20	N	8	12	W
Ballinrobe	34	53	36	N	9	13	W
Ballycastle	34	55	12	N	6	15	W
Ballymena	34	54	53	N	6	18	W
Ballymoney	34	55	5	N	6	30	W
Ballyshannon	34	54	30	N	8	10	W
Balmaceda	192	46	0	S	71	50	W
Balmoral	33	57	3	N	3	13	W
Balrampur	92	27	30	N	82	20	E
Balranald	117	34	38	S	143	33	E
Balsas, R. ~►	177	17	55	N	102	10	W
Baltic Sea	16	56	0	N	20	0	E
Baltimore	164	39	18	N	76	37	W
Baluchistan □	88	27	30	N	65	0	E
Bamako	130	12	34	N	7	55	W
Bambari	129	5	40	N	20	35	E
Bamberg	43	49	54	N	10	53	E
Bāmiān □	87	35	0	N	67	0	E
Ban Aranyaprathet	95	13	41	N	102	30	E
Ban Don = Surat Thani	96	9	6	N	99	20	E
Ban Houei Sai	95	20	22	N	100	32	E
Ban Khe Bo	95	19	10	N	104	39	E
Ban Khun Yuam	94	18	49	N	97	57	E
Ban Nong Pling	94	15	40	N	100	10	E
Ban Phai	95	16	4	N	102	44	E
Banaras = Varanasi	92	25	22	N	83	0	E
Banbridge	34	54	21	N	6	17	W
Banbury	25	52	4	N	1	21	W
Bancroft	151	45	3	N	77	51	W
Banda	91	25	30	N	80	26	E
Banda, Kepulauan	113	4	37	S	129	50	E
Banda Aceh	111	5	35	N	95	20	E
Banda Banda, Mt.	116	31	10	S	152	28	E
Banda Sea	113	6	0	S	130	0	E
Bandar = Machilipatnam	92	16	12	N	81	8	E
Bandär 'Abbās	85	27	15	N	56	15	E
Bandar-e Anzalī	81	37	30	N	49	30	E
Bandar-e Khomeyni	84	30	30	N	49	5	E
Bandar-e Lengeh	85	26	35	N	54	58	E
Bandar-e Nakhīlū	85	26	58	N	53	30	E
Bandar-e Torkeman	86	37	0	N	54	10	E
Bandar Seri Begawan	112	4	52	N	115	0	E
Bandeira, Pico da	188	20	26	S	41	47	W
Bandirma	80	40	20	N	28	0	E
Bandon	35	51	44	N	8	45	W
Bandung	111	6	54	S	107	36	E
Banes	178	21	0	N	75	42	W
Banff, Canada	155	51	10	N	115	34	W
Banff, U.K.	33	57	40	N	2	32	W
Bangalore	90	12	59	N	77	40	E
Bangassou	129	4	55	N	23	7	E
Banggai	113	1	40	S	123	30	E
Banghāzī	128	32	11	N	20	3	E
Bangka, Selat	111	2	30	S	105	30	E
Bangkok	94	13	45	N	100	35	E
Bangladesh ■	92	24	0	N	90	0	E
Bangor, N. Ireland, U.K.	34	54	40	N	5	40	W
Bangor, Wales, U.K.	26	53	13	N	4	9	W
Bangor, U.S.A.	148	44	48	N	68	42	W
Bangui	131	4	23	N	18	35	E
Bangweulu, L.	135	11	0	S	30	0	E
Bani	180	18	16	N	70	22	W
Banja Luka	52	44	49	N	17	11	E
Banjarmasin	111	3	20	S	114	35	E
Banjul	130	13	28	N	16	40	W
Bankipore	92	25	35	N	85	10	E
Banks I., B.C., Canada	154	53	20	N	130	0	W
Banks I., N.W.T., Canada	145	73	15	N	121	30	W
Banks Pen.	123	43	45	S	173	15	E
Banks Str.	119	40	40	S	148	10	E
Bann ~►	34	54	30	N	6	31	W
Banning	173	33	58	N	116	52	W
Bannockburn	31	56	5	N	3	55	W
Bannu	89	33	0	N	70	18	E
Bantry	35	51	40	N	9	28	W
Baoding	98	38	50	N	115	28	E
Baoji	99	34	20	N	107	5	E
Baotou	98	40	32	N	110	2	E
Ba'qūbah	81	33	45	N	44	50	E
Bar	52	42	8	N	19	8	E
Bar Harbor	148	44	15	N	68	20	W
Baraboo	166	43	28	N	89	46	W
Baracoa	178	20	20	N	74	30	W
Barahona	180	18	13	N	71	7	W
Barail Range	93	25	15	N	93	20	E
Baramula	89	34	15	N	74	20	E
Baran	91	25	9	N	76	40	E
Baranof I.	143	57	0	N	135	10	W
Baranovichi	68	53	10	N	26	0	E

BAR

Barbacoas	**184**	1 45N	78	0W
Barbados ■	**180**	13 0N	59	30W
Barbuda I.	**180**	17 30N	61	40W
Barca, La	**175**	20 17N	102	34W
Barcaldine	**121**	23 43S	145	6 E
Barcelona, Spain	**51**	41 21N	2	10 E
Barcelona, Venezuela	**185**	10 10N	64	40W
Barcelos	**185**	1 0S	63	0W
Barddhaman	**92**	23 14N	87	39 E
Bardera	**133**	2 20N	42	27 E
Bardsey I.	**26**	52 46N	4	47W
Bareilly	**89**	28 22N	79	27 E
Barentin	**38**	49 33N	0	58 E
Barents Sea	**13**	73 0N	39	0 E
Bargara	**121**	24 50S	152	25 E
Bari	**49**	41 6N	16	52 E
Bari Doab	**89**	30 20N	73	0 E
Barīm	**82**	12 39N	43	25 E
Barinas	**184**	8 36N	70	15W
Barisal	**92**	22 45N	90	20 E
Barito →	**111**	4 0S	114	50 E
Barlee, L.	**120**	29 15S	119	30 E
Barletta	**49**	41 20N	16	17 E
Barmer	**91**	25 45N	71	20 E
Barmera	**119**	34 15S	140	28 E
Barmouth	**26**	52 44N	4	3W
Barnard Castle	**28**	54 33N	1	55W
Barnaul	**71**	53 20N	83	40 E
Barneveld	**41**	52 7N	5	36 E
Barnsley	**28**	53 33N	1	29W
Barnstaple	**27**	51 5N	4	3W
Baro	**131**	8 35N	6	18 E
Baroda = Vadodara	**91**	22 20N	73	10 E
Barpeta	**93**	26 20N	91	10 E
Barquisimeto	**184**	10 4N	69	19W
Barra	**32**	57 0N	7	30W
Barra Hd.	**32**	56 47N	7	40W
Barraba	**116**	30 21S	150	35 E
Barranca	**186**	10 45S	77	50W
Barrancabermeja	**184**	7 0N	73	50W
Barrancas	**185**	8 55N	62	5W
Barranqueras	**190**	27 30S	59	0W
Barranquilla	**184**	11 0N	74	50W
Barre	**151**	44 15N	72	30W
Barreiros	**188**	8 49S	35	12W
Barrhead	**155**	54 10N	114	24W
Barrie	**151**	44 24N	79	40W
Barrier Ra.	**118**	31 0S	141	30 E
Barrington Tops	**116**	32 6S	151	28 E
Barrow →	**35**	52 10N	6	57W
Barrow, Pt.	**138**	71 22N	156	30W
Barrow-in-Furness	**28**	54 8N	3	15W
Barry	**27**	51 23N	3	19W
Barry's Bay	**151**	45 29N	77	41W
Barsi	**91**	18 10N	75	50 E
Barstow	**173**	34 58N	117	2W
Bartica	**185**	6 25N	58	40W
Bartow	**170**	27 53N	81	49W
Basel	**44**	47 35N	7	35 E
Bashi Channel	**99**	21 15N	122	0 E
Bashkir A.S.S.R. □	**69**	54 0N	57	0 E
Basilan	**112**	6 35N	122	0 E
Basildon	**25**	51 34N	0	29 E
Basilicata □	**49**	40 30N	16	0 E
Basim = Washim	**91**	20 3N	77	0 E
Basle = Basel	**44**	47 35N	7	35 E
Basoka	**134**	1 16N	23	40 E
Basque Provinces = Vascongadas	**50**	42 50N	2	45W
Basra = Al Basrah	**84**	30 30N	47	50 E
Bass Rock	**31**	56 5N	2	40W
Bass Str.	**117**	39 15S	146	30 E
Bassano	**155**	50 48N	112	20W
Basse-Terre	**180**	16 0N	61	40W
Bassein	**93**	16 45N	94	30 E
Basseterre	**180**	17 17N	62	43W
Basti	**92**	26 52N	82	55 E
Bastia	**36**	42 40N	9	30 E
Batabanó	**178**	22 40N	82	20W
Batamay	**74**	63 30N	129	15 E
Batan Is.	**112**	20 25N	121	59 E

Batang	**101**	30 1N	99	0 E
Batavia	**164**	43 0N	78	10W
Batemans Bay	**117**	35 44S	150	11 E
Batesville	**168**	35 48N	91	40W
Bath, U.K.	**27**	51 22N	2	22W
Bath, Maine, U.S.A.	**148**	43 50N	69	49W
Bath, N.Y., U.S.A.	**164**	42 20N	77	17W
Bathurst = Banjul	**130**	13 28N	16	40W
Bathurst, Australia	**117**	33 25S	149	31 E
Bathurst, Canada	**148**	47 37N	65	43W
Bathurst, C.	**145**	70 34N	128	0W
Bathurst Inlet	**145**	66 50N	108	1W
Batlow	**117**	35 31S	148	9 E
Batman	**81**	37 55N	41	5 E
Batna	**127**	35 34N	6	15 E
Baton Rouge	**168**	30 30N	91	5W
Batopilas	**174**	27 1N	107	44W
Battambang	**95**	13 7N	103	12 E
Batticaloa	**90**	7 43N	81	45 E
Battle	**25**	50 55N	0	30 E
Battle Creek	**167**	42 20N	85	6W
Battle Harbour	**147**	52 16N	55	35W
Battleford	**152**	52 45N	108	15W
Batu Gajah	**96**	4 28N	101	3 E
Batu Is.	**111**	0 30S	98	25 E
Batumi	**70**	41 30N	41	30 E
Bauchi	**131**	10 22N	9	48 E
Bauru	**188**	22 10S	49	0W
Bavaria = Bayern □	**43**	49 7N	11	30 E
Bawdwin	**93**	23 5N	97	20 E
Bawean	**111**	5 46S	112	35 E
Bawku	**130**	11 3N	0	19W
Bay City	**167**	43 35N	83	51W
Bay Shore	**164**	40 44N	73	15W
Bayamo	**178**	20 20N	76	40W
Bayamón	**180**	18 24N	66	10W
Bayan Har Shan	**101**	34 0N	98	0 E
Bayan Hot = Alxa Zuoqi	**98**	38 50N	105	40 E
Bayern □	**43**	49 7N	11	30 E
Bayeux	**36**	49 17N	0	42W
Bayfield	**150**	43 34N	81	42W
Baykal, Oz.	**74**	53 0N	108	0 E
Baykonur	**71**	47 48N	65	50 E
Bayonne	**36**	43 30N	1	28W
Bayreuth	**43**	49 56N	11	35 E
Bayrūt	**80**	33 53N	35	31 E
Baytown	**168**	29 42N	94	57W
Beachy Head	**25**	50 44N	0	16 E
Beagle, Canal	**192**	55 0S	68	30W
Béarn	**36**	43 8N	0	36W
Beauce, Plaine de la	**37**	48 10N	1	45 E
Beaudesert	**116**	27 59S	153	0 E
Beaufort	**170**	32 25N	80	40W
Beaufort Sea	**12**	72 0N	140	0W
Beaugency	**39**	47 47N	1	38 E
Beauharnois	**151**	45 20N	73	52W
Beauly	**33**	57 29N	4	27W
Beaumaris	**26**	53 16N	4	7W
Beaumont	**168**	30 5N	94	8W
Beaumont-sur-Oise	**39**	49 9N	2	17 E
Beauséjour	**153**	50 5N	96	35W
Beauvais	**38**	49 25N	2	8 E
Beauval	**152**	55 9N	107	37W
Beaver	**142**	66 20N	147	30W
Beaver →	**152**	55 26N	107	45W
Beaver Falls	**164**	40 44N	80	20W
Beaverlodge	**155**	55 11N	119	29W
Beawar	**91**	26 3N	74	18 E
Bečej	**52**	45 36N	20	3 E
Béchar	**127**	31 38N	2	18W
Beckley	**165**	37 50N	81	8W
Bedford, U.K.	**25**	52 8N	0	29W
Bedford, U.S.A.	**167**	38 50N	86	30W
Bedford □	**25**	52 4N	0	28W
Beenleigh	**116**	27 43S	153	10 E
Be'er Sheva'	**80**	31 15N	34	48 E
Beersheba = Be'er Sheva'	**80**	31 15N	34	48 E
Beeston	**29**	52 55N	1	11W
Bega	**117**	36 41S	149	51 E
Behbehān	**84**	30 30N	50	15 E
Beibei	**99**	29 47N	106	22 E

10

Beihai	**99**	21 28N	109 6 E
Beijing	**98**	39 55N	116 20 E
Beira	**137**	19 50S	34 52 E
Beira-Alta	**50**	40 35N	7 35W
Beira-Baixa	**50**	40 2N	7 30W
Beira-Litoral	**50**	40 5N	8 30W
Beirut = Bayrūt	**80**	33 53N	35 31 E
Bejaia	**127**	36 42N	5 2 E
Békéscsaba	**59**	46 40N	21 5 E
Bela	**92**	25 50N	82 0 E
Bela Crkva	**52**	44 55N	21 27 E
Belaya Tserkov	**68**	49 45N	30 10 E
Belcher Is.	**140**	56 15N	78 45W
Belém	**188**	1 20S	48 30W
Belfast, U.K.	**34**	54 35N	5 56W
Belfast, U.S.A.	**148**	44 30N	69 0W
Belfort	**37**	47 38N	6 50 E
Belgaum	**91**	15 55N	74 35 E
Belgium ■	**42**	50 30N	5 0 E
Belgorod	**68**	50 35N	36 35 E
Belgrade = Beograd	**52**	44 50N	20 37 E
Belitung	**111**	3 10S	107 50 E
Belize ■	**177**	17 0N	88 30W
Belize City	**177**	17 25N	88 0W
Bell Peninsula	**146**	63 50N	82 0W
Bell Ville	**190**	32 40S	62 40W
Bella Coola	**154**	52 25N	126 40W
Bellaire	**164**	40 1N	80 46W
Bellary	**90**	15 10N	76 56 E
Belle Fourche →	**163**	44 25N	102 19W
Belle Glade	**170**	26 43N	80 38W
Belle Isle	**147**	51 57N	55 25W
Belle Isle, Str. of	**141**	51 30N	56 30W
Bellefontaine	**167**	40 20N	83 45W
Belleville, Canada	**151**	44 10N	77 23W
Belleville, U.S.A.	**166**	38 30N	90 0W
Bellevue	**155**	49 35N	114 22W
Bellin	**146**	60 0N	70 0W
Bellingham	**171**	48 45N	122 27W
Bellingshausen Sea	**14**	66 0S	80 0W
Belmont	**117**	33 4S	151 42 E
Belmopan	**177**	17 18N	88 30W
Belo Horizonte	**188**	19 55S	43 56W
Belogorsk	**75**	51 0N	128 20 E
Beloit	**166**	42 35N	89 0W
Belomorsk	**68**	64 35N	34 30 E
Belovo	**71**	54 30N	86 0 E
Beloye More	**69**	66 30N	38 0 E
Beloye Ozero	**68**	45 15N	46 50 E
Belper	**28**	53 2N	1 29W
Belukha	**71**	49 50N	86 50 E
Belyy, Ostrov	**69**	73 30N	71 0 E
Bemidji	**156**	47 30N	94 50W
Ben Lomond, N.S.W., Australia	**116**	30 1S	151 40 E
Ben Lomond, Tas., Australia	**119**	41 38S	147 42 E
Ben Macdhui	**33**	57 4N	3 40W
Ben More, Central, U.K.	**32**	56 23N	4 31W
Ben More, Strathclyde, U.K.	**30**	56 26N	6 2W
Ben More Assynt	**32**	58 7N	4 51W
Ben Nevis	**32**	56 48N	5 0W
Benalla	**117**	36 30S	146 0 E
Benares = Varanasi	**92**	25 22N	83 0 E
Benbecula	**32**	57 26N	7 21W
Benbonyathe, Mt.	**118**	30 25S	139 11 E
Bencubbin	**120**	30 48S	117 52 E
Bend	**171**	44 2N	121 15W
Bendemeer	**116**	30 53S	151 8 E
Bender Beila	**133**	9 30N	50 48 E
Bendigo	**117**	36 40S	144 15 E
Benevento	**49**	41 7N	14 45 E
Bengal, Bay of	**92**	15 0N	90 0 E
Bengbu	**99**	32 58N	117 20 E
Benghazi = Banghāzī	**128**	32 11N	20 3 E
Benguela	**134**	12 37S	13 25 E
Beni →	**187**	10 23S	65 24W
Beni Suef	**128**	29 5N	31 6 E
Benidorm	**51**	38 33N	0 9W
Benin ■	**131**	10 0N	2 0 E
Benin, Bight of	**131**	5 0N	3 0 E
Benin City	**131**	6 20N	5 31 E
Benjamin Constant	**187**	4 40S	70 15W
Bennett	**144**	59 56N	134 53W
Bennettsville	**165**	34 38N	79 39W
Benton	**168**	34 30N	92 35W
Benue →	**131**	7 48N	6 46 E
Benxi	**98**	41 20N	123 48 E
Beograd	**52**	44 50N	20 37 E
Beppu	**108**	33 15N	131 30 E
Berau, Teluk	**113**	2 30S	132 30 E
Berber	**129**	18 0N	34 0 E
Berbera	**133**	10 30N	45 2 E
Berck-sur-Mer	**38**	50 25N	1 36 E
Berezniki	**69**	59 24N	56 46 E
Bérgamo	**46**	45 42N	9 40 E
Bergen, Neth.	**40**	52 40N	4 43 E
Bergen, Norway	**60**	60 23N	5 20 E
Bergen-op-Zoom	**40**	51 30N	4 18 E
Bergerac	**36**	44 51N	0 30 E
Berhala, Selat	**111**	1 0S	104 15 E
Berhampore = Baharampur	**92**	24 2N	88 27 E
Berhampur	**92**	19 15N	84 54 E
Bering Sea	**142**	58 0N	167 0 E
Bering Str.	**142**	66 0N	170 0W
Berkeley	**172**	37 52N	122 20W
Berkshire □	**25**	51 30N	1 20W
Berkshire Downs	**24**	51 30N	1 30W
Berlin, Germany	**43**	52 32N	13 24 E
Berlin, U.S.A.	**148**	44 29N	71 10W
Bermuda ■	**180**	32 45N	65 0W
Bern	**44**	46 57N	7 28 E
Bernay	**39**	49 5N	0 35 E
Berne = Bern	**44**	46 57N	7 28 E
Berri	**119**	34 14S	140 35 E
Berry	**37**	47 0N	2 0 E
Bertoua	**131**	4 30N	13 45 E
Berwick-upon-Tweed	**31**	55 47N	2 0W
Berwyn Mts.	**26**	52 54N	3 26W
Besançon	**37**	47 15N	6 0 E
Bessemer, Ala., U.S.A.	**169**	33 25N	86 57W
Bessemer, Mich., U.S.A.	**156**	46 27N	90 0W
Bethel	**142**	60 50N	161 50W
Bethlehem	**164**	40 39N	75 24W
Béthune	**38**	50 30N	2 38 E
Betsiboka →	**137**	16 3S	46 36 E
Beverley	**29**	53 52N	0 26W
Beverly Hills	**173**	34 4N	118 29W
Beverwijk	**40**	52 28N	4 38 E
Bexhill	**24**	50 51N	0 29 E
Beyneu	**70**	45 10N	55 3 E
Beyşehir Gölü	**80**	37 40N	31 45 E
Béziers	**37**	43 20N	3 12 E
Bezwada = Vijayawada	**92**	16 31N	80 39 E
Bhadravati	**90**	13 49N	75 40 E
Bhagalpur	**92**	25 10N	87 0 E
Bhakra Dam	**89**	31 30N	76 45 E
Bhandara	**91**	21 5N	79 42 E
Bhanrer Ra.	**91**	23 40N	79 45 E
Bharat = India ■	**78**	20 0N	78 0 E
Bharatpur	**89**	27 15N	77 30 E
Bharuch	**91**	21 47N	73 0 E
Bhatpara	**92**	22 50N	88 25 E
Bhaunagar = Bhavnagar	**91**	21 45N	72 10 E
Bhavnagar	**91**	21 45N	72 10 E
Bhilwara	**91**	25 25N	74 38 E
Bhima →	**91**	16 25N	77 17 E
Bhiwandi	**91**	19 20N	73 0 E
Bhiwani	**89**	28 50N	76 9 E
Bhopal	**91**	23 20N	77 30 E
Bhubaneshwar	**92**	20 15N	85 50 E
Bhusaval	**91**	21 3N	75 46 E
Bhutan ■	**92**	27 25N	90 30 E
Biafra, B. of = Bonny, Bight of	**131**	3 30N	9 20 E
Biała Podlaska	**58**	52 4N	23 6 E
Białystok	**58**	53 10N	23 10 E
Biarritz	**36**	43 29N	1 33W
Bibai	**103**	43 19N	141 52 E
Bicester	**25**	51 53N	1 9W
Biche, L. la	**155**	54 50N	112 3W
Bidar	**91**	17 55N	77 35 E
Biddeford	**148**	43 30N	70 28W

Name	Page	Lat°	Lat'	N/S	Lon°	Lon'	E/W
Bideford	27	51	1	N	4	13	W
Bié, Planalto de	136	12	0	S	16	0	E
Bieber	172	41	4	N	121	6	W
Biel	44	47	8	N	7	14	E
Bielé Karpaty	59	49	5	N	18	0	E
Bielefeld	42	52	2	N	8	31	E
Bielsko-Biała	59	49	50	N	19	2	E
Bien Hoa	95	10	57	N	106	49	E
Bienne = Biel	44	47	8	N	7	14	E
Bienville, L.	146	55	5	N	72	40	W
Big Belt Mts.	163	46	50	N	111	30	W
Big Cypress Swamp	170	26	12	N	81	10	W
Big Horn Mts. = Bighorn Mts.	163	44	30	N	107	30	W
Big Rapids	167	43	42	N	85	27	W
Big Sioux →	156	42	30	N	96	25	W
Big Spring	161	32	10	N	101	25	W
Big Stone Gap	165	36	52	N	82	45	W
Big Trout L.	153	53	40	N	90	0	W
Biggar, Canada	152	52	4	N	108	0	W
Biggar, U.K.	31	55	38	N	3	31	W
Bighorn →	163	46	9	N	107	28	W
Bighorn Mts.	163	44	30	N	107	30	W
Bihar	92	25	5	N	85	40	E
Bihar □	92	25	0	N	86	0	E
Bijagós, Arquipélago dos	130	11	15	N	16	10	W
Bijapur	91	16	50	N	75	55	E
Bijeljina	52	44	46	N	19	17	E
Bikaner	89	28	2	N	73	18	E
Bikin	75	46	50	N	134	20	E
Bilaspur	92	22	2	N	82	15	E
Bilauk Taungdan	94	13	0	N	99	0	E
Bilbao	50	43	16	N	2	56	W
Billingham	29	54	36	N	1	18	W
Billings	163	45	43	N	108	29	W
Billiton Is. = Belitung	111	3	10	S	107	50	E
Bilma	127	18	50	N	13	30	E
Biloela	121	24	24	S	150	31	E
Biloxi	169	30	24	N	88	53	W
Bina-Etawah	91	24	13	N	78	14	E
Bīnālūd, Kūh-e	86	36	30	N	58	30	E
Bindi Bindi	120	30	37	S	116	22	E
Bingara	116	29	52	S	150	36	E
Bingerville	130	5	18	N	3	49	W
Bingham	148	45	5	N	69	50	W
Binghamton	164	42	9	N	75	54	W
Binh Dinh = An Nhon	95	13	55	N	109	7	E
Binnaway	116	31	28	S	149	24	E
Binzert = Bizerte	127	37	15	N	9	50	E
Bioko	131	3	30	N	8	40	E
Bir Mogrein	126	25	10	N	11	25	W
Birchip	119	35	56	S	142	55	E
Bird I. = Aves, I. de	181	15	45	N	63	55	W
Birdum	114	15	39	S	133	13	E
Birkenhead	28	53	24	N	3	1	W
Birmingham, U.K.	24	52	30	N	1	55	W
Birmingham, U.S.A.	169	33	31	N	86	50	W
Birobidzhan	75	48	50	N	132	50	E
Birr	35	53	7	N	7	55	W
Bisai	106	35	16	N	136	44	E
Biscay, B. of	36	45	0	N	2	0	W
Biscostasing	150	47	18	N	82	9	W
Bishop Auckland	28	54	40	N	1	40	W
Bishop's Stortford	25	51	52	N	0	11	E
Bismarck	163	46	49	N	100	49	W
Bismarck Arch.	115	2	30	S	150	0	E
Bissagos = Bijagós, Arquipélago dos	130	11	15	N	16	10	W
Bissau	130	11	45	N	15	45	W
Bitola	52	41	5	N	21	10	E
Bitolj = Bitola	52	41	5	N	21	10	E
Bitterroot Range	162	46	0	N	114	20	W
Biu	131	10	40	N	12	3	E
Biwa-Ko	106	35	15	N	136	10	E
Biysk	71	52	40	N	85	0	E
Bizen	109	34	43	N	134	8	E
Bizerte	127	37	15	N	9	50	E
Bjørnøya	13	74	30	N	19	0	E
Black → = Da →	95	21	15	N	105	20	E
Black Diamond	155	50	45	N	114	14	W
Black Forest = Schwarzwald	42	48	0	N	8	0	E
Black Hills	163	44	0	N	103	50	W
Black Mts.	26	51	52	N	3	5	W
Black Sea	17	43	30	N	35	0	E
Blackall	121	24	25	S	145	45	E
Blackburn	28	53	44	N	2	30	W
Blackpool	28	53	48	N	3	3	W
Blackwater	121	23	35	S	148	53	E
Blackwater →, Meath, Ireland	34	53	46	N	7	0	W
Blackwater →, Munster, Ireland	35	51	55	N	7	50	W
Blackwater →, U.K.	34	54	31	N	6	35	W
Blackwell	168	36	55	N	97	20	W
Blaenau Ffestiniog	26	53	0	N	3	57	W
Blagoveshchensk	75	50	20	N	127	30	E
Blair Atholl	33	56	46	N	3	50	W
Blairmore	155	49	40	N	114	25	W
Blanc, Mont	37	45	48	N	6	50	E
Blanca Peak	163	37	35	N	105	29	W
Blanche L.	118	29	15	S	139	40	E
Blanco, C.	171	42	50	N	124	40	W
Blandford Forum	24	50	52	N	2	10	W
Blantyre	137	15	45	S	35	0	E
Blarney	35	51	57	N	8	35	W
Blaydon	28	54	56	N	1	47	W
Blayney	117	33	32	S	149	14	E
Blekinge län □	61	56	20	N	15	20	E
Blenheim	123	41	38	S	173	57	E
Bletchley	25	51	59	N	0	44	W
Blida	127	36	30	N	2	49	E
Blind River	150	46	10	N	82	58	W
Blitar	111	8	5	S	112	11	E
Bloemfontein	137	29	6	S	26	14	E
Blois	36	47	35	N	1	20	E
Bloody Foreland	34	55	10	N	8	18	W
Bloomington, Ill., U.S.A.	166	40	27	N	89	0	W
Bloomington, Ind., U.S.A.	167	39	10	N	86	30	W
Bloomsburg	164	41	0	N	76	30	W
Blue Mts., Oreg., U.S.A.	171	45	15	N	119	0	W
Blue Mts., Pa., U.S.A.	164	40	30	N	76	30	W
Blue Nile = Nîl el Azraq →	129	15	38	N	32	31	E
Blue Ridge Mts.	165	36	30	N	80	15	W
Bluefield	165	37	18	N	81	14	W
Bluefields	179	12	20	N	83	50	W
Bluestack, mt.	34	54	46	N	8	5	W
Bluff	123	46	37	S	168	20	E
Blumenau	191	27	0	S	49	0	W
Blyth	28	55	8	N	1	32	W
Bo	130	7	55	N	11	50	W
Bo Hai	98	39	0	N	120	0	E
Boa Vista	185	2	48	N	60	30	W
Boaco	179	12	29	N	85	35	W
Bobadah	116	32	19	S	146	41	E
Bobcaygeon	151	44	33	N	78	33	W
Bobo-Dioulasso	130	11	8	N	4	13	W
Bobraomby, Tanjon' i	137	12	40	S	49	10	E
Bobruysk	68	53	10	N	29	15	E
Bôca do Acre	187	8	50	S	67	27	W
Boca Raton	170	26	21	N	80	5	W
Bocas del Toro	179	9	15	N	82	20	W
Bocholt	42	51	50	N	6	35	E
Bochum	42	51	28	N	7	12	E
Boden	67	65	50	N	21	42	E
Bodensee	44	47	35	N	9	25	E
Bodhan	91	18	40	N	77	44	E
Bodmin	27	50	28	N	4	44	W
Bodmin Moor	27	50	33	N	4	36	W
Bodø	64	67	17	N	14	24	E
Bogalusa	169	30	50	N	89	55	W
Boggabilla	116	28	36	S	150	24	E
Boggabri	116	30	45	S	150	0	E
Boggeragh Mts.	35	52	2	N	8	55	W
Bognor Regis	25	50	47	N	0	40	W
Bogong, Mt.	117	36	47	S	147	17	E
Bogor	111	6	36	S	106	48	E
Bogotá	184	4	34	N	74	0	W
Boguchany	74	58	40	N	97	30	E
Bohain	38	49	59	N	3	28	E
Bohemian Forest = Böhmerwald	43	49	30	N	12	40	E
Böhmerwald	43	49	30	N	12	40	E
Bohol	112	9	50	N	124	10	E

Name	Page	°	′		°	′	
Bohol Sea	112	9	0N	124	0	E
Bohotleh	133	8	20N	46	25	E
Boise	162	43	43N	116	9	W
Boissevain	153	49	15N	100	5	W
Boké	130	10	56N	14	17	W
Bolan Pass	88	29	50N	67	20	E
Bolaños, R. →	175	21	12N	104	5	W
Bolbec	38	49	30N	0	30	E
Bolgatanga	130	10	44N	0	53	W
Bolívar	190	36	15S	60	53	W
Bolivia ■	187	17	6S	64	0	W
Bollnäs	60	61	21N	16	24	E
Bollon	116	28	2S	147	29	E
Bologna	47	44	30N	11	20	E
Boloven, Cao Nguyen	95	15	10N	106	30	E
Bolsena, L. di	46	42	35N	11	55	E
Bolshevik, Ostrov	72	78	30N	102	0	E
Bolshoi Kavkas	70	42	50N	44	0	E
Bolshoy Begichev, Ostrov	72	74	20N	112	30	E
Bolsward	41	53	3N	5	32	E
Bolton	28	53	35N	2	26	W
Bolzano	47	46	30N	11	20	E
Boma	134	5	50S	13	4	E
Bombala	117	36	56S	149	15	E
Bombay	91	18	55N	72	50	E
Bomu →	129	4	40N	23	30	E
Bon, C.	127	37	1N	11	2	E
Bonaire	181	12	10N	68	15	W
Bonavista	149	48	40N	53	5	W
Bonifacio, Bouches de	48	41	12N	9	15	E
Bonn	42	50	43N	7	6	E
Bonneval	39	48	11N	1	24	E
Bonnie Rock	120	30	29S	118	22	E
Bonny, Bight of	131	3	30N	9	20	E
Bonnyville	152	54	20N	110	45	W
Bonthe	130	7	30N	12	33	W
Boonah	116	27	58S	152	41	E
Boone	166	42	5N	93	53	W
Boonville	167	38	3N	87	13	W
Boorowa	117	34	28S	148	44	E
Boothia, Gulf of	146	71	0N	90	0	W
Boothia Pen.	145	71	0N	94	0	W
Bootle	28	53	28N	3	1	W
Bôr	129	6	10N	31	40	E
Borås	60	57	43N	12	56	E
Borāzjān	85	29	22N	51	10	E
Bordeaux	36	44	50N	0	36	W
Borders □	31	55	35N	2	50	W
Bordertown	119	36	19S	140	45	E
Bordj Omar Driss	127	28	10N	6	40	E
Borger	161	35	40N	101	20	W
Borja	186	4	20S	77	40	W
Borlänge	60	60	29N	15	26	E
Borneo	111	1	0N	115	0	E
Bornholm	61	55	10N	15	0	E
Borujerd	84	33	55N	48	50	E
Borzya	74	50	24N	116	31	E
Boscastle	27	50	42N	4	42	W
Boshan	98	36	28N	117	49	E
Bosna →	52	45	4N	18	29	E
Bosna i Hercegovina □	52	44	0N	18	0	E
Bosnia = Bosna i Hercegovina □	52	44	0N	18	0	E
Bösö-Hantö	107	35	20N	140	20	E
Bosporus = Karadeniz Boğazı	80	41	10N	29	10	E
Bossangoa	131	6	35N	17	30	E
Bossembélé	131	5	25N	17	40	E
Bossier City	168	32	28N	93	48	W
Bosten Hu	100	41	55N	87	40	E
Boston, U.K.	29	52	59N	0	2	W
Boston, U.S.A.	164	42	20N	71	0	W
Bothnia, G. of	67	63	0N	20	0	E
Botletle →	136	20	10S	23	15	E
Botoşani	57	47	42N	26	41	E
Botswana ■	136	22	0S	24	0	E
Botucatu	188	22	55S	48	30	W
Bou Djébéha	126	18	25N	2	45	W
Bouaké	130	7	40N	5	2	W
Bougie = Bejaia	127	36	42N	5	2	E
Boulogne-sur-Mer	38	50	42N	1	36	E
Bourbonnais	37	46	28N	3	0	E
Bourem	130	17	0N	0	24	W
Bourg-en-Bresse	37	46	13N	5	12	E
Bourges	37	47	9N	2	25	E
Bourgogne	37	47	0N	4	30	E
Bourke	116	30	8S	145	55	E
Bournemouth	24	50	43N	1	53	W
Bousso	131	10	34N	16	52	E
Bouvet I. = Bouvetøya	14	54	26S	3	24	E
Bouvetøya	14	54	26S	3	24	E
Bowen	121	20	0S	148	16	E
Bowland, Forest of	28	54	0N	2	30	W
Bowling Green, Ky., U.S.A.	169	37	0N	86	25	W
Bowling Green, Ohio, U.S.A.	167	41	22N	83	40	W
Bowling Green, C.	121	19	19S	147	25	E
Bowmanville	151	43	55N	78	41	W
Bowral	117	34	26S	150	27	E
Boyle	34	53	58N	8	19	W
Boyne →	34	53	43N	6	15	W
Boyne City	150	45	13N	85	1	W
Boyup Brook	120	33	50S	116	23	E
Bozeman	163	45	40N	111	0	W
Bozen = Bolzano	47	46	30N	11	20	E
Brač	52	43	20N	16	40	E
Bracciano, L. di	46	42	8N	12	11	E
Bracebridge	151	45	2N	79	19	W
Bräcke	66	62	45N	15	26	E
Brad	56	46	10N	22	50	E
Bradenton	170	27	25N	82	35	W
Bradford, U.K.	28	53	47N	1	45	W
Bradford, U.S.A.	164	41	58N	78	41	W
Braemar	33	57	2N	3	20	W
Braga	50	41	35N	8	25	W
Bragança, Brazil	188	1	0S	47	2	W
Bragança, Portugal	50	41	48N	6	50	W
Brahmanbaria	93	23	58N	91	15	E
Brahmani →	92	20	39N	86	46	E
Brahmaputra →	93	24	2N	90	59	E
Braidwood	117	35	27S	149	49	E
Bråila	57	45	19N	27	59	E
Brainerd	156	46	20N	94	10	W
Braintree	25	51	53N	0	34	E
Brampton	151	43	45N	79	45	W
Branco →	185	1	20S	61	50	W
Branco, Cabo	182	7	9S	34	47	W
Brandenburg	43	52	24N	12	33	E
Brandon	153	49	50N	99	57	W
Brantford	151	43	10N	80	15	W
Brasil, Planalto	188	18	0S	46	30	W
Brasília	188	15	47S	47	55	E
Braşov	57	45	38N	25	35	E
Brassey, Banjaran	111	5	0N	117	15	E
Brasstown Bald, Mt.	165	34	54N	83	45	W
Bratislava	59	48	10N	17	7	E
Bratsk	74	56	10N	101	30	E
Brattleboro	164	42	53N	72	37	W
Braunschweig	43	52	17N	10	28	E
Brava	133	1	20N	44	8	E
Bravo del Norte →	174	25	57N	97	9	W
Brawley	173	32	58N	115	30	W
Bray	35	53	12N	6	6	W
Brazil	167	39	32N	87	8	W
Brazil ■	188	10	0S	50	0	W
Brazilian Highlands = Brasil, Planalto	188	18	0S	46	30	W
Brazos →	168	28	53N	95	23	W
Brazzaville	134	4	9S	15	12	E
Brčko	52	44	54N	18	46	E
Breadalbane	31	56	30N	4	15	W
Bream Bay	122	35	56S	174	28	E
Brecon	26	51	57N	3	23	W
Brecon Beacons	26	51	53N	3	27	W
Breda	40	51	35N	4	45	E
Breiðafjörður	64	65	15N	23	15	W
Bremen	42	53	4N	8	47	E
Bremerhaven	42	53	34N	8	35	E
Bremerton	171	47	30N	122	38	W
Brenham	168	30	5N	96	27	W
Brentwood	25	51	37N	0	19	E
Bréscia	46	45	33N	10	13	E
Breslau = Wrocław	58	51	5N	17	5	E

Brest, France **36** 48 24N 4 31W
Brest, U.S.S.R. .... **68** 52 10N 23 40 E
Bretagne **36** 48 0N 3 0W
Bretçu .... **57** 46 7N 26 18 E
Breton Sd. **169** 29 40N 89 12W
Brett, C. .... **122** 35 10S 174 20 E
Brewer **148** 44 43N 68 50W
Brewster **171** 48 10N 119 51W
Brewton **169** 31 9N 87 2W
Brezhnev .... **68** 55 42N 52 19 E
Briançon .... **37** 44 54N 6 39 E
Bridgend **27** 51 30N 3 35W
Bridgeport **164** 41 12N 73 12W
Bridgeton **164** 39 29N 75 10W
Bridgetown, Australia .... **120** 33 58S 116 7 E
Bridgetown, Barbados **180** 13 0N 59 30W
Bridgnorth **24** 52 33N 2 25W
Bridgwater **27** 51 7N 3 0W
Bridlington **29** 54 6N 0 11W
Bridport **27** 50 43N 2 45W
Brigham City **163** 41 30N 112 1W
Bright .... **117** 36 42S 146 56 E
Brighton, Australia .... **119** 42 42S 147 16 E
Brighton, U.K. **25** 50 50N 0 9W
Brindisi .... **49** 40 39N 17 55 E
Brisbane .... **116** 27 25S 153 2 E
Bristol, U.K. **27** 51 26N 2 35W
Bristol, Conn., U.S.A. **164** 41 44N 72 57W
Bristol, Tenn., U.S.A. **165** 36 36N 82 11W
Bristol B. **142** 58 0N 160 0W
Bristol Channel **27** 51 18N 4 30W
Bristow **168** 35 55N 96 28W
British Columbia □ **154** 55 0N 125 15W
British Guiana = Guyana ■ **185** 5 0N 59 0W
British Honduras = Belize ■ .. **177** 17 0N 88 30W
British Isles **18** 55 0N 4 0W
Brittany = Bretagne **36** 48 0N 3 0W
Brive-la-Gaillarde .... **36** 45 10N 1 32 E
Brlik .... **71** 44 0N 74 5 E
Brno .... **59** 49 10N 16 35 E
Broach = Bharuch .... **91** 21 47N 73 0 E
Broad Law **31** 55 30N 3 22W
Broad Sd. .... **121** 22 0S 149 45 E
Broads, The .... **29** 52 45N 1 30 E
Brochet **145** 57 53N 101 40W
Brockton **164** 42 8N 71 2W
Brockville **151** 44 35N 75 41W
Brod .... **52** 41 35N 21 17 E
Brodeur Pen. **146** 72 30N 88 10W
Broken Hill = Kabwe .... **135** 14 30S 28 29 E
Broken Hill .... **118** 31 58S 141 29 E
Bromley .... **25** 51 20N 0 5 E
Brookhaven **169** 31 40N 90 25W
Brooks **155** 50 35N 111 55W
Brooks Ra. **142** 68 40N 147 0W
Brosna →— **35** 53 8N 8 0W
Brough **28** 54 32N 2 19W
Broughty Ferry **31** 56 29N 2 50W
Brouwershaven .... **40** 51 45N 3 55 E
Brownsville **158** 25 56N 97 25W
Brownwood **161** 31 45N 99 0W
Bruay-en-Artois .... **38** 50 29N 2 33 E
Bruce, Mt. .... **114** 22 37S 118 8 E
Bruce Rock .... **120** 31 52S 118 8 E
Bruck an der Leitha .... **45** 48 1N 16 47 E
Bruges = Brugge .... **42** 51 13N 3 13 E
Brugge .... **42** 51 13N 3 13 E
Brunei = Bandar Seri
  Begawan .... **112** 4 52N 115 0 E
Brunei ■ .... **111** 4 50N 115 0 E
Bruno **152** 52 20N 105 30W
Brunswick = Braunschweig .... **43** 52 17N 10 28 E
Brunswick, Ga., U.S.A. **170** 31 10N 81 30W
Brunswick, Maine, U.S.A. **148** 43 53N 69 50W
Bruny I. .... **119** 43 20S 147 15 E
Brussel .... **42** 50 51N 4 21 E
Bruthen .... **117** 37 42S 147 50 E
Bruton **27** 51 6N 2 28W
Bryan, Ohio, U.S.A. **167** 41 30N 84 30W
Bryan, Tex., U.S.A. **168** 30 40N 96 27W
Bryan, Mt. .... **119** 33 30S 139 0 E

Bryansk .... **68** 53 13N 34 25 E
Brzeg .... **58** 50 52N 17 30 E
Bucaramanga **184** 7 0N 73 0W
Buchan **33** 57 32N 2 8W
Buchan Ness **33** 57 29N 1 48W
Buchanan **130** 5 57N 10 2W
Buchans **149** 48 50N 56 52W
Bucharest = Bucureşti .... **57** 44 27N 26 10 E
Buckhannon **165** 39 2N 80 10W
Buckhaven **31** 56 10N 3 2W
Buckingham, Canada **151** 45 37N 75 24W
Buckingham, U.K. **25** 52 0N 0 59W
Buckingham □ **25** 51 50N 0 55W
Buckleboo .... **118** 32 54S 136 12 E
Bucureşti .... **57** 44 27N 26 10 E
Bucyrus **167** 40 48N 83 0W
Budalin .... **93** 22 20N 95 10 E
Budapest .... **59** 47 29N 19 5 E
Budaun .... **89** 28 5N 79 10 E
Bude **27** 50 49N 4 33W
Budgewoi Lake .... **117** 33 13S 151 34 E
Buenaventura, Colombia **184** 3 53N 77 4W
Buenaventura, Mexico **174** 29 51N 107 29W
Buenos Aires **190** 34 30S 58 20W
Buffalo **164** 42 55N 78 50W
Bug →— .... **58** 52 31N 21 5 E
Buga **184** 4 0N 76 15W
Bugun Shara .... **100** 49 0N 104 0 E
Builth Wells **26** 52 10N 3 26W
Buir Nur .... **98** 47 50N 117 42 E
Bujumbura .... **135** 3 16S 29 18 E
Bukachacha .... **74** 52 55N 116 50 E
Bukavu .... **23** 2 20S 28 52 E
Bukhara .... **70** 39 48N 64 25 E
Bukit Mertajam .... **96** 5 22N 100 28 E
Bukittinggi .... **111** 0 20S 100 20 E
Bukoba .... **135** 1 20S 31 49 E
Bukuru .... **131** 9 42N 8 48 E
Bulahdelah .... **117** 32 23S 152 13 E
Bulandshahr .... **89** 28 28N 77 51 E
Bulawayo .... **137** 20 7S 28 32 E
Bulgaria ■ .... **53** 42 35N 25 30 E
Bull Shoals L. **168** 36 40N 93 5W
Bully-les-Mines .... **38** 50 27N 2 44 E
Bulsar = Valsad .... **91** 20 40N 72 58 E
Bulun .... **72** 70 37N 127 30 E
Bunbury .... **120** 33 20S 115 35 E
Buncrana **34** 55 8N 7 28W
Bundaberg .... **116** 24 54S 152 22 E
Bundi .... **91** 25 30N 75 35 E
Bundoran **34** 54 24N 8 17W
Bungo-Suidō .... **109** 33 0N 132 15 E
Buorkhaya, Mys .... **72** 71 50N 132 40 E
Bûr Sa'īd .... **128** 31 16N 32 18 E
Bûr Sûdân .... **129** 19 32N 37 9 E
Buraymī, Al Wāhāt al .... **83** 24 10N 55 43 E
Burbank **173** 34 9N 118 23W
Burdur .... **80** 37 45N 30 22 E
Burdwan = Barddhaman .... **92** 23 14N 87 39 E
Burgas .... **53** 42 33N 27 29 E
Burgenland □ .... **45** 47 20N 16 20 E
Burgos **50** 42 21N 3 41W
Burgundy = Bourgogne .... **37** 47 0N 4 30 E
Burin **149** 47 1N 55 14W
Burkina Faso ■ **130** 12 0N 1 0W
Burlington, Canada **151** 43 18N 79 45W
Burlington, Iowa, U.S.A. **166** 40 50N 91 5W
Burlington, N.C., U.S.A. **165** 36 7N 79 27W
Burlington, N.J., U.S.A. **164** 40 5N 74 50W
Burlington, Vt., U.S.A. **151** 44 27N 73 14W
Burma ■ .... **93** 21 0N 96 30 E
Burnie .... **119** 41 4S 145 56 E
Burnley **28** 53 47N 2 15W
Burns **171** 43 40N 119 4W
Burns Lake **154** 54 20N 125 45W
Burra .... **119** 33 40S 138 55 E
Bursa .... **80** 40 15N 29 5 E
Burton-upon-Trent **28** 52 48N 1 39W
Buru .... **113** 3 30S 126 30 E
Burundi ■ .... **135** 3 15S 30 0 E
Bury **28** 53 36N 2 19W

Name	Map	Lat	Long
Bury St. Edmunds	25	52 15N	0 42 E
Buryat A.S.S.R. □	74	53 0N	110 0 E
Buskerud fylke □	60	60 13N	9 0 E
Busselton	120	33 42S	115 15 E
Bussum	40	52 16N	5 10 E
Bute	30	55 48N	5 2W
Butiaba	132	1 50N	31 20 E
Butler	164	40 52N	79 52W
Butte	163	46 0N	112 31W
Butterworth	96	5 24N	100 23 E
Butuan	112	8 57N	125 33 E
Butung	113	5 0S	122 45 E
Buxton	28	53 16N	1 54W
Buyaga	74	59 50N	127 0 E
Buzău	57	45 10N	26 50 E
Buzen	108	33 35N	131 5 E
Buzzards Bay	164	41 45N	70 38W
Bydgoszcz	58	53 10N	18 0 E
Byelorussian S.S.R. □	68	53 30N	27 0 E
Bylot I.	146	73 13N	78 34W
Byrd Land	15	79 30S	125 0W
Byron Bay	116	28 43S	153 37 E
Byrranga, Gory	72	75 0N	100 0 E
Bytom	58	50 25N	18 54 E
Cabimas	184	10 23N	71 25W
Cabinda	134	5 33S	12 11 E
Cabinda □	134	5 0S	12 30 E
Cabo Pantoja	184	1 0S	75 10W
Cabonga, Réservoir	151	47 20N	76 40W
Caboolture	116	27 5S	152 58 E
Cabora Bassa Dam	137	15 20S	32 50 E
Caborca	174	30 40N	112 10W
Cabot Strait	149	47 15N	59 40W
Cabrera, I.	51	39 8N	2 57 E
Cabri	152	50 35N	108 25W
Čačak	52	43 54N	20 20 E
Cáceres	50	39 26N	6 23W
Cache Bay	151	46 22N	80 0W
Cachoeira	189	12 30S	39 0W
Cachoeira de Itapemirim	189	20 51S	41 7W
Cachoeira do Sul	191	30 3S	52 53W
Cader Idris	26	52 43N	3 56W
Cadibarrawirracanna, L.	118	28 52S	135 27 E
Cadillac, Canada	151	48 14N	78 23W
Cadillac, U.S.A.	167	44 16N	85 25W
Cádiz	50	36 30N	6 20W
Cádiz, G. de	50	36 40N	7 0W
Caen	36	49 10N	0 22W
Caernarfon	26	53 8N	4 17W
Caernarfon B.	26	53 4N	4 40W
Caernarvon = Caernarfon	26	53 8N	4 17W
Caerphilly	27	51 34N	3 13W
Cagayan de Oro	112	8 30N	124 40 E
Cágliari	48	39 15N	9 6 E
Caguas	180	18 14N	66 4W
Caha Mts.	35	51 45N	9 40W
Caher	35	52 23N	7 56W
Cahors	36	44 27N	1 27 E
Cahuapanas	186	5 15S	77 0W
Caibarién	178	22 30N	79 30W
Caicos Is.	180	21 40N	71 40W
Cairngorm Mts.	33	57 6N	3 42W
Cairns	121	16 57S	145 45 E
Cairo = El Qâhira	128	30 1N	31 14 E
Cairo	169	37 0N	89 10W
Cajamarca	186	7 5S	78 28W
Calabar	131	4 57N	8 20 E
Calabozo	184	9 0N	67 28W
Calábria □	49	39 24N	16 30 E
Calais, France	38	50 57N	1 56 E
Calais, U.S.A.	148	45 11N	67 20W
Calama, Brazil	187	8 0S	62 50W
Calama, Chile	190	22 30S	68 55W
Calamar	184	10 15N	74 55W
Calamian Group	112	11 50N	119 55 E
Calca	187	13 22S	72 0W
Calcutta	92	22 36N	88 24 E
Caldwell	171	43 45N	116 42W
Calgary	155	51 0N	114 10W
Cali	184	3 25N	76 35W
Calicut	90	11 15N	75 43 E
California □	172	37 25N	120 0W
California, Golfo de	174	28 0N	112 0W
Callander	31	56 15N	4 14W
Callao	186	12 0S	77 0W
Caloundra	116	26 45S	153 10 E
Caltanissetta	49	37 30N	14 3 E
Cam Lam	95	11 54N	109 10 E
Cam Ranh	95	11 54N	109 12 E
Camagüey	178	21 20N	78 0W
Camaná	186	16 30S	72 50W
Camargue	37	43 34N	4 34 E
Camarones	192	44 50S	65 40W
Cambay = Khambhat	91	22 23N	72 33 E
Cambodia ■	95	12 15N	105 0 E
Camborne	27	50 13N	5 18W
Cambrai	38	50 11N	3 14 E
Cambrian Mts.	26	52 25N	3 52W
Cambridge, Canada	151	43 23N	80 15W
Cambridge, N.Z.	122	37 54S	175 29 E
Cambridge, U.K.	25	52 13N	0 8 E
Cambridge, Mass., U.S.A.	164	42 20N	71 8W
Cambridge, Md., U.S.A.	164	38 33N	76 2W
Cambridge, Ohio, U.S.A.	167	40 1N	81 35W
Cambridge Bay	145	69 10N	105 0W
Cambridge Gulf	114	14 55S	128 15 E
Cambridgeshire □	25	52 12N	0 7 E
Camden, Ark., U.S.A.	168	33 40N	92 50W
Camden, N.J., U.S.A.	164	39 57N	75 7W
Camden, S.C., U.S.A.	165	34 17N	80 34W
Cameroon ■	131	6 0N	12 30 E
Cameroun, Mt.	131	4 13N	9 10 E
Cametá	188	2 12S	49 30W
Camiri	187	20 3S	63 31W
Camocim	189	2 55S	40 50W
Campagna	46	40 40N	15 5 E
Campania □	49	40 50N	14 45 E
Campbell I.	15	52 30S	169 0 E
Campbell River	154	50 5N	125 20W
Campbellton	148	47 57N	66 43W
Campbelltown, Australia	117	34 4S	150 49 E
Campbeltown, U.K.	30	57 34N	4 2W
Campeche	177	19 51N	90 32W
Campeche □	177	19 0N	90 30W
Campeche, B. de	177	20 0N	94 0W
Camperdown	119	38 14S	143 9 E
Camperville	153	51 59N	100 9W
Campina Grande	189	7 20S	35 47W
Campinas	188	22 50S	47 0W
Campo Grande	188	20 25S	54 40W
Campos	188	21 50S	41 20W
Camrose	155	53 0N	112 50W
Can Tho	95	10 2N	105 46 E
Canada ■	139	60 0N	100 0W
Cañada de Gómez	190	32 40S	61 30W
Canadian →	158	35 27N	95 3W
Çanakkale Boğazi	80	40 0N	26 0 E
Cananea	174	30 57N	110 18W
Canarias, Islas	126	28 30N	16 0W
Canary Is. = Canarias, Islas	126	28 30N	16 0W
Canaveral, C.	170	28 28N	80 31W
Canberra	117	35 15S	149 8 E
Candala	133	11 30N	49 58 E
Candia = Iráklion	55	35 20N	25 12 E
Canea = Khaniá	55	35 30N	24 4 E
Çankiri	80	40 40N	33 37 E
Canmore	155	51 7N	115 18W
Canna	32	57 3N	6 33W
Cannanore	90	11 53N	75 27 E
Cannes	37	43 32N	7 0 E
Cannock	28	52 42N	2 2W
Canora	152	51 40N	102 30W
Canowindra	117	33 35S	148 38 E
Canso	149	45 20N	61 0W
Cantabrian Mts. = Cantábrica, Cordillera	50	43 0N	5 10W
Cantábrica, Cordillera	50	43 0N	5 10W
Canterbury	25	51 17N	1 5 E
Canterbury □	123	43 45S	171 19 E

Canterbury Bight .... **123** 44 16S 171 55 E
Canterbury Plains .... **123** 43 55S 171 22 E
Canton = Guangzhou .... **99** 23 5N 113 10 E
Canton, Ill., U.S.A. **166** 40 32N 90 0W
Canton, Miss., U.S.A. **169** 32 40N 90 1W
Canton, Ohio, U.S.A. **167** 40 47N 81 22W
Canutama **185** 6 30S 64 20W
Cap-Chat **148** 49 6N 66 40W
Cap-de-la-Madeleine **151** 46 22N 72 31W
Cap-Haïtien **180** 19 40N 72 20W
Cape Barren I. .... **119** 40 25S 148 15 E
Cape Breton I. **149** 46 0N 60 30W
Cape Coast **130** 5 5N 1 15W
Cape Dorset **146** 64 14N 76 32W
Cape Fear ➔ **165** 34 30N 78 25W
Cape Girardeau **169** 37 20N 89 30W
Cape May **164** 39 1N 74 53W
Cape Montague **149** 46 5N 62 25W
Cape Province □ .... **136** 32 0S 23 0 E
Cape Town .... **136** 33 55S 18 22 E
Cape Verde Is. ■ **9** 17 10N 25 20W
Cape York Peninsula .... **115** 12 0S 142 30 E
Caquetá ➔ **184** 1 15S 69 15W
Caracal .... **57** 44 8N 24 22 E
Caracas **184** 10 30N 66 55W
Caratinga **188** 19 50S 42 10W
Carberry **153** 49 50N 99 25W
Carbonara, C. .... **48** 39 8N 9 30 E
Carbondale **166** 37 45N 89 10W
Carbonear **149** 47 42N 53 13W
Carcassonne .... **37** 43 13N 2 20 E
Carcross **144** 60 13N 134 45W
Cárdenas, Cuba **178** 23 0N 81 30W
Cárdenas, Mexico **177** 21 0N 99 40W
Cardiff **27** 51 28N 3 11W
Cardigan **26** 52 6N 4 41W
Cardigan B. **26** 52 30N 4 30W
Cardston **155** 49 15N 113 20W
Cardwell .... **121** 18 14S 146 2 E
Caribbean Sea **181** 15 0N 75 0W
Cariboo Mts. **155** 53 0N 121 0W
Caribou **148** 46 55N 68 0W
Caribou Mts. **145** 59 12N 115 40W
Carinhanha **188** 14 15S 44 46W
Carinthia □ = Kärnten □... **45** 46 52N 13 30 E
Carlisle, U.K. **28** 54 54N 2 55W
Carlisle, U.S.A. **164** 40 12N 77 10W
Carlow **35** 52 50N 6 58W
Carlow □ **35** 52 43N 6 50W
Carlsbad, Calif., U.S.A. **173** 33 11N 117 25W
Carlsbad, N. Mex., U.S.A. ... **161** 32 20N 104 14W
Carlyle **152** 49 40N 102 20W
Carmacks **144** 62 5N 136 16W
Carman **153** 49 30N 98 0W
Carmarthen **26** 51 52N 4 20W
Carmarthen B. **27** 51 40N 4 30W
Carnarvon .... **120** 24 51S 113 42 E
Carnegie, L. .... **114** 26 5S 122 30 E
Carniche, Alpi .... **47** 46 36N 13 0 E
Carnsore Pt. **35** 52 10N 6 20W
Caroline Is. .... **122** 8 0N 150 0 E
Caroona .... **116** 31 24S 150 26 E
Carpathians, Mts. .... **17** 49 50N 21 0 E
Carpaţii Meridionali .... **57** 45 30N 25 0 E
Carpentaria, G. of .... **115** 14 0S 139 0 E
Carrara .... **46** 44 5N 10 7 E
Carrick-on-Shannon **34** 53 57N 8 7W
Carrick-on-Suir **35** 52 22N 7 30W
Carrickfergus **34** 54 43N 5 50W
Carrickmacross **34** 54 0N 6 43W
Carroll **166** 42 2N 94 55W
Carrollton **170** 33 36N 85 5W
Carse of Gowrie **31** 56 30N 3 10W
Carson City **172** 39 12N 119 46W
Carstairs **31** 55 42N 3 41W
Cartagena, Colombia **184** 10 25N 75 33W
Cartagena, Spain **51** 37 38N 0 59W
Cartago, Colombia **184** 4 45N 75 55W
Cartago, C. Rica **179** 9 50N 85 52W
Cartersville **169** 34 11N 84 48W
Carthage **168** 37 10N 94 20W

Cartwright **147** 53 41N 56 58W
Caruaru **189** 8 15S 35 55W
Carúpano **185** 10 39N 63 15W
Caruthersville **169** 36 10N 89 40W
Carvin .... **38** 50 30N 2 57 E
Casablanca **126** 33 36N 7 36W
Casas Grandes **174** 30 22N 107 57W
Cascade Ra. **171** 47 0N 121 30W
Casilda **190** 33 10S 61 10W
Casino .... **116** 28 52S 153 3 E
Casiquiare ➔ **184** 2 1N 67 7W
Casma **186** 9 30S 78 20W
Casper **163** 42 52N 106 20W
Caspian Sea .... **70** 43 0N 50 0 E
Cassiar Mts. **144** 59 30N 130 30W
Castellón de la Plana **51** 39 58N 0 3W
Castelsarrasin .... **36** 44 2N 1 7 E
Casterton .... **119** 37 30S 141 30 E
Castilla La Nueva **50** 39 45N 3 20W
Castilla La Vieja **50** 41 55N 4 0W
Castle Douglas **31** 54 57N 3 57W
Castlebar **34** 53 52N 9 17W
Castleblaney **34** 54 7N 6 44W
Castlegar **155** 49 20N 117 40W
Castlemaine .... **117** 37 2S 144 12 E
Castlereagh **34** 53 47N 8 30W
Castletown **28** 58 35N 3 22W
Castletown Bearhaven **35** 51 40N 9 54W
Castor **155** 52 15N 111 50W
Castres .... **37** 43 37N 2 13 E
Castricum .... **40** 52 33N 4 40 E
Castries **180** 14 0N 60 50W
Castro **192** 42 30S 73 50W
Cat I. **178** 24 30N 75 30W
Catacáos **186** 5 20S 80 45W
Catalonia = Cataluña □ ... **51** 41 40N 1 15 E
Cataluña □ .... **51** 41 40N 1 15 E
Catamarca .... **·190** 28 30S 65 50W
Catanduanes .... **112** 13 50N 124 20 E
Catánia .... **49** 37 31N 15 4 E
Catanzaro .... **49** 38 54N 16 38 E
Catoche, C. **177** 21 35N 87 5W
Catskill Mts. **164** 42 15N 74 15W
Cauca ➔ **184** 8 54N 74 28W
Caucasus Mts. = Bolshoi
  Kavkas .... **70** 42 50N 44 0 E
Caudry .... **38** 50 7N 3 22 E
Cauquenes **190** 36 0S 72 22W
Cavaillon .... **37** 43 50N 5 2 E
Cavan **34** 54 0N 7 22W
Cawnpore = Kanpur ...... **91** 26 28N 80 20 E
Caxias **188** 4 55S 43 20W
Caxias do Sul **191** 29 10S 51 10W
Cayenne **185** 5 0N 52 18W
Cayes, Les **180** 18 15S 73 46W
Cayman Is. **178** 19 40N 80 30W
Ceanannus Mor **34** 53 42N 6 53W
Ceará = Fortaleza **189** 3 45S 38 35W
Ceará □ **189** 5 0S 40 0W
Cebu .... **112** 10 18N 123 54 E
Cedar ➔ **166** 41 17N 91 21W
Cedar City **162** 37 41N 113 3W
Cedar Falls **166** 42 39N 92 29W
Cedar L. **152** 53 10N 100 0W
Cedar Rapids **166** 42 0N 91 38W
Cedartown **169** 34 1N 85 15W
Ceduna .... **118** 32 7S 133 46 E
Cegléd .... **59** 47 11N 19 47 E
Ceiba, La **179** 15 40N 86 50W
Celaya **177** 20 31N 100 37W
Celebes = Sulawesi □ .... **113** 2 0S 120 0 E
Celebes Sea .... **113** 3 0N 123 0 E
Center **168** 31 50N 94 10W
Centerville **166** 40 45N 92 57W
Central □ **31** 56 10N 4 30W
Central, Cordillera **184** 5 0N 75 0W
Central African Republic ■.. **129** 7 0N 20 0 E
Central Auckland □ ...... **122** 37 30S 175 30 E
Central Makran Range .... **88** 26 30N 64 15 E
Central Russian Uplands .. **17** 54 0N 36 0 E
Central Siberian Plateau ... **77** 65 0N 105 0 E

Centralia	**166**	38 32N	89 5W
Cephalonia = Kefallinía	**54**	38 20N	20 30 E
Ceram = Seram	**113**	3 10S	129 0 E
Ceram Sea = Seram Sea	**113**	2 30S	128 30 E
Cerignola	**49**	41 17N	15 53 E
Cerigo = Kíthira	**55**	36 9N	23 0 E
Cerritos	**177**	22 26N	100 17W
Cesena	**47**	44 9N	12 14 E
Českomoravská Vrchovina	**59**	49 30N	15 40 E
Český Těšin	**59**	49 45N	18 39 E
Cessnock	**117**	32 50S	151 21 E
Cetinje	**52**	42 23N	18 59 E
Ceuta	**126**	35 52N	5 18W
Cévennes	**37**	44 10N	3 50 E
Ceylon = Sri Lanka ■	**90**	7 30N	80 50 E
Chachapoyas	**186**	6 15S	77 50W
Chachoengsao	**95**	13 42N	101 5 E
Chad ■	**131**	15 0N	17 15 E
Chad, L. = Tchad, L.	**131**	13 30N	14 30 E
Chadron	**163**	42 50N	103 0W
Chagos Arch.	**76**	6 0S	72 0 E
Chāh Bahār	**85**	25 20N	60 40 E
Chakradharpur	**92**	22 45N	85 40 E
Chala	**186**	15 48S	74 20W
Chalcis = Khalkís	**55**	38 27N	23 42 E
Chalhuanca	**186**	14 15S	73 15W
Chalisgaon	**91**	20 30N	75 10 E
Challapata	**187**	18 53S	66 50W
Chalon-sur-Saône	**37**	46 48N	4 50 E
Châlons-sur-Marne	**37**	48 58N	4 20 E
Chambal →	**91**	26 29N	79 15 E
Chambersburg	**164**	39 53N	77 41W
Chambéry	**37**	45 34N	5 55 E
Chamonix	**37**	45 55N	6 51 E
Champagne	**37**	49 0N	4 40 E
Champaign	**167**	40 8N	88 14W
Champlain, L.	**151**	44 30N	73 20W
Chañaral	**190**	26 23S	70 40W
Chandigarh	**89**	30 43N	76 47 E
Chandler	**118**	27 0S	133 19 E
Chang Jiang →	**99**	31 48N	121 10 E
Changchiak'ou = Zhangjiakou	**98**	40 48N	114 55 E
Ch'angchou = Changzhou	**99**	31 47N	119 58 E
Changchun	**98**	43 57N	125 17 E
Changde	**99**	29 4N	111 35 E
Changhai = Shanghai	**99**	31 15N	121 26 E
Changsha	**99**	28 12N	113 0 E
Changzhi	**98**	36 10N	113 6 E
Changzhou	**99**	31 47N	119 58 E
Channel Is.	**36**	49 30N	2 40W
Channel-Port aux Basques	**149**	47 30N	59 9W
Chanthaburi	**95**	12 38N	102 12 E
Chantilly	**39**	49 12N	2 29 E
Chanute	**166**	37 45N	95 25W
Chao Phraya →	**94**	13 32N	100 36 E
Ch'aoan	**99**	23 41N	116 33 E
Chapala, L. de	**175**	20 15N	103 0W
Chapayevsk	**68**	53 0N	49 40 E
Chapel Hill	**165**	35 53N	79 3W
Chapleau	**150**	47 50N	83 24W
Charagua	**187**	19 45S	63 10W
Charaña	**187**	17 30S	69 25W
Chard	**27**	50 52N	2 59W
Chardzhou	**70**	39 6N	63 34 E
Chari →	**131**	12 58N	14 31 E
Chārīkār	**87**	35 0N	69 10 E
Charleroi	**42**	50 24N	4 27 E
Charles, C.	**165**	37 10N	75 59W
Charles City	**166**	43 2N	92 41W
Charleston, S.C., U.S.A.	**170**	32 47N	79 56W
Charleston, W. Va., U.S.A.	**165**	38 24N	81 36W
Charleville = Rath Luirc	**35**	52 21N	8 40W
Charleville	**116**	26 24S	146 15 E
Charleville-Mézières	**37**	49 44N	4 40 E
Charlotte, Mich., U.S.A.	**167**	42 36N	84 48W
Charlotte, N.C., U.S.A.	**165**	35 16N	80 46W
Charlotte Amalie	**180**	18 22N	64 56W
Charlotte Harbor	**170**	26 58N	82 4W
Charlottenburg	**43**	52 31N	13 15 E
Charlottesville	**165**	38 1N	78 30W
Charlottetown	**149**	46 14N	63 8W
Charlton, Australia	**117**	36 16S	143 24 E
Charlton, U.S.A.	**166**	40 59N	93 20W
Charters Towers	**121**	20 5S	146 13 E
Chartres	**39**	48 29N	1 30 E
Chascomús	**191**	35 30S	58 0W
Château-du-Loir	**39**	47 40N	0 25 E
Château-Thierry	**39**	49 3N	3 20 E
Châteaubriant	**36**	47 43N	1 23W
Châteaudun	**39**	48 3N	1 20 E
Châteauroux	**37**	46 50N	1 40 E
Châtellerault	**36**	46 50N	0 30 E
Chatham, N.B., Canada	**148**	47 2N	65 28W
Chatham, Ont., Canada	**141**	42 24N	82 11W
Chatham, U.K.	**25**	51 22N	0 32 E
Chatta-Hantō	**106**	34 45N	136 55 E
Chattahoochee →	**170**	30 43N	84 51W
Chattanooga	**169**	35 2N	85 17W
Chaumont	**37**	48 7N	5 8 E
Chauny	**38**	49 37N	3 12 E
Cheboksary	**68**	56 8N	47 12 E
Cheboygan	**150**	45 38N	84 29W
Checheno-Ingush A.S.S.R. □	**70**	43 30N	45 29 E
Chegdomyn	**75**	51 7N	133 1 E
Chegga	**126**	25 27N	5 40W
Chehalis	**171**	46 44N	122 59W
Cheju Do	**99**	33 29N	126 34 E
Chekiang = Zhejiang □	**99**	29 0N	120 0 E
Chelforó	**190**	39 0S	66 33W
Chelkar Tengiz, Solonchak	**70**	48 0N	62 30 E
Chełm	**58**	51 8N	23 30 E
Chełmża	**58**	53 10N	18 39 E
Cheltenham	**24**	51 55N	2 5W
Chelyabinsk	**71**	55 10N	61 24 E
Chemainus	**154**	48 55N	123 42W
Chemnitz = Karl-Marx-Stadt	**43**	50 50N	12 55 E
Chemult	**171**	43 14N	121 47W
Chen, Gora	**73**	65 16N	141 50 E
Chencha	**132**	6 15N	37 32 E
Chenchiang = Zhenjiang	**99**	32 11N	119 26 E
Chengchou = Zhengzhou	**99**	34 45N	113 34 E
Chengde	**98**	40 59N	117 58 E
Chengdu	**99**	30 38N	104 2 E
Ch'engtu = Chengdu	**99**	30 38N	104 2 E
Cheo Reo	**95**	13 25N	108 28 E
Chepstow	**27**	51 38N	2 40W
Cher →	**36**	47 21N	0 29 E
Cherbourg	**36**	49 39N	1 40W
Cheremkhovo	**74**	53 8N	103 1 E
Cherepovets	**68**	59 5N	37 55 E
Cherkassy	**68**	49 27N	32 4 E
Chernigov	**68**	51 28N	31 20 E
Chernovtsy	**68**	48 15N	25 52 E
Chernoye	**72**	70 30N	89 10 E
Cherokee	**166**	42 40N	95 30W
Cherrapunji	**93**	25 17N	91 47 E
Cherskiy	**73**	68 45N	161 18 E
Cherskogo Khrebet	**73**	65 0N	143 0 E
Cherwell →	**25**	51 46N	1 18W
Chesapeake	**165**	36 43N	76 15W
Chesapeake Bay	**165**	38 0N	76 12W
Cheshire □	**28**	53 14N	2 30W
Cheshskaya Guba	**69**	67 20N	47 0 E
Chester, U.K.	**28**	53 12N	2 53W
Chester, Pa., U.S.A.	**164**	39 54N	75 20W
Chester, S.C., U.S.A.	**165**	34 44N	81 13W
Chesterfield	**28**	53 14N	1 26W
Chesterfield Inlet	**145**	63 30N	90 45W
Chetumal	**177**	18 30N	88 18W
Cheviot, The	**31**	55 29N	2 8W
Cheviot Hills	**31**	55 20N	2 30W
Chew Bahir	**132**	4 40N	36 50 E
Cheyenne	**163**	41 9N	104 49W
Cheyenne →	**163**	44 40N	101 15W
Chhapra	**92**	25 48N	84 44 E
Chiamussu = Jiamusi	**98**	46 40N	130 26 E
Chiang Mai	**94**	18 47N	98 59 E
Chiapa →	**177**	16 42N	93 0W
Chiapas □	**177**	16 30N	92 30W
Chiba	**107**	35 30N	140 7 E
Chibougamau	**151**	49 56N	74 24W

Chicago	**167**	41 53N	87	40W
Chicago Heights	**167**	41 29N	87	37W
Chichagof I.	**143**	58 0N	136	0W
Chichester	**25**	50 50N	0	47W
Chichibu	**107**	36 5N	139	10 E
Ch'ich'ihaerh = Qiqihar	**98**	47 26N	124	0 E
Chiclayo	**186**	6 42S	79	50W
Chico	**172**	39 45N	121	54W
Chicopee	**164**	42 6N	72	37W
Chicoutimi	**148**	48 28N	71	5W
Chidambaram	**90**	11 20N	79	45 E
Chidley C.	**146**	60 23N	64	26W
Chigasaki	**107**	35 19N	139	24 E
Chihli, G. of = Bo Hai	**98**	39 0N	120	0 E
Chihuahua	**174**	28 38N	106	5W
Chihuahua □	**174**	28 30N	106	0W
Chikugo	**108**	33 14N	130	28 E
Chilapa	**177**	17 40N	99	11W
Childress	**161**	34 30N	100	15W
Chile ■	**190**	35 0S	72	0W
Chilin = Jilin	**98**	43 44N	126	30 E
Chilka L.	**92**	19 40N	85	25 E
Chillán	**190**	36 40S	72	10W
Chillicothe, Mo., U.S.A.	**166**	39 45N	93	30W
Chillicothe, Ohio, U.S.A.	**167**	39 20N	82	58W
Chilliwack	**154**	49 10N	121	54W
Chiloé, I. de	**192**	42 30S	73	50W
Chilpancingo	**177**	17 30N	99	30W
Chiltern Hills	**25**	51 44N	0	42W
Chimborazo	**184**	1 29S	78	55W
Chimbote	**186**	9 0S	78	35W
Chimkent	**71**	42 18N	69	36 E
Chin □	**93**	22 0N	93	0 E
China ■	**79**	30 0N	110	0 E
Chinan = Jinan	**98**	36 38N	117	1 E
Chinandega	**179**	12 35N	87	12W
Chincha Alta	**186**	13 25S	76	7W
Chinchilla	**116**	26 45S	150	38 E
Chinchou = Jinzhou	**98**	41 5N	121	3 E
Chindwin ~→	**93**	21 26N	95	15 E
Ch'ingtao = Qingdao	**98**	36 5N	120	20 E
Chinju	**98**	35 12N	128	2 E
Chinnampo	**98**	38 52N	125	10 E
Chino	**107**	35 59N	138	9 E
Chinon	**36**	47 10N	0	15 E
Chippenham	**24**	51 27N	2	7W
Chippewa Falls	**166**	44 55N	91	22W
Chiquián	**186**	10 10S	77	0W
Chiquimula	**177**	14 51N	89	37W
Chiquinquira	**184**	5 37N	73	50W
Chirala	**90**	15 50N	80	26 E
Chirchik	**71**	41 29N	69	35 E
Chita	**74**	52 0N	113	35 E
Chitral	**89**	35 50N	71	56 E
Chitré	**179**	7 59N	80	27W
Chittagong	**93**	22 19N	91	48 E
Chittagong □	**93**	24 5N	91	0 E
Chivilcoy	**190**	34 55S	60	0W
Chkalov = Orenburg	**70**	51 45N	55	6 E
Chōfu	**107**	35 39N	139	33 E
Choix	**174**	26 43N	108	17W
Chojnice	**58**	53 42N	17	32 E
Cholet	**36**	47 4N	0	52W
Choluteca	**179**	13 20N	87	14W
Chon Buri	**95**	13 21N	101	1 E
Chongjin	**98**	41 47N	129	50 E
Chŏngju	**98**	36 39N	127	27 E
Chongqing	**99**	29 35N	106	25 E
Chŏnju	**98**	35 50N	127	4 E
Chonos, Arch. de los	**192**	45 0S	75	0W
Chorley	**28**	53 39N	2	39W
Chorzów	**58**	50 18N	18	57 E
Chōshi	**107**	35 45N	140	51 E
Christchurch, N.Z.	**123**	43 33S	172	47 E
Christchurch, U.K.	**24**	50 44N	1	33W
Christianshåb	**147**	68 50N	51	18W
Christmas I. = Kiritimati	**123**	1 58N	157	27W
Christmas I.	**111**	10 30S	105	40 E
Ch'uanchou = Quanzhou	**99**	24 55N	118	34 E
Chūbu □	**106**	36 45N	137	30 E
Chubut ~→	**192**	43 20S	65	5W

Chūgoku □	**109**	35 0N	133	0 E
Chūgoku-Sanchi	**109**	35 0N	133	0 E
Chukotskiy Khrebet	**73**	68 0N	175	0 E
Chukotskoye More	**73**	68 0N	175	0W
Chula Vista	**173**	32 39N	117	8W
Chulman	**74**	56 52N	124	52 E
Chulucanas	**186**	5 8S	80	10W
Chumikan	**75**	54 40N	135	10 E
Chumphon	**94**	10 35N	99	14 E
Chunchŏn	**98**	37 58N	127	44 E
Chungking = Chongqing	**99**	29 35N	106	25 E
Chuquibamba	**186**	15 47S	72	44W
Chur	**44**	46 52N	9	32 E
Churchill ~→, Man., Canada	**143**	58 47N	94	12W
Churchill ~→, Nfld., Canada	**147**	53 19N	60	10W
Churchill, C.	**143**	58 46N	93	12W
Churchill Falls	**147**	53 36N	64	19W
Churchill Pk.	**144**	58 10N	125	10W
Churu	**89**	28 20N	74	50 E
Chuvash A.S.S.R.□	**68**	55 30N	47	0 E
Chuxiong	**101**	25 2N	101	28 E
Cicero	**167**	41 48N	87	48W
Ciego de Avila	**178**	21 50N	78	50W
Ciénaga	**184**	11 1N	74	15W
Cienfuegos	**178**	22 10N	80	30W
Cimarron ~→	**161**	36 10N	96	17W
Cincinnati	**167**	39 10N	84	26W
Cinto, Mt.	**36**	42 24N	8	54 E
Ciotat, La	**37**	43 12N	5	36 E
Circle	**142**	65 50N	144	10W
Circleville	**167**	39 35N	82	57W
Cirebon	**111**	6 45S	108	32 E
Cirencester	**24**	51 43N	1	59W
Citlaltépetl, Volcán	**177**	19 1N	97	16W
Ciudad Acuña	**174**	29 20N	100	58W
Ciudad Bolívar	**185**	8 5N	63	36W
Ciudad Camargo, Chihuahua, Mexico	**174**	27 40N	105	10W
Ciudad Camargo, Tamaulipas, Mexico	**176**	26 19N	98	50W
Ciudad de Valles	**177**	21 59N	99	1W
Ciudad del Carmen	**177**	18 38N	91	50W
Ciudad Guayana	**185**	8 0N	62	30W
Ciudad Guzmán	**175**	19 41N	103	29W
Ciudad Juárez	**174**	31 44N	106	29W
Ciudad Madero	**177**	22 16N	97	50W
Ciudad Mante	**177**	22 44N	98	57W
Ciudad Obregón	**174**	27 29N	109	56W
Ciudad Real	**50**	38 59N	3	55W
Ciudad Rodrigo	**50**	40 35N	6	32W
Ciudad Trujillo = Santo Domingo	**180**	18 30N	64	54W
Ciudad Victoria	**177**	23 44N	99	8W
Civril	**80**	38 20N	29	43 E
Cizre	**81**	37 19N	42	10 E
Clare	**119**	33 50S	138	37 E
Clare □	**35**	52 20N	9	0W
Clare ~→	**35**	53 22N	9	5W
Clare I.	**34**	53 48N	10	0W
Claremont	**164**	43 23N	72	20W
Claremore	**168**	36 40N	95	37W
Claremorris	**34**	53 45N	9	0W
Claresholm	**155**	50 0N	113	33W
Clark Fork ~→	**162**	48 9N	116	15W
Clarksburg	**164**	39 18N	80	21W
Clarksdale	**169**	34 12N	90	33W
Clarkston	**171**	46 28N	117	2W
Clarksville	**169**	36 32N	87	20W
Clear, C.	**20**	51 26N	9	30W
Clearwater, Canada	**155**	51 38N	120	2W
Clearwater, U.S.A.	**170**	27 58N	82	45W
Cleburne	**168**	32 18N	97	25W
Clee Hills	**24**	52 26N	2	35W
Cleethorpes	**29**	53 33N	0	2W
Cleeve Hill	**24**	51 54N	2	0W
Clermont, Australia	**121**	22 49S	147	39 E
Clermont, France	**39**	49 23N	2	24 E
Clermont-Ferrand	**37**	45 46N	3	4 E
Clevedon	**27**	51 26N	2	52W
Cleveland, Miss., U.S.A.	**169**	33 43N	90	43W
Cleveland, Ohio, U.S.A.	**167**	41 28N	81	43W

Cleveland, Tenn., U.S.A.	169	35 9N	84 52W
Cleveland, Tex., U.S.A.	169	30 18N	95 0W
Cleveland □	29	54 35N	1 8 E
Cleveleys	28	53 52N	3 3W
Clew B.	34	53 54N	9 50W
Clifton Beach	121	16 46S	145 39 E
Clifton Forge	165	37 49N	79 51W
Clinton, Canada	150	43 37N	81 32W
Clinton, Iowa, U.S.A.	166	41 50N	90 12W
Clinton, Mass., U.S.A.	164	42 26N	71 40W
Clinton, Mo., U.S.A.	166	38 20N	93 46W
Clinton, Okla., U.S.A.	161	35 30N	99 0W
Clinton, S.C., U.S.A.	165	34 30N	81 54W
Clinton Colden L.	145	63 58N	107 27W
Clonakilty	35	51 37N	8 53W
Cloncurry	115	20 40S	140 28 E
Clones	34	54 10N	7 13W
Clonmel	35	52 22N	7 42W
Clovis	161	34 20N	103 10W
Cluj-Napoca	56	46 47N	23 38 E
Clunes	117	37 20S	143 45 E
Clwyd □	26	53 5N	3 20W
Clyde →	31	55 56N	4 29W
Clyde, Firth of	30	55 20N	5 0W
Clydebank	31	55 54N	4 25W
Coahuila □	174	27 20N	102 0W
Coaldale	155	49 45N	112 35W
Coalinga	173	36 10N	120 21W
Coalville	29	52 43N	1 21W
Coast Mts.	144	55 0N	129 0W
Coast Ranges	173	41 0N	123 0W
Coatbridge	31	55 52N	4 2W
Coatepeque	177	14 46N	91 55W
Coats I.	146	62 30N	83 0W
Coats Land	14	77 0S	25 0W
Coatzacoalcos	177	18 9N	94 25W
Cobalt.	151	47 25N	79 42W
Cobán	177	15 30N	90 21W
Cobar	116	31 27S	145 48 E
Cóbh.	35	51 50N	8 18W
Cobham	118	30 18S	142 7 E
Cobourg.	151	43 58N	78 10W
Cobram	117	35 54S	145 40 E
Cocanada = Kakinada	92	16 57N	82 11 E
Cochabamba	187	17 26S	66 10W
Cochin China = Nam-Phan	95	10 30N	106 0 E
Cochran	170	32 25N	83 23W
Cochrane	151	49 0N	81 0W
Cockburn, Canal	192	54 30S	72 0W
Coco →	179	15 0N	83 8W
Coco Chan.	94	13 50N	93 25 E
Cocos Is.	111	12 10S	96 55 E
Cod, C.	164	42 8N	70 10W
Codajás	185	3 55S	62 0W
Codó.	185	4 30S	43 55W
Cœur d'Alene	171	47 45N	116 51W
Coffs Harbour	116	30 16S	153 5 E
Cohoes.	164	42 47N	73 42W
Cohuna	117	35 45S	144 15 E
Coiba, I.	179	7 30N	81 40W
Coihaique	192	45 30S	71 45W
Coimbatore	90	11 2N	76 59 E
Coimbra.	50	40 15N	8 27W
Cojimies	184	0 20N	80 0W
Cojutepequé	177	13 41N	88 54W
Colac	117	38 21S	143 35 E
Colchester	25	51 54N	0 55 E
Coldstream	31	55 39N	2 14W
Coleman	155	49 40N	114 30W
Coleraine, Australia	119	37 36S	141 40 E
Coleraine, U.K.	34	55 8N	6 40W
Colima	175	19 14N	103 43W
Colima □	175	19 10N	104 0W
Coll	30	56 40N	6 35W
College Park	170	33 42N	84 27W
Collie	120	33 22S	116 8 E
Collingwood	151	44 29N	80 13W
Collinsville	121	20 30S	147 56 E
Collooney	34	54 11N	8 28W
Colmar	37	48 5N	7 20 E
Colne	28	53 51N	2 11W
Cologne = Köln	42	50 56N	6 58 E
Colomb-Béchar = Béchar	127	31 38N	2 18W
Colômbia	188	20 10S	48 40W
Colombia ■	184	3 45N	73 0W
Colombo	90	6 56N	79 58 E
Colón, Cuba	178	22 42N	80 54W
Colón, Panama	179	9 20N	79 54W
Colonia	191	34 25S	57 50W
Colonsay	30	56 4N	6 12W
Colorado □	163	37 40N	106 0W
Colorado →, Argentina	190	39 50S	62 8W
Colorado →, Calif., U.S.A.	173	34 45N	114 40W
Colorado →, Tex., U.S.A.	161	28 36N	95 58W
Colorado Desert	160	34 20N	116 0W
Colorado Plateau	161	36 40N	110 30W
Colorado Springs	163	38 55N	104 50W
Columbia, Miss., U.S.A.	169	31 16N	89 50W
Columbia, Mo., U.S.A.	166	38 58N	92 20W
Columbia, S.C., U.S.A.	165	34 0N	81 0W
Columbia, Tenn., U.S.A.	169	35 40N	87 0W
Columbia →	171	46 15N	124 5W
Columbia Basin	171	47 30N	118 30W
Columbretes, Is.	51	39 50N	0 50 E
Columbus, Ga., U.S.A.	170	32 30N	84 58W
Columbus, Ind., U.S.A.	167	39 14N	85 55W
Columbus, Miss., U.S.A.	169	33 30N	88 26W
Columbus, Ohio, U.S.A.	167	39 57N	83 1W
Colwyn Bay	26	53 17N	3 44W
Comeragh Mts.	35	52 17N	7 35W
Comilla	93	23 28N	91 10 E
Comitán	177	16 18N	92 9W
Committee B.	146	68 30N	86 30W
Communism Pk. = Kommunizma, Pik	71	39 0N	72 2 E
Como	46	45 48N	9 5 E
Como, L. di	46	46 5N	9 17 E
Comodoro Rivadavia	192	45 50S	67 40W
Comorin, C.	90	8 3N	77 40 E
Comoro Is. ■	125	12 10S	44 15 E
Comox	154	49 42N	124 55W
Compiègne	38	49 24N	2 50 E
Côn Dao	95	8 45N	106 45 E
Conakry	130	9 29N	13 49W
Conceição da Barra	189	18 35S	39 45W
Concepción, Argentina	191	27 20S	65 35W
Concepción, Chile	190	36 50S	73 0W
Concepción, Est. de	192	50 30S	74 55W
Concepción del Oro	174	24 38N	101 25W
Concepción del Uruguay	190	32 35S	58 20W
Conchos, R. →	174	29 35N	104 25W
Concord, Calif., U.S.A.	172	37 59N	122 2W
Concord, N.C., U.S.A.	165	35 28N	80 35W
Concord, N.H., U.S.A.	164	43 12N	71 30W
Concordia, Argentina	190	31 20S	58 2W
Concordia, U.S.A.	161	39 35N	97 40W
Condamine	155	26 56S	150 9 E
Condé	38	50 26N	3 34 E
Condobolin	117	33 4S	147 6 E
Congleton	28	53 10N	2 12W
Congo = Zaïre →	134	6 4S	12 24 E
Congo (Kinshasa) ■ = Zaïre ■	134	3 0S	23 0 E
Congo ■	134	1 0S	16 0 E
Congo Basin	124	0 10S	24 30 E
Conjeeveram = Kanchipuram	90	12 52N	79 45 E
Connacht	34	53 23N	8 40W
Conneaut	164	41 55N	80 32W
Connecticut □	164	41 40N	72 40W
Connecticut →	157	41 17N	72 21W
Connemara	34	53 29N	9 45W
Connors Ra.	121	21 40S	149 10 E
Consett.	28	54 52N	1 50W
Constance = Konstanz	44	47 39N	9 10 E
Constance, L. = Bodensee	44	47 35N	9 25 E
Constanța	57	44 14N	28 38 E
Constantine	127	36 25N	6 42 E
Contamana	186	7 19S	74 55W
Conway = Conwy	26	53 17N	3 50W
Conway = Conwy →	26	53 18N	3 50W
Conway, N.H., U.S.A.	148	43 58N	71 8W
Conway, S.C., U.S.A.	165	33 49N	79 2W

Conwy	**26** 53 17N	3 50W
Conwy →	**26** 53 18N	3 50W
Cook, Mt.	**123** 43 36S	170 9 E
Cook Inlet	**142** 59 0N	151 0W
Cook Is.	**123** 17 0S	160 0W
Cook Strait	**123** 41 15S	174 29 E
Cookeville	**169** 36 12N	85 30W
Cookstown	**34** 54 40N	6 43W
Coolah	**116** 31 48S	149 41 E
Coolamon	**117** 34 46S	147 8 E
Coolangatta	**116** 28 11S	153 29 E
Coolgardie	**120** 30 55S	121 8 E
Cooma	**117** 36 12S	149 8 E
Coonabarabran	**116** 31 14S	149 18 E
Coonamble	**116** 30 56S	148 27 E
Cooper Cr. →	**118** 12 7S	132 41 E
Coorong, The	**119** 35 50S	139 20 E
Coorow	**120** 29 53S	116 2 E
Coos Bay	**171** 43 26N	124 7W
Cootamundra	**117** 34 36S	148 1 E
Copenhagen = København ..	**61** 55 41N	12 34 E
Copiapó	**190** 27 30S	70 20W
Copper Center	**142** 62 10N	145 25W
Coppermine	**145** 67 50N	115 5W
Coppermine →	**145** 67 49N	116 4W
Coquilhatville = Mbandaka ..	**134** 0 1N	18 18 E
Coquimbo	**190** 30 0S	71 20W
Coracora	**186** 15 5S	73 45W
Coral Gables	**170** 25 45N	80 16W
Coral Harbour	**146** 64 8N	83 10W
Coral Sea	**121** 15 0S	150 0 E
Corbeil-Essonnes	**39** 48 36N	2 26 E
Corbin	**165** 37 0N	84 3W
Corby	**25** 52 29N	0 41W
Cordele	**170** 31 55N	83 49W
Córdoba, Argentina	**190** 31 20S	64 10W
Córdoba, Mexico	**177** 18 53N	96 56W
Córdoba, Spain	**50** 37 50N	4 50W
Córdoba, Sierra de	**190** 31 10S	64 25W
Cordova	**142** 60 36N	145 45W
Corfu = Kérkira	**54** 39 38N	19 50 E
Corinth = Kórinthos	**54** 37 56N	22 55 E
Corinth	**169** 34 54N	88 30W
Corinth, G. of = Korinthiakós Kólpos	**54** 38 16N	22 30 E
Corinto, Brazil	**188** 18 20S	44 30W
Corinto, Nic.	**179** 12 30N	87 10W
Cork	**35** 51 54N	8 30W
Cork □	**35** 51 50N	8 50W
Corlu	**80** 41 11N	27 49 E
Corn Is. = Maíz, Islas del	**179** 12 15N	83 4W
Corner Brook	**140** 48 57N	57 58W
Cornwall	**151** 45 2N	74 44W
Cornwall □	**27** 50 26N	4 40W
Coro	**184** 11 25N	69 41W
Coroatá	**188** 4 8S	44 0W
Corocoro	**187** 17 15S	68 28W
Coroico	**187** 16 0S	67 50W
Coromandel Coast	**90** 12 30N	81 0 E
Corona	**173** 33 49N	117 36W
Coronado	**173** 32 45N	117 9W
Coronation Gulf	**145** 68 25N	110 0W
Coronel	**190** 37 0S	73 10W
Coronel Pringles	**190** 38 0S	61 30W
Corowa	**117** 35 58S	146 21 E
Corozal	**177** 9 19N	75 18W
Corpus Christi	**161** 27 50N	97 28W
Corrib, L.	**34** 53 5N	9 10W
Corrientes	**190** 27 30S	58 45W
Corrientes, C., Colombia . .	**184** 5 30N	77 34W
Corrientes, C., Cuba	**178** 21 43N	84 30W
Corrientes, C., Mexico	**175** 20 25N	105 42W
Corrigin	**120** 32 20S	117 53 E
Corse	**36** 42 0N	9 0 E
Corsica = Corse	**36** 42 0N	9 0 E
Corsicana	**168** 32 5N	96 30W
Cortez	**163** 37 24N	108 35W
Cortland	**164** 42 35N	76 11W
Corum	**80** 40 30N	34 57 E
Corumbá	**187** 19 0S	57 30W
Coruña, La	**50** 43 20N	8 25W
Corunna = Coruña, La	**50** 43 20N	8 25W
Corvallis	**171** 44 36N	123 15W
Cosamaloapan	**177** 18 23N	95 50W
Cosenza	**49** 39 17N	16 14 E
Coshocton	**167** 40 17N	81 51W
Costa Blanca	**51** 38 25N	0 10W
Costa Brava	**51** 41 30N	3 0 E
Costa del Sol	**50** 36 30N	4 30W
Costa Dorada	**51** 40 45N	1 15 E
Costa Rica ■	**179** 10 0N	84 0W
Cotagaita	**187** 20 45S	65 40W
Côte d'Or	**37** 47 10N	4 50 E
Coteau des Prairies	**156** 44 30N	97 0W
Cotonou	**131** 6 20N	2 25 E
Cotopaxi, Vol.	**184** 0 40S	78 30W
Cotswold Hills	**24** 51 42N	2 10W
Cottbus	**43** 51 44N	14 20 E
Coulommiers	**39** 48 50N	3 3 E
Council	**142** 64 55N	163 45W
Council Bluffs	**166** 41 20N	95 50W
Courantyne →	**185** 5 55N	57 5W
Courtrai = Kortrijk	**42** 50 50N	3 17 E
Coventry	**24** 52 25N	1 31W
Covington, Ga., U.S.A.	**170** 33 36N	83 50W
Covington, Ky., U.S.A.	**167** 39 5N	84 30W
Cowdenbeath	**31** 56 7N	3 20W
Cowes	**25** 50 45N	1 18W
Cowra	**117** 33 49S	148 42 E
Coxim	**188** 18 30S	54 55W
Cracow = Kraków	**58** 50 4N	19 57 E
Craigavon = Lurgan	**34** 54 28N	6 20W
Craiova	**57** 44 21N	23 48 E
Cranbrook, Australia	**120** 34 18S	117 33 E
Cranbrook, Canada	**155** 49 30N	115 46W
Crateús	**189** 5 10S	40 39W
Crato	**189** 7 10S	39 25W
Crawfordsville	**167** 40 2N	86 51W
Crawley	**24** 51 7N	0 10W
Creil	**39** 49 15N	2 34 E
Cremona	**46** 45 8N	10 2 E
Crépy-en-Valois	**39** 49 14N	2 54 E
Cres	**52** 44 58N	14 25 E
Crescent City	**172** 41 45N	124 12W
Creston, Canada	**155** 49 10N	116 31W
Creston, U.S.A.	**166** 41 0N	94 20W
Crestview	**169** 30 45N	86 35W
Crete = Kríti	**55** 35 15N	25 0 E
Creuse →	**36** 47 0N	0 34 E
Creusot, Le	**37** 46 50N	4 24 E
Crewe	**28** 53 6N	2 28W
Criciúma	**191** 28 40S	49 23W
Crieff	**31** 56 22N	3 50W
Crimea = Krymskiy P-ov.	**68** 45 0N	34 0 E
Crişul Alb →	**56** 46 42N	21 17 E
Crişul Negru →	**56** 46 38N	22 26 E
Crna Gora	**52** 42 10N	21 30 E
Crna Gora □	**52** 42 40N	19 20 E
Croatia = Hrvatska □	**52** 45 20N	18 0 E
Crockett	**168** 31 20N	95 30W
Cromarty	**33** 57 40N	4 2W
Cromer	**29** 52 56N	1 18 E
Crooked I.	**180** 22 50N	74 10W
Crookwell	**117** 34 28S	149 24 E
Cross Fell	**28** 54 44N	2 29W
Cross L.	**153** 54 45N	97 30W
Crosse, La	**166** 43 48N	91 13W
Crowley	**168** 30 15N	92 20W
Crowsnest Pass	**155** 49 40N	114 40W
Cruz, C.	**178** 19 50N	77 50W
Cruz Alta	**191** 28 45S	53 40W
Cruz del Eje	**190** 30 45S	64 50W
Cruzeiro do Sul	**186** 7 35S	72 35W
Crystal Brook	**119** 33 21S	138 12 E
Cu Lao Hon	**95** 10 54N	108 18 E
Cuando →	**134** 14 0S	19 30 E
Cuanza →	**134** 9 2S	13 30 E
Cuba ■	**178** 22 0N	79 0W
Cubango →	**134** 18 50S	22 25 E
Cucui	**184** 1 12N	66 50W
Cúcuta	**184** 7 54N	72 31W
Cuddalore	**90** 11 46N	79 45 E

Cuddapah	**90**	14 30N	78 47 E
Cue	**120**	27 25S	117 54 E
Cuenca, Ecuador	**184**	2 50S	79 9W
Cuenca, Spain	**51**	40 5N	2 10W
Cuenca, Serranía de	**51**	39 55N	1 50W
Cuernavaca	**177**	18 55N	99 15W
Cuevo	**187**	20 15S	63 30W
Cuiabá	**188**	15 30S	56 0W
Cuillin Hills	**32**	57 14N	6 15W
Cuitzeo, L. de	**175**	19 55N	101 5W
Culcairn	**117**	35 41S	147 3 E
Culiacán	**174**	24 48N	107 24W
Cullarin Range	**117**	34 30S	149 30 E
Culloden Moor	**33**	57 29N	4 7W
Culverden	**123**	42 47S	172 49 E
Cumaná	**185**	10 30N	64 5W
Cumberland	**164**	39 40N	78 43W
Cumberland →	**169**	36 15N	87 0W
Cumberland Is.	**121**	20 35S	149 10 E
Cumberland Pen.	**146**	67 0N	64 0W
Cumberland Plat.	**169**	36 0N	84 30W
Cumberland Sd.	**146**	65 30N	66 0W
Cumbria □	**28**	54 35N	2 55W
Cumbrian Mts.	**28**	54 30N	3 0W
Cumbum	**90**	15 40N	79 10 E
Cummins	**119**	34 16S	135 43 E
Cumnock	**31**	55 27N	4 18W
Cunene →	**134**	17 20S	11 50 E
Cunnamulla	**116**	28 2S	145 38 E
Curaçao	**181**	12 10N	69 0W
Curaray →	**184**	2 20S	74 5W
Curiapo	**185**	8 33N	61 5W
Curicó	**190**	34 55S	71 20W
Curitiba	**191**	25 20S	49 10W
Curtis Group	**117**	39 30S	146 37 E
Curuá →	**188**	5 23S	54 22W
Curuçá	**188**	0 43S	47 50W
Curuzú Cuatiá	**191**	29 50S	58 5W
Cushing	**168**	35 59N	96 46W
Cusihuiriáchic	**174**	28 14N	106 50W
Cuthbert	**170**	31 47N	84 47W
Cuttack	**92**	20 25N	85 57 E
Cuxhaven	**42**	53 51N	8 41 E
Cuyahoga Falls	**167**	41 8N	81 30W
Cuzco, Bolivia	**187**	20 0S	66 50W
Cuzco, Peru	**186**	13 32S	72 0W
Cwmbran	**27**	51 39N	3 0W
Cypress Hills	**152**	49 40N	109 30W
Cyprus ■	**80**	35 0N	33 0 E
Cyrenaica	**124**	27 0N	23 0 E
Czechoslovakia ■	**59**	49 0N	17 0 E
Czeremcha	**58**	52 31N	23 21 E
Częstochowa	**58**	50 49N	19 7 E
Da →	**95**	21 15N	105 20 E
Da Hinggan Ling	**98**	48 0N	121 0 E
Da Nang	**95**	16 4N	108 13 E
Da Yunhe →	**99**	34 25N	120 5 E
Daba Shan	**99**	32 0N	109 0 E
Dacca = Dhaka	**92**	23 43N	90 26 E
Dacca □ = Dhaka □	**93**	24 25N	90 25 E
Dadanawa	**185**	2 50N	59 30W
Dadra and Nagar Haveli □	**91**	20 5N	73 0 E
Daghestan A.S.S.R. □	**70**	42 30N	47 0 E
Dahomey = Benin ■	**131**	10 0N	2 0 E
Dai-Sen	**109**	35 22N	133 32 E
Daiō-Misaki	**106**	34 15N	136 45 E
Daisetsu-Zan	**103**	43 30N	142 57 E
Daito	**109**	35 19N	132 58 E
Dajarra	**115**	21 42S	139 30 E
Dakar	**130**	14 34N	17 29W
Dakhla	**126**	23 50N	15 53W
Dakhla, El Wâhât el-	**128**	25 30N	28 50 E
Đakovica	**52**	42 22N	20 26 E
Dalandzadgad	**98**	43 27N	104 30 E
Dalbeattie	**31**	54 55N	3 50W
Dalby	**116**	27 10S	151 17 E
Dalhousie	**148**	48 5N	66 26W
Dali	**99**	25 40N	100 10 E
Dalian	**98**	38 50N	121 40 E
Daliang Shan	**99**	28 0N	102 45 E
Dallas, Oreg., U.S.A.	**171**	45 0N	123 15W
Dallas, Tex., U.S.A.	**168**	32 50N	96 50W
Dalmacija □	**52**	43 20N	17 0 E
Dalmatia = Dalmacija □	**52**	43 20N	17 0 E
Daloa	**130**	7 0N	6 30W
Dalton	**169**	34 47N	84 58W
Daly Waters	**114**	16 15S	133 24 E
Daman	**91**	20 25N	72 57 E
Damaraland	**136**	21 0S	17 0 E
Damascus = Dimashq	**80**	33 30N	36 18 E
Damāvand	**86**	35 47N	52 0 E
Damāvand, Qolleh-ye	**86**	35 56N	52 10 E
Dampier	**114**	20 41S	116 42 E
Dampier Arch.	**114**	20 38S	116 32 E
Danbury	**164**	41 23N	73 29W
Dandenong	**117**	38 0S	145 15 E
Dandong	**98**	40 10N	124 20 E
Dangriga	**177**	17 0N	88 13W
Dannevirke	**122**	40 12S	176 8 E
Dansville	**164**	42 32N	77 41W
Danville, Ill., U.S.A.	**167**	40 10N	87 40W
Danville, Ky., U.S.A.	**167**	37 40N	84 45W
Danville, Va., U.S.A.	**165**	36 40N	79 20W
Danzig = Gdańsk	**58**	54 22N	18 40 E
Dar es Salaam	**135**	6 50S	39 12 E
Darbhanga	**92**	26 15N	85 55 E
Dardanelles = Çanakkale Boğazi	**80**	40 0N	26 0 E
Dârfûr	**129**	13 40N	24 0 E
Dargan Ata	**70**	40 29N	62 10 E
Dargaville	**122**	35 57S	173 52 E
Darién, G. del	**184**	9 0N	77 0W
Darjeeling = Darjiling	**92**	27 3N	88 18 E
Darjiling	**92**	27 3N	88 18 E
Darling →	**119**	34 4S	141 54 E
Darling Downs	**116**	27 30S	150 30 E
Darling Ra.	**120**	32 30S	116 0 E
Darlington	**28**	54 33N	1 33W
Darmstadt	**42**	49 51N	8 40 E
Darnley, C.	**14**	68 0S	69 0 E
Dart →	**27**	50 24N	3 36W
Dartmoor	**27**	50 36N	4 0W
Dartmouth, Canada	**149**	44 40N	63 30W
Dartmouth, U.K.	**27**	50 21N	3 35W
Darwin	**114**	12 25S	130 51 E
Dasht-e Kavīr	**86**	34 30N	55 0 E
Dasht-e Lūt	**85**	31 30N	58 0 E
Dasht-e Mārgow	**87**	30 40N	62 30 E
Datia	**91**	25 39N	78 27 E
Datong	**98**	40 6N	113 18 E
Daugavpils	**68**	55 53N	26 32 E
Dauphin	**153**	51 9N	100 5W
Dauphiné	**37**	45 15N	5 25 E
Davangere	**90**	14 25N	75 55 E
Davao	**112**	7 0N	125 40 E
Davenport	**166**	41 30N	90 40W
Daventry	**24**	52 16N	1 10W
David	**179**	8 30N	82 30W
Davis Sea	**15**	66 0S	92 0 E
Davis Str.	**146**	65 0N	58 0W
Davos	**44**	46 48N	9 49 E
Dawson	**144**	64 10N	139 30W
Dawson Creek	**155**	55 45N	120 15W
Dawson Range	**121**	24 30S	149 48 E
Daylesford	**117**	37 21S	144 9 E
Dayr az Zawr	**81**	35 20N	40 5 E
Dayton, Ohio, U.S.A.	**167**	39 45N	84 10W
Dayton, Wash., U.S.A.	**171**	46 20N	118 10W
Daytona Beach	**170**	29 14N	81 0W
De Aar	**136**	30 39S	24 0 E
De Land	**170**	29 1N	81 19W
De Ridder	**168**	30 48N	93 15W
De Soto	**166**	38 7N	90 33W
Deakin	**114**	30 46S	128 0 E
Deal	**25**	51 13N	1 25 E
Dean, Forest of	**24**	51 50N	2 35W
Deán Funes	**190**	30 20S	64 20W
Dease →	**144**	59 56N	128 32W
Dease Lake	**144**	58 25N	130 6W

Death Valley **173** 36 19N 116 52W
Deauville . . . . **38** 49 23N 0 2 E
Debar . . . . **52** 41 31N 20 30 E
Debre Markos . . . . **132** 10 20N 37 40 E
Debre Tabor . . . . **132** 11 50N 38 26 E
Debrecen . . . . **59** 47 33N 21 42 E
Decatur, Ala., U.S.A. **169** 34 35N 87 0W
Decatur, Ga., U.S.A. **170** 33 47N 84 17W
Decatur, Ill., U.S.A. **166** 39 50N 89 0W
Deccan . . . . **76** 18 0N 79 0 E
Dedéagach =
  Alexandroúpolis . . . . **55** 40 50N 25 54 E
Dee →, Scotland, U.K. **33** 57 4N 2 7W
Dee →, Wales, U.K. **26** 53 15N 3 7W
Deepwater . . . . **116** 29 25S 151 51 E
Deer Lake **149** 49 11N 57 27W
Defiance **167** 41 20N 84 20W
Deh Bīd . . . . **85** 30 39N 53 11 E
Dehra Dun . . . . **89** 30 20N 78 4 E
Dej . . . . **56** 47 10N 23 52 E
Del Rio **161** 29 23N 100 50W
Delano **173** 35 48N 119 13W
Delaware □ **164** 39 0N 75 40W
Delaware → **164** 39 20N 75 25W
Delaware B. **157** 38 50N 75 0W
Delft . . . . **40** 52 1N 4 22 E
Delfzijl. . . . . **41** 53 20N 6 55 E
Delgado, C. . . . . **137** 10 45S 40 40 E
Delgo . . . . **129** 20 6N 30 40 E
Delhi . . . . **89** 28 38N 77 17 E
Delice → . . . . **80** 39 45N 34 15 E
Delicias **174** 28 13N 105 28W
Delong, Ostrova . . . . **72** 76 40N 149 20 E
Deloraine . . . . **119** 41 30S 146 40 E
Delray Beach **170** 26 27N 80 4W
Demanda, Sierra de la **50** 42 15N 3 0W
Dembidolo . . . . **132** 8 34N 34 50 E
Deming **161** 32 10N 107 50W
Demopolis **169** 32 30N 87 48W
Den Burg . . . . **40** 53 3N 4 47 E
Den Haag = 's-Gravenhage. . **40** 52 7N 4 17 E
Den Helder . . . . **40** 52 57N 4 45 E
Den Oever . . . . **40** 52 56N 5 2 E
Denain . . . . **38** 50 20N 3 22 E
Denbigh **26** 53 12N 3 26W
Denham . . . . **120** 25 56S 113 31 E
Deniliquin . . . . **117** 35 30S 144 58 E
Denison **168** 33 50N 96 40W
Denizli . . . . **80** 37 42N 29 2 E
Denmark ■ . . . . **120** 34 59S 117 25 E
Denmark ■ . . . . **61** 55 30N 9 0 E
Denmark Str. **13** 66 0N 30 0W
Denton **168** 33 12N 97 10W
D'Entrecasteaux Is. . . . . **115** 9 0S 151 0 E
Denver **163** 39 45N 105 0W
Deolali . . . . **91** 19 58N 73 50 E
Deoria . . . . **92** 26 31N 83 48 E
Deosai Mts. . . . . **89** 35 40N 75 0 E
Dera Ghazi Khan . . . . **89** 30 5N 70 43 E
Dera Ismail Khan . . . . **89** 31 50N 70 50 E
Derby **28** 52 55N 1 28W
Derby □ **28** 52 55N 1 28W
Derg, L. **35** 53 0N 8 20W
Derry = Londonderry **34** 55 0N 7 20W
Derryveagh Mts. **34** 55 0N 8 40W
Derwent →, Cumbria, U.K. . . **28** 54 42N 3 22W
Derwent →, Derby, U.K. **29** 52 53N 1 17W
Derwent →, N. Yorks., U.K. . **29** 53 45N 0 57W
Derwent Water, L. **28** 54 35N 3 9W
Des Moines **166** 41 35N 93 37W
Des Moines → **166** 40 23N 91 25W
Deschutes → **171** 45 30N 121 0W
Dese . . . . **133** 11 5N 39 40 E
Despeñaperros, Paso **50** 38 24N 3 30W
Dessau . . . . **43** 51 49N 12 15 E
Dessye = Dese . . . . **133** 11 5N 39 40 E
Desvrès . . . . **38** 50 40N 1 48 E
Detroit **167** 42 23N 83 5W
Deurne . . . . **41** 51 27N 5 49 E
Deutsche Bucht . . . . **42** 54 10N 7 51 E
Devakottai . . . . **90** 9 55N 78 45 E

Deventer . . . . **41** 52 15N 6 10 E
Devizes **24** 51 21N 2 0W
Devon I. **13** 75 10N 85 0W
Devonport, Australia . . . . **119** 41 10S 146 22 E
Devonport, N.Z. . . . . **122** 36 49S 174 49 E
Devonport, U.K. **27** 50 23N 4 11W
Devonshire □ **27** 50 50N 3 40W
Dewsbury **28** 53 42N 1 38W
Dezfūl . . . . **84** 32 20N 48 30 E
Dezhneva, Mys **73** 66 5N 169 40W
Dhahran = Aẓ Ẕahrān . . . . **84** 26 10N 50 7 E
Dhaka . . . . **92** 23 43N 90 26 E
Dhaka □ . . . . **93** 24 25N 90 25 E
Dhamar . . . . **83** 14 30N 44 20 E
Dhar . . . . **91** 22 35N 75 26 E
Dharmapuri . . . . **90** 12 10N 78 10 E
Dharwad . . . . **90** 15 22N 75 15 E
Dhidhimótikhon . . . . **55** 41 22N 26 29 E
Dhikti . . . . **55** 35 8N 25 22 E
Dhodhekánisos . . . . **55** 36 35N 27 0 E
Dhuburi . . . . **92** 26 2N 89 59 E
Dhule . . . . **91** 20 58N 74 50 E
Di Linh, Cao Nguyen . . . . **95** 11 30N 108 0 E
Diamantina **188** 18 17S 43 40W
Diamantina → . . . . **115** 26 45S 139 10 E
Diamantino **188** 14 30S 56 30W
Dibrugarh . . . . **93** 27 29N 94 55 E
Dickinson **163** 46 50N 102 48W
Didsbury **155** 51 35N 114 10W
Diefenbaker L. **152** 51 0N 106 55W
Dieppe . . . . **38** 49 54N 1 4 E
Dieren . . . . **41** 52 3N 6 6 E
Digby **148** 44 38N 65 50W
Digne . . . . **37** 44 5N 6 12 E
Dijlah, Nahr → . . . . **81** 31 0N 47 25 E
Dijon . . . . **37** 47 20N 5 0 E
Dila . . . . **133** 6 21N 38 22 E
Dillon **165** 34 26N 79 20W
Dimashq . . . . **80** 33 30N 36 18 E
Dimboola . . . . **119** 36 28S 142 7 E
Dîmbovița → . . . . **57** 44 14N 26 13 E
Dimitrovgrad . . . . **53** 42 5N 25 35 E
Dimitrovo = Pernik . . . . **53** 42 35N 23 2 E
Dinan **36** 48 28N 2 2W
Dinara Planina . . . . **52** 44 0N 16 30 E
Dinaric Alps = Dinara Planina **52** 44 0N 16 30 E
Dindigul . . . . **90** 10 25N 78 0 E
Dingle **35** 52 9N 10 17W
Dingle B. **35** 52 3N 10 20W
Dingwall **33** 57 36N 4 26W
Dinuba **173** 36 31N 119 22W
Dire Dawa . . . . **133** 9 35N 41 45 E
Diriamba **179** 11 51N 86 19W
Dirranbandi . . . . **116** 28 33S 148 17 E
Disappointment L. . . . . **114** 23 20S 122 40 E
Discovery B. . . . . **119** 38 10S 140 40 E
Disko **146** 69 45N 53 30W
Diss . . . . **25** 52 23N 1 6 E
District of Columbia □ **164** 38 55N 77 0W
Diu . . . . **91** 20 45N 70 58 E
Dives-sur-Mer **39** 49 18N 0 8W
Dixon **166** 41 50N 89 30W
Dixon Entrance **154** 54 30N 132 0W
Diyarbakir . . . . **81** 37 55N 40 18 E
Djakarta = Jakarta . . . . **111** 6 9S 106 49 E
Djelfa . . . . **130** 34 40N 3 15 E
Djerid, Chott . . . . **127** 33 42N 8 30 E
Djibouti . . . . **133** 11 30N 43 5 E
Djibouti ■ . . . . **133** 12 0N 43 0 E
Djoum . . . . **131** 2 41N 12 35 E
Dmitriya Lapteva, Proliv. . . . . . **72** 73 0N 140 0 E
Dnepr → . . . . **68** 46 30N 32 18 E
Dnepropetrovsk . . . . **68** 48 30N 35 0 E
Dnestr → . . . . **68** 46 18N 30 17 E
Dnestrovski = Belgorod . . . . . **68** 50 35N 36 35 E
Dnieper = Dnepr → . . . . **68** 46 30N 32 18 E
Dniester = Dnestr → . . . . **68** 46 18N 30 17 E
Dobruja . . . . **57** 44 30N 28 15 E
Dodecanese =
  Dhodhekánisos . . . . **55** 36 35N 27 0 E
Dodge City **161** 37 42N 100 0W

Dodoma . . . . **135** 6 8S 35 45 E
Doesburg . . . . **41** 52 1N 6 9 E
Doetinchem . . . . **41** 51 59N 6 18 E
Dogger Bank . . . . **124** 54 50N 2 0 E
Doi Luang . . . . **95** 18 30N 101 0 E
Dojran . . . . **54** 41 10N 22 45 E
Dokkum . . . . **41** 53 20N 5 59 E
Dolbeau **148** 48 53N 72 18W
Dole . . . . **37** 47 7N 5 31 E
Dolgellau **26** 52 44N 3 53W
Dolgelley = Dolgellau **26** 52 44N 3 53W
Dolomites = Dolomiti . . . . **47** 46 30N 11 40 E
Dolomiti . . . . **47** 46 30N 11 40 E
Dolores **191** 36 20S 57 40W
Dolphin and Union Str. **145** 69 5N 114 45W
Domel I. = Letsôk-aw Kyun . . **94** 11 30N 98 25 E
Dominica ■ **180** 15 20N 61 20W
Dominican Rep. ■ **180** 19 0N 70 30W
Don →, U.K. **33** 57 14N 2 5W
Don →, U.S.S.R. . . . . **68** 47 4N 39 18 E
Donaghadee **34** 54 38N 5 32W
Donau → . . . . **42** 48 10N 17 0 E
Doncaster **29** 53 31N 1 9W
Dondra Head . . . . **90** 5 55N 80 40 E
Donegal **34** 54 39N 8 8W
Donegal □ **34** 54 53N 8 0W
Donegal B. **34** 54 30N 8 35W
Donetsk . . . . **68** 48 0N 37 45 E
Dongara . . . . **120** 29 14S 114 57 E
Dongen . . . . **40** 51 38N 4 56 E
Dongting Hu . . . . **99** 29 18N 112 45 E
Donnelly's Crossing . . . . **122** 35 42S 173 38 E
Donnybrook . . . . **120** 33 34S 115 48 E
Doon → **31** 55 26N 4 41W
Dorada, La **184** 5 30N 74 40W
Dorchester **27** 50 42N 2 28W
Dorchester, C. **146** 65 27N 77 27W
Dordogne □ . . . . **36** 45 5N 0 40 E
Dordrecht . . . . **40** 51 48N 4 39 E
Dornoch **33** 57 52N 4 0W
Dorrigo . . . . **116** 30 20S 152 44 E
Dorris **172** 41 59N 121 58W
Dorset □ **27** 50 48N 2 25W
Dortmund . . . . **42** 51 32N 7 28 E
Dothan **169** 31 10N 85 25W
Douai . . . . **38** 50 21N 3 4 E
Douala . . . . **131** 4 0N 9 45 E
Douarnenez **36** 48 6N 4 21W
Douglas, U.K. **28** 54 9N 4 29W
Douglas, U.S.A. **170** 31 32N 82 52W
Doullens . . . . **38** 50 10N 2 20 E
Dounreay **33** 58 34N 3 44W
Dourados **188** 22 9S 54 50W
Douro → **50** 41 8N 8 40W
Douro Litoral □ **50** 41 10N 8 20W
Dove → **28** 52 51N 1 36W
Dover, U.K. . . . . **25** 51 7N 1 19 E
Dover, Del., U.S.A. **164** 39 10N 75 31W
Dover, N.H., U.S.A. **164** 43 12N 70 51W
Dover, Str. of . . . . **38** 51 0N 1 30 E
Dovey → **26** 52 32N 4 0W
Downham Market . . . . **25** 52 36N 0 22 E
Downpatrick **34** 54 20N 5 43W
Drachten . . . . **41** 53 7N 6 5 E
Dragoman, Prokhod . . . . **53** 43 0N 22 53 E
Draguignan . . . . **37** 43 30N 6 27 E
Drakensberg . . . . **137** 31 0S 28 0 E
Dráma . . . . **55** 41 9N 24 10 E
Drammen . . . . **60** 59 42N 10 12 E
Drau = Drava → . . . . **59** 45 33N 18 55 E
Drava → . . . . **59** 45 33N 18 55 E
Drayton Valley **155** 53 12N 114 58W
Drenthe □ . . . . **41** 52 52N 6 40 E
Dresden . . . . **43** 51 2N 13 45 E
Dreux . . . . **39** 48 44N 1 23 E
Driffield **29** 54 0N 0 25W
Drin i zi → . . . . **52** 41 37N 20 28 E
Drina → . . . . **52** 44 53N 19 21 E
Drogheda **34** 53 45N 6 20W
Droitwich **24** 52 16N 2 10W
Dronne → **36** 45 2N 0 9W

Dronning Maud Land . . . . **14** 72 30S 12 0 E
Drumheller **155** 51 25N 112 40W
Drummond Ra. . . . . **121** 23 45S 147 10 E
Drummondville **151** 45 55N 72 25W
Dryden **153** 49 47N 92 50W
Du Bois **164** 41 8N 78 46W
Du Quoin **166** 38 0N 89 10W
Dubai = Dubayy . . . . **85** 25 18N 55 20 E
Dubawnt → **145** 64 33N 100 6W
Dubawnt, L. **143** 63 4N 101 42W
Dubayy . . . . **85** 25 18N 55 20 E
Dubbo . . . . **116** 32 11S 148 35 E
Dublin, Ireland **35** 53 20N 6 18W
Dublin, U.S.A. **170** 32 30N 82 34W
Dublin □ **34** 53 24N 6 20W
Dubrovnik . . . . **52** 42 39N 18 6 E
Dubuque **166** 42 30N 90 41W
Dudley **24** 52 30N 2 5W
Dugi Otok . . . . **52** 44 0N 15 0 E
Duisburg . . . . **42** 51 27N 6 42 E
Duluth **150** 46 48N 92 10W
Dumbarton **31** 55 58N 4 35W
Dumfries **31** 55 4N 3 37W
Dumfries & Galloway □ **31** 55 0N 4 0W
Dun Laoghaire **35** 53 17N 6 9W
Dunârea → . . . . **57** 45 30N 8 15 E
Dunaújváros . . . . **59** 47 0N 18 57 E
Dunbar **31** 56 0N 2 32W
Dunblane **31** 56 10N 3 58W
Duncan, Canada **154** 48 45N 123 40W
Duncan, U.S.A. **161** 34 25N 98 0W
Duncan Pass. . . . . **94** 11 0N 92 30 E
Dundalk **34** 54 1N 6 25W
Dundas, Canada **151** 43 17N 79 59W
Dundas, Greenland **13** 77 0N 69 0W
Dundee **31** 56 29N 3 0W
Dundrum **34** 54 17N 5 50W
Dunedin . . . . **123** 45 50S 170 33 E
Dunedoo . . . . **116** 32 0S 149 25 E
Dunfermline **31** 56 5N 3 28W
Dungannon **34** 54 30N 6 47W
Dungarvan **35** 52 6N 7 40W
Dungeness . . . . **25** 50 54N 0 59 E
Dungog . . . . **117** 32 22S 151 46 E
Dunhuang . . . . **100** 40 8N 94 36 E
Dunkeld **33** 56 34N 3 36W
Dunkerque . . . . **38** 51 2N 2 20 E
Dunkery Beacon **27** 51 15N 3 37W
Dunkirk = Dunkerque . . . . **38** 51 2N 2 20 E
Dunkirk **164** 42 30N 79 18W
Dúnleary = Dun Laoghaire . . . **35** 53 17N 6 9W
Dunmore **164** 41 27N 75 38W
Dunn **165** 35 18N 78 36W
Dunnet Hd. **33** 58 38N 3 22W
Duns **31** 55 47N 2 20W
Dunsmuir **172** 41 10N 122 18W
Dunstan Mts. . . . . **123** 44 53S 169 35 E
Durance → . . . . **37** 43 55N 4 45 E
Durango, Mexico **174** 24 3N 104 39W
Durango, U.S.A. **163** 37 16N 107 50W
Durango □ **174** 24 50N 104 50W
Durant **168** 34 0N 96 25W
Durazno **191** 33 25S 56 31W
Durban . . . . **137** 29 49S 31 1 E
Durg . . . . • **92** 21 15N 81 22 E
Durham, U.K. **28** 54 47N 1 34W
Durham, U.S.A. **165** 36 0N 78 55W
Durham □ **28** 54 42N 1 45W
Durmitor . . . . **52** 43 10N 19 0 E
Durness **32** 58 34N 4 45W
D'Urville I. . . . . **122** 40 50S 173 55 E
Dushanbe . . . . **71** 38 33N 68 48 E
Düsseldorf . . . . **42** 51 15N 6 46 E
Duwādimi . . . . **82** 24 35N 44 15 E
Duyun . . . . **99** 26 18N 107 29 E
Düzce . . . . **80** 40 50N 31 10 E
Duzdab = Zāhedān . . . . **86** 29 30N 60 50 E
Dvina, Sev. → . . . . **69** 64 32N 40 30 E
Dvinsk = Daugavpils . . . . **68** 55 53N 26 32 E
Dyer, C. **146** 66 40N 61 0W
Dyersburg **169** 36 2N 89 20W

Name	Map	Lat°	Lat′	N/S	Long°	Long′	E/W
Dyfed □	**26**	52	0	N	4	30	W
Dysart	**121**	22	32	S	148	23	E
Dzamin Üüd	**98**	43	50	N	111	58	E
Dzerzhinsk	**68**	53	40	N	27	1	E
Dzhalal-Abad	**71**	40	56	N	73	0	E
Dzhalinda	**75**	53	26	N	124	0	E
Dzhambul	**71**	42	54	N	71	22	E
Dzhardzhan	**72**	68	10	N	124	10	E
Dzhetygara	**71**	52	11	N	61	12	E
Dzhezkazgan	**71**	47	44	N	67	40	E
Dzhugdzur, Khrebet	**75**	57	30	N	138	0	E
Dzuumod	**98**	47	45	N	106	58	E
Eagle	**142**	64	44	N	141	7	W
Eagle Pass	**161**	28	45	N	100	35	W
Eagle River	**150**	45	55	N	89	17	W
Ealing	**25**	51	30	N	0	19	W
Earn ~►	**31**	56	20	N	3	19	W
Easley	**165**	34	52	N	82	35	W
East Angus	**148**	45	30	N	71	40	W
East Bengal	**92**	24	0	N	90	0	E
East Beskids = Vychodné Beskydy	**59**	49	30	N	22	0	E
East C.	**122**	37	42	S	178	35	E
East Chicago	**167**	41	40	N	87	30	W
East China Sea	**99**	30	5	N	126	0	E
East Falkland	**192**	51	30	S	58	30	W
East Indies	**77**	0	0		120	0	E
East Kilbride	**31**	55	46	N	4	10	W
East Liverpool	**164**	40	39	N	80	35	W
East London	**137**	33	0	S	27	55	E
East Main = Eastmain	**140**	52	10	N	78	30	W
East Pakistan = Bangladesh ■	**92**	24	0	N	90	0	E
East Point	**170**	33	40	N	84	28	W
East St. Louis	**166**	38	37	N	90	4	W
East Schelde ~► = Oosterschelde	**40**	51	33	N	4	0	E
East Siberian Sea	**73**	73	0	N	160	0	E
East Sussex □	**25**	51	0	N	0	20	E
Eastbourne, N.Z.	**123**	41	19	S	174	55	E
Eastbourne, U.K.	**25**	50	46	N	0	18	E
Eastern Ghats	**90**	14	0	N	78	50	E
Eastleigh	**25**	50	58	N	1	21	W
Eastmain	**140**	52	10	N	78	30	W
Eastmain ~►	**140**	52	27	N	78	26	W
Easton	**164**	40	41	N	75	15	W
Eau Claire	**166**	44	46	N	91	30	W
Eau Claire, L. à l'	**146**	56	10	N	74	25	W
Ebbw Vale	**26**	51	47	N	3	12	W
Eboli	**49**	40	39	N	15	2	E
Ebro ~►	**51**	40	43	N	0	54	E
Echizen-Misaki	**106**	35	59	N	135	57	E
Echo Bay	**145**	46	29	N	84	4	W
Echuca	**117**	36	10	S	144	20	E
Ecuador ■	**184**	2	0	S	78	0	W
Ed Dâmer	**129**	17	27	N	34	0	E
Edam	**40**	52	31	N	5	3	E
Eddystone	**27**	50	11	N	4	16	W
Ede	**41**	52	4	N	5	40	E
Eden	**117**	37	3	S	149	55	E
Eden ~►	**28**	54	57	N	3	2	W
Edenhope	**119**	37	4	S	141	19	E
Edge Hill	**24**	52	7	N	1	28	W
Edhessa	**54**	40	48	N	22	5	E
Edinburgh	**31**	55	57	N	3	12	W
Edirne	**80**	41	40	N	26	34	E
Edmonton, Australia	**121**	17	2	S	145	46	E
Edmonton, Canada	**155**	53	30	N	113	30	W
Edmundston	**148**	47	23	N	68	20	W
Edson	**155**	53	35	N	116	28	W
Edward, L.	**132**	0	25	S	29	40	E
Edward VII Land	**15**	80	0	S	150	0	W
Edwards Plat.	**161**	30	30	N	101	5	W
Effingham	**167**	39	8	N	88	30	W
Égadi, Ísole	**48**	37	55	N	12	16	E
Eger	**59**	47	53	N	20	27	E
Egmont, Mt.	**122**	39	17	S	174	5	E
Eğridir Gölü	**80**	37	53	N	30	50	E
Egypt ■	**128**	28	0	N	31	0	E
Eifel	**42**	50	10	N	6	45	E
Eigg	**32**	56	54	N	6	10	W
Eil	**133**	8	0	N	49	50	E
Eindhoven	**41**	51	26	N	5	30	E
Eirunepé	**187**	6	35	S	69	53	W
El Aaiún	**126**	27	9	N	13	12	W
El Cajon	**173**	32	49	N	117	0	W
El Callao	**185**	7	18	N	61	50	W
El Centro	**173**	32	50	N	115	40	W
El Cerro	**187**	17	30	S	61	40	W
El Dere	**133**	3	50	N	47	8	E
El Djouf	**126**	20	0	N	11	30	E
El Dorado	**168**	33	10	N	92	40	W
El Escorial	**50**	40	35	N	4	7	W
El Faiyûm	**128**	29	19	N	30	50	E
El Fâsher	**129**	13	33	N	25	26	E
El Ferrol	**50**	43	29	N	8	15	W
El Fuerte	**174**	26	25	N	108	39	W
El Geteina	**129**	14	50	N	32	27	E
El Iskandarîya	**128**	31	0	N	30	0	E
El Jadida	**126**	33	11	N	8	17	W
El Khârga	**128**	25	30	N	30	33	E
El Khartûm	**129**	15	31	N	32	35	E
El Mahalla el Kubra	**128**	31	0	N	31	0	E
El Minyâ	**128**	28	7	N	30	33	E
El Obeid	**129**	13	8	N	30	10	E
El Oro :	**177**	27	15	N	103	30	W
El Paso	**161**	31	50	N	106	30	W
El Progreso	**177**	15	26	N	87	51	W
El Qâhira	**128**	30	1	N	31	14	E
El Qasr	**128**	25	44	N	28	42	E
El Salvador ■	**177**	13	50	N	89	0	W
El Suweis	**128**	29	58	N	32	31	E
El Tigre	**185**	8	44	N	64	15	W
El Turbio	**192**	51	45	S	72	5	W
Elat	**80**	29	30	N	34	56	E
Elâzığ	**81**	38	37	N	39	14	E
Elba	**46**	42	48	N	10	15	E
Elbasani	**52**	41	9	N	20	9	E
Elbe ~►	**42**	53	50	N	9	0	E
Elbert, Mt.	**163**	39	5	N	106	27	W
Elberton	**165**	34	7	N	82	51	W
Elbeuf	**39**	49	17	N	1	2	E
Elbing = Elbląg	**58**	54	10	N	19	25	E
Elbląg	**58**	54	10	N	19	25	E
Elbrus	**70**	43	21	N	42	30	E
Elburg	**41**	52	26	N	5	50	E
Elburz Mts. = Alborz, Reshteh-ye Kūhhā-ye	**86**	36	0	N	52	0	E
Elche	**51**	38	15	N	0	42	W
Eldorado	**174**	24	20	N	107	22	W
Eldorado Springs	**166**	37	54	N	93	59	W
Eldoret	**132**	0	30	N	35	17	E
Eleanora, Peak	**120**	32	57	S	121	9	E
Electra	**161**	34	0	N	99	0	W
Elephant Butte Res.	**161**	33	45	N	107	30	W
Eleuthera	**178**	25	0	N	76	20	W
Elgin, U.K.	**33**	57	39	N	3	20	W
Elgin, Ill., U.S.A.	**167**	42	0	N	88	20	W
Elgin, Oreg., U.S.A.	**171**	45	37	N	118	0	W
Elgon, Mt.	**132**	1	10	N	34	30	E
Elisabethville = Lubumbashi	**135**	11	40	S	27	28	E
Elizabeth, Australia	**119**	34	42	S	138	41	E
Elizabeth, U.S.A.	**164**	40	37	N	74	12	W
Elizabeth City	**165**	36	18	N	76	16	W
Elizabethton	**165**	36	20	N	82	13	W
Elizabethtown	**167**	37	40	N	85	54	W
Elk Point	**152**	53	54	N	110	55	W
Elkhart	**167**	41	42	N	85	55	W
Elkins	**165**	38	53	N	79	53	W
Elko	**172**	40	50	N	115	50	W
Ellensburg	**171**	47	0	N	120	30	W
Ellery, Mt.	**117**	37	28	S	148	47	E
Ellesmere I.	**13**	79	30	N	80	0	W
Ellesmere Port	**28**	53	17	N	2	55	W
Ellice Is. = Tuvalu ■	**122**	8	0	S	178	0	E
Elliot Lake	**150**	46	25	N	82	35	W
Ellore = Eluru	**92**	16	48	N	81	8	E
Ellsworth Land	**14**	76	0	S	89	0	W

Ellsworth Mts.	**14**	78 30S	85 0W
Elmhurst	**167**	41 52N	87 58W
Elmira	**164**	42 8N	76 49W
Elrose	**152**	51 12N	108 0W
Eluru	**92**	16 48N	81 8 E
Elvas	**50**	38 50N	7 10W
Elwood	**167**	40 20N	85 50W
Ely	**172**	39 10N	114 50W
Elyria	**167**	41 22N	82 8W
Emāmrūd	**86**	36 30N	55 0 E
Emba →	**70**	46 38N	53 14 E
Emden	**42**	53 22N	7 12 E
Emerald	**121**	23 32S	148 10 E
Emilia-Romagna □	**46**	44 33N	10 40 E
Emmeloord	**41**	52 44N	5 46 E
Emmen	**41**	52 48N	6 57 E
Empalme	**174**	27 58N	110 51W
Emporia, Kans., U.S.A.	**158**	38 25N	96 10W
Emporia, Va., U.S.A.	**165**	36 41N	77 32W
Ems →	**42**	52 37N	9 26 E
En Nahud	**129**	12 45N	28 25 E
Ena	**106**	35 25N	137 25 E
Ena-San	**106**	35 26N	137 36 E
Encarnación	**191**	27 15S	55 50W
Encarnación de Díaz	**175**	21 31N	102 14W
Encontrados	**184**	9 3N	72 14W
Enderby	**155**	50 35N	119 10W
Enderby Land	**14**	66 0S	53 0 E
Endicott	**164**	42 6N	76 2W
Engaño, C.	**180**	18 30N	68 20W
Engels	**68**	51 28N	46 6 E
Enggano	**111**	5 20S	102 40 E
England □	**21**	53 0N	2 0W
English Bazar = Ingraj Bazar	**92**	24 58N	88 10 E
English Channel	**16**	50 0N	2 0W
Enid	**161**	36 26N	97 52W
Enkhuizen	**40**	52 42N	5 17 E
Ennedi	**129**	17 15N	22 0 E
Ennis	**35**	52 51N	8 59W
Enniscorthy	**35**	52 30N	6 35W
Enniskillen	**34**	54 20N	7 40W
Enriquillo, L.	**180**	18 20N	72 5W
Enschede	**41**	52 13N	6 53 E
Ensenada	**174**	31 52N	116 37W
Enshū-Nada	**106**	34 27N	137 38 E
Entebbe	**132**	0 4N	32 28 E
Enterprise	**171**	45 30N	117 18W
Entre Ríos □	**190**	30 30S	58 30W
Enugu	**131**	6 20N	7 30 E
Enzan	**107**	35 42N	138 44 E
Eólie, I.	**49**	38 30N	14 50 E
Epe	**41**	52 21N	5 59 E
Épernay	**39**	49 3N	3 56 E
Ephesus	**80**	37 50N	27 33 E
Épinal	**37**	48 10N	6 27 E
Epping	**25**	51 42N	0 8 E
Equatorial Guinea ■	**134**	2 0S	8 0 E
Er Rif	**126**	35 1N	4 1W
Erāwadī Myit → = Irrawaddy →	**93**	15 50N	95 6 E
Ercha	**73**	69 45N	147 20 E
Erciyaş Dağı	**80**	38 30N	35 30 E
Erebus, Mt.	**15**	77 35S	167 0 E
Erechim	**191**	27 35S	52 15W
Ereğli	**80**	41 15N	31 30 E
Erfurt	**43**	50 58N	11 2 E
Erg Chech	**126**	50 59N	11 0 E
Erie	**164**	42 10N	80 7W
Erie, L.	**151**	42 15N	81 0W
Erímanthos	**54**	37 57N	21 50 E
Erimo-misaki	**103**	41 50N	143 15 E
Eritrea □	**132**	14 0N	41 0 E
Ermoúpolis = Síros	**55**	37 28N	24 57 E
Erne, Lough	**34**	54 26N	7 46W
Erode	**90**	11 24N	77 45 E
Erramala Hills	**90**	15 30N	78 15 E
Erris Hd.	**34**	54 19N	10 0W
Erzgebirge	**43**	50 25N	13 0 E
Erzincan	**81**	39 46N	39 30 E
Erzurum	**81**	39 57N	41 15 E
Es Sînâ'	**128**	29 0N	34 0 E
Esan-Misaki	**103**	41 40N	141 10 E
Esashi	**103**	41 52N	140 7 E
Esbjerg	**61**	55 29N	8 29 E
Escanaba	**150**	45 44N	87 5W
Escondido	**173**	33 9N	117 4W
Escuintla	**177**	14 20N	90 48W
Eşfahān	**85**	33 0N	53 0 E
Esh Sham = Dimashq	**80**	33 30N	36 18 E
Esk →	**29**	54 27N	0 36W
Eskilstuna	**60**	59 22N	16 32 E
Eskimo Pt.	**145**	61 10N	94 15W
Eskişehir	**80**	39 50N	30 35 E
Eslāmābād-e Gharb	**84**	34 10N	46 30 E
Esmeraldas	**184**	1 0N	79 40W
Espanola	**151**	46 15N	81 46W
Esperance	**114**	33 45S	121 55 E
Espinazo, Sierra del = Espinhaço, Serra do	**188**	17 30S	43 30W
Espinhaço, Serra do	**188**	17 30S	43 30W
Espírito Santo □	**189**	20 0S	40 45W
Essaouira	**126**	31 32N	9 42W
Essen	**42**	51 28N	6 59 E
Essequibo →	**185**	6 50N	58 30W
Essex □	**25**	51 48N	0 30 E
Estados, I. de los	**192**	54 40S	64 30W
Estelí	**179**	13 9N	86 22W
Estevan	**152**	49 10N	102 59W
Estherville	**166**	43 25N	94 50W
Estonian S.S.R. □	**68**	58 30N	25 30 E
Estoril	**50**	38 42N	9 23W
Estrêla, Serra da	**50**	40 10N	7 45W
Estremadura	**50**	39 0N	9 0W
Étampes	**39**	48 26N	2 10 E
Étaples	**38**	50 30N	1 39 E
Etawah	**91**	26 48N	79 6 E
Ethiopia ■	**133**	8 0N	40 0 E
Ethiopian Highlands	**132**	10 0N	37 0 E
Etna	**49**	37 45N	15 0 E
Etosha Pan	**136**	18 40S	16 30 E
Etzatlán	**175**	20 46N	104 5W
Euboea = Évvoia	**55**	38 30N	24 0 E
Euclid	**167**	41 32N	81 31W
Eucumbene, L.	**117**	36 2S	148 40 E
Eufaula	**169**	35 20N	95 33W
Eugene	**171**	44 0N	123 8W
Eupen	**42**	50 37N	6 3 E
Euphrates = Furāt, Nahr al →	**84**	31 0N	47 25 E
Eureka, Calif., U.S.A.	**172**	40 50N	124 0W
Eureka, Nev., U.S.A.	**172**	39 32N	116 2W
Euroa	**117**	36 44S	145 35 E
Europa, Pta. de	**50**	36 3N	5 21W
Europa Pt. = Europa, Pta. de	**50**	36 3N	5 21W
Europoort	**40**	51 57N	4 10 E
Euston	**119**	34 30S	142 46 E
Eutsuk L.	**154**	53 20N	126 45W
Evans Head	**116**	29 7S	153 27 E
Evanston	**167**	42 0N	87 40W
Evansville	**167**	38 0N	87 35W
Everard, L.	**118**	31 30S	135 0 E
Everest, Mt.	**92**	28 5N	86 58 E
Everett	**171**	48 0N	122 10W
Everglades	**170**	26 0N	80 30W
Evesham	**24**	52 6N	1 57W
Évora	**50**	38 33N	7 57W
Évreux	**39**	49 0N	1 8 E
Évvoia	**55**	38 30N	24 0 E
Excelsior Springs	**166**	39 20N	94 10W
Exe →	**27**	50 38N	3 27W
Exeter	**27**	50 43N	3 31W
Exmoor	**27**	51 10N	3 59W
Exmouth	**27**	50 37N	3 26W
Extremadura □	**50**	39 30N	6 5W
Eyasi, L.	**135**	3 30S	35 0 E
Eye Pen.	**32**	58 13N	6 10W
Eyre, L.	**118**	29 30S	137 26 E
Eyre Mts.	**123**	45 25S	168 25 E
Eyre Pen.	**119**	33 30S	137 17 E

Facatativá	**184**	4 49N	74 22W
Faddeyevskiy, Ostrov	**72**	76 0N	150 0 E
Fair Hd.	**34**	55 14N	6 10W
Fairbanks	**142**	64 50N	147 50W
Fairfield, N.Z.	**123**	45 54S	170 24 E
Fairfield, Ala., U.S.A.	**169**	33 30N	87 0W
Fairfield, Calif., U.S.A.	**172**	38 14N	122 1W
Fairfield, Tex., U.S.A.	**168**	31 40N	96 0W
Fairmont, Minn., U.S.A.	**166**	43 37N	94 30W
Fairmont, W. Va., U.S.A.	**164**	39 29N	80 10W
Fairview	**155**	56 5N	118 25W
Fairweather, Mt.	**143**	58 55N	137 45W
Faisalabad	**89**	31 30N	73 5 E
Faizabad	**92**	26 45N	82 10 E
Fajardo	**180**	18 20N	65 39W
Fakenham	**29**	52 50N	0 51 E
Falam	**93**	23 0N	93 45 E
Falkirk	**31**	56 0N	3 47W
Falkland Is.	**192**	51 30S	59 0W
Falköping	**60**	58 12N	13 33 E
Fall River	**164**	41 45N	71 5W
Falls City	**166**	40 0N	95 40W
Falmouth, Jamaica	**180**	18 30N	77 40W
Falmouth, U.K.	**27**	50 9N	5 5W
Famagusta	**80**	35 8N	33 55 E
Farāh	**87**	32 20N	62 7 E
Farāh □	**87**	32 25N	62 10 E
Fareham	**25**	50 52N	1 11W
Farewell, C.	**122**	40 29S	172 43 E
Farewell C. = Farvel, Kap	**147**	59 48N	43 55W
Fargo	**156**	46 52N	96 40W
Farmington, N.H., U.S.A.	**157**	43 25N	71 3W
Farmington, N. Mex., U.S.A.	**161**	36 45N	108 28W
Farnborough	**25**	51 17N	0 46W
Faro	**50**	37 2N	7 55W
Faroe Is.	**16**	62 0N	7 0W
Fars □	**85**	29 30N	55 0 E
Fársala	**54**	39 17N	22 23 E
Farvel, Kap	**147**	59 48N	43 55W
Fāryāb □	**87**	36 0N	65 0 E
Fatehgarh	**89**	27 25N	79 35 E
Fatehpur, Raj., India	**92**	28 0N	74 40 E
Fatehpur, Ut. P., India	**89**	25 56N	81 13 E
Faxaflói	**64**	64 29N	23 0W
Fayetteville, Ark., U.S.A.	**168**	36 0N	94 5W
Fayetteville, N.C., U.S.A.	**165**	35 0N	78 58W
Fazilka	**89**	30 27N	74 2 E
Fdérik	**126**	22 40N	12 45W
Fear, C.	**165**	33 51N	78 0W
Fécamp	**38**	49 45N	0 22 E
Feilding	**122**	40 13S	175 35 E
Feira de Santana	**189**	12 15S	38 57W
Felixstowe	**25**	51 58N	1 22 E
Fengjie	**99**	31 5N	109 36 E
Fens, The	**29**	52 45N	0 2 E
Fenyang	**98**	37 19N	111 46 E
Ferfer	**133**	5 4N	45 9 E
Fergana	**71**	40 23N	71 19 E
Fergus Falls	**156**	46 18N	96 7W
Fermoy	**35**	52 4N	8 18W
Fernando de Noronha	**189**	4 0S	33 10W
Fernando Póo = Bioko	**131**	3 30N	8 40 E
Fernie	**155**	49 30N	115 5W
Ferrara	**47**	44 50N	11 36 E
Ferté-Bernard, La	**39**	48 10N	0 40 E
Fès	**126**	34 0N	5 0W
Feuilles —►	**146**	58 47N	70 4W
Feyzābād	**87**	37 7N	70 33 E
Fezzan	**124**	27 0N	15 0 E
Fianarantsoa	**137**	21 26S	47 5 E
Fichtelgebirge	**43**	50 10N	12 0 E
Fife □	**31**	56 13N	3 2W
Fife Ness	**31**	56 17N	2 35W
Fiji ■	**122**	17 20S	179 0 E
Filey	**29**	54 13N	0 18W
Findlay	**167**	41 0N	83 41W
Finisterre, C.	**50**	42 50N	9 19W
Finland ■	**67**	63 0N	27 0 E
Finland, G. of	**67**	60 0N	26 0 E
Finlay —►	**144**	57 0N	125 10W
Finley	**117**	35 38S	145 35 E
Firenze	**47**	43 47N	11 15 E
Firozabad	**89**	27 10N	78 25 E
Fishguard	**26**	51 59N	4 59W
Fiskenæsset	**147**	63 5N	50 45W
Fitchburg	**164**	42 35N	71 47W
Fitzgerald	**170**	31 45N	83 16W
Fitzroy —►	**121**	23 32S	150 52 E
Fiume = Rijeka	**52**	45 20N	14 21 E
Flagstaff	**160**	35 10N	111 40W
Flamborough Hd.	**29**	54 8N	0 4W
Flannan Is.	**32**	58 9N	7 52W
Flattery, C.	**171**	48 21N	124 43W
Flèche, La	**39**	47 42N	0 4W
Fleetwood	**28**	53 55N	3 1W
Flekkefjord	**60**	58 18N	6 39 E
Flensburg	**43**	54 46N	9 28 E
Flers	**36**	48 47N	0 33W
Flin Flon	**152**	54 46N	101 53W
Flinders I.	**117**	40 0S	148 0 E
Flinders Ranges	**118**	31 30S	138 30 E
Flinders Reefs	**121**	17 37S	148 31 E
Flint, U.K.	**26**	53 15N	3 7W
Flint, U.S.A.	**167**	43 5N	83 40W
Flint —►	**170**	30 52N	84 38W
Flodden	**31**	55 37N	2 8W
Flora	**167**	38 40N	88 30W
Florence = Firenze	**47**	43 47N	11 15 E
Florence, Ala., U.S.A.	**169**	34 50N	87 40W
Florence, S.C., U.S.A.	**165**	34 12N	79 44W
Flores, Guat.	**177**	16 59N	89 50W
Flores, Indonesia	**113**	8 35S	121 0 E
Flores Sea	**113**	6 30S	124 0 E
Floriano	**188**	6 50S	43 0W
Florianópolis	**191**	27 30S	48 30W
Florida	**191**	34 7S	56 10W
Florida □	**170**	28 30N	82 0W
Florida, Straits of	**159**	25 0N	80 0W
Florida B.	**159**	25 0N	81 20W
Florida Keys	**159**	25 0N	80 40W
Flórina	**54**	40 48N	21 26 E
Flushing = Vlissingen	**40**	51 26N	3 34 E
Fly —►	**115**	8 25S	143 0 E
Foam Lake	**152**	51 40N	103 32W
Fóggia	**49**	41 28N	15 31 E
Foix	**36**	42 58N	1 38 E
Folda	**64**	64 41N	10 50 E
Folkestone	**25**	51 5N	1 11 E
Follette, La	**169**	36 23N	84 9W
Fond-du-Lac, Canada	**145**	59 19N	107 12W
Fond-du-Lac, U.S.A.	**167**	43 46N	88 26W
Fontainebleau	**39**	48 24N	2 40 E
Fonte Boa	**184**	2 33S	66 0W
Foochow = Fuzhou	**99**	26 5N	119 16 E
Forbes	**117**	33 22S	148 0 E
Forestburg	**155**	52 35N	112 1W
Forestville	**148**	48 48N	69 2W
Forfar	**33**	56 40N	2 53W
Forlì	**47**	44 14N	12 2 E
Formby Pt.	**28**	53 33N	3 7W
Formentera	**51**	38 43N	1 27 E
Formosa = Taiwan ■	**99**	23 30N	121 0 E
Formosa	**191**	26 15S	58 10W
Forrest City	**169**	35 0N	90 50W
Fort Albany	**140**	52 15N	81 35W
Fort Augustus	**32**	57 9N	4 40W
Fort Chipewyan	**145**	58 42N	111 8W
Fort Collins	**163**	40 30N	105 4W
Fort-Coulonge	**151**	45 50N	76 45W
Fort-de-France	**180**	14 36N	61 2W
Fort Dodge	**166**	42 29N	94 10W
Fort Frances	**153**	48 36N	93 24W
Fort Franklin	**145**	65 10N	123 30W
Fort George	**140**	53 50N	79 0W
Fort Good-Hope	**144**	66 14N	128 40W
Fort Hertz = Putao	**93**	27 28N	97 30 E
Fort Kent	**148**	47 12N	68 30W
Fort-Lamy = Ndjamena	**131**	12 10N	14 59 E
Fort Lauderdale	**170**	26 10N	80 5W
Fort Liard	**144**	60 14N	123 30W
Fort Mackay	**143**	57 12N	111 41W
Fort Macleod	**155**	49 45N	113 30W

Fort McMurray 155 56 44N 111 7W
Fort McPherson 144 67 30N 134 55W
Fort Madison 166 40 39N 91 20W
Fort Morgan 163 40 10N 103 50W
Fort Myers 170 26 39N 81 51W
Fort Nelson 144 58 50N 122 44W
Fort Nelson → 144 59 32N 124 0W
Fort Payne 169 34 25N 85 44W
Fort Peck L. 163 47 40N 107 0W
Fort Pierce 170 27 29N 80 19W
Fort Providence 145 61 3N 117 40W
Fort Qu'Appelle 152 50 45N 103 50W
Fort Resolution 145 61 10N 113 40W
Fort Rupert 140 51 30N 78 40W
Fort St. James 154 54 30N 124 10W
Fort St. John 155 56 15N 120 50W
Fort Sandeman . . . . . . 88 31 20N 69 31 E
Fort Saskatchewan 155 53 40N 113 15W
Fort Scott 166 37 50N 94 40W
Fort Severn 140 56 0N 87 40W
Fort Shevchenko . . . . . . 70 43 40N 51 20 E
Fort Simpson 144 61 45N 121 15W
Fort Smith, Canada 145 60 0N 111 51W
Fort Smith, U.S.A. 168 35 25N 94 25W
Fort Smith Region □ 145 63 0N 120 0W
Fort Trinquet = Bir Mogrein . . 126 25 10N 11 25W
Fort Valley 170 32 33N 83 52W
Fort Vermilion 145 58 24N 116 0W
Fort Wayne 167 41 5N 85 10W
Fort William 32 56 48N 5 8W
Fort Worth 168 32 45N 97 25W
Fort Yukon 142 66 35N 145 20W
Fortaleza 189 3 45S 38 35W
Forth → 31 56 9N 4 18W
Forth, Firth of 31 56 5N 2 55W
Fortuna 172 40 38N 124 8W
Foshan . . . . . . 99 23 4N 113 5 E
Foster . . . . . . 117 38 40S 146 15 E
Fougères 36 48 21N 1 14W
Foula, I. 30 60 10N 2 5W
Foulness I. . . . . . . 24 51 36N 0 55 E
Fourmies . . . . . . 38 50 1N 4 2 E
Foúrnoi . . . . . . 55 37 36N 26 32 E
Fouta Djalon 130 11 20N 12 10W
Foveaux Str. . . . . . . 123 46 42S 168 10 E
Fowey 27 50 20N 4 39W
Foxe Basin 146 66 0N 77 0W
Foxe Chan. 146 65 0N 80 0W
Foxe Pen. 146 65 0N 76 0W
Foxton . . . . . . 122 40 29S 175 18 E
Foyle, Lough 34 55 6N 7 8W
Foynes 35 52 37N 9 5W
Franca 188 20 33S 47 30W
France ■ . . . . . . 37 47 0N 3 0 E
Franche-Comté . . . . . . 37 46 30N 5 50 E
François 180 14 38N 60 57W
Franeker . . . . . . 41 53 12N 5 33 E
Frankfort, Ind., U.S.A. 167 40 20N 86 33W
Frankfort, Ky., U.S.A. 165 38 12N 84 52W
Frankfurt am Main . . . . . . 42 50 7N 8 40 E
Frankfurt an der Oder . . . . . . 43 52 50N 14 31 E
Fränkische Alb . . . . . . 43 49 20N 11 30 E
Franklin, La., U.S.A. 168 29 45N 91 30W
Franklin, N.H., U.S.A. 164 43 28N 71 39W
Franklin, W. Va., U.S.A. 165 38 38N 79 21W
Franklin D. Roosevelt L. 162 48 30N 118 16W
Franklin Mts. 145 65 0N 125 0W
Franklin Str. 145 72 0N 96 0W
Frankston . . . . . . 117 38 8S 145 8 E
Franz 150 48 25N 84 30W
Fraser → 154 49 7N 123 11W
Fraser, Mt. . . . . . . 120 25 35S 118 20 E
Fraser I. . . . . . . 116 25 15S 153 10 E
Fraserburgh 33 57 41N 2 0W
Fray Bentos 190 33 10S 58 15W
Frederick 164 39 25N 77 23W
Fredericksburg 165 38 16N 77 29W
Fredericton 148 45 57N 66 40W
Frederikshavn . . . . . . 61 57 28N 10 31 E
Fredrikstad . . . . . . 60 59 13N 10 57 E
Freeport, Bahamas 178 26 30N 78 47W
Freeport, Ill., U.S.A. 166 42 18N 89 40W
Freeport, N.Y., U.S.A. 164 40 39N 73 35W
Freeport, Tex., U.S.A. 158 28 55N 95 22W
Freetown 130 8 30N 13 17W
Freiberg . . . . . . 42 50 55N 13 20 E
Freibourg = Fribourg . . . . . . 44 46 49N 7 9 E
Fréjus . . . . . . 37 43 25N 6 44 E
Fremantle . . . . . . 120 32 7S 115 47 E
Fremont, Calif., U.S.A. 172 37 32N 122 1W
Fremont, Nebr., U.S.A. 166 41 30N 96 30W
French Guiana ■ 185 4 0N 53 0W
French Pass . . . . . . 123 40 55S 173 55 E
French Terr. of Afars & Issas
= Djibouti ■ . . . . . . 133 12 0N 43 0 E
Fresnillo 175 23 10N 102 53W
Fresno 173 36 47N 119 50W
Fria, C. . . . . . . 136 18 0S 12 0 E
Frías 190 28 40S 65 5W
Fribourg . . . . . . 44 46 49N 7 9 E
Friendly, Is. = Tonga ■ 123 19 50S 174 30W
Friesland □ . . . . . . 41 53 5N 5 50 E
Frio, C. 182 22 50S 41 50W
Friuli-Venezia Giulia □ . . . . . . 47 46 0N 13 0 E
Frobisher B. 146 62 30N 66 0W
Frobisher Bay 146 63 44N 68 31W
Frobisher L. 152 56 20N 108 15W
Frome 27 51 16N 2 17W
Frome, L. . . . . . . 118 30 45S 139 45 E
Frome Downs . . . . . . 118 31 13S 139 45 E
Front Range 163 40 0N 105 40W
Front Royal 164 38 55N 78 10W
Frontera 177 18 32N 92 38W
Frostburg 164 39 43N 78 57W
Frunze . . . . . . 71 42 54N 74 46 E
Frutal 188 20 0S 49 0W
Fuchou = Fuzhou . . . . . . 99 26 5N 119 16 E
Fuchū, Hiroshima, Japan . . . . . . 109 34 34N 133 14 E
Fuchū, Tōkyō, Japan . . . . . . 107 35 40N 139 29 E
Fuerte, R. → 174 25 54N 109 22W
Fuji . . . . . . 107 35 9N 138 39 E
Fuji-no-miya . . . . . . 107 35 10N 138 40 E
Fuji-San . . . . . . 107 35 22N 138 44 E
Fuji-yoshida . . . . . . 107 35 30N 138 46 E
Fujian □ . . . . . . 99 26 0N 118 0 E
Fujieda . . . . . . 107 34 52N 138 16 E
Fujisawa . . . . . . 107 35 22N 139 29 E
Fukaya . . . . . . 107 36 12N 139 12 E
Fukien = Fujian □ . . . . . . 99 26 0N 118 0 E
Fukuchiyama . . . . . . 106 35 19N 135 9 E
Fukue-Shima . . . . . . 104 32 40N 128 45 E
Fukui . . . . . . 106 36 0N 136 10 E
Fukuoka . . . . . . 108 33 39N 130 21 E
Fukushima . . . . . . 103 37 44N 140 28 E
Fukuyama . . . . . . 109 34 35N 133 20 E
Fulton, Mo., U.S.A. 166 38 50N 91 55W
Fulton, N.Y., U.S.A. 164 43 20N 76 22W
Funabashi . . . . . . 107 35 45N 140 0 E
Funchal 126 32 38N 16 54W
Fundación 184 10 31N 74 11W
Fundy, B. of 148 45 0N 66 0W
Furāt, Nahr al → . . . . . . 84 31 0N 47 25 E
Furneaux Group . . . . . . 119 40 10S 147 50 E
Furness 28 54 14N 3 8W
Fürth . . . . . . 43 49 29N 11 0 E
Fury and Hecla Str. 146 69 56N 84 0W
Fushun . . . . . . 98 41 50N 123 55 E
Fuxin . . . . . . 98 42 5N 121 48 E
Fuzhou . . . . . . 99 26 5N 119 16 E
Fylde 28 53 50N 2 58W
Fyn . . . . . . 61 55 20N 10 30 E
Fyne, L. 30 56 0N 5 20W

Gabès, Golfe de . . . . . . 127 34 0N 10 30 E
Gabon ■ . . . . . . 134 0 10S 10 0 E
Gaborone . . . . . . 137 24 45S 25 57 E
Gachsārān . . . . . . 85 30 15N 50 45 E
Gadag . . . . . . 90 15 30N 75 45 E
Gadsden 169 34 1N 86 0W
Gaeta . . . . . . 49 41 12N 13 35 E

Gaffney	**165**	35 3N	81 40W
Gagnon	**141**	51 50N	68 5W
Gainesville, Fla., U.S.A.	**170**	29 38N	82 20W
Gainesville, Ga., U.S.A.	**165**	34 17N	83 47W
Gainesville, Tex., U.S.A.	**168**	33 40N	97 10W
Gainsborough	**29**	53 23N	0 46W
Gairdner L.	**118**	31 30S	136 0 E
Galápagos	**10**	0 0	89 0W
Galas —▸	**96**	4 55N	101 57 E
Galashiels	**31**	55 37N	2 50W
Galaţi	**57**	45 27N	28 2 E
Galatina	**49**	40 10N	18 10 E
Galdhøpiggen	**60**	61 38N	8 18 E
Galesburg	**166**	40 57N	90 23W
Galicia □	**50**	42 43N	7 45W
Galilee, L.	**121**	22 20S	145 50 E
Gallatin	**169**	36 24N	86 27W
Galle	**90**	6 5N	80 10 E
Gallinas, Pta.	**184**	12 28N	71 40W
Gallipoli = Gelibolu	**80**	40 28N	26 43 E
Gallípoli	**49**	40 8N	18 0 E
Gällivare	**66**	67 9N	20 40 E
Galloway	**31**	55 0N	4 25W
Galloway, Mull of	**30**	54 38N	4 50W
Gallup	**161**	35 30N	108 45W
Galty Mts.	**35**	52 22N	8 10W
Galveston	**168**	29 15N	94 48W
Galveston B.	**168**	29 30N	94 50W
Galway	**35**	53 16N	9 4W
Galway □	**34**	53 16N	9 3W
Gamagóri	**106**	34 50N	137 14 E
Gambia ■	**130**	13 25N	16 0W
Gambia —▸	**130**	13 28N	16 0W
Gand = Gent	**42**	51 2N	3 42 E
Gander	**149**	48 58N	54 35W
Gandhi Sagar	**91**	24 40N	75 40 E
Gandi	**131**	12 55N	5 49 E
Ganga —▸	**92**	23 20N	90 30 E
Ganges = Ganga —▸	**92**	23 20N	90 30 E
Gangtok	**92**	27 20N	88 37 E
Gannett Pk.	**163**	43 15N	109 38W
Gansu □	**98**	36 0N	104 0 E
Ganzhou	**99**	25 51N	114 56 E
Gao	**130**	16 15N	0 5W
Gaoxiong	**99**	22 38N	120 18 E
Garachiné	**179**	8 0N	78 12W
Garanhuns	**189**	8 50S	36 30W
Garberville	**172**	40 11N	123 50W
Garda, L. di	**46**	45 40N	10 40 E
Garden City	**161**	38 0N	100 45W
Garden Grove	**173**	33 47N	117 55W
Gardēz	**87**	33 37N	69 9 E
Garmsār	**86**	35 20N	52 25 E
Garonne —▸	**36**	45 2N	0 36W
Garoua	**131**	9 19N	13 21 E
Garrison Res. = Sakakawea, L.	**163**	47 30N	102 0W
Garry L.	**145**	65 58N	100 18W
Garvie Mts.	**123**	45 30S	168 50 E
Garwa = Garoua	**131**	9 19N	13 21 E
Gary	**167**	41 35N	87 20W
Garzón	**184**	2 10N	75 40W
Gascogne	**36**	43 45N	0 20 E
Gascony = Gascogne	**36**	43 45N	0 20 E
Gaspé	**148**	48 52N	64 30W
Gaspé, C. de	**148**	48 48N	64 7W
Gaspé, Pén. de	**148**	48 45N	65 40W
Gastonia	**165**	35 17N	81 10W
Gastre	**192**	42 20S	69 15W
Gata, C. de	**51**	36 41N	2 13W
Gateshead	**28**	54 57N	1 37W
Gauhati	**93**	26 10N	91 45 E
Gävle	**60**	60 40N	17 9 E
Gävleborgs län □	**60**	61 30N	16 15 E
Gawilgarh Hills	**91**	21 15N	76 45 E
Gawler	**119**	34 30S	138 42 E
Gawler Ranges	**114**	32 30S	135 45 E
Gaxun Nur	**100**	42 22N	100 30 E
Gaya	**92**	24 47N	85 4 E
Gaylord	**150**	45 1N	84 41W
Gayndah	**116**	25 35S	151 32 E
Gaza	**80**	31 30N	34 28 E
Gaziantep	**80**	37 6N	37 23 E
Gdańsk	**58**	54 22N	18 40 E
Gdańska, Zatoka	**58**	54 30N	19 20 E
Gdynia	**58**	54 35N	18 33 E
Gedaref	**129**	14 2N	35 28 E
Geelong	**117**	38 10S	144 22 E
Gejiu	**99**	23 20N	103 10 E
Gelderland □	**41**	52 5N	6 10 E
Geldermalsen	**40**	51 53N	5 17 E
Geldrop	**41**	51 25N	5 32 E
Geleen	**41**	50 57N	5 49 E
Gelibolu	**80**	40 28N	26 43 E
Gelsenkirchen	**42**	51 30N	7 5 E
Gemert	**41**	51 33N	5 41 E
General Alvear	**190**	35 0S	67 40W
General Pico	**190**	35 45S	63 50W
Geneva = Genève	**44**	46 12N	6 9 E
Geneva	**164**	42 53N	77 0W
Geneva, L. = Léman, Lac	**44**	46 26N	6 30 E
Genève	**44**	46 12N	6 9 E
Genk	**41**	50 58N	5 32 E
Genkai-Nada	**108**	34 0N	130 0 E
Gennargentu, Mti. del	**48**	40 0N	9 10 E
Genoa = Génova	**46**	44 24N	8 56 E
Génova	**46**	44 24N	8 56 E
Génova, Golfo di	**46**	44 0N	9 0 E
Gent	**42**	51 2N	3 42 E
George, L.	**132**	0 5N	30 10 E
George River = Port Nouveau-Québec	**146**	58 30N	65 59W
George Town	**96**	5 25N	100 15 E
Georgetown, Australia	**119**	18 17S	143 33 E
Georgetown, Canada	**151**	43 40N	79 56W
Georgetown, Guyana	**185**	6 50N	58 12W
Georgetown, U.S.A.	**170**	33 22N	79 15W
Georgia □	**170**	32 0N	82 0W
Georgian B.	**151**	45 15N	81 0W
Georgian S.S.R. □	**70**	42 0N	43 0 E
Gera	**43**	50 53N	12 11 E
Geraldton, Australia	**120**	28 48S	114 32 E
Geraldton, Canada	**150**	49 44N	86 59W
Gereshk	**87**	31 47N	64 35 E
Germany, ■	**18**	52 0N	12 0 E
Germiston	**137**	26 15S	28 10 E
Gerona	**51**	41 58N	2 46 E
Ghana ■	**130**	6 0N	1 0W
Ghat	**127**	24 59N	10 11 E
Ghawdex = Gozo	**49**	36 0N	14 13 E
Ghaziabad	**89**	28 42N	77 26 E
Ghazipur	**92**	25 38N	83 35 E
Ghaznī	**87**	33 30N	68 28 E
Ghaznī □	**87**	32 10N	68 20 E
Ghent = Gent	**42**	51 2N	3 42 E
Ghowr □	**87**	34 0N	64 20 E
Ghulam Mohammad Barrage	**88**	25 30N	68 20 E
Giant's Causeway	**34**	55 15N	6 30W
Gibara	**178**	21 9N	76 11W
Gibraltar	**50**	36 7N	5 22W
Gibraltar, Str. of	**50**	35 55N	5 40W
Gien	**39**	47 40N	2 36 E
Gifu	**106**	35 30N	136 45 E
Gigha	**30**	55 42N	5 45W
Gijón	**50**	43 32N	5 42W
Gila —▸	**173**	32 43N	114 33W
Gīlān □	**81**	37 0N	50 0 E
Gilbert Is. = Kiribati ■	**122**	1 0N	176 0 E
Gilford I.	**154**	50 40N	126 30W
Gilgandra	**116**	31 43S	148 39 E
Gilgit	**89**	35 50N	74 15 E
Gillingham	**25**	51 23N	0 34 E
Gingin	**120**	31 22S	115 54 E
Gippsland	**117**	37 45S	147 15 E
Girardot	**184**	4 18N	74 48W
Giresun	**81**	40 55N	38 30 E
Gironde —▸	**36**	45 32N	1 7W
Girvan	**30**	55 15N	4 50W
Gisborne	**122**	38 39S	178 5 E
Gisors	**39**	49 15N	1 47 E
Gizhiga	**73**	62 3N	160 30 E

Gizhiginskaya, Guba .... **73** 61 0N 158 0 E
Giżycko .... **58** 54 2N 21 48 E
Gjoa Haven **145** 68 20N 96 8W
Glace Bay **149** 46 11N 59 58W
Gladstone, Queens., Australia **121** 23 52S 151 16 E
Gladstone, S. Austral.,
  Australia .... **118** 33 15S 138 22 E
Gláma **64** 65 48N 23 0W
Glasgow, U.K. **31** 55 52N 4 14W
Glasgow, U.S.A. **169** 37 2N 85 55W
Glastonbury **27** 51 9N 2 42W
Gleiwitz = Gliwice .... **58** 50 22N 18 41 E
Glen Coe **32** 56 40N 5 0W
Glen Innes .... **116** 29 44S 151 44 E
Glen Mor .... **33** 57 12N 4 37 E
Glenburgh .... **120** 25 26S 116 6 E
Glendale **173** 34 7N 118 18W
Glendive **163** 47 7N 104 40W
Glenelg .... **119** 34 58S 138 31 E
Glenns Ferry **172** 43 0N 115 15W
Glenorchy .... **119** 42 49S 147 18 E
Glenrothes **31** 56 12N 3 11W
Glens Falls **164** 43 20N 73 40W
Gliwice .... **58** 50 22N 18 41 E
Głogów .... **58** 51 37N 16 5 E
Glossop **28** 53 27N 1 56W
Gloucester **24** 51 52N 2 15W
Gloucestershire □ **24** 51 44N 2 10W
Gloversville **164** 43 5N 74 18W
Gniezno .... **58** 52 30N 17 35 E
Go Cong .... **95** 10 22N 106 40 E
Goa .... **91** 15 33N 73 59 E
Goa □ .... **90** 15 33N 73 59 E
Goat Fell **30** 55 37N 5 11W
Goba .... **133** 7 1N 39 59 E
Gobi .... **98** 44 0N 111 0 E
Gobō .... **106** 33 53N 135 10 E
Godavari → .... **91** 16 25N 82 18 E
Godbout **148** 49 20N 67 38W
Goderich **150** 43 45N 81 41W
Godhra .... **91** 22 49N 73 40 E
Gods L. **153** 54 40N 94 15W
Godthåb **147** 64 10N 51 35W
Goeie Hoop, Kaap die ..... **136** 34 24S 18 30 E
Goeree .... **40** 51 50N 4 0 E
Goes .... **40** 51 30N 3 55 E
Gogama **151** 47 35N 81 43W
Goiânia **188** 16 43S 49 20W
Goiás □ **188** 12 10S 48 0W
Goirle .... **40** 51 31N 5 4 E
Gojō .... **106** 34 21N 135 42 E
Gökçeada .... **55** 40 10N 25 50 E
Gold Coast, Australia ..... **116** 28 0S 153 25 E
Gold Coast, W. Afr. **124** 4 0N 1 40W
Golden Bay .... **122** 40 40S 172 50 E
Golden Gate **172** 37 54N 122 30W
Golden Hinde **154** 49 40N 125 44W
Golden Vale **35** 52 33N 8 17W
Goldfield **172** 37 45N 117 13W
Goldsboro **165** 35 24N 77 59W
Goldsworthy .... **114** 20 21S 119 30 E
Golfo Aranci .... **48** 41 0N 9 35 E
Gomel .... **68** 52 28N 31 0 E
Gómez Palacio **174** 25 34N 103 30W
Gonābād .... **86** 34 15N 58 45 E
Gonaïves **180** 19 20N 72 42W
Gonda .... **92** 27 9N 81 58 E
Gonder .... **132** 12 39N 37 30 E
Good Hope, C. of = Goeie
  Hoop, Kaap die .... **136** 34 24S 18 30 E
Goole **29** 53 42N 0 52W
Goondiwindi .... **116** 28 30S 150 21 E
Goose Bay **147** 53 15N 60 20W
Gorakhpur .... **92** 26 47N 83 23 E
Gordonvale .... **121** 17 5S 145 50 E
Gore, Ethiopia .... **132** 8 12N 35 32 E
Gore, N.Z. .... **123** 46 5S 168 58 E
Gorey **35** 52 41N 6 18W
Gorinchem .... **40** 51 50N 4 59 E
Gorki = Gorkiy .... **68** 56 20N 44 0 E

Gorkiy .... **68** 56 20N 44 0 E
Görlitz .... **43** 51 10N 14 59 E
Gorna Oryakhovitsa .... **53** 43 7N 25 40 E
Gort **35** 53 4N 8 50W
Gorzów Wielkopolski ...... **58** 52 43N 15 15 E
Gosford .... **117** 33 23S 151 18 E
Gospić .... **52** 44 35N 15 23 E
Gosport **25** 50 48N 1 8W
Göteborg .... **60** 57 43N 11 59 E
Göteborgs och Bohus län □ . **60** 58 30N 11 30 E
Gotemba .... **107** 35 18N 138 56 E
Gotha .... **43** 50 56N 10 42 E
Gotland .... **60** 57 30N 18 33 E
Gōtsu .... **109** 35 0N 132 14 E
Gottwaldov .... **59** 49 14N 17 40 E
Gouda .... **40** 52 1N 4 42 E
Gouin, Rés. **151** 48 35N 74 40W
Goulburn .... **117** 34 44S 149 44 E
Goundam **130** 16 25N 3 45W
Gournay-en-Bray .... **38** 49 29N 1 44 E
Governador Valadares **188** 18 15S 41 57W
Governor's Harbour **178** 25 10N 76 14W
Gower, The **27** 51 35N 4 10W
Goya **190** 29 10S 59 10W
Gozo .... **49** 36 0N 14 13 E
Graaff-Reinet .... **136** 32 13S 24 32 E
Gracias a Dios, C. **179** 15 0N 83 10W
Grafton .... **116** 29 38S 152 58 E
Graham **165** 36 5N 79 22W
Graham I. **154** 53 40N 132 30W
Graham Land **14** 65 0S 64 0W
Grahamstown .... **137** 33 19S 26 31 E
Grain Coast **124** 4 20N 10 0W
Grampian □ **33** 57 0N 3 0W
Grampian Mts. **33** 56 50N 4 0W
Grampians, The .... **119** 37 0S 142 20 E
Gran Chaco **190** 25 0S 61 0W
Gran Sasso d'Italia ...... **47** 42 25N 13 30 E
Granada, Nic. **179** 11 58N 86 0W
Granada, Spain **50** 37 10N 3 35W
Granby **151** 45 25N 72 45W
Grand Bah **149** 47 6N 55 48W
Grand Bassam **130** 5 10N 3 49W
Grand Canyon **160** 36 3N 112 9W
Grand Cayman **178** 19 20N 81 20W
Grand Cess **130** 4 40N 8 12W
Grand Falls **149** 48 56N 55 40W
Grand Forks, Canada **155** 49 0N 118 30W
Grand Forks, U.S.A. **156** 48 0N 97 3W
Grand Island **163** 40 59N 98 25W
Grand Junction **163** 39 0N 108 30W
Grand Mère **151** 46 36N 72 40W
Grand Portage **150** 47 58N 89 41W
Grand Rapids, Canada **153** 53 12N 99 19W
Grand Rapids, U.S.A. **167** 42 57N 86 40W
Grand St.-Bernard, Col. du .. **44** 45 53N 7 11 E
Grand Teton **163** 43 54N 111 50W
Grand View **153** 51 10N 100 42W
Grande →, Bolivia **187** 15 51S 64 39W
Grande →, Brazil **188** 20 6S 51 4W
Grande, B. **192** 50 30S 68 20W
Grande, La **171** 45 15N 118 0W
Grande, La → **140** 53 50N 79 0W
Grande Baleine, R. de la → . **140** 55 16N 77 47W
Grande de Santiago, R. → . **175** 21 36N 105 26W
Grande Prairie **155** 55 10N 118 50W
Grande-Rivière **148** 48 26N 64 30W
Grange, La **170** 33 4N 85 0W
Grangemouth **31** 56 1N 3 43W
Grangeville **162** 45 57N 116 4W
Granite City **166** 38 45N 90 3W
Grant, Mt. **172** 38 34N 118 48W
Grantham **29** 52 55N 0 39W
Grantown-on-Spey **33** 57 19N 3 36W
Grants Pass **171** 42 30N 123 22W
Grass Valley **172** 39 18N 121 0W
Grasse .... **37** 43 38N 6 56 E
Gravelbourg **152** 49 50N 106 35W
Gravelines .... **38** 51 0N 2 10 E
's-Gravenhage .... **40** 52 7N 4 17 E

Gravesend	**25**	51 25N	0	22 E
Grayling	**167**	44 40N	84	42W
Graz	**45**	47 4N	15	27 E
Great Abaco I.	**178**	26 25N	77	10W
Great Australian Bight	**114**	33 30S	130	0 E
Great Bahama Bank	**178**	23 15N	78	0W
Great Barrier I.	**122**	36 11S	175	25 E
Great Barrier Reef	**121**	18 0S	146	50 E
Great Basin	**172**	40 0N	116	30W
Great Bear L.	**145**	65 30N	120	0W
Great Britain	**16**	54 0N	2	15W
Great Divide, The	**117**	35 0S	149	17 E
Great Dividing Ra.	**121**	23 0S	146	0 E
Great Exuma I.	**178**	23 30N	75	50W
Great Falls	**163**	47 27N	111	12W
Great Inagua I.	**180**	21 0N	73	20W
Great Indian Desert = Thar Desert.	**89**	28 0N	72	0 E
Great Orme's Head	**26**	53 20N	3	52W
Great Ouse ⟶	**29**	52 47N	0	22 E
Great Plains	**138**	47 0N	105	0W
Great Salt Lake	**162**	41 0N	112	30W
Great Salt Lake Desert	**162**	40 20N	113	50W
Great Slave L.	**145**	61 23N	115	38W
Great Wall	**98**	38 30N	109	30 E
Great Whernside	**28**	54 9N	1	59W
Great Yarmouth	**29**	52 40N	1	45 E
Greater Antilles	**181**	17 40N	74	0W
Greater Manchester □	**28**	53 30N	2	15W
Greater Sunda Is.	**111**	2 30S	110	0 E
Gredos, Sierra de	**50**	40 20N	5	0W
Greece ■	**54**	40 0N	23	0 E
Greeley	**163**	40 30N	104	40W
Green ⟶, Ky., U.S.A.	**167**	37 54N	87	30W
Green ⟶, Utah, U.S.A.	**163**	38 11N	109	53W
Green Bay	**167**	44 30N	88	0W
Greenfield	**164**	42 38N	72	38W
Greenland □	**147**	66 0N	45	0W
Greenland Sea	**13**	73 0N	10	0W
Greenock	**30**	55 57N	4	46W
Greensboro	**165**	36 7N	79	46W
Greenville, Ala., U.S.A.	**169**	31 50N	86	37W
Greenville, Mich., U.S.A.	**167**	43 12N	85	14W
Greenville, Miss., U.S.A.	**168**	33 25N	91	0W
Greenville, N.C., U.S.A.	**165**	35 37N	77	26W
Greenville, S.C., U.S.A.	**165**	34 54N	82	24W
Greenville, Tenn., U.S.A.	**165**	36 13N	82	51W
Greenwood, Miss., U.S.A.	**169**	33 30N	90	4W
Greenwood, S.C., U.S.A.	**165**	34 13N	82	13W
Grenada	**169**	33 45N	89	50W
Grenada ■	**180**	12 10N	61	40W
Grenoble	**37**	45 12N	5	42 E
Grenville	**117**	37 46S	143	52 E
Gretna Green	**31**	55 0N	3	3W
Grey Range	**116**	27 0S	143	30 E
Grey Res.	**149**	48 20N	56	30W
Greymouth	**123**	42 29S	171	13 E
Griffin	**170**	33 17N	84	14W
Griffith	**117**	34 18S	146	2 E
Grimsby	**29**	53 35N	0	5W
Grimshaw	**155**	56 10N	117	40W
Grinnell	**166**	41 45N	92	43W
Grodno	**68**	53 42N	23	52 E
Groningen	**41**	53 15N	6	35 E
Groningen □	**41**	53 16N	6	40 E
Grootfontein	**136**	19 31S	18	6 E
Groznyy	**70**	43 20N	45	45 E
Grudziądz	**58**	53 30N	18	47 E
Grytviken	**14**	53 50S	37	10W
Gt. Stour = Stour ⟶	**25**	51 15N	1	20 E
Guadalajara, Mexico	**175**	20 40N	103	20W
Guadalajara, Spain	**50**	40 37N	3	12W
Guadalquivir ⟶	**50**	36 47N	6	22W
Guadalupe = Guadeloupe ■	**180**	16 20N	61	40W
Guadalupe Bravos	**174**	31 23N	106	7W
Guadarrama, Sierra de	**50**	41 0N	4	0W
Guadeloupe ■	**180**	16 20N	61	40W
Guadiana ⟶	**50**	37 14N	7	22W
Guadix	**50**	37 18N	3	11W
Guaíra	**191**	24 5S	54	10W

Guajará-Mirim	**187**	10 50S	65	20W
Gualeguay	**190**	33 10S	59	14W
Gualeguaychú	**190**	33 3S	59	31W
Guam	**10**	13 27N	144	45 E
Guanabacoa	**178**	23 8N	82	18W
Guanacaste, Cordillera del	**179**	10 40N	85	4W
Guanahani = San Salvador	**178**	24 0N	74	40W
Guanajay	**178**	22 56N	82	42W
Guanajuato	**177**	21 1N	101	15W
Guanajuato □	**177**	21 0N	101	0W
Guanare	**184**	8 42N	69	12W
Guangdong □	**99**	23 0N	113	0 E
Guangxi Zhuangzu Zizhiqu □	**99**	24 0N	109	0 E
Guangzhou	**99**	23 5N	113	10 E
Guantánamo	**178**	20 10N	75	14W
Guaporé ⟶	**187**	11 55S	65	4W
Guaqui	**187**	16 41S	68	54W
Guarapuava	**191**	25 20S	51	30W
Guarda	**50**	40 32N	7	20W
Guardafui, C. = Asir, Ras	**133**	11 55N	51	10 E
Guatemala	**177**	14 40N	90	22W
Guatemala ■	**177**	15 40N	90	30W
Guaviare ⟶	**184**	4 3N	67	44W
Guayama	**180**	17 59N	66	7W
Guayaquil	**184**	2 15S	79	52W
Guayaquil, G. de	**186**	3 10S	81	0W
Guaymas	**174**	27 56N	110	54W
Guddu Barrage	**89**	28 30N	69	50 E
Gudur	**90**	14 12N	79	55 E
Guelph	**151**	43 35N	80	20W
Guernica	**50**	43 19N	2	40W
Guernsey	**36**	49 30N	2	35W
Guerrero □	**177**	17 40N	100	0W
Guilin	**99**	25 18N	110	15 E
Guimarães	**188**	2 9S	44	42W
Guinea ■	**130**	10 20N	10	0W
Guinea, Gulf of	**130**	3 0N	2	30 E
Guinea-Bissau ■	**130**	12 0N	15	0W
Güines	**178**	22 50N	82	0W
Guiyang	**99**	26 32N	106	40 E
Guizhou □	**99**	27 0N	107	0 E
Gujarat □	**91**	23 20N	71	0 E
Gujranwala	**89**	32 10N	74	12 E
Gujrat	**89**	32 40N	74	2 E
Gulbarga	**91**	17 20N	76	50 E
Gulf, The	**85**	27 0N	50	0 E
Gulfport	**169**	30 21N	89	3W
Gulgong	**116**	32 20S	149	49 E
Gull Lake	**152**	50 10N	108	29W
Gümüsane	**81**	40 30N	39	30 E
Guna	**91**	24 40N	77	19 E
Gundagai	**117**	35 3S	148	6 E
Gunnedah	**116**	30 59S	150	15 E
Gunningbar Cr. ⟶	**116**	31 14S	147	6 E
Guntakal	**90**	15 11N	77	27 E
Guntersville	**169**	34 18N	86	16W
Guntur	**92**	16 23N	80	30 E
Gurdaspur	**89**	32 5N	75	31 E
Gurgaon	**89**	28 27N	77	1 E
Gurkha	**92**	28 5N	84	40 E
Gurupi ⟶	**188**	1 13S	46	6W
Guryev	**70**	47 5N	52	0 E
Gusau	**131**	12 12N	6	40 E
Guthrie	**168**	35 55N	97	30W
Guyana ■	**185**	5 0N	59	0W
Guyenne	**36**	44 30N	0	40 E
Guyra	**116**	30 15S	151	40 E
Gwalior	**91**	'26 12N	78	10 E
Gwent □	**27**	51 45N	2	55W
Gweru	**137**	19 28S	29	45 E
Gwynedd □	**26**	53 0N	4	0W
Gyaring Hu	**101**	34 50N	97	40 E
Gydanskiy P-ov.	**69**	70 0N	78	0 E
Gympie	**116**	26 11S	152	38 E
Gyoda	**107**	36 10N	139	30 E
Gyöngyös	**59**	47 48N	20	0 E
Györ	**59**	47 41N	17	40 E
Gypsumville	**153**	51 45N	98	40W

Ha 'Arava	**80**	30	50N	35	20 E
Ha Giang	**95**	22	50N	104	59 E
Haarlem	**40**	52	23N	4	39 E
Habana, La	**178**	23	8N	82	22W
Hachijō-Jima	**105**	33	5N	139	45 E
Hachinohe	**103**	40	30N	141	29 E
Hachiōji	**107**	35	40N	139	20 E
Hadera	**80**	32	27N	34	55 E
Hadhramaut = Haḍramawt	**83**	15	30N	49	30 E
Hadiya	**82**	25	30N	36	56 E
Haḍramawt	**83**	15	30N	49	30 E
Hadrians Wall	**28**	55	0N	2	30W
Haeju	**98**	38	3N	125	45 E
Haerhpin = Harbin	**98**	45	48N	126	40 E
Hafar al Bāṭin	**82**	28	25N	46	0 E
Hafnarfjörður	**64**	64	4N	21	57W
Haft-Gel	**84**	31	30N	49	32 E
Hagen	**42**	51	21N	7	29 E
Hagerstown	**164**	39	39N	77	46W
Hagi	**108**	34	30N	131	22 E
Hags Hd.	**35**	52	57N	9	30W
Hague, The = 's-Gravenhage	**40**	52	7N	4	17 E
Hai'an	**99**	32	37N	120	27 E
Haifa = Ḥefa	**80**	32	46N	35	0 E
Haikou	**99**	20	1N	110	16 E
Ḥā'il	**82**	27	28N	41	45 E
Hailar	**98**	49	10N	119	38 E
Hailey	**162**	43	30N	114	15W
Haileybury	**151**	47	30N	79	38W
Hainan	**99**	19	0N	110	0 E
Hainan Dao	**99**	19	0N	109	30 E
Haiphong	**95**	20	47N	106	41 E
Haiti ■	**180**	19	0N	72	30W
Hakken-Zan	**106**	34	10N	135	54 E
Hakodate	**103**	41	45N	140	44 E
Ḥalab	**80**	36	10N	37	15 E
Halaib	**129**	22	12N	36	30 E
Halberstadt	**43**	51	53N	11	2 E
Halfmoon Bay	**123**	46	50S	168	5 E
Halifax, Canada	**148**	44	38N	63	35W
Halifax, U.K.	**28**	53	43N	1	51W
Halifax B.	**121**	18	50S	147	0 E
Hallands län □	**61**	56	50N	12	50 E
Halle	**43**	51	29N	12	0 E
Halls Creek	**114**	18	16S	127	38 E
Halmahera	**113**	0	40N	128	0 E
Halmstad	**61**	56	41N	12	52 E
Hälsingborg = Helsingborg	**61**	56	3N	12	42 E
Hamada	**109**	34	56N	132	4 E
Hamadān	**81**	34	52N	48	32 E
Hamadān □	**81**	35	0N	49	0 E
Hamāh	**80**	35	5N	36	40 E
Hamakita	**107**	34	45N	137	47 E
Hamamatsu	**106**	34	45N	137	45 E
Hamar	**60**	60	48N	11	7 E
Hamburg	**43**	53	32N	9	59 E
Hämeenlinna	**67**	61	0N	24	28 E
Hamelin Pool	**120**	26	22S	114	20 E
Hameln	**42**	52	7N	9	24 E
Hamhung	**98**	39	54N	127	30 E
Hamilton, Australia	**119**	37	45S	142	2 E
Hamilton, Bermuda	**180**	32	15N	64	45W
Hamilton, Canada	**151**	43	15N	79	50W
Hamilton, N.Z.	**122**	37	47S	175	19 E
Hamilton, U.K.	**31**	55	47N	4	2W
Hamilton, U.S.A.	**167**	39	20N	84	35W
Hamm	**42**	51	40N	7	49 E
Hammerfest	**67**	70	39N	23	41 E
Hammond, Ind., U.S.A.	**167**	41	40N	87	30W
Hammond, La., U.S.A.	**169**	30	32N	90	30W
Hampshire □	**25**	51	3N	1	20W
Hampshire Downs	**25**	51	10N	1	10W
Hampton	**165**	37	4N	76	18W
Hanamaki	**103**	39	23N	141	7 E
Hancock	**150**	47	10N	88	40W
Handa	**106**	34	53N	137	0 E
Handan	**98**	36	35N	114	28 E
Haney	**154**	49	12N	122	40W
Hanford	**173**	36	23N	119	39W
Hangayn Nuruu	**100**	47	30N	100	0 E
Hangchou = Hangzhou	**99**	30	18N	120	11 E

Hangö	**67**	59	50N	22	57 E
Hangu	**98**	39	18N	117	53 E
Hangzhou	**99**	30	18N	120	11 E
Hanna	**155**	51	40N	111	54W
Hannibal	**166**	39	42N	91	22W
Hannover	**42**	52	23N	9	43 E
Hanoi	**95**	21	5N	105	55 E
Hanover = Hannover	**42**	52	23N	9	43 E
Hanover, N.H., U.S.A.	**148**	43	43N	72	17W
Hanover, Pa., U.S.A.	**164**	39	46N	76	59W
Hansi	**89**	29	10N	75	57 E
Hanyū	**107**	36	10N	139	32 E
Hanzhong	**99**	33	10N	107	1 E
Haora	**92**	22	37N	88	20 E
Haparanda	**67**	65	52N	24	8 E
Haraḍ, Si. Arabia	**83**	24	22N	49	0 E
Ḥaraḍ, Yemen	**83**	16	26N	43	5 E
Harare	**137**	17	43S	31	2 E
Harbin	**98**	45	48N	126	40 E
Harbour Breton	**149**	47	29N	55	50W
Harbour Grace	**149**	47	40N	53	22W
Hardap Dam	**136**	24	32S	17	50 E
Hardenberg	**41**	52	34N	6	37 E
Harderwijk	**41**	52	21N	5	38 E
Hardinxveld	**40**	51	49N	4	53 E
Hardwar = Haridwar	**89**	29	58N	78	9 E
Harer	**133**	9	20N	42	8 E
Harfleur	**38**	49	30N	0	10 E
Hargeisa	**133**	9	30N	44	2 E
Hari →	**111**	1	16S	104	5 E
Haridwar	**89**	29	58N	78	9 E
Harima-Nada	**109**	34	30N	134	35 E
Harīrūd →	**86**	34	20N	62	30 E
Harlech	**26**	52	52N	4	7W
Harlingen, Neth.	**41**	53	11N	5	25 E
Harlingen, U.S.A.	**161**	26	20N	97	50W
Harlow	**25**	51	47N	0	9 E
Harney Basin	**171**	43	30N	119	0W
Härnösand	**66**	62	38N	18	0 E
Harriman	**169**	36	0N	84	35W
Harris	**32**	57	50N	6	55W
Harris L.	**118**	31	10S	135	10 E
Harrisburg, Ill., U.S.A.	**167**	37	42N	88	30W
Harrisburg, Pa., U.S.A.	**164**	40	18N	76	52W
Harrison	**168**	36	10N	93	4W
Harrison, C.	**147**	54	55N	57	55W
Harrison B.	**142**	70	25N	151	30W
Harrisonburg	**165**	38	28N	78	52W
Harrogate	**28**	53	59N	1	32W
Harrow	**25**	51	35N	0	15W
Hartford	**164**	41	47N	72	41W
Hartland Pt.	**27**	51	2N	4	32W
Hartlepool	**29**	54	42N	1	11W
Hartsville	**165**	34	23N	80	2W
Harvey, Australia	**120**	33	5S	115	54 E
Harvey, U.S.A.	**167**	41	40N	87	40W
Harwich	**25**	51	56N	1	18 E
Haryana □	**89**	29	0N	76	10 E
Hashima	**106**	35	20N	136	40 E
Hashimoto	**106**	34	19N	135	37 E
Hastings, N.Z.	**122**	39	39S	176	52 E
Hastings, U.K.	**25**	50	51N	0	36 E
Hastings, U.S.A.	**163**	40	34N	98	22W
Hastings Ra.	**116**	31	15S	152	14 E
Hatano	**107**	35	22N	139	14 E
Hathras	**89**	27	36N	78	6 E
Hatteras, C.	**165**	35	10N	75	30W
Hattiesburg	**169**	31	20N	89	20W
Hatvan	**59**	47	40N	19	45 E
Hau Bon = Cheo Reo	**95**	13	25N	108	28 E
Hauraki Gulf	**122**	36	35S	175	5 E
Haut Atlas	**126**	32	30N	5	0W
Havana = Habana, La	**178**	23	8N	82	22W
Havant	**25**	50	51N	0	59W
Havelock	**151**	44	26N	77	53W
Haverfordwest	**26**	51	48N	4	59W
Haverhill	**164**	42	50N	71	2W
Havre	**163**	48	34N	109	40W
Havre, Le	**38**	49	30N	0	5 E
Hawaii □	**160**	20	30N	157	0W
Hawaiian Is.	**160**	20	30N	156	0W

Hawea Lake	**123**	44 28S	169	19 E
Hawera	**122**	39 35S	174	19 E
Hawick	**31**	55 25N	2	48W
Hawke B.	**122**	39 25S	177	20 E
Hawke's Bay □	**122**	39 45S	176	35 E
Hawkesbury	**151**	45 37N	74	37W
Hawthorne	**172**	38 31N	118	37W
Hay, Australia	**117**	34 30S	144	51 E
Hay, U.K.	**26**	52 4N	3	9W
Hay River	**145**	60 51N	115	44W
Hayward's Heath	**25**	51 0N	0	5W
Hazard	**165**	37 18N	83	10W
Hazaribag	**92**	23 58N	85	26 E
Hazebrouck	**38**	50 42N	2	31 E
Hazelton	**154**	55 20N	127	42W
Hazleton	**164**	40 58N	76	0W
Healdsburg	**172**	38 33N	122	51W
Healesville	**117**	37 35S	145	30 E
Heanor	**29**	53 1N	1	20W
Hearst	**150**	49 40N	83	41W
Hebei □	**98**	39 0N	116	0 E
Hebel	**116**	28 58S	147	47 E
Hebrides	**16**	57 30N	7	0W
Hebron = Al Khalīl	**80**	31 32N	35	6 E
Hebron	**147**	58 5N	62	30W
Hecate Str.	**154**	53 10N	130	30W
Hechuan	**99**	30 2N	106	12 E
Hedmark fylke □	**60**	61 17N	11	40 E
Heemstede	**40**	52 22N	4	37 E
Heerenveen	**41**	52 57N	5	55 E
Heerlen	**41**	50 55N	6	0 E
Hefa	**80**	32 46N	35	0 E
Hefei	**99**	31 52N	117	18 E
Hegang	**98**	47 20N	130	19 E
Heidelberg	**42**	49 23N	8	41 E
Heilbronn	**42**	49 8N	9	13 E
Heilongjiang □	**98**	48 0N	126	0 E
Heilunkiang = Heilongjiang □	**98**	48 0N	126	0 E
Heinze Is.	**94**	14 25N	97	45 E
Hekimhan	**81**	38 50N	38	0 E
Hekinan	**106**	34 52N	137	0 E
Hekla	**16**	63 56N	19	35W
Helena, Ark., U.S.A.	**169**	34 30N	90	35W
Helena, Mont., U.S.A.	**163**	46 40N	112	0W
Helensburgh	**30**	56 0N	4	44W
Helmand →	**87**	31 12N	61	34 E
Helmond	**41**	51 29N	5	41 E
Helmsdale	**33**	58 7N	3	40W
Helsingborg	**61**	56 3N	12	42 E
Helsinki	**67**	60 15N	25	3 E
Helston	**27**	50 7N	5	17W
Helvellyn	**28**	54 31N	3	1W
Hemel Hempstead	**25**	51 45N	0	28W
Hempstead	**164**	30 5N	96	5W
Henan □	**99**	34 0N	114	0 E
Henderson	**165**	36 20N	78	25W
Hendersonville	**165**	35 21N	82	28W
Hengelo	**41**	52 16N	6	48 E
Hengyang	**99**	26 51N	112	30 E
Hénin-Beaumont	**38**	50 25N	2	58 E
Hennebont	**36**	47 49N	3	19W
Henrietta Maria C.	**140**	55 9N	82	20W
Henty	**117**	35 30S	147	0 E
Henzada	**93**	17 38N	95	26 E
Herät	**87**	34 20N	62	7 E
Herät □	**87**	35 0N	62	0 E
Herbert →	**121**	18 31S	146	17 E
Herbiers, Les	**36**	46 52N	1	0W
Hercegnovi	**52**	42 30N	18	33 E
Hercegovina = Bosna i Hercegovina □	**52**	44 0N	18	0 E
Hereford	**24**	52 4N	2	42W
Hereford and Worcester □	**24**	52 10N	2	30W
Herford	**42**	52 7N	8	40 E
Hermosillo	**174**	29 4N	110	58W
Heroica = Caborca	**174**	30 40N	112	10W
Heroica Nogales = Nogales	**174**	31 20N	110	56W
Heron Bay	**150**	48 40N	86	25W
Herrin	**166**	37 50N	89	0W
Hertford □	**25**	51 51N	0	5W
's-Hertogenbosch	**40**	51 42N	5	17 E
Hesse = Hessen □	**42**	50 40N	9	20 E
Hessen □	**42**	50 40N	9	20 E
Hewett, C.	**146**	70 16N	67	45W
Hexham	**28**	54 58N	2	7W
Heysham	**28**	54 5N	2	53W
Heywood	**119**	38 8S	141	37 E
Hi-no-Misaki	**109**	35 26N	132	38 E
Hialeach	**170**	25 49N	80	17W
Hibiki-Nada	**108**	34 0N	130	0 E
Hickory	**165**	35 46N	81	17W
Hida-Gawa →	**106**	35 26N	137	3 E
Hida-Sammyaku	**106**	36 30N	137	40 E
Hida-Sanchi	**106**	36 10N	137	0 E
Hidaka	**109**	35 30N	134	44 E
Hidalgo □	**177**	20 30N	99	0W
Hidalgo del Parral	**174**	26 56N	105	40W
Higashi-matsuyama	**107**	36 2N	139	25 E
Higashiōsaka	**106**	34 40N	135	37 E
Higasi-Suidō	**108**	34 0N	129	30 E
High Atlas = Haut Atlas	**126**	32 30N	5	0W
High Point	**165**	35 57N	79	58W
High Prairie	**155**	55 30N	116	30W
Highland □	**32**	57 30N	5	0W
Highland Park	**167**	42 10N	87	50W
Hijārah, Şahrā' al	**84**	30 25N	44	30 E
Hikari	**108**	33 58N	131	58 E
Hikone	**106**	35 15N	136	10 E
Hildesheim	**43**	52 9N	9	55 E
Hillegom	**40**	52 18N	4	35 E
Hillsboro	**171**	45 31N	123	0W
Hillston	**117**	33 30S	145	31 E
Hilo	**160**	19 44N	155	5W
Hilversum	**40**	52 14N	5	10 E
Himachal Pradesh □	**89**	31 30N	77	0 E
Himalaya, Mts.	**101**	29 0N	84	0 E
Hime-Jima	**108**	33 43N	131	40 E
Himeji	**109**	34 50N	134	40 E
Himi	**106**	36 50N	137	0 E
Himş	**80**	34 40N	36	45 E
Hinchinbrook I.	**121**	18 20S	146	15 E
Hinckley	**25**	52 33N	1	21W
Hindmarsh	**119**	34 54S	138	34 E
Hindu Kush	**89**	36 0N	71	0 E
Hindupur	**90**	13 49N	77	32 E
Hines Creek	**155**	56 20N	118	40W
Hingoli	**91**	19 41N	77	15 E
Hinton	**185**	37 40N	80	51W
Hirado	**108**	33 22N	129	33 E
Hirakarta	**106**	34 48N	135	40 E
Hirakud Dam	**92**	21 32N	83	45 E
Hirata	**109**	35 24N	132	49 E
Hiratsuka	**107**	35 19N	139	21 E
Hirosaki	**103**	40 34N	140	28 E
Hiroshima	**109**	34 24N	132	30 E
Hirson	**38**	49 55N	4	4 E
Hispaniola	**180**	19 0N	71	0W
Hita	**108**	33 20N	130	58 E
Hitachi	**107**	36 36N	140	39 E
Hitachiota	**107**	36 30N	140	30 E
Hitchin	**25**	51 57N	0	16W
Hitoyoshi	**108**	32 13N	130	45 E
Hitra	**65**	63 30N	8	45 E
Hiuchi-Nada	**109**	34 5N	133	20 E
Ho Chi Minh City = Thanh Pho Ho Chi Minh	**95**	10 58N	106	40 E
Hoa Binh	**95**	20 50N	105	20 E
Hobart	**119**	42 50S	147	21 E
Hobbs	**161**	32 40N	103	3W
Hodaka-Dake	**106**	36 17N	137	39 E
Hódmezóvásárhely	**59**	46 28N	20	22 E
Hoek van Holland	**40**	52 0N	4	7 E
Hofsjökull	**64**	64 49N	18	48W
Hōfu	**108**	34 3N	131	34 E
Hogan Group	**117**	39 13S	147	1 E
Hoh Xil Shan	**101**	35 0N	89	0 E
Hohhot	**98**	40 52N	111	40 E
Hōjō	**109**	33 58N	132	46 E
Hokitika	**123**	42 42S	171	0 E
Hokkaidō □	**103**	43 30N	143	0 E
Holbrook	**117**	35 42S	147	18 E
Holderness	**29**	53 45N	0	5W

Holdrege **163** 40 26N 99 22W
Holguín **178** 20 50N 76 20W
Holland **167** 42 47N 86 7W
Holly Springs **169** 34 45N 89 25W
Hollywood, Calif., U.S.A. **173** 34 7N 118 25W
Hollywood, Fla., U.S.A. **170** 26 0N 80 9W
Holsteinsborg **147** 66 40N 53 30W
Holsworthy **27** 50 48N 4 21W
Holt **64** 63 33N 19 48W
Holy I., Scotland, U.K. **31** 55 31N 5 4W
Holy I., Wales, U.K. **26** 53 17N 4 37W
Holyhead **26** 53 18N 4 38W
Holyoke **164** 42 14N 72 37W
Hombori **130** 15 20N 1 38W
Home Hill **121** 19 43S 147 25 E
Homer **142** 59 40N 151 35W
Homs = Ḥimş **80** 34 40N 36 45 E
Honan = Henan □ **99** 34 0N 114 0 E
Hondo **108** 32 27N 130 12 E
Honduras ■ **179** 14 40N 86 30W
Honduras, Golfo de **177** 16 50N 87 0W
Hong Kong ■ **99** 22 11N 114 14 E
Hongha → **95** 22 0N 104 0 E
Hongshui He → **99** 23 48N 109 30 E
Honiton **27** 50 48N 3 11W
Honolulu **160** 21 19N 157 52W
Honshū **106** 36 0N 138 0 E
Hoogeveen **41** 52 44N 6 30 E
Hook Hd. **35** 52 8N 6 57W
Hook of Holland = Hoek van Holland **40** 52 0N 4 7 E
Hoorn **40** 52 38N 5 4 E
Hope, Canada **154** 49 25N 121 25 E
Hope, U.S.A. **168** 33 40N 93 36W
Hope Town **178** 26 35N 76 57W
Hopedale **147** 55 28N 60 13W
Hopei = Hebei □ **98** 39 0N 116 0 E
Hopelchén **177** 19 46N 89 51W
Hopetoun, Vic., Australia **119** 35 42S 142 22 E
Hopetoun, W. Austral., Australia **120** 33 57S 120 7 E
Hopkinsville **169** 36 52N 87 26W
Hoquiam **171** 46 50N 123 55W
Hordaland fylke □ **60** 60 25N 6 15 E
Hormoz **85** 27 35N 55 0 E
Hormuz Str. **85** 26 30N 56 30 E
Horn, Cape = Hornos, Cabo de **192** 55 50S 67 30W
Hornavan **66** 66 15N 17 30 E
Hornell **164** 42 23N 77 41W
Hornos, Cabo de **192** 55 50S 67 30W
Hornsby **117** 33 42S 151 2 E
Hornsea **29** 53 55N 0 10W
Horqin Youyi Qianqi **98** 46 5N 122 3 E
Horsens **61** 55 52N 9 51 E
Horsham **119** 36 44S 142 13 E
Horton → **145** 69 56N 126 52W
Hoshiarpur **89** 31 30N 75 58 E
Hospet **90** 15 15N 76 20 E
Hospitalet de Llobregat **51** 41 21N 2 6 E
Hoste, I. **192** 55 0S 69 0W
Hot Springs **168** 34 30N 93 0W
Houghton **150** 47 9N 88 39W
Houghton-le-Spring **28** 54 51N 1 28W
Houhora **122** 34 49S 173 9 E
Houlton **148** 46 5N 67 50W
Houma **169** 29 35N 90 44W
Houston, Canada **154** 54 25N 126 39W
Houston, U.S.A. **168** 29 50N 95 20W
Houtman Abrolhos **120** 28 43S 113 48 E
Hovd **100** 48 2N 91 37 E
Hove **25** 50 50N 0 10W
Howe, C. **117** 37 30S 150 0 E
Howrah = Haora **92** 22 37N 88 20 E
Hoy I. **33** 58 50N 3 15W
Hrádec Králové **58** 50 15N 15 50 E
Hrvatska □ **52** 45 20N 18 0 E
Hsiamen = Xiamen **99** 24 25N 118 4 E
Hsian = Xi'an **99** 34 15N 109 0 E
Hsinhailien = Lianyungang **99** 34 40N 119 11 E
Hsüchou = Xuzhou **99** 34 18N 117 10 E
Hua Hin **94** 12 34N 99 58 E
Huacho **186** 11 10S 77 35W
Huainan **99** 32 38N 116 58 E
Huallaga → **186** 5 0S 75 30W
Huambo **134** 12 42S 15 54 E
Huancane **187** 15 10S 69 44W
Huancavelica **186** 12 50S 75 5W
Huancayo **186** 12 5S 75 12W
Huanchaca **187** 20 15S 66 40W
Huang Hai = Yellow Sea **99** 35 0N 123 0 E
Huang Ho → **98** 37 30N 118 50 E
Huangshi **99** 30 10N 115 3 E
Huánuco **186** 9 55S 76 15W
Huaraz **186** 9 30S 77 32W
Huascarán **186** 9 8S 77 36W
Huasco **190** 28 30S 71 15W
Huatabampo **174** 26 50N 109 38W
Huautla **177** 17 51N 100 5W
Hubei □ **99** 31 0N 112 0 E
Hubli-Dharwad = Dharwad **90** 15 22N 75 15 E
Huddersfield **28** 53 38N 1 49W
Hudiksvall **66** 61 43N 17 10 E
Hudson **164** 42 15N 73 46W
Hudson → **164** 40 42N 74 2W
Hudson Bay **146** 52 51N 102 23W
Hudson Str. **146** 62 0N 70 0W
Hudson's Hope **155** 56 0N 121 54W
Hue **95** 16 30N 107 35 E
Huehuetenango **177** 15 20N 91 28W
Huelva **50** 37 18N 6 57W
Huesca **51** 42 8N 0 25W
Hughenden **121** 20 52S 144 10 E
Huila, Nevado del **184** 3 0N 76 0W
Huinca Renancó **190** 34 51S 64 22W
Huixtla **177** 15 9N 92 28W
Huizen **40** 52 18N 5 14 E
Hukawng Valley **93** 26 30N 96 30 E
Hull, Canada **151** 45 25N 75 44W
Hull, U.K. **29** 53 45N 0 20W
Hulst **40** 51 17N 4 2 E
Hulun Nur **98** 49 0N 117 30 E
Humaitá **187** 27 2S 58 31W
Humber → **29** 53 40N 0 10W
Humberside □ **29** 53 50N 0 30W
Humboldt, Canada **152** 52 15N 105 9W
Humboldt, U.S.A. **169** 35 50N 88 55W
Humboldt → **172** 40 2N 118 31W
Hume, L. **117** 36 0S 147 0 E
Húnaflói **64** 65 50N 20 50W
Hunan □ **99** 27 30N 111 30 E
Hunedoara **56** 45 40N 22 50 E
Hungary ■ **59** 47 20N 19 20 E
Hungary, Plain of **17** 47 0N 20 0 E
Hungnam **98** 39 49N 127 45 E
Hunsrück **42** 49 30N 7 0 E
Hunstanton **29** 52 57N 0 30 E
Hunter Ra. **117** 32 45S 150 15 E
Huntingdon **25** 52 20N 0 11W
Huntington, Ind., U.S.A. **167** 40 52N 85 30W
Huntington, W. Va., U.S.A. **165** 38 20N 82 30W
Huntington Beach **173** 33 40N 118 0W
Huntly **122** 37 34S 175 11 E
Huntsville, Canada **151** 45 20N 79 14W
Huntsville, Ala., U.S.A. **169** 34 45N 86 35W
Huntsville, Tex., U.S.A. **168** 30 45N 95 35W
Huonville **119** 43 0S 147 5 E
Hupeh □ = Hubei □ **99** 31 0N 112 0 E
Huron, L. **150** 45 0N 83 0W
Hurricane **173** 37 10N 113 12W
Húsavík **64** 66 3N 17 21W
Hutchinson **161** 38 3N 97 59W
Hvar **52** 43 11N 16 28 E
Hwang Ho = Huang Ho → **98** 37 30N 118 50 E
Hwange **137** 18 18S 26 30 E
Hyden **120** 32 24S 118 53 E
Hyderabad, India **91** 17 22N 78 29 E
Hyderabad, Pakistan **88** 25 23N 68 24 E
Hyères **37** 43 8N 6 9 E
Hyndman Pk. **162** 43 50N 114 10W
Hythe **24** 51 4N 1 5 E
Hyūga **108** 32 25N 131 35 E

Iaşi	**57**	47 10N	27 40 E
Ibadan	**131**	7 22N	3 58 E
Ibagué	**184**	4 20N	75 20W
Ibara	**109**	34 36N	133 28 E
Ibaraki	**106**	34 49N	135 34 E
Ibarra	**184**	0 21N	78 7W
Iberian Peninsula	**16**	40 0N	5 0W
Ibiza	**51**	38 54N	1 26 E
Ibuki-Sanchi	**106**	35 25N	136 18 E
Ibusuki	**108**	31 12N	130 40 E
Icá	**186**	14 0S	75 48W
Iça →	**184**	2 55S	67 58W
Iceland ■	**64**	65 0N	19 0W
Icha	**73**	55 30N	156 0 E
Ich'ang = Yichang	**99**	30 40N	111 20 E
Ichchapuram	**92**	19 10N	84 40 E
Ichihara	**107**	35 28N	140 5 E
Ichikawa	**107**	35 44N	139 55 E
Ichinomiya	**106**	35 18N	136 48 E
Ichinoseki	**103**	38 55N	141 8 E
Idaho □	**162**	44 10N	114 0W
Idaho Falls	**163**	43 30N	112 1W
Ídhi Óros	**55**	35 15N	24 45 E
Ídhra	**55**	37 20N	23 28 E
Ierápetra	**55**	35 0N	25 44 E
Ife	**131**	7 30N	4 31 E
Igloolik	**146**	69 20N	81 49W
Iguaçu →	**191**	25 36S	54 36W
Iguaçu, Cat. del	**191**	25 41S	54 26W
Iguaçu Falls = Iguaçu, Cat. del	**191**	25 41S	54 26W
Iguala de la Independencia	**177**	18 21N	99 32W
Iguassu = Iguaçu →	**191**	25 36S	54 36W
Iida	**107**	35 35N	137 50 E
Iisalmi	**67**	63 32N	27 10 E
Iizuka	**108**	33 38N	130 42 E
IJmuiden	**40**	52 28N	4 35 E
IJsselmeer	**40**	52 45N	5 20 E
IJsselstein	**40**	52 1N	5 2 E
Ikaría	**55**	37 35N	26 10 E
Ikeda	**109**	34 1N	133 48 E
Iki	**108**	33 45N	129 42 E
Iki-Kaikyō	**108**	33 40N	129 45 E
Île-de-France	**37**	49 0N	2 20 E
Ilebo	**134**	4 17S	20 55 E
Ilfracombe	**27**	51 13N	4 8W
Ilhéus	**189**	14 49S	39 2W
Ili →	**71**	45 53N	77 10 E
Iliamna L.	**142**	59 35N	155 30W
Iliodhrómia	**55**	39 12N	23 50 E
Ilkeston	**29**	52 59N	1 19W
Illampu = Ancohuma, Nevada	**187**	16 0S	68 50W
Illinois □	**166**	40 15N	89 30W
Illinois →	**166**	38 55N	90 28W
Ilo	**187**	17 40S	71 20W
Iloilo	**112**	10 45N	122 33 E
Ilorin	**131**	8 30N	4 35 E
Imabari	**109**	34 4N	133 0 E
Imari	**108**	33 15N	129 52 E
Imatra	**67**	61 12N	28 48 E
Immingham	**29**	53 37N	0 12W
Imperial	**152**	51 21N	105 28W
Imphal	**92**	24 48N	93 56 E
Imroz = Gökçeada	**55**	40 10N	25 50 E
Ina	**107**	35 50N	138 0 E
Iñapari	**187**	11 0S	69 40W
Inari	**67**	68 54N	27 5 E
Inarijärvi	**67**	69 0N	28 0 E
Inazawa	**106**	35 15N	136 47 E
Inchon	**98**	37 27N	126 40 E
Indalsälven →	**66**	62 36N	17 30 E
Independence, Kans., U.S.A.	**166**	37 10N	95 43W
Independence, Mo., U.S.A.	**166**	39 3N	94 25W
India ■	**78**	20 0N	78 0 E
Indian Head	**152**	50 30N	103 41W
Indiana	**164**	40 38N	79 9W
Indiana □	**167**	40 0N	86 0W
Indianapolis	**167**	39 42N	86 10W
Indigirka →	**73**	70 48N	148 54 E
Indonesia ■	**111**	5 0S	115 0 E
Indore	**91**	22 42N	75 53 E
Indre →	**36**	47 16N	0 19 E
Indus →	**88**	24 20N	67 47 E
Indus, Mouth of the	**88**	24 0N	68 0 E
İnebolu	**80**	41 55N	33 40 E
İnegöl	**80**	40 5N	29 31 E
Ingersoll	**151**	43 4N	80 55W
Ingham	**121**	18 43S	146 10 E
Ingleborough	**28**	54 11N	2 23W
Inglewood, N.Z.	**122**	39 9S	174 14 E
Inglewood, U.S.A.	**173**	33 58N	118 21W
Ingolstadt	**43**	48 45N	11 26 E
Ingraj Bazar	**92**	24 58N	88 10 E
Inhambane	**137**	23 54S	35 30 E
Ining = Yining	**100**	43 58N	81 10 E
Inishmore	**35**	53 8N	9 45W
Inishowen	**34**	55 14N	7 15W
Inn →	**43**	48 35N	13 28 E
Innamincka	**118**	27 44S	140 46 E
Inner Hebrides	**32**	57 0N	6 30W
Inner Mongolia = Nei Monggol Zizhiqu □	**98**	42 0N	112 0 E
Innisfail, Australia	**121**	17 33S	146 5 E
Innisfail, Canada	**155**	52 0N	113 57W
In'no-shima	**109**	34 19N	133 10 E
Innsbruck	**45**	47 16N	11 23 E
Inoucdjouac	**146**	58 25N	78 15W
Inowrocław	**58**	52 50N	18 12 E
Inquisivi	**187**	16 50S	67 10W
Insein	**93**	16 50N	96 5 E
Interlaken	**44**	46 41N	7 50 E
Inuvik	**144**	68 16N	133 40W
Inuvik □	**144**	70 0N	130 0W
Inuyama	**106**	35 23N	136 56 E
Inveraray	**30**	56 13N	5 5W
Invercargill	**123**	46 24S	168 24 E
Inverell	**116**	29 45S	151 8 E
Invergordon	**33**	57 41N	4 10W
Inverness	**33**	57 29N	4 12W
Investigator Group	**119**	34 45S	134 20 E
Investigator Str.	**119**	35 30S	137 0 E
Ioánnina	**54**	39 42N	20 47 E
Iola	**166**	38 0N	95 20W
Iona	**30**	56 20N	6 25W
Ionian Is. = Iónioi Nísoi	**54**	38 40N	20 0 E
Ionian Sea	**54**	37 30N	17 30 E
Iónioi Nísoi	**54**	38 40N	20 0 E
Íos	**55**	36 41N	25 20 E
Iowa □	**166**	42 18N	93 30W
Iowa City	**166**	41 40N	91 35W
Iowa Falls	**166**	42 30N	93 15W
Ipiales	**184**	0 50N	77 37W
Ipin = Yibin	**99**	28 45N	104 32 E
Ípiros □	**54**	39 30N	20 30 E
Ipoh	**96**	4 35N	101 5 E
Ipswich, Australia	**116**	27 35S	152 40 E
Ipswich, U.K.	**25**	52 4N	1 9 E
Iquique	**187**	20 19S	70 5W
Iquitos	**186**	3 45S	73 10W
Iracoubo	**185**	5 30N	53 10W
Iráklion	**55**	35 20N	25 12 E
Iran ■	**86**	33 0N	53 0 E
Iran Ra.	**111**	2 20N	114 50 E
Irapuato	**177**	20 41N	101 28W
Iraq ■	**81**	33 0N	44 0 E
Irbid	**80**	32 35N	35 48 E
Ireland ■	**34**	53 0N	8 0W
Irian Jaya □	**113**	4 0S	137 0 E
Iriri →	**188**	3 52S	52 37W
Irish Republic ■	**20**	53 0N	8 0W
Irish Sea	**20**	54 0N	5 0W
Irkutsk	**74**	52 18N	104 20 E
Irō-Zaki	**107**	34 36N	138 51 E
Iron Gate = Portile de Fier	**56**	44 42N	22 30 E
Iron Knob	**118**	32 46S	137 8 E
Iron Mountain	**150**	45 49N	88 4W
Ironbridge	**24**	52 38N	2 29W
Ironton	**167**	38 35N	82 40W
Ironwood	**150**	46 30N	90 10W

Iroquois Falls	**151**	48 46N	80 41W
Irrawaddy →	**93**	15 50N	95 6 E
Irtysh →	**69**	61 4N	68 52 E
Irumu	**135**	1 32N	29 53 E
Irún	**51**	43 20N	1 52W
Irvine	**31**	55 37N	4 40W
Irvinestown	**34**	54 28N	7 38W
Ísafjörður	**64**	66 5N	23 9W
Isahaya	**108**	32 52N	130 2 E
Íschia	**49**	40 45N	13 51 E
Ise	**106**	34 25N	136 45 E
Ise-Wan	**106**	34 43N	136 43 E
Isère →	**37**	44 59N	4 51 E
Isesaki	**107**	36 19N	139 12 E
Ishikari-Wan	**103**	43 25N	141 1 E
Ishinomaki	**103**	38 32N	141 20 E
Ishioka	**107**	36 11N	140 16 E
Ishkuman	**89**	36 30N	73 50 E
Ishpeming	**150**	46 30N	87 40W
Iskenderun	**80**	36 32N	36 10 E
Islamabad	**89**	33 40N	73 10 E
Island L.	**153**	53 47N	94 25W
Island Pond	**148**	48 25N	56 23W
Islay	**30**	55 46N	6 10W
Isle-Adam, L'	**39**	49 6N	2 14 E
Isle Royale	**150**	48 0N	88 50W
Isparta	**80**	37 47N	30 30 E
Israel ■	**80**	32 0N	34 50 E
Issoire	**37**	45 32N	3 15 E
Issyk-Kul, Ozero	**71**	42 25N	77 15 E
Istanbul	**80**	41 0N	29 0 E
Istra	**52**	45 10N	14 0 E
Istria = Istra	**52**	45 10N	14 0 E
Itabuna	**189**	14 48S	39 16W
Itaituba	**185**	4 10S	55 50W
Itajaí	**191**	27 50S	48 39W
Italy ■	**19**	42 0N	13 0 E
Itaquatiara	**185**	2 58S	58 30W
Itaquí	**191**	29 8S	56 30W
Itchen →	**24**	50 57N	1 20W
Ithaca = Itháki	**54**	38 25N	20 40 E
Ithaca	**164**	42 25N	76 30W
Itháki	**54**	38 25N	20 40 E
Ito	**107**	34 58N	139 5 E
Ituaçu	**189**	13 50S	41 18W
Ituiutaba	**188**	19 0S	49 25W
Iturup, Ostrov	**75**	45 0N	148 0 E
Ivano-Frankovsk	**68**	48 40N	24 40 E
Ivanovo, Byelorussian S.S.R., U.S.S.R.	**68**	52 7N	25 29 E
Ivanovo, R.S.F.S.R., U.S.S.R.	**68**	57 5N	41 0 E
Ivigtut	**147**	61 14N	48 12W
Iviza = Ibiza	**51**	38 54N	1 26 E
Ivory Coast ■	**130**	7 30N	5 0W
Iwai-Jima	**108**	33 47N	131 58 E
Iwaki	**105**	37 3N	140 55 E
Iwakuni	**109**	34 15N	132 8 E
Iwami	**109**	35 32N	134 15 E
Iwamizawa	**103**	43 12N	141 46 E
Iwanuma	**103**	38 7N	140 51 E
Iwata	**107**	34 42N	137 51 E
Iwo	**131**	7 39N	4 9 E
Ixiamas	**187**	13 50S	68 5W
Ixtepec	**177**	16 34N	95 6W
Ixtlán	**175**	20 11N	102 24W
Ixtlán de Juárez	**177**	17 23N	96 28W
Iyo	**109**	33 45N	132 45 E
Iyo-mishima	**109**	33 58N	133 30 E
Iyo-Nada	**109**	33 40N	132 20 E
Izamal	**177**	20 56N	89 1W
Izhevsk = Ustinov	**69**	56 51N	53 14 E
İzmir	**80**	38 25N	27 8 E
İzmit	**80**	40 45N	29 50 E
Izu-Hantō	**107**	34 45N	139 0 E
Izumi	**108**	32 5N	130 22 E
Izumi-sano	**106**	34 23N	135 18 E
Izumiotsu	**106**	34 30N	135 24 E
Izumo	**109**	35 20N	132 46 E

Jabalpur	**91**	23 9N	79 58 E
Jacarèzinho	**191**	23 5S	50 0W
Jackson, Mich., U.S.A.	**167**	42 18N	84 25W
Jackson, Miss., U.S.A.	**169**	32 20N	90 10W
Jackson, Tenn., U.S.A.	**169**	35 40N	88 50W
Jacksonville, Fla., U.S.A.	**170**	30 15N	81 38W
Jacksonville, Ill., U.S.A.	**166**	39 42N	90 15W
Jacksonville, N.C., U.S.A.	**165**	34 50N	77 29W
Jacksonville, Tex., U.S.A.	**168**	31 58N	95 19W
Jacmel	**180**	18 14N	72 32W
Jacobabad	**88**	28 20N	68 29 E
Jacques Cartier, Dét. de	**149**	50 0N	63 30W
Jadotville = Likasi	**135**	10 55S	26 48 E
Jaén, Peru	**186**	5 25S	78 40W
Jaén, Spain	**50**	37 44N	3 43W
Jaffa = Tel Aviv-Yafo	**80**	32 4N	34 48 E
Jaffna	**90**	9 45N	80 2 E
Jagdalpur	**92**	19 3N	82 0 E
Jaguariaíva	**191**	24 10S	49 50W
Jagüey Grande	**178**	22 35N	81 7W
Jahrom	**85**	28 30N	53 31 E
Jaipur	**91**	27 0N	75 50 E
Jakarta	**111**	6 9S	106 49 E
Jalalabad	**87**	34 30N	70 29 E
Jalapa, Guat.	**177**	14 39N	89 59W
Jalapa, Mexico	**177**	17 43N	92 49W
Jalgaon	**91**	21 0N	75 42 E
Jalisco □	**175**	20 20N	103 40W
Jalna	**91**	19 48N	75 38 E
Jalón →	**51**	41 47N	1 4W
Jalpaiguri	**92**	26 32N	88 46 E
Jamaica ■	**180**	18 10N	77 30W
Jamalpur, Bangla.	**92**	24 52N	89 56 E
Jamalpur, India	**92**	25 18N	86 28 E
Jambi	**111**	1 38S	103 30 E
James →	**163**	42 52N	97 18W
James B.	**140**	51 30N	80 0W
Jamestown, Australia	**118**	33 10S	138 32 E
Jamestown, N. Dak., U.S.A.	**163**	46 54N	98 42W
Jamestown, N.Y., U.S.A.	**164**	42 5N	79 18W
Jamkhandi	**91**	16 30N	75 15 E
Jammu	**89**	32 43N	74 54 E
Jammu & Kashmir □	**89**	34 25N	77 0 E
Jamnagar	**90**	22 30N	70 6 E
Jamshedpur	**92**	22 44N	86 12 E
Jan Mayen Is.	**13**	71 0N	9 0W
Janesville	**166**	42 39N	89 1W
Januária	**188**	15 25S	44 25W
Jaora	**91**	23 40N	75 10 E
Japan ■	**79**	36 0N	136 0 E
Japan, Sea of	**102**	40 0N	135 0 E
Japurá →	**185**	3 8S	64 46W
Jargalant = Hovd	**100**	48 2N	91 37 E
Jargeau	**39**	47 50N	2 1 E
Jarosław	**58**	50 2N	22 42 E
Jāsk	**85**	25 38N	57 45 E
Jasło	**59**	49 45N	21 30 E
Jasper, Canada	**155**	52 55N	118 5W
Jasper, U.S.A.	**169**	33 48N	87 16W
Jassy = Iaşi	**57**	47 10N	27 40 E
Jataí	**188**	17 58S	51 48W
Jaú	**188**	22 10S	48 30W
Jaunpur	**92**	25 46N	82 44 E
Java, I.	**111**	7 0S	110 0 E
Java Sea	**111**	4 35S	107 15 E
Javhlant = Ulyasutay	**100**	47 56N	97 28 E
Jean Marie River	**144**	61 32N	120 38W
Jean Rabel	**180**	19 50N	73 5W
Jedburgh	**31**	55 28N	2 33W
Jędrzejów	**58**	50 35N	20 15 E
Jefferson, Mt.	**171**	44 45N	121 50W
Jefferson City	**166**	38 34N	92 10W
Jeffersonville	**167**	38 20N	85 42W
Jelenia Góra	**58**	50 50N	15 45 E
Jena	**43**	50 56N	11 33 E
Jenkins	**165**	37 13N	82 41W
Jennings	**168**	30 10N	92 45W
Jeparit	**119**	36 8S	142 1 E
Jequié	**189**	13 51S	40 5W
Jequitinhonha	**189**	16 30S	41 0W
Jérémie	**180**	18 40N	74 10W

Name	Map	Lat °	′	N/S	Long °	′	E/W
Jerez de García Salinas	175	22	39	N	103	0	W
Jerez de la Frontera	50	36	41	N	6		7W
Jerez de los Caballeros	50	38	20	N	6	45	W
Jericho	121	23	38	S	146	6	E
Jerilderie	117	35	20	S	145	41	E
Jerome	148	47	37	N	82	14	W
Jersey, I.	36	49	13	N	2		7W
Jersey City	164	40	41	N	74		8W
Jerseyville	166	39	5	N	90	20	W
Jerusalem	80	31	47	N	35	10	E
Jesselton = Kota Kinabalu	112	6	0	N	116	4	E
Jhang Maghiana	89	31	15	N	72	22	E
Jhansi	91	25	30	N	78	36	E
Jharsuguda	92	21	56	N	84	5	E
Jhelum →	89	31	20	N	72	10	E
Jhunjhunu	89	28	10	N	75	30	E
Jiamusi	98	46	40	N	130	26	E
Ji'an	99	27	6	N	114	59	E
Jiangmen	99	22	32	N	113	0	E
Jiangsu □	99	33	0	N	120	0	E
Jiangxi □	99	27	30	N	116	0	E
Jian'ou	99	27	3	N	118	17	E
Jiao Xian	98	36	18	N	120	1	E
Jiaozuo	99	35	16	N	113	12	E
Jiaxing	99	30	49	N	120	45	E
Jiayi	99	23	30	N	120	24	E
Jibuti = Djibouti ■	133	12	0	N	43	0	E
Jiddah	82	21	29	N	39	10	E
Jido	93	29	2	N	94	58	E
Jihlava	59	49	28	N	15	35	E
Jilin	98	43	44	N	126	30	E
Jilong	99	25	8	N	121	42	E
Jima	132	7	40	N	36	47	E
Jiménez	174	27	8	N	104	54	W
Jinan	98	36	38	N	117	1	E
Jingdezhen	99	29	20	N	117	11	E
Jining, Nei Mongol Zizhiqu, China	98	41	5	N	113	0	E
Jining, Shandong, China	99	35	22	N	116	34	E
Jinja	132	0	25	N	33	12	E
Jinnah Barrage	89	32	58	N	71	33	E
Jinotega	179	13	6	N	85	59	W
Jinotepe	179	11	50	N	86	10	W
Jinshi	99	29	40	N	111	50	E
Jinzhou	98	41	5	N	121	3	E
Jipijapa	184	1	0	S	80	40	W
Jiquilpan de Juárez	175	19	59	N	102	43	W
Jisr ash Shughūr	80	35	49	N	36	18	E
Jiujiang	99	29	42	N	115	58	E
Jixi	98	45	20	N	130	50	E
João Pessoa	189	7	10	S	34	52	W
Jodhpur	91	26	23	N	73	8	E
Joensuu	67	62	37	N	29	49	E
Jogjakarta = Yogyakarta	111	7	49	S	110	22	E
Jōhana	106	36	30	N	136	57	E
Johannesburg	137	26	10	S	28	2	E
John o' Groats	33	58	39	N	3		3W
Johnson City, N.Y., U.S.A.	164	42	7	N	75	57	W
Johnson City, Tenn., U.S.A.	165	36	18	N	82	21	W
Johnston	31	51	45	N	5		5W
Johnstown, N.Y., U.S.A.	164	43	1	N	74	20	W
Johnstown, Pa., U.S.A.	164	40	19	N	78	53	W
Johor □	96	2	5	N	103	20	E
Johor Baharu	96	1	28	N	103	46	E
Joigny	39	48	0	N	3	20	E
Joinvile	191	26	15	S	48	55	E
Joliet	167	41	30	N	88	0	W
Joliette	151	46	3	N	73	24	W
Jolo	112	6	0	N	121	0	E
Jonesboro	169	35	50	N	90	45	W
Jönköping	60	57	45	N	14	10	E
Jönköpings län □	61	57	30	N	14	30	E
Jonquière	148	48	27	N	71	14	W
Joplin	168	37	0	N	94	31	W
Jordan ■	80	31	0	N	36	0	E
Jordan →	80	31	48	N	35	32	E
Jorhat	93	26	45	N	94	12	E
José de San Martín	192	44	4	S	70	26	W
Jowzjān □	87	36	10	N	66	0	E
Juan de Fuca Str.	142	48	15	N	124	0	W
Juan Fernández, Arch. de	183	33	50	S	80	0	W
Juàzeiro	189	9	30	S	40	30	W
Juàzeiro do Norte	189	7	10	S	39	18	W
Jubbulpore = Jabalpur	91	23	9	N	79	58	E
Júcar →	51	39	5	N	0	10	W
Juchitán de Zaragoza	177	16	26	N	95	1	W
Jugoslavia = Yugoslavia ■	52	44	0	N	20	0	E
Juiz de Fora	188	21	43	S	43	19	W
Juli	187	16	10	S	69	25	W
Juliaca	187	15	25	S	70	10	W
Julianeháb	147	60	43	N	46	0	W
Jullundur	89	31	20	N	75	40	E
Jumla	92	29	15	N	82	13	E
Jumna = Yamuna →	92	25	30	N	81	53	E
Junagadh	91	21	30	N	70	30	E
Jundiaí	191	24	30	S	47	0	W
Juneau	143	58	20	N	134	20	W
Junee	117	34	53	S	147	35	E
Junggar Pendi	100	44	30	N	86	0	E
Junín	190	34	33	S	60	57	W
Jura, Europe	37	46	35	N	6	5	E
Jura, U.K.	30	56	0	N	5	50	W
Jurado	184	7	7	N	77	46	W
Juruá →	184	2	37	S	65	44	W
Juruena	187	13	0	S	58	10	W
Juruena →	187	7	20	S	58		3W
Juticalpa	179	14	40	N	86	12	W
Jutland = Jylland	61	56	25	N	9	30	E
Juventud, I. de la	178	21	40	N	82	40	W
Jylland	61	56	25	N	9	30	E
Jyväskylä	67	62	14	N	25	50	E
Kaapstad = Cape Town	136	33	55	S	18	22	E
Kabala	130	9	38	N	11	37	W
Kabardino-Balkar-A.S.S.R. □	70	43	30	N	43	30	E
Kabarega Falls	132	2	15	N	31	30	E
Kabīr Kūh	84	33	0	N	47	30	E
Kābul	87	34	28	N	69	11	E
Kābul □	87	34	30	N	69	0	E
Kabwe	135	14	30	S	28	29	E
Kachin □	93	26	0	N	97	30	E
Kadan Kyun	94	12	30	N	98	20	E
Kadina	119	34	0	S	137	43	E
Kaduna	131	10	30	N	7	21	E
Kaédi	126	16	9	N	13	28	W
Kāf	80	31	25	N	37	29	E
Kafirévs, Ákra	55	38	9	N	24	38	E
Kafue →	135	15	30	S	26	0	E
Kaga	106	36	16	N	136	15	E
Kagoshima	108	31	35	N	130	33	E
Kagoshima-Wan	108	31	25	N	130	40	E
Kai, Kepulauan	113	5	55	S	132	45	W
Kaieteur Falls	185	5	1	N	59	10	W
Kaifeng	99	34	49	N	114	30	E
Kaikoura Ra.	123	41	59	S	173	41	E
Kailua	160	19	39	N	156	0	W
Kaimanawa Mts.	122	39	15	S	175	56	E
Kainan	106	34	9	N	135	12	E
Kainji Res.	131	10	1	N	4	40	E
Kaipara Harbour	122	36	25	S	174	14	E
Kaiserslautern	42	49	30	N	7	43	E
Kaitaia	122	35	8	S	173	17	E
Kajaani	67	64	17	N	27	46	E
Kajana = Kajaani	67	64	17	N	27	46	E
Kakabeka Falls	150	48	24	N	89	37	W
Kakamigahara	106	35	28	N	136	48	E
Kakanui Mts.	123	45	10	S	170	30	E
Kakegawa	107	34	45	N	138	1	E
Kakinada	92	16	57	N	82	11	E
Kakogawa	109	34	46	N	134	51	E
Kalabáka	54	39	42	N	21	39	E
Kalahari	136	24	0	S	21	30	E
Kalamata	54	37	3	N	22	10	E
Kalamazoo	167	42	20	N	85	35	W
Kalamazoo →	167	42	40	N	86	12	W
Kalat	88	29	8	N	66	31	E
Kalaupapa	160	21	12	N	156	59	W
Kalemie	135	5	55	S	29	9	E
Kalgan = Zhangjiakou	98	40	48	N	114	55	E
Kalgoorlie-Boulder	120	30	40	S	121	22	E

Name	Page	Lat		Long	
Kálimnos	55	37 0N		27 0 E	
Kalinin	68	56 55N		35 55 E	
Kaliningrad	68	54 42N		20 32 E	
Kalispell	162	48 10N		114 22W	
Kalisz	58	51 45N		18 8 E	
Kalmar	61	56 40N		16 20 E	
Kalmar län □	61	57 25N		16 0 E	
Kalmyk A.S.S.R. □	70	46 5N		46 1 E	
Kalocsa	59	46 32N		19 0 E	
Kaluga	68	54 35N		36 10 E	
Kama ⟶	68	55 45N		52 0 E	
Kamaishi	103	39 16N		141 53 E	
Kamakura	107	35 19N		139 33 E	
Kamaran	82	15 21N		42 35 E	
Kamchatka, P-ov.	73	57 0N		160 0 E	
Kamenka	69	53 10N		44 5 E	
Kamensk Uralskiy	69	56 25N		62 2 E	
Kamenskoye	73	62 45N		165 30 E	
Kameoka	106	35 0N		135 35 E	
Kameyama	106	34 51N		136 27 E	
Kami-koshiki-Jima	108	31 50N		129 52 E	
Kamioka	106	36 25N		137 15 E	
Kamloops	155	50 40N		120 20W	
Kampala	132	0 20N		32 30 E	
Kampar	96	4 18N		101 9 E	
Kampen	41	52 33N		5 53 E	
Kampot	95	10 36N		104 10 E	
Kampuchea = Cambodia ■	95	12 15N		105 0 E	
Kamsack	152	51 34N		101 54W	
Kamui-Misaki	103	43 20N		140 21 E	
Kamyshin	68	50 10N		45 24 E	
Kananga	134	5 55S		22 18 E	
Kanawha ⟶	165	38 50N		82 8W	
Kanazawa	106	36 30N		136 38 E	
Kanchenjunga	92	27 50N		88 10 E	
Kanchipuram	90	12 52N		79 45 E	
Kandahar = Qandahār	87	31 32N		65 30 E	
Kandalaksha	69	67 9N		32 30 E	
Kandi	131	11 7N		2 55 E	
Kandos	117	32 45S		149 58 E	
Kandy	90	7 18N		80 43 E	
Kangar	97	6 27N		100 12 E	
Kangaroo I.	119	35 45S		137 0 E	
Kangean Is.	113	6 55S		115 23 E	
Kangnŭng	98	37 45N		128 54 E	
Kangto	93	27 50N		92 35 E	
Kaniapiskau ⟶	146	56 40N		69 30W	
Kanin, P-ov.	69	68 0N		45 0 E	
Kaniva	119	36 22S		141 18 E	
Kankakee	167	41 6N		87 50W	
Kankakee ⟶	167	41 23N		88 16W	
Kankan	130	10 23N		9 15W	
Kanmuri-Yama	109	34 30N		132 4 E	
Kannapolis	165	35 32N		80 37W	
Kano	131	12 2N		8 30 E	
Kan'onji	109	34 7N		133 39 E	
Kanoya	108	31 25N		130 50 E	
Kanpur	91	26 28N		80 20 E	
Kansas □	161	38 40N		98 0W	
Kansas ⟶	158	39 7N		94 36W	
Kansas City, Kans., U.S.A.	166	39 0N		94 40W	
Kansas City, Mo., U.S.A.	166	39 3N		94 30W	
Kansk	74	56 20N		95 37 E	
Kansu = Gansu □	98	36 0N		104 0 E	
Kantō □	107	36 15N		139 30 E	
Kantō-Sanchi	107	35 59N		138 50 E	
Kanuma	107	36 34N		139 42 E	
Kaohsiung = Gaoxiong	99	22 38N		120 18 E	
Kaolack	130	14 5N		16 8W	
Kāpīsā □	87	35 0N		69 20 E	
Kapoeta	129	4 50N		33 35 E	
Kapuas ⟶	111	0 25S		109 20 E	
Kapunda	119	34 20S		138 56 E	
Kapuskasing	150	49 25N		82 30W	
Kaputar, Mt.	116	30 15S		150 10 E	
Kara Bogaz Gol, Zaliv	70	41 0N		53 30 E	
Kara Kalpak A.S.S.R. □	70	43 0N		60 0 E	
Kara Kum = Karakum, Peski	70	39 30N		60 0 E	
Kara Sea	69	75 0N		70 0 E	
Karabük	80	41 12N		32 37 E	
Karachi	88	24 53N		67 0 E	
Karad	91	17 15N		74 10 E	
Karadeniz Boğazı	80	41 10N		29 10 E	
Karaganda	71	49 50N		73 10 E	
Karaj	86	35 48N		51 0 E	
Karakoram Pass	89	35 33N		77 50 E	
Karakoram Ra.	89	35 30N		77 0 E	
Karakum, Peski	70	39 30N		60 0 E	
Karaman	80	37 14N		33 13 E	
Karamea Bight	123	41 22S		171 40 E	
Karasuk	71	53 44N		78 2 E	
Karatau, Khrebet	71	43 30N		69 30 E	
Karbalā	84	32 36N		44 3 E	
Karelian A.S.S.R. □	68	65 30N		32 30 E	
Karen	94	12 49N		92 53 E	
Kariba Lake	137	16 40S		28 25 E	
Karimata I.	111	1 40S		109 0 E	
Karimnagar	91	18 26N		79 10 E	
Karimunjawa, Kepulauan	111	5 50S		110 30 E	
Kariya	106	34 58N		137 1 E	
Karl-Marx-Stadt	43	50 50N		12 55 E	
Karlskrona	61	56 10N		15 35 E	
Karlsruhe	42	49 3N		8 23 E	
Karlstad	60	59 23N		13 30 E	
Karnal	89	29 42N		77 2 E	
Karnaphuli Res.	93	22 40N		92 20 E	
Karnataka □	90	13 15N		77 0 E	
Kärnten □	45	46 52N		13 30 E	
Kárpathos	55	35 37N		27 10 E	
Kars	81	40 40N		43 5 E	
Karshi	70	38 53N		65 48 E	
Kasai ⟶	134	3 30S		16 10 E	
Kasaoka	109	34 30N		133 30 E	
Kaseda	108	31 25N		130 19 E	
Kāshān	86	34 5N		51 30 E	
Kashi	100	39 30N		76 2 E	
Kashihara	106	34 27N		135 46 E	
Kashima	108	33 7N		130 6 E	
Kashima-Nada	107	36 0N		140 45 E	
Kashiwa	107	35 52N		139 59 E	
Kāshmar	86	35 16N		58 26 E	
Kashmir	78	34 0N		76 0 E	
Kashun Noerh = Gaxun Nur.	100	42 22N		100 30 E	
Kásos	55	35 20N		26 55 E	
Kassala	129	16 0N		36 0 E	
Kassel	42	51 19N		9 32 E	
Kastoría	54	40 30N		21 19 E	
Kasugai	106	35 12N		136 59 E	
Kasukabe	107	35 58N		139 49 E	
Kasumiga-Ura	107	36 0N		140 25 E	
Kasur	89	31 5N		74 25 E	
Katanning	120	33 40S		117 33 E	
Katha	93	24 10N		96 30 E	
Katherîna, Gebel	128	28 30N		33 57 E	
Katherine	114	14 27S		132 20 E	
Kathiawar	91	22 20N		71 0 E	
Katihar	92	25 34N		87 36 E	
Katmandu	92	27 45N		85 20 E	
Katoomba	117	33 41S		150 19 E	
Katowice	58	50 17N		19 5 E	
Katsuta	107	36 25N		140 31 E	
Katsuura	107	35 10N		140 20 E	
Katsuyama	106	36 3N		136 30 E	
Kattegatt	61	57 0N		11 20 E	
Katwijk-aan-Zee	40	52 12N		4 24 E	
Kauai	160	22 0N		159 30W	
Kaukauna	167	44 20N		88 13W	
Kaunas	68	54 54N		23 54 E	
Kawachi-Nagano	106	34 28N		135 31 E	
Kawagoe	107	35 55N		139 29 E	
Kawaguchi	107	35 52N		139 45 E	
Kawanoe	109	34 1N		133 34 E	
Kawarau	122	45 3S		168 45 E	
Kawasaki	107	35 35N		139 42 E	
Kayah □	93	19 15N		97 15 E	
Kayes	130	14 25N		11 30W	
Kayseri	80	38 45N		35 30 E	
Kazachinskoye	74	56 16N		107 36 E	
Kazachye	72	70 52N		135 58 E	
Kazakh S.S.R. □	71	50 0N		70 0 E	
Kazan	68	55 48N		49 3 E	
Kazanlŭk	53	42 38N		25 20 E	

Kāzerūn	**85**	29 38N	51 40 E
Kazo	**107**	36 7N	139 36 E
Kéa	**55**	37 35N	24 22 E
Keaau	**160**	19 37N	155 3W
Kebnekaise	**66**	67 53N	18 33 E
Kecskemét	**59**	46 57N	19 42 E
Kedah □	**96**	5 50N	100 40 E
Kediri	**111**	7 51S	112 1 E
Keeling Is. = Cocos Is.	**111**	12 10S	96 55 E
Keene	**164**	42 57N	72 17W
Keetmanshoop	**136**	26 35S	18 8 E
Keewatin	**153**	49 46N	94 34W
Keewatin □	**145**	63 20N	95 0W
Kefallinía	**54**	38 20N	20 30 E
Keflavík	**64**	64 2N	22 35W
Keighley	**28**	53 52N	1 54W
Keith, Australia	**119**	36 6S	140 20 E
Keith, U.K.	**33**	57 33N	2 58W
Kelang	**96**	3 2N	101 26 E
Kelantan □	**96**	5 10N	102 0 E
Kelantan →	**96**	6 13N	102 14 E
Kellerberrin	**120**	31 36S	117 38 E
Kellogg	**162**	47 30N	116 5W
Kells = Ceanannus Mor	**34**	53 42N	6 53W
Kelowna	**155**	49 50N	119 25W
Kelso, U.K.	**31**	55 36N	2 27W
Kelso, U.S.A.	**171**	46 10N	122 57W
Keluang	**96**	2 3N	103 18 E
Kelvington	**152**	52 10N	103 30W
Kemerovo	**71**	55 20N	86 5 E
Kemi	**67**	65 44N	24 34 E
Kemi →	**67**	67 30N	28 30 E
Kempsey	**116**	31 1S	152 50 E
Kendal	**28**	54 19N	2 44W
Keng Tung	**93**	21 0N	99 30 E
Kenitra	**126**	34 15N	6 40W
Kenmare	**35**	51 52N	9 35W
Kennewick	**171**	46 11N	119 2W
Keno Hill	**144**	63 57N	135 18W
Kenora	**153**	49 47N	94 29W
Kenosha	**167**	42 33N	87 48W
Kent	**164**	41 8N	81 20W
Kent □	**25**	51 12N	0 40 E
Kent Group	**117**	39 30S	147 20 E
Kent Pen.	**145**	68 30N	107 0W
Kentucky □	**167**	37 20N	85 0W
Kentucky →	**167**	38 41N	85 11W
Kenya ■	**133**	1 0N	38 0 E
Kenya, Mt.	**132**	0 10S	37 18 E
Keokuk	**166**	40 25N	91 24W
Kepsut	**80**	39 40N	28 9 E
Kerala □	**90**	11 0N	76 15 E
Kerang	**117**	35 40S	143 55 E
Kerch	**68**	45 20N	36 20 E
Kerki	**70**	37 50N	65 12 E
Kérkira	**54**	39 38N	19 50 E
Kerkrade	**41**	50 53N	6 4 E
Kermadec Is.	**122**	30 0S	178 15W
Kermān	**85**	30 15N	57 1 E
Kermān □	**85**	30 0N	57 0 E
Kermānshāh = Bākhtarān	**84**	34 23N	47 0 E
Kerrobert	**152**	52 0N	109 11W
Kerry □	**35**	52 7N	9 35W
Kerulen →	**98**	48 48N	117 0 E
Kestenga	**68**	66 0N	31 50 E
Keswick	**28**	54 35N	3 9W
Ketchikan	**143**	55 25N	131 40W
Kettering	**156**	39 41N	84 10W
Kewanee	**166**	41 18N	89 55W
Keweenaw B.	**150**	46 56N	88 23W
Key West	**159**	24 33N	82 0W
Keyser	**164**	39 26N	79 0W
Khabarovsk	**75**	48 30N	135 5 E
Khalkhāl	**81**	37 37N	48 32 E
Khalkís	**55**	38 27N	23 42 E
Khalmer Yu	**69**	67 58N	65 1 E
Khambhat	**91**	22 23N	72 33 E
Khambhat, G. of	**91**	20 45N	72 30 E
Khamir	**82**	16 0N	44 0 E
Khānābād	**87**	36 45N	69 5 E
Khānaqīn	**81**	34 23N	45 25 E
Khandwa	**91**	21 49N	76 22 E
Khanewal	**89**	30 20N	71 55 E
Khaniá	**55**	35 30N	24 4 E
Khanka, Ozero	**75**	45 0N	132 24 E
Kharagpur	**92**	22 20N	87 25 E
Kharkov	**68**	49 58N	36 20 E
Khartoum = El Khartûm	**129**	15 31N	32 35 E
Khashm el Girba	**129**	14 59N	35 58 E
Khaskovo	**53**	41 56N	25 30 E
Khatanga	**72**	72 0N	102 20 E
Khatanga →	**72**	72 55N	106 0 E
Khenchela	**127**	35 28N	7 11 E
Kherson	**68**	46 35N	32 35 E
Kheta →	**72**	71 54N	102 6 E
Khíos, I.	**55**	38 20N	26 0 E
Khmer Rep. = Cambodia ■	**95**	12 15N	105 0 E
Khojak P.	**88**	30 55N	66 30 E
Kholm	**87**	36 45N	67 40 E
Khon Kaen	**95**	16 30N	102 47 E
Khoper →	**68**	49 30N	42 20 E
Khorāsān □	**86**	34 0N	58 0 E
Khorat = Nakhon Ratchasima	**95**	14 59N	102 12 E
Khorat, Cao Nguyen	**95**	15 30N	102 50 E
Khorog	**71**	37 30N	71 36 E
Khorramābād	**84**	33 30N	48 25 E
Khorrāmshahr	**84**	30 29N	48 15 E
Khulna	**92**	22 45N	89 34 E
Khulna □	**92**	22 25N	89 35 E
Khushab	**89**	32 20N	72 20 E
Khūzestān □	**84**	31 0N	49 0 E
Khvor	**86**	33 45N	55 0 E
Khvoy	**81**	38 35N	45 0 E
Khyber Pass	**89**	34 10N	71 8 E
Kiama	**117**	34 40S	150 50 E
Kiangsi = Jiangxi □	**99**	27 30N	116 0 E
Kiangsu = Jiangsu □	**99**	33 0N	120 0 E
Kichiga	**73**	59 50N	163 5 E
Kicking Horse Pass	**155**	51 28N	116 16W
Kidderminster	**24**	52 24N	2 13W
Kidnappers, C.	**122**	39 38S	177 5 E
Kiel	**43**	54 16N	10 8 E
Kielce	**58**	50 52N	20 42 E
Kieler Bucht	**42**	54 30N	10 30 E
Kiev = Kiyev	**68**	50 30N	30 28 E
Kigali	**135**	1 59S	30 4 E
Kii-Hantō	**106**	34 0N	135 45 E
Kii-Sanchi	**106**	34 20N	136 0 E
Kii-Suidō	**109**	33 40N	135 0 E
Kikládhes □	**55**	37 0N	25 0 E
Kikuchi	**108**	32 59N	130 47 E
Kilcoy	**116**	26 59S	152 30 E
Kildare □	**35**	53 10N	6 50W
Kilimanjaro	**132**	3 7S	37 20 E
Kilis	**80**	36 50N	37 10 E
Kilkenny	**35**	52 40N	7 17W
Kilkenny □	**35**	52 35N	7 15W
Killala B.	**34**	54 20N	9 12W
Killarney, Canada	**153**	49 10N	99 40W
Killarney, Ireland	**35**	52 2N	9 30W
Killary Harbour	**34**	53 38N	9 52W
Killiecrankie, Pass of	**33**	56 44N	3 46W
Kilmarnock	**31**	55 36N	4 30W
Kilmore	**117**	37 25S	144 53 E
Kilrush	**35**	52 39N	9 30W
Kimba	**118**	33 8S	136 23 E
Kimberley, Australia	**114**	16 20S	127 0 E
Kimberley, Canada	**155**	49 40N	115 59W
Kimberley, S. Africa	**136**	28 43S	24 46 E
Kinabalu	**112**	6 3N	116 14 E
Kincardine	**150**	44 10N	81 40W
Kindersley	**152**	51 30N	109 10W
Kindia	**130**	10 0N	12 52W
King Frederick VI Land = Kong Frederik VI.s Kyst	**147**	63 0N	43 0W
King George Is.	**140**	57 20N	80 30W
King I. = Kadan Kyun	**94**	12 30N	98 20 E
King I., Australia	**119**	39 50S	144 0 E
King I., Canada	**154**	52 10N	127 40W
King Sd.	**114**	16 50S	123 20 E
King William I.	**145**	69 10N	97 25W
Kingaroy	**116**	26 32S	151 51 E

Kingman 173 35 12N 114 2W
King's Lynn 29 52 45N 0 25 E
Kingscote 119 35 40S 137 38 E
Kingsport 165 36 33N 82 36W
Kingston, Canada 151 44 14N 76 30W
Kingston, Jamaica 180 18 0N 76 50W
Kingston, N.Z. 123 45 20S 168 43 E
Kingston, U.S.A. 164 41 55N 74 0W
Kingston South East 119 36 51S 139 55 E
Kingstown 180 13 10N 61 10W
Kingsville 150 42 2N 82 45W
Kingussie 33 57 5N 4 2W
Kinistino 152 52 57N 105 2W
Kinki □ 106 33 30N 136 0 E
Kinnairds Hd. 33 57 40N 2 0W
Kinsale, Old Hd. of 35 51 37N 8 32W
Kinshasa 134 4 20S 15 15 E
Kinston 165 35 18N 77 35W
Kintyre 30 55 30N 5 35W
Kintyre, Mull of 30 55 17N 5 55W
Kinu-Gawa → 107 35 36N 139 57 E
Kiparissía 54 37 15N 21 40 E
Kirensk 74 57 50N 107 55 E
Kirgiz S.S.R. □ 71 42 0N 75 0 E
Kiribati ■ 122 1 0N 176 0 E
Kırıkkale 80 39 51N 33 32 E
Kirin = Jilin 98 43 44N 126 30 E
Kiritimati 123 1 58N 157 27W
Kirkcaldy 31 56 7N 3 10W
Kirkcudbright 31 54 50N 4 3W
Kirkee 91 18 34N 73 56 E
Kirkintilloch 31 55 57N 4 10W
Kirkland Lake 151 48 9N 80 2W
Kirksville 166 40 8N 92 35W
Kirkūk 81 35 30N 44 21 E
Kirkwall 33 58 59N 2 59W
Kirov 69 58 35N 49 40 E
Kirovabad 70 40 45N 46 20 E
Kirovograd 68 48 35N 32 20 E
Kirthar Range 88 27 0N 67 0 E
Kiruna 66 67 52N 20 15 E
Kiryū 107 36 24N 139 20 E
Kisangani 135 0 35N 25 15 E
Kisarazu 107 35 23N 139 55 E
Kiselevsk 71 54 5N 86 39 E
Kishangarh 89 27 50N 70 30 E
Kishinev 68 47 0N 28 50 E
Kishiwada 106 34 28N 135 22 E
Kiskunfelégyháza 59 46 42N 19 53 E
Kiso-Gawa → 106 35 20N 136 45 E
Kisumu 132 0 3S 34 45 E
Kita 130 13 5N 9 25W
Kita-Ura 107 36 0N 140 34 E
Kitakami-Gawa → 103 38 25N 141 19 E
Kitakyūshū 108 33 50N 130 50 E
Kitale 132 1 0N 35 0 E
Kitami 103 43 48N 143 54 E
Kitchener 151 43 27N 80 29W
Kíthira 55 36 9N 23 0 E
Kíthnos 55 37 26N 24 27 E
Kitikmeot □ 145 70 0N 110 0W
Kitimat 154 54 3N 128 38W
Kitsuki 108 33 25N 131 37 E
Kittakittaooloo, L. 118 28 3S 138 14 E
Kitwe 135 12 54S 28 13 E
Kiyev 68 50 30N 30 28 E
Klagenfurt 45 46 38N 14 20 E
Klaipeda 68 55 43N 21 10 E
Klamath → 172 41 40N 124 4W
Klamath Falls 171 42 20N 121 50W
Klamath Mts. 172 41 20N 123 0W
Kleena Kleene 154 52 0N 124 59W
Klondike 144 64 0N 139 26W
Kluane L. 144 61 15N 138 40W
Klyuchevsk, mt. 73 55 50N 160 30 E
Knaresborough 28 54 1N 1 29W
Knockmealdown Mts. 35 52 16N 8 0W
Knossos 55 35 16N 25 10 E
Knoxville, Iowa, U.S.A. 166 41 20N 93 5W
Knoxville, Tenn., U.S.A. 165 35 58N 83 57W
Ko Chang 95 12 0N 102 20 E
Ko Kut 95 11 40N 102 32 E
Koartac 146 60 55N 69 40W
Kobarid 52 46 15N 13 30 E
Kobayashi 108 31 56N 130 59 E
Kobdo = Hovd 100 48 2N 91 37 E
Kōbe 106 34 45N 135 10 E
København 61 55 41N 12 34 E
Koblenz 42 50 21N 7 36 E
Kobroor, Kepulauan 113 6 10S 134 30 E
Kočani 53 41 55N 22 25 E
Kōchi 109 33 30N 133 35 E
Kochiu = Gejiu 99 23 20N 103 10 E
Kodaira 107 35 44N 139 29 E
Kodiak I. 142 57 30N 152 45W
Kōfu 107 35 40N 138 30 E
Koga 107 36 11N 139 43 E
Kogota 103 38 33N 141 3 E
Koh-i-Bābā 87 34 30N 67 0 E
Kohat 89 33 40N 71 29 E
Kokand 71 40 30N 70 57 E
Kokchetav 71 53 20N 69 25 E
Koko Kyunzu 94 14 10N 93 25 E
Kokomo 167 40 30N 86 6W
Kokopo 115 4 22S 152 19 E
Koksoak → 146 58 30N 68 10W
Kokubu 108 31 44N 130 46 E
Kola Pen. = Kolskiy Poluostrov 69 67 30N 38 0 E
Kolar 90 13 12N 78 15 E
Kolar Gold Fields 90 12 58N 78 16 E
Kolarovgrad 53 43 18N 26 55 E
Kolding 61 55 30N 9 29 E
Kolguyev, Ostrov 69 69 20N 48 30 E
Kolhapur 91 16 43N 74 15 E
Köln 42 50 56N 6 58 E
Koło 58 52 14N 18 40 E
Kolomna 68 55 8N 38 45 E
Kolskiy Poluostrov 69 67 30N 38 0 E
Kolyma → 73 69 30N 161 0 E
Komagene 107 35 44N 137 58 E
Komaki 106 35 17N 136 55 E
Komandorskiye, Is. 73 55 0N 167 0 E
Komárno 59 47 49N 18 5 E
Komatsu 106 36 25N 136 30 E
Komatsujima 109 34 0N 134 35 E
Komi A.S.S.R. □ 69 64 0N 55 0 E
Kommunizma, Pik 71 39 0N 72 2 E
Komoro 107 36 19N 138 26 E
Kompong Cham 95 12 0N 105 30 E
Kompong Chhnang 95 12 20N 104 35 E
Kompong Som 95 10 38N 103 30 E
Komsomolets, Ostrov 72 80 30N 95 0 E
Komsomolsk 75 50 30N 137 0 E
Konarhá □ 87 35 30N 71 3 E
Kong 130 8 54N 4 36W
Kong, Koh 95 11 20N 103 0 E
Kong Christian X.s Land 13 74 0N 29 0W
Kong Frederik VI.s Kyst 147 63 0N 43 0W
Kong Frederik VIII.s Land 13 78 30N 26 0W
Kongor 129 7 1N 31 27 E
Königsberg = Kaliningrad 68 54 42N 20 32 E
Konin 58 52 12N 18 15 E
Konjic 52 43 42N 17 58 E
Konosha 68 61 0N 40 5 E
Konstanz 44 47 39N 9 10 E
Kontagora 131 10 23N 5 27 E
Konya 80 37 52N 32 35 E
Konya Ovasi 80 38 30N 33 0 E
Koolyanobbing 120 30 48S 119 36 E
Kopaonik Planina 52 43 10N 21 50 E
Kopeysk 71 55 7N 61 37 E
Kopparberg 60 59 52N 15 0 E
Koppeh Dāgh 86 38 0N 58 0 E
Korab 52 41 44N 20 40 E
Korça 52 40 37N 20 50 E
Korčula 52 42 57N 17 8 E
Kordestān □ 81 36 0N 47 0 E
Korea Bay 98 39 0N 124 0 E
Korea Strait 104 34 0N 129 30 E
Korhogo 130 9 29N 5 28W
Korinthiakós Kólpos 54 38 16N 22 30 E

Kórinthos	**54**	37 56N	22 55 E
Kōriyama	**105**	37 24N	140 23 E
Koroit	**119**	38 18S	142 24 E
Kortrijk	**42**	50 50N	3 17 E
Koryakskiy Khrebet	**73**	61 0N	171 0 E
Kos	**55**	36 50N	27 15 E
Kosciusko	**169**	33 3N	89 34W
Kosciusko, Mt.	**117**	36 27S	148 16 E
Koshigaya	**107**	35 54N	139 48 E
K'oshih = Kashi	**100**	39 30N	76 2 E
Koshiki-Rettō	**108**	31 45N	129 49 E
Kōshoku	**107**	36 38N	138 6 E
Košice	**59**	48 42N	21 15 E
Kosovska-Mitrovica	**52**	42 54N	20 52 E
Kôstî	**129**	13 8N	32 43 E
Kostroma	**68**	57 50N	40 58 E
Koszalin	**58**	53 50N	16 8 E
Kota	**91**	25 14N	75 49 E
Kota Baharu	**96**	6 7N	102 14 E
Kota Kinabalu	**112**	6 0N	116 4 E
Kotelnich	**68**	58 20N	48 10 E
Kotka	**67**	60 28N	26 58 E
Kotlas	**69**	61 15N	47 0 E
Kotor	**52**	42 25N	18 47 E
Kotuy →	**77**	71 54N	102 6 E
Kotzebue	**142**	66 50N	162 40W
Kowloon	**99**	22 20N	114 15 E
Kōyama	**108**	31 20N	130 56 E
Koyukuk →	**142**	64 56N	157 30W
Kozáni	**55**	40 19N	21 47 E
Kozhikode = Calicut	**90**	11 15N	75 43 E
Kōzu-Shima	**107**	34 13N	139 10 E
Kra, Isthmus of = Kra, Kho Khot	**94**	10 15N	99 30 E
Kra, Kho Khot	**94**	10 15N	99 30 E
Kragujevac	**52**	44 2N	20 56 E
Kraków	**58**	50 4N	19 57 E
Kraljevo	**52**	43 44N	20 41 E
Krasnodar	**68**	45 5N	39 0 E
Krasnovodsk	**70**	40 0N	52 52 E
Krasnoyarsk	**74**	56 8N	93 0 E
Krasnyy Kut	**68**	50 50N	47 0 E
Kratie	**95**	12 32N	106 10 E
Kravanh, Chuor Phnum	**95**	12 0N	103 32 E
Krefeld	**42**	51 20N	6 32 E
Kremenchug	**68**	49 5N	33 25 E
Krishna →	**91**	15 57N	80 59 E
Krishnanagar	**92**	23 24N	88 33 E
Kristiansand	**60**	58 9N	8 1 E
Kristianstad	**61**	56 2N	14 9 E
Kristianstads län □	**61**	56 15N	14 0 E
Kristiansund	**65**	63 7N	7 45 E
Kríti	**55**	35 15N	25 0 E
Krivoy Rog	**68**	47 51N	33 20 E
Krk	**52**	45 8N	14 40 E
Kronobergs län □	**61**	56 45N	14 30 E
Kronshtadt	**68**	60 5N	29 45 E
Krotoszyn	**58**	51 42N	17 23 E
Krugersdorp	**137**	26 5S	27 46 E
Krung Thep = Bangkok	**94**	13 45N	100 35 E
Kruševac	**52**	43 35N	21 28 E
Krymskiy P-ov.	**68**	45 0N	34 0 E
Kuala Dungun	**96**	4 45N	103 25 E
Kuala Kangsar	**96**	4 46N	100 56 E
Kuala Lipis	**96**	4 10N	102 3 E
Kuala Lumpur	**96**	3 9N	101 41 E
Kuala Pilah	**96**	2 45N	102 15 E
Kuala Trengganu	**96**	5 20N	103 8 E
Kuangchou = Guangzhou	**99**	23 5N	113 10 E
Kuantan	**96**	3 49N	103 20 E
Kubak	**88**	27 10N	63 10 E
Kuban →	**68**	45 20N	37 30 E
Kubokawa	**109**	33 12N	133 8 E
Kuchinoerabu-Jima	**104**	30 28N	130 11 E
Kucing	**111**	1 33N	110 25 E
Kudamatsu	**108**	34 0N	131 52 E
Kueiyang = Guiyang	**99**	26 32N	106 40 E
Kūh-e-Jebāl Bārez	**85**	29 0N	58 0 E
Kūh-e Sorkh	**86**	35 30N	58 45 E
Kūhhā-ye-Bashākerd	**85**	26 45N	59 0 E
Kūhhā-ye Sabalān	**81**	38 15N	47 45 E
Kuji	**103**	40 11N	141 46 E
Kuldja = Yining	**100**	43 58N	81 10 E
Kulunda	**71**	52 35N	78 57 E
Kumagaya	**107**	36 9N	139 22 E
Kumamoto	**108**	32 45N	130 45 E
Kumano	**106**	33 54N	136 5 E
Kumano-Nada	**106**	33 47N	136 20 E
Kumasi	**130**	6 41N	1 38W
Kumon Bum	**93**	26 30N	97 15 E
Kunashir, Ostrov	**75**	44 0N	146 0 E
Kunimi-Dake	**109**	32 33N	131 1 E
Kunlun Shan	**100**	36 0N	86 30 E
Kunming	**101**	25 1N	102 41 E
Kunsan	**98**	35 59N	126 45 E
Kuopio	**67**	62 53N	27 35 E
Kupang	**113**	10 19S	123 39 E
Kurashiki	**109**	34 40N	133 50 E
Kurayoshi	**109**	35 26N	133 50 E
Kure	**109**	34 14N	132 32 E
Kurgan	**71**	55 26N	65 18 E
Kuril Is. = Kurilskiye Ostrova	**75**	45 0N	150 0 E
Kurilskiye Ostrova	**75**	45 0N	150 0 E
Kurnool	**90**	15 45N	78 0 E
Kurobe-Gawe →	**106**	36 55N	137 25 E
Kurri Kurri	**117**	32 50S	151 28 E
Kursk	**68**	51 42N	36 11 E
Kuršumlija	**52**	43 9N	21 19 E
Kurume	**108**	33 15N	130 30 E
Kurunegala	**90**	7 30N	80 23 E
Kusatsu	**106**	34 58N	135 57 E
Kushikino	**108**	31 44N	130 16 E
Kushima	**108**	31 29N	131 14 E
Kushimoto	**106**	33 28N	135 47 E
Kushiro	**103**	43 0N	144 25 E
Kushka	**70**	35 20N	62 18 E
Kushtia	**92**	23 55N	89 5 E
Kuskokwim Bay	**142**	59 50N	162 56W
Kustanay	**71**	53 10N	63 35 E
Kusu	**108**	33 16N	131 9 E
Kütahya	**80**	39 30N	30 2 E
Kutaisi	**70**	42 19N	42 40 E
Kutaraja = Banda Aceh	**111**	5 35N	95 20 E
Kutno	**58**	52 15N	19 23 E
Kuujjuaq	**146**	58 6N	68 15W
Kuwait = Al Kuwayt	**84**	29 30N	47 30 E
Kuwait ■	**84**	29 30N	47 30 E
Kuwana	**106**	35 0N	136 43 E
Kuybyshev	**68**	53 8N	50 6 E
Kwakoegron	**185**	5 12N	55 25W
Kwangju	**98**	35 9N	126 54 E
Kwangsi-Chuang = Guangxi Zhuangzu Zizhiqu □	**99**	24 0N	109 0 E
Kwangtung = Guangdong □	**99**	23 0N	113 0 E
Kweichow = Guizhou □	**99**	27 0N	107 0 E
Kwinana New Town	**120**	32 15S	115 47 E
Kyabram	**117**	36 19S	145 4 E
Kyaukpadaung	**93**	20 52N	95 8 E
Kyle of Lochalsh	**32**	57 17N	5 43W
Kyneton	**117**	37 10S	144 29 E
Kyō-ga-Saki	**106**	35 45N	135 15 E
Kyoga, L.	**132**	1 35N	33 0 E
Kyogle	**116**	28 40S	153 0 E
Kyōto	**106**	35 0N	135 45 E
Kyrenia	**80**	35 20N	33 20 E
Kyūshū	**108**	33 0N	131 0 E
Kyūshū □	**108**	33 0N	131 0 E
Kyūshū-Sanchi	**108**	32 35N	131 17 E
Kyustendil	**53**	42 16N	22 41 E
Kyzyl	**74**	51 50N	94 30 E
Kyzylkum, Peski	**70**	42 30N	65 0 E
Kzyl-Orda	**71**	44 48N	65 28 E
Labe = Elbe →	**42**	53 50N	9 0 E
Laboulaye	**190**	34 10S	63 30W
Labrador, Coast of □	**147**	53 20N	61 0W
Lábrea	**187**	7 15S	64 51W
Lac la Martre	**145**	63 8N	117 16W
Laccadive Is. = Lakshadweep Is.	**78**	10 0N	72 30 E

Name	Page	Lat.	Long.
Lachine	**151**	45 30N	73 40W
Lachute	**151**	45 39N	74 21W
Lackawanna	**164**	42 49N	78 50W
Lacombe	**155**	52 30N	113 44W
Laconia	**148**	43 32N	71 30W
Ladakh Ra.	**89**	34 0N	78 0E
Ladoga, L. = Ladozhskoye Ozero	**68**	61 15N	30 30E
Ladozhskoye Ozero	**68**	61 15N	30 30E
Ladysmith	**154**	49 0N	123 49W
Lae	**115**	6 40S	147 2E
Lafayette, Ind., U.S.A.	**167**	40 25N	86 54W
Lafayette, La., U.S.A.	**168**	30 18N	92 0W
Laghmān □	**87**	34 20N	70 0E
Laghouat	**127**	33 50N	2 59E
Lagny	**39**	48 52N	2 40E
Lagos, Nigeria	**131**	6 25N	3 27E
Lagos, Portugal	**50**	37 5N	8 41W
Lagos de Moreno	**175**	21 21N	101 55W
Laguna	**191**	28 30S	48 50W
Laguna Beach	**173**	33 31N	117 52W
Laguna Madre	**158**	27 0N	97 20W
Lagunas, Chile	**187**	21 0S	69 45W
Lagunas, Peru	**186**	5 10S	75 35W
Lahore	**89**	31 32N	74 22E
Lahti	**67**	60 58N	25 40E
Lahtis = Lahti	**67**	60 58N	25 40E
Laï	**131**	9 25N	16 18E
Laidley	**116**	27 39S	152 20E
Lairg	**33**	58 1N	4 24W
Laja, R. de la →	**177**	20 55N	100 46W
Lajes	**191**	27 48S	50 20W
Lake Cargelligo	**117**	33 15S	146 22E
Lake Charles	**168**	30 15N	93 10W
Lake City, Fla., U.S.A.	**170**	30 10N	82 40W
Lake City, S.C., U.S.A.	**165**	33 51N	79 44W
Lake Grace	**120**	33 7S	118 28E
Lake Harbour	**146**	62 50N	69 50W
Lake Worth	**170**	26 36N	80 3W
Lakeland	**170**	28 0N	82 0W
Lakes Entrance	**117**	37 50S	148 0E
Lakewood	**167**	41 28N	81 50W
Lakshadweep Is.	**78**	10 0N	72 30E
Lala Ghat	**93**	24 30N	92 40E
Lalitpur	**91**	24 42N	78 28E
Lamar	**163**	38 9N	102 35W
Lambi Kyun	**96**	10 50N	98 20E
Lameroo	**119**	35 19S	140 33E
Lamía	**54**	38 55N	22 26E
Lammermuir Hills	**31**	55 50N	2 40W
Lamon Bay	**112**	14 30N	122 20E
Lampa	**187**	15 22S	70 22W
Lampang	**94**	18 16N	99 32E
Lampeter	**26**	52 6N	4 6W
Lamu	**133**	2 16S	40 55E
Lanark	**31**	55 40N	3 48W
Lancang Jiang →	**101**	21 40N	101 10E
Lancashire □	**28**	53 40N	2 30W
Lancaster, U.K.	**28**	54 3N	2 48W
Lancaster, U.S.A.	**164**	40 4N	76 19W
Lancaster Sd.	**146**	74 13N	84 0W
Lanchow = Lanzhou	**99**	36 1N	103 52E
Landes, Les	**36**	44 20N	1 0W
Land's End	**27**	50 4N	5 43W
Landskrona	**61**	55 53N	12 50E
Lanett	**169**	33 0N	85 15W
Langjökull	**64**	64 39N	20 12W
Langlade	**149**	46 50N	56 20W
Langøya	**64**	68 45N	14 50E
Langres, Plateau de	**37**	47 45N	5 3E
Languedoc	**37**	43 58N	4 0E
Lannion	**36**	48 46N	3 29W
Lansing	**167**	42 47N	84 40W
Lanzhou	**99**	36 1N	103 52E
Laois □	**35**	53 0N	7 20W
Laon	**38**	49 33N	3 35E
Laona	**150**	45 32N	88 41W
Laos ■	**95**	17 45N	105 0E
Lapeer	**167**	43 3N	83 20W
Lapland = Lappland	**67**	68 7N	24 0E
Lappland	**67**	68 7N	24 0E
Laptev Sea	**72**	76 0N	125 0E
Laramie	**163**	41 20N	105 38W
Laramie Mts.	**163**	42 0N	105 30W
Laredo	**161**	27 34N	99 29W
Laren	**40**	52 16N	5 14E
Largs	**30**	55 48N	4 51W
Lárisa	**54**	39 49N	22 28E
Larkana	**88**	27 32N	68 18E
Larnaca	**80**	35 0N	33 35E
Larne	**34**	54 52N	5 50W
Laryak	**69**	61 15N	80 0E
Las Cruces	**161**	32 18N	106 50W
Las Lajas	**190**	38 30S	70 25W
Las Palmas	**126**	28 7N	15 26W
Las Vegas, N. Mex., U.S.A.	**161**	35 35N	105 10W
Las Vegas, Nev., U.S.A.	**173**	36 10N	115 5W
Lashio	**93**	22 56N	97 45E
Latacunga	**184**	0 50S	78 35W
Latakia = Al Lādhiqīyah	**80**	35 30N	35 45E
Latium = Lazio □	**46**	42 10N	12 30E
Latrobe	**119**	41 14S	146 30E
Latur	**91**	18 25N	76 40E
Latvian S.S.R. □	**68**	56 50N	24 0E
Lauchhammer	**43**	51 35N	13 48E
Launceston, Australia	**119**	41 24S	147 8E
Launceston, U.K.	**27**	50 38N	4 21W
Launglon Bok	**94**	13 50N	97 54E
Laurel	**169**	31 41N	89 9W
Laurens	**165**	34 32N	82 2W
Laurentian Plat.	**138**	52 0N	70 0W
Laurinburg	**165**	34 50N	79 25W
Lausanne	**44**	46 32N	6 38E
Laut, Pulau	**111**	3 40S	116 10E
Laut Ketil, Kepulauan	**113**	4 45S	115 40E
Lauzon	**148**	46 48N	71 10W
Laval	**36**	48 4N	0 48W
Lávrion	**55**	37 40N	24 4E
Lawrence, Kans., U.S.A.	**166**	39 0N	95 10W
Lawrence, Mass., U.S.A.	**164**	42 40N	71 9W
Lawrenceburg	**169**	35 12N	87 19W
Lawton	**161**	34 33N	98 25W
Lazio □	**46**	42 10N	12 30E
Lea →	**25**	51 30N	0 10W
Leader	**152**	50 50N	109 30W
Leadhills	**31**	55 25N	3 47W
Leadville	**163**	39 17N	106 23W
Leamington, Canada	**150**	42 3N	82 36W
Leamington, U.K.	**24**	52 18N	1 32W
Leavenworth	**166**	39 25N	95 0W
Lebanon, Mo., U.S.A.	**166**	37 40N	92 40W
Lebanon, Oreg., U.S.A.	**171**	44 31N	122 57W
Lebanon, Pa., U.S.A.	**164**	40 20N	76 28W
Lebanon, Tenn., U.S.A.	**169**	36 15N	86 20W
Lebanon ■	**80**	34 0N	36 0E
Lecce	**49**	40 20N	18 10E
Ledbury	**24**	52 3N	2 25W
Leduc	**155**	53 15N	113 30W
Leeds	**28**	53 48N	1 34W
Leek	**28**	53 7N	2 2W
Leerdam	**40**	51 54N	5 6E
Leesburg	**170**	28 47N	81 52W
Leeton	**117**	34 33S	146 23E
Leeuwarden	**41**	53 15N	5 48E
Leeuwin, C.	**120**	34 20S	115 9E
Leeward Is.	**181**	16 30N	63 30W
Leghorn = Livorno	**46**	43 32N	10 18E
Legnica	**58**	51 12N	16 10E
Leicester	**25**	52 39N	1 9W
Leicester □	**25**	52 40N	1 10W
Leichhardt	**121**	33 53S	151 9E
Leiden	**40**	52 9N	4 30E
Leigh Creek South	**118**	30 38S	138 26E
Leinster	**120**	27 51S	120 36E
Leinster □	**35**	53 0N	7 10W
Leinster, Mt.	**35**	52 38N	6 47W
Leipzig	**43**	51 20N	12 23E
Leith	**31**	55 59N	3 10W
Leith Hill	**24**	51 10N	0 23W
Leitrim	**34**	54 0N	8 5W
Lek →	**40**	51 54N	4 35E
Leleque	**192**	42 28S	71 0W

Léman, Lac	**44**	46 26N	6 30 E
Lemmer	**41**	52 51N	5 43 E
Lena →	**72**	72 52N	126 40 E
Leninabad	**71**	40 17N	69 37 E
Leninakan	**70**	40 47N	43 50 E
Leningrad	**68**	59 55N	30 20 E
Leninsk-Kuznetskiy	**71**	54 44N	86 10 E
Leninskoye	**75**	47 56N	132 38 E
Lenoir City	**165**	35 40N	84 20W
Lens, Belgium	**38**	50 33N	3 54 E
Lens, France	**37**	50 26N	2 50 E
Lensk	**74**	60 48N	114 55 E
Leominster, U.K.	**24**	52 15N	2 43W
Leominster, U.S.A.	**164**	42 32N	71 45W
León, Mexico	**177**	21 7N	101 40W
León, Nic.	**179**	12 20N	86 51W
León, Spain	**50**	42 38N	5 34W
León □	**50**	42 40N	5 55W
Leongatha	**117**	38 30S	145 58 E
Léopold II, Lac = Mai-Ndombe, L.	**134**	2 0S	18 20 E
Léopoldville = Kinshasa	**134**	4 20S	15 15 E
Lérida	**51**	41 37N	0 39 E
Lerwick	**30**	60 10N	1 10W
Lesbos, I. = Lésvos	**55**	39 10N	26 20 E
Lesotho ■	**137**	29 40S	28 0 E
Lesozavodsk	**75**	45 30N	133 29 E
Lesser Antilles	**181**	15 0N	61 0W
Lesser Slave L.	**155**	55 30N	115 25W
Lésvos	**55**	39 10N	26 20 E
Letchworth	**25**	51 58N	0 13W
Lethbridge	**155**	49 45N	112 45W
Leti, Kepulauan	**113**	8 10S	128 0 E
Leticia	**184**	4 9S	70 0W
Letsôk-aw Kyun	**94**	11 30N	98 25 E
Letterkenny	**34**	54 57N	7 42W
Leuven	**42**	50 52N	4 42 E
Levanger	**65**	63 45N	11 19 E
Levin	**122**	40 37S	175 18 E
Lévis	**148**	46 48N	71 9W
Levkás	**54**	38 40N	20 43 E
Levkôsia = Nicosia	**80**	35 10N	33 25 E
Lewes	**25**	50 53N	0 2 E
Lewis	**32**	58 10N	6 40W
Lewis, Butt of	**32**	58 30N	6 12W
Lewis Ra.	**162**	48 0N	113 15W
Lewisporte	**149**	49 15N	55 3W
Lewiston	**148**	44 3N	70 10 E
Lexington, Ky., U.S.A.	**165**	38 6N	84 30W
Lexington, Mo., U.S.A.	**166**	39 7N	93 55W
Lexington, N.C., U.S.A.	**165**	35 50N	80 13W
Lexington, Oreg., U.S.A.	**171**	45 29N	119 46W
Lexington Park	**165**	38 16N	76 27W
Leyte	**112**	11 0N	125 0 E
Lhasa	**101**	29 50N	91 3 E
Lhazê	**101**	29 5N	87 38 E
Lianyungang	**99**	34 40N	119 11 E
Liaoning □	**98**	41 40N	122 30 E
Liaoyuan	**98**	42 58N	125 2 E
Liard →	**144**	61 51N	121 18W
Libau = Liepaja	**68**	56 30N	21 0 E
Liberec	**58**	50 47N	15 7 E
Liberia ■	**130**	6 30N	9 30W
Lîbîya, Sahrâ'	**128**	27 35N	25 0 E
Libreville	**134**	0 25N	9 26 E
Libya ■	**127**	27 0N	17 0 E
Lichfield	**28**	52 40N	1 50W
Liechtenstein ■	**44**	47 8N	9 35 E
Liège	**42**	50 38N	5 35 E
Liegnitz = Legnica	**58**	51 12N	16 10 E
Lienyünchiangshih = Lianyungang	**99**	34 40N	119 11 E
Liepaja	**68**	56 30N	21 0 E
Liévin	**38**	50 24N	2 47 E
Liffey →	**35**	53 21N	6 20W
Lifford	**34**	54 50N	7 30W
Liguria □	**46**	44 30N	9 0 E
Ligurian Sea	**46**	43 20N	9 0 E
Lihou Reefs and Cays	**121**	17 25S	151 40 E
Lihue	**160**	21 59N	159 24W
Likasi	**135**	10 55S	26 48 E
Lille, Belgium	**38**	51 15N	4 50 E
Lille, France	**37**	50 38N	3 3 E
Lille Bælt	**61**	55 20N	9 45 E
Lillehammer	**60**	61 8N	10 30 E
Lillers	**38**	50 35N	2 28 E
Lillooet	**154**	50 44N	121 57W
Lilongwe	**137**	14 0S	33 48 E
Lima, Peru	**186**	12 0S	77 0W
Lima, U.S.A.	**167**	40 42N	84 5W
Limassol	**80**	34 42N	33 1 E
Limavady	**34**	55 3N	6 58W
Limbe	**137**	15 55S	35 2 E
Limburg □	**41**	51 20N	5 55 E
Limeira	**188**	22 35S	47 28W
Limerick	**35**	52 40N	8 38W
Limerick □	**35**	52 30N	8 50W
Limfjorden	**61**	56 55N	9 0 E
Límnos	**55**	39 50N	25 5 E
Limoges	**36**	45 50N	1 15 E
Limón	**179**	10 0N	83 2W
Limousin	**36**	46 0N	1 0 E
Limpopo →	**137**	25 15S	33 30 E
Linares, Chile	**190**	35 50S	71 40W
Linares, Mexico	**176**	24 50N	99 40W
Linares, Spain	**50**	38 10N	3 40W
Lincoln, Argentina	**190**	34 55S	61 30W
Lincoln, U.K.	**29**	53 14N	0 32W
Lincoln, Ill., U.S.A.	**166**	40 10N	89 20W
Lincoln, Maine, U.S.A.	**148**	45 27N	68 29W
Lincoln, Nebr., U.S.A.	**156**	40 50N	96 42W
Lincoln □	**29**	53 14N	0 32W
Lincoln Sea	**12**	84 0N	55 0W
Lincoln Wolds	**29**	53 20N	0 5W
Lindsay, Canada	**151**	44 22N	78 43W
Lindsay, U.S.A.	**173**	36 14N	119 6W
Línea de la Concepción, La	**50**	36 15N	5 23W
Lingga, Kepulauan	**111**	0 10S	104 30 E
Linguéré	**130**	15 25N	15 5W
Linköping	**60**	58 28N	15 36 E
Linlithgow	**31**	55 58N	3 38W
Linxia	**99**	35 36N	103 10 E
Linz	**45**	48 18N	14 18 E
Lion, G. du	**37**	43 0N	4 0 E
Lípari, Is.	**49**	38 30N	14 50 E
Lipetsk	**68**	52 37N	39 35 E
Lippe →	**42**	51 39N	6 38 E
Lisboa	**50**	38 42N	9 10W
Lisbon = Lisboa	**50**	38 42N	9 10W
Lisburn	**34**	54 30N	6 9W
Lisburne, C.	**142**	68 50N	166 0W
Lisieux	**39**	49 10N	0 12 E
Lismore	**116**	28 44S	153 21 E
Lister, Mt.	**15**	78 0S	162 0 E
Listowel	**35**	52 27N	9 30W
Litchfield	**166**	39 10N	89 40W
Lithgow	**117**	33 25S	150 8 E
Lithuanian S.S.R. □	**68**	55 30N	24 0 E
Little Andaman I.	**94**	10 40N	92 15 E
Little Barrier I.	**122**	36 12S	175 8 E
Little Current	**150**	45 55N	82 0W
Little Falls	**164**	43 3N	74 50W
Little Minch	**32**	57 35N	6 45W
Little Rann	**91**	23 25N	71 25 E
Little Rock	**168**	34 41N	92 10W
Littlehampton	**25**	50 48N	0 32W
Liuzhou	**99**	24 22N	109 22 E
Liverpool, Australia	**117**	33 54S	150 58 E
Liverpool, Canada	**148**	44 5N	64 41W
Liverpool, U.K.	**28**	53 25N	3 0W
Liverpool Plains	**116**	31 15S	150 15 E
Livingston, Guat.	**177**	15 50N	88 50W
Livingston, U.K.	**31**	55 52N	3 33W
Livingston, Mont., U.S.A.	**163**	45 40N	110 40W
Livingston, Tex., U.S.A.	**168**	30 44N	94 54W
Livingstone	**135**	17 46S	25 52 E
Livonia	**167**	42 25N	83 23W
Livorno	**46**	43 32N	10 18 E
Lizard Pt.	**27**	49 57N	5 11W
Ljubljana	**52**	46 4N	14 33 E
Ljusnan →	**66**	61 12N	17 8 E
Llandeilo	**26**	51 53N	4 0W

Llandovery	26	51 59N	3 49W
Llandrindod Wells	26	52 15N	3 23W
Llandudno	26	53 19N	3 51W
Llanelli	27	51 41N	4 11W
Llanes	50	43 25N	4 50W
Llangollen	26	52 58N	3 10W
Llanidloes	26	52 28N	3 31W
Llano Estacado	161	34 0N	103 0W
Llanos	184	5 0N	71 35W
Lloydminster	152	53 17N	110 0W
Loc Ninh	95	11 50N	106 34 E
Lochaber	32	56 55N	5 0W
Lochboisdale	32	57 10N	7 20W
Lochem	41	52 9N	6 26 E
Lochgilphead	30	56 2N	5 37W
Lochinver	32	58 9N	5 15W
Lochmaddy	32	57 36N	7 10W
Lochy, L.	32	56 58N	4 55W
Lock Haven	164	41 7N	77 31W
Lockhart	117	35 14S	146 40 E
Lockport	164	43 12N	78 42W
Lodi	172	38 12N	121 16W
Łódź	58	51 45N	19 27 E
Lofoten	64	68 30N	15 0 E
Logan, Utah, U.S.A.	163	41 45N	111 50W
Logan, W. Va., U.S.A.	165	37 51N	81 59W
Logan, Mt	144	60 31N	140 22W
Logansport	167	40 45N	86 21W
Logroño	51	42 28N	2 27W
Loire ~→	36	47 16N	2 10W
Loja	184	3 59S	79 16W
Lokka	67	67 55N	27 35 E
Lolland	61	54 45N	11 30 E
Lom	53	43 48N	23 12 E
Lomami ~→	134	0 46N	24 16 E
Lombardia □	46	45 35N	9 45 E
Lombardy = Lombardia □	46	45 35N	9 45 E
Lombok	113	8 45S	116 30 E
Lomé	130	6 9N	1 20 E
Lomond, L.	31	56 8N	4 38W
Lompoc	173	34 41N	120 32W
Łomża	58	53 10N	22 2 E
London, Canada	150	42 59N	81 15W
London, U.K.	25	51 30N	0 5W
Londonderry	34	55 0N	7 20W
Londrina	191	23 18S	51 10W
Long Beach	173	33 46N	118 12W
Long I., Bahamas	178	23 20N	75 10W
Long I., U.S.A.	164	40 50N	73 20W
Long Range Mts.	149	49 30N	57 30W
Long Xuyen	95	10 19N	105 28 E
Longford, Australia	119	41 32S	147 3 E
Longford, Ireland	34	53 43N	7 50W
Longford □	34	53 42N	7 45W
Longlac	150	49 45N	86 25W
Longmont	163	40 10N	105 4W
Longreach	121	23 28S	144 14 E
Longview, Tex., U.S.A.	168	32 30N	94 45W
Longview, Wash., U.S.A.	171	46 9N	122 58W
Looe	27	50 24N	4 25W
Loop Hd.	35	52 34N	9 55W
Lop Nor	100	40 20N	90 10 E
Lopez, C.	134	0 47S	8 40 E
Lorain	167	41 28N	82 55W
Lorca	51	37 41N	1 42W
Lord Howe I.	122	31 33S	159 6 E
Lordsburg	161	32 22N	108 45W
Lorient	36	47 45N	3 23W
Lorn	30	56 26N	5 10W
Lorn, Firth of	30	56 20N	5 40W
Lorraine	37	49 0N	6 0 E
Los Alamos	161	35 57N	106 17W
Los Andes	190	32 50S	70 40W
Los Angeles, Chile	190	37 28S	72 23W
Los Angeles, U.S.A.	173	34 0N	118 10W
Los Angeles Aqueduct	173	35 25N	118 0W
Los Hermanos	181	11 45N	84 25W
Los Mochis	174	25 45N	108 57W
Los Testigos	181	11 23N	63 6W
Lošinj	52	44 30N	14 30 E
Lossiemouth	33	57 43N	3 17W
Lot ~→	36	44 18N	0 20 E
Lota	190	37 5S	73 10W
Lothian □	31	55 50N	3 0W
Loughborough	29	52 46N	1 11W
Loughrea	35	53 11N	8 33W
Louisbourg	149	45 55N	60 0W
Louise I.	154	52 55N	131 50W
Louisiana □	168	30 50N	92 0W
Louisville, Ky., U.S.A.	167	38 15N	85 45W
Louisville, Miss., U.S.A.	169	33 7N	89 3W
Lourdes	36	43 6N	0 3W
Lourenço-Marques = Maputo	137	25 58S	32 32 E
Louth	29	53 23N	0 0 E
Louth □	34	53 55N	6 30W
Louvain = Leuven	42	50 52N	4 42 E
Louviers	39	49 12N	1 10 E
Lowell	164	42 38N	71 19W
Lower Austria = Niederösterreich □	45	48 25N	15 40 E
Lower California = Baja California	174	31 10N	115 12W
Lower Hutt	123	41 10S	174 55 E
Lower Saxony = Niedersachsen □	42	52 45N	9 0 E
Lowestoft	25	52 29N	1 44 E
Łowicz	58	52 6N	19 55 E
Loxton	119	34 28S	140 31 E
Loyalty Is. = Loyauté, Is.	122	21 0S	167 30 E
Loyang = Luoyang	99	34 40N	112 26 E
Loyauté, Is.	122	21 0S	167 30 E
Lualaba ~→	135	0 26N	25 20 E
Luan Chau	95	21 38N	103 24 E
Luanda	134	8 50S	13 15 E
Luang Prabang	95	19 52N	102 10 E
Luarca	50	43 32N	6 32W
Lubbock	161	33 40N	101 53W
Lübeck	43	53 52N	10 41 E
Lublin	58	51 12N	22 38 E
Lubnän, L.	80	33 50N	35 45 E
Lubumbashi	135	11 40S	27 28 E
Lucca	46	43 50N	10 30 E
Luce Bay	30	54 45N	4 48W
Lučenec	59	48 18N	19 42 E
Lucerne = Luzern	44	47 3N	8 18 E
Lucknow	92	26 50N	81 0 E
Lüda = Dalian	98	38 50N	121 40 E
Lüderitz	136	26 41S	15 8 E
Ludhiana	89	30 57N	75 56 E
Ludington	167	43 58N	86 27W
Ludlow	24	52 23N	2 42W
Ludwigshafen	42	49 27N	8 27 E
Lufkin	168	31 25N	94 40W
Lugano	44	46 0N	8 57 E
Lugansk = Voroshilovgrad	68	48 38N	39 15 E
Lugo	50	43 2N	7 35W
Lugovoye	71	42 55N	72 43 E
Luján	190	34 45S	59 5W
Łuków	58	51 55N	22 23 E
Lule älv ~→	67	65 35N	22 10 E
Luleå	67	65 35N	22 10 E
Lüleburgaz	80	41 23N	27 22 E
Lulua ~→	134	6 30S	22 50 E
Luluabourg = Kananga	134	5 55S	22 18 E
Lumberton	165	34 37N	78 59W
Lundy	27	51 10N	4 41W
Lune ~→	28	54 0N	2 51W
Lüneburg	43	53 15N	10 23 E
Lüneburg Heath = Lüneburger Heide	43	53 0N	10 0 E
Lüneburger Heide	43	53 0N	10 0 E
Lüni ~→	91	24 41N	71 14 E
Luoyang	99	34 40N	112 26 E
Lurgan	34	54 28N	6 20W
Lusaka	135	15 28S	28 16 E
Luta = Dalian	98	38 50N	121 40 E
Luton	25	51 53N	0 24W
Lutsk	68	50 50N	25 15 E
Luvua ~→	135	6 50S	27 30 E
Luxembourg	42	49 37N	6 9 E
Luxembourg ■	42	50 0N	6 0 E
Luzern	44	47 3N	8 18 E

Luzhou	**99**	28 52N	105	20 E
Luziânia	**188**	16 20S	48	0W
Luzon	**112**	16 0N	121	0 E
Lvov	**68**	49 50N	24	0 E
Lyakhovskiye, Ostrova	**72**	73 40N	141	0 E
Lyallpur = Faisalabad	**89**	31 30N	73	5 E
Lyell I.	**154**	52 40N	131	35W
Lyell Range	**123**	41 38S	172	20 E
Lyme Regis	**27**	50 44N	2	57W
Lymington	**24**	50 46N	1	32W
Lynchburg	**165**	37 23N	79	10W
Lynn	**164**	42 28N	70	57W
Lynn Lake	**152**	56 51N	101	3W
Lynton	**27**	51 14N	3	50W
Lyon	**37**	45 46N	4	50 E
Lyons = Lyon	**37**	45 46N	4	50 E
Lytham St. Anne's	**28**	53 45N	2	58W
Lyttelton	**122**	43 35S	172	44 E
Ma'ãn	**80**	30 12N	35	44 E
Ma'anshan	**99**	31 44N	118	29 E
Ma'arrat an Nu'mãn	**80**	35 43N	36	43 E
Maas ~	**40**	51 45N	4	32 E
Maaseik	**41**	51 6N	5	45 E
Maastricht	**41**	50 50N	5	40 E
Mablethorpe	**29**	53 21N	0	14 E
McAlester	**168**	34 57N	95	46W
Macao = Macau ■	**99**	22 16N	113	35 E
Macapá	**185**	0 5N	51	4W
Macau	**189**	5 0S	36	40W
Macau ■	**99**	22 16N	113	35 E
McBride	**155**	53 20N	120	19W
Macclesfield	**28**	53 16N	2	9W
McClure Str.	**12**	75 0N	119	0W
McComb	**169**	31 13N	90	30W
McCook	**163**	40 15N	100	35W
McDermitt	**172**	42 0N	117	45W
Macdonald L.	**114**	23 30S	129	0 E
Macdonnell Ranges	**114**	23 40S	133	0 E
McDouall Peak	**118**	29 51S	134	55 E
Macduff	**33**	57 40N	2	30W
Macedonia = Makedhonía □	**55**	40 39N	22	0 E
Maceió	**189**	9 40S	35	41W
Macfarlane, L.	**118**	32 0S	136	40 E
Macgillycuddy's Reeks	**35**	52 2N	9	45W
Machala	**184**	3 20S	79	57W
Machida	**107**	35 28N	139	23 E
Machilipatnam	**92**	16 12N	81	8 E
Machiques	**184**	10 4N	72	34W
Machynlleth	**26**	52 36N	3	51W
Mackay	**121**	21 8S	149	11 E
Mackay, L.	**114**	22 30S	129	0 E
McKeesport	**164**	40 21N	79	50W
Mackenzie ~	**144**	69 10N	134	20W
Mackenzie Bay	**12**	69 0N	137	30W
Mackenzie Mts.	**144**	64 0N	130	0W
McKinley, Mt.	**142**	63 2N	151	0W
McKinley Sea	**13**	84 0N	10	0W
McKinney	**168**	33 10N	96	40W
Macksville	**116**	30 40S	152	56 E
Maclean	**116**	29 26S	153	16 E
McLennan	**155**	55 42N	116	50W
MacLeod Lake	**154**	54 58N	123	0W
M'Clintock Chan.	**145**	72 0N	102	0W
McMinnville, Oreg., U.S.A.	**171**	45 16N	123	11W
McMinnville, Tenn., U.S.A.	**169**	35 43N	85	45W
McMurdo Sd.	**15**	77 0S	170	0 E
McMurray = Fort McMurray	**155**	56 44N	111	7W
McNaughton L.	**155**	52 0N	118	10W
Macomb	**166**	40 25N	90	40W
Mâcon, France	**37**	46 19N	4	50 E
Mâcon, U.S.A.	**170**	32 50N	83	37W
McPherson	**161**	38 25N	97	40W
Macpherson Ra.	**116**	28 15S	153	15 E
Macquarie ~	**116**	30 5S	147	30 E
Macquarie Is.	**15**	54 36S	158	55 E
MacRobertson Land	**14**	71 0S	64	0 E
Macroom	**35**	51 54N	8	57W
Madagascar ■	**137**	20 0S	47	0 E
Madang	**115**	5 12S	145	49 E
Madaripur	**93**	23 19N	90	15 E
Made	**40**	51 41N	4	49 E
Madeira	**126**	32 50N	17	0W
Madeira ~	**185**	3 22S	58	45W
Madeleine, Îs. de la	**149**	47 30N	61	40W
Madera	**173**	37 0N	120	1W
Madhya Pradesh □	**91**	21 50N	81	0 E
Madison, Fla., U.S.A.	**170**	30 29N	83	39W
Madison, Ind., U.S.A.	**167**	38 42N	85	20W
Madison, Wis., U.S.A.	**166**	43 5N	89	25W
Madisonville	**167**	37 20N	87	30W
Madiun	**111**	7 38S	111	32 E
Madras = Tamil Nadu □	**90**	11 0N	77	0 E
Madras, India	**90**	13 8N	80	19 E
Madras, U.S.A.	**171**	44 40N	121	10W
Madre, Laguna	**176**	25 0N	97	30W
Madre de Dios ~	**187**	10 59S	66	8W
Madre del Sur, Sa.	**177**	17 0N	100	0W
Madre Occidental, Sa.	**174**	25 0N	105	0W
Madre Oriental, Sa.	**177**	22 0N	99	30W
Madrid	**50**	40 25N	3	45W
Madura, Selat	**111**	7 30S	113	20 E
Madurai	**90**	9 55N	78	10 E
Madurantakam	**90**	12 30N	79	50 E
Mae Rim	**94**	18 54N	98	57 E
Maebashi	**107**	36 24N	139	4 E
Maesteg	**27**	51 36N	3	40W
Maestra, Sierra	**178**	20 15N	77	0W
Mafeking	**152**	52 40N	101	10W
Maffra	**117**	37 53S	146	58 E
Mafia	**135**	7 45S	39	50 E
Mafikeng	**136**	25 50S	25	38 E
Mafra	**191**	26 10S	50	0W
Magadan	**73**	59 38N	150	50 E
Magallanes, Estrecho de	**192**	52 30S	75	0W
Magangué	**184**	9 14N	74	45W
Magdalena, Bolivia	**187**	13 13S	63	57W
Magdalena, Mexico	**174**	30 38N	110	57W
Magdalena ~	**184**	11 6N	74	51W
Magdeburg	**43**	52 8N	11	36 E
Magelang	**111**	7 29S	110	13 E
Magellan's Str. = Magallanes, Estrecho de	**192**	52 30S	75	0W
Magherafelt	**34**	54 44N	6	37W
Magnitogorsk	**71**	53 27N	59	4 E
Magog	**148**	45 18N	72	9W
Magosa = Famagusta	**80**	35 8N	33	55 E
Magrath	**155**	49 25N	112	50W
Mahābād	**81**	36 50N	45	45 E
Mahajanga □	**137**	17 0S	47	0 E
Mahakam ~	**111**	0 35S	117	17 E
Mahallāt	**86**	33 55N	50	30 E
Mahanadi ~	**92**	20 20N	86	25 E
Maharashtra □	**91**	20 30N	75	30 E
Mahbubnagar	**91**	16 45N	77	59 E
Mahia Pen.	**122**	39 9S	177	55 E
Mahón	**51**	39 53N	4	16 E
Mahone Bay	**148**	44 30N	64	20W
Mahukona	**160**	20 11N	155	52W
Mai-Ndombe, L.	**134**	2 0S	18	20 E
Maidenhead	**25**	51 31N	0	42W
Maiduguri	**131**	12 0N	13	20 E
Maikala Ra.	**92**	22 0N	81	0 E
Main ~	**42**	50 0N	8	18 E
Maine	**36**	48 0N	0	0 E
Maine □	**148**	45 20N	69	0W
Mainland, Orkney, U.K.	**33**	59 0N	3	10W
Mainland, Shetland, U.K.	**30**	60 15N	1	22W
Mainpuri	**89**	27 18N	79	4 E
Mainz	**42**	50 0N	8	17 E
Maiquetía	**184**	10 36N	66	57W
Maisí, Pta. de	**178**	20 10N	74	10W
Maitland, N.S.W., Australia	**117**	32 33S	151	36 E
Maitland, S. Austral., Australia	**119**	34 23S	137	40 E
Maíz, Islas del	**179**	12 15N	83	4W
Maizuru	**106**	35 25N	135	22 E
Majorca, I. = Mallorca	**51**	39 30N	3	0 E
Makarikari = Makgadikgadi Salt Pans	**136**	20 40S	25	45 E
Makasar = Ujung Pandang	**113**	5 10S	119	20 E

Makasar, Selat	**113**	1 0S	118 20 E
Makedhonía □	**55**	40 39N	22 0 E
Makena	**160**	20 39N	156 27W
Makeyevka	**68**	48 0N	38 0 E
Makgadikgadi Salt Pans	**136**	20 40S	25 45 E
Makhachkala	**70**	43 0N	47 30 E
Makkah	**82**	21 30N	39 54 E
Makó	**59**	46 14N	20 33 E
Makran Coast Range	**88**	25 40N	64 0 E
Makurazaki	**108**	31 15N	130 20 E
Makurdi	**131**	7 43N	8 35 E
Malabar Coast	**90**	11 0N	75 0 E
Malacca, Str. of	**111**	3 0N	101 0 E
Malad City	**162**	42 10N	112 20 E
Málaga	**50**	36 43N	4 23W
Malakal	**129**	9 33N	31 50 E
Malang	**111**	7 59S	112 45 E
Mälaren	**60**	59 30N	17 10 E
Malatya	**81**	38 25N	38 20 E
Malawi ■	**137**	13 0S	34 0 E
Malawi, L.	**137**	12 30S	34 30 E
Malay Pen.	**97**	7 25N	100 0 E
Malāyer	**84**	34 19N	48 51 E
Malaysia ■	**111**	5 0N	110 0 E
Malbaie, La	**148**	47 40N	70 10W
Malbork	**58**	54 3N	19 1 E
Malcolm	**120**	28 51S	121 25 E
Maldives ■	**78**	7 0N	73 0 E
Maldonado	**191**	35 0S	55 0W
Malebo, Pool	**134**	4 17S	15 20 E
Malegaon	**91**	20 30N	74 38 E
Mali ■	**130**	15 0N	2 0W
Mali Kyun	**94**	13 0N	98 20 E
Malin Hd.	**34**	55 18N	7 24W
Malindi	**133**	3 12S	40 5 E
Malines = Mechelen	**42**	51 2N	4 29 E
Mallaig	**32**	57 0N	5 50W
Mallorca	**51**	39 30N	3 0 E
Mallow	**35**	52 8N	8 40W
Malmédy	**42**	50 25N	6 2 E
Malmö	**61**	55 36N	12 59 E
Malmöhus län □	**61**	55 45N	13 30 E
Malone	**151**	44 50N	74 19W
Malta ■	**49**	35 50N	14 30 E
Malton	**29**	54 9N	0 48W
Maluku	**113**	1 0S	127 0 E
Malvern, U.K.	**24**	52 7N	2 19W
Malvern, U.S.A.	**168**	34 22N	92 50W
Malvern Hills	**24**	52 0N	2 19W
Malvinas, Is. = Falkland Is.	**192**	51 30S	59 0W
Mamers	**39**	48 21N	0 22 E
Mamoré →	**187**	10 23S	65 53W
Mamou	**130**	10 15N	12 0W
Man	**130**	7 30N	7 40W
Man, I. of	**28**	54 15N	4 30W
Mana, Fr. Gui.	**185**	5 45N	53 55W
Mana, U.S.A.	**160**	22 3N	159 45W
Manaar, Gulf of = Mannar, G. of	**90**	8 30N	79 0 E
Manacapuru	**185**	3 16S	60 37W
Manado	**113**	1 29N	124 51 E
Managua	**179**	12 6N	86 20W
Manaos = Manaus	**185**	3 0S	60 0W
Manapouri	**123**	45 34S	167 39 E
Manaung	**93**	18 45N	93 40 E
Manaus	**185**	3 0S	60 0W
Mancha, La	**50**	39 10N	2 54W
Manchester, U.K.	**28**	53 30N	2 15W
Manchester, U.S.A.	**164**	42 58N	71 29W
Mandalay	**93**	22 0N	96 4 E
Mandale = Mandalay	**93**	22 0N	96 4 E
Mandurah	**120**	32 36S	115 48 E
Manfredónia, G. di	**49**	41 30N	16 10 E
Mangalore	**90**	12 55N	74 47 E
Mangla Dam	**89**	33 9N	73 44 E
Mangole	**113**	1 50S	125 55 E
Mangonui	**122**	35 1S	173 32 E
Mangyshlak P-ov.	**70**	44 30N	52 30 E
Manhattan	**158**	39 10N	96 40W
Manicoré	**185**	5 48S	61 16W
Manicouagan →	**148**	49 30N	68 30W
Manila	**112**	14 40N	121 3 E
Manilla	**116**	30 45S	150 43 E
Manipur □	**93**	25 0N	94 0 E
Manisa	**80**	38 38N	27 30 E
Manistee	**167**	44 15N	86 20W
Manistique	**150**	45 59N	86 18W
Manitoba □	**153**	55 30N	97 0W
Manitoba, L.	**153**	51 0N	98 45W
Manitoulin I.	**150**	45 40N	82 30W
Manitowoc	**167**	44 8N	87 40W
Manizales	**184**	5 5N	75 32W
Manjil	**81**	36 46N	49 30 E
Manjimup	**120**	34 15S	116 6 E
Mankato	**166**	44 8N	93 59W
Manly	**117**	33 48S	151 17 E
Mannar, G. of	**90**	8 30N	79 0 E
Mannar I.	**90**	9 5N	79 45 E
Mannheim	**42**	49 28N	8 29 E
Mannum	**119**	34 50S	139 20 E
Manosque	**37**	43 49N	5 47 E
Manouane, L.	**148**	50 45N	70 45W
Mans, Le	**39**	48 0N	0 10 E
Mansel I.	**146**	62 0N	80 0W
Mansfield, Australia	**117**	37 4S	146 6 E
Mansfield, U.K.	**29**	53 8N	1 12W
Mansfield, U.S.A.	**167**	40 45N	82 30W
Manta	**184**	1 0S	80 40W
Mantes-la-Jolie	**39**	49 0N	1 41 E
Mantiqueira, Serra da	**188**	22 0S	44 0W
Mántova	**46**	45 20N	10 42 E
Mantua = Mántova	**46**	45 20N	10 42 E
Manu	**187**	12 10S	70 51W
Manukau	**122**	35 14S	173 13 E
Manyara, L.	**135**	3 40S	35 50 E
Manzanillo, Cuba	**178**	20 20N	77 31W
Manzanillo, Mexico	**175**	19 3N	104 20W
Manzhouli	**98**	49 35N	117 25 E
Mapimí	**174**	25 49N	103 51W
Maple	**152**	43 51N	79 31W
Maputo	**137**	25 58S	32 32 E
Maquinchao	**192**	41 15S	68 50W
Mar, Serra do	**191**	25 30S	49 0W
Mar Chiquita, L.	**190**	30 40S	62 50W
Mar del Plata	**191**	38 0S	57 30W
Mar Menor, L.	**51**	37 40N	0 45W
Marabá	**188**	5 20S	49 5W
Maracaibo	**184**	10 40N	71 37W
Maracaibo, Lago de	**184**	9 40N	71 30W
Maracay	**184**	10 15N	67 28W
Marajó, Ilha de	**188**	1 0S	49 30W
Maranhão = São Luís	**188**	2 39S	44 15W
Maranhão □	**188**	5 0S	46 0W
Marañón →	**186**	4 30S	73 35W
Maraş	**80**	37 37N	36 53 E
Marathón	**55**	38 11N	23 58 E
Marbella	**50**	36 30N	4 57W
Marble Bar	**114**	21 9S	119 44 E
March	**25**	52 33N	0 5 E
Marché	**36**	46 0N	1 20 E
Marche □	**47**	43 22N	13 10 E
Marchena	**50**	37 18N	5 23W
Marches = Marche □	**47**	43 22N	13 10 E
Mardan	**89**	34 20N	72 0 E
Mardin	**81**	37 20N	40 43 E
Mareeba	**121**	16 59S	145 28 E
Margarita	**175**	9 20N	79 55W
Margarita I.	**185**	11 0N	64 0W
Margate	**25**	51 23N	1 24 E
Mari, A.S.S.R. □	**68**	56 30N	48 0 E
Maria van Diemen, C.	**122**	34 29S	172 40 E
Marianao	**178**	23 8N	82 24W
Marianna	**169**	30 45N	85 15W
Maribor	**52**	46 36N	15 40 E
Maricourt	**146**	61 30N	72 0W
Marie-Galante	**180**	15 56N	61 16W
Marienberg	**41**	52 30N	6 35 E
Marietta, Ga., U.S.A.	**169**	34 0N	84 30W
Marietta, Ohio, U.S.A.	**164**	39 27N	81 27W
Marília	**188**	22 13S	50 0W
Marín	**50**	42 23N	8 42W
Marinette	**167**	45 4N	87 40W

Maringá	**191**	23 26S	52	2W
Marion, Ill., U.S.A.	**166**	37 45N	88	55W
Marion, Ind., U.S.A.	**167**	40 35N	85	40W
Marion, Ohio, U.S.A.	**167**	40 38N	83	8W
Marken	**40**	52 26N	5	12 E
Market Drayton	**28**	52 55N	2	30W
Market Harborough	**25**	52 29N	0	55W
Market Rasen	**29**	53 24N	0	20W
Markham Mt.	**15**	83 0S	164	0 E
Marlborough	**24**	51 26N	1	44W
Marlborough □	**123**	41 45S	173	33 E
Marlborough Downs	**24**	51 25N	1	55W
Marlin	**168**	31 25N	96	50W
Marmagao	**91**	15 25N	73	56 E
Marmara, Sea of = Marmara				
Denizi	**80**	40 45N	28	15 E
Marmara Denizi	**80**	40 45N	28	15 E
Marmaris	**80**	36 50N	28	14 E
Marne ⭢	**39**	8 23N	18	36 E
Maroochydore	**116**	26 29S	153	5 E
Marquesas Is.	**123**	9 30S	140	0W
Marquette	**150**	46 30N	87	21W
Marrakech	**126**	31 9N	8	0W
Marree	**118**	29 39S	138	1 E
Marsabit	**133**	2 18N	38	0 E
Marseille	**37**	43 18N	5	23 E
Marseilles = Marseille	**37**	43 18N	5	23 E
Marshall, Minn., U.S.A.	**166**	44 25N	95	45W
Marshall, Mo., U.S.A.	**166**	39 8N	93	15W
Marshall, Tex., U.S.A.	**168**	32 29N	94	20W
Marshalltown	**166**	42 5N	92	56W
Marshfield	**166**	44 42N	90	10W
Martaban, G. of	**93**	16 5N	96	30 E
Martha's Vineyard	**164**	41 25N	70	35W
Martigues	**37**	43 24N	5	4 E
Martinique	**180**	14 40N	61	0W
Martinsburg	**164**	39 30N	77	57W
Martinsville, Ind., U.S.A.	**167**	39 29N	86	23W
Martinsville, Va., U.S.A.	**165**	36 41N	79	52W
Marton	**122**	40 4S	175	23 E
Marugame	**109**	34 15N	133	40 E
Maruoka	**106**	36 9N	136	16 E
Marwar	**91**	25 43N	73	45 E
Mary	**70**	37 40N	61	50 E
Maryborough = Port Laoise	**35**	53 2N	7	20W
Maryborough, Queens.,				
Australia	**116**	25 31S	152	37 E
Maryborough, Vic., Australia	**117**	37 0S	143	44 E
Maryland □	**164**	39 10N	76	40W
Maryport	**28**	54 43N	3	30W
Marysville	**172**	39 14N	121	40W
Maryville	**165**	35 50N	84	0W
Marzūq	**127**	25 53N	13	57 E
Masan	**98**	35 11N	128	32 E
Masaya	**179**	12 0N	86	7W
Masbate, I.	**112**	12 21N	123	36 E
Mascota	**175**	20 32N	104	49W
Maseru	**137**	29 18S	27	30 E
Mashhad	**86**	36 20N	59	35 E
Masisea	**186**	8 35S	74	22W
Masjed Soleyman	**84**	31 55N	49	18 E
Mask, L.	**34**	53 36N	9	24W
Mason City	**166**	43 9N	93	12W
Masqat	**83**	23 37N	58	36 E
Massachusetts □	**164**	42 25N	72	0W
Massawa = Mitsiwa	**132**	15 35N	39	25 E
Massena	**151**	44 52N	74	55W
Massif Central	**37**	45 30N	2	21 E
Massillon	**167**	40 47N	81	30W
Mastanli = Momchilgrad	**53**	41 33N	25	23 E
Masterton	**123**	40 56S	175	39 E
Mastūrah	**82**	23 7N	38	52 E
Masuda	**108**	34 40N	131	51 E
Matachewan	**151**	47 56N	80	39W
Matadi	**134**	5 52S	13	31 E
Matagalpa	**179**	13 0N	85	58W
Matamoros, Coahuila, Mexico	**174**	25 32N	103	15W
Matamoros, Puebla, Mexico	**177**	18 2N	98	17W
Matane	**148**	48 50N	67	33W
Matanzas	**178**	23 0N	81	40W
Matapan, C. = Taínaron, Ákra	**54**	36 22N	22	27 E
Matarani	**186**	77 0S	72	10W
Matehuala	**177**	23 39N	100	39W
Mathura	**89**	27 30N	77	40 E
Matlock	**28**	53 8N	1	32W
Mato Grosso □	**188**	14 0S	55	0W
Mato Grosso, Planalto do	**188**	15 0S	59	57W
Matopo Hills	**137**	20 36S	28	20 E
Matrah	**83**	23 37N	58	30 E
Matsubara	**106**	34 33N	135	34 E
Matsudo	**107**	35 47N	139	54 E
Matsue	**109**	35 25N	133	10 E
Matsumoto	**107**	36 15N	138	0 E
Matsusaka	**106**	34 34N	136	32 E
Matsutō	**106**	36 31N	136	34 E
Matsuura	**108**	33 20N	129	49 E
Matsuyama	**109**	33 45N	132	45 E
Mattancheri	**90**	9 50N	76	15 E
Mattawa	**151**	46 20N	78	45W
Matterhorn	**44**	45 58N	7	39 E
Matucana	**186**	11 55S	76	25W
Maturín	**185**	9 45N	63	11W
Mau Ranipur	**91**	25 16N	79	8 E
Maubeuge	**38**	50 17N	3	57 E
Maudin Sun	**93**	16 0N	94	30 E
Maui	**160**	20 45N	156	20 E
Maulamyaing	**93**	16 30N	97	40 E
Mauna Kea	**160**	19 50N	155	28W
Mauna Loa	**160**	21 8N	157	10W
Maungmagan Kyunzu	**94**	14 0N	97	48 E
Mauritania ■	**126**	20 50N	10	0W
Mauritius ■	**9**	20 0S	57	0 E
Mawlaik	**93**	23 40N	94	26 E
May Pen	**180**	17 58N	77	15W
Maya ⭢	**75**	54 31N	134	41 E
Mayagüez	**180**	18 12N	67	9W
Mayerthorpe	**155**	53 57N	115	8W
Mayfield	**169**	36 45N	88	40W
Maykop	**70**	44 35N	40	25 E
Maynooth	**34**	53 22N	6	38W
Mayo	**144**	63 38N	135	57W
Mayo □	**34**	53 47N	9	7W
Mayor I.	**122**	37 16S	176	17 E
Maysville	**167**	38 39N	83	46W
Mazagán = El Jadida	**126**	33 11N	8	17W
Mazán	**186**	3 30S	73	0W
Mazar-e Sharīf	**87**	36 41N	67	0 E
Mazarredo	**192**	47 10S	66	50W
Mazatenango	**177**	14 35N	91	30W
Mazatlán	**175**	23 13N	106	25W
Mbandaka	**134**	0 1N	18	18 E
Mdina	**49**	35 51N	14	25 E
Mead, L.	**173**	36 11N	114	44W
Meadville	**164**	41 39N	80	9W
Meander River	**145**	59 2N	117	42W
Meath □	**34**	53 32N	6	40W
Meaux	**39**	48 58N	2	50 E
Mecca = Makkah	**82**	21 30N	39	54 E
Mechelen	**42**	51 2N	4	29 E
Mecklenburger Bucht	**42**	54 20N	11	40 E
Medan	**111**	3 40N	98	38 E
Medellín	**184**	6 15N	75	35W
Medford	**171**	42 20N	122	52W
Mediaş	**57**	46 9N	24	22 E
Medicine Hat	**152**	50 0N	110	45W
Medina = Al Madīnah	**82**	24 35N	39	52 E
Medina	**167**	41 9N	81	50W
Medina del Campo	**50**	41 18N	4	55W
Mediterranean Sea	**124**	35 0N	15	0 E
Medley	**152**	54 25N	110	16W
Médoc	**36**	45 10N	0	56W
Medvezhi, Ostrava	**73**	71 0N	161	0 E
Medway ⭢	**25**	51 28N	0	45 E
Meekatharra	**120**	26 32S	118	29 E
Meerut	**89**	29 1N	77	42 E
Mega	**133**	3 57N	38	19 E
Mégantic, L.	**148**	45 32N	70	53W
Mégara	**55**	37 58N	23	22 E
Meghalaya □	**93**	25 50N	91	0 E
Mei Xian	**99**	24 16N	116	6 E
Meknès	**126**	33 57N	5	33W
Mekong ⭢	**95**	9 30N	106	15 E

Melaka	**96**	2 15N	102	15 E
Melaka □	**96**	2 15N	102	15 E
Melanesia	**122**	4 0S	155	0 E
Melbourne	**117**	37 50S	145	0 E
Melchor Muzquiz	**174**	27 53N	101	31W
Melfort	**152**	52 50N	104	37W
Melilla	**126**	35 21N	2	57W
Melitopol	**68**	46 50N	35	22 E
Melo	**191**	32 20S	54	10W
Melrose	**31**	53 35N	2	44W
Melton Mowbray	**29**	52 46N	0	52W
Melun	**39**	48 32N	2	39 E
Melville	**152**	50 55N	102	50W
Melville, L.	**147**	53 30N	60	0W
Melville I., Australia	**114**	11 30S	131	0 E
Melville I., Canada	**12**	75 30N	112	0W
Melville Pen.	**146**	68 0N	84	0W
Memel = Klaipeda	**68**	55 43N	21	10 E
Memphis	**169**	35 7N	90	0W
Menai Strait	**26**	53 14N	4	10W
Ménaka	**131**	15 59N	2	18 E
Menan = Chao Phraya →	**94**	13 32N	100	36 E
Menasha	**167**	44 13N	88	27W
Mende	**37**	44 31N	3	30 E
Mendip Hills	**27**	51 17N	2	40W
Mendocino	**172**	39 26N	123	50W
Mendoza	**190**	32 50S	68	52W
Menindee	**118**	32 20S	142	25 E
Menindee, L.	**118**	32 20S	142	25 E
Menominee	**150**	45 9N	87	39W
Menorca	**51**	40 0N	4	0 E
Mentawai, Kepulauan	**111**	2 0S	99	0 E
Menzies	**120**	29 40S	120	58 E
Meppel	**41**	52 42N	6	12 E
Merbein	**119**	34 10S	142	2 E
Merca	**133**	1 48N	44	50 E
Merced	**172**	37 18N	120	30W
Mercedes, Buenos Aires, Argentina	**190**	34 40S	59	30W
Mercedes, Corrientes, Argentina	**191**	29 10S	58	5W
Mercedes, San Luis, Argentina	**190**	33 40S	65	21W
Mercedes, Uruguay	**191**	33 12S	58	0W
Mere	**24**	51 5N	2	16W
Mergui Arch. = Myeik Kyunzu	**94**	11 30N	97	30 E
Mérida, Mexico	**177**	20 58N	89	37W
Mérida, Spain	**50**	38 55N	6	25W
Mérida, Venezuela	**184**	8 24N	71	8W
Mérida, Cord. de	**182**	9 0N	71	0W
Meriden	**164**	41 33N	72	47W
Meridian	**169**	32 20N	88	42W
Merowe	**129**	18 29N	31	46 E
Merredin	**120**	31 28S	118	18 E
Merrill	**156**	45 11N	89	41W
Merritt	**155**	50 10N	120	45W
Merriwa	**116**	32 6S	150	22 E
Mersey →	**28**	53 20N	2	56W
Merseyside □	**28**	53 25N	2	55W
Mersin	**80**	36 51N	34	36 E
Merthyr Tydfil	**27**	51 45N	3	23W
Méru	**39**	49 13N	2	8 E
Merville	**38**	50 38N	2	38 E
Mesa	**160**	33 20N	111	56W
Mesa, La	**173**	32 48N	117	5W
Meshed = Mashhad	**86**	36 20N	59	35 E
Mesolóngion	**54**	38 21N	21	28 E
Mesopotamia = Al Jazirah	**81**	33 30N	44	0 E
Mesquite	**173**	36 47N	114	6W
Messina, Italy	**49**	38 10N	15	32 E
Messina, S. Africa	**137**	22 20S	30	0 E
Messina, Str. di	**49**	38 5N	15	35 E
Messíni	**54**	37 4N	22	1 E
Meta →	**184**	6 12N	67	28W
Metairie	**169**	29 59N	90	9W
Metán	**190**	25 30S	65	0W
Metropolis	**169**	37 10N	88	47W
Metz	**37**	49 8N	6	10 E
Meuse →	**42**	50 45N	5	41 E
Mexia	**168**	31 38N	96	32W
Mexicali	**174**	32 40N	115	29W
México, Mexico	**177**	19 20N	99	10W
México, U.S.A.	**166**	39 10N	91	55W
México □	**177**	19 20N	99	30W
Mexico ■	**174**	20 0N	100	0W
Mexico, G. of	**138**	25 0N	90	0W
Mezen →	**69**	66 11N	43	59 E
Mhow	**91**	22 33N	75	50 E
Miahuatlán	**177**	16 21N	96	36W
Miami	**170**	25 45N	80	15W
Miami Beach	**170**	25 49N	80	6W
Miāneh	**81**	37 30N	47	40 E
Mianwali	**89**	32 38N	71	28 E
Miaoli	**99**	24 37N	120	49 E
Miass	**69**	54 59N	60	6 E
Michigan □	**167**	44 40N	85	40W
Michigan, L.	**150**	44 0N	87	0W
Michigan City	**167**	41 42N	86	56W
Michikamau L.	**147**	54 20N	63	10W
Michipicoten	**150**	47 55N	84	55W
Michoacán □	**175**	19 10N	101	50W
Michurinsk	**68**	52 58N	40	27 E
Micronesia	**122**	11 0N	160	0 E
Mid Glamorgan □	**27**	51 40N	3	25W
Middelburg	**40**	51 30N	3	36 E
Middle Andaman I.	**94**	12 30N	92	30 E
Middlesboro	**165**	36 36N	83	43W
Middlesbrough	**29**	54 35N	1	14W
Middleton	**148**	44 57N	65	4W
Middletown, Conn., U.S.A.	**164**	41 37N	72	40W
Middletown, N.Y., U.S.A.	**164**	41 28N	74	28W
Middletown, Ohio, U.S.A.	**167**	39 29N	84	25W
Midland, Canada	**151**	44 45N	79	50W
Midland, Mich., U.S.A.	**167**	43 37N	84	17W
Midland, Tex., U.S.A.	**161**	32 0N	102	3W
Międzyrzec Podlaski	**58**	51 58N	22	45 E
Miercurea Ciuc	**57**	46 21N	25	48 E
Mieres	**50**	43 18N	5	48W
Migennes	**39**	47 58N	3	31 E
Mihara	**109**	34 24N	133	5 E
Miki	**109**	34 48N	134	59 E
Míkonos	**55**	37 30N	25	25 E
Mikuni-Tōge	**107**	36 50N	138	50 E
Mikura-Jima	**107**	33 52N	139	36 E
Milagro	**184**	2 11S	79	36W
Milan = Milano	**46**	45 28N	9	10 E
Milano	**46**	45 28N	9	10 E
Milås	**80**	37 20N	27	50 E
Mildura	**119**	34 13S	142	9 E
Miles	**116**	26 40S	150	9 E
Miles City	**163**	46 24N	105	50W
Milford	**164**	38 52N	75	27W
Milford Haven	**27**	51 43N	5	2W
Milk →	**163**	48 5N	106	15W
Millau	**37**	44 8N	3	4 E
Millicent	**119**	37 34S	140	21 E
Millinocket	**148**	45 45N	68	45W
Millmerran	**116**	27 53S	151	16 E
Millom	**28**	54 13N	3	16W
Millville	**164**	39 22N	75	0W
Milne Inlet	**146**	72 30N	80	0W
Mílos	**55**	36 44N	24	25 E
Milton Keynes	**25**	52 3N	0	42W
Milwaukee	**167**	43 9N	87	58W
Milwaukie	**171**	45 27N	122	39W
Minamata	**108**	32 10N	130	30 E
Minas	**191**	34 20S	55	10W
Minas Gerais □	**188**	18 50S	46	0W
Minatitlán	**177**	17 59N	94	31W
Mindanao	**112**	8 0N	125	0 E
Mindanao Sea = Bohol Sea	**112**	9 0N	124	0 E
Minden	**168**	32 40N	93	20W
Mindoro	**112**	13 0N	121	0 E
Mindoro Strait	**112**	12 30N	120	30 E
Mine	**108**	34 12N	131	7 E
Minehead	**27**	51 12N	3	29W
Mineral Wells	**161**	32 50N	98	5W
Mingan	**148**	50 20N	64	0W
Mingenew	**120**	29 12S	115	21 E
Minho □	**50**	41 25N	8	20W
Minneapolis	**166**	44 58N	93	20W
Minnedosa	**153**	50 14N	99	50W

Minnesota □	**156**	46 40N	94 0W
Mino	**106**	35 32N	136 55 E
Mino-Kamo	**106**	35 23N	137 2 E
Mino-Mikawa-Kōgen	**106**	35 10N	137 23 E
Minorca = Menorca	**51**	40 0N	4 0 E
Minot	**163**	48 10N	101 15W
Minsk	**68**	53 52N	27 30 E
Mintaka Pass	**89**	37 0N	74 58 E
Miquelon, I.	**149**	47 2N	56 20W
Miraj	**91**	16 50N	74 45 E
Miranda do Douro	**50**	41 30N	6 16W
Mirpur Khas	**88**	25 30N	69 0 E
Mirzapur	**92**	25 10N	82 34 E
Mirzapur-cum-Vindhyachal = Mirzapur	**92**	25 10N	82 34 E
Miscou I.	**148**	47 57N	64 31W
Mishawaka	**167**	41 40N	86 8W
Mishima	**107**	35 10N	138 52 E
Miskitos, Cayos	**179**	14 26N	82 50W
Miskolc	**59**	48 7N	20 50 E
Misool	**113**	1 52S	130 10 E
Misrātah	**127**	32 24N	15 3 E
Mission City	**154**	49 10N	122 15W
Mississippi □	**169**	33 0N	90 0W
Mississippi →	**169**	29 0N	89 15W
Mississippi, Delta of the	**169**	29 15N	90 30W
Missoula	**162**	46 52N	114 0W
Missouri □	**166**	38 25N	92 30W
Missouri →	**166**	38 50N	90 8W
Mistassini L.	**151**	51 0N	73 30W
Mitaka	**107**	35 40N	139 33 E
Mitchell, Australia	**116**	26 29S	147 58 E
Mitchell, U.S.A.	**163**	43 40N	98 0W
Mitchell →	**115**	15 12S	141 35 E
Mitilíni	**55**	39 6N	26 35 E
Mito	**107**	36 20N	140 30 E
Mitsiwa	**132**	15 35N	39 25 E
Mitsukaidō	**107**	36 1N	139 59 E
Mittagong	**117**	34 28S	150 29 E
Mitú	**184**	1 8N	70 3W
Miura	**107**	35 12N	139 40 E
Miyake-Jima	**107**	34 0N	139 30 E
Miyako	**103**	39 40N	141 59 E
Miyakonojō	**108**	31 40N	131 5 E
Miyanojō	**108**	31 54N	130 27 E
Miyazaki	**108**	31 56N	131 30 E
Miyazu	**106**	35 35N	135 10 E
Miyoshi	**109**	34 48N	132 51 E
Mizamis = Ozamis	**112**	8 15N	123 50 E
Mizen Hd.	**35**	51 27N	9 50W
Mizoram □	**93**	23 30N	92 40 E
Mizunami	**106**	35 22N	137 15 E
Mława	**58**	53 9N	20 25 E
Mobara	**107**	35 25N	140 18 E
Moberley	**166**	39 25N	92 25W
Mobile	**169**	30 41N	88 3W
Mobutu Sese Seko, L.	**132**	1 30N	31 0 E
Moçâmedes = Namibe	**134**	15 7S	12 11 E
Moctezuma, R. →	**177**	21 59N	98 34W
Módena	**46**	44 39N	10 55 E
Modesto	**172**	37 43N	121 0W
Moe	**117**	38 12S	146 19 E
Moei →	**94**	17 25N	98 10 E
Moengo	**185**	5 45N	54 20W
Moffat	**31**	55 20N	3 27W
Mogadishu = Muqdisho	**133**	2 2N	45 25 E
Mogador = Essaouira	**126**	31 32N	9 42W
Mogami →	**103**	38 45N	140 0 E
Mogi das Cruzes	**191**	23 31S	46 11W
Mogilev	**68**	53 55N	30 18 E
Mointy	**71**	47 10N	73 18 E
Moisie	**148**	50 12N	66 1W
Mojave Desert	**173**	35 0N	116 30W
Mold	**26**	53 10N	3 10W
Moldavian S.S.R. □	**68**	47 0N	28 0 E
Molde	**65**	62 45N	7 9 E
Molfetta	**49**	41 12N	16 35 E
Moline	**166**	41 30N	90 30W
Molise □	**49**	41 45N	14 30 E
Mollendo	**187**	17 0S	72 0W
Mölndal	**60**	57 40N	12 3 E
Molong	**117**	33 5S	148 54 E
Molopo →	**136**	28 30S	20 13 E
Molotov = Perm	**69**	58 0N	57 10 E
Molucca Sea	**113**	4 0S	124 0 E
Moluccas = Maluku	**113**	1 0S	127 0 E
Mombasa	**135**	4 2S	39 43 E
Mombetsu	**103**	42 27N	142 4 E
Momchilgrad	**53**	41 33N	25 23 E
Mompós	**184**	9 14N	74 26W
Møn	**61**	54 57N	12 15 E
Mona, Canal de la	**180**	18 30N	67 45W
Monach Is.	**32**	57 32N	7 40W
Monaco ■	**37**	43 46N	7 23 E
Monaghan	**34**	54 15N	6 58W
Monaghan □	**34**	54 10N	7 0W
Monastir = Bitola	**52**	41 5N	21 10 E
Mönchengladbach	**42**	51 12N	6 23 E
Monchique	**50**	37 19N	8 38W
Monclova	**174**	26 50N	101 30W
Moncton	**148**	46 7N	64 51W
Monessen	**164**	40 9N	79 50W
Monforte	**50**	39 6N	7 25W
Mongalla	**129**	5 8N	31 42 E
Monghyr = Munger	**92**	25 23N	86 30 E
Mongolia ■	**98**	47 0N	103 0 E
Monmouth, U.K.	**26**	51 48N	2 43W
Monmouth, U.S.A.	**166**	40 50N	90 40W
Monroe, La., U.S.A.	**168**	32 32N	92 4W
Monroe, Mich., U.S.A.	**167**	41 55N	83 26W
Monroe, N.C., U.S.A.	**165**	35 2N	80 37W
Monrovia, Liberia	**130**	6 18N	10 47W
Monrovia, U.S.A.	**173**	34 7N	118 1W
Mons	**42**	50 27N	3 58 E
Mont-de-Marsan	**36**	43 54N	0 31W
Mont Laurier	**151**	46 35N	75 30W
Montague	**172**	41 47N	122 30W
Montana □	**163**	47 0N	110 0W
Montargis	**39**	48 0N	2 43 E
Montauban	**36**	44 0N	1 21 E
Montbéliard	**37**	47 31N	6 48 E
Montceau-les-Mines	**37**	46 40N	4 23 E
Montdidier	**38**	49 38N	2 35 E
Monte-Carlo	**37**	43 46N	7 23 E
Monte Caseros	**191**	30 10S	57 50W
Montego Bay	**180**	18 30N	78 0W
Montélimar	**37**	44 33N	4 45 E
Montemorelos	**176**	25 11N	99 42W
Montenegro = Crna Gora □	**52**	42 40N	19 20 E
Monterey	**173**	36 35N	121 57W
Montería	**184**	8 46N	75 53W
Monterrey	**176**	25 40N	100 30W
Montes Claros	**188**	16 30S	43 50W
Montevideo, Uruguay	**191**	34 50S	56 11W
Montevideo, U.S.A.	**166**	44 55N	95 40W
Montgomery = Sahiwal	**89**	30 45N	73 8 E
Montgomery, U.K.	**26**	52 34N	3 9W
Montgomery, U.S.A.	**169**	32 20N	86 20W
Montluçon	**37**	46 22N	2 36 E
Montmagny	**148**	46 58N	70 34W
Montmorency	**148**	46 53N	71 11W
Montpelier, Idaho, U.S.A.	**163**	42 15N	111 20W
Montpelier, Vt., U.S.A.	**151**	44 15N	72 38W
Montpellier	**37**	43 37N	3 52 E
Montréal	**151**	45 31N	73 34W
Montrose, U.K.	**33**	56 43N	2 28W
Montrose, U.S.A.	**163**	38 30N	107 52W
Montserrat	**180**	16 40N	62 10W
Monywa	**93**	22 7N	95 11 E
Monze, C.	**88**	24 47N	66 37 E
Mo'oka	**107**	36 26N	140 1 E
Moonta	**119**	34 6S	137 32 E
Moora	**120**	30 37S	115 58 E
Moorfoot Hills	**31**	55 44N	3 8W
Moorhead	**156**	46 51N	96 44W
Mooroopna	**117**	36 25S	145 22 E
Moose Jaw	**152**	50 24N	105 30W
Moosehead L.	**148**	45 34N	69 40W
Moosomin	**152**	50 9N	101 40W
Moosonee	**140**	51 17N	80 39W
Mopti	**130**	14 30N	4 0W
Moradabad	**89**	28 50N	78 50 E

Moranbah	**121** 22	1 S	148	6 E
Moratuwa	**90** 6	45N	79	55 E
Morava →	**59** 48	10N	16	59 E
Moravian Hts. =				
Ceskomoravská Vrchovina	**59** 49	30N	15	40 E
Morawa	**120** 29	13S	116	0 E
Morawhanna	**185** 8	30N	59	40W
Moray Firth	**33** 57	50N	3	30W
Morden	**153** 49	15N	98	10W
Mordovian A.S.S.R.□	**68** 54	20N	44	30 E
Møre og Romsdal fylke □	**65** 62	30N	8	0 E
Morecambe	**28** 54	5N	2	52W
Morecambe B.	**28** 54	7N	3	0W
Moree	**116** 29	28S	149	54 E
Morehead City	**165** 34	46N	76	44W
Morelia	**175** 19	42N	101	7W
Morelos □	**177** 18	45N	99	0W
Morena, Sierra	**50** 38	20N	4	0W
Moresby I.	**154** 52	30N	131	40W
Morgan City	**168** 29	40N	91	15W
Morganton	**165** 35	46N	81	48W
Morgantown	**164** 39	39N	79	58W
Moriguchi	**106** 34	44N	135	34 E
Morlaix	**36** 48	36N	3	52W
Mornington	**117** 38	15S	145	5 E
Moro G.	**112** 6	30N	123	0 E
Morocco ■	**126** 32	0N	5	50W
Moroleón	**177** 20	8N	101	12W
Morón	**178** 22	8N	78	39W
Morotai	**113** 2	10N	128	30 E
Morrilton	**168** 35	10N	92	45W
Morrinhos	**188** 17	45S	49	10W
Morris	**153** 49	25N	97	22W
Morristown	**165** 36	18N	83	20W
Mortes, R. das →	**188** 11	45S	50	44W
Mortlake	**119** 38	5S	142	50 E
Moruya	**117** 35	58S	150	3 E
Morvern	**30** 56	38N	5	44W
Morwell	**117** 38	10S	146	22 E
Moscos Is.	**94** 14	0N	97	30 E
Moscow = Moskva	**68** 55	45N	37	35 E
Moscow	**171** 46	45N	116	59W
Mosel →	**42** 50	22N	7	36 E
Moselle = Mosel →	**42** 50	22N	7	36 E
Mosgiel	**123** 45	53S	170	21 E
Mosjøen	**65** 65	51N	13	12 E
Moskva	**68** 55	45N	37	35 E
Mosquera	**184** 2	35N	78	24W
Mosquitos, Golfo de los	**179** 9	15N	81	10W
Moss Vale	**117** 34	32S	150	25 E
Mosselbaai	**136** 34	11S	22	8 E
Mossman	**121** 16	21S	145	15 E
Mossoró	**189** 5	10S	37	15W
Mostaganem	**127** 35	54N	0	5 E
Mostar	**52** 43	22N	17	50 E
Mosul = Al Mawşil	**81** 36	15N	43	5 E
Motala	**60** 58	32N	15	1 E
Motherwell	**31** 55	48N	4	0W
Motihari	**92** 26	30N	84	55 E
Motueka	**123** 41	7S	173	1 E
Motul	**177** 21	6N	89	17W
Moúdhros	**55** 39	50N	25	18 E
Moule	**180** 16	20N	61	22W
Moulins	**37** 46	35N	3	19 E
Moultrie	**170** 31	11N	83	47W
Moundsville	**164** 39	53N	80	43W
Mount Airy	**165** 36	31N	80	37W
Mount Barker, S. Austral., Australia	**119** 35	5S	138	52 E
Mount Barker, W. Austral., Australia	**120** 34	38S	117	40 E
Mount Carmel	**167** 38	20N	87	48W
Mount Forest	**151** 43	59N	80	43W
Mount Gambier	**119** 37	50S	140	46 E
Mount Isa	**115** 20	42S	139	26 E
Mount Lofty Ra.	**119** 34	35S	139	5 E
Mount Magnet	**120** 28	2S	117	47 E
Mount Maunganui	**122** 37	40S	176	14 E
Mount Morgan	**121** 23	40S	150	25 E
Mount Pearl	**149** 47	31N	52	47W
Mount Pleasant, Mich., U.S.A.	**167** 43	35N	84	47W
Mount Pleasant, Tex., U.S.A.	**168** 33	5N	95	0W
Mount Sterling	**165** 38	0N	84	0W
Mount Vernon, Ill., U.S.A.	**166** 38	17N	88	57W
Mount Vernon, N.Y., U.S.A.	**164** 40	57N	73	49W
Mount Vernon, Wash., U.S.A.	**171** 48	25N	122	20W
Mount Whaleback	**114** 23	18S	119	44 E
Mountain City	**172** 41	54N	116	0W
Mountain View	**172** 37	26N	122	5W
Moura, Australia	**121** 24	35S	149	58 E
Moura, Brazil	**185** 1	32S	61	38W
Mourne →	**34** 54	45N	7	39W
Mourne Mts.	**34** 54	10N	6	0W
Moyale	**133** 3	30N	39	0 E
Mozambique ■	**137** 19	0S	35	0 E
Mozambique Chan.	**137** 20	0S	39	0 E
Mu Us Shamo	**98** 39	0N	109	0 E
Muaná	**188** 1	25S	49	15W
Muang Chiang Rai	**94** 19	52N	99	50 E
Muck	**32** 56	50N	6	15W
Mucuri	**189** 18	0S	39	36W
Mudanjiang	**98** 44	38N	129	30 E
Mudgee	**117** 32	32S	149	31 E
Muğla	**80** 37	15N	28	22 E
Mukden = Shenyang	**98** 41	50N	123	25 E
Mukhtuya = Lensk	**74** 60	48N	114	55 E
Mukinbudin	**120** 30	55S	118	5 E
Muktsar	**89** 30	30N	74	30 E
Mulchén	**190** 37	45S	72	20W
Mulgrave	**149** 45	38N	61	31W
Mulhacén	**50** 37	4N	3	20W
Mülheim	**42** 51	26N	6	53 E
Mulhouse	**37** 47	40N	7	20 E
Mull	**30** 56	27N	6	0W
Muller, Pegunungan	**111** 0	30N	113	30 E
Mullet Pen.	**34** 54	10N	10	2W
Mullewa	**120** 28	29S	115	30 E
Mullingar	**34** 53	31N	7	20W
Mullumbimby	**116** 28	30S	153	30 E
Multan	**89** 30	15N	71	36 E
Muna	**113** 5	0S	122	30 E
München	**43** 48	8N	11	33 E
Munchen-Gladbach = Mönchengladbach	**42** 51	12N	6	23 E
Muncie	**167** 40	10N	85	20W
Mundo Novo	**189** 11	50S	40	29W
Mungana	**121** 17	8S	144	27 E
Munger	**92** 25	23N	86	30 E
Munich = München	**43** 48	8N	11	33 E
Munising	**150** 46	25N	86	39W
Munku-Sardyk	**74** 51	45N	100	20 E
Münster	**42** 51	58N	7	37 E
Munster □	**35** 52	20N	8	40W
Muqdisho	**133** 2	2N	45	25 E
Murallón, Cuerro	**192** 49	48S	73	30W
Murchison →	**120** 27	45S	114	0 E
Murchison Falls = Kabarega Falls	**132** 2	15N	31	30 E
Murcia	**51** 38	20N	1	10W
Murcia □	**51** 37	50N	1	30W
Mureş →	**56** 46	15N	20	13 E
Mureşul = Mureş →	**56** 46	15N	20	13 E
Murfreesboro	**169** 35	50N	86	21W
Murgon	**116** 26	15S	151	54 E
Müritz See	**43** 53	25N	12	40 E
Murmansk	**69** 68	57N	33	10 E
Muroran	**103** 42	25N	141	0 E
Muroto	**109** 33	18N	134	9 E
Muroto-Misaki	**109** 33	15N	134	10 E
Murphysboro	**166** 37	50N	89	20W
Murray	**169** 36	40N	88	20W
Murray →	**119** 35	20S	139	22 E
Murray Bridge	**119** 35	6S	139	14 E
Murrumbidgee →	**117** 34	43S	143	12 E
Murrurundi	**116** 31	42S	150	51 E
Murtoa	**119** 36	35S	142	28 E
Murupara	**122** 38	28S	176	42 E
Murwillumbah	**116** 28	18S	153	27 E
Muş	**81** 38	45N	41	30 E
Musashino	**107** 35	42N	139	34 E
Muscat = Masqaţ	**83** 23	37N	58	36 E
Muscat & Oman = Oman ■	**83** 23	0N	58	0 E

Muscatine	**166**	41 25N	91	5W
Musgrave Ras.	**114**	26 0S	132	0 E
Musi ⟶	**111**	2 20S	104	56 E
Muskegon	**167**	43 15N	86	17W
Muskegon ⟶	**167**	43 25N	86	0W
Muskegon Hts.	**167**	43 12N	86	17W
Muskogee	**168**	35 50N	95	25W
Musselburgh	**31**	55 57N	3	3W
Muswellbrook	**116**	32 16S	150	56 E
Mutare	**137**	18 58S	32	38 E
Mutsu	**103**	41 5N	140	55 E
Mutsu-Wan	**103**	41 5N	140	55 E
Muzaffargarh	**89**	30 5N	71	14 E
Muzaffarnagar	**89**	29 26N	77	40 E
Muzaffarpur	**92**	26 7N	85	23 E
Mwanza	**135**	2 30S	32	58 E
Mweru, L.	**135**	9 0S	28	40 E
My Tho	**95**	10 29N	106	23 E
Myanaung	**93**	18 18N	95	22 E
Myeik Kyunzu	**94**	11 30N	97	30 E
Myingyan	**93**	21 30N	95	20 E
Myitkyina	**93**	25 24N	97	26 E
Mýrdalsjökull	**64**	63 40N	19	6W
Myrtle Point	**171**	43 0N	124	4W
Mysore	**90**	12 17N	76	41 E
Mysore □ = Karnataka □	**90**	13 15N	77	0 E
Naaldwijk	**40**	51 59N	4	13 E
Nabari	**106**	34 37N	136	5 E
Nablus = Nābulus	**80**	32 14N	35	15 E
Nābulus	**80**	32 14N	35	15 E
Nacogdoches	**168**	31 33N	94	39W
Nacozari	**174**	30 24N	109	39W
Nadiad	**91**	22 41N	72	56 E
Nadym	**69**	65 35N	72	42 E
Nagahama	**106**	35 23N	136	16 E
Nagaland □	**93**	26 0N	94	30 E
Nagano	**107**	36 40N	138	10 E
Nagaoka	**105**	37 27N	138	51 E
Nagappattinam	**90**	10 46N	79	51 E
Nagasaki	**108**	32 47N	129	50 E
Nagato	**108**	34 19N	131	5 E
Nagercoil	**90**	8 12N	77	26 E
Nagornyy	**75**	55 58N	124	57 E
Nagoya	**106**	35 10N	136	50 E
Nagpur	**91**	21 8N	79	10 E
Nahanni Butte	**144**	61 2N	123	31W
Nahāvand	**84**	34 10N	48	22 E
Naicam	**152**	52 30N	104	30W
Nain	**147**	56 34N	61	40W
Nainpur	**91**	22 30N	80	10 E
Nairn	**33**	57 35N	3	54W
Nairobi	**132**	1 17S	36	48 E
Naivasha	**132**	0 40S	36	30 E
Najafābād	**85**	32 40N	51	15 E
Najibabad	**89**	29 40N	78	20 E
Naka ⟶	**107**	36 20N	140	36 E
Naka-no-Shima	**104**	29 51N	129	46 E
Nakama	**108**	33 56N	130	43 E
Nakamura	**109**	33 0N	133	0 E
Nakano	**107**	36 45N	138	22 E
Nakanojō	**107**	36 35N	138	51 E
Nakatsu	**108**	33 34N	131	15 E
Nakatsugawa	**106**	35 29N	137	30 E
Nakhichevan A.S.S.R. □	**70**	39 14N	45	30 E
Nakhodka	**75**	42 53N	132	54 E
Nakhon Phanom	**95**	17 23N	104	43 E
Nakhon Ratchasima	**95**	14 59N	102	12 E
Nakhon Sawan	**94**	15 35N	100	10 E
Nakhon Si Thammarat	**96**	8 29N	100	0 E
Nakina	**140**	50 10N	86	40W
Nakskov	**61**	54 50N	11	8 E
Nakuru	**132**	0 15S	36	4 E
Nalchik	**70**	43 30N	43	33 E
Nalgonda	**91**	17 6N	79	15 E
Nam Co	**101**	30 30N	90	45 E
Nam Dinh	**95**	20 25N	106	5 E
Nam-Phan	**95**	10 30N	106	0 E
Nam Tha	**95**	20 58N	101	30 E

Nam Tok	**94**	14 21N	99	4 E
Namaland	**136**	24 30S	17	0 E
Namangan	**71**	41 0N	71	40 E
Nambour	**116**	26 32S	152	58 E
Nambucca Heads	**116**	30 37S	153	0 E
Namerikawa	**106**	36 46N	137	20 E
Namib Desert = Namib-Woestyn	**124**	22 30S	15	0 E
Namib-Woestyn	**124**	22 30S	15	0 E
Namibe	**134**	15 7S	12	11 E
Namibia ■	**136**	22 0S	18	9 E
Nampa	**171**	43 34N	116	34W
Namsos	**65**	64 29N	11	30 E
Namur	**42**	50 27N	4	52 E
Nanaimo	**154**	49 10N	124	0W
Nanango	**116**	26 40S	152	0 E
Nanao	**105**	37 0N	137	0 E
Nanchang	**99**	28 42N	115	55 E
Nanching = Nanjing	**99**	32 2N	118	47 E
Nanching	**99**	32 3N	118	47 E
Nancy	**37**	48 42N	6	12 E
Nanda Devi	**101**	30 23N	79	59 E
Nandan	**109**	34 10N	134	42 E
Nanded	**91**	19 10N	77	20 E
Nandurbar	**91**	21 20N	74	15 E
Nanga Parbat	**89**	35 10N	74	35 E
Nangarhár □	**87**	34 20N	70	0 E
Nanjing	**99**	32 2N	118	47 E
Nanking = Nanching	**99**	32 3N	118	47 E
Nanking = Nanjing	**99**	32 2N	118	47 E
Nankoku	**109**	33 39N	133	44 E
Nanning	**99**	22 48N	108	20 E
Nanping	**99**	26 38N	118	10 E
Nantes	**36**	47 12N	1	33W
Nanticoke	**164**	41 12N	76	1W
Nanton	**155**	50 21N	113	46W
Nanuque	**189**	17 50S	40	21W
Napa	**172**	38 18N	122	17W
Napier	**122**	39 30S	176	56 E
Naples = Nápoli	**49**	40 50N	14	17 E
Napo ⟶	**186**	3 20S	72	40W
Nápoli	**49**	40 50N	14	17 E
Nara, Japan	**106**	34 40N	135	49 E
Nara, Mali	**130**	15 10N	7	20W
Naracoorte	**119**	36 58S	140	45 E
Narasapur	**92**	16 26N	81	40 E
Narayanganj	**92**	23 40N	90	33 E
Narayanpet	**91**	16 45N	77	30 E
Narbonne	**37**	43 11N	3	0 E
Narita	**107**	35 47N	140	19 E
Narmada ⟶	**91**	21 38N	72	36 E
Narooma	**117**	36 14S	150	4 E
Narrabri	**116**	30 19S	149	46 E
Narrandera	**117**	34 42S	146	31 E
Narrogin	**120**	32 58S	117	14 E
Narromine	**116**	32 12S	148	12 E
Naruto	**109**	34 11N	134	37 E
Narvik	**64**	68 28N	17	26 E
Narym	**71**	59 0N	81	30 E
Naser, Buheirat en	**128**	23 0N	32	30 E
Nashua	**164**	42 50N	71	25W
Nashville	**169**	36 12N	86	46W
Nasik	**91**	19 58N	73	50 E
Nasirabad	**91**	26 15N	74	45 E
Nassau	**178**	25 0N	77	20W
Nasser, L. = Naser, Buheirat en	**128**	23 0N	32	30 E
Nässjö	**60**	57 39N	14	42 E
Natal	**189**	5 47S	35	13W
Natal □	**137**	28 30S	30	30 E
Natashquan	**149**	50 14N	61	46W
Natchez	**168**	31 35N	91	25W
Natchitoches	**168**	31 47N	93	4W
Nathalia	**117**	36 1S	145	13 E
National City	**173**	32 39N	117	7W
Natuna Besar, Kepulauan	**111**	4 0N	108	15 E
Natuna Selatan, Kepulauan	**111**	2 45N	109	0 E
Nauru ■	**122**	1 0S	166	0 E
Nauta	**186**	4 31S	73	35W
Nautanwa	**92**	27 20N	83	25 E
Nautla	**177**	20 20N	96	50W

Navarra □	**51**	42 40N	1	40W
Navojoa	**174**	27 0N	109	30W
Navsari	**91**	20 57N	72	59 E
Nawabshah	**88**	26 15N	68	25 E
Nawalgarh	**89**	27 50N	75	15 E
Náxos	**55**	37 8N	25	25 E
Nãy Band	**87**	27 20N	52	40 E
Nayakhan	**73**	61 56N	159	0 E
Nayarit □	**175**	22 0N	105	0W
Ndélé	**129**	8 25N	20	36 E
Ndjamena	**131**	12 10N	14	59 E
Ndola	**135**	13 0S	28	34 E
Neagh, Lough	**34**	54 35N	6	25W
Near Is.	**142**	53 0N	172	0 E
Neath	**27**	51 39N	3	49W
Nebraska □	**163**	41 30N	100	0W
Nebraska City	**166**	40 40N	95	52W
Nebrodi Mts.	**49**	37 55N	14	45 E
Neches ➤	**168**	29 55N	93	52W
Neckar ➤	**42**	49 31N	8	26 E
Necochea	**190**	38 30S	58	50W
Needles, The	**24**	50 39N	1	35W
Neenah	**167**	44 10N	88	30W
Neepawa	**153**	50 15N	99	30W
Negapatam =				
Nagappattinam	**90**	10 46N	79	51 E
Negeri Sembilan □	**96**	2 45N	102	10 E
Negotin	**53**	44 16N	22	37 E
Negra, Pta.	**186**	6 6S	81	10W
Negro ➤, Argentina	**190**	41 2S	62	47W
Negro ➤, Brazil	**185**	3 0S	60	0W
Negros	**112**	9 30N	122	40 E
Nehbandãn	**85**	31 35N	60	5 E
Nei Monggol Zizhiqu □	**98**	42 0N	112	0 E
Neijiang	**99**	29 35N	104	55 E
Neiva	**184**	2 56N	75	18W
Nellore	**90**	14 27N	79	59 E
Nelson, Canada	**155**	49 30N	117	20W
Nelson, N.Z.	**123**	41 18S	173	16 E
Nelson, U.K.	**28**	53 50N	2	14W
Nelson ➤	**153**	54 33N	98	2W
Néma	**126**	16 40N	7	15W
Neman ➤	**68**	55 25N	21	10 E
Nemours	**39**	48 16N	2	40 E
Nemunas = Neman ➤	**68**	55 25N	21	10 E
Nemuro	**103**	43 20N	145	35 E
Nemuro-Kaikyō	**103**	43 30N	145	30 E
Nenagh	**35**	52 52N	8	11W
Nenana	**142**	64 30N	149	20W
Nene ➤	**29**	52 38N	0	13 E
Neosho	**168**	36 56N	94	28W
Neosho ➤	**168**	35 59N	95	10W
Nepal ■	**92**	28 0N	84	30 E
Nephi	**162**	39 43N	111	52W
Ness, Loch	**33**	57 15N	4	30W
Netanya	**80**	32 20N	34	51 E
Netherlands ■	**41**	52 0N	5	30 E
Netherlands Antilles ■	**181**	12 15N	69	0W
Netherlands Guiana =				
Surinam ■	**185**	4 0N	56	0W
Nettilling L.	**146**	66 30N	71	0W
Netzahualcoyotl, Presa	**177**	17 10N	93	30W
Neuchâtel	**44**	47 0N	6	55 E
Neuchâtel, Lac de	**44**	46 53N	6	50 E
Neuquén	**190**	38 55S	68	0 E
Neuse ➤	**165**	35 5N	76	30W
Neusiedler See	**45**	47 50N	16	47 E
Nevada □	**166**	37 51N	94	22W
Nevada □	**172**	39 20N	117	0W
Nevada, Sierra, Spain	**50**	37 3N	3	15W
Nevada, Sierra, U.S.A.	**172**	39 0N	120	30W
Nevada City	**172**	39 20N	121	0W
Nevada de Sta. Marta, Sa.	**184**	10 55N	73	50W
Nevers	**37**	47 0N	3	9 E
New Albany	**167**	38 20N	85	50W
New Amsterdam	**185**	6 15N	57	36W
New Bedford	**164**	41 40N	70	52W
New Bern	**165**	35 8N	77	3W
New Braunfels	**161**	29 43N	98	9W
New Brighton	**123**	43 29S	172	43 E

New Britain, Papua N. G.	**115**	5 50S	150	20 E
New Britain, U.S.A.	**164**	41 41N	72	47W
New Brunswick	**164**	40 30N	74	28W
New Brunswick □	**148**	46 50N	66	30W
New Caledonia = Nouvelle				
Calédonie	**122**	21 0S	165	0 E
New Castile = Castilla La				
Nueva	**50**	39 45N	3	20W
New Castle, Ind., U.S.A.	**164**	39 55N	85	23W
New Castle, Pa., U.S.A.	**164**	41 0N	80	20W
New England Ra.	**116**	30 20S	151	45 E
New Forest	**24**	50 53N	1	40W
New Glasgow	**149**	45 35N	62	36W
New Hampshire □	**164**	43 40N	71	40W
New Haven	**164**	41 20N	72	54W
New Hebrides = Vanuatu ■	**122**	15 0S	168	0 E
New Iberia	**168**	30 2N	91	54W
New Ireland	**115**	3 20S	151	50 E
New Jersey □	**164**	40 30N	74	10W
New Kensington	**164**	40 36N	79	43W
New London	**164**	41 23N	72	8W
New Mexico □	**161**	34 30N	106	0W
New Norfolk	**119**	42 46S	147	2 E
New Orleans	**169**	30 0N	90	5W
New Philadelphia	**164**	40 29N	81	25W
New Plymouth	**122**	39 4S	174	5 E
New Providence	**178**	25 25N	78	35W
New Radnor	**26**	52 15N	3	10W
New Siberian Is. =				
Novosibirskiye Ostrova	**72**	75 0N	142	0 E
New South Wales □	**116**	33 0S	146	0 E
New Ulm	**166**	44 15N	94	30W
New Waterford	**149**	46 13N	60	4W
New Westminster	**154**	49 13N	122	55W
New York □	**164**	42 40N	76	0W
New York City	**164**	40 45N	74	0W
New Zealand ■	**122**	40 0S	176	0 E
Newark, N.J., U.S.A.	**164**	40 41N	74	12W
Newark, N.Y., U.S.A.	**164**	43 2N	77	10W
Newark, Ohio, U.S.A.	**167**	40 5N	82	24W
Newark-on-Trent	**29**	53 6N	0	48W
Newberry, Mich., U.S.A.	**150**	46 20N	85	32W
Newberry, S.C., U.S.A.	**165**	34 17N	81	37W
Newburgh	**164**	41 30N	74	1W
Newburyport	**164**	42 48N	70	50W
Newcastle, Australia	**117**	33 0S	151	46 E
Newcastle, Canada	**148**	47 1N	65	38W
Newcastle, U.K.	**34**	54 13N	5	54W
Newcastle Emlyn	**26**	52 2N	4	29W
Newcastle-under-Lyme	**28**	53 2N	2	15W
Newcastle-upon-Tyne	**28**	54 59N	1	37W
Newfoundland □	**149**	53 0N	58	0W
Newhaven	**25**	50 47N	0	4 E
Newmarket	**25**	52 15N	0	23 E
Newnan	**170**	33 22N	84	48W
Newport, Gwent, U.K.	**27**	51 35N	3	0W
Newport, I. of W., U.K.	**25**	50 42N	1	18W
Newport, Ark., U.S.A.	**168**	35 38N	91	15W
Newport, Ky., U.S.A.	**167**	39 5N	84	23W
Newport, Oreg., U.S.A.	**171**	44 41N	124	2W
Newport, R.I., U.S.A.	**164**	41 13N	71	19W
Newport, Vt., U.S.A.	**148**	44 57N	72	17W
Newport Beach	**173**	33 40N	117	58W
Newport News	**165**	37 2N	76	30W
Newquay	**27**	50 24N	5	6W
Newry	**34**	54 10N	6	20W
Newton, Iowa, U.S.A.	**166**	41 40N	93	3W
Newton, Mass., U.S.A.	**164**	42 21N	71	10W
Newton Abbot	**27**	50 32N	3	37W
Newton Stewart	**31**	54 57N	4	30W
Newtonmore	**33**	57 4N	4	7W
Newtown	**26**	52 31N	3	19W
Newtownards	**34**	54 37N	5	40W
Ngaoundéré	**131**	7 15N	13	35 E
Ngoring Hu	**101**	34 55N	97	5 E
Nguru	**131**	12 56N	10	29 E
Nha Trang	**95**	12 16N	109	10 E
Nhill	**119**	36 18S	141	40 E
Niagara Falls, Canada	**151**	43 7N	79	5W
Niagara Falls, U.S.A.	**164**	43 5N	79	0W

Name	Page	Lat			Long		
Niamey	**131**	13	27N		2	6	E
Nias	**111**	1	0N		97	30	E
Nicaragua ■	**179**	11	40N		85	30W	
Nicaragua, Lago de	**179**	12	0N		85	30W	
Nice	**37**	43	42N		7	14	E
Nichinan	**108**	31	38N		131	23	E
Nicobar Is.	**8**	9	0N		93	0	E
Nicosia	**80**	35	10N		33	25	E
Nicoya, Pen. de	**179**	9	45N		85	40W	
Nidd →	**28**	54	1N		1	32W	
Niederösterreich □	**45**	48	25N		15	40	E
Niedersachsen □	**42**	52	45N		9	0	E
Nieuw Nickerie	**185**	6	0N		56	59W	
Niger ■	**131**	13	30N		10	0	E
Niger →	**131**	5	33N		6	33	E
Nigeria ■	**131**	8	30N		8	0	E
Nii-Jima	**107**	34	20N		139	15	E
Niigata	**103**	37	58N		139	0	E
Niihama	**109**	33	55N		133	16	E
Niimi	**109**	34	59N		133	28	E
Nijkerk	**41**	52	13N		5	30	E
Nijmegen	**41**	51	50N		5	52	E
Nikki	**131**	9	58N		3	12	E
Nikkō	**107**	36	45N		139	35	E
Nikolayev	**68**	46	58N		32	0	E
Nikolayevsk-na-Amur	**75**	53	8N		140	44	E
Nikolskoye	**73**	55	12N		166	0	E
Nikšić	**52**	42	50N		18	57	E
Nîl, Nahr en →	**128**	30	10N		31	6	E
Nîl el Abyad →	**129**	15	38N		32	31	E
Nîl el Azraq →	**129**	15	38N		32	31	E
Nile = Nîl, Nahr en →	**128**	30	10N		31	6	E
Niles	**164**	41	8N		80	40W	
Nîmes	**37**	43	50N		4	23	E
Nimule	**129**	3	32N		32	3	E
Nīnawá	**81**	36	25N		43	10	E
Nineveh = Nīnawá	**81**	36	25N		43	10	E
Ningbo	**99**	29	51N		121	28	E
Ningde	**99**	26	38N		119	23	E
Ningpo = Ningbo	**99**	29	51N		121	28	E
Ningsia Hui A.R. = Ningxia Huizu Zizhiqu □	**98**	38	0N		106	0	E
Ningxia Huizu Zizhiqu □	**98**	38	0N		106	0	E
Niobrara →	**163**	42	45N		98	0W	
Nioro du Sahel	**130**	15	15N		9	30W	
Niort	**36**	46	19N		0	29W	
Nipawin	**152**	53	20N		104	0W	
Nipigon	**150**	49	0N		88	17W	
Nipigon, L.	**150**	49	50N		88	30W	
Niš	**53**	43	19N		21	58	E
Nişāb	**83**	14	25N		46	29	E
Nishinomiya	**106**	34	45N		135	20	E
Nishio	**106**	34	52N		137	3	E
Nishiwaki	**109**	34	59N		134	58	E
Niterói	**188**	22	52S		43	0W	
Nith →	**31**	55	20N		3	5W	
Nitra	**59**	48	19N		18	4	E
Nivernais	**37**	47	0N		3	40	E
Nizamabad	**91**	18	45N		78	7	E
Nizhne Kolymsk	**73**	68	34N		160	55	E
Nizhneudinsk	**74**	54	54N		99	3	E
Nizhnevartovsk	**69**	60	56N		76	38	E
Nizhniy Novgorod = Gorkiy	**68**	56	20N		44	0	E
Nizhniy Tagil	**69**	57	55N		59	57	E
Nizhnyaya Tunguska →	**74**	64	20N		93	0	E
Nizké Tatry	**59**	48	55N		20	0	E
Nkongsamba	**131**	4	55N		9	55	E
Noatak	**142**	67	32N		162	59W	
Nobeoka	**108**	32	36N		131	41	E
Noda	**107**	35	56N		139	52	E
Nogales	**174**	31	20N		110	56W	
Nōgata	**108**	33	48N		130	44	E
Nogent-le-Rotrou	**39**	48	20N		0	50	E
Noi →	**94**	14	50N		100	15	E
Noirmoutier, Î. de	**36**	46	58N		2	10W	
Nojima-Zaki	**107**	34	54N		139	53	E
Nok Kundi	**88**	28	50N		62	45	E
Nome	**142**	64	30N		165	24W	
Nong Khae	**95**	14	29N		100	53	E
Nong Khai	**95**	17	50N		102	46	E
Nonoava	**174**	27	28N		106	44W	
Noord Brabant □	**40**	51	40N		5	0	E
Noord Holland □	**40**	52	30N		4	45	E
Noordbeveland	**40**	51	35N		3	50	E
Noordoostpolder	**41**	52	45N		5	45	E
Noordwijk aan Zee	**40**	52	14N		4	26	E
Nootka I.	**154**	49	32N		126	42W	
Nord-Trøndelag fylke □	**65**	64	20N		12	0	E
Nordaustlandet	**13**	79	14N		23	0	E
Nordegg	**155**	52	29N		116	5W	
Nordkapp	**67**	71	10N		25	44	E
Nordkinn	**67**	71	8N		27	40	E
Nordland fylke □	**65**	65	40N		13	0	E
Nordrhein-Westfalen □	**42**	51	45N		7	30	E
Nordvik	**72**	74	2N		111	32	E
Nore →	**35**	52	40N		7	20W	
Norfolk	**165**	36	40N		76	15W	
Norfolk □	**29**	52	39N		1	0	E
Norfolk I.	**122**	28	58S		168	3	E
Norilsk	**72**	69	20N		88	6	E
Norman	**168**	35	12N		97	30W	
Norman Wells	**144**	65	17N		126	51W	
Normandie	**39**	48	45N		0	10	E
Normandin	**151**	48	49N		72	31W	
Normandy = Normandie	**39**	48	45N		0	10	E
Normanton	**115**	17	40S		141	10	E
Norquinco	**192**	41	51S		70	55W	
Norristown	**164**	40	9N		75	21W	
Norrköping	**60**	58	37N		16	11	E
Norrland □	**66**	66	50N		18	0	E
Norseman	**114**	32	8S		121	43	E
Norsk	**75**	52	30N		130	0	E
North Andaman I.	**94**	13	15N		92	40	E
North Battleford	**152**	52	50N		108	17W	
North Bay	**151**	46	20N		79	30W	
North Bend	**171**	43	28N		124	14W	
North Berwick	**31**	56	4N		2	44W	
North C.	**122**	34	23S		173	4	E
North Carolina □	**165**	35	30N		80	0W	
North Channel, Br. Is.	**30**	55	0N		5	30W	
North Channel, Canada	**150**	46	0N		83	0W	
North Dakota □	**163**	47	30N		100	0W	
North Downs	**25**	51	17N		0	30	E
North European Plain	**17**	55	0N		20	0	E
North I.	**122**	38	0S		175	0	E
North Korea ■	**98**	40	0N		127	0	E
North Minch	**32**	58	5N		5	55W	
North Ossetian A.S.S.R. □	**70**	43	30N		44	30	E
North Platte	**163**	41	10N		100	50W	
North Platte →	**163**	41	15N		100	45W	
North Pole	**12**	90	0N		0	0	E
North Ronaldsay	**33**	59	20N		2	30W	
North Saskatchewan →	**143**	53	15N		105	5W	
North Sea	**16**	56	0N		4	0	E
North Sentinel I.	**94**	11	35N		92	15	E
North Sporades = Voríai Sporádhes	**55**	39	15N		23	30	E
North Sydney	**149**	46	12N		60	15W	
North Tonawanda	**164**	43	5N		78	50W	
North Uist	**32**	57	40N		7	15W	
North Vancouver	**154**	49	25N		123	3W	
North Walsham	**29**	52	49N		1	22	E
North West Frontier □	**89**	34	0N		71	0	E
North West Highlands	**32**	57	35N		5	2W	
North West River	**147**	53	30N		60	10W	
North West Territories □	**145**	67	0N		110	0W	
North York Moors	**29**	54	25N		0	50W	
North Yorkshire □	**28**	54	15N		1	25W	
Northallerton	**28**	54	20N		1	26W	
Northam	**120**	31	35S		116	42	E
Northam, Australia	**120**	28	27S		114	33	E
Northampton, U.K.	**25**	52	14N		0	54W	
Northampton, U.S.A.	**164**	42	22N		72	31W	
Northampton □	**25**	52	16N		0	55W	
Northcliffe	**120**	34	39S		116	7	E
Northern Circars	**92**	17	30N		82	30	E
Northern Ireland □	**34**	54	45N		7	0W	
Northern Territory □	**114**	16	0S		133	0	E
Northfield	**166**	44	30N		93	10W	
Northland □	**122**	35	30S		173	30	E

Northumberland □ 28 55 12N 2 0W
Northumberland Is. 121 21 30S 149 50 E
Northumberland Str. 148 46 20N 64 0W
Northwich 28 53 16N 2 30W
Norton Sd. 142 64 0N 164 0W
Norwalk 164 41 9N 73 25W
Norway ■ 18 63 0N 11 0 E
Norwegian Sea 16 66 0N 1 0 E
Norwich 29 52 38N 1 17 E
Nos Kaliakra 53 43 21N 28 30 E
Noshiro 103 40 12N 140 0 E
Noss Hd. 33 58 29N 3 4W
Nossob → 136 26 55S 20 37 E
Noteć → 58 52 44N 15 26 E
Notre Dame de Koartac = Koartac 146 60 55N 69 40W
Nottaway → 140 51 22N 78 55W
Nottingham 29 52 57N 1 10W
Nottingham □ 29 53 10N 1 0W
Nouâdhibou 126 20 54N 17 0W
Nouâdhibou, Ras 126 20 50N 17 0W
Nouakchott 126 18 9N 15 58W
Noumea 122 22 17S 166 30 E
Nouveau Comptoir 140 53 0N 78 49W
Nouvelle Calédonie 122 21 0S 165 0 E
Nova Friburgo 188 22 16S 42 30W
Nova Granada 188 20 30S 49 20W
Nova Lisboa = Huambo 134 12 42S 15 54 E
Nova Scotia □ 149 45 10N 63 0W
Novara 46 45 27N 8 36 E
Novaya Sibir, Ostrov 72 75 10N 150 0 E
Novaya Zemlya 69 75 0N 56 0 E
Novgorod 68 58 30N 31 25 E
Novi Pazar 52 43 12N 20 28 E
Novi Sad 52 45 18N 19 52 E
Novocherkassk 68 47 27N 40 5 E
Novokuznetsk 71 53 45N 87 10 E
Novomoskovsk 68 54 5N 38 15 E
Novorossiysk 68 44 43N 37 46 E
Novosibirsk 71 55 0N 83 5 E
Novosibirskiye Ostrova 72 75 0N 142 0 E
Nowgong 93 26 20N 92 50 E
Nowra 117 34 53S 150 35 E
Nowy Sącz 59 49 40N 20 41 E
Noyon 38 49 34N 3 0 E
Nûbîya, Es Sahrâ En 129 21 30N 33 30 E
Nueces → 161 27 50N 97 30W
Nueltin L. 145 60 30N 99 30W
Nueva Gerona 178 21 53N 82 49W
Nueva Rosita 174 27 57N 101 13W
Nuevitas 178 21 30N 77 20W
Nuevo Laredo 176 27 30N 99 30W
Nuevo Leon □ 176 25 40N 100 0W
Nuhaka 122 39 3S 177 45 E
Nukey Bluff, Mt. 118 32 26S 135 29 E
Nukus 70 42 20N 59 7 E
Nulato 142 64 40N 158 10W
Nullarbor Plain 114 30 45S 129 0 E
Numan 131 9 29N 12 3 E
Numazu 107 35 7N 138 51 E
Numurkah 117 36 5S 145 26 E
Nuneaton 25 52 32N 1 29W
Nunivak 142 60 0N 166 0W
Nunspeet 41 52 21N 5 45 E
Nuoro 48 40 20N 9 20 E
Nuremburg = Nürnberg 43 49 26N 11 5 E
Nuriootpa 119 34 27S 139 0 E
Nürnberg 43 49 26N 11 5 E
Nurran, L. = Terewah, L. 116 29 52S 147 35 E
Nutak 147 57 28N 61 59W
Nuweveldberge 136 32 10S 21 45 E
Nuyts Arch. 118 32 35S 133 20 E
Nyaake 130 4 52N 7 37W
Nyainqentanglha Shan 101 30 0N 90 0 E
Nyasa, L. = Malawi, L. 137 12 30S 34 30 E
Nyíregyháza 59 47 58N 21 47 E
Nyngan 116 31 30S 147 8 E
Nysa 58 50 30N 17 22 E
Oahe L. 163 45 30N 100 25W
Oahu 160 21 30N 158 0W
Oak Hill 165 38 0N 81 7W
Oak Park 167 41 55N 87 45W
Oak Ridge 169 36 1N 84 12W
Oakengates 28 52 42N 2 29W
Oakey 116 27 25S 151 43 E
Oakham 29 52 40N 0 43W
Oakland 172 37 50N 122 18W
Oakridge 171 43 47N 122 31W
Oamaru 123 45 5S 170 59 E
Oaxaca 177 17 2N 96 40W
Oaxaca □ 177 17 0N 96 30W
Ob → 69 66 45N 69 30 E
Oba 150 49 4N 84 7W
Obama 106 35 30N 135 45 E
Oban 30 56 25N 5 30W
Obbia 133 5 25N 48 30 E
Oberhausen 42 51 28N 6 50 E
Oberon 117 33 45S 149 52 E
Oberösterreich □ 45 48 10N 14 0 E
Obi, Is. 113 1 30S 127 30 E
Obihiro 103 42 56N 143 12 E
Obskaya Guba 69 69 0N 73 0 E
Ocala 170 29 11N 82 5W
Ocampo 174 28 11N 108 23W
Ocaña 184 8 15N 73 20W
Occidental, Cordillera 184 5 0N 76 0W
Ocean City 164 39 18N 74 34W
Oceanside 173 33 13N 117 26W
Ochil Hills 31 56 14N 3 40W
Oconee → 170 31 58N 82 32W
Oconto 167 44 52N 87 53W
Ocotlán 175 20 21N 102 46W
Ōda 109 35 11N 132 30 E
Ódáðahraun 64 65 5N 17 0W
Odate 103 40 16N 140 34 E
Odawara 107 35 20N 139 6 E
Ödemiş 80 38 15N 28 0 E
Odense 61 55 22N 10 23 E
Oder → 58 53 33N 14 38 E
Odessa, U.S.A. 161 31 51N 102 23W
Odessa, U.S.S.R. 68 46 30N 30 45 E
Odra → 58 53 33N 14 38 E
Odžak 52 45 3N 18 18 E
Offaly □ 35 53 15N 7 30W
Offenbach 42 50 6N 8 46 E
Oga-Hantō 103 39 58N 139 47 E
Ogaden 133 7 30N 45 30 E
Ōgaki 106 35 21N 136 37 E
Ogbomosho 131 8 1N 4 11 E
Ogden 163 41 13N 112 1W
Ogdensburg 151 44 40N 75 27W
Ohio □ 167 40 20N 14 10 E
Ohio → 167 38 0N 86 0W
Ohrid 52 41 8N 20 52 E
Ohridsko, Jezero 52 41 8N 20 52 E
Oil City 164 41 26N 79 40W
Oise → 38 49 0N 2 4 E
Oisterwijk 40 51 35N 5 12 E
Ōita 108 33 14N 131 36 E
Ojos del Salado, Cerro 190 27 0S 68 40W
Oka → 68 56 20N 43 59 E
Okawa 108 33 9N 130 21 E
Okaya 107 36 0N 138 10 E
Okayama 109 34 40N 133 54 E
Okazaki 106 34 57N 137 10 E
Okeechobee, L. 170 27 0N 80 50W
Okehampton 27 50 44N 4 1W
Okha 75 53 40N 143 0 E
Okhotsk 75 59 20N 143 10 E
Okhotsk, Sea of 77 55 0N 145 0 E
Okhotsko Kolymskoye 73 63 0N 157 0 E
Oki-no-Shima 109 32 44N 132 33 E
Oki-Shotō 109 36 5N 133 15 E
Okinawa-Jima 99 26 32N 128 0 E
Oklahoma □ 161 35 20N 97 30W
Oklahoma City 161 35 25N 97 30W
Okmulgee 168 35 38N 96 0W
Oktabrsk 70 49 28N 57 25 E
Oktyabrskoy Revolyutsii, Os. 72 79 30N 97 0 E

Oktyabrskoye	**69** 62	28N	66	3 E
Okuchi	**108** 32	4N	130	37 E
Okuru	**123** 43	55S	168	55 E
Okushiri-Tō	**103** 42	15N	139	30 E
Olanchito	**179** 15	30N	86	30W
Öland	**61** 56	45N	16	38 E
Olary	**118** 32	18S	140	19 E
Olavarría	**190** 36	55S	60	20W
Old Castile = Castilla La				
Vieja	**50** 41	55N	4	0W
Old Town	**148** 45	0N	68	41W
Oldenburg	**42** 53	10N	8	10 E
Oldenzaal	**41** 52	19N	6	53 E
Oldham	**28** 53	33N	2	8W
Olds	**155** 51	50N	114	10W
Olekma ~→	**74** 60	22N	120	42 E
Olekminsk	**74** 60	25N	120	30 E
Olenek	**72** 68	28N	112	18 E
Olenek ~→	**72** 73	0N	120	10 E
Oléron, Île d'	**36** 45	55N	1	15W
Oleśnica	**58** 51	13N	17	22 E
Olifants ~→	**137** 24	5S	31	20 E
Ólimbos, Óros	**54** 40	6N	22	23 E
Oliveira	**188** 20	39S	44	50W
Oliver	**155** 49	13N	119	37W
Ollagüe	**187** 21	15S	68	10W
Olney	**167** 38	40N	88	0W
Olomouc	**59** 49	38N	17	12 E
Olsztyn	**58** 53	48N	20	29 E
Olt ~→	**57** 43	50N	24	40 E
Olympia, Greece	**54** 37	39N	21	39 E
Olympia, U.S.A.	**171** 47	0N	122	58W
Olympic Mts.	**171** 47	50N	123	45W
Olympus, Mt. = Ólimbos,				
Óros	**54** 40	6N	22	23 E
Olympus, Mt.	**171** 47	52N	123	40W
Omachi	**107** 36	30N	137	50 E
Omae-Zaki	**107** 34	36N	138	14 E
Omagh	**34** 54	36N	7	20W
Omaha	**166** 41	15N	96	0W
Omak	**171** 48	24N	119	31W
Oman ■	**83** 23	0N	58	0 E
Oman, G. of	**83** 24	30N	58	30 E
Omdurmân	**129** 15	40N	32	28 E
Ome	**107** 35	47N	139	15 E
Omeo	**117** 37	6S	147	36 E
Omihachiman	**106** 35	7N	136	3 E
Omiya	**107** 35	54N	139	38 E
Omo ~→	**132** 6	25N	36	10 E
Omolon ~→	**73** 68	42N	158	36 E
Omono-Gawa ~→	**103** 39	46N	140	3 E
Omsk	**71** 55	0N	73	12 E
Omura	**108** 32	56N	130	0 E
Omuta	**108** 33	0N	130	26 E
Onega	**68** 64	0N	38	10 E
Onega, L. = Onezhskoye				
Ozero	**68** 62	0N	35	30 E
Onehunga	**122** 36	55S	174	48 E
Oneida	**164** 43	5N	75	40W
Onekotan, Ostrov	**75** 49	25N	154	45 E
Onezhskoye Ozero	**68** 62	0N	35	30 E
Ongerup	**120** 33	58S	118	28 E
Ongole	**90** 15	33N	80	2 E
Onguren	**74** 53	38N	107	36 E
Onitsha	**131** 6	6N	6	42 E
Ono, Fukui, Japan	**106** 35	59N	136	29 E
Ono, Hyōgo, Japan	**109** 34	51N	134	56 E
Onoda	**108** 34	2N	131	25 E
Onomichi	**109** 34	25N	133	12 E
Onslow	**114** 21	40S	115	12 E
Onslow B.	**165** 34	20N	77	20W
Ontake-San	**106** 35	53N	137	29 E
Ontario	**173** 34	2N	117	40W
Ontario □	**140** 52	0N	88	10W
Ontario, L.	**151** 43	40N	78	0W
Oodnadatta	**118** 27	33S	135	30 E
Ooldea	**114** 30	27S	131	50 E
Oostende	**42** 51	15N	2	50 E
Oosterhout	**40** 51	39N	4	47 E
Oosterschelde	**40** 51	33N	4	0 E
Opala	**73** 51	58N	156	30 E
Opava	**58** 49	57N	17	58 E
Opelousas	**168** 30	35N	92	7W
Ophir	**142** 63	10N	156	40W
Opole	**58** 50	42N	17	58 E
Oporto = Porto	**50** 41	8N	8	40W
Opp	**169** 31	19N	86	13W
Oppland fylke □	**60** 61	15N	9	40 E
Opua	**122** 35	19S	174	9 E
Oradea	**56** 47	2N	21	58 E
Öræfajökull	**64** 64	2N	16	39W
Orai	**91** 25	58N	79	30 E
Oran, Algeria	**127** 35	45N	0	39W
Oran, Argentina	**190** 23	10S	64	20W
Orange, Australia	**117** 33	15S	149	7 E
Orange, France	**37** 44	8N	4	47 E
Orange, U.S.A.	**168** 30	10N	93	50W
Orange ~→ = Oranje ~→	**136** 28	41S	16	28 E
Orange, C.	**185** 4	20N	51	30W
Orangeburg	**170** 33	35N	80	53W
Oranje ~→	**136** 28	41S	16	28 E
Oraşul Stalin = Braşov	**57** 45	38N	25	35 E
Orbost	**117** 37	40S	148	29 E
Orchies	**38** 50	28N	3	14 E
Ordos = Mu Us Shamo	**98** 39	0N	109	0 E
Ordu	**81** 40	55N	37	53 E
Ordzhonikidze	**70** 43	0N	44	35 E
Ore Mts. = Erzgebirge	**43** 50	25N	13	0 E
Örebro	**60** 59	20N	15	18 E
Oregon □	**171** 44	0N	121	0W
Oregon City	**171** 45	21N	122	35W
Orel	**68** 52	57N	36	3 E
Orenburg	**70** 51	45N	55	6 E
Orense	**50** 42	19N	7	55W
Orepuki	**123** 46	19S	167	46 E
Orford Ness	**24** 52	6N	1	31 E
Oriental, Cordillera	**184** 6	0N	73	0W
Orillia	**151** 44	40N	79	24W
Orinoco ~→	**185** 9	15N	61	30W
Orissa □	**92** 20	0N	84	0 E
Oristano	**48** 39	54N	8	35 E
Oristano, Golfo di	**48** 39	50N	8	22 E
Orizaba	**177** 18	51N	97	6W
Orkney Is.	**33** 59	0N	3	0W
Orland	**172** 39	46N	122	12W
Orlando	**170** 28	30N	81	25W
Orléanais	**39** 48	0N	2	0 E
Orléans	**39** 47	54N	1	52 E
Ormara	**88** 25	16N	64	33 E
Ormskirk	**28** 53	35N	2	53W
Örnsköldsvik	**66** 63	17N	18	40 E
Orocué	**184** 4	48N	71	20W
Oroville	**172** 39	31N	121	30W
Orsha	**68** 54	30N	30	25 E
Orsk	**70** 51	12N	58	34 E
Ortegal, C.	**50** 43	43N	7	52W
Orümīyeh	**81** 37	40N	45	0 E
Orümīyeh, Daryācheh-ye	**81** 37	50N	45	30 E
Oruro	**187** 18	0S	67	9W
Oruzgān □	**87** 33	30N	66	0 E
Oryakhovo	**53** 43	40N	23	57 E
Osage ~→	**166** 38	35N	91	57W
Osaka	**106** 34	40N	135	30 E
Osceola	**169** 35	40N	90	0W
Ösel = Saaremaa	**68** 58	30N	22	30 E
Osh	**71** 40	37N	72	49 E
Oshawa	**151** 43	50N	78	50W
Oshima	**107** 33	55N	132	14 E
Oshkosh	**167** 44	3N	88	35W
Oshogbo	**131** 7	48N	4	37 E
Osijek	**52** 45	34N	18	41 E
Oskaloosa	**166** 41	18N	92	40W
Oslo	**60** 59	55N	10	45 E
Osmaniye	**80** 37	5N	36	10 E
Osnabrück	**42** 52	16N	8	2 E
Osorno	**190** 40	25S	73	0W
Oss	**41** 51	46N	5	32 E
Ossa, Mt.	**119** 41	52S	146	3 E
Ostend = Oostende	**42** 51	15N	2	50 E
Östergötlands län □	**60** 58	35N	15	45 E
Östersund	**66** 63	10N	14	38 E
Østfold fylke □	**60** 59	25N	11	25 E

Ostfriesische Inseln	**42**	53 45N	7 15 E
Ostia	**46**	41 40N	12 20 E
Ostrava	**59**	49 51N	18 18 E
Ostróda	**58**	53 42N	19 58 E
Ostrołeka	**58**	53 4N	21 32 E
Ostrów Mazowiecka	**58**	52 50N	21 51 E
Ostrów Wielkopolski	**58**	51 36N	17 44 E
Ōsumi-Kaikyō	**104**	30 55N	131 0 E
Ōsumi-Shotō	**104**	30 30N	130 0 E
Oswego	**164**	43 29N	76 30W
Oswestry	**28**	52 52N	3 3W
Ōta	**107**	36 18N	139 22 E
Otago □	**123**	44 44S	169 10 E
Ōtake	**109**	34 12N	132 13 E
Otaki	**122**	40 45S	175 10 E
Otaru	**103**	43 10N	141 0 E
Otaru-Wan = Ishikari-Wan	**103**	43 25N	141 1 E
Otira Gorge	**123**	42 53S	171 33 E
Otoineppu	**103**	44 44N	142 16 E
Otranto	**49**	40 9N	18 28 E
Otranto, C. d'	**49**	40 7N	18 30 E
Otranto, Str. of	**52**	40 15N	18 40 E
Ōtsu	**106**	35 0N	135 50 E
Ottawa, Canada	**151**	45 27N	75 42W
Ottawa, U.S.A.	**166**	38 40N	95 6W
Ottawa → = Outaouais →	**140**	45 27N	74 8W
Ottawa Is.	**146**	59 35N	80 10W
Otter Rapids, Ont., Canada	**151**	50 11N	81 39W
Otter Rapids, Sask., Canada	**152**	55 38N	104 44W
Ottumwa	**166**	41 0N	92 25W
Otwock	**58**	52 5N	21 20 E
Ouachita →	**168**	31 38N	91 49W
Ouachita Mts.	**168**	34 50N	94 30W
Ouagadougou	**130**	12 25N	1 30W
Ouahran = Oran	**127**	35 45N	0 39W
Ouargla	**127**	31 59N	5 16 E
Oubangi →	**131**	1 0N	17 50 E
Oudenbosch	**40**	51 35N	4 32 E
Oudtshoorn	**136**	33 35S	22 14 E
Ouessant, Île d'	**36**	48 28N	5 6W
Oujda	**127**	34 41N	1 55W
Oulu	**67**	65 1N	25 29 E
Oulujärvi	**67**	64 25N	27 15 E
Oulujoki →	**67**	65 1N	25 30 E
Ouse →	**29**	54 3N	0 7 E
Outaouais →	**140**	45 27N	74 8W
Outer Hebrides	**32**	57 30N	7 40W
Outlook	**152**	51 30N	107 0W
Outreau	**38**	50 40N	1 36 E
Ouyen	**119**	35 1S	142 22 E
Ovalle	**190**	30 33S	71 18W
Overflakkee	**40**	51 44N	4 10 E
Overijssel □	**41**	52 25N	6 35 E
Oviedo	**50**	43 25N	5 50W
Owaka	**123**	46 27S	169 40 E
Owase	**106**	34 7N	136 12 E
Owatonna	**166**	44 3N	93 10W
Owen Sound	**151**	44 35N	80 55W
Owen Stanley Range	**115**	8 30S	147 0 E
Owensboro	**167**	37 40N	87 5W
Owosso	**167**	43 0N	84 10W
Owyhee →	**171**	43 46N	117 2W
Oxford, U.K.	**25**	51 45N	1 15W
Oxford, U.S.A.	**165**	36 19N	78 36W
Oxford □	**25**	51 45N	1 15W
Oxford L.	**153**	54 51N	95 37W
Oxnard	**173**	34 10N	119 14W
Oyabe	**106**	36 47N	136 56 E
Oyama	**107**	36 18N	139 48 E
Oyana	**108**	32 32N	130 30 E
Oyo	**131**	7 46N	3 56 E
Oyonnax	**37**	46 16N	5 40 E
Ozamis	**112**	8 15N	123 50 E
Ozark	**169**	31 29N	85 39W
Ozark Plateau	**168**	37 20N	91 40W
Ozarks, L. of	**166**	38 10N	92 40W
Ozu, Ehime, Japan	**109**	33 30N	132 33 E
Ozu, Kumamoto, Japan	**108**	32 52N	130 52 E
Paarl	**136**	33 45S	18 56 E
Pabna	**92**	24 1N	89 18 E
Pacaraima, Sierra	**185**	4 0N	62 30W
Pacasmayo	**186**	7 20S	79 35W
Pachuca	**177**	20 10N	98 40W
Padang	**111**	1 0S	100 20 E
Pádova	**47**	45 24N	11 52 E
Padstow	**27**	50 33N	4 57W
Padua = Pádova	**47**	45 24N	11 52 E
Paducah	**169**	37 0N	88 40W
Pag	**52**	44 30N	14 50 E
Pagalu = Annobón	**131**	1 25S	5 36 E
Pagastikós Kólpos	**54**	39 15N	23 0 E
Page	**160**	36 57N	111 27W
Pahala	**160**	19 12N	155 25W
Pahang □	**96**	3 30N	102 45 E
Pahiatua	**122**	40 27S	175 50 E
Paignton	**27**	50 26N	3 33W
Painesville	**167**	41 42N	81 18W
Paint Hills = Nouveau Comptoir	**140**	53 0N	78 49W
Painted Desert	**160**	36 0N	111 30W
Paisley	**31**	55 51N	4 27W
Paita	**186**	5 11S	81 9W
Pak Sane	**95**	18 22N	103 39 E
Pakistan ■	**78**	30 0N	70 0 E
Pakistan, East = Bangladesh ■	**92**	24 0N	90 0 E
Pakokku	**93**	21 20N	95 0 E
Pakse	**95**	15 5N	105 52 E
Paktīā □	**87**	33 0N	69 15 E
Palanpur	**91**	24 10N	72 25 E
Palatka	**170**	29 40N	81 40W
Palawan	**112**	9 30N	118 30 E
Palembang	**111**	3 0S	104 50 E
Palencia	**50**	42 1N	4 34W
Palermo	**48**	38 8N	13 20 E
Palestine	**168**	31 42N	95 35W
Palghat	**90**	10 46N	76 42 E
Pali	**91**	25 50N	73 20 E
Palizada	**177**	18 15N	92 5W
Palk Bay	**90**	9 30N	79 15 E
Palk Strait	**90**	10 0N	79 45 E
Palm Is.	**121**	18 40S	146 35 E
Palm Springs	**173**	33 51N	116 35W
Palma, La	**179**	8 15N	78 0W
Palma de Mallorca	**51**	39 35N	2 39 E
Palma Soriano	**178**	20 15N	76 0W
Palmas, C.	**130**	4 27N	7 46W
Palmer Land	**14**	73 0S	60 0W
Palmerston North	**122**	40 21S	175 39 E
Palmi	**49**	38 21N	15 51 E
Palmira	**184**	3 32N	76 16W
Palmyra = Tudmur	**80**	34 36N	38 15 E
Palo Alto	**172**	37 25N	122 8W
Pamirs	**71**	37 40N	73 0 E
Pamlico Sd.	**165**	35 20N	76 0W
Pampa	**161**	35 35N	100 58W
Pampas	**190**	35 0S	63 0W
Pamplona	**51**	42 48N	1 38W
Panaca	**173**	37 51N	114 23W
Panaji	**91**	15 25N	73 50 E
Panamá	**179**	9 0N	79 25W
Panama ■	**179**	8 48N	79 55W
Panamá, Golfo de	**179**	8 4N	79 20W
Panama Canal	**175**	9 10N	79 37W
Panama City	**169**	30 10N	85 41W
Panay	**112**	11 10N	122 30 E
Pančevo	**52**	44 52N	20 41 E
Pandharpur	**91**	17 41N	75 20 E
Pangfou = Bengbu	**99**	32 58N	117 20 E
Pangkalpinang	**111**	2 0S	106 0 E
Pangnirtung	**146**	66 8N	65 54W
Panjim = Panaji	**91**	15 25N	73 50 E
Panjinad Barrage	**89**	29 22N	71 15 E
Pantelleria	**48**	36 52N	12 0 E
Pánuco	**177**	22 3N	98 10W
Paoting = Baoding	**98**	38 50N	115 28 E
Paot'ou = Baotou	**98**	40 32N	110 2 E
Papien Chiang = Da →	**95**	21 15N	105 20 E
Papua, Gulf of	**115**	9 0S	144 50 E

PAP

Papua New Guinea ■	115	8	0S	145	0 E
Pará = Belém	188	1	20S	48	30W
Pará □	188	3	20S	52	0W
Paracatu	188	17	10S	46	50W
Paragua, La	185	6	50N	63	20W
Paraguay ■	191	23	0S	57	0W
Paraguay ～►	191	27	18S	58	38W
Paraíba = João Pessoa	189	7	10S	34	52W
Paraíba □	189	7	0S	36	0W
Parakou	131	9	25N	2	40 E
Paramaribo	185	5	50N	55	10W
Paraná	190	31	45S	60	30W
Paraná □	191	24	30S	51	0W
Paraná ～►	190	33	43S	59	15W
Paranaguá	191	25	30S	48	30W
Paranaíba ～►	188	20	6S	51	4W
Parbhani	91	19	8N	76	52 E
Parecis, Serra dos	187	13	0S	60	0W
Parent	151	47	55N	74	35W
Paria, Golfo de	180	10	20N	62	0W
Parika	185	6	50N	58	20W
Parintins	185	2	40S	56	50W
Pariparit Kyun	94	14	55S	93	45 E
Paris, France	39	48	50N	2	20 E
Paris, Tenn., U.S.A.	169	36	20N	88	20W
Paris, Tex., U.S.A.	168	33	40N	95	30W
Park Range	163	40	0N	106	30W
Parker	173	34	8N	114	16W
Parkersburg	164	39	18N	81	31W
Parkes	117	33	9S	148	11 E
Parma	46	44	50N	10	20 E
Parnaguá	188	10	10S	44	38W
Parnaíba	189	2	54S	41	47W
Parnaíba ～►	188	3	0S	41	50W
Parnassós	54	38	35N	22	30 E
Pärnu	68	58	28N	24	33 E
Páros	55	37	5N	25	12 E
Parral	190	36	10S	71	52W
Parramatta	117	33	48S	151	1 E
Parras	174	25	30N	102	20W
Parrett ～►	27	51	7N	2	58W
Parry Is.	12	77	0N	110	0W
Parry Sound	151	45	20N	80	0W
Parsons	166	37	20N	95	17W
Paruro	187	13	45S	71	50W
Parvän □	87	35	0N	69	0 E
Pasadena, Calif., U.S.A.	173	34	5N	118	9W
Pasadena, Tex., U.S.A.	168	29	45N	95	14W
Pasaje	184	3	23S	79	50W
Pascagoula	169	30	21N	88	30W
Pasco	171	46	10N	119	0W
Pasco, Cerro de	186	10	45S	76	10W
Paso Robles	173	35	40N	120	45W
Passero, C.	49	36	42N	15	8 E
Passo Fundo	191	28	10S	52	20W
Pasto	184	1	13N	77	17W
Patagonia	192	45	0S	69	0W
Patan	91	23	54N	72	14 E
Patchogue	164	40	46N	73	1W
Paterson	164	40	55N	74	10W
Pathankot	89	32	18N	75	45 E
Patiala	89	30	23N	76	26 E
Patkai Bum	93	27	0N	95	30 E
Pátmos	55	37	21N	26	36 E
Patna	92	25	35N	85	12 E
Patos, Lag. dos	191	31	20S	51	0 E
Patos de Minas	188	18	35S	46	32W
Pátrai	54	38	14N	21	47 E
Patuca ～►	179	15	50N	84	18W
Pátzcuaro	175	19	32N	101	36W
Pau	36	43	19N	0	25W
Paulistana	189	8	9S	41	9W
Paulo Afonso	189	9	21S	38	15W
Pavia	46	45	10N	9	10 E
Pavlodar	71	52	33N	77	0 E
Pavlovo	74	63	5N	115	25 E
Pawtucket	164	41	51N	71	22W
Payette	171	44	0N	117	0W
Payne Bay = Bellin	146	60	0N	70	0W
Payne L.	146	59	30N	74	30W
Paynes Find	120	29	15S	117	42 E
Paysandú	191	32	19S	58	8W
Paz, La, Argentina	190	30	50S	59	45W
Paz, La, Bolivia	187	16	20S	68	10W
Paz, La, Mexico	174	24	10N	110	18W
Pazardzhik	53	42	12N	24	20 E
Peace ～►	145	59	0N	111	25W
Peace River	155	56	15N	117	18W
Peak, The	28	53	24N	1	53W
Peak Hill	116	32	47S	148	11 E
Pearl City	160	21	24N	158	0W
Pearl Harbor	160	21	20N	158	0W
Peary Land	13	82	40N	33	0W
Pebas	186	3	10S	71	46W
Pechenga	69	69	30N	31	25 E
Pechora ～►	69	68	13N	54	15 E
Pechorskaya Guba	69	68	40N	54	0 E
Pecos	161	31	25N	103	35W
Pecos ～►	161	29	42N	102	30W
Pécs	59	46	5N	18	15 E
Pedro Afonso	188	9	0S	48	10W
Pedro Juan Caballero	191	22	30S	55	40W
Peebles	31	55	40N	3	12W
Peekskill	164	41	18N	73	57W
Peel	28	54	14N	4	40W
Peel ～►	144	67	0N	135	0W
Pegasus Bay	123	43	20S	173	10 E
Pegu	93	17	20N	96	29 E
Pegu Yoma	93	19	0N	96	0 E
Pehuajó	190	35	45S	62	0W
Peip'ing = Beijing	98	39	55N	116	20 E
Pekalongan	111	6	53S	109	40 E
Pekan	96	3	30N	103	25 E
Pekanbaru	111	0	30N	101	15 E
Pekin	166	40	35N	89	40W
Peking = Beijing	98	39	55N	116	20 E
Peleng	113	1	20S	123	30 E
Pelly ～►	144	62	47N	137	19W
Pelly Bay	146	68	38N	89	50W
Peloponnes = Pelopónnisos □	54	37	10N	22	0 E
Pelopónnisos □	54	37	10N	22	0 E
Peloro, C.	49	38	15N	15	40 E
Pelorus Sound	123	40	59S	173	59 E
Pelotas	191	31	42S	52	23W
Pelvoux, Massif de	37	44	52N	6	20 E
Pematangsiantar	111	2	57N	99	5 E
Pemba	135	5	0S	39	45 E
Pembroke, Canada	151	45	50N	77	7W
Pembroke, U.K.	27	51	41N	4	57W
Pen-y-Ghent	28	54	10N	2	15W
Penas, G. de	192	47	0S	75	0W
Pench'i = Benxi	98	41	20N	123	48 E
Pendembu	130	9	7N	12	14W
Pendleton	171	45	35N	118	50W
Penetanguishene	151	44	50N	79	55W
Penguin	119	41	8S	146	6 E
Penicuik	31	55	50N	3	14W
Peninsular Malaysia □	96	4	0N	102	0 E
Pennines	28	54	50N	2	20W
Pennsylvania □	164	40	50N	78	0W
Penola	119	37	25S	140	21 E
Penonomé	179	8	31N	80	21W
Penrith, Australia	117	33	43S	150	38 E
Penrith, U.K.	28	54	40N	2	45W
Pensacola	169	30	30N	87	10W
Pensacola Mts.	14	84	0S	40	0W
Penshurst	119	37	49S	142	20 E
Penticton	155	49	30N	119	38W
Pentland Firth	33	58	43N	3	10W
Pentland Hills	31	55	48N	3	25W
Penza	68	53	15N	45	5 E
Penzance	27	50	7N	5	32W
Penzhinskaya Guba	73	61	30N	163	0 E
Peoria	166	40	40N	89	40W
Perak □	96	5	0N	101	0 E
Perche	36	48	31N	1	1 E
Pereira	184	4	49N	75	43W
Perenjori	120	29	26S	116	16 E
Pergamino	190	33	52S	60	30W
Périgueux	36	45	10N	0	42 E
Perlis □	96	6	30N	100	15 E

Perm	**69**	58 0N	57 10 E
Pernambuco = Recife	**189**	8 0S	35 0W
Pernambuco □	**189**	8 0S	37 0W
Pernatty Lagoon	**118**	31 30S	137 12 E
Pernik	**53**	42 35N	23 2 E
Peron Pen.	**120**	26 0S	113 10 E
Péronne	**38**	49 55N	2 57 E
Perouse Str., La	**77**	45 40N	142 0 E
Perpignan	**37**	42 42N	2 53 E
Perry, Iowa, U.S.A.	**166**	41 48N	94 5W
Perry, Okla., U.S.A.	**168**	36 20N	97 20W
Persepolis	**85**	29 55N	52 50 E
Persia = Iran ■	**86**	33 0N	53 0 E
Persian Gulf = Gulf, The	**85**	27 0N	50 0 E
Perth, Australia	**120**	31 57S	115 52 E
Perth, Canada	**151**	44 55N	76 15W
Perth, U.K.	**31**	56 24N	3 27W
Perth Amboy	**164**	40 31N	74 16W
Peru	**167**	40 42N	86 0W
Peru ■	**186**	8 0S	75 0W
Perúgia	**46**	43 6N	12 24 E
Pervouralsk	**69**	56 55N	60 0 E
Pésaro	**47**	43 55N	12 53 E
Pescara	**47**	42 28N	14 13 E
Peshawar	**89**	34 2N	71 37 E
Pesqueria →	**176**	25 54N	99 11W
Petah Tiqwa	**80**	32 6N	34 53 E
Petaling Jaya	**96**	3 4N	101 42 E
Petaluma	**172**	38 13N	122 39W
Petatlán	**177**	17 31N	101 16W
Peterborough, Australia	**118**	32 58S	138 51 E
Peterborough, Canada	**151**	44 20N	78 20W
Peterborough, U.K.	**25**	52 35N	0 14W
Peterhead	**33**	57 30N	1 49W
Peterlee	**29**	54 45N	1 18W
Petersburg, Alaska, U.S.A.	**143**	56 50N	133 0W
Petersburg, Va., U.S.A.	**164**	37 17N	77 26W
Petit Goâve	**180**	18 27N	72 51W
Petitsikapau, L.	**147**	54 37N	66 25W
Petlad	**91**	22 30N	72 45 E
Petone	**123**	41 13S	174 53 E
Petoskey	**150**	45 22N	84 57W
Petrich	**53**	41 24N	23 13 E
Petrolia	**150**	42 54N	82 9W
Petrolina	**189**	9 24S	40 30W
Petropavlovsk	**71**	54 53N	69 13 E
Petropavlovsk-Kamchatskiy	**73**	53 3N	158 43 E
Petrópolis	**188**	22 33S	43 9W
Petrovaradin	**52**	45 16N	19 55 E
Petrozavodsk	**68**	61 41N	34 20 E
Pevek	**73**	69 41N	171 19 E
Pforzheim	**42**	48 53N	8 43 E
Phan Rang	**95**	11 34N	109 0 E
Phangan, Ko	**96**	9 45N	100 0 E
Phenix City	**169**	32 30N	85 0W
Philadelphia	**164**	40 0N	75 10W
Philippi	**55**	41 1N	24 16 E
Philippines ■	**112**	12 0N	123 0 E
Philippopolis = Plovdiv	**53**	42 8N	24 44 E
Phitsanulok	**94**	16 50N	100 12 E
Phnom Penh	**95**	11 33N	104 55 E
Phoenix	**160**	33 30N	112 10W
Phoenix Is.	**123**	3 30S	172 0W
Phra Chedi Sam Ong	**94**	15 16N	98 23 E
Phuket	**96**	7 52N	98 22 E
Piacenza	**46**	45 2N	9 42 E
Piauí □	**188**	7 0S	43 0W
Picardie	**38**	50 0N	2 15 E
Picardie, Plaine de	**37**	50 0N	2 0 E
Picardy = Picardie	**38**	50 0N	2 15 E
Picayune	**169**	30 31N	89 40W
Pickering	**29**	54 15N	0 46W
Picton, Australia	**117**	34 12S	150 34 E
Picton, N.Z.	**123**	41 18S	174 3 E
Pictou	**149**	45 41N	62 42W
Pidurutalagala	**90**	7 10N	80 50 E
Piedad, La	**175**	20 20N	102 1W
Piedmont = Piemonte □	**46**	45 0N	7 30 E
Piedmont Plat.	**165**	34 0N	81 30W
Piedras Negras	**174**	28 42N	100 31W
Piemonte □	**46**	45 0N	7 30 E
Pierre	**163**	44 23N	100 20W
Pietermaritzburg	**137**	29 35S	30 25 E
Pietrosul	**57**	47 35N	24 43 E
Pikeville	**165**	37 30N	82 30W
Pilcomayo →	**190**	25 21S	57 42W
Pilsen = Plzen	**43**	49 45N	13 22 E
Pimenta Bueno	**187**	11 35S	61 10W
Pinang □	**96**	5 20N	100 20 E
Pinar del Río	**178**	22 26N	83 40W
Pinaroo	**119**	35 17S	140 53 E
Pinawa	**153**	50 9N	95 50W
Pincher Creek	**155**	49 30N	113 57W
Pinczów	**58**	50 30N	20 35 E
Pindos Óros	**54**	40 0N	21 0 E
Pindus Mts. = Pindos Óros	**54**	40 0N	21 0 E
Pine Bluff	**168**	34 10N	92 0W
Pine Pass	**155**	55 25N	122 42W
Pineville	**168**	31 22N	92 30W
Ping →	**94**	15 42N	100 9 E
Pingdong	**99**	22 39N	120 30 E
Pingliang	**99**	35 35N	106 31 E
Pingxiang	**99**	22 6N	106 46 E
Piniós →	**54**	37 48N	21 20 E
Pinjarra	**120**	32 37S	115 52 E
Piombino	**46**	42 54N	10 30 E
Piotrków Trybunalski	**58**	51 23N	19 43 E
Piqua	**167**	40 10N	84 10W
Piracicaba	**188**	22 45S	47 40W
Pirœus = Piraiévs	**55**	37 57N	23 42 E
Piraiévs	**55**	37 57N	23 42 E
Pirapora	**188**	17 20S	44 56W
Pírgos	**54**	37 40N	21 27 E
Pirin Planina	**53**	41 40N	23 30 E
Pirineos	**51**	42 40N	1 0 E
Pisa	**46**	43 43N	10 23 E
Pisagua	**187**	19 40S	70 15W
Pisco	**186**	13 50S	76 12W
Pistóia	**46**	43 57N	10 53 E
Pitcairn I.	**10**	25 5S	130 5W
Piteå	**67**	65 20N	21 25 E
Piteşti	**57**	44 52N	24 54 E
Pithiviers	**39**	48 10N	2 13 E
Pitlochry	**33**	56 43N	3 43W
Pitt I.	**154**	53 30N	129 50W
Pittsburg, Kans., U.S.A.	**166**	37 21N	94 43W
Pittsburg, Tex., U.S.A.	**168**	32 59N	94 58W
Pittsburgh	**164**	40 25N	79 55W
Pittsfield	**164**	42 28N	73 17W
Pittsworth	**116**	27 41S	151 37 E
Piura	**186**	5 15S	80 38W
Placentia	**149**	47 20N	54 0W
Placerville	**172**	38 47N	120 51W
Placetas	**178**	22 15N	79 44W
Plainfield	**164**	40 37N	74 28W
Plainview	**161**	34 10N	101 40W
Plaster Rock	**148**	46 53N	67 22W
Plata, La	**191**	35 0S	57 55W
Plata, Río de la	**191**	34 45S	57 30W
Platte →	**163**	39 16N	94 50W
Plattsburg	**151**	44 41N	73 30W
Plauen	**43**	50 29N	12 9 E
Pleasantville	**164**	39 25N	74 30W
Plenty, Bay of	**122**	37 45S	177 0 E
Plessisville	**148**	46 14N	71 47W
Pleven	**53**	43 26N	24 37 E
Płock	**58**	52 32N	19 40 E
Ploieşti	**57**	44 57N	26 5 E
Plovdiv	**53**	42 8N	24 44 E
Plymouth	**27**	50 23N	4 9W
Plzen	**43**	49 45N	13 22 E
Po →	**47**	44 57N	12 4 E
Po Hai = Bo Hai	**98**	39 0N	120 0 E
Pobeda	**73**	65 12N	146 12 E
Pobedy Pik	**71**	40 45N	79 58 E
Pocatello	**163**	42 50N	112 25W
Pochutla	**177**	15 50N	96 31W
Poços de Caldas	**188**	21 50S	46 33W
Podgorica = Titograd	**52**	42 30N	19 19 E
Podkamennaya Tunguska →	**74**	61 50N	90 13 E
Point Edward	**150**	43 0N	82 30W

Pointe-à-Pitre **180** 16 10N 61 30W
Pointe Noire **134** 4 48S 11 53 E
Poissy **39** 48 55N 2 0 E
Poitiers **36** 46 35N 0 20 E
Poitou, Plaines et Seuil du **36** 46 30N 0 1W
Pokaran **91** 27 0N 71 50 E
Pola = Pula **52** 44 54N 13 57 E
Poland ■ **58** 52 0N 20 0 E
Polden Hills **27** 51 7N 2 50W
Polesye **17** 52 0N 28 10 E
Polillo Is. **112** 14 56N 122 0 E
Políyiros **55** 40 23N 23 25 E
Pollachi **90** 10 35N 77 0 E
Polotsk **68** 55 30N 28 50 E
Poltava **68** 49 35N 34 35 E
Polynesia **123** 10 0S 162 0W
Pomona **173** 34 2N 117 49W
Pompano Beach **170** 26 12N 80 6W
Ponca City **168** 36 40N 97 5W
Ponce **180** 18 1N 66 37W
Pond Inlet **146** 72 40N 77 0W
Pondicherry **90** 11 59N 79 50 E
Ponnyadaung **93** 22 0N 94 10 E
Ponoka **155** 52 42N 113 40W
Pont-Audemer **39** 49 21N 0 30 E
Ponta Grossa **191** 25 7S 50 10W
Ponta Pora **188** 22 20S 55 35W
Pontchartrain, L. **169** 30 12N 90 0W
Pontefract **29** 53 42N 1 19W
Pontevedra **50** 42 26N 8 40W
Pontiac **167** 42 40N 83 20W
Pontianak **111** 0 3S 109 15 E
Pontine Is. = Ponziane, Isole **48** 40 55N 13 0 E
Pontoise **39** 49 3N 2 5 E
Pontypool **27** 51 42N 3 1W
Pontypridd **27** 51 36N 3 21W
Ponziane, Isole **48** 40 55N 13 0 E
Poochera **118** 32 43S 134 51 E
Poole **24** 50 42N 1 58W
Pooley I. **154** 52 45N 128 15W
Poona = Pune **91** 18 29N 73 57 E
Poopó, Lago de **187** 18 30S 67 35W
Popayán **184** 2 27N 76 36W
Poplar Bluff **169** 36 45N 90 22W
Popocatépetl, Volcán **177** 19 2N 98 38W
Porcher I. **154** 53 50N 130 30W
Porcupine → **142** 66 35N 145 15W
Pori **67** 61 29N 21 48 E
Porkkala **67** 59 59N 24 26 E
Port Adelaide **119** 34 46S 138 30 E
Port Alberni **154** 49 40N 124 50W
Port Albert **115** 38 42S 146 42 E
Port Alfred **148** 48 18N 70 53W
Port Angeles **171** 48 7N 123 30W
Port Antonio **180** 18 10N 76 30W
Port Arthur **168** 30 0N 94 0W
Port-au-Prince **180** 18 40N 72 20W
Port Augusta **118** 32 30S 137 50 E
Port Blair **94** 11 40N 92 30 E
Port-Cartier **148** 50 2N 66 50W
Port Chalmers **123** 45 49S 170 30 E
Port Colborne **151** 42 50N 79 10W
Port Coquitlam **154** 49 15N 122 45W
Port Darwin **192** 51 50S 59 0W
Port-de-Paix **180** 19 50N 72 50W
Port Elgin **150** 44 25N 81 25W
Port Elizabeth **136** 33 58S 25 40 E
Port Erin **28** 54 5N 4 45W
Port Etienne = Nouâdhibou **126** 20 54N 17 0W
Port Fairy **119** 38 22S 142 12 E
Port Glasgow **30** 55 57N 4 40W
Port Harcourt **131** 4 40N 7 10 E
Port Harrison = Inoucdjouac **146** 58 25N 78 15W
Port Hawkesbury **149** 45 36N 61 22W
Port Hope **151** 43 56N 78 20W
Port Huron **167** 43 0N 82 28W
Port Kembla **117** 34 52S 150 49 E
Port Laoise **35** 53 2N 7 20W
Port Lavaca **158** 28 38N 96 38W
Port Lincoln **119** 34 42S 135 52 E
Port Lyautey = Kenitra **126** 34 15N 6 40W
Port Macquarie **116** 31 25S 152 25 E
Port Morant **180** 17 54N 76 19W
Port Moresby **115** 9 24S 147 8 E
Port Nelson **143** 57 3N 92 36W
Port Nolloth **136** 29 17S 16 52 E
Port Nouveau-Québec **146** 58 30N 65 59W
Port of Spain **180** 10 40N 61 31W
Port Phillip B. **117** 38 10S 144 50 E
Port Pirie **118** 33 10S 138 1 E
Port Said = Bûr Sa'îd **128** 31 16N 32 18 E
Port Simpson **154** 54 30N 130 20W
Port Stanley **150** 42 40N 81 10W
Port Sudan = Bûr Sûdân **129** 19 32N 37 9 E
Port Talbot **27** 51 35N 3 48W
Port Townsend **171** 48 7N 122 50W
Portadown **34** 54 27N 6 26W
Portage La Prairie **153** 49 58N 98 18W
Portarlington **35** 53 10N 7 10W
Porte, La **167** 41 36N 86 43W
Porterville **173** 36 5N 119 0W
Porthcawl **27** 51 28N 3 42W
Porthmadog **26** 52 55N 4 13W
Portile de Fier **56** 44 42N 22 30 E
Portland, Australia **119** 38 20S 141 35 E
Portland, Maine, U.S.A. **148** 43 40N 70 15W
Portland, Oreg., U.S.A. **171** 45 35N 122 40W
Portland, Bill of **24** 50 31N 2 27W
Portland Prom. **146** 58 40N 78 33W
Porto **50** 41 8N 8 40W
Pôrto Alegre **191** 30 5S 51 10W
Porto Empédocle **48** 37 18N 13 30 E
Porto Mendes **191** 24 30S 54 15W
Porto Novo **131** 6 23N 2 42 E
Pôrto Seguro **189** 16 26S 39 5W
Pôrto Velho **187** 8 46S 63 54W
Portoferráio **46** 42 50N 10 20 E
Portoscuso **48** 39 12N 8 22 E
Portovlejo **184** 1 7S 80 28W
Portpatrick **30** 54 50N 5 7W
Portree **32** 57 25N 6 11W
Portrush **34** 55 13N 6 40W
Portsmouth, Domin. **180** 15 34N 61 27W
Portsmouth, U.K. **25** 50 48N 1 6W
Portsmouth, N.H., U.S.A. **164** 43 5N 70 45W
Portsmouth, Ohio, U.S.A. **167** 38 45N 83 0W
Portsmouth, Va., U.S.A. **165** 36 50N 76 20W
Porttipahta **67** 68 5N 26 40 E
Portugal ■ **50** 40 0N 7 0W
Portuguese-Guinea = Guinea-Bissau ■ **130** 12 0N 15 0W
Portuguese Timor ■ = Timor **113** 9 0S 125 0 E
Portumna **35** 53 5N 8 12W
Porvenir **192** 53 10S 70 16W
Posadas **191** 27 30S 55 50W
Poshan = Boshan **98** 36 28N 117 49 E
Poste-de-la-Baleine **140** 55 17N 77 45W
Potchefstroom **137** 26 41S 27 7 E
Potenza **49** 40 40N 15 50 E
Potomac → **165** 38 0N 76 23W
Potosí **187** 19 38S 65 50W
Potsdam, Germany **43** 52 23N 13 4 E
Potsdam, U.S.A. **151** 44 40N 74 59W
Pottsville **164** 40 39N 76 12W
Pouce Coupé **155** 55 40N 120 10W
Poughkeepsie **164** 41 40N 73 57W
Poulaphouca Res. **35** 53 8N 6 30W
Póvoa de Varzim **50** 41 25N 8 46W
Powell, L. **163** 37 25N 110 45W
Powell River **154** 49 50N 124 35W
Powys □ **26** 52 20N 3 20W
Poyang Hu **99** 29 10N 116 10 E
Poyarkovo **75** 49 36N 128 41 E
Poznań **58** 52 25N 16 55 E
Prachuap Khiri Khan **94** 11 49N 99 48 E
Prague = Praha **58** 50 5N 14 22 E
Praha **58** 50 5N 14 22 E
Prainha, Amazonas, Brazil **187** 7 10S 60 30W
Prainha, Pará, Brazil **185** 1 45S 53 30W
Prairie du Chien **166** 43 1N 91 9W
Prato **46** 43 53N 11 5 E
Pratt **161** 37 40N 98 45W

Prepansko Jezero	**52**	40 55N	21	0 E
Preparis North Channel	**94**	15 12N	93	40 E
Preparis South Channel	**94**	14 36N	93	40 E
Prescott	**160**	34 35N	112	30W
Preservation Inlet	**123**	46 8S	166	35 E
Presidencia Roque Saenz				
Peña	**190**	26 45S	60	30W
Presidente Prudente	**188**	22 5S	51	25W
Presidio	**161**	29 30N	104	20W
Prespa, L. = Prepansko				
Jezero	**52**	40 55N	21	0 E
Presque Isle	**148**	46 40N	68	0W
Preston, Borders, U.K.	**28**	55 48N	2	18W
Preston, Lancs., U.K.	**21**	53 46N	2	42W
Prestonpans	**31**	55 58N	3	0W
Prestwick	**31**	55 30N	4	38W
Pretoria	**137**	25 44S	28	12 E
Préveza	**55**	38 57N	20	47 E
Prichard	**169**	30 47N	88	5W
Prilep	**52**	41 21N	21	37 E
Prince Albert	**152**	53 15N	105	50W
Prince Albert Pen.	**145**	72 30N	116	0W
Prince Albert Sd.	**145**	70 25N	115	0W
Prince Charles I.	**146**	67 47N	76	12W
Prince Edward I. □	**148**	46 20N	63	20W
Prince George	**154**	53 55N	122	50W
Prince of Wales I., Canada	**145**	73 0N	99	0W
Prince of Wales I., U.S.A.	**143**	55 30N	133	0W
Prince Patrick I.	**12**	77 0N	120	0W
Prince Rupert	**154**	54 20N	130	20W
Princess Royal I.	**154**	53 0N	128	40W
Princeton	**155**	49 27N	120	30W
Principe, I. de	**131**	1 37N	7	27 E
Principe da Beira	**187**	12 20S	64	30W
Pripet = Pripyat →	**68**	51 20N	30	9 E
Pripet Marshes = Polesye	**17**	52 0N	28	10 E
Pripyat →	**68**	51 20N	30	9 E
Pripyat Marshes = Polesye	**17**	52 0N	28	10 E
Priština	**52**	42 40N	21	13 E
Privolzhskaya Vozvyshennost	**17**	51 0N	46	0 E
Prizren	**52**	42 13N	20	45 E
Proddatur	**90**	14 45N	78	30 E
Progreso	**177**	21 17N	89	40W
Prokopyevsk	**71**	54 0N	86	45 E
Proserpine	**121**	20 21S	148	36 E
Provence	**37**	43 40N	5	46 E
Providence	**164**	41 50N	71	28W
Provo	**163**	40 16N	111	37W
Prudhoe Bay	**142**	70 20N	148	20W
Pruszków	**58**	52 9N	20	49 E
Prut →	**57**	46 3N	28	10 E
Przemyśl	**58**	49 50N	22	45 E
Przeworsk	**58**	50 6N	22	32 E
Pskov	**68**	57 50N	28	25 E
Pucallpa	**186**	8 25S	74	30W
Puebla	**177**	19 3N	98	12W
Puebla □	**177**	18 50N	98	0W
Pueblo	**163**	38 20N	104	40W
Puelches	**190**	38 5S	65	51W
Puente Alto	**190**	33 32S	70	35W
Puerto Armuelles	**179**	8 20N	82	51W
Puerto Ayacucho	**184**	5 40N	67	35W
Puerto Barrios	**177**	15 40N	88	32W
Puerto Cabello	**184**	10 28N	68	1W
Puerto Cabezas	**179**	14 0N	83	30W
Puerto Castilla	**179**	16 0N	86	0W
Puerto Cortes, C. Rica	**179**	8 55N	84	0W
Puerto Cortes, Hond.	**177**	15 51N	88	0W
Puerto Heath	**187**	12 34S	68	39W
Puerto La Cruz	**185**	10 13N	64	38W
Puerto Libertad	**174**	29 55N	112	41W
Puerto Lobos	**192**	42 0S	65	3W
Puerto Maldonado	**187**	12 30S	69	10W
Puerto Montt	**190**	41 28S	73	0W
Puerto Padre	**178**	21 13N	76	35W
Puerto Pinasco	**191**	22 36S	57	50W
Puerto Plata	**180**	19 48N	70	45W
Puerto Quepos	**179**	9 29N	84	6W
Puerto Rico ■	**180**	18 15N	66	45W
Puerto Vallarta	**175**	20 37N	105	15W
Puertollano	**50**	38 43N	4	7W
Puget Sd.	**171**	47 15N	122	30W
Pùglia □	**49**	41 0N	16	30 E
Pula	**52**	44 54N	13	57 E
Pulaski, Tenn., U.S.A.	**169**	35 10N	87	0W
Pulaski, Va., U.S.A.	**165**	37 4N	80	49W
Pulicat, L.	**90**	13 40N	80	15 E
Pullman	**171**	46 49N	117	10W
Punakha	**92**	27 42N	89	52 E
Punata	**187**	17 32S	65	50W
Pune	**91**	18 29N	73	57 E
Punjab □, India	**89**	31 0N	76	0 E
Punjab □, Pakistan.	**89**	30 0N	72	0 E
Puno	**187**	15 55S	70	3W
Punta Alta	**190**	38 53S	62	4W
Punta Arenas	**192**	53 10S	71	0W
Punta Gorda	**177**	16 10N	88	45W
Puntabie	**118**	32 12S	134	13 E
Puntarenas	**179**	10 0N	84	50W
Punto Fijo	**184**	11 50N	70	13W
Puquio	**186**	14 45S	74	10W
Pur →	**69**	67 31N	77	55 E
Purbeck, Isle of	**24**	50 40N	2	5W
Purmerend	**40**	52 30N	4	58 E
Purnia	**92**	25 45N	87	31 E
Pursat	**95**	12 34N	103	50 E
Purus →	**185**	3 42S	61	28W
Pusan	**98**	35 5N	129	0 E
Putao	**93**	27 28N	97	30 E
Putorana, Gory	**72**	69 0N	95	0 E
Putumayo →	**184**	3 7S	67	58W
Puy, Le	**37**	45 2N	3	53 E
Puy-de-Dôme	**37**	45 46N	2	57 E
Puyallup	**171**	47 10N	122	22W
Pwllheli	**26**	52 54N	4	26W
Pyasina →	**72**	73 30N	87	0 E
Pyatigorsk	**70**	44 2N	43	6 E
Pyinmana	**93**	19 45N	96	12 E
Pyŏngyang	**98**	39 0N	125	30 E
Pyramid L.	**172**	40 0N	119	30W
Pyrénées	**124**	42 45N	0	18 E
Qā'emshahr	**86**	36 30N	52	55 E
Qahremānshahr = Bākhtarān	**84**	34 23N	47	0 E
Qaidam Pendi	**100**	37 0N	95	0 E
Qal'at al Akhḍar	**82**	28 0N	37	10 E
Qamar, Ghubbat al	**83**	16 20N	52	30 E
Qamdo	**101**	31 15N	97	6 E
Qandahār	**87**	31 32N	65	30 E
Qaşr-e Qand	**85**	26 15N	60	45 E
Qatar ■	**85**	25 30N	51	15 E
Qāyen	**86**	33 40N	59	10 E
Qazvin	**81**	36 15N	50	0 E
Qena	**128**	26 10N	32	43 E
Qeshm	**85**	26 55N	56	10 E
Qilian Shan	**100**	38 30N	96	0 E
Qingdao	**98**	36 5N	120	20 E
Qinghai □	**101**	36 0N	98	0 E
Qinghai Hu	**100**	36 40N	100	10 E
Qinhuangdao	**98**	39 56N	119	30 E
Qiqihar	**98**	47 26N	124	0 E
Qom	**86**	34 40N	51	0 E
Qomsheh	**85**	32 0N	51	55 E
Qondūz □	**87**	36 50N	68	50 E
Qu Xian	**99**	30 48N	106	58 E
Quang Ngai	**95**	15 13N	108	58 E
Quantock Hills	**27**	51 8N	3	10W
Quanzhou	**99**	24 55N	118	34 E
Quatsino	**154**	50 30N	127	40W
Queanbeyan	**117**	35 17S	149	14 E
Québec	**148**	46 52N	71	13W
Québec □	**140**	50 0N	70	0W
Queen Alexandra Ra.	**15**	85 0S	170	0 E
Queen Charlotte	**154**	53 15N	132	2W
Queen Charlotte Is.	**154**	53 20N	132	10W
Queen Charlotte Str.	**154**	51 0N	128	0W
Queen Elizabeth Is.	**138**	76 0N	95	0W
Queen Mary Land	**15**	70 0S	95	0 E
Queen Maud G.	**145**	68 15N	102	30W
Queen Maud Mts.	**15**	86 0S	160	0W

Queenscliff . . . . **117** 38 16S 144 39 E
Queensland □ . . . . **115** 22 0S 142 0 E
Queenstown, Australia . . . . . **119** 42 4S 145 35 E
Queenstown, N.Z. . . . . **123** 45 1S 168 40 E
Quelimane . . . . **137** 17 53S 36 58 E
Quelpart = Cheju Do . . . . . . **99** 33 29N 126 34 E
Querétaro **177** 20 36N 100 23W
Querétaro □ **177** 21 0N 99 55W
Quesnel **154** 53 0N 122 30W
Quetta . . . . **88** 30 15N 66 55 E
Quezaltenango **177** 14 50N 91 30W
Quezon City . . . . **112** 14 38N 121 0 E
Qui Nhon . . . . **95** 13 40N 109 13 E
Quibdo **184** 5 42N 76 40W
Quillabamba **186** 12 50S 72 50W
Quilon . . . . **90** 8 50N 76 38 E
Quilpie . . . . **116** 26 35S 144 11 E
Quimper **36** 48 0N 4 9W
Quincy, Calif., U.S.A. **172** 39 56N 121 0W
Quincy, Fla., U.S.A. **170** 30 34N 84 34W
Quincy, Ill., U.S.A. **166** 39 55N 91 20W
Quincy, Mass., U.S.A. **164** 42 14N 71 0W
Quintana Roo □ **177** 19 40N 88 30W
Quirindi . . . . **116** 31 28S 150 40 E
Quitman **170** 30 49N 83 35W
Quito **184** 0 15S 78 35W
Quixadá **189** 4 55S 39 0W
Quorn . . . . **118** 32 25S 138 0 E
Quseir . . . . **128** 26 7N 34 16 E

Raahe . . . . **67** 64 40N 24 28 E
Raasay **32** 57 25N 6 4W
Rabat **126** 34 2N 6 48W
Rabaul . . . . **115** 4 24S 152 18 E
Rābigh . . . . **82** 22 50N 39 5 E
Race, C. **149** 46 40N 53 5W
Rach Gia . . . . **95** 10 5N 105 5 E
Racibórz . . . . **58** 50 7N 18 18 E
Racine **167** 42 41N 87 51W
Radium Hot Springs **155** 50 35N 116 2W
Radnor Forest **26** 52 17N 3 10W
Radom . . . . **58** 51 23N 21 12 E
Radomir . . . . **53** 42 37N 23 4 E
Radstock **27** 51 17N 2 25W
Radville **152** 49 30N 104 15W
Rae **145** 62 50N 116 3W
Rae Bareli . . . . **92** 26 18N 81 20 E
Raetihi . . . . **122** 39 25S 175 17 E
Rafaela **190** 31 10S 61 30W
Rafḥā . . . . **82** 29 35N 43 35 E
Rafsanjān . . . . **85** 30 30N 56 5 E
Ragama . . . . **90** 7 0N 79 50 E
Raglan . . . . **122** 37 55S 174 55 E
Ragusa . . . . **49** 36 56N 14 42 E
Rahaeng = Tak . . . . **94** 16 52N 99 8 E
Raichur . . . . **91** 16 10N 77 20 E
Rainier, Mt. **171** 46 50N 121 50W
Rainy L. **153** 48 42N 93 10W
Rainy River **153** 48 43N 94 29W
Raipur . . . . **92** 21 17N 81 45 E
Rajahmundry . . . . **92** 17 1N 81 48 E
Rajapalaiyam . . . . **90** 9 25N 77 35 E
Rajasthan □ . . . . **91** 26 45N 73 30 E
Rajasthan Canal . . . . **89** 28 0N 72 0 E
Rajkot . . . . **91** 22 15N 70 56 E
Rajshahi □ . . . . **92** 25 0N 89 0 E
Raleigh **165** 35 47N 78 39W
Raleigh B. **165** 34 50N 76 15W
Rambouillet . . . . **39** 48 40N 1 48 E
Rampur . . . . **89** 28 50N 79 5 E
Ramsey **28** 54 20N 4 21W
Rancagua **190** 34 10S 70 50W
Ranchi . . . . **92** 23 19N 85 27 E
Rangiora . . . . **123** 43 19S 172 36 E
Rangoon . . . . **93** 16 45N 96 20 E
Rangpur . . . . **92** 25 42N 89 22 E
Raniwara . . . . **91** 24 50N 72 10 E
Rankin Inlet **145** 62 30N 93 0W
Rankins Springs . . . . **117** 33 49S 146 14 E

Rannoch, L. **33** 56 41N 4 20W
Rannoch Moor **30** 56 38N 4 48W
Rapid City **163** 44 0N 103 0W
Ras Dashen . . . . **132** 13 8N 38 26 E
Rasa, Punta **192** 40 50S 62 15W
Rasht . . . . **81** 37 20N 49 40 E
Rat Is. . . . . **142** 51 50N 178 15 E
Ratangarh . . . . **89** 28 5N 74 35 E
Rath Luirc **35** 52 21N 8 40W
Rathlin I. **34** 55 18N 6 14W
Ratibor = Racibórz . . . . **58** 50 7N 18 18 E
Ratlam . . . . **91** 23 20N 75 0 E
Ratnagiri . . . . **91** 16 57N 73 18 E
Rattray Hd. **33** 57 38N 1 50W
Raub . . . . **96** 3 47N 101 52 E
Raukumara Ra. . . . . **122** 38 5S 177 55 E
Ravenna . . . . **47** 44 28N 12 15 E
Ravenshoe . . . . **121** 17 37S 145 29 E
Ravensthorpe . . . . **120** 33 35S 120 2 E
Rawalpindi . . . . **89** 33 38N 73 8 E
Rawlins **163** 41 50N 107 20W
Ray, C. **149** 47 33N 59 15W
Raymond **155** 49 30N 112 35W
Razgrad . . . . **53** 43 33N 26 34 E
Ré, Ile de **36** 46 12N 1 30W
Reading, U.K. **25** 51 27N 0 57W
Reading, U.S.A. **164** 40 20N 75 53W
Reay Forest **32** 58 20N 4 55W
Rebun-Tō . . . . **103** 45 23N 141 2 E
Recife **189** 8 0S 35 0W
Reconquista **190** 29 10S 59 45W
Recreo **190** 29 25S 65 10W
Red → **168** 31 0N 91 40W
Red Bluff **172** 40 11N 122 11W
Red Cliffs . . . . **119** 34 19S 142 11 E
Red Deer **155** 52 20N 113 50W
Red Lake **153** 51 3N 93 49W
Red Oak **166** 41 0N 95 10W
Red Sea . . . . **128** 25 0N 36 0 E
Red Tower Pass = Turnu
    Rosu Pasul . . . . **57** 45 33N 24 17 E
Red Wing **166** 44 32N 92 35W
Redcar **29** 54 37N 1 4W
Redcliff **152** 50 10N 110 50W
Redcliffe . . . . **116** 27 12S 153 0 E
Redding **172** 40 30N 122 25W
Redditch **24** 52 18N 1 57W
Redlands **173** 34 0N 117 11W
Redruth **27** 50 14N 5 14W
Redwater **155** 53 55N 113 6W
Redwood City **172** 37 30N 122 15W
Ree, L. **34** 53 35N 8 0W
Reedley **173** 36 36N 119 27W
Regensburg . . . . **43** 49 1N 12 7 E
Réggio di Calábria . . . . **49** 38 7N 15 38 E
Réggio nell' Emilia . . . . **46** 44 42N 10 38 E
Regina **152** 50 27N 104 35W
Rehovot . . . . **80** 31 54N 34 48 E
Reichenbach . . . . **43** 50 36N 12 19 E
Reidsville **165** 36 21N 79 40W
Reims . . . . **39** 49 15N 4 0 E
Reina Adelaida, Arch. **192** 52 20S 74 0W
Reindeer L. **143** 57 15N 102 15W
Reliance **145** 63 0N 109 20W
Remanso **189** 9 41S 42 4W
Remarkable, Mt. . . . . **118** 32 48S 138 10 E
Remscheid . . . . **42** 51 11N 7 12 E
Rendsburg . . . . **42** 54 18N 9 41 E
Renfrew, Canada **151** 45 30N 76 40W
Renfrew, U.K. **31** 55 52N 4 24W
Renkum . . . . **41** 51 58N 5 43 E
Renmark . . . . **119** 34 11S 140 43 E
Rennes **36** 48 7N 1 41W
Reno **172** 39 30N 119 50W
Republic **150** 46 25N 87 59W
Republican → **163** 39 3N 96 48W
Repulse Bay **146** 66 30N 86 30W
Requena **186** 5 5S 73 52W
Resht = Rasht . . . . **81** 37 20N 49 40 E
Resistencia **190** 27 30S 59 0W
Resolution I., Canada **146** 61 30N 65 0W

Resolution I., N.Z.	**123**	45 40S	166 40 E
Retalhuleu	**177**	14 33N	91 46W
Réthímnon	**55**	35 18N	24 30 E
Réunion	**9**	22 0S	56 0 E
Reval = Tallinn	**68**	59 22N	24 48 E
Revelstoke	**155**	51 0N	118 10W
Revilla Gigedo, Is.	**139**	18 40N	112 0W
Rewa	**92**	24 33N	81 25 E
Rewari	**89**	28 15N	76 40 E
Rexburg	**163**	43 55N	111 50W
Rey Malabo	**131**	3 45N	8 50 E
Reykjavík	**64**	64 10N	21 57 E
Reynosa	**176**	26 5N	98 18W
Rhayader	**26**	52 19N	3 30W
Rhein →	**42**	51 52N	6 20 E
Rheinland-Pfalz □	**42**	50 0N	7 0 E
Rhin = Rhein →	**42**	51 52N	6 20 E
Rhine = Rhein →	**42**	51 52N	6 20 E
Rhineland-Palatinate □ = Rheinland-Pfalz □	**42**	50 0N	7 0 E
Rhinelander	**150**	45 38N	89 29W
Rhode Island □	**164**	41 38N	71 37W
Rhodes = Ródhos	**55**	36 15N	28 10 E
Rhodesia = Zimbabwe ■	**137**	20 0S	30 0 E
Rhodope Mts. = Rhodopi Planina	**53**	41 40N	24 20 E
Rhodopi Planina	**53**	41 40N	24 20 E
Rhön	**42**	50 24N	9 58 E
Rhondda	**27**	51 39N	3 30W
Rhône →	**37**	43 28N	4 42 E
Rhum	**32**	57 0N	6 20W
Rhyl	**26**	53 19N	3 29W
Rhymney	**27**	51 45N	3 17W
Riachão	**188**	7 20S	46 37W
Riau, Kepulauan	**111**	0 30N	104 20 E
Ribatejo □	**50**	39 15N	8 30W
Ribble →	**28**	54 13N	2 20W
Ribeirão Prêto	**188**	21 10S	47 50W
Riberalta	**187**	11 0S	66 0W
Riccarton	**123**	43 32S	172 37 E
Richland	**171**	46 15N	119 15W
Richmond, Australia	**116**	20 43S	143 8 E
Richmond, N.Z.	**123**	41 20S	173 12 E
Richmond, N. Yorks., U.K.	**28**	54 24N	1 43W
Richmond, Surrey, U.K.	**25**	51 28N	0 18W
Richmond, Calif., U.S.A.	**172**	37 58N	122 21W
Richmond, Ind., U.S.A.	**167**	39 50N	84 50W
Richmond, Ky., U.S.A.	**165**	37 40N	84 20W
Richmond, Va., U.S.A.	**165**	37 33N	77 27W
Richwood	**165**	38 17N	80 32W
Ridgeway	**164**	42 56S	147 16 E
Riga	**68**	56 53N	24 8 E
Rīgestān □	**87**	30 15N	65 0 E
Rigolet	**147**	54 10N	58 23W
Rijeka	**52**	45 20N	14 21 E
Rijssen	**41**	52 19N	6 30 E
Rijswijk	**40**	52 4N	4 22 E
Rímini	**47**	44 3N	12 33 E
Rîmnicu Vîlcea	**57**	45 9N	24 21 E
Rimouski	**148**	48 27N	68 30W
Rinía	**55**	37 23N	25 13 E
Rio Branco	**187**	9 58S	67 49W
Rio Claro	**180**	10 20N	61 25W
Río Cuarto	**190**	33 10S	64 25W
Rio de Janeiro	**188**	23 0S	43 12W
Rio de Janeiro □	**188**	22 50S	43 0W
Río Gallegos	**192**	51 35S	69 15W
Rio Grande	**191**	32 0S	52 20W
Rio Grande →	**161**	25 57N	97 9W
Rio Grande do Norte □	**189**	5 40S	36 0W
Rio Grande do Sul □	**191**	30 0S	53 0W
Río Mulatos	**187**	19 40S	66 50W
Rio Negro	**191**	26 0S	50 0W
Rio Verde	**188**	17 50S	51 0W
Ríobamba	**184**	1 50S	78 45W
Ríohacha	**184**	11 33N	72 55W
Rioja, La	**190**	29 20S	67 0W
Rioja, La □	**50**	42 20N	2 20W
Ríosucio	**184**	7 27N	77 7W
Ripon	**28**	54 8N	1 31W
Rishiri-Tō	**103**	45 11N	141 15 E
Ritchies Archipelago	**94**	12 5N	94 0 E
Rivas	**179**	11 30N	85 50W
Riverhead	**164**	40 53N	72 40W
Riverside	**173**	34 0N	117 22W
Riverton	**153**	51 1N	97 0W
Riviera di Levante	**46**	44 23N	9 15 E
Riviera di Ponente	**46**	43 50N	7 58 E
Rivière-du-Loup	**148**	47 50N	69 30W
Riyadh = Ar Riyāḑ	**83**	24 41N	46 42 E
Roanne	**37**	46 3N	4 4 E
Roanoke, Ala., U.S.A.	**169**	33 9N	85 23W
Roanoke, Va., U.S.A.	**165**	37 19N	79 55W
Roanoke →	**165**	35 56N	76 43W
Roanoke Rapids	**165**	36 28N	77 42W
Robinvale	**119**	34 40S	142 45 E
Roblin	**152**	51 14N	101 21W
Roboré	**187**	18 10S	59 45W
Robson, Mt.	**155**	53 10N	119 10W
Roca, C. da	**50**	38 40N	9 31W
Rocha	**191**	34 30S	54 25W
Rochdale	**28**	53 36N	2 10W
Roche-sur-Yon, La	**36**	46 40N	1 25W
Rochefort	**36**	45 56N	0 57W
Rochelle, La	**36**	46 10N	1 9W
Rochester, Minn., U.S.A.	**166**	44 1N	92 28W
Rochester, N.H., U.S.A.	**164**	43 19N	70 57W
Rochester, N.Y., U.S.A.	**164**	43 10N	77 40W
Rock Hill	**165**	34 55N	81 2W
Rock Island	**166**	41 30N	90 35W
Rock Sprs.	**163**	41 40N	109 10W
Rockall	**16**	57 37N	13 42W
Rockford	**166**	42 20N	89 0W
Rockglen	**152**	49 11N	105 57W
Rockhampton	**119**	23 22S	150 32 E
Rockingham	**120**	32 15S	115 38 E
Rockland	**148**	44 6N	69 6W
Rocky Mount	**165**	35 55N	77 48W
Rocky Mountain House	**155**	52 22N	114 55W
Rocky Mts.	**138**	55 0N	121 0W
Ródhos	**55**	36 15N	28 10 E
Roebourne	**114**	20 44S	117 9 E
Roermond	**41**	51 12N	6 0 E
Roes Welcome Sd.	**146**	65 0N	87 0W
Rogaland fylke □	**60**	59 12N	6 20 E
Rogers	**168**	36 20N	94 5W
Rohri	**88**	27 45N	68 51 E
Rohtak	**89**	28 55N	76 43 E
Rojo, C.	**177**	21 33N	97 20W
Rolla	**166**	37 56N	91 42W
Roma, Australia	**116**	26 32S	148 49 E
Roma, Italy	**46**	41 54N	12 30 E
Romaine →	**141**	50 18N	63 47W
Roman	**57**	46 57N	26 55 E
Romana, La	**180**	18 27N	68 57W
Romania ■	**57**	46 0N	25 0 E
Romans	**37**	45 3N	5 3 E
Romanzof, C.	**142**	62 0N	165 50W
Rome = Roma	**46**	41 54N	12 30 E
Rome, Ga., U.S.A.	**169**	34 20N	85 0W
Rome, N.Y., U.S.A.	**164**	43 14N	75 29W
Romilly	**39**	48 31N	3 44 E
Romney Marsh	**25**	51 0N	1 0 E
Rona	**32**	57 33N	6 0W
Rondônia □	**187**	11 0S	63 0W
Rong, Koh	**95**	10 45N	103 15 E
Ronge, L. la	**152**	55 6N	105 17W
Roosendaal	**40**	51 32N	4 29 E
Roraima □	**185**	2 0N	61 30W
Roraima, Mt.	**185**	5 10N	60 40W
Rosario, Argentina	**190**	33 0S	60 40W
Rosario, Brazil	**188**	3 0S	44 15W
Rosario, Mexico	**175**	22 58N	105 53W
Rosario, Paraguay	**191**	24 30S	57 35W
Rosário do Sul	**191**	30 15S	54 55W
Roscommon	**34**	53 38N	8 11W
Roscommon □	**34**	53 40N	8 15W
Roscrea	**35**	52 58N	7 50W
Roseau	**180**	15 20N	61 24W
Roseburg	**171**	43 10N	123 20W
Rosenberg	**168**	29 30N	95 48W
Rosendaël	**38**	51 3N	2 24 E

Rosetown **152** 51 35N 107 59W
Roseville **172** 38 46N 121 17W
Rosewood . . . . **116** 27 38S 152 36 E
Roskilde . . . . **61** 55 38N 12 3 E
Ross on Wye **24** 51 55N 2 34W
Ross Sea . . . . **15** 74 0S 178 0 E
Rossan Pt. **34** 54 42N 8 47W
Rossland **155** 49 6N 117 50W
Rosslare **35** 52 17N 6 23W
Røssvatnet . . . . **65** 65 45N 14 5 E
Rosthern **152** 52 40N 106 20W
Rostock . . . . **43** 54 4N 12 9 E
Rostov . . . . **68** 47 15N 39 45 E
Roswell. **161** 33 26N 104 32W
Rosyth **31** 56 2N 3 26W
Rother ⟶ . . . . **25** 50 59N 0 40 E
Rotherham **29** 53 26N 1 21W
Rothesay **30** 55 50N 5 3W
Roto . . . . **117** 33 0S 145 30 E
Rotorua . . . . **122** 38 9S 176 16 E
Rotorua, L. . . . . **122** 38 5S 176 18 E
Rotterdam . . . . **40** 51 55N 4 30 E
Rotuma . . . . **122** 12 25S 177 5 E
Roubaix . . . . **37** 50 40N 3 10 E
Rouen . . . . **38** 49 27N 1 4 E
Round Mt. . . . . **116** 30 26S 152 16 E
Roussillon . . . . **37** 42 30N 2 35 E
Rouyn **151** 48 20N 79 0W
Rovaniemi . . . . **67** 66 29N 25 41 E
Rovno . . . . **68** 50 40N 26 10 E
Ruahine Ra. . . . . **122** 39 55S 176 2 E
Ruapehu . . . . **122** 39 17S 175 35 E
Rub' al Khali . . . . **83** 18 0N 48 0 E
Rubh a' Mhail **30** 55 55N 6 10W
Rubio **184** 7 43N 72 22W
Rubtsovsk . . . . **71** 51 30N 81 10 E
Rudnyy . . . . **71** 52 57N 63 7 E
Rudolf, Ostrov . . . . **69** 81 45N 58 30 E
Rufiji ⟶ . . . . **135** 7 50S 39 15 E
Rufino **190** 34 20S 62 50W
Rugby. **25** 52 23N 1 16W
Rügen. . . . . **43** 54 22N 13 25 E
Ruhr ⟶ . . . . **42** 51 25N 6 44 E
Rukwa L. . . . . **135** 8 0S 32 20 E
Rumania = Romania ■ . . . . **57** 46 0N 25 0 E
Rumford **148** 44 30N 70 30W
Rumoi **103** 43 56N 141 39W
Runcorn **28** 53 20N 2 44W
Rupat . . . . **111** 1 45N 101 40 E
Rupert ⟶ **140** 51 29N 78 45W
Rupert House = Fort Rupert . . **140** 51 30N 78 40W
Ruschuk = Ruse. . . . . **53** 43 48N 25 59 E
Ruse . . . . **53** 43 48N 25 59 E
Russell **152** 50 50N 101 20W
Russellville, Ala., U.S.A. **169** 34 30N 87 44W
Russellville, Ark., U.S.A. **168** 35 15N 93 8W
Ruston **168** 32 30N 92 58W
Rutherglen. **31** 55 50N 4 11W
Rutland I. . . . . **94** 11 25N 92 40 E
Ruwenzori . . . . **132** 0 30N 29 55 E
Rwanda ■ . . . . **135** 2 0S 30 0 E
Ryan, L. **30** 55 0N 5 2W
Ryazan . . . . **68** 54 40N 39 40 E
Rybache . . . . **71** 46 40N 81 20 E
Rybinsk = Andropov . . . . . . **68** 58 5N 38 50 E
Ryde **25** 50 44N 1 9W
Rye . . . . **25** 50 57N 0 46 E
Rylstone . . . . **117** 32 46S 149 58 E
Ryōhaku-Sanchi . . . . **106** 36 9N 136 49 E
Ryūgasaki . . . . **107** 35 54N 140 11 E
Rzeszów . . . . **58** 50 5N 21 58 E

Sa Dec . . . . **95** 10 20N 105 46 E
Saar ⟶ . . . . **42** 49 41N 6 32 E
Saarbrücken . . . . **42** 49 15N 6 58 E
Saaremaa . . . . **68** 58 30N 22 30 E
Saarland □ . . . . **42** 49 15N 7 0 E
Sabadell. . . . . **51** 41 28N 2 7 E
Sabae. . . . . **106** 35 57N 136 11 E

Sabah □ . . . . **112** 6 0N 117 0 E
Sábana de la Mar **180** 19 7N 69 24W
Sabhah . . . . **127** 27 9N 14 29 E
Sabi ⟶ . . . . **137** 18 50S 31 40 E
Sabinas **174** 27 51N 101 7W
Sabinas Hidalgo, R. ⟶ **176** 26 50N 99 35W
Sabine ⟶ **158** 30 0N 93 35W
Sable, C., Canada **148** 43 29N 65 38W
Sable, C., U.S.A. **159** 25 13N 81 0W
Sable I. **149** 44 0N 60 0W
Sabrina Coast . . . . **15** 68 0S 120 0 E
Sabzevār . . . . **86** 36 15N 57 40 E
Saco **148** 43 30N 70 27W
Sacramento. . . . . **172** 38 33N 121 30 E
Sacramento ⟶ **172** 38 3N 121 56W
Sacramento Mts. **161** 32 30N 105 30W
Sado, Shima . . . . **103** 38 15N 138 30 E
Safed Koh . . . . **87** 34 0N 70 0 E
Saffron Walden . . . . **25** 52 2N 0 15 E
Safi **126** 32 18N 9 20W
Saga . . . . **108** 33 15N 130 16 E
Sagami-Nada . . . . **107** 34 58N 139 30 E
Sagami-Wan . . . . **107** 35 15N 139 25 E
Sagamihara . . . . **107** 35 33N 139 25 E
Sagar . . . . **91** 14 14N 75 6 E
Sagara . . . . **107** 34 41N 138 12 E
Saginaw **167** 43 26N 83 55W
Saginaw B. **167** 43 50N 83 40W
Saglouc **146** 62 14N 75 38W
Sagres **50** 37 0N 8 58W
Sagua la Grande **178** 22 50N 80 10W
Saguenay ⟶ **148** 48 22N 71 0W
Sahara . . . . **126** 23 0N 5 0 E
Saharanpur . . . . **89** 29 58N 77 33 E
Saharien, Atlas . . . . **127** 33 30N 1 0 E
Sahiwal. . . . . **89** 30 45N 73 8 E
Sahuaripa **174** 29 3N 109 14W
Saigō . . . . **109** 36 12N 133 20 E
Saigon = Thanh Pho Ho Chi
Minh . . . . **95** 10 58N 106 40 E
Saijō, Ehime, Japan . . . . **109** 33 55N 133 11 E
Saijō, Hiroshima, Japan . . . . . **109** 34 25N 132 45 E
Saikhoa Ghat. . . . . **93** 27 50N 95 40 E
Saiki . . . . **108** 32 58N 131 51 E
Saimaa . . . . **67** 61 15N 28 15 E
Sa'in Dezh . . . . **81** 36 40N 46 25 E
St. Abb's Head **31** 55 55N 2 10W
St. Albans, U.K. **25** 51 44N 0 19W
St. Albans, U.S.A. **151** 44 49N 73 7W
St. Alban's Head **24** 50 34N 2 3W
St. Albert **155** 53 37N 113 32W
St. Andrews **31** 56 20N 2 48W
St. Arnaud . . . . **119** 36 40S 143 16 E
St. Asaph **26** 53 15N 3 27W
St-Augustin-Saguenay **141** 51 13N 58 38W
St. Augustine **170** 29 52N 81 20W
St. Austell **27** 50 20N 4 48W
St. Bee's Hd. . . . . **28** 54 30N 3 38 E
St. Boniface **153** 49 53N 97 5W
St. Bride's B. **26** 51 48N 5 15W
St-Brieuc **36** 48 30N 2 46W
St. Catharines **151** 43 10N 79 15W
St. Charles **166** 38 46N 90 30W
St. Christopher-Nevis ■ **180** 17 20N 62 40W
St. Cloud **156** 45 30N 94 11W
St. Croix **180** 17 45N 64 45W
St. David's **26** 51 54N 5 16W
St. David's Head **26** 51 55N 5 16W
St-Denis . . . . **39** 48 56N 2 22 E
St-Dizier . . . . **37** 48 40N 5 0 E
St. Elias, Mt. **144** 60 14N 140 50W
St. Elias Mts. **144** 60 33N 139 28W
St-Étienne . . . . **37** 45 27N 4 22 E
St-Félicien **151** 48 40N 72 25W
St. Gallen . . . . **44** 47 25N 9 20 E
St. George, Australia . . . . **116** 28 1S 148 30 E
St. George, Bermuda. **180** 32 24N 64 42W
St. Georges, Fr. Gui. **185** 4 0N 52 0W
St. Georges, Grenada **180** 12 5N 61 43W
St. George's Channel **20** 52 0N 6 0W

St. Gotthard P. = San Gottardo, Paso del	**44**	46 33N	8 33 E
St. Helena	**125**	15 55S	5 44W
St. Helena B.	**136**	32 40S	18 10 E
St. Helens, Australia	**119**	41 20S	148 15 E
St. Helens, U.K.	**28**	53 28N	2 44W
St. Helens, U.S.A.	**171**	45 55N	122 50W
St. Helier	**36**	49 11N	2 6W
St-Hyacinthe	**151**	45 40N	72 58W
St. Ives, Cambs., U.K.	**25**	52 20N	0 5W
St. Ives, Cornwall, U.K.	**27**	50 13N	5 29W
St-Jean	**151**	45 20N	73 20W
St-Jérôme	**151**	45 47N	74 0W
St. John	**148**	45 20N	66 8W
St. John's	**149**	47 35N	52 40W
St. John's →	**170**	30 20N	81 30W
St. Johnsbury	**148**	44 25N	72 1W
St. Joseph, Mich., U.S.A.	**167**	42 5N	86 30W
St. Joseph, Mo., U.S.A.	**166**	39 46N	94 50W
St. Kilda, N.Z.	**123**	45 53S	170 31 E
St. Kilda, U.K.	**22**	57 9N	8 34W
St. Lawrence	**149**	46 54N	55 23W
St. Lawrence →	**148**	49 30N	66 0W
St. Lawrence, Gulf of	**149**	48 25N	62 0W
St. Lawrence I.	**142**	63 0N	170 0W
St. Leonard	**148**	47 12N	67 58W
St-Louis	**130**	16 8N	16 27W
St. Louis	**166**	38 40N	90 12W
St. Lucia ■	**180**	14 0N	60 50W
St. Maarten	**180**	18 0N	63 5W
St-Malo	**36**	48 39N	2 1W
St-Marc	**180**	19 10N	72 41W
St-Martin, I.	**180**	18 0N	63 0W
St. Mary Pk.	**118**	31 32S	138 34 E
St. Marys	**164**	41 27N	78 33W
St. Matthews, I. = Zadetkyi Kyun	**94**	10 0N	98 25 E
St. Michael's Mt.	**27**	50 7N	5 30W
St. Moritz	**44**	46 30N	9 51 E
St-Nazaire	**36**	47 17N	2 12W
St. Neots	**25**	52 14N	0 16W
St-Omer	**38**	50 45N	2 15 E
St. Pascal	**148**	47 32N	69 48W
St. Paul	**166**	44 54N	93 5W
St. Paul, I.	**149**	47 12N	60 9W
St. Petersburg	**170**	27 45N	82 40W
St-Pierre et Miquelon □	**149**	46 55N	56 10W
St-Quentin	**38**	49 50N	3 16 E
St-Raphaël	**37**	43 25N	6 46 E
St-Servan-sur-Mer	**36**	48 38N	2 0W
St. Thomas, Canada	**151**	42 45N	81 10W
St. Thomas, W. Indies	**180**	18 21N	64 55W
St-Tropez	**37**	43 17N	6 38 E
St. Vincent and the Grenadines ■	**180**	13 0N	61 10W
Ste-Adresse	**38**	49 31N	0 5 E
Ste Anne de Beaupré	**148**	47 2N	70 58W
Ste Marie	**180**	14 48N	61 1W
Ste-Rose	**180**	16 20N	61 45W
Ste. Rose du lac	**153**	51 4N	99 30W
Saintes	**36**	45 45N	0 37W
Saintonge	**36**	45 40N	0 50W
Saito	**108**	32 3N	131 24 E
Sajama	**187**	18 7S	69 0W
Sakai	**106**	34 30N	135 30 E
Sakaide	**109**	34 15N	133 50 E
Sakaiminato	**109**	35 38N	133 11 E
Sakakawea, L.	**163**	47 30N	102 0W
Sakata	**103**	38 55N	139 50 E
Sakhalin	**79**	51 0N	143 0 E
Sakhalinskiy Zaliv	**75**	54 0N	141 0 E
Saku	**107**	36 17N	138 31 E
Sakura	**107**	35 43N	140 14 E
Sakurai	**106**	34 30N	135 51 E
Salaberry-de-Valleyfield	**151**	45 15N	74 8W
Salado →	**190**	31 40S	60 41W
Salado, R. →	**176**	26 52N	99 19W
Salamanca, Spain	**50**	40 58N	5 39W
Salamanca, U.S.A.	**164**	42 10N	78 42W
Salamis	**55**	37 56N	23 30 E
Salcombe	**27**	50 14N	3 47W
Sale	**117**	38 6S	147 6 E
Salem, India	**90**	11 40N	78 11 E
Salem, Mass., U.S.A.	**164**	42 29N	70 53W
Salem, Oreg., U.S.A.	**171**	45 0N	123 0W
Salem, Va., U.S.A.	**165**	37 19N	80 8W
Salerno	**49**	40 40N	14 44 E
Salford	**28**	53 30N	2 17W
Salida	**163**	38 35N	106 0W
Salina, Italy	**49**	38 35N	14 50 E
Salina, U.S.A.	**161**	38 50N	97 40W
Salina Cruz	**177**	16 10N	95 12W
Salinas, Ecuador	**184**	2 10S	80 58W
Salinas, U.S.A.	**173**	36 40N	121 41W
Salinas →	**173**	36 45N	121 48W
Salinas Grandes	**190**	30 0S	65 0W
Salisbury = Harare	**137**	17 43S	31 2 E
Salisbury, U.K.	**24**	51 4N	1 48W
Salisbury, Md., U.S.A.	**165**	38 20N	75 38W
Salisbury, N.C., U.S.A.	**165**	35 20N	80 29W
Salisbury Plain	**24**	51 13N	1 50W
Salle, La	**166**	41 20N	89 6W
Salmon	**162**	45 12N	113 56W
Salmon →	**171**	45 51N	116 46W
Salmon Arm	**155**	50 40N	119 15W
Salmon River Mts.	**162**	45 0N	114 30W
Salon-de-Provence	**37**	43 39N	5 6 E
Salonica = Thessaloníki	**54**	40 38N	22 58 E
Salop = Shropshire □	**24**	52 36N	2 45W
Salt Fork →	**161**	36 37N	97 7W
Salt Lake City	**163**	40 45N	111 58W
Salta	**190**	24 57S	65 25W
Saltcoats	**30**	55 38N	4 47W
Saltillo	**174**	25 25N	101 0W
Salto	**191**	31 27S	57 50W
Salton Sea	**173**	33 20N	115 50W
Salûm	**128**	31 31N	25 7 E
Salvador	**189**	13 0S	38 30W
Salween →	**93**	16 31N	97 37 E
Salzburg	**45**	47 48N	13 2 E
Salzburg □	**45**	47 15N	13 0 E
Salzgitter	**43**	52 13N	10 22 E
Sam Neua	**95**	20 29N	104 0 E
Sama	**69**	60 12N	60 22 E
Samangán □	**87**	36 15N	68 3 E
Samar	**112**	12 0N	125 0 E
Samarkand	**70**	39 40N	66 55 E
Sāmarrā	**81**	34 12N	43 52 E
Sambalpur	**92**	21 28N	84 4 E
Sambhal	**89**	28 35N	78 37 E
Sámos	**55**	37 45N	26 50 E
Samothráki	**55**	40 28N	25 28 E
Samsun	**80**	41 15N	36 22 E
Samut Prakan	**95**	13 32N	100 40 E
Samut Sakhon	**94**	13 31N	100 13 E
Samut Songkhram →	**94**	13 24N	100 1 E
San Andreas	**172**	38 0N	120 39W
San Andres Mts.	**161**	33 0N	106 45W
San Andrés Tuxtla	**177**	18 27N	95 13W
San Angelo	**161**	31 30N	100 30W
San Antonio, Chile	**190**	33 40S	71 40W
San Antonio, U.S.A.	**161**	29 30N	98 30W
San Antonio, C., Argentina	**191**	36 15S	56 40W
San Antonio, C., Cuba	**178**	21 50N	84 57W
San Antonio de los Baños	**178**	22 54N	82 31W
San Antônio Falls	**182**	9 30S	65 0W
San Antonio Oeste	**192**	40 40S	65 0W
San Bernardino	**173**	34 7N	117 18W
San Bernardino Str.	**112**	13 0N	125 0 E
San Bernardo	**190**	33 40S	70 50W
San Blas, C.	**169**	29 40N	85 12W
San Carlos, Chile	**190**	36 10S	72 0W
San Carlos, Mexico	**174**	29 1N	100 51W
San Carlos, Nic.	**179**	11 12N	84 50W
San Carlos de Bariloche	**192**	41 10S	71 25W
San Clemente I.	**173**	32 53N	118 30W
San Cristóbal, Argentina	**190**	30 20S	61 10W
San Cristóbal, Dom. Rep.	**180**	18 25N	70 6W
San Cristóbal, Venezuela	**184**	16 50N	92 40W
San Cristóbal de las Casas	**177**	16 45N	92 38W
San Diego	**173**	32 43N	117 10W
San Felipe, Chile	**190**	32 43S	70 42W

San Felipe, Colombia	**184**	1 55N	67 6W
San Fernando, Chile	**190**	34 30S	71 0W
San Fernando, Mexico	**174**	30 0N	115 10W
San Fernando, Trin. & Tob.	**180**	10 20N	61 30W
San Fernando, U.S.A.	**173**	34 15N	118 29W
San Fernando de Apure	**184**	7 54N	67 15W
San Francisco	**172**	37 47N	122 30W
San Francisco de Macorís	**180**	19 19N	70 15W
San Francisco del Oro	**174**	26 52N	105 51W
San Gabriel	**191**	0 36N	77 49W
San Gottardo, Paso del	**44**	46 33N	8 33 E
San Ignacio	**187**	16 20S	60 55W
San Joaquin →	**172**	37 4N	121 51W
San Jorge, Golfo	**192**	46 0S	66 0W
San Jorge, G. de	**51**	40 50N	0 55W
San José, Bolivia	**187**	17 53S	60 50W
San José, C. Rica	**179**	10 0N	84 2W
San José, U.S.A.	**172**	37 20N	121 53W
San José de Mayo	**191**	34 27S	56 40W
San José del Cabo	**175**	23 3N	109 41W
San José del Guaviare	**184**	2 35N	72 38W
San Juan, Argentina	**190**	31 30S	68 30W
San Juan, Dom. Rep.	**180**	18 49N	71 12W
San Juan, Puerto Rico	**180**	18 28N	66 8W
San Juan →	**179**	10 56N	83 42W
San Juan de los Morros	**184**	9 55N	67 21W
San Juan Mts.	**163**	38 30N	108 30W
San Julián	**192**	49 15S	67 45W
San Leandro	**172**	37 40N	122 6W
San Lorenzo	**184**	1 15N	78 50W
San Lucas, C. de	**175**	22 50N	110 0W
San Luis	**190**	33 20S	66 20W
San Luis de la Paz	**177**	21 18N	100 31W
San Luis Obispo	**173**	35 21N	120 38W
San Luis Potosí	**177**	22 9N	100 59W
San Luis Potosí □	**177**	22 30N	100 30W
San Marcos	**177**	14 59N	91 52W
San Marino ■	**47**	43 56N	12 25 E
San Mateo	**172**	37 32N	122 19W
San Matías	**187**	16 25S	58 20W
San Matías, Golfo	**192**	41 30S	64 0W
San Miguel	**177**	13 30N	88 12W
San Miguel de Tucumán	**190**	26 50S	65 20W
San Pedro →	**175**	21 45N	105 30W
San Pedro de las Colonias	**174**	25 45N	102 59W
San Pedro de Macorís	**180**	18 30N	69 18W
San Pedro Sula	**177**	15 30N	88 0W
San Rafael, Argentina	**190**	34 40S	68 21W
San Rafael, U.S.A.	**172**	37 59N	122 32W
San Roque	**190**	28 25S	58 45W
San Salvador, Bahamas	**178**	24 0N	74 40W
San Salvador, El Salv.	**177**	13 40N	89 10W
San Salvador de Jujuy	**190**	24 10S	64 48W
San Sebastián	**51**	43 17N	1 58W
San Valentin, Mte.	**192**	46 30S	73 30W
Sana'	**82**	15 27N	44 12 E
Sanandaj	**81**	35 18N	47 1 E
Sancti-Spíritus	**178**	21 52N	79 33W
Sanda	**106**	34 53N	135 14 E
Sandgate	**116**	27 18S	153 3 E
Sandomierz	**58**	50 40N	21 43 E
Sandpoint	**171**	48 20N	116 34W
Sandringham	**29**	52 50N	0 30 E
Sandstone	**120**	27 59S	119 16 E
Sandusky	**167**	41 25N	82 40W
Sandwip Chan.	**93**	22 35N	91 35 E
Sandy C.	**119**	41 25S	144 45 E
Sandy Lake	**153**	53 0N	93 15W
Sanford, Fla., U.S.A.	**170**	28 45N	81 20W
Sanford, Maine, U.S.A.	**148**	43 28N	70 47W
Sanford, N.C., U.S.A.	**165**	35 30N	79 10W
Sangay	**184**	2 0S	78 20W
Sangihe, P.	**113**	3 45N	125 30 E
Sangli	**91**	16 55N	74 33 E
Sangre de Cristo Mts.	**161**	37 0N	105 0W
Sankuru →	**134**	4 17S	20 25 E
Sano	**107**	36 19N	139 35 E
Sanok	**59**	49 35N	22 10 E
Sanquhar	**31**	55 21N	3 56W
Sanshui	**99**	23 10N	112 56 E
Santa Ana, Bolivia	**187**	13 50S	65 40W
Santa Ana, Mexico	**174**	30 33N	111 7W
Santa Ana, U.S.A.	**173**	33 48N	117 55W
Santa Bárbara, Mexico	**174**	26 48N	105 49W
Santa Bárbara, U.S.A.	**173**	34 25N	119 40W
Santa Barbara I.	**160**	33 29N	119 2W
Santa Catarina □	**191**	27 25S	48 30W
Santa Clara, Cuba	**178**	22 20N	80 0W
Santa Clara, U.S.A.	**162**	37 21N	122 0W
Santa Clotilde	**186**	2 33S	73 45W
Santa Cruz, Bolivia	**187**	17 43S	63 10W
Santa Cruz, U.S.A.	**172**	36 55N	122 1W
Santa Cruz, Is.	**122**	10 30S	166 0 E
Sta. Cruz de Tenerife	**126**	28 28N	16 15W
Santa Cruz del Sur	**178**	20 44N	78 0W
Santa Cruz do Sul	**191**	29 42S	52 25W
Santa Fe, Argentina	**190**	31 35S	60 41W
Santa Fe, U.S.A.	**161**	35 40N	106 0W
Santa Inés, I.	**192**	54 0S	73 0W
Santa Isabel = Rey Malabo	**131**	3 45N	8 50 E
Santa Lucia Range	**173**	36 0N	121 20W
Santa Maria, Brazil	**191**	29 40S	53 48W
Santa Maria, U.S.A.	**173**	34 58N	120 29W
Santa Maria da Vitória	**188**	13 24S	44 12W
Santa Maria di Leuca, C.	**49**	39 48N	18 20 E
Santa Marta	**184**	11 15N	74 13W
Santa Maura = Levkás	**54**	38 40N	20 43 E
Santa Monica	**173**	34 0N	118 30W
Santa Rosa, Argentina	**190**	36 40S	64 17W
Santa Rosa, U.S.A.	**172**	38 26N	122 43W
Santa Rosa I., Calif., U.S.A.	**173**	34 0N	120 6W
Santa Rosa I., Fla., U.S.A.	**169**	30 23N	87 0W
Santa Rosalía	**174**	27 19N	112 17W
Santana do Livramento	**191**	30 55S	55 30W
Santander	**50**	43 27N	3 51W
Santander Jiménez	**176**	24 13N	98 28W
Santarém, Brazil	**185**	2 25S	54 42W
Santarém, Portugal	**50**	39 12N	8 42W
Santiago, Brazil	**191**	29 11S	54 52W
Santiago, Chile	**190**	33 24S	70 40W
Santiago, Panama	**179**	8 0N	81 0W
Santiago de Compostela	**50**	42 52N	8 37W
Santiago de Cuba	**178**	20 0N	75 49W
Santiago de los Cabelleros	**180**	19 30N	70 40W
Santiago del Estero	**190**	27 50S	64 15W
Santiago Ixcuintla	**175**	21 50N	105 11W
Santo Amaro	**189**	12 30S	38 43W
Santo Ângelo	**191**	28 15S	54 15W
Santo Domingo	**180**	18 30N	64 54W
Santo Tomé	**191**	28 40S	56 5W
Santoña	**50**	43 29N	3 27W
Santos	**191**	24 0S	46 20W
São Borja	**191**	28 39S	56 0W
São Carlos	**188**	22 0S	47 50W
São Francisco →	**189**	10 30S	36 24W
São Francisco do Sul	**191**	26 15S	48 36W
São João del Rei	**188**	21 8S	44 15W
São José do Rio Prêto	**188**	20 50S	49 20W
São Leopoldo	**191**	29 50S	51 10W
São Lourenço	**188**	22 7S	45 3W
São Luís	**188**	2 39S	44 15W
São Paulo	**191**	23 32S	46 37W
São Paulo □	**188**	22 0S	49 0W
São Paulo de Olivença	**184**	3 27S	68 48W
São Roque, C. de	**189**	5 30S	35 16W
São Tomé	**131**	0 10N	6 39 E
São Tomé & Principe ■	**131**	0 12N	6 39 E
São Vicente, Cabo de	**50**	37 0N	9 0W
Saône →	**37**	45 44N	4 50 E
Sapporo	**103**	43 0N	141 21 E
Sapulpa	**168**	36 0N	96 0W
Saqqez	**81**	36 15N	46 20 E
Sar Planina	**52**	42 10N	21 0 E
Saragossa = Zaragoza	**51**	41 39N	0 53W
Sarajevo	**52**	43 52N	18 26 E
Saranac Lake	**151**	44 20N	74 10W
Sarangani B.	**112**	6 0N	125 13 E
Saransk	**68**	54 10N	45 10 E
Sarapul	**69**	56 28N	53 48 E
Sarasota	**165**	27 20N	82 30W
Saratoga Springs	**164**	43 5N	73 47W
Saratov	**68**	51 30N	46 2 E

Sarawak □	**111**	2	0N	113 0 E
Sardegna	**48**	39	57N	9 0 E
Sardinia = Sardegna	**48**	39	57N	9 0 E
Sargodha	**89**	32	10N	72 40 E
Sarh	**131**	9	5N	18 23 E
Sārī	**86**	36	30N	53 4 E
Sarina	**121**	21	22S	149 13 E
Sarmiento	**192**	45	35S	69 5W
Sarnia	**150**	42	58N	82 23W
Saronikós Kólpos	**55**	37	45N	23 45 E
Sarre = Saar ⇢	**42**	49	41N	6 32 E
Sarre, La	**151**	48	45N	79 15W
Sarthe ⇢	**36**	47	33N	0 31W
Sasaram	**92**	24	57N	84 5 E
Sasebo	**108**	33	10N	129 43 E
Saskatchewan □	**152**	54	40N	106 0W
Saskatchewan ⇢	**152**	53	37N	100 40W
Saskatoon	**152**	52	10N	106 38W
Sassandra	**130**	5	0N	6 8W
Sássari	**48**	40	44N	8 33 E
Sata-Misaki	**108**	30	59N	130 40 E
Satara	**91**	17	44N	73 58 E
Satmala Hills	**91**	20	15N	74 40 E
Satna	**92**	24	35N	80 50 E
Satpura Ra.	**91**	21	25N	76 10 E
Sattahip	**95**	12	41N	100 54 E
Satu Mare	**56**	47	46N	22 55 E
Sauðarkrókur	**64**	65	45N	19 40W
Saudi Arabia ■	**82**	26	0N	44 0 E
Sault Ste. Marie, Canada	**150**	46	30N	84 20W
Sault Ste. Marie, U.S.A.	**150**	46	27N	84 22W
Saumur	**36**	47	15N	0 5W
Sava ⇢	**52**	44	50N	20 26 E
Savanna la Mar	**180**	18	10N	78 10W
Savannah	**170**	32	4N	81 4W
Savannah ⇢	**170**	32	2N	80 53W
Savannakhet	**95**	16	30N	104 49 E
Savoie □	**37**	45	26N	6 35 E
Savona	**46**	44	19N	8 29 E
Sawankhalok	**94**	17	19N	99 50 E
Sawara	**107**	35	55N	140 30 E
Sawatch Mts.	**163**	38	30N	106 30W
Sawu, I.	**113**	10	35S	121 50 E
Sawu Sea	**113**	9	30S	121 50 E
Saxony, Lower = Niedersachsen □	**42**	52	45N	9 0 E
Sayan, Zapadnyy	**77**	52	30N	94 0 E
Saydā	**80**	33	35N	35 25 E
Sayḥut	**83**	15	12N	51 10 E
Sayula	**175**	19	52N	103 36W
Sazan	**52**	40	30N	19 20 E
Scafell Pikes	**28**	54	26N	3 14W
Scalloway	**30**	60	9N	1 16W
Scandinavia	**16**	64	0N	12 0 E
Scapa Flow	**33**	58	52N	3 6W
Scarborough	**29**	54	17N	0 24W
Schaffhausen	**44**	47	42N	8 39 E
Schefferville	**146**	54	48N	66 50W
Schelde ⇢	**42**	51	15N	4 16 E
Schenectady	**164**	42	50N	73 58W
Scheveningen	**40**	52	6N	4 16 E
Schiedam	**40**	51	55N	4 25 E
Schiermonnikoog	**41**	53	30N	6 15 E
Schleswig-Holstein □	**42**	54	10N	9 40 E
Schouten I.	**119**	42	20S	148 20 E
Schouten Is.	**113**	1	0S	136 0 E
Schouwen	**40**	51	43N	3 45 E
Schreiber	**150**	48	45N	87 20W
Schwäbische Alb	**42**	48	30N	9 30 E
Schwarzwald	**42**	48	0N	8 0 E
Schwerin	**43**	53	37N	11 22 E
Schwyz	**44**	47	2N	8 39 E
Scilly, Isles of	**20**	49	55N	6 15W
Scone, Australia	**116**	32	5S	150 52 E
Scone, U.K.	**31**	56	25N	3 26W
Scoresbysund	**13**	70	20N	23 0W
Scotia Sea	**14**	56	5S	56 0W
Scotland □	**23**	57	0N	4 0W
Scottsbluff	**163**	41	55N	103 35W
Scottsdale	**119**	41	9S	147 31 E
Scranton	**164**	41	22N	75 41W
Scunthorpe	**29**	53	35N	0 38W
Scutari = Üsküdar	**80**	41	0N	29 5 E
Seaforth	**150**	43	35N	81 25W
Searcy	**168**	35	15N	91 45W
Seascale	**28**	54	24N	3 29W
Seattle	**171**	47	41N	122 15W
Sebastián Vizcaíno, B.	**174**	28	0N	114 30W
Sebastopol = Sevastopol	**68**	44	35N	33 30 E
Sebring	**170**	27	30N	81 26W
Sebta = Ceuta	**126**	35	52N	5 18W
Sebuku, Teluk	**111**	4	0N	118 10 E
Sechura, Desierto de	**186**	6	0S	80 30W
Seclin	**38**	50	33N	3 2 E
Sedalia	**166**	38	40N	93 18W
Segamat	**96**	2	30N	102 50 E
Ségou	**130**	13	30N	6 16W
Segovia = Coco ⇢	**179**	15	0N	83 8W
Segovia	**50**	40	57N	4 10W
Séguéla	**130**	7	55N	6 40W
Segura ⇢	**51**	38	6N	0 54W
Seine ⇢	**38**	49	26N	0 26 E
Seistan	**85**	30	50N	61 0 E
Seki	**106**	35	29N	136 55 E
Sekondi-Takoradi	**130**	4	58N	1 45W
Selangor □	**96**	3	10N	101 30 E
Selby	**29**	53	47N	1 5W
Sélibabi	**130**	15	10N	12 15W
Selkirk, Canada	**153**	50	10N	96 55W
Selkirk, U.K.	**31**	55	33N	2 50W
Selkirk Mts.	**155**	51	15N	117 40W
Selma, Ala., U.S.A.	**169**	32	30N	87 0W
Selma, Calif., U.S.A.	**173**	36	39N	119 39W
Selsey Bill	**24**	50	44N	0 47W
Selvas	**187**	6	30S	67 0W
Semarang	**111**	7	0S	110 26 E
Seminole	**168**	35	15N	96 45W
Semipalatinsk	**71**	50	30N	80 10 E
Semnān	**86**	35	55N	53 25 E
Semnān □	**86**	36	0N	54 0 E
Sendai, Kagoshima, Japan	**108**	31	50N	130 20 E
Sendai, Miyagi, Japan	**103**	38	15N	140 53 E
Senegal ■	**130**	14	30N	14 30W
Senegal ⇢	**126**	15	48N	16 32W
Senge Khambab = Indus ⇢	**88**	24	20N	67 47 E
Senhor-do-Bonfim	**189**	10	30S	40 10W
Senja I.	**64**	69	15N	17 30 E
Senlis	**39**	49	13N	2 35 E
Sennâr	**129**	13	30N	33 35 E
Senneterre	**151**	48	25N	77 15W
Sens	**39**	48	11N	3 15 E
Senta	**52**	45	55N	20 3 E
Seoul = Sŏul	**98**	37	31N	126 58 E
Sept-Îles	**148**	50	13N	66 22W
Seram	**113**	3	10S	129 0 E
Seram Sea	**113**	2	30S	128 30 E
Seremban	**96**	2	43N	101 53 E
Serena, La	**190**	29	55S	71 10W
Sereth = Siret ⇢	**57**	47	58N	26 5 E
Sergipe □	**189**	10	30S	37 30W
Sérifos	**55**	37	9N	24 30 E
Serny Zavod	**70**	39	59N	58 50 E
Serov	**69**	59	29N	60 35 E
Serowe	**137**	22	25S	26 43 E
Serpukhov	**68**	54	55N	37 28 E
Serra do Navio	**185**	0	59N	52 3W
Sérrai	**55**	41	5N	23 31 E
Sesheke	**134**	17	29S	24 13 E
Setana	**103**	42	26N	139 51 E
Sète	**37**	43	25N	3 42 E
Sétif	**127**	36	9N	5 26 E
Seto	**106**	35	14N	137 6 E
Setonaikai	**109**	34	20N	133 30 E
Settle	**28**	54	5N	2 18W
Setúbal	**50**	38	30N	8 58W
Sevastopol	**68**	44	35N	33 30 E
Seven Sisters	**154**	54	56N	128 10W
Severn ⇢, Canada	**140**	56	2N	87 36W
Severn ⇢, U.K.	**24**	51	35N	2 38W
Severnaya Zemlya	**72**	79	0N	100 0 E
Severodinsk	**69**	64	27N	39 58 E

Place	Page	Lat.	Long.
Sevilla	**50**	37 23N	6 0W
Seville = Sevilla	**50**	37 23N	6 0W
Seward	**142**	60 6N	149 26W
Seward Pen.	**142**	65 0N	164 0W
Seychelles ■	**78**	5 0S	56 0E
Seyðisfjörður	**64**	65 16N	14 0W
Seymour	**117**	37 0S	145 10E
Seyne-sur-Mer, La	**37**	43 7N	5 52E
Sézanne	**39**	48 40N	3 40E
Sfax	**127**	34 49N	10 48E
Sfîntu Gheorghe	**57**	45 52N	25 48E
Shaanxi □	**99**	35 0N	109 0E
Shaba □	**135**	8 0S	25 0E
Shache	**100**	38 20N	77 10E
Shaftesbury	**24**	51 0N	2 12W
Shahdād	**85**	30 30N	57 40E
Shakhty	**68**	47 40N	40 16E
Shamo = Gobi	**98**	44 0N	111 0E
Shamokin	**164**	40 47N	76 33W
Shan □	**93**	21 30N	98 30E
Shandong □	**99**	36 0N	118 0E
Shanghai	**99**	31 15N	121 26E
Shangqiu	**99**	34 26N	115 36E
Shangrao	**99**	28 25N	117 59E
Shangshui	**99**	33 42N	114 35E
Shannon →	**35**	52 35N	9 30W
Shansi = Shanxi □	**98**	37 0N	112 0E
Shantou	**99**	23 18N	116 40E
Shantung = Shandong □	**99**	36 0N	118 0E
Shanxi □	**98**	37 0N	112 0E
Shaoguan	**99**	24 48N	113 35E
Shaoxing	**99**	30 0N	120 35E
Shaoyang	**99**	27 14N	111 25E
Shap	**28**	54 32N	2 40W
Sharjah = Ash Shāriqah	**85**	25 23N	55 26E
Shark B.	**120**	25 55S	113 32E
Sharon	**164**	41 18N	80 30W
Shashi	**99**	30 25N	112 14E
Shasta, Mt.	**172**	41 30N	122 12W
Shasta L.	**172**	40 50N	122 15W
Shaunavon	**152**	49 35N	108 25W
Shawano	**167**	44 45N	88 38W
Shawinigan	**151**	46 35N	72 50W
Shawnee	**168**	35 15N	97 0W
Shcherbakov = Andropov	**68**	58 5N	38 50E
Shebele, Wabi →	**133**	2 0N	44 0E
Sheboygan	**167**	43 46N	87 45W
Sheerness	**24**	51 26N	0 47E
Sheffield	**28**	53 23N	1 28W
Shekhupura	**89**	31 42N	73 58E
Shelburne	**148**	43 47N	65 20W
Shelby, Mont., U.S.A.	**163**	48 30N	111 52W
Shelby, N.C., U.S.A.	**165**	35 18N	81 34W
Shelbyville, Ind., U.S.A.	**167**	39 30N	85 42W
Shelbyville, Tenn., U.S.A.	**169**	35 30N	86 25W
Shelikhova, Zaliv	**73**	59 30N	157 0E
Shellharbour	**117**	34 31S	150 51E
Shelton	**171**	47 15N	123 6W
Shenandoah	**166**	40 50N	95 25W
Shensi = Shaanxi □	**99**	35 0N	109 0E
Shenyang	**98**	41 50N	123 25E
Shepparton	**117**	36 23S	145 26E
Sheppey, I. of	**24**	51 23N	0 50E
Sherborne	**27**	50 56N	2 31W
Sherbrooke	**148**	45 28N	71 57W
Sheridan	**163**	44 50N	107 0W
Sherman	**168**	33 40N	96 35W
Sherridon	**152**	55 8N	101 5W
Sherwood Forest	**29**	53 5N	1 5W
Shetland Is.	**30**	60 30N	1 30W
Shibām	**83**	16 0N	48 36E
Shibata	**103**	37 57N	139 20E
Shibetsu	**103**	44 10N	142 23E
Shibukawa	**107**	36 29N	139 0E
Shibushi-Wan	**108**	31 24N	131 8E
Shiel, L.	**32**	56 48N	5 32W
Shihchiachuangi = Shijiazhuang	**98**	38 2N	114 28E
Shijiazhuang	**98**	38 2N	114 28E
Shikarpur	**88**	27 57N	68 39E
Shikine-Jima	**107**	34 19N	139 13E
Shikoku	**109**	33 30N	133 30E
Shikoku □	**109**	33 30N	133 30E
Shikoku-Sanchi	**109**	33 30N	133 30E
Shillong	**93**	25 35N	91 53E
Shimabara	**108**	32 48N	130 20E
Shimada	**107**	34 49N	138 10E
Shimizu	**107**	35 0N	138 30E
Shimo-Jima	**108**	32 15N	130 7E
Shimo-Koshiki-Jima	**108**	31 40N	129 43E
Shimoda	**107**	34 40N	138 57E
Shimodate	**107**	36 20N	139 55E
Shimoga	**90**	13 57N	75 32E
Shimonoseki	**108**	33 58N	131 0E
Shin, L.	**33**	58 7N	4 30W
Shin-Tone →	**107**	35 44N	140 51E
Shinano →	**105**	36 50N	138 30E
Shingū	**106**	33 40N	135 55E
Shinji Ko	**109**	35 26N	132 57E
Shinjō	**103**	38 46N	140 18E
Shinminato	**106**	36 47N	137 4E
Shinshiro	**106**	34 54N	137 30E
Shio-no-Misaki	**106**	33 25N	135 45E
Shiogama	**103**	38 19N	141 1E
Shiojiri	**107**	36 6N	137 58E
Shipka	**53**	42 46N	25 33E
Shirane-San, Gumma, Japan	**107**	36 48N	139 22E
Shirane-San, Yamanashi, Japan	**107**	35 42N	138 9E
Shīrāz	**85**	29 42N	52 30E
Shire →	**137**	17 42S	35 19E
Shiriya-Zaki	**103**	41 25N	141 30E
Shivpuri	**91**	25 26N	77 42E
Shizuoka	**107**	35 0N	138 24E
Shkoder = Shkodra	**52**	42 6N	19 20E
Shkodra	**52**	42 6N	19 20E
Shkumbini →	**52**	41 5N	19 50E
Shō-Gawa →	**106**	36 47N	137 4E
Shōbara	**109**	34 51N	133 1E
Shoeburyness	**24**	51 31N	0 49E
Sholapur = Solapur	**91**	17 43N	75 56E
Shoshone	**172**	43 0N	114 27W
Shreveport	**168**	32 30N	93 50W
Shrewsbury	**28**	52 42N	2 45W
Shrirampur	**92**	22 44N	88 21E
Shropshire □	**24**	52 36N	2 45W
Shuangyashan	**98**	46 37N	131 22E
Siahan Range	**88**	27 30N	64 40E
Sialkot	**89**	32 32N	74 30E
Siam = Thailand ■	**95**	16 0N	102 0E
Sian = Xi'an	**99**	34 15N	109 0E
Siberia	**77**	60 0N	100 0E
Siberut	**111**	1 30S	99 0E
Sibi	**88**	29 30N	67 54E
Sibiu	**57**	45 45N	24 9E
Sichuan □	**99**	31 0N	104 0E
Sicilia	**49**	37 30N	14 30E
Sicily = Sicilia	**49**	37 30N	14 30E
Sicuani	**187**	14 21S	71 10W
Sidi-bel-Abbès	**127**	35 13N	0 39W
Sidlaw Hills	**31**	56 32N	3 10W
Sidley, Mt.	**15**	77 2S	126 2W
Sidmouth	**27**	50 40N	3 13W
Sidney	**154**	48 39N	123 24W
Sidon = Saydā	**80**	33 35N	35 25E
Sidra, G. of = Surt, Khalīj	**127**	31 40N	18 30E
Siedlce	**58**	52 10N	22 20E
Siena	**46**	43 20N	11 20E
Sierra Blanca Pk.	**161**	33 20N	105 54W
Sierra Leone ■	**130**	9 0N	12 0W
Sífnos	**55**	37 0N	24 45E
Siglufjörður	**64**	66 12N	18 55W
Sihanoukville = Kompong Som	**95**	10 38N	103 30E
Siirt	**81**	37 57N	41 55E
Sikar	**89**	27 33N	75 10E
Sikeston	**169**	36 52N	89 35W
Sikhote Alin, Khrebet	**75**	46 0N	136 0E
Síkinos	**55**	36 40N	25 8E
Sikkim □	**92**	27 50N	88 30E
Silchar	**93**	24 49N	92 48E
Silesia = Slask	**58**	51 0N	16 30E

Siling Co **101** 31 50N 89 20 E
Silloth **28** 54 53N 3 25W
Simcoe **151** 42 50N 80 20W
Simenga **74** 62 42N 108 25 E
Simeulue **111** 2 45N 95 45 E
Simferopol **68** 44 55N 34 3 E
Simi Valley **173** 34 16N 118 47W
Simla **89** 31 2N 77 9 E
Simplon Pass **44** 46 15N 8 0 E
Simushir, Ostrov **75** 46 50N 152 30 E
Sinai = Es Sînâ' **128** 29 0N 34 0 E
Sinaloa **174** 25 50N 108 20W
Sinaloa □ **174** 25 0N 107 30W
Sincelejo **184** 9 18N 75 24W
Sinclair Mills **155** 54 5N 121 40W
Sind □ **88** 26 0N 69 0 E
Sind Sagar Doab **89** 32 0N 71 30 E
Singa **129** 13 10N 33 57 E
Singapore ■ **96** 1 17N 103 51 E
Singapore, Straits of **96** 1 15N 104 0 E
Singkaling Hkamti **92** 26 0N 95 39 E
Singleton **117** 32 33S 151 0 E
Singora = Songkhla **97** 7 13N 100 37 E
Sinkiang Uighur = Xinjiang Uygur Zizhiqu □ **100** 42 0N 86 0 E
Sioux City **166** 42 32N 96 25W
Sioux Falls **166** 43 35N 96 40W
Sioux Lookout **153** 50 10N 91 50W
Siping **98** 43 8N 124 21 E
Sipora **111** 2 18S 99 40 E
Siracusa **49** 37 4N 15 17 E
Sirajganj **92** 24 25N 89 47 E
Siret → **57** 47 58N 26 5 E
Síros **55** 37 28N 24 57 E
Sitapur **92** 27 38N 80 45 E
Sitka **143** 57 9N 135 20W
Sittard **41** 51 0N 5 52 E
Sivas **80** 39 43N 36 58 E
Siverek **81** 37 50N 39 19 E
Sivrihisar **80** 39 30N 31 35 E
Sîwa **128** 29 11N 25 31 E
Siwalik Range **92** 28 0N 83 0 E
Sizewell **24** 52 13N 1 38 E
Sjumen = Kolarovgrad **53** 43 18N 26 55 E
Skadarsko Jezero **52** 42 10N 19 20 E
Skagerrak **60** 57 30N 9 0 E
Skagway **143** 59 23N 135 20W
Skaraborgs län □ **60** 58 20N 13 30 E
Skeena → **154** 54 9N 130 5W
Skegness **29** 53 9N 0 20 E
Skellefte → **66** 65 30N 18 30 E
Skellefteå **67** 64 45N 20 58 E
Skerries, The **26** 53 27N 4 40W
Skiddaw **28** 54 39N 3 9W
Skien **60** 59 12N 9 35 E
Skierniewice **58** 51 58N 20 10 E
Skikda **127** 36 50N 6 58 E
Skipton **28** 53 57N 2 1W
Skíros **55** 38 55N 24 34 E
Skopje **52** 42 1N 21 32 E
Skowhegan **148** 44 49N 69 40W
Skull **35** 51 32N 9 40W
Skye **32** 57 15N 6 10W
Skyros = Skíros **55** 38 55N 24 34 E
Slaney → **35** 52 52N 6 45W
Slask **58** 51 0N 16 30 E
Slave → **145** 61 18N 113 39W
Slave Coast **124** 6 0N 2 30 E
Sleaford **29** 53 0N 0 22W
Sliedrecht **40** 51 50N 4 45 E
Slieve Aughty **35** 53 4N 8 30W
Slieve Bloom **35** 53 4N 7 40W
Slieve Donard **34** 54 10N 5 57W
Slieve Mish **35** 52 12N 9 50W
Slievenamon **35** 52 25N 7 37W
Sligo **34** 54 17N 8 28W
Sligo □ **34** 54 10N 8 35W
Sliven **53** 42 42N 26 19 E
Slovakian Ore Mts. = Slovenské Rudohorie **59** 48 45N 20 0 E
Slovenia = Slovenija □ **52** 45 58N 14 30 E
Slovenija □ **52** 45 58N 14 30 E
Slovenské Rudohorie **59** 48 45N 20 0 E
Słupsk **58** 54 30N 17 3 E
Slyne Hd. **34** 53 25N 10 10W
Smara **126** 32 9N 8 16W
Smithers **154** 54 45N 127 10W
Smithfield **165** 35 31N 78 16W
Smiths Falls **151** 44 55N 76 0W
Smithton **119** 40 53S 145 6 E
Smolensk **68** 54 45N 32 0 E
Smolikas, Óros **54** 40 9N 20 58 E
Smyrna = İzmir **80** 38 25N 27 8 E
Snœfell, Iceland **64** 64 48N 15 34W
Snœfell, U.K. **28** 54 18N 4 26W
Snœfellsjökull **64** 64 49N 23 46W
Snake → **171** 46 12N 119 2W
Sneek **41** 53 2N 5 40 E
Snowdon **26** 53 4N 4 8W
Snowdrift **145** 62 24N 110 44W
Snowy Mts. **117** 36 30S 148 20 E
Sobat → **129** 8 32N 32 40 E
Sobral **177** 3 50S 40 20W
Soch'e = Shache **100** 38 20N 77 10 E
Sochi **70** 43 35N 39 40 E
Société, Is. de la **123** 17 0S 151 0W
Society Is. = Société, Is. de la **123** 17 0S 151 0W
Socorro **161** 34 4N 106 54W
Socotra **78** 12 30N 54 0 E
Söderhamn **60** 61 18N 17 10 E
Södermanlands län □ **60** 59 10N 16 30 E
Södertälje **60** 59 12N 17 39 E
Sodo **132** 7 0N 37 41 E
Sofala **137** 33 4S 149 43 E
Sofia = Sofiya **53** 42 45N 23 20 E
Sofiya **53** 42 45N 23 20 E
Sogn og Fjordane fylke □ **60** 61 40N 6 0 E
Soissons **39** 49 25N 3 19 E
Sōja **109** 34 40N 133 45 E
Söke **80** 37 48N 27 28 E
Sol Iletsk **70** 51 10N 55 0 E
Solapur **91** 17 43N 75 56 E
Soledad, Colombia **184** 10 55N 74 46W
Soledad, Venezuela **185** 8 10N 63 34W
Solent, The **24** 50 45N 1 25W
Solesmes **38** 50 10N 3 30 E
Solikamsk **69** 59 38N 56 50 E
Solimões → = Amazonas → **185** 0 5S 50 0W
Sóller **51** 39 46N 2 43 E
Sololá **177** 14 49N 91 10 E
Solomon Is. ■ **122** 6 0S 155 0 E
Solṭānābād **86** 36 29N 58 5 E
Solway Firth **31** 54 45N 3 38W
Somali Rep. ■ **133** 7 0N 47 0 E
Sombor **52** 45 46N 19 9 E
Sombrerete **175** 23 38N 103 39W
Somerset, Bermuda **180** 32 16N 64 55W
Somerset, U.S.A. **169** 37 5N 84 40W
Somerset □ **27** 51 9N 3 0W
Somerset I. **145** 73 30N 93 0W
Somme □ **36** 50 0N 2 20 E
Somport, Puerto de **51** 42 48N 0 31W
Søndre Strømfjord **147** 66 59N 50 40W
Songkhla **97** 7 13N 100 37 E
Sonora □ **174** 29 20N 110 40W
Soochow = Suzhou **99** 31 19N 120 38 E
Sop's Arm **149** 49 46N 56 56W
Sør-Rondane **14** 72 0S 25 0 E
Sør-Trøndelag fylke □ **65** 63 0N 10 0 E
Sorata **187** 15 50S 68 40W
Sorel **151** 46 0N 73 10W
Soria **51** 41 43N 2 32W
Sorocaba **191** 23 31S 47 27W
Sørøya **67** 70 40N 22 30 E
Sorsogon **112** 13 0N 124 0 E
Sosnowiec **58** 50 20N 19 10 E
Sotteville-lès-Rouen **38** 49 24N 1 5 E
Sŏul **98** 37 31N 126 58 E
Souris, Man., Canada **153** 49 40N 100 20W
Souris, P.E.I., Canada **149** 46 21N 62 15W

South Africa, Rep. of ■	**136**	32 0S	17 0E
South Auckland & Bay of Plenty □	**122**	38 30S	177 0E
South Australia □	**118**	32 0S	139 0E
South Bend	**167**	41 38N	86 20W
South Carolina □	**165**	33 45N	81 0W
South Charleston	**165**	38 20N	81 40W
South China Sea	**77**	10 0N	113 0E
South Dakota □	**163**	45 0N	100 0W
South Downs	**25**	50 53N	0 10W
South Georgia	**183**	54 30S	37 0W
South Glamorgan □	**27**	51 30N	3 20W
South Haven	**167**	42 22N	86 20W
South Island	**123**	44 0S	170 0E
South Korea ■	**98**	36 0N	128 0E
South Orkney Is.	**14**	63 0S	45 0W
South Platte →	**163**	41 7N	100 42W
South Pole	**14**	90 0S	0 0E
South Porcupine	**151**	48 30N	81 12W
South Ronaldsay	**33**	58 46N	2 58W
South Sandwich Is.	**14**	57 0S	27 0W
South Sentinel I.	**94**	11 1N	92 16E
South Shetland Is.	**14**	62 0S	59 0W
South Shields	**28**	54 59N	1 26W
South Taranaki Bight	**122**	39 40S	174 5E
South Uist	**32**	57 20N	7 15W
South West Africa = Namibia ■	**136**	22 0S	18 9E
South West Cape	**123**	47 16S	167 31E
South Yorkshire □	**29**	53 30N	1 20W
Southampton	**25**	50 54N	1 23W
Southampton I.	**146**	64 30N	84 0W
Southend-on-Sea	**25**	51 32N	0 42E
Southern Alps	**123**	43 41S	170 11E
Southern Cross	**120**	31 12S	119 15E
Southern Indian L.	**143**	57 10N	98 30W
Southern Uplands	**31**	55 30N	3 3W
Southland □	**123**	45 51S	168 13E
Southport, Australia	**116**	27 58S	153 25E
Southport, U.K.	**28**	53 38N	3 1W
Southwold	**25**	52 19N	1 41E
Sovetskaya Gavan	**75**	48 50N	140 0E
Soviet Union ■ = Union of Soviet Socialist Republics ■	**79**	60 0N	100 0E
Sōya-Kaikyō = Perouse Str., La	**77**	45 40N	142 0E
Spain ■	**50**	40 0N	5 0W
Spalding	**29**	52 47N	0 9W
Spandau	**43**	52 35N	13 7E
Spanish Fork	**163**	40 10N	111 37W
Spanish Town	**180**	18 0N	76 57W
Sparks	**172**	39 30N	119 45W
Sparta = Spárti	**54**	37 5N	22 25E
Sparta	**166**	43 55N	90 47W
Spartanburg	**165**	35 0N	82 0W
Spárti	**54**	37 5N	22 25E
Spartivento, C., Calabria, Italy	**49**	37 56N	16 4E
Spartivento, C., Sard., Italy	**48**	38 52N	8 50E
Spassk-Dalniy	**75**	44 40N	132 48E
Speightstown	**180**	13 15N	59 39W
Spence Bay	**145**	69 32N	93 32W
Spencer	**166**	43 5N	95 19W
Spencer G.	**119**	34 0S	137 20E
Spenser Mts.	**123**	42 15S	172 45E
Sperrin Mts.	**34**	54 50N	7 0W
Spessart	**42**	50 10N	9 20E
Spey →	**33**	57 26N	3 25W
Spézia, La	**46**	44 8N	9 50E
Spinazzola	**49**	40 58N	16 5E
Spithead	**25**	50 43N	1 5W
Spitzbergen = Svalbard	**13**	78 0N	17 0E
Split	**52**	43 31N	16 26E
Splügenpass	**44**	46 30N	9 20E
Spokane	**171**	47 45N	117 25W
Sporyy Navolok, Mys	**69**	75 50N	68 40E
Spratly, I.	**112**	8 20N	112 0E
Spring Mts.	**173**	36 20N	115 43W
Springfield, Ill., U.S.A.	**166**	39 48N	89 40W
Springfield, Mass., U.S.A.	**164**	42 8N	72 37W
Springfield, Mo., U.S.A.	**168**	37 15N	93 20W
Springfield, Ohio, U.S.A.	**167**	39 58N	83 48W
Springfield, Oreg., U.S.A.	**171**	44 2N	123 0W
Springfield, Tenn., U.S.A.	**169**	36 35N	86 55W
Springfield, Vt., U.S.A.	**164**	43 20N	72 30W
Springhill	**148**	45 40N	64 4W
Springs	**137**	26 13S	28 25E
Springwood	**117**	33 41S	150 33E
Spurn Hd.	**29**	53 34N	0 8E
Squamish	**154**	49 45N	123 10W
Sredinnyy Khrebet	**73**	57 0N	160 0E
Srednekolymsk	**73**	67 27N	153 40E
Sremska Mitrovica	**52**	44 59N	19 33E
Srepok →	**95**	13 33N	106 16E
Sretensk	**74**	52 10N	117 40E
Sri Lanka ■	**90**	7 30N	80 50E
Srinagar	**89**	34 5N	74 50E
Stadskanaal	**41**	53 4N	6 55E
Staffa	**30**	56 26N	6 21W
Stafford	**28**	52 49N	2 9W
Stafford □	**28**	52 53N	2 10W
Staines	**25**	51 26N	0 30W
Stalingrad = Volgograd	**68**	48 40N	44 25E
Stalino = Donetsk	**68**	48 0N	37 45E
Stalinogorsk = Novomoskovsk	**68**	54 5N	38 15E
Stalybridge	**28**	53 29N	2 4W
Stamford, U.K.	**25**	52 39N	0 29W
Stamford, U.S.A.	**164**	41 5N	73 30W
Stanislav = Ivano-Frankovsk	**68**	48 40N	24 40E
Stanley, Canada	**152**	55 24N	104 22W
Stanley, Falk. Is.	**192**	51 40S	59 51W
Stanovoy Khrebet	**75**	55 0N	130 0E
Stanthorpe	**116**	28 36S	151 59E
Stara Planina	**53**	43 15N	23 0E
Stara Zagora	**53**	42 26N	25 39E
Starkville	**169**	33 26N	88 48W
Start Pt.	**27**	50 13N	3 38W
State College	**164**	40 47N	77 49W
Staten, I. = Estados, I. de los	**192**	54 40S	64 30W
Statesboro	**170**	32 26N	81 46W
Statesville	**165**	35 48N	80 51W
Staunton	**165**	38 7N	79 4W
Stavanger	**60**	58 57N	5 40E
Staveren	**40**	52 53N	5 22E
Stavropol	**70**	45 5N	42 0E
Stawell	**119**	37 6S	142 47E
Steenwijk	**41**	52 47N	6 7E
Stefanie L. = Chew Bahir	**132**	4 40N	36 50E
Steiermark □	**45**	47 26N	15 0E
Steinbach	**153**	49 32N	96 40W
Steinkjer	**65**	63 59N	11 31E
Stellarton	**149**	45 32N	62 30W
Stephenville	**149**	48 31N	58 35W
Stereá Ellas □	**54**	38 50N	22 0E
Sterling, Colo., U.S.A.	**163**	40 40N	103 15W
Sterling, Ill., U.S.A.	**166**	41 45N	89 45W
Sterlitamak	**71**	53 40N	56 0E
Stettin = Szczecin	**58**	53 27N	14 27E
Stettler	**155**	52 19N	112 40W
Steubenville	**164**	40 21N	80 39W
Stevens Port	**166**	44 32N	89 34W
Stewart	**144**	63 19N	139 26W
Stewart I.	**123**	46 58S	167 54E
Stikine →	**144**	56 40N	132 30W
Stillwater, Minn., U.S.A.	**166**	45 3N	92 47W
Stillwater, Okla., U.S.A.	**168**	36 5N	97 3W
Stillwater Ra.	**172**	39 45N	118 6W
Stip	**53**	41 42N	22 10E
Stirling	**31**	56 7N	3 57W
Stirling Ra.	**120**	34 23S	118 0E
Stockholm	**60**	59 20N	18 3E
Stockholms län □	**60**	59 30N	18 20E
Stockport	**28**	53 25N	2 11W
Stockton	**172**	38 0N	121 20W
Stockton-on-Tees	**29**	54 34N	1 20W
Stoke-on-Trent	**28**	53 1N	2 11W
Stonehaven	**33**	56 58N	2 11W
Stonehenge	**24**	51 9N	1 45W
Stonewall	**153**	50 10N	97 19W
Stora Lulevatten	**66**	67 10N	19 30E

Storavan	**66**	65 45N	18 10 E
Store Bælt	**61**	55 20N	11 0 E
Storm B.	**119**	43 10S	147 30 E
Storm Lake	**166**	42 35N	95 11W
Stornoway	**32**	58 12N	6 23W
Storsjön	**66**	63 12N	14 18 E
Storuman	**66**	65 5N	17 10 E
Stour →, Hereford & Worcs., U.K.	**24**	52 25N	2 13W
Stour →, Kent, U.K.	**25**	51 15N	1 20 E
Stour →, Suffolk, U.K.	**25**	51 55N	1 5 E
Stourbridge	**24**	52 28N	2 8W
Stowmarket	**25**	52 11N	1 0 E
Strabane	**34**	54 50N	7 28W
Stralsund	**43**	54 17N	13 5 E
Strangford, L.	**34**	54 30N	5 37W
Stranraer	**30**	54 54N	5 0W
Strasbourg	**37**	48 35N	7 42 E
Stratford, Canada	**151**	43 23N	81 0W
Stratford, N.Z.	**122**	39 20S	174 19 E
Stratford-on-Avon	**24**	52 12N	1 42W
Strath Spey	**33**	57 15N	3 40W
Strathalbyn	**119**	35 13S	138 53 E
Strathclyde □	**30**	56 0N	4 50W
Strathmore	**33**	56 40N	3 4W
Strathy Pt.	**33**	58 35N	4 0W
Streaky B.	**118.**	32 51S	134 18 E
Streator	**167**	41 9N	88 52W
Strómboli	**49**	38 48N	15 12 E
Stromeferry	**32**	57 20N	5 33W
Stromness	**33**	58 58N	3 18W
Stronsay	**33**	59 8N	2 38W
Stroud	**24**	51 44N	2 12W
Strumica	**53**	41 28N	22 41 E
Stuart L.	**154**	54 30N	124 30W
Stung Treng	**95**	13 31N	105 58 E
Sturgeon Bay	**167**	44 52N	87 20W
Sturgeon Falls	**151**	46 25N	79 57W
Stuttgart, Germany	**42**	48 46N	9 10 E
Stuttgart, U.S.A.	**168**	34 30N	91 33W
Styria = Steiermark □	**45**	47 26N	15 0 E
Suakin	**129**	19 8N	37 20 E
Subotica	**52**	46 6N	19 49 E
Suchitoto	**177**	13 56N	89 0W
Suchou = Suzhou	**99**	31 19N	120 38 E
Süchow = Xuzhou	**99**	34 18N	117 10 E
Sucre	**187**	19 0S	65 15W
Sudan ■	**129**	15 0N	30 0 E
Sudbury, Canada	**151**	46 30N	81 0W
Sudbury, U.K.	**25**	52 2N	0 44 E
Sudetan Mts. = Sudety	**58**	50 20N	16 45 E
Sudety	**58**	50 20N	16 45 E
Suez = El Suweis	**128**	29 58N	32 31 E
Suez Canal = Suweis, Qanâl es	**128**	31 0N	32 20 E
Suffolk	**165**	36 47N	76 33W
Suffolk □	**25**	52 16N	1 0 E
Sugluk = Saglouc	**146**	62 14N	75 38W
Suhbaatar	**98**	50 17N	106 10 E
Suir →	**35**	52 15N	7 10W
Suita	**106**	34 45N	135 32 E
Sukhona →	**68**	60 30N	45 0 E
Sukhumi	**70**	43 0N	41 0 E
Sukkertoppen	**147**	65 26N	52 55W
Sukkur	**88**	27 42N	68 54 E
Sukkur Barrage	**88**	27 40N	68 50 E
Sukumo	**109**	32 56N	132 44 E
Sulaiman Range	**89**	30 30N	69 50 E
Sulawesi □	**113**	2 0S	120 0 E
Sulina	**57**	45 10N	29 40 E
Sulitjelma	**66**	67 9N	16 3 E
Sullana	**186**	4 52S	80 39W
Sullivan	**167**	39 5N	87 26W
Sullivan I. = Lambi Kyun	**96**	10 50N	98 20 E
Sulphur Springs	**168**	33 5N	95 36W
Sulu Arch.	**112**	6 0N	121 0 E
Sulu Sea	**112**	8 0N	120 0 E
Suluq	**128**	31 44N	20 14 E
Sumatera □	**111**	0 40N	100 20 E
Sumatra = Sumatera □	**111**	0 40N	100 20 E
Sumba	**113**	9 45S	119 35 E
Sumbawa	**113**	8 26S	117 30 E
Sumburgh Hd.	**30**	59 52N	1 17W
Summerland	**155**	49 32N	119 41W
Summerside	**148**	46 24N	63 47W
Sumoto	**109**	34 21N	134 54 E
Sumter	**165**	33 55N	80 22W
Sumy	**68**	50 57N	34 50 E
Sunbury, Australia	**117**	37 35S	144 44 E
Sunbury, U.S.A.	**164**	40 50N	76 46W
Sunda, Selat	**111**	6 20S	105 30 E
Sundarbans, The	**92**	22 0N	89 0 E
Sunderland	**28**	54 54N	1 22W
Sundsvall	**66**	62 23N	17 17 E
Sungei Patani	**96**	5 38N	100 29 E
Sungei Siput	**96**	4 51N	101 6 E
Sungurlu	**80**	40 12N	34 21 E
Sunnyside	**171**	46 24N	120 2W
Sunnyvale	**172**	37 23N	122 2W
Suntar	**74**	62 15N	117 30 E
Suō-Nada	**108**	33 50N	131 30 E
Superior	**150**	46 45N	92 5W
Superior, L.	**150**	47 40N	87 0W
Suphan Daği	**81**	38 54N	42 48 E
Sūr	**80**	22 34N	59 32 E
Surabaja = Surabaya	**111**	7 17S	112 45 E
Surabaya	**111**	7 17S	112 45 E
Surakarta	**111**	7 35S	110 48 E
Surat	**91**	21 12N	72 55 E
Surat Thani	**96**	9 6N	99 20 E
Suratgarh	**89**	29 18N	73 55 E
Surgut	**69**	61 14N	73 20 E
Surin	**95**	14 50N	103 34 E
Surinam ■	**185**	4 0N	56 0W
Surrey □	**25**	51 16N	0 30W
Surt	**127**	31 11N	16 39 E
Surt, Khalīj	**127**	31 40N	18 30 E
Suruga-Wan	**107**	34 45N	138 30 E
Susaki	**109**	33 22N	133 17 E
Susanville	**172**	40 28N	120 40W
Susquehanna →	**164**	39 33N	76 5W
Sutherland Falls	**123**	44 48S	167 46 E
Sutlej →	**89**	29 23N	71 3 E
Sutton-in-Ashfield	**29**	53 7N	1 20W
Suva	**122**	18 6S	178 30 E
Suwa	**107**	36 2N	138 8 E
Suwa-Ko	**107**	36 3N	138 5 E
Suwannee →	**170**	29 18N	83 9W
Suwanose-Jima	**104**	29 38N	129 43 E
Suweis, Qanâl es	**128**	31 0N	32 20 E
Suzaka	**107**	36 39N	138 19 E
Suzhou	**99**	31 19N	120 38 E
Suzu-Misaki	**105**	37 31N	137 21 E
Svalbard	**13**	78 0N	17 0 E
Svartenhuk Halvø	**146**	71 50N	54 30W
Svendborg	**61**	55 4N	10 35 E
Sverdlovsk	**69**	56 50N	60 30 E
Sverdrup Is.	**12**	79 0N	97 0W
Svishtov	**53**	43 36N	25 23 E
Svobodnyy	**75**	51 20N	128 0 E
Swabian Alps = Schwäbische Alb	**42**	48 30N	9 30 E
Swakopmund	**136**	22 37S	14 30 E
Swale →	**28**	54 5N	1 20W
Swan Hill	**117**	35 20S	143 33 E
Swan Hills	**155**	54 42N	115 24W
Swan Islands	**178**	17 22N	83 57W
Swan River	**152**	52 10N	101 16W
Swanage	**24**	50 36N	1 59W
Swansea	**27**	51 37N	3 57W
Swartberge	**136**	33 20S	22 0 E
Swatow = Shantou	**99**	23 18N	116 40 E
Swaziland ■	**137**	26 30S	31 30 E
Sweden ■	**66**	57 0N	15 0 E
Sweetwater	**161**	32 30N	100 28W
Swift Current	**152**	50 20N	107 45W
Swindon	**24**	51 33N	1 47W
Switzerland ■	**44**	46 30N	8 0 E
Swords	**34**	53 27N	6 15W
Sydney, Australia	**117**	33 53S	151 10 E
Sydney, Canada	**149**	46 7N	60 7W
Sydney Mines	**149**	46 18N	60 15W

Sydprøven	**147**	60 30N	45 35W
Sydra G. of = Surt, Khalīj	**127**	31 40N	18 30 E
Syktyvkar	**69**	61 45N	50 40 E
Sylacauga	**169**	33 10N	86 15W
Sylhet	**92**	24 54N	91 52 E
Sylvan Lake	**155**	52 20N	114 3W
Syracuse	**164**	43 4N	76 11W
Syrdarya →	**71**	46 3N	61 0 E
Syria ■	**80**	35 0N	38 0 E
Syrian Desert	**76**	31 0N	40 0 E
Syzran	**68**	53 12N	48 30 E
Szczecin	**58**	53 27N	14 27 E
Szechwan = Sichuan □	**99**	31 0N	104 0 E
Szeged	**59**	46 16N	20 10 E
Székesfehérvár	**59**	47 15N	18 25 E
Szolnok	**59**	47 10N	20 15 E
Szombathely	**59**	47 14N	16 38 E
Tabacal	**190**	23 15S	64 15W
Ṭābah	**82**	26 55N	42 38 E
Tabasco □	**177**	18 0N	92 40W
Taber	**155**	49 47N	112 8W
Tablas	**112**	12 25N	122 2 E
Table Mt.	**136**	34 0S	18 22 E
Table Top, Mt.	**121**	23 24S	147 11 E
Tabora	**135**	5 2S	32 50 E
Tabrīz	**81**	38 7N	46 20 E
Tabūk	**82**	28 23N	36 36 E
Tachibana-Wan	**108**	32 45N	130 7 E
Tachikawa	**107**	35 42N	139 25 E
Tacna	**187**	18 0S	70 20W
Tacoma	**171**	47 15N	122 30W
Tacuarembó	**191**	31 45S	56 0W
Tademaït, Plateau du	**127**	28 30N	2 30 E
Tadoussac	**148**	48 11N	69 42W
Tadzhik S.S.R. □	**71**	35 30N	70 0 E
Taegu	**98**	35 50N	128 37 E
Taejŏn	**98**	36 20N	127 28 E
Taganrog	**68**	47 12N	38 50 E
Tagish	**144**	60 19N	134 16W
Tagua, La	**184**	0 3N	74 40W
Tagus = Tajo →	**50**	38 40N	9 24W
Tahiti	**123**	17 37S	149 27W
Tahoua	**131**	14 57N	5 16 E
Taibei	**99**	25 4N	121 29 E
T'aichung = Taizhong	**99**	24 12N	120 35 E
Taidong	**99**	22 43N	121 9 E
Taihape	**122**	39 41S	175 48 E
Tailem Bend	**119**	35 12S	139 29 E
Taimyr = Taymyr, Poluostrov	**72**	75 0N	100 0 E
Tain	**33**	57 49N	4 4W
Tainan	**99**	23 17N	120 18 E
Taínaron, Ákra	**54**	36 22N	22 27 E
T'aipei = Taibei	**99**	25 4N	121 29 E
Taiping	**96**	4 51N	100 44 E
Taisha	**109**	35 24N	132 40 E
Taitao, Pen. de	**192**	46 30S	75 0W
Taiwan ■	**99**	23 30N	121 0 E
Taiyuan	**98**	37 52N	112 33 E
Taizhong	**99**	24 12N	120 35 E
Ta'izz	**83**	13 35N	44 2 E
Tajimi	**106**	35 19N	137 8 E
Tajo →	**50**	38 40N	9 24W
Tak	**94**	16 52N	99 8 E
Takachiho	**108**	32 42N	131 18 E
Takada	**105**	37 7N	138 15 E
Takahashi	**109**	34 51N	133 39 E
Takamatsu	**109**	34 20N	134 5 E
Takaoka	**106**	36 47N	137 0 E
Takapuna	**122**	36 47S	174 47 E
Takasago	**109**	34 45N	134 48 E
Takasaki	**107**	36 20N	139 0 E
Takatsuki	**106**	34 51N	135 37 E
Takawa	**108**	33 38N	130 51 E
Takayama	**106**	36 18N	137 11 E
Takayama-Bonchi	**106**	36 0N	137 18 E
Takefu	**106**	35 50N	136 10 E
Takehara	**109**	34 21N	132 55 E
Taketa	**108**	32 58N	131 24 E
Takhār □	**87**	36 40N	70 0 E
Takla Landing	**154**	55 30N	125 50W
Takla Makan	**76**	39 0N	83 0 E
Taku	**108**	33 18N	130 3 E
Talara	**186**	4 38S	81 18 E
Talaud, Kepulauan	**113**	4 30N	127 10 E
Talca	**190**	35 28S	71 40W
Talcahuano	**190**	36 40S	73 10W
Ṭalesh, Kūhhā-ye	**81**	39 0N	48 30 E
Talguppa	**90**	14 10N	74 45 E
Taliabu	**113**	1 45S	125 0 E
Talkeetna	**142**	62 20N	150 9W
Tall 'Afar	**81**	36 22N	42 27 E
Talladega	**169**	33 28N	86 2W
Tallahassee	**170**	30 25N	84 15W
Tallangatta	**117**	36 15S	147 19 E
Tallinn	**68**	59 22N	24 48 E
Tallulah	**168**	32 25N	91 12W
Tamale	**130**	9 22N	0 50W
Tamana	**108**	32 58N	130 32 E
Tamano	**109**	34 29N	133 59 E
Tamanrasset	**127**	22 50N	5 30 E
Tamar →	**27**	50 33N	4 15W
Tamaulipas □	**176**	24 0N	98 45W
Tambellup	**120**	34 4S	117 37 E
Tambov	**68**	52 45N	41 28 E
Tamgak, Mts.	**127**	19 12N	8 35 E
Tamil Nadu □	**90**	11 0N	77 0 E
Tammerfors = Tampere	**67**	61 30N	23 50 E
Tamo Abu, Pegunungan	**111**	3 10N	115 0 E
Tampa	**170**	27 57N	82 38W
Tampa B.	**170**	27 40N	82 40W
Tampere	**67**	61 30N	23 50 E
Tampico	**177**	22 20N	97 50W
Tamrah	**83**	20 24N	45 25 E
Tamsagbulag	**98**	47 14N	117 21 E
Tamworth, Australia	**116**	31 7S	150 58 E
Tamworth, U.K.	**24**	52 38N	1 41W
Tana →, Kenya	**133**	2 32S	40 31 E
Tana →, Norway	**67**	70 30N	28 23 E
Tana, L.	**132**	13 5N	37 30 E
Tanabe	**106**	33 44N	135 22 E
Tanana	**142**	65 10N	152 15W
Tananarive = Antananarivo	**137**	18 55S	47 31 E
Tanba-Sanchi	**106**	35 7N	135 48 E
Tandil	**190**	37 15S	59 6W
Tando Adam	**88**	25 45N	68 40 E
Tane-ga-Shima	**104**	30 30N	131 0 E
Tanen Tong Dan	**93**	16 30N	98 30 E
Tanezrouft	**127**	23 9N	0 11 E
Tanga	**135**	5 5S	39 2 E
Tanganyika, L.	**135**	6 40S	30 0 E
Tanger	**126**	35 50N	5 49W
Tanggula Shan	**101**	32 40N	92 10 E
Tangier = Tanger	**126**	35 50N	5 49W
Tangshan	**98**	39 38N	118 10 E
Tanimbar, Kepulauan	**113**	7 30S	131 30 E
Taniyama	**108**	31 31N	130 31 E
Tanjore = Thanjavur	**90**	10 48N	79 12 E
Tannu Ola	**74**	51 0N	94 0 E
Tanout	**131**	14 50N	8 55 E
Tanta	**128**	30 45N	30 57 E
Tantung = Dandong	**98**	40 10N	124 20 E
Tanunda	**119**	34 30S	139 0 E
Tanzania ■	**135**	6 40S	34 0 E
Tapa Shan = Daba Shan	**99**	32 0N	109 0 E
Tapachula	**177**	14 54N	92 17W
Tapajós →	**185**	2 24S	54 41W
Tapanui	**123**	45 56S	169 18 E
Tapi →	**91**	21 8N	72 41 E
Tara →	**71**	56 42N	74 36 E
Tarabagatay, Khrebet	**71**	48 0N	83 0 E
Tarābulus, Lebanon	**80**	34 31N	35 50 E
Tarābulus, Libya	**127**	32 49N	13 7 E
Taranaki □	**122**	39 5S	174 51 E
Táranto	**49**	40 30N	17 11 E
Táranto, G. di	**49**	40 0N	17 15 E
Tarapoto	**186**	6 30S	76 20W
Tarare	**37**	45 54N	4 26 E
Tararua Range	**123**	40 45S	175 25 E
Tarauacá	**187**	8 6S	70 48W

Tarbela Dam	**89**	34 8N	72 52 E
Tarbert	**32**	57 54N	6 49W
Tarbes	**36**	43 15N	0 3 E
Tarcoola	**118**	30 44S	134 36 E
Taree	**116**	31 50S	152 30 E
Tarfaya	**126**	27 55N	12 55W
Tarifa	**50**	36 1N	5 36W
Tarija	**187**	21 30S	64 40W
Tarim →	**100**	41 5N	86 40 E
Tarim Pendi	**100**	40 0N	84 0 E
Tarko Sale	**69**	64 55N	77 50 E
Tarn →	**36**	44 5N	1 6 E
Tarnobrzeg	**58**	50 35N	21 41 E
Tarnów	**58**	50 3N	21 0 E
Tarragona	**51**	41 5N	1 17 E
Tarrasa	**51**	41 34N	2 1 E
Tarsus	**80**	36 58N	34 55 E
Tartagal	**190**	22 30S	63 50W
Tarṭūs	**80**	34 55N	35 55 E
Tarumizu	**108**	31 29N	130 42 E
Tarutao, Ko	**96**	6 33N	99 40 E
Taschereau	**151**	48 40N	78 40W
Tashi Chho Dzong = Thimphu	**92**	27 31N	89 45 E
Tashkent	**71**	41 20N	69 10 E
Tasman B.	**123**	40 59S	173 25 E
Tasman Mts.	**123**	41 3S	172 25 E
Tasman Sea	**122**	36 0S	160 0 E
Tasmania □	**119**	42 0S	146 30 E
Tatabánya	**59**	47 32N	18 25 E
Tatarsk	**71**	55 14N	76 0 E
Tateshina-Yama	**107**	36 8N	138 11 E
Tateyama	**107**	35 0N	139 50 E
Tatra = Tatry	**59**	49 20N	20 0 E
Tatry	**59**	49 20N	20 0 E
Tatsuno	**109**	34 52N	134 33 E
Tat'ung = Datong	**98**	40 6N	113 18 E
Taubaté	**191**	23 0S	45 36W
Tauern	**45**	47 15N	12 40 E
Taumarunui	**122**	38 53S	175 15 E
Taunggyi	**93**	20 50N	97 0 E
Taungup Taunggya	**93**	18 20N	93 40 E
Taunton, U.K.	**27**	51 1N	3 7W
Taunton, U.S.A.	**164**	41 54N	71 6W
Taunus	**42**	50 15N	8 20 E
Taupo	**122**	38 41S	176 7 E
Taupo, L.	**122**	38 46S	175 55 E
Tauranga	**122**	37 42S	176 11 E
Taurus Mts. = Toros Daglari	**80**	37 0N	35 0 E
Taverny	**39**	49 2N	2 13 E
Tavistock	**27**	50 33N	4 9W
Tavoy	**94**	14 2N	98 12 E
Tawas City	**167**	44 16N	83 31W
Tay →	**33**	56 37N	3 38W
Tayabamba	**186**	8 15S	77 16W
Taylor Mt.	**161**	35 16N	107 36W
Taymā	**82**	27 35N	38 45 E
Taymyr, Poluostrov	**72**	75 0N	100 0 E
Tayshet	**74**	55 58N	98 1 E
Tayside □	**31**	56 25N	3 30W
Taz →	**69**	67 32N	78 40 E
Tbilisi	**70**	41 43N	44 50 E
Tchad ■ = Chad ■	**131**	15 0N	17 15 E
Tchad, L.	**131**	13 30N	14 30 E
Tch'eng-tou = Chengdu	**99**	30 38N	104 2 E
Tch'ong-k'ing = Chongqing	**99**	29 35N	106 25 E
Te Anau, L.	**123**	45 15S	167 45 E
Te Kuiti	**122**	38 20S	175 11 E
Tecuala	**175**	22 23N	105 27W
Tefé	**185**	3 25S	64 50W
Tegal	**111**	6 52S	109 8 E
Tegucigalpa	**179**	14 5N	87 14W
Tehachapi Mts.	**173**	35 0N	118 40W
Tehrān	**86**	35 44N	51 30 E
Tehuacán	**177**	18 27N	97 23W
Tehuantepec	**177**	16 21N	95 13W
Tehuantepec, G. de	**177**	16 0N	94 50W
Tehuantepec, Istmo de	**177**	17 0N	94 30W
Teifi →	**26**	52 4N	4 14W
Teignmouth	**27**	50 33N	3 30W
Tejo →	**50**	38 40N	9 24W
Tekax	**177**	20 12N	89 17W
Tekeli	**71**	44 50N	79 0 E
Tekirdağ	**80**	40 58N	27 30 E
Tel Aviv-Yafo	**80**	32 4N	34 48 E
Tela	**179**	15 40N	87 28W
Telanaipura = Jambi	**111**	1 38S	103 30 E
Telegraph Cr. →	**144**	58 0N	131 10W
Telemark fylke □	**60**	59 25N	8 30 E
Teles Pires →	**187**	7 21S	58 3W
Telford	**28**	52 42N	2 31W
Tell City	**167**	38 0N	86 44W
Teme →	**24**	52 23N	2 15W
Temerloh	**96**	3 27N	102 25 E
Temirtau	**71**	50 5N	72 56 E
Temora	**117**	34 30S	147 30 E
Temosachic	**174**	28 57N	107 51W
Temple	**158**	31 5N	97 22W
Temuco	**190**	38 45S	72 40W
Temuka	**123**	44 14S	171 17 E
Tenali	**91**	16 15N	80 35 E
Tenancingo	**177**	19 0N	99 33W
Tenango	**177**	19 7N	99 33W
Tenby	**27**	51 40N	4 42W
Tenerife	**126**	28 15N	16 35W
Teng Xian	**99**	35 5N	117 10 E
Tennessee □	**169**	36 0N	86 30W
Tennessee →	**169**	37 4N	88 34W
Tenri	**106**	34 39N	135 49 E
Tenryū	**107**	34 52N	137 49 E
Tenryū-Gawa →	**107**	35 39N	137 48 E
Tenterfield	**116**	29 0S	152 0 E
Teófilo Otoni	**189**	17 50S	41 30W
Tepic	**175**	21 30N	104 54W
Terang	**119**	38 15S	142 55 E
Terek →	**70**	44 0N	47 30 E
Terengganu □	**96**	4 55N	103 0 E
Teresina	**188**	5 9S	42 45W
Terewah, L.	**116**	29 52S	147 35 E
Termez	**70**	37 15N	67 15 E
Términos, L. de	**177**	18 37N	91 33W
Terneuzen	**40**	51 20N	3 50 E
Terni	**46**	42 34N	12 38 E
Terrace	**154**	54 30N	128 35W
Terre Haute	**167**	39 28N	87 24W
Terrell	**168**	32 44N	96 19W
Terschelling	**40**	53 25N	5 20 E
Teruel	**51**	40 22N	1 8W
Teshio	**103**	44 53N	141 44 E
Teslin	**144**	60 10N	132 43W
Test →	**24**	51 7N	1 30W
Tete	**137**	16 13S	33 33 E
Teteven	**53**	42 58N	24 17 E
Tétouan	**126**	35 35N	5 21W
Tetuán = Tétouan	**126**	35 35N	5 21W
Teuco →	**190**	25 35S	60 11W
Teutoburger Wald	**42**	52 5N	8 20 E
Tevere →	**46**	41 44N	12 14 E
Tewkesbury	**24**	51 59N	2 8W
Texarkana, Ark., U.S.A.	**168**	33 25N	94 0W
Texarkana, Tex., U.S.A.	**168**	33 25N	94 3W
Texas □	**161**	31 40N	98 30W
Texel	**40**	53 5N	4 50 E
Teziutlán	**177**	19 49N	97 21W
Tezpur	**93**	26 40N	92 45 E
Thabana Ntlenyana	**137**	29 30S	29 16 E
Thailand ■	**95**	16 0N	102 0 E
Thailand, G. of	**95**	11 30N	101 0 E
Thal Desert	**89**	31 10N	71 30 E
Thame →	**24**	51 35N	1 8W
Thames	**122**	37 7S	175 34 E
Thames →	**25**	51 30N	0 35 E
Thane	**91**	19 12N	72 59 E
Thanh Hoa	**95**	19 48N	105 46 E
Thanh Pho Ho Chi Minh	**95**	10 58N	106 40 E
Thanjavur	**90**	10 48N	79 12 E
Thar Desert	**89**	28 0N	72 0 E
Thásos	**55**	40 40N	24 40 E
Thaungdut	**93**	24 30N	94 40 E
Thazi	**93**	21 0N	96 5 E
The Dalles	**171**	45 40N	121 11W
The Grenadines, Is.	**180**	12 40N	61 20W

THE

The Hague = 's-Gravenhage . **40** 52 7N 4 17 E
The Macumba ~► .... **118** 27 52S 137 12 E
The Neales —► .... **118** 28 8S 136 47 E
The Pas **152** 53 45N 101 15W
The Rock .... **117** 35 15S 147 2 E
The Warburton ~► .... **118** 28 4S 137 28 E
Thebes = Thívai .... **55** 38 19N 23 19 E
Thermaïkos Kólpos .... **54** 40 15N 22 45 E
Thermopolis **163** 43 35N 108 10W
Thessalía □ .... **54** 39 30N 22 0 E
Thessalon **150** 46 20N 83 30W
Thessaloníki .... **54** 40 38N 22 58 E
Thessaly = Thessalía □ ..... **54** 39 30N 22 0 E
Thetford Mines........... **148** 46 8N 71 18W
Thicket Portage........... **153** 55 19N 97 42W
Thies **130** 14 50N 16 51W
Thimphu................. **92** 27 31N 89 45 E
Thionville .... **37** 49 20N 6 10 E
Thíra .... **55** 36 23N 25 27 E
Thirsk **29** 54 15N 1 20W
Thisted .... **61** 56 58N 8 40 E
Thívai .... **55** 38 19N 23 19 E
Thomaston............... **170** 32 54N 84 20W
Thomasville, Ga., U.S.A. ... **170** 30 50N 84 0W
Thomasville, N.C., U.S.A. ... **165** 35 55N 80 4W
Thon Buri .... **94** 13 43N 100 29 E
Thornaby on Tees **29** 54 36N 1 19W
Thrace = Thráki □ .... **55** 41 9N 25 30 E
Thráki □ .... **55** 41 9N 25 30 E
Three Hills **155** 51 43N 113 15W
Three Hummock I. .... **119** 40 25S 144 55 E
Thule **13** 77 40N 69 0W
Thundelarra.............. **120** 28 53S 117 7 E
Thunder B. **150** 45 0N 83 20W
Thunder Bay **150** 48 20N 89 15W
Thüringer Wald .... **43** 50 35N 11 0 E
Thurles **35** 52 40N 7 53W
Thursday I. .... **115** 10 30S 142 3 E
Thurso **33** 58 34N 3 31W
Tian Shan .... **100** 43 0N 84 0 E
Tianjin .... **98** 39 8N 117 10 E
Tianshui .... **99** 34 32N 105 40 E
Tiber = Tevere ~► .... **46** 41 44N 12 14 E
Tibesti.................. **127** 21 0N 17 30 E
Tibet = Xizang □ .... **101** 32 0N 88 0 E
Tibooburra .... **118** 29 26S 142 1 E
Ticul **177** 20 24N 89 32W
Tiel .... **40** 51 53N 5 26 E
Tien Shan .... **76** 42 0N 80 0 E
Tien-tsin = Tianjin .... **98** 39 8N 117 10 E
T'ienching = Tianjin ...... **98** 39 8N 117 10 E
Tientsin = Tianjin .... **98** 39 8N 117 10 E
Tierra de Campos......... **50** 42 10N 4 50W
Tierra del Fuego □ **192** 54 0S 67 45W
Tiffin **167** 41 8N 83 10W
Tiflis = Tbilisi .... **70** 41 43N 44 50 E
Tifton................... **170** 31 28N 83 32W
Tignish **148** 46 58N 64 2W
Tigris = Dijlah, Nahr ~► ... **81** 31 0N 47 25 E
Tijuana **174** 32 32N 117 1W
Tiksi .... **72** 71 40N 128 45 E
Tilburg .... **40** 51 31N 5 6 E
Tilbury .... **25** 51 27N 0 24 E
Tillsonburg.............. **151** 42 53N 80 44W
Tílos .... **55** 36 27N 27 27 E
Timaru .... **123** 44 23S 171 14 E
Timbuktu = Tombouctou **130** 16 50N 3 0W
Timişoara .... **56** 45 43N 21 15 E
Timmins **151** 48 28N 81 25W
Timor .... **113** 9 0S 125 0 E
Timor Sea............... **113** 10 0S 127 0 E
Tinaca Pt................ **112** 5 30N 125 25 E
Tindouf................. **126** 27 42N 8 10W
Tinnevelly = Tirunelveli ... **90** 8 45N 77 45 E
Tinogasta **190** 28 5S 67 32W
Tínos .... **55** 37 33N 25 8 E
Tioman, Pulau .... **96** 2 50N 104 10 E
Tipperary **35** 52 28N 8 10W
Tipperary □.............. **35** 52 37N 7 55W
Tipton **24** 52 32N 2 4W
Tirana .... **52** 41 18N 19 49 E

Tiraspol .... **68** 46 55N 29 35 E
Tire .... **80** 38 5N 27 50 E
Tirebolu .... **81** 40 58N 38 45 E
Tiree **30** 56 31N 6 55W
Tîrgu Mureş .... **57** 46 31N 24 38 E
Tirol □ .... **45** 47 3N 10 43 E
Tiruchchirappalli .... **90** 10 45N 78 45 E
Tirunelveli .... **90** 8 45N 77 45 E
Tisa ~► .... **59** 45 15N 20 17 E
Tisdale **152** 52 50N 104 0W
Titicaca, L. **187** 15 30S 69 30W
Titograd .... **52** 42 30N 19 19 E
Titov Veles .... **53** 41 46N 21 47 E
Titovo Užice............. **52** 43 55N 19 50 E
Tiverton **27** 50 54N 3 30W
Tívoli .... **46** 41 58N 12 45 E
Tizimín **177** 21 9N 88 9W
Tjirebon = Cirebon .... **111** 6 45S 108 32 E
Tlaxcala □ **177** 19 25N 98 10W
Tlaxiaco **177** 17 18N 97 40W
Tlemcen **127** 34 52N 1 21W
To-Shima .... **107** 34 31N 139 17 E
Toamasina.............. **137** 18 10S 49 25 E
Toba Kakar .... **88** 31 30N 69 0 E
Tobago **180** 11 10N 60 30W
Tobermory **30** 56 37N 6 4W
Tobolsk .... **69** 58 15N 68 10 E
Tobruk = Tubruq .... **128** 32 7N 23 55 E
Tocantins —► **188** 1 45S 49 10W
Toccoa **165** 34 32N 83 17W
Tochigi .... **107** 36 25N 139 45 E
Tocopilla **190** 22 5S 70 10W
Todos Santos **175** 23 27N 110 13W
Tōgane .... **107** 35 33N 140 22 E
Togliatti .... **68** 53 32N 49 24 E
Togo ■ .... **130** 6 15N 1 35 E
Tōhoku □ .... **103** 39 50N 141 45 E
Tōjō .... **109** 34 53N 133 16 E
Tokai .... **106** 35 2N 136 55 E
Tokaj .... **58** 48 8N 21 27 E
Tokara Kaikyō .... **104** 30 0N 130 0 E
Tokat.................. **80** 40 22N 36 35 E
Tokelau Is. **123** 9 0S 171 45W
Toki .... **106** 35 18N 137 8 E
Tokoname .... **106** 34 53N 136 51 E
Tokorozawa............. **107** 35 47N 139 28 E
Tokushima .... **109** 34 4N 134 34 E
Tokuyama .... **108** 34 3N 131 50 E
Tōkyō .... **107** 35 45N 139 45 E
Tōkyō-Wan .... **107** 35 25N 139 47 E
Tolbukhin .... **53** 43 37N 27 49 E
Toledo, Spain **50** 39 50N 4 2W
Toledo, U.S.A. **167** 41 37N 83 33W
Tolga .... **127** 34 40N 5 22 E
Tolima, Vol. **184** 4 40N 75 19W
Toluca **177** 19 20N 99 40W
Tomakomai .... **103** 42 38N 141 36 E
Tombigbee —► **169** 31 4N 87 58W
Tombouctou **130** 16 50N 3 0W
Tomini, Teluk .... **113** 0 10S 122 0 E
Tomsk.................. **71** 56 30N 85 5 E
Tonalá **177** 16 4N 93 45W
Tonantins **184** 2 45S 67 45W
Tonbridge .... **25** 51 12N 0 18 E
Tong Xian............... **98** 39 55N 116 35 E
Tonga ■ **123** 19 50S 174 30W
Tongchuan .... **99** 35 6N 109 3 E
Tonghua................ **98** 41 42N 125 58 E
Tongking, G. of .... **95** 20 0N 108 0 E
Tongue **33** 58 29N 4 25W
Tonk .... **91** 26 6N 75 54 E
Tonkin = Bac Phan .... **95** 22 0N 105 0 E
Tonlé Sap............... **95** 13 0N 104 0 E
Tonopah................ **172** 38 4N 117 14W
Tonoshō .... **109** 34 29N 134 11 E
Tooele **162** 40 30N 112 20W
Toowoomba .... **116** 27 32S 151 56 E
Topeka **166** 39 3N 95 40W
Toppenish **171** 46 27N 120 16W
Torbay **27** 50 26N 3 31W
Torino .... **46** 45 4N 7 40 E

Tormes →	**50**	41 18N	6 29W
Torne älv →	**67**	65 50N	24 12 E
Torneå = Tornio	**67**	65 50N	24 12 E
Torneträsk	**66**	68 24N	19 15 E
Tornio	**67**	65 50N	24 12 E
Toro, Cerro del	**190**	29 10S	69 50W
Toronto, Australia	**117**	33 0S	151 30 E
Toronto, Canada	**151**	43 39N	79 20W
Toros Daglari	**80**	37 0N	35 0 E
Torquay	**27**	50 27N	3 31W
Torre Annunziata	**49**	40 45N	14 26 E
Tôrre de Moncorvo	**50**	41 12N	7 8W
Torremolinos	**50**	36 38N	4 30W
Torrens, L.	**119**	31 0S	137 50 E
Torreón	**174**	25 33N	103 26W
Torres Vedras	**50**	39 5N	9 15W
Torridge →	**27**	50 51N	4 10W
Torrington	**164**	41 50N	73 9W
Tortosa	**51**	40 49N	0 31 E
Tortosa, C.	**51**	40 41N	0 52 E
Toruń	**58**	53 0N	18 39 E
Tory I.	**34**	55 17N	8 12W
Tosa-Shimizu	**109**	32 52N	132 58 E
Tosa-Wan	**109**	33 15N	133 30 E
Toscana	**46**	43 30N	11 5 E
Tostado	**190**	29 15S	61 50W
Tosu	**109**	33 22N	130 31 E
Totnes	**27**	50 26N	3 41W
Totonicapán	**177**	14 58N	91 12W
Tottori	**109**	35 30N	134 15 E
Toubkal, Djebel	**126**	31 0N	8 0W
Touggourt	**127**	33 6N	6 4 E
Toulon	**37**	43 10N	5 55 E
Toulouse	**36**	43 37N	1 27 E
Toungoo	**93**	19 0N	96 30 E
Touraine	**36**	47 20N	0 30 E
Tourane = Da Nang	**95**	16 4N	108 13 E
Tourcoing	**38**	50 42N	3 10 E
Tournai	**42**	50 35N	3 25 E
Tours	**36**	47 22N	0 40 E
Townsville	**121**	19 15S	146 45 E
Towson	**164**	39 26N	76 34W
Toyama	**106**	36 40N	137 15 E
Toyama-Wan	**105**	37 0N	137 30 E
Toyohashi	**106**	34 45N	137 25 E
Toyokawa	**106**	34 48N	137 27 E
Toyonaka	**106**	34 50N	135 28 E
Toyooka	**109**	35 35N	134 48 E
Toyota	**106**	35 3N	137 7 E
Tozeur	**127**	33 56N	8 8 E
Trabzon	**81**	41 0N	39 45 E
Tracy	**172**	37 46N	121 27W
Trafalgar, C.	**50**	36 10N	6 2W
Trail	**155**	49 5N	117 40W
Tralee	**35**	52 16N	9 42W
Tralee B.	**35**	52 17N	9 55W
Tran Ninh, Cao Nguyen	**95**	19 30N	103 10 E
Trangan	**113**	6 40S	134 20 E
Trangie	**116**	32 4S	148 0 E
Transantarctic Mts.	**15**	85 0S	170 0W
Transcona	**153**	49 55N	97 0W
Transilvania	**57**	46 19N	25 0 E
Transkei	**137**	32 15S	28 15 E
Transvaal □	**137**	25 0S	29 0 E
Transylvania = Transilvania	**57**	46 19N	25 0 E
Transylvanian Alps	**17**	45 30N	25 0 E
Trápani	**48**	38 1N	12 30 E
Traralgon	**117**	38 12S	146 34 E
Trasimeno, L.	**46**	43 10N	12 5 E
Travers, Mt.	**123**	42 1S	172 45 E
Traverse City	**167**	44 45N	85 39W
Travnik	**52**	44 17N	17 39 E
Tredegar	**27**	51 47N	3 16W
Tregaron	**26**	52 14N	3 56W
Treinta y Tres	**191**	33 16S	54 17W
Trelew	**192**	43 10S	65 20W
Trenque Lauquen	**190**	36 5S	62 45W
Trent →	**29**	53 33N	0 44W
Trentino-Alto Adige □	**47**	46 30N	11 0 E
Trento	**47**	46 5N	11 8 E
Trenton, Canada	**151**	44 10N	77 34W
Trenton, Mo., U.S.A.	**166**	40 5N	93 37W
Trenton, N.J., U.S.A.	**164**	40 15N	74 41W
Tréport, Le	**38**	50 3N	1 20 E
Tres Arroyos	**190**	38 26S	60 20W
Três Lagoas	**188**	20 50S	51 43W
Tres Montes, C.	**192**	46 50S	75 30W
Tres Puntas, C.	**192**	47 0S	66 0W
Treviso	**47**	45 40N	12 15 E
Trichinopoly = Tiruchchirappalli	**90**	10 45N	78 45 E
Trichur	**90**	10 30N	76 18 E
Trier	**42**	49 45N	6 37 E
Trieste	**47**	45 39N	13 45 E
Tríkkala	**54**	39 34N	21 47 E
Trincomalee	**90**	8 38N	81 15 E
Trinidad, Bolivia	**187**	14 46S	64 50W
Trinidad, Colombia	**184**	5 25N	71 40W
Trinidad, Cuba	**178**	21 48N	80 0W
Trinidad, Uruguay	**191**	33 30S	56 50W
Trinidad, U.S.A.	**163**	37 15N	104 30W
Trinidad & Tobago ■	**180**	10 30N	61 20W
Trinity →	**168**	30 30N	95 0W
Trinity Mts.	**172**	40 20N	118 50W
Tripoli = Tarābulus, Lebanon	**80**	34 31N	35 50 E
Tripoli = Tarābulus, Libya	**127**	32 49N	13 7 E
Trípolis	**54**	37 31N	22 25 E
Tripura □	**93**	24 0N	92 0 E
Trivandrum	**90**	8 41N	77 0 E
Trois-Riviéres	**151**	46 25N	72 34W
Troitsk	**71**	54 10N	61 35 E
Trollhättan	**60**	58 17N	12 20 E
Tromsø	**66**	69 40N	18 56 E
Trondheim	**65**	63 36N	10 25 E
Trossachs, The	**31**	56 14N	4 24W
Trotternish	**32**	57 32N	6 15W
Trouville	**38**	49 21N	0 5 E
Trowbridge	**24**	51 18N	2 12W
Troy, Ala., U.S.A.	**169**	31 50N	85 58W
Troy, N.Y., U.S.A.	**164**	42 45N	73 39W
Troyes	**39**	48 19N	4 3 E
Trucial States = United Arab Emirates ■	**85**	23 50N	54 0 E
Trujillo, Hond.	**179**	16 0N	86 0W
Trujillo, Peru	**186**	8 6S	79 0W
Trujillo, Venezuela	**184**	9 22N	70 38W
Trundle	**117**	32 53S	147 35 E
Trung-Phan	**95**	16 0N	108 0 E
Truro, Canada	**149**	45 21N	63 14W
Truro, U.K.	**27**	50 17N	5 2W
Tselinograd	**71**	51 10N	71 30 E
Tsinan = Jinan	**98**	36 38N	117 1 E
Tsinghai = Qinghai □	**101**	36 0N	98 0 E
Tsingtao = Qingdao	**98**	36 5N	120 20 E
Tsu	**106**	34 45N	136 25 E
Tsuchiura	**107**	36 5N	140 15 E
Tsugaru-Kaikyō	**103**	41 35N	141 0 E
Tsukumi	**108**	33 4N	131 52 E
Tsukushi-Sanchi	**108**	33 25N	130 30 E
Tsuruga	**106**	35 45N	136 2 E
Tsurugi-San	**109**	33 51N	134 6 E
Tsuruoka	**103**	38 44N	139 50 E
Tsushima, Gifu, Japan	**106**	35 10N	136 43 E
Tsushima, Nagasaki, Japan	**104**	34 20N	129 20 E
Tuamotu Arch.	**123**	17 0S	144 0W
Tubarão	**191**	28 30S	49 0W
Tubruq	**128**	32 7N	23 55 E
Tubuai Is.	**123**	25 0S	150 0W
Tucacas	**184**	10 48N	68 19W
Tucson	**160**	32 14N	110 59W
Tucumcari	**161**	35 12N	103 45W
Tucupita	**185**	9 2N	62 3W
Tucuruí	**188**	3 42S	49 44W
Tudmur	**80**	34 36N	38 15 E
Tuktoyaktuk	**144**	69 27N	133 2W
Tula, Mexico	**177**	23 0N	99 43W
Tula, U.S.S.R.	**68**	54 13N	37 38 E
Tulare	**173**	36 15N	119 26W
Tulcán	**184**	0 48N	77 43W
Tullahoma	**169**	35 23N	86 12W
Tullamore	**35**	53 17N	7 30W
Tully	**121**	17 56S	145 55 E

Tulsa	**168**	36	10N	96	0W
Tulua	**184**	4	6N	76	11W
Tuma —→	**179**	13	6N	84	35W
Tumaco	**184**	1	50N	78	45W
Tumatumari	**185**	5	20N	58	55W
Tumbarumba	**117**	35	44S	148	0 E
Túmbes	**186**	3	37S	80	27W
Tumkur	**90**	13	18N	77	6 E
Tummel, L.	**33**	56	43N	3	55W
Tummo	**127**	22	45N	14	8 E
Tump	**88**	26	7N	62	16 E
Tumucumaque, Serra	**188**	2	0N	55	0W
Tumut	**117**	35	16S	148	13 E
Tunbridge Wells	**25**	51	7N	0	16 E
Tundzha —→	**53**	41	40N	26	35 E
Tunis	**127**	36	50N	10	11 E
Tunisia ■	**127**	33	30N	9	10 E
Tunja	**184**	5	33N	73	25W
Tunxi	**99**	29	42N	118	25 E
Tupelo	**169**	34	15N	88	42W
Tupiza	**187**	21	30S	65	40W
Tupper L.	**151**	44	18N	74	30W
Tuque, La	**151**	47	30N	72	50W
Túquerres	**184**	1	5N	77	37W
Tura	**92**	25	30N	90	16 E
Turayf	**82**	31	41N	38	39 E
Turfan = Turpan	**100**	43	58N	89	10 E
Turfan Depression = Turpan					
Hami	**100**	42	40N	89	25 E
Türgovishte	**53**	43	17N	26	38 E
Turgutlu	**80**	38	30N	27	48 E
Turin = Torino	**46**	45	4N	7	40 E
Turkana, L.	**132**	3	30N	36	5 E
Turkestan	**71**	43	17N	68	16 E
Turkey ■	**80**	39	0N	36	0 E
Turkmen S.S.R. □	**70**	39	0N	59	0 E
Turks Is.	**180**	21	20N	71	20W
Turku	**67**	60	30N	22	19 E
Turlock	**172**	37	30N	120	55W
Turnagain, C.	**122**	40	28S	176	38 E
Turnhout	**42**	51	19N	4	57 E
Türnovo	**53**	43	5N	25	41 E
Turnu Rosu Pasul	**57**	45	33N	24	17 E
Turnu-Severin	**56**	44	39N	22	41 E
Turpan	**100**	43	58N	89	10 E
Turpan Hami	**100**	42	40N	89	25 E
Turukhansk	**74**	65	21N	88	5 E
Tuscaloosa	**169**	33	13N	87	31W
Tuscany = Toscana	**46**	43	30N	11	5 E
Tuskegee	**169**	32	24N	85	39W
Tutrakan	**53**	44	2N	26	40 E
Tuvalu ■	**122**	8	0S	178	0 E
Tuxpan	**177**	20	57N	97	24W
Tuxtla Gutiérrez	**177**	16	45N	93	7W
Tuy Hoa	**95**	13	5N	109	10 E
Tuyen Hoa	**95**	17	50N	106	10 E
Tuz Gölü	**80**	38	45N	33	30 E
Tüz Khurmātū	**81**	34	56N	44	38 E
Tuzla	**52**	44	34N	18	41 E
Tweed —→	**31**	55	42N	2	10W
Tweed Heads	**116**	28	10S	153	31 E
Twin Falls	**172**	42	30N	114	30W
Two Harbors	**156**	47	1N	91	40W
Tyler	**168**	32	18N	95	18W
Tyne —→	**28**	54	58N	1	28W
Tyne & Wear □	**28**	54	55N	1	35W
Tynemouth	**28**	55	1N	1	27W
Tyrol = Tirol □	**45**	47	3N	10	43 E
Tyrrhenian Sea	**48**	40	0N	12	30 E
Tyumen	**69**	57	11N	65	29 E
Tzukong = Zigong	**99**	29	15N	104	48 E
Uaupés	**184**	0	8S	67	5W
Ubangi = Oubangi —→	**131**	1	0N	17	50 E
Ube	**108**	33	56N	131	15 E
Uberaba	**188**	19	50S	47	55W
Uberlândia	**188**	19	0S	48	20W
Ubon Ratchathani	**95**	15	15N	104	50 E
Ucayali —→	**186**	4	30S	73	30W
Uchi Lake	**153**	51	5N	92	35W
Uchiura-Wan	**103**	42	25N	140	40 E
Uchur —→	**75**	58	48N	130	35 E
Udaipur	**91**	24	36N	73	44 E
Uddevalla	**60**	58	21N	11	55 E
Údine	**47**	46	5N	13	10 E
Udmurt A.S.S.R. □	**69**	57	30N	52	30 E
Udon Thani	**95**	17	29N	102	46 E
Ueda	**107**	36	24N	138	16 E
Uelen	**73**	66	10N	170	0W
Uelzen	**43**	53	0N	10	33 E
Ueno	**106**	34	45N	136	8 E
Ufa	**69**	54	45N	55	55 E
Uganda ■	**132**	2	0N	32	0 E
Uinta Mts.	**163**	40	45N	110	30W
Uithuizen	**41**	53	24N	6	41 E
Uji	**106**	34	53N	135	48 E
Ujjain	**91**	23	9N	75	43 E
Ujpest	**59**	47	32N	19	6 E
Ujung Pandang	**113**	5	10S	119	20 E
Ukiah	**172**	39	10N	123	9W
Ukrainian S.S.R. □	**68**	49	0N	32	0 E
Ulaanbaatar	**98**	47	55N	106	53 E
Ulan Bator = Ulaanbaatar	**98**	47	55N	106	53 E
Ulan Ude	**74**	51	45N	107	40 E
Ulcinj	**52**	41	58N	19	10 E
Ulhasnagar	**91**	19	15N	73	10 E
Ulladulla	**117**	35	21S	150	29 E
Ullapool	**32**	57	54N	5	10W
Ullswater	**28**	54	35N	2	52W
Ulm	**42**	48	23N	10	0 E
Ulster □	**34**	54	35N	6	30W
Ulverston	**28**	54	13N	3	7W
Ulverstone	**119**	41	11S	146	11 E
Ulyanovsk	**68**	54	20N	48	25 E
Ulyasutay	**100**	47	56N	97	28 E
Umbrella Mts	**123**	45	35S	169	5 E
Umbria □	**46**	42	53N	12	30 E
Ume älv —→	**66**	63	45N	20	20 E
Umeå	**66**	63	45N	20	20 E
Umm al Qaywayn	**85**	25	30N	55	35 E
Umm Lajj	**82**	25	0N	37	23 E
Umnak	**142**	53	20N	168	20W
Umpang	**94**	16	3N	98	54 E
Umtata	**137**	31	36S	28	49 E
Unalaska	**142**	53	40N	166	40W
Ungava B.	**146**	59	30N	67	30W
Ungava Pen.	**146**	60	0N	74	0W
União da Vitória	**191**	26	13S	51	5W
Unimak	**142**	55	0N	164	0W
Union City	**169**	36	25N	89	0W
Union of Soviet Socialist					
Republics ■	**79**	60	0N	100	0 E
Uniontown	**164**	39	54N	79	45W
United Arab Emirates ■	**85**	23	50N	54	0 E
United Kingdom ■	**18**	55	0N	3	0W
United States of America ■	**139**	37	0N	96	0W
Unity	**152**	52	30N	109	5W
Unnao	**92**	26	35N	80	30 E
Unst	**30**	60	50N	0	55W
Uozu	**106**	36	48N	137	24 E
Upata	**185**	8	1N	62	24W
Upper Austria =					
Oberösterreich □	**45**	48	10N	14	0 E
Upper Hutt	**123**	41	8S	175	5 E
Upper Taimyr —→	**72**	74	15N	99	48 E
Upper Volta ■ = Burkina					
Faso ■	**130**	12	0N	1	0W
Uppsala	**60**	59	53N	17	38 E
Uppsala län □	**60**	60	0N	17	30 E
Ur	**84**	30	55N	46	25 E
Uracara	**185**	2	20S	57	50W
Urakawa	**103**	42	9N	142	47 E
Ural —→	**70**	47	0N	51	48 E
Ural Mts. = Uralskie Gory	**69**	60	0N	59	0 E
Uralsk	**70**	51	20N	51	20 E
Uralskie Gory	**69**	60	0N	59	0 E
Uranium City	**145**	59	34N	108	37W
Urawa	**107**	35	50N	139	40 E
Urbana, Ill., U.S.A.	**167**	40	7N	88	12W
Urbana, Ohio, U.S.A.	**167**	40	9N	83	44W

Urbana, La	**184**	7 8N	66 56W
Urcos	**187**	13 40S	71 38W
Ures	**174**	29 26N	110 24W
Urfa	**81**	37 12N	38 50 E
Urgench	**70**	41 40N	60 41 E
Uribia	**184**	11 43N	72 16W
Urk	**41**	52 39N	5 36 E
Urmia = Orūmīyeh	**81**	37 40N	45 0 E
Urmia, L. = Orūmīyeh, Daryācheh-ye	**81**	37 50N	45 30 E
Uruapan	**175**	19 30N	102 0W
Uruçuí	**188**	7 20S	44 28W
Uruguaiana	**191**	29 50S	57 0W
Uruguay ■	**191**	32 30S	56 30W
Uruguay →	**191**	34 12S	58 18W
Urumchi = Ürümqi	**100**	43 45N	87 45 E
Ürümqi	**100**	43 45N	87 45 E
Urup, Os.	**75**	46 0N	151 0 E
Usa	**108**	33 31N	131 21 E
Uşak	**80**	38 43N	29 28 E
Usfan	**82**	21 58N	39 27 E
Ushant = Ouessant, Île d'	**36**	48 28N	5 6W
Ushibuka	**108**	32 11N	130 1 E
Ushuaia	**192**	54 50S	68 23W
Usk →	**26**	51 37N	2 56W
Üsküdar	**80**	41 0N	29 5 E
Usolye Sibirskoye	**74**	52 48N	103 40 E
Uspenskiy	**71**	48 41N	72 43 E
Ussuriysk	**75**	43 48N	131 59 E
Ust-Aldan = Batamay	**74**	63 30N	129 15 E
Ust-Ilimsk	**74**	58 3N	102 39 E
Ust-Kamchatsk	**73**	56 10N	162 28 E
Ust-Kamenogorsk	**71**	50 0N	82 36 E
Ust Maya	**75**	60 30N	134 28 E
Ust Olenek	**72**	73 0N	119 48 E
Ust Port	**69**	69 40N	84 26 E
Ust Urt = Ustyurt, Plato	**70**	44 0N	55 0 E
Ust Vorkuta	**69**	67 24N	64 0 E
Ústí nad Labem	**58**	50 41N	14 3 E
Ustica	**48**	38 42N	13 10 E
Ustinov	**69**	56 51N	53 14 E
Ustyurt, Plato	**70**	44 0N	55 0 E
Usu	**100**	44 27N	84 40 E
Usuki	**108**	33 8N	131 49 E
Usumbura = Bujumbura	**135**	3 16S	29 18 E
Utah □	**163**	39 30N	111 30W
Utah, L.	**163**	40 10N	111 58W
Uthai Thani	**94**	15 22N	100 3 E
Utica	**164**	43 5N	75 18W
Uto	**108**	32 41N	130 40 E
Utrecht	**40**	52 5N	5 8 E
Utrecht □	**40**	52 6N	5 7 E
Utrera	**50**	37 12N	5 48W
Utsunomiya	**107**	36 30N	139 50 E
Uttar Pradesh □	**92**	27 0N	80 0 E
Uttoxeter	**28**	52 53N	1 50W
Uusikaupunki	**66**	60 47N	21 25 E
Uvalde	**161**	29 15N	99 48W
Uvs Nuur	**74**	50 20N	92 30 E
Uwajima	**109**	33 10N	132 35 E
Uzbek S.S.R. □	**70**	41 30N	65 0 E
Vaal →	**137**	29 4S	23 38 E
Vaals	**41**	50 46N	6 1 E
Vaasa	**67**	63 6N	21 38 E
Vác	**58**	47 49N	19 10 E
Vach →	**69**	60 45N	76 45 E
Vadodara	**91**	22 20N	73 10 E
Vadsø	**67**	70 3N	29 50 E
Váh →	**59**	47 55N	18 0 E
Vaigach	**69**	70 10N	59 0 E
Val d'Or	**151**	48 7N	77 47W
Valahia	**57**	44 35N	25 0 E
Valcheta	**192**	40 40S	66 8W
Valdés, Pen.	**192**	42 30S	63 45W
Valdez	**142**	61 14N	146 17W
Valdivia	**190**	39 50S	73 14W
Valdosta	**170**	30 50N	83 20W
Valence	**37**	44 57N	4 54 E
Valencia, Spain	**51**	39 27N	0 23W
Valencia, Venezuela	**184**	10 11N	68 0W
Valencia □	**51**	39 20N	0 40W
Valencia, Albufera de	**51**	39 20N	0 27W
Valencia, G. de	**51**	39 30N	0 20 E
Valencia de Alcántara	**50**	39 25N	7 14W
Valenciennes	**38**	50 20N	3 34 E
Valentia I.	**35**	51 54N	10 22W
Valera	**184**	9 19N	70 37W
Valkenswaard	**41**	51 21N	5 29 E
Valladolid, Mexico	**177**	20 41N	88 12W
Valladolid, Spain	**50**	41 38N	4 43W
Valle d'Aosta □	**46**	45 45N	7 22 E
Valle de la Pascua	**184**	9 13N	66 0W
Valle de Santiago	**177**	20 23N	101 12W
Vallecas	**50**	40 23N	3 41W
Vallejo	**172**	38 12N	122 15W
Valletta	**49**	35 54N	14 30 E
Valley City	**163**	46 57N	98 0W
Valley View	**155**	40 39N	76 33W
Valona = Vlóra	**52**	40 32N	19 28 E
Valparaíso, Chile	**190**	33 2S	71 40W
Valparaíso, Mexico	**175**	22 46N	103 34W
Valsad	**91**	20 40N	72 58 E
Van	**81**	38 30N	43 20 E
Van, L. = Van Gölü	**81**	38 30N	43 0 E
Van Buren, Canada	**148**	47 10N	67 55W
Van Buren, U.S.A.	**168**	35 28N	94 18W
Van Gölü	**81**	38 30N	43 0 E
Van Wert	**167**	40 52N	84 31W
Vancouver, Canada	**154**	49 15N	123 10W
Vancouver, U.S.A.	**171**	45 44N	122 41W
Vancouver I.	**154**	49 50N	126 0W
Vandalia	**166**	38 57N	89 4W
Vanderhoof	**154**	54 0N	124 0W
Vänern	**60**	58 47N	13 30 E
Vanier	**151**	45 27N	75 40W
Vankarem	**73**	67 51N	175 50 E
Vännäs	**66**	63 58N	19 48 E
Vannes	**36**	47 40N	2 47W
Vanua Levu	**122**	16 33S	179 15 E
Vanuatu ■	**122**	15 0S	168 0 E
Varanasi	**92**	25 22N	83 0 E
Varangerfjorden	**67**	70 3N	29 25 E
Varaždin	**52**	46 20N	16 20 E
Vardak □	**87**	34 0N	68 0 E
Vardø	**67**	70 23N	31 5 E
Värmland	**60**	60 0N	13 30 E
Varna	**53**	43 13N	27 56 E
Vascongadas	**50**	42 50N	2 45W
Västerås	**60**	59 37N	16 38 E
Västmanlands län □	**60**	59 45N	16 20 E
Vatnajökull	**64**	64 30N	16 48W
Vatra-Dornei	**57**	47 22N	25 22 E
Vättern	**60**	58 25N	14 30 E
Vaygach, Ostrov	**69**	70 0N	60 0 E
Veendam	**41**	53 5N	6 52 E
Vega, La	**180**	19 20N	70 30W
Veghel	**41**	51 37N	5 32 E
Vegreville	**155**	53 30N	112 5W
Vela, La	**184**	11 27N	69 34W
Vellore	**90**	12 57N	79 10 E
Venado Tuerto	**190**	33 50S	62 0W
Vendôme	**39**	47 47N	1 3 E
Véneto □	**47**	45 40N	12 0 E
Venézia	**47**	45 27N	12 20 E
Venézia, Golfo di	**47**	45 20N	13 0 E
Venezuela ■	**184**	8 0N	65 0W
Venezuela, Golfo de	**184**	11 30N	71 0W
Vengurla	**91**	15 53N	73 45 E
Venice = Venézia	**47**	45 27N	12 20 E
Venlo	**41**	51 22N	6 11 E
Venraij	**41**	51 31N	6 0 E
Ventnor	**24**	50 35N	1 12W
Ventoux	**37**	44 10N	5 17 E
Ventura	**173**	34 16N	119 18W
Veracruz	**177**	19 10N	96 10W
Veracruz □	**177**	19 20N	96 40W
Verde, R. →	**175**	15 59N	97 50W
Verdun	**37**	49 12N	5 24 E
Vereeniging	**137**	26 38S	27 57 E

Verkhoyansk	**72**	67 35N	133 25 E
Verkhoyanskiy Khrebet	**72**	66 0N	129 0 E
Vermilion	**152**	53 20N	110 50W
Vermont □	**164**	43 40N	72 50W
Verneuil-sur-Avre	**39**	48 45N	0 55 E
Vernon, Canada	**155**	50 20N	119 15W
Vernon, France	**39**	49 5N	1 30 E
Vernon, U.S.A.	**161**	34 10N	99 20W
Verona	**46**	45 27N	11 0 E
Versailles	**39**	48 48N	2 8 E
Vert, C.	**130**	14 45N	17 30W
Verviers	**42**	50 37N	5 52 E
Vest-Agder fylke □	**60**	58 30N	7 15 E
Vesterålen	**64**	68 45N	15 0 E
Vestfjorden	**64**	67 55N	14 0 E
Vestfold fylke □	**60**	59 15N	10 0 E
Vestspitsbergen	**13**	78 40N	17 0 E
Vesuvio	**49**	40 50N	14 22 E
Vesuvius, Mt. = Vesuvio	**49**	40 50N	14 22 E
Viacha	**187**	16 39S	68 18W
Viborg	**61**	56 27N	9 23 E
Vicenza	**47**	45 32N	11 31 E
Vichy	**37**	46 9N	3 26 E
Vicksburg	**169**	32 22N	90 56W
Victor Harbor	**119**	35 30S	138 37 E
Victoria, Canada	**154**	48 30N	123 25W
Victoria, Chile	**190**	38 13S	72 20W
Victoria, U.S.A.	**158**	28 50N	97 0W
Victoria □	**117**	37 0S	144 0 E
Victoria, L.	**132**	1 0S	33 0 E
Victoria de las Tunas	**178**	20 58N	76 59W
Victoria Falls	**137**	17 58S	25 52 E
Victoria I.	**145**	71 0N	111 0W
Victoria Ld.	**15**	75 0S	160 0 E
Victoriaville	**148**	46 4N	71 56W
Vidalia	**170**	32 13N	82 25W
Vidin	**53**	43 59N	22 50 E
Viedma	**192**	40 50S	63 0W
Vienna = Wien	**45**	48 12N	16 22 E
Vienne	**37**	45 31N	4 53 E
Vienne →	**36**	47 13N	0 5 E
Vientiane	**95**	17 58N	102 36 E
Vientos, Paso de los	**180**	20 0N	74 0W
Vietnam ■	**95**	19 0N	106 0 E
Vigo	**50**	42 12N	8 41W
Vijayawada	**92**	16 31N	80 39 E
Vila Real de Santo António	**50**	37 10N	7 28W
Vilhelmina	**66**	64 35N	16 39 E
Vilhena	**187**	12 40S	60 5W
Villa Bella	**187**	10 25S	65 22W
Villa Bens = Tarfaya	**126**	27 55N	12 55W
Villa Cisneros = Dakhla	**126**	23 50N	15 53W
Villa Dolores	**190**	31 58S	65 15W
Villa María	**190**	32 20S	63 10W
Villa Montes	**187**	21 10S	63 30W
Villaguay	**190**	32 0S	59 0W
Villahermosa	**177**	17 59N	92 55W
Villanueva de la Serena	**50**	38 59N	5 50W
Villarreal	**51**	39 55N	0 3W
Villarrica	**191**	39 15S	72 15W
Villazón	**187**	22 0S	65 35W
Ville Platte	**168**	30 45N	92 17W
Villefranche-sur-Saône	**37**	45 59N	4 43 E
Villers-Cotterêts	**39**	49 15N	3 4 E
Vilnius	**68**	54 38N	25 19 E
Vilskutskogo, Proliv	**72**	78 0N	103 0 E
Vilyuy →	**74**	64 24N	126 26 E
Vilyuysk	**74**	63 40N	121 35 E
Viña del Mar	**190**	33 0S	71 30W
Vincennes	**167**	38 42N	87 29W
Vindhya Ra.	**91**	22 50N	77 0 E
Vinh	**95**	18 45N	105 38 E
Vinita	**168**	36 40N	95 12W
Vinkovci	**52**	45 19N	18 48 E
Vinnitsa	**68**	49 15N	28 30 E
Viramgam	**91**	23 5N	72 0 E
Virden	**153**	49 50N	100 56W
Vire	**36**	48 50N	0 53W
Vírgenes, C.	**192**	52 19S	68 21W
Virgin →	**173**	36 50N	114 10W
Virgin Is.	**180**	18 40N	64 30W
Virginia	**156**	47 30N	92 32W
Virginia □	**165**	37 45N	78 0W
Virginia Beach	**165**	36 54N	75 58W
Visalia	**173**	36 25N	119 18W
Visby	**60**	57 37N	18 18 E
Viscount Melville Sd.	**145**	74 10N	108 0W
Višegrad	**52**	43 47N	19 17 E
Vishakhapatnam	**92**	17 45N	83 20 E
Vistula = Wisła →	**58**	54 22N	18 55 E
Vitebsk	**68**	55 10N	30 15 E
Viti Levu	**122**	17 30S	177 30 E
Vitim →	**74**	59 26N	112 34 E
Vitória, Brazil	**189**	20 20S	40 22W
Vitória, Spain	**50**	42 50N	2 41W
Vitória da Conquista	**189**	14 51S	40 51W
Vizianagaram	**92**	18 6N	83 30 E
Vlaardingen	**40**	51 55N	4 21 E
Vladimir	**68**	56 15N	40 30 E
Vladivostok	**75**	43 10N	131 53 E
Vlieland	**40**	53 16N	4 55 E
Vlissingen	**40**	51 26N	3 34 E
Vlóra	**52**	40 32N	19 28 E
Vltava →	**59**	50 21N	14 30 E
Vogelkop	**113**	1 25S	133 0 E
Vogels Berg, mt.	**42**	50 37N	9 30 E
Vohimena, Tanjon' i	**137**	25 36S	45 8 E
Voi	**133**	3 25S	38 32 E
Volendam	**40**	52 30N	5 4 E
Volga →	**68**	48 30N	46 0 E
Volga Hts. = Privolzhskaya Vozvyshennost	**17**	51 0N	46 0 E
Volgograd	**68**	48 40N	44 25 E
Vollenhove	**41**	52 40N	5 58 E
Vologda	**68**	59 10N	40 0 E
Vólos	**54**	39 24N	22 59 E
Volsk	**68**	52 5N	47 22 E
Volta →	**130**	5 46N	0 41 E
Volta, L.	**130**	7 30N	0 15 E
Volta Redonda	**188**	22 31S	44 5W
Voorburg	**40**	52 5N	4 24 E
Vopnafjörður	**64**	65 45N	14 40W
Voríai Sporádhes	**55**	39 15N	23 30 E
Voronezh	**68**	51 40N	39 10 E
Voroshilovgrad	**68**	48 38N	39 15 E
Vosges	**37**	48 20N	7 10 E
Vostochnyy Sayan	**74**	54 0N	96 0 E
Vrangelya, Ostrov	**73**	71 0N	180 0 E
Vranje	**53**	42 34N	21 54 E
Vratsa	**53**	43 13N	23 30 E
Vršac	**52**	45 8N	21 18 E
Vught	**40**	51 38N	5 20 E
Vulcan	**155**	50 25N	113 15W
Vyborg	**68**	60 43N	28 47 E
Vychegda →	**69**	61 18N	46 36 E
Vychodné Beskydy	**59**	49 30N	22 0 E
Wa	**130**	10 7N	2 25W
Waal →	**41**	51 59N	4 30 E
Waalwijk	**40**	51 42N	5 4 E
Wabash	**167**	40 48N	85 46W
Wabash →	**167**	37 46N	88 2W
Wąbrzeźno	**58**	53 16N	18 57 E
Waco	**168**	31 33N	97 5W
Wâd Medanî	**129**	14 28N	33 30 E
Waddenzee	**40**	53 6N	5 10 E
Waddington, Mt.	**154**	51 23N	125 15W
Waddinxveen	**40**	52 2N	4 40 E
Wadena	**152**	51 57N	103 47W
Wadi Halfa	**129**	21 53N	31 19 E
Wageningen	**41**	51 58N	5 40 E
Wager Bay	**146**	65 56N	90 49W
Wagga Wagga	**117**	35 7S	147 24 E
Wagin	**120**	33 17S	117 25 E
Waigeo	**113**	0 20S	130 40 E
Waihi	**122**	37 23S	175 52 E
Waikerie	**119**	34 9S	140 0 E
Waikokopu	**122**	39 3S	177 52 E
Waimate	**123**	44 45S	171 3 E
Wainwright, Canada	**152**	52 50N	110 50W

Wainwright, U.S.A.	**142**	70 39N	160 1W
Waipara	**123**	43 3S	172 46 E
Waipu	**122**	35 59S	174 29 E
Waipukurau	**122**	40 1S	176 33 E
Wairoa	**122**	39 3S	177 25 E
Waitara	**122**	38 59S	174 15 E
Wajima	**105**	37 30N	137 0 E
Wajir	**133**	1 42N	40 5 E
Wakasa-Wan	**106**	35 40N	135 30 E
Wakatipu, L.	**123**	45 5S	168 33 E
Wakayama	**106**	34 15N	135 15 E
Wakefield, N.Z.	**123**	41 24S	173 5 E
Wakefield, U.K.	**28**	53 41N	1 31W
Wakkanai	**103**	45 28N	141 35 E
Wałbrzych	**58**	50 45N	16 18 E
Walcha	**116**	30 55S	151 31 E
Walcheren	**40**	51 30N	3 35 E
Wales □	**26**	52 30N	3 30W
Walgett	**116**	30 0S	148 5 E
Walkerton	**151**	44 10N	81 10W
Walla Walla	**171**	46 3N	118 25W
Wallaceburg	**150**	42 34N	82 23W
Wallachia = Valahia	**57**	44 35N	25 0 E
Wallangarra	**116**	28 56S	151 58 E
Wallaroo	**119**	33 56S	137 39 E
Wallasey	**28**	53 26N	3 2W
Wallerawang	**117**	33 25S	150 4 E
Wallis & Futuna	**122**	13 18S	176 10W
Wallowa, Mts.	**171**	45 20N	117 30W
Wallsend, Australia	**117**	32 55S	151 40 E
Wallsend, U.K.	**28**	54 59N	1 30W
Walney, Isle of	**28**	54 5N	3 15W
Walpole	**120**	34 58S	116 44 E
Walsall	**24**	52 36N	1 59W
Walvis Bay	**136**	23 0S	14 28 E
Wana	**88**	32 20N	69 32 E
Wanaka L.	**123**	44 33S	169 7 E
Wang Saphung	**95**	17 18N	101 46 E
Wanganui	**122**	39 56S	175 3 E
Wangaratta	**117**	36 21S	146 19 E
Wanxian	**99**	30 42N	108 20 E
Warabi	**107**	35 49N	139 41 E
Warangal	**91**	17 58N	79 35 E
Warburton	**117**	37 47S	145 42 E
Wardha	**91**	20 45N	78 39 E
Wardha →	**91**	19 57N	79 11 E
Warialda	**116**	29 29S	150 33 E
Warley	**24**	52 30N	2 0W
Warner Mts.	**172**	41 30N	120 20W
Waroona	**120**	32 50S	115 58 E
Warracknabeal	**119**	36 9S	142 26 E
Warragul	**117**	38 10S	145 58 E
Warrego →	**116**	30 24S	145 21 E
Warrego Ra.	**121**	24 58S	146 0 E
Warren, Australia	**116**	31 42S	147 51 E
Warren, Ark., U.S.A.	**168**	33 35N	92 3W
Warren, Mich., U.S.A.	**167**	42 31N	83 2W
Warren, Ohio, U.S.A.	**164**	41 18N	80 52W
Warren, Pa., U.S.A.	**164**	41 52N	79 10W
Warrenpoint	**34**	54 7N	6 15W
Warrensburg	**166**	38 45N	93 45W
Warrington, U.K.	**28**	53 25N	2 38W
Warrington, U.S.A.	**169**	30 22N	87 16W
Warrnambool	**119**	38 25S	142 30 E
Warsaw = Warszawa	**58**	52 13N	21 0 E
Warszawa	**58**	52 13N	21 0 E
Warta →	**58**	52 35N	14 39 E
Warthe = Warta →	**58**	52 35N	14 39 E
Warwick, Australia	**116**	28 10S	152 1 E
Warwick, U.K.	**24**	52 17N	1 36W
Warwick, U.S.A.	**164**	41 43N	71 25W
Warwick □	**24**	52 20N	1 30W
Wasatch Ra.	**163**	40 30N	111 15W
Wasco	**173**	35 37N	119 16W
Wash, The	**29**	52 58N	0 20 E
Washim	**91**	20 3N	77 0 E
Washington, D.C., U.S.A.	**165**	38 52N	77 0W
Washington, Ind., U.S.A.	**167**	38 40N	87 8W
Washington, Mo., U.S.A.	**166**	38 35N	91 1W
Washington, Pa., U.S.A.	**164**	40 10N	80 20W
Washington □	**171**	47 45N	120 30W
Wassenaar	**40**	52 8N	4 24 E
Waterbury	**164**	41 32N	73 0W
Waterford	**35**	52 16N	7 8W
Waterford □	**35**	52 10N	7 40W
Waterloo, Canada	**151**	43 30N	80 32W
Waterloo, U.S.A.	**166**	42 27N	92 20W
Watertown, N.Y., U.S.A.	**151**	43 58N	75 57W
Watertown, Wis., U.S.A.	**167**	43 15N	88 45W
Waterville	**148**	44 35N	69 40W
Watling I. = San Salvador	**178**	24 0N	74 40W
Watrous	**152**	51 40N	105 25W
Watson Lake	**144**	60 6N	128 49W
Watsonville	**173**	36 55N	121 49W
Watubela, Kepulauan	**113**	4 28S	131 35 E
Wauchope	**116**	31 28S	152 45 E
Waukegan	**167**	42 22N	87 54W
Waukesha	**167**	43 0N	88 15W
Wausau	**166**	44 57N	89 40W
Wauwatosa	**167**	43 6N	87 59W
Waveney →	**25**	52 24N	1 20 E
Wâw	**129**	7 45N	28 1 E
Waxahachie	**168**	32 22N	96 53W
Waycross	**170**	31 12N	82 25W
Waynesboro, Pa., U.S.A.	**164**	39 46N	77 32W
Waynesboro, Va., U.S.A.	**165**	38 4N	78 57W
Waynesville	**165**	35 31N	83 0W
Wazirabad	**89**	32 30N	74 8 E
Weald, The	**25**	51 7N	0 9 E
Webo = Nyaake	**130**	4 52N	7 37W
Weddell Sea	**14**	72 30S	40 0W
Wedderburn	**117**	36 26S	143 33 E
Wee Waa	**116**	30 11S	149 26 E
Weert	**41**	51 15N	5 43 E
Weesp	**40**	52 18N	5 2 E
Weifang	**98**	36 47N	119 10 E
Weiser	**171**	44 10N	117 0W
Welbourn Hill	**118**	27 21S	134 6 E
Welch	**165**	37 29N	81 36W
Welland	**151**	43 0N	79 15W
Welland →	**29**	52 43N	0 10W
Wellingborough	**25**	52 18N	0 41W
Wellington, Australia	**116**	32 35S	148 59 E
Wellington, N.Z.	**123**	41 19S	174 46 E
Wellington, Salop, U.K.	**28**	52 42N	2 31W
Wellington, Somerset, U.K.	**27**	50 58N	3 13W
Wellington □	**123**	40 8S	175 36 E
Wellington, I.	**192**	49 30S	75 0W
Wells, Norfolk, U.K.	**29**	52 57N	0 51 E
Wells, Somerset, U.K.	**27**	51 12N	2 39W
Wells, U.S.A.	**172**	41 8N	115 0W
Wellsville, N.Y., U.S.A.	**164**	42 9N	77 53W
Wellsville, Ohio, U.S.A.	**164**	40 36N	80 40W
Welshpool	**26**	52 40N	3 9W
Wem	**28**	52 52N	2 45W
Wenatchee	**171**	47 30N	120 17W
Wenchow = Wenzhou	**99**	28 0N	120 38 E
Wensleydale	**28**	54 18N	2 0W
Wentworth	**119**	34 2S	141 54 E
Wenzhou	**99**	28 0N	120 38 E
Werribee	**117**	37 54S	144 40 E
Werris Creek	**116**	31 18S	150 38 E
Weser →	**42**	53 33N	8 30 E
West Bengal □	**92**	23 0N	88 0 E
West Bromwich	**24**	52 32N	2 1W
West Falkland	**192**	51 40S	60 0W
West Frankfort	**166**	37 56N	89 0W
West Glamorgan □	**27**	51 40N	3 55W
West Memphis	**169**	35 5N	90 11W
West Midlands □	**24**	52 30N	1 55W
West Palm Beach	**170**	26 44N	80 3W
West Schelde → = Westerschelde →	**40**	51 25N	3 25 E
West Siberian Plain	**76**	62 0N	75 0 E
West Sussex □	**25**	50 55N	0 30W
West Virginia □	**165**	39 0N	81 0W
West Yorkshire □	**28**	53 45N	1 40W
Western Australia □	**114**	25 0S	118 0 E
Western Ghats	**90**	14 0N	75 0 E
Western Isles □	**32**	57 30N	7 10W
Western Sahara ■	**126**	25 0N	13 0W

Western Samoa ■	**123**	14	0S 172	0W
Westerschelde ⤳	**40**	51	25N	3 25 E
Westerwald	**42**	50	39N	8 0 E
Westfriesche Eilanden	**40**	53	20N	5 10 E
Westland □	**123**	43	33S 169	59 E
Westland Bight	**123**	42	55S 170	5 E
Westlock	**155**	54	9N 113	55W
Westmeath □	**34**	53	30N	7 30W
Westminster	**164**	39	34N	77 1W
Weston	**165**	39	3N	80 29W
Weston-super-Mare	**27**	51	20N	2 59W
Westport	**123**	41	46S 171	37 E
Westray	**33**	59	18N	3 0W
Wetar	**113**	7	30S 126	30 E
Wetaskiwin	**155**	52	55N 113	24W
Wewaka	**168**	35	10N	96 35W
Wexford	**35**	52	20N	6 28W
Wexford □	**35**	52	20N	6 25W
Weyburn	**152**	49	40N 103	50W
Weymouth	**27**	50	36N	2 28W
Whakatane	**122**	37	57S 177	1 E
Whale Cove	**145**	62	11N	92 36W
Whalsay	**30**	60	22N	1 0W
Whangamomona	**122**	39	8S 174	44 E
Whangarei	**122**	35	43S 174	21 E
Wharfe ⤳	**29**	53	55N	1 30W
Wheeler Pk.	**172**	38	57N 114	15W
Wheeling	**164**	40	2N	80 41W
Whernside	**28**	54	14N	2 24W
Whitby	**29**	54	29N	0 37W
Whitchurch	**28**	52	58N	2 42W
White ⤳, Ark., U.S.A.	**168**	33	53N	91 3W
White ⤳, Ind., U.S.A.	**167**	38	25N	87 45W
White ⤳, S. Dak., U.S.A.	**163**	43	45N	99 30W
White Cliffs	**118**	30	50S 143	10 E
White Mts.	**157**	44	15N	71 15W
White Nile = Nîl el Abyad ⤳	**129**	15	38N	32 31 E
White Russia = Byelorussian S.S.R. □	**68**	53	30N	27 0 E
White Sea = Beloye More	**69**	66	30N	38 0 E
Whitecliffs	**123**	43	26S 171	55 E
Whitehaven	**28**	54	33N	3 35W
Whitehorse	**144**	60	43N 135	3W
Whitney, Mt.	**173**	36	35N 118	14W
Whitstable	**25**	51	21N	1 2 E
Whitsunday I.	**121**	20	15S 149	4 E
Whittier	**142**	60	46N 148	48W
Whyalla	**118**	33	2S 137	30 E
Wichita	**158**	37	40N	97 20W
Wichita Falls	**161**	33	57N	98 30W
Wick	**33**	58	26N	3 5W
Wickepin	**120**	32	50S 117	30 E
Wicklow	**35**	53	0N	6 2W
Wicklow □	**35**	52	59N	6 25W
Wicklow Mts.	**35**	53	0N	6 30W
Widnes	**28**	53	22N	2 44W
Wieluń	**58**	51	15N	18 34 E
Wien	**45**	48	12N	16 22 E
Wiesbaden	**42**	50	7N	8 17 E
Wigan	**28**	53	33N	2 38W
Wight, I. of	**25**	50	40N	1 20W
Wigtown	**31**	54	52N	4 27W
Wigtown B.	**31**	54	46N	4 15W
Wilcannia	**118**	31	30S 143	26 E
Wildwood	**164**	38	59N	74 46W
Wilhelmshaven	**42**	53	30N	8 9 E
Wilkes Barre	**164**	41	15N	75 52W
Wilkes Sub-Glacial Basin	**15**	75	0S 130	0 E
Wilkie	**152**	52	27N 108	42W
Willamina	**171**	45	9N 123	32W
Willemstad	**181**	12	5N	69 0W
Williams L.	**154**	51	48N	90 45W
Williamsburg	**165**	37	17N	76 44W
Williamson	**165**	37	46N	82 17W
Williamsport	**164**	41	18N	77 1W
Williamstown	**117**	37	51S 144	52 E
Williston	**163**	48	10N 103	35W
Willits	**172**	39	28N 123	17W
Willmar	**156**	45	5N	95 0W
Wilmette	**167**	42	6N	87 44W
Wilmington, Del., U.S.A.	**164**	39	45N	75 32W
Wilmington, N.C., U.S.A.	**165**	34	14N	77 54W
Wilson	**165**	35	44N	77 54W
Wilsons Promontory	**117**	38	55S 146	25 E
Wilton	**24**	51	5N	1 52W
Wiltshire □	**24**	51	20N	2 0W
Wiluna	**120**	26	36S 120	14 E
Wimereux	**38**	50	45N	1 37 E
Winchester, U.K.	**25**	51	4N	1 19W
Winchester, Ind., U.S.A.	**167**	40	10N	84 56W
Winchester, Ky., U.S.A.	**165**	38	0N	84 8W
Winchester, Va., U.S.A.	**164**	39	14N	78 8W
Wind River Range	**163**	43	0N 109	30W
Windermere	**28**	54	24N	2 56W
Windermere, L.	**28**	54	20N	2 57W
Windhoek	**136**	22	35S	17 4 E
Windsor, Australia	**117**	33	37S 150	50 E
Windsor, Nfld., Canada	**149**	48	57N	55 40W
Windsor, Ont., Canada	**150**	42	18N	83 0W
Windsor, U.K.	**25**	51	28N	0 36W
Windward Is.	**181**	13	0N	63 0W
Windward Passage = Vientos, Paso de los	**180**	20	0N	74 0W
Winisk ⤳	**140**	55	17N	85 5W
Winkler	**153**	49	10N	97 56W
Winnemucca	**172**	41	0N 117	45W
Winnfield	**168**	31	57N	92 38W
Winnipeg	**153**	49	54N	97 9W
Winnipeg, L.	**153**	52	0N	97 0W
Winnipegosis L.	**153**	52	30N 100	0W
Winona	**166**	44	2N	91 39W
Winooski	**151**	44	31N	73 11W
Winschoten	**41**	53	9N	7 3 E
Winslow	**161**	35	2N 110	41W
Winston-Salem	**165**	36	7N	80 15W
Winter Haven	**170**	28	0N	81 42W
Winter Park	**170**	28	34N	81 19W
Winterswijk	**41**	51	58N	6 43 E
Winterthur	**44**	47	30N	8 44 E
Wirral	**28**	53	25N	3 0W
Wisbech	**29**	52	39N	0 10 E
Wisconsin □	**166**	44	30N	90 0W
Wisconsin ⤳	**166**	43	0N	91 15W
Wisconsin Rapids	**166**	44	25N	89 50W
Wishaw	**31**	55	46N	3 55W
Wisła ⤳	**58**	54	22N	18 55 E
Witham ⤳	**29**	53	3N	0 8W
Withernsea	**29**	53	43N	0 2 E
Witney	**24**	51	47N	1 29W
Włocławek	**58**	52	40N	19 3 E
Wodonga	**117**	36	5S 146	50 E
Wokam	**113**	5	45S 134	28 E
Woking	**25**	51	18N	0 33W
Wolin	**58**	53	50N	14 37 E
Wollaston L.	**145**	58	7N 103	10W
Wollaston Pen.	**145**	69	30N 115	0W
Wollongong	**117**	34	25S 150	54 E
Wolverhampton	**24**	52	35N	2 6W
Wondai	**116**	26	20S 151	49 E
Wŏnsan	**98**	39	11N 127	27 E
Wonthaggi	**117**	38	37S 145	37 E
Woodburn	**116**	29	6S 153	23 E
Woodenbong	**116**	28	24S 152	39 E
Woodend	**117**	37	20S 144	33 E
Woodland	**172**	38	40N 121	50W
Woods, L. of the	**153**	49	15N	94 45W
Woodstock, N.B., Canada	**148**	46	11N	67 37W
Woodstock, Ont., Canada	**151**	43	10N	80 45W
Woolgoolga	**116**	30	6S 153	11 E
Woomera	**118**	31	30S 137	10 E
Woonsocket	**164**	42	0N	71 30W
Wooroloo	**120**	31	48S 116	18 E
Worcester, U.K.	**24**	52	12N	2 12W
Worcester, U.S.A.	**164**	42	14N	71 49W
Workington	**28**	54	39N	3 34W
Worksop	**29**	53	19N	1 9W
Wormerveer	**40**	52	30N	4 46 E
Worms	**42**	49	37N	8 21 E
Worthing	**25**	50	49N	0 21W
Worthington	**166**	43	35N	95 36W
Wou-han = Wuhan	**99**	30	31N 114	18 E

Woy Woy	**117**	33 30S	151 19 E
Wrangel I.	**138**	71 0N	180 0 E
Wrangell	**143**	56 30N	132 25W
Wrangell Mts.	**142**	61 40N	143 30W
Wrath, C.	**32**	58 38N	5 0W
Wrekin, The	**28**	52 41N	2 35W
Wrexham	**26**	53 5N	3 0W
Wrigley	**144**	63 16N	123 37W
Wrocław	**58**	51 5N	17 5 E
Września	**58**	52 21N	17 36 E
Wu Jiang →	**99**	29 40N	107 20 E
Wubin	**120**	30 6S	116 37 E
Wuhan	**99**	30 31N	114 18 E
Wuhsi = Wuxi	**99**	31 33N	120 18 E
Wuhu	**99**	31 22N	118 21 E
Wulumuchi = Ürümqi	**100**	43 45N	87 45 E
Wuppertal	**42**	51 15N	7 8 E
Würzburg	**42**	49 46N	9 55 E
Wutongqiao	**99**	29 22N	103 50 E
Wuxi	**99**	31 33N	120 18 E
Wuzhong	**98**	38 2N	106 12 E
Wuzhou	**99**	23 30N	111 18 E
Wyalkatchem	**120**	31 8S	117 22 E
Wyandotte	**167**	42 14N	83 13W
Wycheproof	**119**	36 0S	143 17 E
Wye →	**27**	51 36N	2 40W
Wyndham	**114**	15 33S	128 3 E
Wynnum	**116**	27 27S	153 9 E
Wynyard	**152**	51 45N	104 10W
Wyoming □	**163**	42 48N	109 0W
Wytheville	**165**	37 0N	81 3W
Xánthi	**55**	41 10N	24 58 E
Xapuri	**187**	10 35S	68 35W
Xenia	**167**	39 42N	83 57W
Xiamen	**99**	24 25N	118 4 E
Xi'an	**99**	34 15N	109 0 E
Xiangfan	**99**	32 2N	112 8 E
Xiangtan	**99**	27 51N	112 54 E
Xiao Hinggan Ling	**98**	49 0N	127 0 E
Xigazê	**101**	29 5N	88 45 E
Xingtai	**98**	37 3N	114 32 E
Xingu →	**188**	1 30S	51 53W
Xining	**98**	36 34N	101 40 E
Xinjiang Uygur Zizhiqu □	**100**	42 0N	86 0 E
Xinxiang	**99**	35 18N	113 50 E
Xinyang	**99**	32 6N	114 3 E
Xinzhu	**99**	24 49N	120 57 E
Xique-Xique	**188**	10 50S	42 40W
Xizang □	**101**	32 0N	88 0 E
Xuanhua	**98**	40 40N	115 2 E
Xuchang	**99**	34 2N	113 48 E
Xuzhou	**99**	34 18N	117 10 E
Ya'an	**99**	29 58N	103 5 E
Yablonovy Khrebet	**74**	53 0N	114 0 E
Yablonovy Ra. = Yablonovy Khrebet	**74**	53 0N	114 0 E
Yacuiba	**187**	22 0S	63 43W
Yaizu	**107**	34 52N	138 20 E
Yakima	**171**	46 42N	120 30W
Yaku-Jima	**104**	30 20N	130 30 E
Yakut A.S.S.R. □	**72**	62 0N	130 0 E
Yakutat	**143**	59 29N	139 44W
Yakutsk	**75**	62 5N	129 50 E
Yalgoo	**120**	28 16S	116 39 E
Yalinga	**129**	6 33N	23 10 E
Yamaga	**108**	33 1N	130 41 E
Yamagata	**103**	38 15N	140 15 E
Yamaguchi	**108**	34 10N	131 32 E
Yamal, Poluostrov	**69**	71 0N	70 0 E
Yamato	**107**	35 27N	139 25 E
Yamatotakada	**106**	34 31N	135 45 E
Yamazaki	**109**	35 0N	134 32 E
Yamba	**116**	29 26S	153 23 E
Yambol	**53**	42 30N	26 36 E
Yamdena	**113**	7 45S	131 20 E
Yame	**108**	33 13N	130 35 E
Yamma-Yamma, L.	**118**	26 16S	141 20 E
Yampa →	**163**	40 37N	108 59W
Yamuna →	**92**	25 30N	81 53 E
Yamzho Yumco	**101**	28 48N	90 35 E
Yana →	**72**	71 30N	136 0 E
Yanagawa	**108**	33 10N	130 24 E
Yanai	**109**	33 58N	132 7 E
Yanco	**117**	34 38S	146 27 E
Yangch'ü = Taiyuan	**98**	37 52N	112 33 E
Yangquan	**98**	37 58N	113 31 E
Yangtze Kiang = Chang Jiang →	**99**	31 48N	121 10 E
Yanji	**98**	42 59N	129 30 E
Yantai	**98**	37 34N	121 22 E
Yao	**106**	34 32N	135 36 E
Yaoundé	**131**	3 50N	11 35 E
Yaqui →	**174**	27 37N	110 39W
Yare →	**25**	52 36N	1 28 E
Yarensk	**69**	61 10N	49 8 E
Yarkand = Shache	**100**	38 20N	77 10 E
Yarmouth	**148**	43 50N	66 7W
Yaroslavl	**68**	57 35N	39 55 E
Yarram	**117**	38 29S	146 9 E
Yashiro-Jima	**109**	33 55N	132 15 E
Yass	**117**	34 49S	148 54 E
Yasugi	**109**	35 26N	133 15 E
Yatsushiro	**108**	32 30N	130 40 E
Yavari →	**186**	4 21S	70 2W
Yavatmal	**91**	20 20N	78 15 E
Yawatahama	**109**	33 27N	132 24 E
Yazd	**85**	31 55N	54 27 E
Yazoo →	**169**	32 35N	90 50W
Yazoo City	**169**	32 48N	90 28W
Ye Xian	**98**	37 8N	119 57 E
Yegros	**191**	26 20S	56 25W
Yell	**30**	60 35N	1 5W
Yellow Sea	**99**	35 0N	123 0 E
Yellowhead P.	**155**	52 53N	118 25W
Yellowknife	**145**	62 27N	114 29W
Yellowstone →	**163**	47 58N	103 59W
Yellowstone National Park	**163**	44 35N	110 0W
Yemen ■	**82**	15 0N	44 0 E
Yenisey →	**69**	71 50N	82 40 E
Yeniseyskiy Zaliv	**69**	72 20N	81 0 E
Yeo →	**27**	51 10N	3 0W
Yeola	**91**	20 0N	74 30 E
Yeovil	**27**	50 57N	2 38W
Yeppoon	**121**	23 5S	150 47 E
Yerevan	**70**	40 10N	44 31 E
Yes Tor	**27**	50 41N	3 59W
Yetman	**116**	28 56S	150 48 E
Yezd = Yazd	**85**	31 55N	54 27 E
Yiannitsa	**54**	40 46N	22 24 E
Yibin	**99**	28 45N	104 32 E
Yichang	**99**	30 40N	111 20 E
Yichun	**98**	47 44N	128 52 E
Yilan	**99**	24 51N	121 44 E
Yinchuan	**98**	38 30N	106 15 E
Yingkou	**98**	40 37N	122 18 E
Yingtan	**99**	28 12N	117 0 E
Yining	**100**	43 58N	81 10 E
Yíthion	**54**	36 46N	22 34 E
Yiyang	**99**	28 45N	112 16 E
Yogyakarta	**111**	7 49S	110 22 E
Yōkaichiba	**107**	35 42N	140 33 E
Yokkaichi	**106**	35 0N	136 38 E
Yokohama	**107**	35 27N	139 28 E
Yokosuka	**107**	35 20N	139 40 E
Yokote	**103**	39 20N	140 30 E
Yonago	**109**	35 25N	133 19 E
Yoneshiro →	**103**	40 15N	140 15 E
Yonezawa	**103**	37 57N	140 4 E
Yongji	**99**	34 52N	110 28 E
Yonkers	**164**	40 57N	73 51W
York, Australia	**120**	31 52S	116 47 E
York, U.K.	**29**	53 58N	1 7W
York, U.S.A.	**164**	39 57N	76 43W
Yorke Pen.	**119**	34 50S	137 40 E
Yorkshire Wolds	**29**	54 0N	0 30W
Yorkton	**152**	51 11N	102 28W

Yosemite National Park **172** 38 0N 119 30W
Youghal **35** 51 58N 7 51W
Young .... **117** 34 19S 148 18 E
Younghusbànd Pen. .... **119** 36 0S 139 25 E
Youngstown **164** 41 7N 80 41W
Yuba City **172** 39 12N 121 37W
Yūbari.................... **103** 43 4N 141 59 E
Yūbetsu .... **103** 43 13N 144 5 E
Yucatán □ **177** 20 50N 89 0W
Yucatán, Canal de **178** 22 0N 86 30W
Yucatan Str. = Yucatán,
Canal de **178** 22 0N 86 30W
Yuci..................... **98** 37 42N 112 46 E
Yugoslavia ■ .... **52** 44 0N 20 0 E
Yukon ⇀ **142** 65 30N 150 0W
Yukon Territory □ **144** 63 0N 135 0W
Yuma **173** 32 45N 114 37W
Yunnan □ .... **101** 25 0N 102 30 E
Yuribei .... **69** 71 8N 76 58 E
Yurimaguas **186** 5 55S 76 7W
Yushu .... **101** 33 5N 96 55 E
Yuzhno-Sakhalinsk........ **75** 46 58N 142 45 E
Yvetot .... **38** 49 37N 0 44 E

Zaandam .... **40** 52 26N 4 49 E
Zabaykalskiy .... **74** 49 40N 117 25 E
Zabid .... **82** 14 0N 43 10 E
Zábol .... **85** 31 0N 61 32 E
Zābol □ .... **87** 32 0N 67 0 E
Zabrze .... **58** 50 18N 18 50 E
Zacapa................... **177** 14 59N 89 31W
Zacatecas **175** 22 47N 102 35W
Zacatecas □ **175** 23 0N 103 0W
Zacatecoluca **177** 13 29N 88 51W
Zadar .... **52** 44 8N 15 14 E
Zadetkyi Kyun .... **94** 10 0N 98 25 E
Zagreb .... **52** 45 50N 16 0 E
Zähedän .... **86** 29 30N 60 50 E
Zahlah .... **80** 33 52N 35 50 E
Zaïre ■ .... **134** 3 0S 23 0 E
Zaïre ⇀ .... **134** 6 4S 12 24 E
Zákinthos .... **54** 37 47N 20 57 E
Zambeze ⇀ .... **135** 18 55S 36 4 E
Zambezi = Zambeze ⇀ .... **135** 18 55S 36 4 E
Zambia ■ .... **135** 15 0S 28 0 E
Zamboanga............... **112** 6 59N 122 3 E
Zamora, Mexico **175** 20 0N 102 21W
Zamora, Spain **50** 41 30N 5 45W
Zandvoort .... **40** 52 22N 4 32 E
Zanesville **167** 39 56N 82 2W
Zanjan .... **81** 36 40N 48 35 E
Zante = Zákinthos .... **54** 37 47N 20 57 E
Zanzibar................. **135** 6 12S 39 12 E
Zaouiet El-Kala = Bordj Omar
Driss .... **127** 28 10N 6 40 E
Zaouiet Reggane .... **127** 26 32N 0 3 E
Zapadnaya Dvina ⇀ .... **68** 57 4N 24 3 E
Západné Beskydy ⇀ .... **59** 49 30N 19 0 E
Zapala **190** 39 0S 70 5W
Zaporozhye .... **68** 47 50N 35 10 E
Zaragoza, Mexico **174** 28 29N 100 55W

Zaragoza, Spain **51** 41 39N 0 53W
Zaranj .... **87** 30 55N 61 55 E
Zaria .... **131** 11 0N 7 40 E
Zaruma **184** 3 40S 79 38W
Zaskar Mountains .... **89** 33 15N 77 30 E
Zavitinsk............... **75** 50 10N 129 20 E
Zaysan, Oz.............. **71** 48 0N 83 0 E
Zayü .... **101** 28 48N 97 27 E
Zduńska Wola .... **58** 51 37N 18 59 E
Zeebrugge .... **42** 51 19N 3 12 E
Zeeland □ .... **40** 51 30N 3 50 E
Zeila .... **133** 11 21N 43 30 E
Zeist .... **40** 52 5N 5 15 E
Zemlya Frantsa Iosifa........ **13** 81 0N 55 0 E
Zentsūji .... **109** 34 14N 133 47 E
Zeya .... **75** 53 48N 127 14 E
Zêzere ⇀ **50** 39 28N 8 20W
Zhanghua .... **99** 24 6N 120 29 E
Zhangjiakou .... **98** 40 48N 114 55 E
Zhangzhou .... **99** 24 30N 117 35 E
Zhanjiang............... **99** 21 15N 110 20 E
Zhdanov................. **68** 47 5N 37 31 E
Zhejiang □ .... **99** 29 0N 120 0 E
Zhengzhou .... **99** 34 45N 113 34 E
Zhenjiang............... **99** 32 11N 119 26 E
Zhenyuan............... **99** 27 4N 108 21 E
Zhijiang .... **99** 27 27N 109 42 E
Zhitomir .... **68** 50 20N 28 40 E
Zhumadian .... **99** 32 59N 114 2 E
Zhupanovo............... **73** 53 40N 159 52 E
Zhuzhou................. **99** 27 49N 113 12 E
Zibo .... **98** 36 47N 118 3 E
Zielona Góra .... **58** 51 57N 15 31 E
Zierikzee .... **40** 51 40N 3 55 E
Zigong .... **99** 29 15N 104 48 E
Zile .... **80** 40 15N 35 52 E
Žilina .... **59** 49 12N 18 42 E
Zimbabwe .... **137** 20 16S 30 54 E
Zimbabwe ■ .... **137** 20 0S 30 0 E
Zinder .... **131** 13 48N 9 0 E
Zipaquirá **184** 5 0N 74 0W
Zitácuaro **175** 19 24N 100 22W
Zlatograd .... **53** 41 22N 25 7 E
Zlatoust .... **69** 55 10N 59 40 E
Zlin = Gottwaldov....... **59** 49 14N 17 40 E
Zomba .... **137** 15 22S 35 19 E
Zonguldak .... **80** 41 28N 31 50 E
Zorritos **186** 3 43S 80 40W
Zoutkamp .... **41** 53 20N 6 18 E
Zrenjanin .... **52** 45 22N 20 23 E
Zufar .... **83** 17 40N 54 0 E
Zug .... **44** 47 10N 8 31 E
Zuid-Holland □ .... **40** 52 0N 4 35 E
Zuidhorn .... **41** 53 15N 6 23 E
Zungeru .... **131** 9 48N 6 8 E
Zunyi.................. **99** 27 42N 106 53 E
Zürich .... **44** 47 22N 8 32 E
Zutphen .... **41** 52 9N 6 12 E
Zuwārah .... **127** 32 58N 12 1 E
Zvolen .... **59** 48 33N 19 10 E
Zwickau .... **43** 50 43N 12 30 E
Zwolle .... **41** 52 31N 6 6 E
Zyryanovsk .... **71** 49 43N 84 20 E